The United Nations Declaration on the Rights of Indigenous Peoples

The development and adoption of the United Nations Declaration on the Rights of Indigenous Peoples (UNDRIP) was a huge success for the global indigenous movement. This book offers an insightful and nuanced contemporary evaluation of the progress and challenges that indigenous peoples have faced in securing the implementation of this new instrument, as well as its normative impact, at both the national and international levels.

The chapters in this collection offer a multi-disciplinary analysis of the UNDRIP as it enters the second decade since its adoption by the UN General Assembly in 2007. Following centuries of resistance by Indigenous peoples to state, and state sponsored, dispossession, violence, cultural appropriation, murder, neglect and derision, the UNDRIP is an achievement with deep implications in international law, policy and politics. In many ways, it also represents just the beginning – the opening of new ways forward that include advocacy, activism, and the careful and hard-fought crafting of new relationships between Indigenous peoples and states and their dominant populations and interests.

This book was originally published as a special issue of *The International Journal of Human Rights.*

Damien Short is Co-Director of the Human Rights Consortium at the School of Advanced Study, University of London, UK and a Professor in Human Rights. He has spent much of his career researching and writing on indigenous peoples' rights and reconciliation debates issues in Australia, a monograph on which, *Reconciliation and Colonial Power: indigenous rights in Australia,* was published by Ashgate in 2008. Since then he has researched memory and genocide in Australia, publishing his work in *Memory Studies*, the *International Journal of Human Rights* and the *Journal of Genocide Research*. More recently, he has researched the impacts of Tar Sands production in Alberta, Canada on downstream indigenous communities. He is a frequent contributor to the United Nations Expert Mechanism on the Rights of Indigenous Peoples and is the Editor in Chief of the *International Journal of Human Rights.*

Corinne Lennox is Senior Lecturer in Human Rights at the Institute of Commonwealth Studies, and Co-Director of the Human Rights Consortium, School of Advanced Study, University of London, UK. Her research focuses on issues of minority and indigenous peoples' rights protection, civil society mobilisation for human rights, and on human rights and development. She has worked for many years as a human rights practitioner and trainer with various NGOs, including at Minority Rights Group International (MRG). She has been a consultant on minority and indigenous peoples' rights for the UNDP, the UN Office of the High Commissioner for Human Rights and several governments. She is a regular contributor to the annual *State of the World's Minorities and Indigenous Peoples Report* (MRG) and has published on transnational dimensions of minority and indigenous peoples' rights, including in her recent book *Transnational Social Mobilisation and Minority Rights: Identity, Advocacy and Norms* (Routledge 2020).

Julian Burger is Fellow of the Human Rights Consortium, School of Advanced Study, University of London and Visiting Professor at the Human Rights Centre at the University of Essex in the UK. He is also Visiting Professor at the University of Alcala de Henares, Spain. Before taking up his University appointments, he worked at the United Nations Office of the High Commissioner for Human Rights for 20 years during which time he headed the programme on indigenous peoples and minorities. During this period, he organized the discussions on the Declaration on the Rights of Indigenous Peoples and helped launch the principle human rights mechanisms on indigenous peoples - the Special Rapporteur, Permanent Forum on Indigenous Issues and the Expert Mechanism on the Rights of Indigenous Peoples. He also helped establish inter-agency networks of UN organizations to improve integration of indigenous and minority rights into development programmes. He has visited indigenous and minority communities in many parts of the world and has published books and articles on indigenous peoples and human rights since the 1980s.

Jessie Hohmann has broad research and teaching interests in the areas of international law, human rights (with a particular focus on the right to housing), Indigenous peoples in international law, and the material and visual culture of international law. She is currently Associate Professor in the Faculty of Law at the University of Technology Sydney, Australia. She has degrees from Sydney University, Osgoode Hall Law School of York University, Canada, and the University of Guelph. She has previously held appointments at Queen Mary, University of London, the University of Cambridge, King's College, London and Macquarie University in Sydney.

The United Nations Declaration on the Rights of Indigenous Peoples

A Contemporary Evaluation

Edited by
Damien Short, Corinne Lennox, Julian Burger and Jessie Hohmann

Routledge
Taylor & Francis Group
LONDON AND NEW YORK

First published 2021
by Routledge
2 Park Square, Milton Park, Abingdon, Oxon, OX14 4RN

and by Routledge
52 Vanderbilt Avenue, New York, NY 10017

Routledge is an imprint of the Taylor & Francis Group, an informa business

British Library Cataloguing-in-Publication Data
A catalogue record for this book is available from the British Library

ISBN-13: 978-0-367-47670-0 (hbk)
ISBN-13: 978-0-367-61980-0 (pbk)
ISBN-13: 978-1-003-03577-0 (ebk)

DOI: 10.4324/9781003035770

Typeset in Minion Pro
by codeMantra

Publisher's Note
The publisher accepts responsibility for any inconsistencies that may have arisen during the conversion of this book from journal articles to book chapters, namely the inclusion of journal terminology.

Disclaimer
Every effort has been made to contact copyright holders for their permission to reprint material in this book. The publishers would be grateful to hear from any copyright holder who is not here acknowledged and will undertake to rectify any errors or omissions in future editions of this book.

Contents

Citation Information

The chapters in this book were originally published in *The International Journal of Human Rights*, volume 23, issue 1–2 (2019). When citing this material, please use the original page numbering for each article, as follows:

Chapter 1
Introduction
Jessie Hohmann
The International Journal of Human Rights, volume 23, issue 1–2 (2019) pp. 1–6

Chapter 2
The UNDRIP: an increasingly robust legal parameter
Felipe Gómez Isa
The International Journal of Human Rights, volume 23, issue 1–2 (2019) pp. 7–21

Chapter 3
After the Declaration: next steps for the protection of indigenous peoples' rights
Julian Burger
The International Journal of Human Rights, volume 23, issue 1–2 (2019) pp. 22–33

Chapter 4
The UNDRIP and the legal significance of the right of indigenous peoples to self-determination: a human rights approach with a multidimensional perspective
Dorothée Cambou
The International Journal of Human Rights, volume 23, issue 1–2 (2019) pp. 34–50

Chapter 5
Implementation of the UNDRIP around the world: achievements and future perspectives. The outcome of the work of the ILA Committee on the Implementation of the Rights of Indigenous Peoples
Federico Lenzerini
The International Journal of Human Rights, volume 23, issue 1–2 (2019) pp. 51–62

Chapter 6
The World Bank's new Environmental and Social Framework: some progress but many gaps regarding the rights of indigenous peoples
Corinne Lewis and Carl Söderbergh
The International Journal of Human Rights, volume 23, issue 1–2 (2019) pp. 63–86

Chapter 7

Implementing free prior and informed consent: the United Nations Declaration on the Rights of Indigenous Peoples (2007), the challenges of REDD+ and the case for the precautionary principle
Malayna Raftopoulos and Damien Short
The International Journal of Human Rights, volume 23, issue 1–2 (2019) pp. 87–103

Chapter 8

Towards new development paradigms: the United Nations Declaration on the Rights of Indigenous Peoples as a tool to support self-determined development
Jérémie Gilbert and Corinne Lennox
The International Journal of Human Rights, volume 23, issue 1–2 (2019) pp. 104–124

Chapter 9

Creating a space for indigenous rights: the Universal Periodic Review as a mechanism for promoting the rights of indigenous peoples
Noelle Higgins
The International Journal of Human Rights, volume 23, issue 1–2 (2019) pp. 125–148

Chapter 10

Looking back to move forward: the status of environmental rights under the UN Declaration on the Rights of Indigenous Peoples
Adriana Giunta
The International Journal of Human Rights, volume 23, issue 1–2 (2019) pp. 149–173

Chapter 11

Treaty making and the UN Declaration on the Rights of Indigenous Peoples: lessons from emerging negotiations in Australia
Harry Hobbs
The International Journal of Human Rights, volume 23, issue 1–2 (2019) pp. 174–192

Chapter 12

The self divided: the problems of contradictory claims to Indigenous peoples' self-determination in Australia
Stephen M. Young
The International Journal of Human Rights, volume 23, issue 1–2 (2019) pp. 193–213

Chapter 13

Indigenous rights and the legal politics of Canadian coloniality: what is happening to free, prior and informed consent in Canada?
Jeremy Patzer
The International Journal of Human Rights, volume 23, issue 1–2 (2019) pp. 214–233

Chapter 14

A critical evaluation of the domestic standards of the right to prior consultation under the UNDRIP: lessons from the Peruvian case
Amelia Alva-Arévalo
The International Journal of Human Rights, volume 23, issue 1–2 (2019) pp. 234–248

Chapter 15

Implementing the rights of indigenous peoples in Japan: implications and challenges of forest certification for the Ainu
Fumiya Nagai
The International Journal of Human Rights, volume 23, issue 1–2 (2019) pp. 249–266

Chapter 16

The approach to UNDRIP within the African Regional Human Rights System
Lucy Claridge
The International Journal of Human Rights, volume 23, issue 1–2 (2019) pp. 267–280

Chapter 17

Indigenous peoples' rights in Morocco: subaltern narratives by Amazigh women
Silvia Gagliardi
The International Journal of Human Rights, volume 23, issue 1–2 (2019) pp. 281–296

Chapter 18

Reflections on indigenous peoples' rights vis-à-vis the law of occupation
Shlomit Stein
The International Journal of Human Rights, volume 23, issue 1–2 (2019) pp. 297–312

Contributors

Amelia Alva-Arévalo Human Rights Centre, Ghent University, Belgium.

Julian Burger Human Rights Centre, School of Law, University of Essex, Colchester, UK Human Rights Consortium, School of Advanced Study, University of London, UK.

Dorothée Cambou Helsinki University, Arts Faculty, HELSUS, Helsinki, Finland.

Lucy Claridge Forest Peoples Programme, UK.

Silvia Gagliardi Irish Centre for Human Rights, National University of Ireland, Galway, Ireland.

Jérémie Gilbert School of Law, University of Roehampton, London, UK.

Adriana Giunta Brunel Law School, Brunel University London, UK.

Felipe Gómez Isa Deusto Law School, Pedro Arrupe Institute of Human Rights, University of Deusto, Bilbao, Spain.

Noelle Higgins Department of Law, Maynooth University, Ireland.

Harry Hobbs Faculty of Law, University of Technology Sydney, Australia.

Jessie Hohmann Faculty of Law, University of Technology Sydney, Australia.

Corinne Lennox School of Advanced Study, University of London, UK.

Federico Lenzerini International Law and Human Rights, University of Siena, Italy.

Corinne Lewis Lex Justi, Brussels, Belgium.

Fumiya Nagai Department of Anthropology, University of British Columbia, Vancouver, Canada.

Jeremy Patzer Department of Sociology and Criminology, University of Manitoba, Winnipeg, Canada.

Malayna Raftopoulos Department of Culture and Global Studies, Aalborg University, Denmark.

Damien Short School of Advanced Study, University of London, UK.

Carl Söderbergh Minority Rights Group International, London, UK.

Shlomit Stein LLM, Yale Law School, USA.

Stephen M. Young University of New South Wales, Sydney, Australia.

Introduction

Jessie Hohmann

The papers collected in this special issue of the International Journal of Human Rights consider the United Nations Declaration on the Rights of Indigenous Peoples (UNDRIP) as it enters the second decade since its adoption by the UN General Assembly in 2007. The adoption of the UNDRIP was the result of years of resistance by Indigenous peoples to state, and state sponsored dispossession, violence, cultural appropriation, murder, neglect and derision. It is an achievement with deep implications in international law and politics. But in many ways it also represents just the beginning – the opening of new ways forward that include advocacy, activism, and the careful and hard-fought crafting of new relationships between Indigenous peoples and states and their dominant populations and interests.

The papers collected here came out of a conference hosted at the School of Advanced Study (SAS), University of London, and jointly sponsored and organised by the SAS; the Centre for European and International Legal Affairs (CEILA) at Queen Mary, University of London; the City Law School, City, University of London; and the University of Lapland, in October 2017. We aimed to bring together a multi-disciplinary group of Indigenous and non-Indigenous scholars with a common interest in UNDRIP to reflect on the achievements, and assess the future challenges for Indigenous peoples, since the adoption of the UNDRIP in 2007.

While there is widespread recognition of the rights of Indigenous peoples, there are still countless areas of conflict in which rights are violated, peoples are displaced and lands despoiled. Indigenous peoples everywhere face numerous challenges and remain some of the most marginalised individuals and communities on earth.[1] The impact, and potential, of the UNDRIP remains contested, and Indigenous peoples and activists face new challenges – political, environmental, existential – while old problems, and their effects, persist. What role has the UNDRIP played in Indigenous struggles since its adoption? To what extent has it been implemented, and with what effects? How can the Declaration best be brought to bear for Indigenous peoples – for instance, as an instrument of international (soft) law, as a platform for advocacy, as a commitment of principle, or in yet other ways? What next steps are needed in international diplomacy, activism and law?

The papers in this volume address these questions in a number of ways. They are written by people from across the world, and shine a light on some of the regional challenges facing Indigenous peoples in their quest to realise the rights under UNDRIP and beyond, at the same time that a number of common themes emerge from the papers as areas of particular importance. This introduction maps out some of the common themes and concerns addressed in the papers included in this special issue.

A number of papers rightly celebrate the achievement of the UNDRIP as the culmination of decades of efforts to decolonise, as Gómez-Iza notes, both international law and the United Nations, and to transform Indigenous persons – and peoples – from objects to subjects of international law.[2] The UNDRIP is recognised as a major effort to redress past injustice, and to force a new framework for the recognition of Indigenous peoples and their rights[3]; as a 'propulsive force' – as Lenzerini puts it – in advancing the rights of Indigenous peoples under international law.[4]

A number of authors also attempt to distil the 'hard' from 'soft' law in the Declaration. These papers take stock of the impact of the declaration as a legal instrument. Specifically, Lenzerini's paper draws on the in-depth studies of the ILA Committee on the Implementation of the UNDRIP, and he notes that states generally treat the declaration as of a binding legal character,[5] while Gomez argues that the UNDRIP has become an unavoidable parameter of reference.[6] But it is particularly notable how many of the papers, while acknowledging the UNDRIP as an important way-marker, are primarily turned toward the future. The authors recognise the work still to be done, and the challenges to overcome, in implementing the UNDRIP, and in otherwise realising and protecting the rights, status, and continuing survival and vitality of Indigenous peoples in the world.

In many papers, it is clear that we need ongoing political and activist struggles, to be carried out nationally and transnationally, to push for the meaningful implementation of the UNDRIP. Several of the papers point to the opportunities at the international level, through various global governance structures, inter-governmental organisations and human rights monitoring mechanisms. Higgins identifies the need for domestic activism around the UN's Universal Periodic Review (UPR) process,[7] while Soderbergh and Lewis demonstrate the importance of activism and engagement with the World Bank in the consultations around – and application of – the new Environmental and Social Framework.[8] Claridge illuminates one of the results of such activist struggles in Africa: the *Okiek* and *Endorois* cases under the African Regional Human Rights system.[9] Gilbert and Lennox also examine the review processes of the Sustainable Development Goals (SDGs) and the 'data revolution' required by the SDGs, which has the potential to meet Indigenous people's 'data sovereignty'[10] demands.

As these papers demonstrate, while these international engagements are valuable, they may not translate into success at the national level. This is partly due to the complexity, political sensitivity, and legal paradoxes of activism around Indigenous rights in the often polarised domestic sphere. This is discussed by Young, who illuminates the contestations over the 'self' that is to be 'self-determined' in the context of the Native Title Act in Australia, and its framework for Indigenous rights.[11] The question over who speaks as the agent of self-determination, this paper shows, is deeply contested within Indigenous groups, and cannot easily be separated from the ongoing effects of colonialism. Gagliardi also illuminates the issue of who has power to speak, or act, as Indigenous with reference to the struggles of Amazigh women in Morocco.[12] Hobbs' contribution also illuminates the legal and political entanglements in the ongoing treaty making process in Australia,[13] while Alva-Arevalo reveals the tense and often violent Peruvian political situation in which Indigenous rights struggles unfold, and its impact on the potential for meaningful rights fulfilment for Indigenous communities, with particular reference to the principle of Free, Prior and Informed Consent (FPIC).[14]

Given the continuing challenges that face Indigenous communities, many authors contributing here suggest that it is time to push for new or complementary inter- and transnational mechanisms to further implement and realise Indigenous rights. Burger asks whether it is time for a binding convention on the rights of Indigenous peoples in international law, which would build on, and potentially strengthen the UNDRIP in a number of key areas.[15] Likewise, Giunta argues that a binding convention could resolve existing tensions among rights to culture, trade, and the environment, and bring added coherence to international law in these areas.[16] Nagai, meanwhile, shows that international forest certification programmes can be used productively as part of a 'business and human rights' approach to protecting the rights of Indigenous peoples, focusing on Japan.[17] Hobbs reflects on treaty making processes between Indigenous peoples and the Australian state, looking at the efforts in the state of Victoria.[18] If successful these would, for the first time, bring into being a new inter-national relationship between Indigenous peoples and the colonial Australian state. Other new paths forward include 'bio-cultural protocols' adopted by Indigenous peoples and operationalised by the Nagoya Protocol. As Lennox and Gilbert argue, these provide important frameworks for implementing FPIC, as well as for achieving self-determined development.[19]

Of the multiple issues facing Indigenous peoples 'on the ground' the effects of extractive industries appear in this volume as one of the most pressing and serious. Alva-Arevalo[20] Patzer,[21] Nagai[22] and Young[23] point to the ways in which extractive industries that exploit natural resources in ways that damage – often in irreparable fashion – the lands and territories of Indigenous communities present some of the biggest challenges facing these communities today. This is partly because of the scale of the impacts of these industries, and the irreparable harm they cause to the land both through the immediate physical despoliation of mining and logging, and the long-term environmental impacts that remain for generations to come, even if the physical marks fade.[24] It is also partly because, as Giunta notes, rights to land, environment, resources and territories of Indigenous peoples cannot be separated from their existence as distinct peoples and their collective identity.[25] In fact, as Indigenous peoples have argued, the land and environment cannot be separated from them as beings.[26] Finally it is because – as Lennox and Gilbert set out in their contribution – the vast majority of these projects are undertaken under a paradigm of 'development as aggression'.[27] That is, dominant development paradigms impose views of what development 'is' that are paternalistic and which bear little relationship to the aspirations and world views of Indigenous peoples. Has the UNDRIP catalysed the concept and practice of self-determined development they ask?[28]

Climate change, to which so many extractive industries (and the dominant development paradigm itself) contribute, will impact on all the world's inhabitants, Indigenous or not, animal or plant. But it is clear that vulnerable human communities – including Indigenous communities – are likely to suffer the most from its impacts. In their contribution, Short and Raftopoulos argue that we can harness the principle of Free, Prior and informed Consent (FPIC) under the UNDRIP, and argue for a need to make the precautionary principle central to implementing FPIC, in order to protect the planet's biodiversity, and help create climate and human rights responsive policies in the face of climate change.[29] Giunta also argues that, in the face of a changing climate, a reframing of land

and resources rights in favour of environmental rights can better protect Indigenous peoples' subsistence rights.[30]

The principle of FPIC enshrined in the UNDRIP is potentially powerful in giving Indigenous peoples a meaningful voice in when – or whether – developmental projects can be carried out on their lands and territories. It is clear that FPIC under the UNDRIP is stronger than it is in other legal contexts.[31] For this reason, FPIC is a major topic of concern in the papers in this volume. Alva considers issues of FPIC in Peru, where the volatile situation on the ground, and the interplay between politics, domestic legislation, and the UNDRIP's standards demonstrate the difficulty of using the UNDRIP as a shield against extractive projects.[32] Patzer also analyses the difficult questions raised by the disparities between FPIC under the UNDRIP, and as conceptualised by domestic courts, in particular in Canada as an 'extractivist' colonial state.[33]

Not far below the surface in a number of the papers is the question of what constitutes meaningful self-determination for Indigenous peoples in the wake of the UNDRIP. For Young, one of the risks for Indigenous peoples engaging in political and legal strategies through UNDRIP lies in the particular conception of the self that must be recognised. In Young's view, the UNDRIP does not succeed in overcoming the perils of recognition of Indigenous peoples within the frame of colonial and imperial law and power.[34] Dorothee Cambou also tackles the question of self-determination head-on, asking what self-determination means in the context of the UNDRIP's explicit preservation of territorial integrity, and suggesting that we need to take a multidimensional approach to self-determination, which is democratic, and which protects autonomy and effective participation in decision making.[35] Lennox and Gilbert examine what meaningful self-determination looks like in the space of development policy, where the concept of self-determined development, advanced by Indigenous peoples at the international level, including through litigation, is finding some realisation through tools like bio-cultural community protocols negotiated by local Indigenous communities. Other Indigenous peoples face particular situations of *legal* difficulty in realising their right to self-determination under the UNDRIP. Stein, for instance, examines the situation of the Bedouin in the West Bank, and asks how the UNDRIP might be made applicable to them in a situation of occupation, where the occupying power is prevented under international law from imposing a new legal regime over occupied territory, and where Indigenous populations cannot exercise self-determination.[36]

If Indigenous peoples, individuals and communities are to flourish, we need to accept that it must be on their own terms. The UNDRIP represents an undeniable step towards decolonising international law and the United Nations, recognising Indigenous peoples as relevant actors and subjects. But it is a step, and there are many more to be taken. While many of us have celebrated the achievement of the UNDRIP, and with good reason, the papers collected in this volume turn their faces to the future, so that invariably, the UNDRIP appears as a platform for departure, rather than a destination. Where might we go now, they ask, and how might we get there? Each offers its own answer, with the author cognisant that each answer is only a partial one. Together, the papers demonstrate that concerted action, on many fronts, is still needed.

To measure the impact of UNDRIP, including its use in the legal and policy spheres, we appeal for more research in this area. If UNDRIP is to serve as an instrument of international law, we need to document better how it is being applied in different contexts.

This will help to build a dataset of state (and non-state actor) practice and influence norm socialisation on the many provisions of UNDRIP. We need to understand and engage with Indigenous worldviews and approaches to the UNDRIP, and to provide support for Indigenous struggles under it, which will take place over the next decades.

Notes

1. See Camilo Pérez-Bustillo and Jessie Hohmann, 'Indigenous Rights to Development, Socio-Economic Rights, and Rights for Groups with Vulnerabilities: Articles 20–22, 24, and 44', in *The Declaration on the Rights of Indigenous Peoples: A Commentary*, ed. Jessie Hohmann and Marc Weller (OUP, 2018) p 485–6.
2. See Felipe Gómez-Isa, 'The UNDRIP: An Increasingly Robust Legal Parameter', 3.
3. See particularly Gómez-Iza (n 2) and Federico Lenzerini, 'Implementation of the UNDRIP Around the world: Achievements and Future Perspectives: The Outcome of the Work of the ILA Committee on the Implementation of the Rights of Indigenous Peoples'.
4. Lenzerini, (n 3) 5.
5. Ibid., 8.
6. Gómez-Iza (n 2).
7. Noelle Higgins, 'Creating a Space for Indigenous Rights: The Universal Periodic Review as a Mechanism for Promoting the Rights of Indigenous Peoples'.
8. Corinne Lewis and Carl Soderbergh 'The World Bank's New Environmental and Social Framework: Some Progress but Many Gaps regarding the Rights of Indigenous Peoples'.
9. Lucy Claridge, 'The Approach to UNDRIP within the African Regional Human Rights System'.
10. Tahu Kukutai and John Taylor, eds., *Indigenous Data Sovereignty: Toward an Agenda* (ANU Press, 2016).
11. Stephen Young, 'The Self Divided: The Problems of Indigenous Peoples' Contradictory Self-determination Claims in Australia'.
12. Silvia Gagliardi, 'Indigenous Peoples' Rights in Morocco: Subaltern Narratives by Amazigh Women'.
13. Harry Hobbs, 'Treaties and the United Nations Declaration on the Rights of Indigenous Peoples in Australia'.
14. Amelia Alva-Arevalo, 'A Critical Evaluation of the Domestic Standards of the Right to Prior Consultation under the UNDRIP. Lessons from the Peruvian Case'.
15. Julian Burger, 'After the Declaration: Next Steps for the Protection of Indigenous Peoples' Rights'.
16. Adriana Giunta, 'The Status of Environmental Rights under the UN Declaration on the Rights of Indigenous Peoples on the Occasion of Its Tenth Anniversary: Looking Back to Move Forward'.
17. Fumiya Nagai, 'Implementing the Rights of Indigenous Peoples in Japan: Implications and Challenges of Forest Certification for the Ainu'.
18. Hobbs (n 13).
19. Jérémie Gilbert and Corinne Lennox, 'The UNDRIP and Self-Determined Development: Analysing the Sustainable Development Goals (SDGs), Adjudication and Community Protocols'.
20. Alva-Arevalo, (n 14).
21. Jeremy Patzer 'Indigenous Rights and the Legal Politics of Canadian Coloniality: What Is Happening to Free, Prior, and Informed Consent in Canada?'
22. Nagai (n 17).
23. Young (n 11).
24. See for example 'Report of the Special Rapporteur on the Rights of Indigenous Peoples, James Anaya: Extractive Industries Operating Within or Near Indigenous Territories' A/HRC/18/

35 11 July 2011 and Jerry Mander and Victoria Tauli-Corpuz, *Paradigm Wars: Indigenous Peoples' Resistance to Globalization* (Sierra Club Books 2006).
25. Giunta (n 16) 2.
26. See for example, in the context of Australia, Irene Watson, *Aboriginal Peoples, Colonialism and International Law: Raw Law* (Routledge, 2015); C. F. Black, *The Land Is the Source of the Law: A Dialogic Encounter with Indigenous Jurisprudence* (Routledge, 2011). See also Mander and Tauli-Corpuz, (n 24).
27. Lennox and Gilbert (n 19) 1.
28. Ibid.
29. Malayna Raftopolous and Damien Short, 'Implementing Free Prior and Informed Consent: The United Nations Declaration on the Rights of Indigenous Peoples, the Challenges of REDD+ and the Case for the Precautionary Principle'.
30. Giunta (n 16).
31. See Mauro Barelli, 'Free, Prior, and Informed Consent in the UNDRIP: Articles 10, 19, 29(2) and 32(2)', in Jessie Hohmann and Marc Weller, eds., (n 1).
32. Alva-Arevalo, (n 14).
33. Patzer, (n 21).
34. Young, (n 11).
35. Dorothée Cambou 'The UNDRIP and the Legal Significance of Self-Determination: A Multi-dimensional Approach'.
36. Shlomit Stein, 'Reflections on Indigenous Peoples Rights vis-à-vis the Law of Occupation'.

Disclosure statement

No potential conflict of interest was reported by the author.

The UNDRIP: an increasingly robust legal parameter

Felipe Gómez Isa

ABSTRACT
Indigenous peoples have lived through a process of invisibility and systematic exclusion practically ever since the era of conquest. The arrival of republican States in Latin America following the decolonisation process did not involve a substantial change in the traditional relationship of subjection and submission endured by native peoples in the Americas. In the mid-twentieth century, the international community began to pay attention to the marginalised situation of indigenous peoples. The main objective was to integrate some peoples that were considered to be backward and in need of protection. It was within this paradigm that most of the interactions with indigenous peoples have occurred, such as the first international treaty adopted in this field, Convention No. 107 of the International Labour Organisation (ILO, 1957). This situation began to change with the adoption of Convention No. 169 by the ILO in 1989, and especially with the recently adopted United Nations Declaration on the Rights of Indigenous Peoples (UNDRIP, 2007). The UNDRIP has to be seen as the culmination of a long and difficult journey in which indigenous peoples themselves and their representatives have been key participants. Irrespective of the uncertain legal nature of the UNDRIP *per se*, one can conclude that it has become an unavoidable parameter of reference when dealing with indigenous peoples' rights, an increasingly robust legal instrument.

Indigenous peoples under international law: from exclusion to inclusion

Traditional international law has played a major role in the dramatic history of conquest, usurpation of indigenous peoples' sovereignty, and dispossesion of their lands, territories and resources.[1] The emerging international legal order in Europe became a powerful instrument in the hands of conquerors to dominate and subjugate indigenous peoples in the Americas.[2] Since its inception, given the role played by the main European powers in its creation, and the subordinate position of indigenous peoples and other non-Western countries and societies, international law could be characterised as a hegemonic discourse and as a source of domination.[3] Accordingly, Elvira Pulitano[4] has referred to international law as 'quintessentially Eurocentric'. At the same time, in a highly contradictory move, the so-called *Spanish School of International Law*,[5] based on the Aristotelian and Thomist idea of the natural sociability and rationality of human beings, defended the essential humanity and freedom of the Indians in the context of the Spanish conquest of the Americas.[6] The ideas of scholars such as Francisco de Vitoria[7] or Bartolomé de las Casas opened the door to the consideration of the Indians as full human beings in need of protection.[8] But, unfortunately, the Conquest of the Americas did not follow in practice the teachings of these precursors of contemporary human rights law.

This situation continued unaltered until very recently, when contemporary international law progressively changed its approach to indigenous peoples. But it is highly shocking that even in the first half of the twentieth century the West still believed that it was entrusted with a 'civilizing mission' to save non-European peoples from ignorance and backwardness.[9] In line with this approach, the first international treaty adopted by the International Labour Organisation (ILO) in 1957 to deal specifically with indigenous issues was still dominated by an assimilationist paradigm.[10] As stated in Article 2 of the Indigenous and Tribal Populations Convention (Convention No. 107, 1957), 'Governments shall have the primary responsibility for developing co-ordinated and systematic action for the protection of the populations concerned and their *progressive integration* into the life of their respective countries' (emphasis added).[11]

The 1970s and the 1980s witnessed the so-called 'indigenous emergence',[12] and International law, particularly international human rights law, became a very powerful discursive resource for indigenous peoples to advance their demands both at domestic and at international fora. In Rhiannon Morgan's view, 'the global indigenous movement is just one example of a movement that has grasped the transformative, dynamic potential lodged in the discourse of human rights, drawing on its manipulability and malleability to foster the reform of human rights'.[13] But the human rights discourse has also some inherent contradictions when approached from an indigenous perspective. We have to admit that the very idea of human rights has certain reminiscences of colonialism. Like colonialism,

> human rights discourse contains implicit assumptions about the nature of civilized and backward societies … Concepts of civilization and savagery, rationality and passion, that were fundamental binaries of thinking during the imperialist era creep back into debates over human rights and social justice. The practice of human rights is burdened by a colonialist understanding of culture … .[14]

Along the same lines, Makau Mutua[15] sees the way the most dominant proponents have constructed human rights as 'part of the colonial project that forms the unbroken chain of the Christian missionary, the early merchant of capital, and the colonial administrator'.

Postcolonial scholars[16] have underlined that, in spite of the formal end of colonialism both in the American continent in the eighteenth century and in Africa and Asia in the twentieth century, most indigenous peoples still suffer the pervasive influence of what Eve Darian-Smith calls 'new forms of colonialism'[17] that lead to 'soft imperialism' over sites of former colonial control.[18] As has been critically emphasised by Antony Anghie, 'imperialism has always been part of the international system',[19] therefore colonial relations still dominate the global relations between the North and the South,[20] and the internal relations between dominant societies and indigenous peoples within the boundaries of nation-states that emerged from the processes of decolonisation.

An illustrative example of the continuation of colonial relations *vis-à-vis* indigenous peoples is the application of the rule of *uti possidetis*. According to this international legal principle, the borders drawn by colonisers should be maintained during and after the process of decolonisation.[21] The main consequence of this policy was that the new states 'had the same borders as the former colonies, and indigenous peoples continuously enjoyed no rights over their traditional territories'.[22] In the case of Africa, the straight lines drawn by the colonial powers at the Berlin Conference in 1884 'cut right through the heartlands of very distinct linguistic and ethnic groups, creating problems that persist to the present day'.[23] In practice, decolonisation and emergence of new independent states did not make any meaningful difference for indigenous peoples; on the contrary, they continued experiencing oppressive and exclusionary colonial relations, particularly as regards their lands and territories.

The continuation of colonial and imperial relations as applied to indigenous peoples in Latin America has given rise to the concept of *coloniality of power*.[24] This concept influences not only power relations, but also the production and reproduction of knowledge,[25] and the construction of subjectivities and collective identities. As highlighted by a distinguished indigenous scholar, 'while colonialism is the territorial occupation by coercive means … , coloniality refers to the imposition of the Western cultural imaginary',[26] an advanced form of cultural imperialism.[27] Coloniality of power implies that indigenous peoples are still in a situation of vulnerability and symbolic domination through the internalisation of the logics of the coloniality of power. As a consequence, most legacies of colonialism still prevail in the relations between indigenous peoples and dominant sectors of society. The most influential consequence of the coloniality of power is the colonisation of minds and hearts of sub-altern groups such as indigenous peoples.[28] In this process of naturalisation of domination, education and law play a remarkable role; they form a 'constitutive link to the coloniality of power'.[29]

In spite of this critical approach, and as part of the process of empowerment of indigenous peoples, since the 1970s the United Nations has been increasingly receptive to the claims by indigenous peoples,[30] opening institutional spaces and avenues for their participation and for the advance of their demands.[31] Indigenous peoples used the United Nations as a mobilising structure to increase visibility of their marginalised position and to pursue some strategic goals in terms of recognition and protection.[32] In a sense, we witnessed a very promising process of *decolonisation* of both international law and the United Nations.[33] This process has allowed indigenous peoples to transform from solely victims to actors, and from objects of protection to subjects of rights, thus opening the door to their acquisition of some forms of international legal personality.[34] The culmination of this legal and institutional development is the creation of the UN Permanent Forum on Indigenous Issues in 2000, a unique body in which states and indigenous representatives participate on an equal footing,[35] and, above all, the adoption of the UNDRIP in 2007. As the Committee on the Rights of Indigenous Peoples of the International Law Association has affirmed, all these developments demonstrate that 'indigenous persons and peoples are back not only as fully entitled holders of individual human rights, but as collective actors with distinct rights and status under international law'.[36]

Progressive recognition of indigenous people's rights

One of the most significant developments in the field of human rights in recent decades has been the gradual recognition of the rights of indigenous peoples, both in the domestic and in the international legal arenas. The ILO was the first international organisation to pay attention to the situation of marginalisation and exclusion suffered by indigenous peoples. The adoption of ILO Convention 169 in 1989 substituting ILO Convention No. 107 (1957)[37] was a relevant step forward for the recognition of indigenous rights,[38] but states have been very reluctant to ratify it.[39] Against the background of the negative experience with the two existing ILO Conventions, the global indigenous movement established as a priority the adoption of a declaration of universal reach to recognise its rights. After a lengthy process of negotiation in which indigenous peoples themselves were key participants,[40] the UNDRIP was finally adopted on 13 September 2007 by the UN General Assembly by an overwhelming majority. The negotiation process was unique, since it involved negotiations between states, on the one hand, and indigenous peoples' representatives, on the other. It is fair to say that this is significantly new for the process of negotiation of human rights instruments.

Main innovations of the UNDRIP

The UNDRIP has incorporated a whole range of new rights, thus expanding significantly the scope of existing human rights. The main conceptual innovation refers to the recognition of *collective rights* as complementary to the classical individual rights. Collective rights have been alien to the process of emergence and recognition of human rights in Western legal culture.[41] The multiculturalism that indigenous peoples advocate in addressing human rights clearly challenges, and eventually enriches, a concept of human rights that has been essentially mono-cultural so far. As recognised and reaffirmed in the Preamble of the UNDRIP,

> indigenous individuals are entitled without discrimination to all human rights recognized in international law, and that indigenous peoples possess *collective rights which are indispensable for their existence, well-being and integral development as peoples* (emphasis added).

The second expansion of rights put forward by the UNDRIP is the recognition of the right to self-determination, one of the key demands by the global indigenous movement. Against the background of the fierce opposition by many governments, in the end Article 3 of the UNDRIP reads as follows:

> Indigenous peoples have the right to self-determination. By virtue of that right they freely determine their political status and freely pursue their economic, social and cultural development.

But Article 3 of the UNDRIP has to be read and interpreted in light of Article 4. According to this provision, 'indigenous peoples, in exercising their right to self-determination, have the right to autonomy or self-government in matters relating to their internal and local affairs … '. The exercise of the right to self-determination has to take place mainly through autonomy and self-government. A final provision that has to be mentioned in this context is Article 46.1, the so-called African clause, since most African governments paved the way for the adoption of the UNDRIP provided that it would never open the door to questioning the territorial integrity of states.[42] As established in this Article,

> Nothing in this Declaration may be interpreted as implying for any State, people, group or person any right to engage in any activity or to perform any act contrary to the Charter of the United Nations or construed as authorizing or encouraging any action which would

dismember or impair, totally or in part, the territorial integrity or political unity of sovereign and independent States.

A highly significant innovation by the UNDRIP is the recognition of some so-called *third generation human rights*, also known as solidarity rights. As we all know, these rights emerged in the 1980s but faced strong opposition from Western countries. The most relevant solidarity right enshrined in the UNDRIP is the right to development.[43] In light of Article 23 of the UNDRIP, 'indigenous peoples have the right to determine and develop priorities and strategies for exercising their right to development'. Along the same lines, Article 29.1 of the UNDRIP establishes that 'indigenous peoples have the right to the conservation and protection of the environment and the productive capacity of their lands or territories and resources'.

A very relevant step forward by the UNDRIP is the recognition of the need of the *free, prior and informed consent* of indigenous peoples when states take legislative or administrative measures that may affect them.[44] While ILO Convention 169 is mainly based on consultation with indigenous peoples,[45] the UNDRIP takes a new step and requires that consultation must be led to obtaining their free, prior and informed consent. As stated in Article 19 of the UNDRIP,

> States shall consult and cooperate in good faith with the indigenous peoples concerned through their own representative institutions in order to obtain their free, prior and informed consent before adopting and implementing legislative or administrative measures that may affect them.

Another major innovation of the UNDRIP is the recognition of historical injustices as an impediment to the enjoyment of human rights by indigenous peoples. Actually, it is one of the first references to this issue that can be found in an international legal instrument.

The adoption of the UNDRIP in 2007 reflects the deepest aspirations of the world's indigenous peoples and their confidence in international law and human rights law as powerful tools to modify entrenched patterns of domination and exclusion that have affected indigenous peoples since colonial times.[46] The very adoption of the UNDRIP can be interpreted as an attempt to repair historical wrongs suffered by indigenous peoples.[47] Significantly, the wording of the Declaration includes an explicit reference to historical injustices. In the preamble of this Declaration, the General Assembly of the United Nations emphasised that

> indigenous peoples have suffered from *historic injustices* as a result of, inter alia, their colonisation and dispossession of their lands, territories and resources, thus preventing them from exercising, in particular, their right to development in accordance with their own needs and interests (emphasis added).[48]

In addition to the concern about historic injustices expressed by the General Assembly, we can also see a cause–effect link between colonisation and the dispossession of land, territories and resources suffered by indigenous peoples in the past, and the inability to effectively exercise their right to development, the consequences of which are still being felt.[49]

The UNDRIP and existing international law

To a great extent, many of the provisions embodied in the UNDRIP do not create new rights, but can be considered as an elaboration of previous human rights, and as a reaffirmation of existing customary international law.[50] As James Anaya,[51] former Special Rapporteur on the situation of human rights and fundamental freedoms of indigenous people, has argued, the Declaration 'reflects the existing international consensus regarding the individual and collective rights of indigenous peoples in a way that is coherent with, and expands upon, international developments, including the interpretations of other human rights instruments by international bodies and mechanisms'. The same conclusion can be found in a recent resolution adopted by the International Law Association.[52] According to this very authoritative opinion, 'the 2007 UNDRIP as a whole cannot yet be considered as a statement of existing customary international law. However it includes several key provisions which correspond to existing state obligations under customary international law'. Among the norms of the UNDRIP that can be regarded as evidence of customary international law, the ILA included the following: the right of indigenous peoples to self-determination, autonomy and self-government; the right to participate in national decision-making with respect to decisions that may affect them; the right to free, prior and informed consent (FPIC) on projects significantly impacting their rights and ways of life; the right to cultural identity; the right to lands, territories and resources, including restitution of ancestral lands of which they have been deprived in the past; the right to establish their own educational institutions and media; and the right to reparation and redress for wrongs indigenous peoples have suffered.

This position was explicitly rejected by those states that voted against the UNDRIP (United States, Canada, Australia and New Zealand). The clearest opposition came from the United States (US), denying

> any possibility that this document is or can become customary international law ... As this declaration does not describe current state practice or actions that states feel obliged to take as a matter of legal obligation, it cannot be cited as evidence of the evolution of customary international law.[53]

The Canadian representative also shared this approach, when it stated that the Declaration 'has no legal effect in Canada, and its provisions do not represent customary international'.[54] In the same vein, the Australian government emphasised that the UNDRIP 'is an aspirational declaration with political and moral force but no legal force ... , it is not intended itself to be legally binding or reflective of international law'.[55] While recognising the relevance of the position of these states, we must underline that they 'represent only a minority of states specially affected by the Declaration'.[56] It seems quite clear that the position of these states would not be able to prevent the emergence of international customary law,[57] but they probably could have been considered as persistent objectors, given that they opposed the text of the UNDRIP since the very early stages of its drafting. Although, fortunately for the cause of indigenous peoples, these 4 states have changed their official positions *vis-à-vis* the UNDRIP and have endorsed it, they have repeatedly reiterated that the Declaration is neither legally binding nor a statement of current international law. According to the US, 'while not legally binding or a statement of current international law', the Declaration 'has both moral and political force', and 'expresses both the aspirations of indigenous peoples around the world and those of States in seeking to improve their relations with indigenous peoples'.[58] Along the same lines, Australia declared that 'while it is non-binding and does not affect existing Australian law, it sets important international principles for nations to aspire to'. And, more importantly from an international legal perspective, 'Australia's existing obligations under international human rights treaties are mirrored in the Declaration's fundamental principles'.[59] Irrespective of the legal nuances expressed by these countries, we must recognise that these endorsements, an unprecedented move as regards an instrument of this nature, represents a clear signal of the growing acceptance of indigenous peoples' rights as an integral part of the contemporary human rights regime.[60] In this sense, the words by the Minister of Maori Affairs of New Zealand when she announced its support to the UNDRIP are very illustrative: 'New Zealand now adds its support to the Declaration both as an affirmation of fundamental rights and in its expression of new and widely supported aspirations'.[61]

Legal scope and implementation of the UNDRIP

When trying to ascertain the legal value of the UNDRIP, three elements are of utmost importance: the circumstances of adoption of the instrument, the precision and normative nature of its content, and the existence of implementation mechanisms.

The adoption of the UNDRIP in 2007 is the result of more than twenty-five years of intense and controversial negotiations in which indigenous peoples and their close allies achieved very significant levels of participation. We can affirm that the way in which this process was conducted, and the very positive outcomes, will eventually influence international norm-creation exercises in other areas of international law, in general, and international human rights law, in particular. H. Patrick Glenn[62] situates the Declaration as part of a broader movement of international law. In his view, the Declaration 'would represent not simply a use or application of international law, in novel circumstances, but a major shift in the nature and direction of international law itself'. The inclusiveness of the process and the support from a number of bodies and instances within the UN, and from states themselves, provides the Declaration with high degrees of legitimacy that will definitely increase compliance.

The final vote on the UNDRIP at the UN General Assembly is also an indication of the international consensus around the document. As we know, 144 states voted in favour of the Declaration, 11 abstained,[63] and 4 voted against. An interesting evolution has taken place since 2007, and the 4 states that voted against have all endorsed the Declaration. Along the same lines, two of the abstaining states, Colombia and Samoa, have also made up their mind. This overwhelming support to the UNDRIP shows a clear commitment on the part of the international community to support the protection of the rights enshrined in the Declaration and promote compliance, and can be considered as a clear evidence of *opinio iuris* that, if accompanied by consistent state practice, may give rise to new rules of customary international law.

The final determining factor to calibrate the legal value of the UNDRIP is the existence of mechanisms for its implementation. The UNDRIP does not create specific follow-up mechanisms, but it relies on existing bodies both at international and at state level. The only body explicitly mentioned is the Permanent Forum on Indigenous Issues (PFII), thus placing it 'at the forefront in ensuring the effective implementation of the Declaration'.[64] In light of Article 42 of the Declaration,

> The United Nations, its bodies, including the Permanent Forum on Indigenous Issues, and specialized agencies, including at the country level, and States shall promote respect for and full application of the provisions of this Declaration and follow up the effectiveness of this Declaration.

According to the interpretation developed by Luis Rodríguez-Piñero,[65] the main goal of this provision is 'mainstreaming and operationalizing' the promotion of the rights enshrined in the Declaration within the activities of UN bodies, specialised agencies, regional organisations and states. Therefore, implementation measures of the UNDRIP will need to be taken at three parallel and inte-related levels: international, regional, and national.

At the *international level*, it must be acknowledged that a high number of UN bodies and specialised agencies are increasingly using the UNDRIP as a *parameter of reference* when interpreting international legal standards and their mandates. First of all, the mechanisms created to specifically address indigenous issues refer explicitly to the UNDRIP as an interpretive guide. Given the relevant coordinating role of the PFII aimed at mainstreaming indigenous issues throughout the whole UN system,[66] its position is key for the implementation of the UNDRIP. In its 2008 session, the PFII welcomed the adoption of the Declaration and stated that it will be 'its legal framework'.[67] Similarly, the Special Rapporteur on the situation of human rights and fundamental freedoms of indigenous people (SR) was also entrusted with the mandate of promoting the UNDRIP,[68] and it has worked very hard to make it possible. As James Anaya,[69] former SR, stated, the UNDRIP

> represents an authoritative common understanding, at the global level, of the minimum content of the rights of indigenous peoples, upon a foundation of various sources of international human rights law ... The principles and rights affirmed in the Declaration constitute or add to the normative frameworks for the activities of United Nations human rights institutions, mechanisms and specialized agencies as they relate to indigenous peoples.

Finally, the recently created Expert Mechanism on the Rights of Indigenous Peoples (EMRIP) is also a body that can significantly contribute to the implementation of the UNDRIP. Given its technical and advisory function as a body composed by 5 independent experts, the EMRIP is in a 'privileged position to contribute to promoting authoritative interpretations of the standards of the Declaration'.[70]

The UN human rights treaty bodies have also gradually interpreted the human rights conventions incorporating indigenous peoples' rights,[71] and more recently they have referred explicitly to the UNDRIP as a parameter of reference when interpreting the international human rights legal standards. Along these lines, the recent World Conference on Indigenous Peoples invited the human rights treaty bodies 'to consider the Declaration in accordance with their respective mandates', and encouraged states 'to include ... information on the situation of the rights of indigenous peoples, including measures taken to pursue the objectives of the Declaration, in reports to those bodies'.[72]

At the *regional level*, both the Inter-American Court of Human Rights and the African Commission on Human and Peoples' Rights are using the UNDRIP as one of the legal basis for their findings and decisions. The UNDRIP, and the positive vote by Suriname at the UN General Assembly, were used by the Inter-American Court of Human Rights in its judgement on *Saramaka People vs. Suriname*,[73] a case in which the Court affirmed the indigenous peoples' rights over land, territories and natural resources. The Court affirmed that states have the obligation 'to obtain the consent of indigenous and tribal peoples to carry out large-scale development or investment projects that have a significant impact on the right of use and enjoyment of their ancestral territories'.[74] This is a very far-reaching decision, since the Court is implicitly recognising that these standards are operative principles of international law irrespective of the normative scope of the Declaration and despite the fact that the state involved in this specific case is not a party to ILO Convention 169.

The African Commission on Human and Peoples' Rights (ACHPR) has also been open to incorporate the UNDRIP in the legal framework it has to apply. Just some two months after the approval of the UNDRIP, the ACHPR welcomed its adoption and stated that 'the Declaration will become a very valuable tool and a point of reference for its efforts to ensure that promotion and protection of indigenous peoples' rights on the African continent'.[75] In a memorable decision dated May 2009,[76] the African Commission stated that the forcible eviction of the Endorois people from their traditional lands near Lake Bogoria by the Government of Kenya without prior consultation and with no provision for compensation was a violation of a number of rights under the African Charter on Human and Peoples' Rights (ACHPR) and under the UNDRIP.[77] In a more recent decision on the Ogiek Case, the African Court on Human and Peoples' Rights has established that Article 22 of the African Charter on Human and Peoples' Rights 'should be read in light of Article 23 of the UNDRIP'.[78] As can be seen, the African Court is using the UNDRIP as an interpretive source when applying the African Charter.

At the *national level*, indigenous peoples' rights have also been gradually recognised both at the legislative and at the judicial level,[79] opening avenues for their effective implementation. First of all, many states, especially in Latin America, have gone through constitutional changes to incorporate indigenous peoples' rights. The most significant development took place in Bolivia,[80] where a law[81] was adopted to explicitly incorporate the UNDRIP in its domestic legal system. At the judicial level, both the Colombian Constitutional Court,[82] the Constitutional Court of Peru[83] and the Supreme Court of Belize have used the UNDRIP in some of their decisions. It is worth noting that the Supreme Court of Belize issued 'the first court judgment ever to apply the UNDRIP … barely a month after its adoption'.[84] The Supreme Court referred specifically to Belize's vote in favour of the UNDRIP as a clear commitment on future compliance in the *Case of the Maya Villages of Belize*. As stated by the Supreme Court, 'General Assembly resolutions are not ordinarily binding on member states. But where these resolutions or Declarations contain principles of general international law, states are not expected to disregard them'.[85] And the Court continues emphasising that 'it is of some signal importance … that Belize voted in favour of the Declaration'.[86] Finally, the Court is of the view that Article 26 of the UNDRIP reflects 'the growing consensus and the general principles of international law on indigenous peoples and their lands and resources'.[87]

In sum, there is a significant emerging practice at international, regional and domestic level that constitute a solid basis to defend that the UNDRIP has become a parameter of reference when interpreting and applying indigenous rights, and that at least some of the key provisions of the UNDRIP have already become customary international law, or are in the process of emerging as new rules of customary law.

Conclusions

Indigenous peoples have used contemporary international law and international institutions as very close allies in their struggle for recognition and in their efforts to put an end to historically rooted patterns of subjugation, dispossession and cultural assimilation. As part of this evolution, indigenous peoples have become subjects of rights under international law rather than objects of protection, thus becoming protagonists of a far-reaching process of expansion of human rights. The UNDRIP, adopted in 2007 by the UN General Assembly, has to be seen as the culmination of a long and difficult journey in which indigenous peoples themselves and their representatives have been key participants. Irrespective of the uncertain legal nature of the UNDRIP *per se*, one can conclude that it has become an unavoidable parameter of reference when dealing with indigenous peoples' rights. The recent experience of UN bodies, specialised agencies, human rights treaty bodies, regional human rights courts and commissions, and some domestic courts, clearly shows the strong persuasive authority and the interpretive function of the UNDRIP. But in spite of all these promising legal and institutional developments, indigenous peoples' rights still face what Rodolfo Stavenhagen[88] has termed as 'the implementation gap'. Indigenous peoples continue to suffer from situations of vulnerability and poverty in most countries where they live, as well as growing threats to their lands, territories and natural resources. There is a huge gap between the formal proclamations at the UN and other international organisations, and the harsh realities encountered by indigenous peoples in their daily life.

Notes

1. Paul Keal, *European Conquest and the Rights of Indigenous Peoples: The Moral Backwardness of International Society* (New York: Cambridge University Press, 2003).
2. James Anaya, *Indigenous Peoples in International Law* (Oxford: Oxford University Press, 2004); Antony Anghie, *Imperialism, Sovereignty and the Making of International Law* (Cambridge: Cambridge University Press, 2004).
3. Balakrishnan Rajagopal, *International Law from Below. Development, Social Movements and Third World Resistance* (Cambridge: Cambridge University Press, 2003).
4. Elvira Pulitano, 'Indigenous Rights and International Law: An Introduction', in *Indigenous Rights in the Age of the UN Declaration*, ed. E. Pulitano (Cambridge: Cambridge University Press, 2012), 4.
5. James Brown Scott, *The Spanish Origin of International Law: Francisco de Vitoria and his Law of Nations* (London: Clarendon Press, 1934).
6. Felipe Gómez Isa, 'The First Cry for Justice in the Americas-from Antonio de Montesinos to the Laws of Burgos (1512)', in *First Fundamental Rights Documents in Europe. Commemorating 800 Years of Magna Carta*, ed. M. Suksi et al. (Cambridge: Intersentia, 2015), 93–105.
7. See the refreshing analysis by Ignacio de la Rasilla del Moral, *In the Shadow of Vitoria: A History of International Law in Spain (1770–1953)* (Brill/Nijhoff, 2018).
8. Paolo G. Carozza, 'From Conquest to Constitutions: Retrieving a Latin American Tradition of the Idea of Human Rights', *Human Rights Quarterly* 25 (2003): 291.
9. This is the essence of some provisions found in the *Covenant of the League of Nations* (1919), the constitutive treaty of the first international organization. According to Article 22, a provision that has to be read in a colonial context, 'to those colonies and territories which as a consequence of the late war have ceased to be under the sovereignty of the States which formerly governed them and which are inhabited by *peoples not yet able to stand by themselves* under the strenuous conditions of the modern world, there should be applied the principle that the well-being and development of such peoples form a *sacred trust of civilization* … ' (emphasis added).
10. Patrick Thornberry, *Indigenous Peoples and Human Rights* (Manchester: Manchester University Press, 2002), 329–33.

11. Besides, ILO Convention No. 107 refers to indigenous 'populations' instead of peoples. The recognition as true peoples and nations is one of the main claims of the global indigenous movement. See the leading work by Luis Rodríguez-Piñero, *Indigenous Peoples, Post-colonialism and International Law. The ILO Regime (1919–1989)* (Oxford: Oxford University Press, 2005).
12. José Bengoa, *La emergencia indígena en América Latina* (México: Fondo de Cultura Económica, 2000); Alison Brysk, *From Tribal Village to Global Village. Indian Rights and International Relations in Latin America* (Stanford, CA: Stanford University Press, 2000).
13. Rhiannon Morgan, *Transforming Law and Institution. Indigenous Peoples, the United Nations and Human Rights* (Farnham: Ashgate, 2011), 43.
14. Salle Engle Merry, *Human Rights and Gender Violence. Translating International Law into Local Justice* (Chicago, IL: The University of Chicago Press, 2006), 226.
15. Makau Mutua, 'The Transformation of Africa. A Critique of the Rights Discourse', in *International Human Rights Law in a Global Context*, ed. F. Gómez Isa and K. De Feyter (Bilbao: Deusto Univesity Press, 2009), 901.
16. Edward Said, *Orientalism* (London: Penguin, 1978); Gayatri Chakravorty Spivak, *A Critique of Postcolonial Reason* (Cambridge, MA: Harvard University Press, 1999).
17. Eve Darian-Smith, 'Postcolonial Theories of Law', in *An Introduction to Law and Social Theory*, ed. R. Banakar and M. Travers (Oxford: Hart Publishing, 2013), 247.
18. Kwame Nkrumah, *Neo-colonialism: The Last Stage of Imperialism* (New York: International Publishers, 1966).
19. Antony Anghie, 'The Evolution of International Law: Colonial and Postcolonial Realities', *Third World Quarterly* 27 (2006): 749.
20. On the role that International Financial and Trade Institutions such as the International Monetary Fund (IMF), the World Bank (WB) or the World Trade Organization (WTO) play in the maintenance of colonial relations between the North and the South aiming at the imposition of a neoliberal global order, see David Fidler, 'A Kinder, Gentler System of Capitulations? International Law, Structural Adjustment Policies, and the Standard of Liberal, Globalized, Civilization', *Texas International Law Journal* 35 (2000): 387–413; Chimni, 'International Institutions Today: An Imperial Global State in the Making', *European Journal of International Law* 15 (2004): 1–37.
21. Malcolm Shaw, 'The Heritage of States: The Principle of *Uti Possidetis Juris* Today', *British YearBook of International Law* 67 (1997): 97–151.
22. Mattias Ahrén, *Indigenous Peoples' Status in the International Legal System* (Oxford: Oxford University Press, 2016), 19.
23. Siegfried Wiessner, 'Indigenous Self-determination, Culture, and Land: A Reassessment in Light of the 2007 UN Declaration on the Rights of Indigenous Peoples', in E. Pulitano see note 4 above, 36. A critical account of the influence of the principle of *uti possidetis* in today's Africa can be found in Makau Mutua, 'Why Redraw the Map of Africa: A Moral and Legal Inquiry', *Michigan Journal of International Law* 16 (1995): 1113–76. See also Steven Ratner, 'Drawing a Better Line: *Uti Possidetis* and the Borders of New States', *American Journal of International Law* 90 (1996): 590–624.
24. See the seminal work by Aníbal Quijano, 'Colonialidad y Modernidad/Racionalidad', in *Los conquistados. 1492 y la población indígena de las Américas*, comp H. Bonilla (Bogotá: Tercer Mundo-Libri Mundi, 1992), 437–47. See also Enrique Dussel, *1492. El Encubrimiento del Otro: hacia el Origen del Mito de la Modernidad* (La Paz: Plural Editores-UMSA, 1994); Walter Mignolo, 'El desprendimiento: pensamiento crítico y giro descolonial', in *Interculturalidad, Descolonización del Estado y del Conocimiento*, ed. C. Walsh, A. García Linera y W. Mignolo (Buenos Aires: Ediciones del Signo, 2006), 9–20.
25. See Boaventura de Sousa Santos, ed., *Another Knowledge is Possible: Beyond Northern Epistemologies* (London: Verso, 2007).
26. Pedro Garzón López, *Ciudadanía Indígena. Del multiculturalismo a la colonialidad del poder* (Madrid: Centro de Estudios Políticos y Constitucionales, 2016), 279.

27. Iris Marion Young, *Justice and the Politics of Difference* (Princeton, NJ: Princeton University Press, 1990); Asier Martínez de Bringas, *La cultura como derecho en América Latina. Ensayo sobre la realidad postcolonial en la globalización* (Bilbao: Universidad de Deusto, 2005).
28. Santiago Castro-Gómez, *La poscolonialidad explicada a los niños* (Bogotá: Universidad Javeriana de Bogotá, 2005), 59.
29. Catherine Walsh, *Interculturalidad, estado y sociedad. Luchas (de)coloniales de nuestra época* (Quito: Universidad Andina Simón Bolívar, 2009), 167.
30. Augusto Willemsen-Diaz, 'How Indigenous Peoples' Rights Reached the UN', in *Making the Declaration Work. The United Nations Declaration on the Rights of Indigenous Peoples*, ed. C. Chartres and R. Stavenhagen (Copenhagen: IWGIA, 2009), 16–31.
31. A number of bodies were created to deal specifically with indigenous issues (Working Group on Indigenous Peoples; Working Group on a Draft Declaration on indigenous peoples' rights; Permanent Forum on Indigenous Issues; Special Rapporteur on the rights of indigenous peoples, and Expert Mechanism on the Rights of Indigenous Peoples). The General Assembly of the UN also proclaimed two consecutive UN Decades on Indigenous Peoples (1994–2003 and 2005–2014). The UN Permanent Forum on Indigenous Issues has recently called for a Third International Decade of the World's Indigenous Peoples. In its view, 'over the course of the two Decades, we have seen some progress ... However, we need to ensure and reinvigorate momentum to genuinely implement the UN Declaration ... A Third Decade can provide a framework and consolidate clear milestones for the achievement of the UN Declaration ... ', *A Third International Decade of the World's Indigenous Peoples*, United Nations Permanent Forum on Indigenous Issues, Dalee Sambo Dorough, Chairperson, 7 November 2014, http://www.un.org/esa/socdev/unpfii/documents/Communication-UNPFII%20Chair-3decade.pdf.
32. Irène Bellier and Martin Préaud, 'Emerging Issues in Indigenous Rights: Transformative Effects of the Recognition of Indigenous Peoples', *The International Journal of Human Rights* 16, no. 3 (2012): 474–88.
33. Post-1945 international law and institutions have been used by the West (an imagined community itself) to construct and impose a new set of rational truths based on particular values, norms and socio-political organizations that were defined as universal. Post-colonial studies have demonstrated that international law and institutions, among many other structures of power, were used by the West to maintain its hierarchies and modes of domination. Indigenous peoples' struggles have aimed to decolonize both the theory and practice of the 'ideological-institutional complex' known as international law. On this challenging processes see the illuminating essay by Sundhya Pahuja, *Decolonising International Law. Development, Economic Growth and the Politics of Universality* (Cambridge: Cambridge University Press, 2011).
34. Dalee Sambo Dorough, 'The Significance of the Declaration on the Rights of Indigenous Peoples and Its Future Implementation', in note 30 above, 264–79.
35. Lola García-Alix, *The Permanent Forum on Indigenous Issues* (Copenhagen: IWGIA, 2003).
36. International Law Association, *Rights of Indigenous Peoples*, Report of the Hague Conference (2010), 2.
37. 27 states ratified this convention. Since the adoption of ILO Convention 169, Convention 107 is no longer open for ratification. However, it is still in force in 18 countries that have not ratified yet Convention 169.
38. Rodríguez-Piñero, note 11 above.
39. As of February 2018, only 22 states have ratified ILO Convention No. 169 (Argentina, Plurinational State of Bolivia, Brazil, Central African Republic, Chile, Colombia, Costa Rica, Denmark, Dominica, Ecuador, Fiji, Guatemala, Honduras, Mexico, Nepal, Netherlands, Nicaragua, Norway, Paraguay, Peru, Spain and Bolivarian Republic of Venezuela), http://www.ilo.org/dyn/normlex/en/f?p=1000:11300:0::NO:11300:P11300_INSTRUMENT_ID:312314.
40. Irène Bellier, 'Les peuples autochtones aux Nations Unies: un nouvel acteur dans la fabrique des normes internationales', *Critique Internationale* 54, no. 1 (2012): 61–80.

41. Some governments are still reluctant to recognise the very category of collective rights in the context of indigenous peoples' rights. In the view of the United Kingdom, 'with the exception of the right to self-determination, the United Kingdom did not accept the concept of collective human rights in international law', https://www.un.org/press/en/2007/ga10612.doc.htm.
42. Albert K. Barume, 'Responding to the Concerns of African States', in note 30 above, 180–81.
43. Felipe Gómez Isa, 'The Right to Development, Translating Indigenous Voice(s) into Development Theory and Practice', in *The World Bank Legal Review Volume 6. Improving Delivery in Development: The Role of Voice, Social Contract, and Accountability*, ed. J. Wouters et al. (Washington, DC: World Bank Publications, 2015), 91–102.
44. Sebastiaan Johannes Rombouts, *Having a Say. Indigenous Peoples, International Law and Free, Prior and Informed Consent* (Oisterwijk: Wolf Legal Publishers, 2014).
45. Free, prior and informed consent can also be arguably found in Art. 6.2 of ILO Convention 169. According to this provision, 'The consultations carried out in application of this Convention shall be undertaken, in good faith and in a form appropriate to the circumstances, with the objective of achieving agreement or consent to the proposed measures'.
46. Patrick Glenn, 'The Three Ironies of the UN Declaration on the Rights of Indigenous Peoples', in *Reflections on the UN Declaration on the Rights of Indigenous Peoples*, ed. S. Allen and A. Xanthaki (Oxford: Hart Publishing, 2011), 174.
47. Felipe Gómez Isa, 'Repairing Historical Injustices: Indigenous Peoples in Post-conflict Scenarios', in *Rethinking Transitions. Equality and Social Justice in Societies Emerging from Conflict*, ed. G. Oré Aguilar and F. Gómez Isa (Cambridge: Intersentia, 2011), 265–300.
48. Paragraph 6 of the Preamble.
49. Miguel Concha Malo, 'Lucha por la dignidad y los derechos humanos individuales y colectivos de los pueblos de América Latina', in *Responsabilidad Histórica. Preguntas del nuevo al viejo mundo*, ed. R. Mate (Barcelona: Anthropos, 2007), 321.
50. James Anaya and Sigfried Wiessner, 'The UN Declaration on the Rights of Indigenous Peoples: Towards Re-empowement', *Jurist*, October 3, 2007, http://jurist.org/forum/2007/10/un-declaration-on-rights-of-indigenous.php.
51. James Anaya, *Report of the Special Rapporteur on the situation of human rights and fundamental freedoms of indigenous people, S. James Anaya*, UN Doc. A/HRC/9/9, 11 August (2008), 43.
52. International Law Association, Resolution No. 5/2012, 75th Conference of the ILA, Sofia, 26–30 August (2012): para. 2.
53. United States, 'Observations of the United States with respect to the Declaration on the Rights of Indigenous Peoples: Explanation of Vote by Robert Hagen, U.S. Advisor, on the Declaration on the Rights of Indigenous Peoples, to the UN General Assembly', 13 September (2007).
54. UN Doc. A/61/PV.107, 13.
55. Ibid., 12.
56. Mauro Barelli, 'The Role of Soft Law in the International Legal System: The Case of the United Nations Declaration on the Rights of Indigenous Peoples', *International and Comparative Law Quarterly* 58, no. 4 (2009): 967.
57. Matías Meza-Lopehandía, 'El Derecho Internacional de los Derechos Humanos y los Pueblos Indígenas', in *Los Pueblos Indígenas y el Derecho*, coord. J. Aylwin (Santiago de Chile: LOM Ediciones, 2013), 466.
58. *Announcement of U.S. Support for the United Nations Declaration on the Rights of Indigenous Peoples*, 16 December 2010, http://www.state.gov/documents/organization/184099.pdf. A very similar position was expressed by the Canadian government. In its view, '… the Declaration is a non-legally binding document that does not reflect customary international law nor change Canadian laws … In 2007, at the time of the vote during the United Nations General Assembly, and since, Canada placed on record its concerns with various provisions of the Declaration … These concerns are well known and remain. However, we have since listened to Aboriginal leaders who have urged Canada to endorse the Declaration and we have also learned from the experience of other countries. We are now confident that

Canada can interpret the principles expressed in the Declaration in a manner that is consistent with our Constitution and legal framework', *Canada's Statement of Support on the United Nations Declaration on the Rights of Indigenous Peoples*, 12 November 2010, http://www.aadnc-aandc.gc.ca/eng/1309374239861/1309374546142.

59. *Statement on the United Nations Declaration on the Rights of Indigenous Peoples*, Parliament House, Canberra, 3 April 2009, http://www.un.org/esa/socdev/unpfii/documents/Australia_official_statement_endorsement_UNDRIP.pdf.
60. A less optimistic view has been expressed by some scholars. In relation to Australia's endorsement, 'it remains to be seen whether the international legislation underpinning the UNDRIP can be brought to bear on Australia, or whether the current government's endorsement of UNDRIP is indeed little more than an empty gesture designed to enhance the country's reputation in the eyes of the world', Sheila Collingwood-Whittick, 'Australia's Northern Territory Intervention and Indigenous Rights on Language, Education and Culture: An Ethnocidal Solution to Aboriginal 'Dysfunction'?', in Pulitano, note 4 above, 136.
61. *Statement by Hon Dr Pita Sharples, Minister of Maori Affairs, Announcement of New Zealand's support for the Declaration on the Rights of Indigenous Peoples*, 19 April 2010, http://www.mfat.govt.nz/Media-and-publications/Media/MFAT-speeches/2010/0-19-April-2010.php.
62. Glenn note 46 above, 174.
63. Azerbaijan, Bangladesh, Bhutan, Burundi, Colombia, Georgia, Kenya, Nigeria, Russian Federation, Samoa and Ukraine.
64. Barelli note 56 above, 978.
65. Luis Rodríguez-Piñero, 'La "implementación" de la Declaración: las implicaciones del Artículo 42', in *La Declaración sobre los derechos de los pueblos indígenas. Hacia un mundo intercultural y sostenible*, ed. N. Álvarez et al. (Madrid: Los Libros de la Catarata, 2009), 74–5.
66. In 2002, the *Inter-Agency Support Group on Indigenous Issues* (IASG) was created to support the PFII in the goal of promoting dialogue and cooperation between UN bodies and agencies dealing with indigenous issues. The IASG is composed by 31 bodies, departments, funds and agencies of the UN. See Julian Burger, in Chartres and Stavenhagen note 30 above, 309–10.
67. UN Permanent Forum on Indigenous Issues, 'Report of the Seventh Session', UN Doc. E/C.19/2008/23, 2008. Some members of the PFII have claimed that, given the special legitimacy and radical novelty of the UNDRIP, it should have some legally binding effects. This view has been expressed, among others, by Bartolomé Clavero, for whom 'although the Declaration is not a treaty between states, it constitutes a convention or covenant between states and peoples, between the member states of the United Nations and indigenous peoples', Bartolomé Clavero, *Nota sobre el Alcance del Mandato contenido en el Artículo 42 de la Declaración sobre los Derechos de los Pueblos Indígenas y el Mejor Modo de Satisfacerlo por parte del Foro Permanente para las Cuestiones Indígenas*, UN Doc. E/C.19/2008/CRP.6, 26 March 2008, 9.
68. Human Rights Council, Resolution 6/12, 28 September 2007.
69. Anaya note 51 above, para. 85.
70. Luis Rodríguez-Piñero, 'Where Appropriate: Monitoring/Implementing of Indigenous Peoples' Rights Under the Declaration', in Chartres and Stavenhagen note 29 above, 334.
71. Thornberry note 10 above, 116.
72. World Conference on Indigenous Peoples, *Outcome Document of the High-level Plenary Meeting of the General Assembly Known as the World Conference on Indigenous Peoples*, UN Doc. A/RES/69/2, 22 September 2014, para. 29.
73. Inter-American Court of Human Rights, *Saramaka People v. Suriname (Preliminary Objections, Merits, Reparations, and Costs)*, Judgement of 28 November 2007, Series C No. 172, paras. 131 and 138.
74. Ibid., para 129.
75. ACHPR, Resolution 121 (XXXXII) on the UN Declaration on the Rights of Indigenous Peoples, 28 November 2007.

76. *Centre for Minority Rights Development (Kenya) and Minority Rights Group International on behalf of Endorois Welfare Council v. Kenya*, Communication 276/2003, para. 232. The African Commission relied to a great extent on the indigenous jurisprudence of the Inter-American Court of Human Rights, in a clear example of cross-fertilization between regional human rights systems.
77. Patricia Borraz, 'The Endorois Case: Indigenous Peoples' Rights in the African regional human rights system', in *Indigenous Peoples' Human Rights in Domestic Courts*, ed. L. Ferrer and P. Borraz (Madrid: Almaciga, 2013), 211–6.
78. *African Commission on Human and Peoples' Rights v. Republic of Kenya*, Application No. 006/2012 Judgment, 26 May 2017, para. 209. See more references to the UNDRIP in paras. 126, 127 and 181.
79. Countries that have affirmed the right of indigenous peoples to their cultural identity, their cultural rights, land rights, right to autonomy and participatory rights include Argentina, Australia, Bangladesh, Botswana, Brazil, Cambodia, Canada, Chile, Colombia, Costa Rica, India, Laos, Malaysia, Mexico, New Zealand, Nicaragua, Norway, Paraguay, Peru, South Africa and Taiwan, among many others, ILA note 35 above, 49–50.
80. The new Constitutions of Bolivia (2009) and Ecuador (2008) are leading examples of a new wave of constitutionalism known as *plurinational constitutionalism*. See Almut Schilling-Vacaflor and René Kuppe, 'Plurinational Constitutionalism: A New Era of Indigenous-state Relations?' in *New Constitutionalism in Latin America: Promises and Practices*, ed. D. Nolte and A. Schilling-Vacaflor (Farnham: Ashgate, 2012), 347–70.
81. *Ley 3760 de los derechos de los pueblos indígenas*, 7 November 2007.
82. Felipe Gómez Isa, 'Cultural Diversity, Legal Pluralism, and Human Rights from an Indigenous Perspective: The Approach by the Colombian Constitutional Court and the Inter-American Court of Human Rights', *Human Rights Quarterly* 36, no. 2 (2014): 722–55.
83. The Constitutional Court of Peru has also referred to ILO Convention 169, the jurisprudence of the Inter-American Court of Human Rights and the UNDRIP to reaffirm the rights of indigenous peoples to their lands and territories in the *Tres Islas indigenous community Case*, Sentencia del Tribunal Constitucional, Exp. No. 01126-2011-HC/TC, 11 September 2012, para. 23.
84. Maia Campbell and James Anaya, 'The Case of the Maya Villages of Belize: Reversing the Trend of Government Neglect to Secure Indigenous Land Rights', *Human Rights Law Review* 8, no. 2 (2008): 377.
85. *Manuel Coy, Maya Village of Conejo, Manuel Caal, Perfecto Makin, Melina Makin Claimants v. Attorney General of Belize, Minister of Natural Resources, and Environmental Defendants*, Supreme Court of Belize, 18 October 2007, para. 131.
86. Ibid.
87. Ibid.
88. Rodolfo Stavenhagen, *Report of the Special Rapporteur on the Situation of Human Rights and Fundamental Freedoms of Indigenous People*, UN Doc. E/CN.4/2006/78, 16 February 2006.

Disclosure statement

No potential conflict of interest was reported by the author.

After the Declaration: next steps for the protection of indigenous peoples' rights

Julian Burger

ABSTRACT
The article presents arguments in favour of beginning the process of elaborating a convention on the rights of indigenous peoples.

When the UN General Assembly finally adopted the Declaration on the Rights of Indigenous Peoples in September 2007, there was a metaphorical sigh of relief from many who had been engaged in the process of drafting. Nearly 25 years had passed since the UN formally began its work on elaborating its provisions. Negotiations had sometimes been acrimonious. When small steps had been taken and consensus achieved around an article, there was a sense of euphoria; when there was no progress year after year, there was disappointment and frustration. In the end, the Declaration was voted on and those indigenous experts and lobbyists who had spent years at the Geneva meetings could rightly feel a sense of achievement. There were parts that were not as strong as hoped for but in general the Declaration contained the minimum standards that indigenous peoples called for. It was natural that those involved in the negotiations should feel that the work of standard-setting was over and they could move on to other matters, not least of all the implementation of the rights in practice.

But is the adoption of the Declaration the end of the affair? Is the Declaration as comprehensive as it can be? How helpful is it for the protection of indigenous peoples' rights to have a document that states describe as non-binding?[1] Is a document that has none of the standard means for monitoring States compliance enough? Should indigenous peoples be satisfied with what they have got or strive for something better?[2]

In general, indigenous peoples who were active on the Declaration are not in favour of lobbying for a legally binding convention on the rights of indigenous peoples. There is of course an understandable 'battle fatigue' after the lengthy, expensive and time-consuming discussions that took place over more than two decades. But there is also a political evaluation. Governments, they say, are not ready for further protracted negotiations over indigenous peoples' rights. There is a fear that embarking on a new negotiation may lead to weaker rights. The American Declaration on the Rights of Indigenous Peoples adopted in 2016 appears to substantiate that position in so far as it does not provide an unqualified right of indigenous peoples to self-determination as recognised in the UN Declaration.[3]

Furthermore, for certain experts, the UN Declaration is establishing itself as legally-binding through its association with existing UN treaties and through the developing jurisprudence of the UN treaty bodies and the regional human rights bodies such as the Inter-American Court and Commission of Human Rights and the African Court and Commission of Human and Peoples' Rights.[4] The Declaration is used by experts of UN treaty bodies and regional human rights courts as well as domestic courts as a reference and a means of determining rights and corresponding state responsibilities. There is an expectation that the UNDRIP will establish itself as customary law.[5]

It may also be argued that ILO Convention 169 on tribal and indigenous peoples, a legally binding convention when ratified, was adopted in 1989 and has succeeded in gaining only 22 ratifications, mostly in Latin America and with the last ratification more than 10 years ago.[6] If that is the case, it is legitimate to argue that there is little appetite on behalf of states to commit themselves to ratifying a new Convention, even if it should be elaborated.

One feature of UNDRIP is that it offers some flexibility and ambiguity which may be seen as politically useful. The formulation around free, prior and informed consent, for example, which in its article 32 talks of consultation to obtain the consent of the indigenous peoples concerned is clearly open to interpretation – Governments stressing the consultation aspect and indigenous peoples the consent element. It may be, at this time, and with the multitudinous land rights conflicts with indigenous peoples that the right needs to remain a broad principle that allows states and indigenous peoples to find a mutually acceptable and pragmatic interpretation. In the United Nations, there is something to be said for a degree of ambiguity, allowing positions to mature and adapt themselves and eventually bringing differing views around a modus vivendi.

There is also an argument that when indigenous peoples ask for more, states may seize the opportunity to impose some new limitations. This appears to be the case regarding the recommendation arising from the so-called world conference on indigenous peoples of 2016 to give indigenous peoples a new and distinct status and means of participation at intergovernmental meetings including the General Assembly.[7] The response of some states has been to insist on defining indigenous peoples and creating a mechanism for determining who and who should not be understood as indigenous.[8] Thus, a debate about definition has re-emerged and threatens to undermine the principle of self-identification. This was a discussion that took up some time during the negotiations on the Declaration but eventually was abandoned in favour of self-identification as a criterion for determining indigenous identity.[9] It does appear to illustrate though that demanding more may sometimes result in obtaining less.

Notwithstanding these concerns, there are good reasons for engaging in a more focused discussion on the value of pressing for negotiations to begin on elaborating a convention. The purpose of this article is to set out the technical and political rationale for drafting a convention. But before doing so, let us start with the human rights argument.

Human rights

Despite over a decade since the UNDRIP was adopted by the General Assembly, there has been no respite from the violations of human rights experienced by indigenous peoples in their legitimate struggles to protect their lands, resources, livelihoods and cultures. Indeed, what is notable is that there may even have been increases in violence against indigenous peoples and certainly no let-up in conflicts arising from governmental or corporate activities on indigenous lands. Anecdotally, one has only to note the aggressive policies of the Philippines President Duterte towards indigenous peoples in general and human rights defenders in particular or the militarisation of the Standing Rock conflict in the US under President Trump to be concerned at the way indigenous peoples' rights remain as tenuous as ever.[10] More substantive studies, such as that undertaken by Global Witness point to the increased violence against indigenous environmental defenders in Latin America and elsewhere.[11] Of course, Presidents Trump and Duterte are examples of Heads of State with apparently little interest in global opinion about their actions but indigenous rights appear to be on the defensive in other states. Efforts are in place in Brazil to push back indigenous peoples' land rights.[12] The Pinochet laws on terrorism are still being used to prosecute and incarcerate Mapuche human rights activists and threaten all those who peacefully protest in favour of their rights. In Bolivia, the honeymoon for Evo Morales as the country's first indigenous leader is long past and indigenous peoples, particularly from the lowlands, having already confronted the authorities to defend their lands in the TIPNIS events, are now facing up to the changes in the mining laws that undermine the principle of free, prior and informed consent.[13]

Curiously, the places where these violations can be denounced at the United Nations have been restricted even as the institutions dealing with indigenous peoples' issues have been given higher status, additional funding and greater indigenous membership. While the Special Rapporteur on the rights of indigenous peoples continues single-handedly to try to serve as a mouth-piece for the victims of human rights around the world, the Permanent Forum on Indigenous Issues and the Expert Mechanism on the Rights of Indigenous Peoples are largely engaged in thematic discussions with limited opportunity for indigenous representatives to bring to international attention abuses affecting their own communities. EMRIP's new mandate authorising it to provide technical assistance to states at their request may in the future provide a form of monitoring of implementation of the Declaration. At present, however, there is no complaints mechanism for indigenous peoples when rights have been violated nor any formal and periodic monitoring of how governments apply and implement the rights presently contained in the UNDRIP.[14]

A proposal was made by the Permanent Forum to establish a monitoring mechanism through the establishment of an optional protocol to the Declaration. The idea was discussed at a meeting of experts in 2015 but has not been formalised.[15] In that meeting the former Special Rapporteur on the rights of indigenous peoples, James Anaya writes: 'I believe it can hardly be debated that there exists on a global scale a wide gap between the standards expressed in the Declaration and their implementation.' And further he writes:

> In my work during two terms as the United Nations Human Rights Council's Special Rapporteur on the rights of indigenous peoples, I came across numerous situations, in numerous countries, in which the conditions of indigenous peoples and the relevant domestic legal and

policy regimes were far from what the Declaration aspires to establish. I therefore readily accept and affirm that existing capacities within the international human rights system are insufficient.[16]

The need to establish a monitoring mechanism may not be denied but is the proposal to establish a new kind of voluntary monitoring mechanism possible or desirable? I concur with the indigenous expert Suhas Chakma when he writes:

> If the purpose of establishing a complaints body is to adjudicate breaches of the UNDRIP akin to consideration of individual complaints by the UN Treaty Bodies, there is no escape from the rigours of enacting a new treaty by the UN … A legally binding treaty appears to be the minimum requirement to accept the competence/jurisdiction of an oversight body.[17]

A recent development of the EMRIP mandates the body to 'assist Member States, upon request, in achieving the ends of the Declaration through the promotion, protection and fulfilment of the rights of indigenous peoples'.[18] This positive and useful additional activity has the potential to engage further with states on indigenous peoples' rights and supplements the already existing forms of technical assistance provided more generally by the UN system. It does not, however, offer a mechanism for monitoring states' compliance with human rights and is an entirely voluntary exercise.

The initiative taken by the PFII to come up with an alternative means of monitoring indigenous peoples' rights, laudable though it is, may not be sufficient to address what is a growing concern about the difficulties of applying the articles of the Declaration in practice more than 10 years after its adoption by the General Assembly.

Technical issues

When the draft declaration emerged from the Working Group on Indigenous Populations in 1993 to make its way to the Human Rights Commission, as it was known at that time, the Sub-Commission on the Prevention of Discrimination and Protection of Minorities requested a technical review.[19] A review was subsequently prepared by the secretariat setting out the principles, articles and other references that substantiated the provisions of the draft declaration as well as drawing attention to duplication, possible omissions and structural aspects.[20] The review was appreciated but otherwise ignored by states as the draft declaration moved to the responsibility of the Commission on Human Rights and states. In the course of the 11-year negotiations of the draft under the aegis of the Commission (and finally the Human Rights Council), there were occasional recommendations from a few states and indigenous peoples to undertake a further technical review but no action was ever taken.

As the discussions on the draft progressed and agreements in principle on articles settled, there was reluctance particularly from the Chairperson of the sessions to identify technical issues that might re-open questions about articles that had been tenuously approved. On the indigenous side, the politics from the start had been to insist that the draft declaration approved by the Working Group on Indigenous Populations serve as the basis for negotiations.[21] Hence the rather convoluted title of the annual sessions of the Commission's open-ended inter-sessional working group officially known as the 'working group established in accordance with Commission on Human Rights resolution

1995/32 of 3 March 1995'. This formulation was used to avoid the tricky debate about indigenous peoples/indigenous people which for many years divided the participants, with certain states (the USA in particular) seeking a formulation excluding indigenous peoples with its implications regarding a right of self-determination. These factors combined meant that some technical issues remained unresolved.

What are these issues and do they matter? In certain cases, probably not. For example, it always seemed at odds with practice to place the article on equality of male and female indigenous individuals at the end of the document instead of with the general human rights provisions at the beginning of the Declaration, almost as an afterthought.[22] Elsewhere there are points where the Declaration appears to present different options as in the articles 18 and 19 requiring states to consult with indigenous peoples. Article 18 speaks of indigenous peoples' right to participate in decision-making in matters which would affect their rights. Article 19, in a much stronger formulation, calls upon states 'to consult and cooperate in good faith with the indigenous peoples concerned through their own representative institutions in order to obtain their free, prior and informed consent before adopting and implementing legislative or administrative measures that may affect them'.

The articles dealing with cultural heritage are located in different parts of the declaration (articles 11, 12, 31 and 34) and would perhaps be better placed together so that all the rights associated with culture can be understood as a coherent whole. There is also duplication or rather different formulations of similar ideas. Article 11 states: 'Indigenous peoples have the right to practise and revitalize their cultural traditions and customs'. Article 12 formulates this idea as following: 'Indigenous peoples have the right to manifest, practise, develop and teach their spiritual and religious traditions, customs and ceremonies'. Article 31 begins: 'Indigenous peoples have the right to maintain, control, protect and develop their cultural heritage, traditional knowledge and traditional cultural expressions … '

These points are perhaps niggling and do not detract from the enormous effort of negotiation by states and indigenous delegations, the political compromises that were necessary, and an end result which is largely satisfactory to all parties. Even if ideally the Declaration could be better structured and enjoy some editing to avoid repetition, the essential rights are present. Or are they?

Gaps

Here it is useful to recall the decision taken by indigenous peoples following the adoption of the draft declaration by the Working Group on Indigenous Populations and the Sub-Commission. This was to argue with states that they should not begin a new process of drafting from scratch but to use the draft declaration adopted by UN experts as the basis for discussions and to the extent possible maintain its principal provisions intact. In practice, for some years indigenous peoples argued in favour of a 'no change' policy, fighting off each governmental proposal as it was made.[23] Some states including in particular the Nordic states were broadly able to accept the draft submitted by experts but others, particularly the Asian countries and the so-called CANZUS group (Australia, Canada, New Zealand and USA), were vehemently opposed and had plenty of alternative texts in their pockets to propose. However, even if states could not accept the language of the articles as they stood, they remained within the confines of the 1993 text never proposing wholescale re-drafting of sections. In the end, indigenous peoples' rigidity in defending the 1993 text of the draft declaration as a basis of discussions paid off. The present Declaration remains in many ways the same shape as it was in 1993 and includes most of its key provisions, although often substantially amended over the period of negotiation.

But 1993 is not 2018, the time of writing. In 1993, indigenous peoples' issues were only just emerging on the international agenda. In 1992, the UN Conference on Environment and Development included a chapter on indigenous peoples – the first time a world conference incorporated a substantive section of its final document on indigenous peoples.[24] The following year, the UN instituted the International Year of the World's Indigenous People and in June of that same year a series of far-reaching recommendations on indigenous peoples were made at the World Conference on Human Rights. Thenceforward, indigenous peoples became increasingly engaged in the wider UN processes and the UN itself increasingly initiated activities relevant to indigenous peoples.

In the course of the next decade, indigenous peoples became engaged in many other standard-setting or policy discussions in the UN system. Since the Convention on Biological Diversity, adopted in 1992, contained articles singling out the role of indigenous peoples in protecting and ensuring that they benefit from biodiversity, indigenous delegations pushed for and acquired a space where they could contribute to and monitor the Convention.[25] The achievements for indigenous peoples within the CBD are not reflected in the UNDRIP. Biodiversity as such is not mentioned nor is benefit sharing. The only article dealing with the environment (article 29) is extraordinarily limited, calling on states to protect the environment of indigenous peoples' lands and setting out restrictions for the storing of hazardous materials. The role of indigenous peoples as owners, managers or trustees of critical environmental spaces is not recognised nor, as research is increasingly demonstrating, that they can be more reliable and effective than governments and, therefore, ought to be supported in this role.[26]

The right to the protection of indigenous peoples' traditional knowledge is covered in UNDRIP specifically in article 31. But to what extent might that formulation be modified and expanded in the light of more than 10 years of discussions at WIPO's Intergovernmental Committee on Intellectual Property and Genetic Resources, Traditional Knowledge and Folklore, itself mandated to elaborate a convention? In 2003 UNESCO adopted the Convention for the Safeguarding of the Intangible Cultural Heritage which also sets out to safeguard intangible cultural heritage including traditional knowledge and practices about nature and the universe.[27] There were no indigenous delegations during the discussions of the Convention as was the case in other UN standard-setting activities possibly accounting for an absence of any reference to indigenous peoples in the operative part of the document. Notwithstanding this important text contains recommendations to states, in particular articles 14 on education and capacity-building and article 15 on participation, which are not reflected in texts of the UNDRIP but surely have relevance.[28]

An issue that is specifically unmentioned in the UNDRIP is climate change and the very direct and critical impacts it has on indigenous peoples, especially those in ecologically sensitive living spaces. The magnitude of this global challenge is now well understood but less recognised is how the impacts and the present mitigation policies fall disproportionally on indigenous peoples and are largely negative. The need for full involvement of indigenous peoples in policy-making and the contribution indigenous knowledge and practices can make to international efforts to combat climate change are not reflected in UNDRIP. The Framework Convention on Climate Change was adopted at the time of the 1992 Rio Environment Conference and since then extensive scientific evidence and subsequent commitments by states, most recently though the 2015 Paris Agreement, have recognised the contribution that can be made by indigenous peoples. The Agreement calls on states to base their adaption action on, *inter alia*, 'traditional knowledge, knowledge of indigenous peoples and local knowledge systems'. [29]

The relationship of indigenous peoples to the extractive industries and other invasive kinds of development by non-state actors on indigenous peoples' lands is not touched on in the Declaration though it is the source of the most violent confrontations. While the UNDRIP is the responsibility of states to recognise and implement, it is increasingly important that companies that seek to explore and exploit the resources on indigenous peoples' territories have a clear understanding of their obligations. This is not made explicit in the UNDRIP as it stands. Article 32, for example, requires states to consult with indigenous peoples in order to obtain 'their free and informed consent prior to the approval of any project affecting their lands or territories and other resources, particularly in connection with the development, utilization or exploitation of mineral, water or other resources'. No mention is made of private sector entities and their obligations to comply with the provisions of UNDRIP, a deficiency that in practice leaves many companies unclear about their responsibilities towards indigenous peoples.[30]

Article 32, which particularly refers to free, prior, and informed consent has, as noted earlier, a built-in ambiguity. As states are required to consult to obtain the consent of the affected indigenous peoples, it does leave unanswered what happens if that consent is not granted or indeed is only provided by a part of the community. As states seek to apply this principal in practice, they have opted for a right to be consulted. Peru, for example, in its legislation and regulations regarding FPIC, using ILO Convention 169 as its base, has adopted a law on prior consultation.[31] The Law sets out a process formulated in large part in line with article 32 but with the final decision left in the hands of the state. Its article 15 states that 'the final decision on approval of a legislative or administrative measure belongs to the competent state entity'.[32] Similar outcomes can be found in the legislation in Colombia and in Bolivia's latest Mining Law.[33]

It is probably true to say that indigenous peoples do not understand the Declaration in the same way as these governments. In that they are interestingly joined by some of the development banks notably the International Finance Corporation (IFC) and the European Bank of Reconstruction and Development (EBRD). Performance standard (PS) 7 of the IFC, in its article 12 requires the borrower to provide 'evidence of agreement between the parties as the outcome of the negotiations'. In accordance with PS 7, if the borrower cannot provide clear proof that the community is favourable to the project, financial support cannot be given.[34] The EBRD standard is similarly explicit in requiring their clients 'to obtain the free, prior and informed consent of indigenous peoples before starting with an activity'.[35] Given the experiences both positive and negative of indigenous peoples and private sector activities on their lands, clearer principles and guidance can surely be elaborated. Certainly in the case of the private sector, as in the above-mentioned standards, there should be no ambiguity about the need to obtain the consent of indigenous peoples thereby bringing the UNDRIP up to the higher and less ambiguous formulation contained in these documents.

The world conference on indigenous peoples laid particular stress on the importance of integrating indigenous peoples into the Sustainable Development Goals (2015–30). This was inspired by the general criticism by indigenous peoples that the MDGs had largely ignored indigenous peoples and better and more targeted programmes were needed to address their development needs in the next round of development goals. Several articles in UNDRIP address economic and social rights stressing both the self-determination elements (the rights of indigenous peoples to run their own health, welfare or educational programmes) and the right to existing services without discrimination. Article 14, for example, articulates this by recognising indigenous peoples' rights to education at all levels without discrimination and their right to establish their own educational establishments. What is less well recognised in the UNDRIP is the right of indigenous peoples to benefit from national and international development programmes based on indigenous peoples' own development priorities.

Article 32 of UNDRIP recognises the right of Indigenous peoples 'to determine and develop priorities and strategies for the development or use of their lands or territories and other resources'. The contents of an indigenous development priority is not further expanded upon. However, over the last years indigenous peoples have been challenging not only the fact that they are often excluded from national and international development policy but also questioning the very model of development that is being proposed and implemented. This is expressed through the ideas around the rubric of development with culture and identity.[36] They include the notion that indigenous development takes account of the specificities of distinct cultures, ensures a harmonious relationship with nature and focuses on community well-being rather than economic growth.[37]

A new political project

The present article is not meant to disparage the enormous achievement of the UNDRIP which includes elements, for example recognising the rights of indigenous peoples to self-determination and to land and resource rights, that were ardently resisted by states in the early 1980s. It argues instead that the Declaration provides minimum standards that can and should be enhanced in the light of developments over the last 20 years. It maintains that the drafting of a convention is the preferred means of doing so. This is a standard operating procedure for the UN's human rights work. It is not something far-fetched. Human rights are there to be implemented by states. They should not remain voluntary and aspirational. In that prescient document, the Martinez Cobo report of 1983, the drafting of a declaration was deemed the basis for a future convention and not an end in itself.[38]

Furthermore, indigenous peoples' participation, diversity and experience are markedly different from the 1980s and 1990s. Indigenous peoples are office holders in the UN's institutions with experience as members of high-level advisory bodies, Special Rapporteurs and experts. The new generation of indigenous delegate represents a far wider geo-cultural network than before. It was only from 1993 that indigenous delegates began to participate from Africa and from a large number of Asian states. These delegations are armed with more than 20 years of negotiating experience at international meetings and an increasingly supportive international, regional and national jurisprudence on indigenous peoples' rights to hand.[39] They are infinitely better prepared than the generation that were learning their way through the UN monolith of the 1980s and 1990s. States also come to the table with far greater experience of indigenous peoples' issues as well as some positive and practical national legislation that reflects the provisions of UNDRIP.[40] There is no reason to believe that a number of states would not coalesce around a progressive binding human rights instrument on indigenous peoples, if encouraged to do so by their indigenous constituents.

The final word must be about the UN as an institution. It is an organisation that easily settles into routine and ritual. The advisory bodies established on indigenous issues – the EMRIP and PFII – have to be wary of falling into this trap. There is a need for a new and invigorating political project to re-assert indigenous peoples' rights and serve as a rallying point for a new generation of indigenous peoples and those who support their right to exist, flourish and shape the future.

Notes

1. Certain states recognise that some of the core rights of the UNDRIP are binding since they reflect existing human rights law but only one state, Bolivia, has formally integrated the Declaration into its legal framework.
2. There is an argument that UNDRIP's being binding is a distraction as it is its legitimacy that will determine implementation whether binding as a matter of formal law or not (comment by Dr Claire Charters). See also Luis Rodriguez-Pinero Royo, '"Where Appropriate": Monitoring/Implementing of Indigenous Peoples' Rights Under the Declaration', in *Making the Declaration Work*, eds. C. Charters and R. Stavenhagen (Copenhagen: IWGIA, 2009).
3. The American Declaration on the Rights of Indigenous Peoples was adopted by the Organization of American States on 15 June 2016. It is available at https://www.oas.org/en/sare/documents/DecAmIND.pdf. In the case of Colombia, there are several occasions where the state exempts itself from articles. This is notable in the case of article XXIX (4) covering consultation and consent. See footnote 4 to the Declaration.
4. See, for example, the arguments put forward by the Special Rapporteur James Anaya in his report to the Human Rights Council (A/HRC/9/9) especially paras. 40–1.
5. This appears implicit in the report of the Expert Mechanism on the Rights of Indigenous Peoples on 'Ten Years of Implementation of the UN Declaration on the Rights of indigenous Peoples: good practices and lessons learned', A/HRC/36/56, paras 9 and 10. For example, in paragraph 10 of the report it is stated that ' … many of the rights contained in the Declaration are already guaranteed by major international human rights instruments and have been given significant normative strength, including through the work of the treaty bodies, regional and national courts.'
6. See ILO ratification of conventions available at http://www.ilo.org/dyn/normlex/en/f?p=NORMLEXPUB:11300:0::NO:11300:P11300_INSTRUMENT_ID:312314:NO. Luxembourg has signed the Convention but it will not enter into force until June 2019.
7. See paragraph 33 of the Outcome document of the high-level plenary meeting of the General Assembly known as the World Conference on Indigenous Peoples, A/69/L.1. See also General Assembly resolution A/C.3/70/L.26/Rev.1, paragraph 19.
8. See, for example, the compilation of comments regarding the participation of indigenous peoples in Annex 1 to General Assembly report A/70/990, paragraph 2.
9. Author's observations.
10. An extreme manifestation of President Duterte efforts to delegitimize human rights defenders was the inclusion of the Special Rapporteur Victoria Tauli-Corpuz on a list of terrorist

suspects. See The Guardian: https://www.theguardian.com/world/2018/mar/09/philippines-lists-un-special-rapporteur-on-terrorist-hit-list-rodrigo-duterte.

11. Global Witness, 'Defenders of the Earth: Global Killings of Land and Environment Defenders in 2016'. See also https://www.globalwitness.org/en/blog/new-data-reveals-197-land-and-environmental-defenders-murdered-2017/.
12. For example, in 2017 President Temer's government proposed freezing indigenous land demarcations thereby stopping work on some 700 land claims. See World Resources Institute, 'Land Ruling Threatens Brazil's Indigenous Peoples and Climate Commitments', http://www.wri.org/blog/2017/09/opinion-land-ruling-threatens-brazils-indigenous-peoples-and-its-climate-commitments.
13. In 2011 indigenous peoples living in the TIPNIS national Park protested against the building of a highway through their territory. This led to violent confrontations with the government of Evo Morales. TIPNIS (Isiboro Secure National Park and Indigenous Territory) is in the lowlands region of the country and is home to over 12,000 indigenous people. The 2014 Ley de Mineria y Metalurgia, No.535, articles 207–216 considerably weaken indigenous communities faced with mining activities on their lands, including by criminalising opposition to mining operations and applying penalties for illegal occupation of mine sites. Article 208, for example, referring to the UNDRIP explicitly states that indigenous peoples have no right of veto – 'no otorgan a los sujetos de la consulta previa el derecho a veto a la ejecución de las actividades de la explotación minera'. (Author's translation: 'does not authorize the beneficiaries of prior consultation the right of veto with regard to the implementation of mining exploitation activities').
14. Although the Human Rights Council's Universal Periodic Review is being effectively used by some indigenous delegations it does not constitute either a public space for denunciations of human rights abuses or a monitoring mechanism.
15. Expert Group Meeting, 'Dialogue on an Optional Protocol to the United Nations Declaration on the Rights of Indigenous Peoples', January 28–29, 2015.
16. Expert Group Meeting on an optional protocol to the United Nations Declaration on the Rights of Indigenous Peoples, January 27–29, 2015, paper submitted by James Anaya, PFII/2015/EGM.
17. Ibid, paper submitted by Suhas Chakma, PFII, 2015/EGM.
18. HRC resolution 33/25 of 30 September 2016.
19. Technical reviews are generally undertaken by the secretariat of the United Nations with a view to ensuring conformity with existing norms and instruments, and in terms of language, style and structure. They also provide an opportunity for a neutral body to identify areas of duplication or omission.
20. E/CN.4/Sub.2/1994/2/Add.1.
21. The mandate reads:

    > By resolution 1995/32 of 3 March 1995, the Commission on Human Rights decided to establish an open-ended inter-sessional working group of the Commission on Human Rights with the sole purpose of elaborating a draft declaration, considering the draft contained in the annex to resolution 1994/45 of 26 August 1994 of the Sub-Commission on Prevention of Discrimination and Protection of Minorities (now the Sub-Commission on the Promotion and Protection of Human Rights) entitled "Draft United Nations declaration on the rights of indigenous peoples" for consideration and adoption by the General Assembly within the International Decade of the World's Indigenous People.

22. Article 44 reads: 'All the rights and freedoms recognized herein are equally guaranteed to male and female indigenous individuals.' For an interesting feminist critique of the Declaration see Raunna Kuokkanen, 'Indigenous Women's Rights in International Law: Challenges of the UN Declaration on the Rights of Indigenous Peoples', in *Handbook of indigenous peoples rights*, eds. C. Lennox and D. Short (Routledge, 2016), 129–45.

23. Author's observation. The no change position was a central negotiating strategy agreed upon in the indigenous caucuses that prepared a single indigenous position for the plenary meetings.
24. Conference on Environment and Development, Rio de Janeiro, June 1992, Agenda 21, Chapter 26 and World Conference on Human Rights, Vienna, June 1993.
25. Ad-hoc open-ended working group on article 8 (j) and related articles. For further information on indigenous peoples' participation see https://www.cbd.int/traditional/participation.shtml.
26. 'Toward a Global Baseline of Carbon Storage in Collective Lands', Rights and Resources, November 2016. 'Tropical forest carbon in indigenous territories: a global analysis', a report prepared for UNFCCC COP21, December 2015, by Alianza de Mezoamericana de Pueblos y Bosques and others. et al., December 2015. See also Paola Totaro, 'Indigenous peoples best custodians of threatened forests', Reuters Foundation at https://www.reuters.com/article/us-forests-landrights-conference-idUSKBN16S2QA.
27. Article 2 of the Convention for the Safeguarding of the Intangible Cultural Heritage.
28. Article 14, for example, states:

    Each State Party shall endeavour, by all appropriate means, to: (a) ensure recognition of, respect for, and enhancement of the intangible cultural heritage in society, in particular through: (i) educational, awareness-raising and information programmes, aimed at the general public, in particular young people; (ii) specific educational and training programmes within the communities and groups concerned; (iii) capacity-building activities for the safeguarding of the intangible cultural heritage, in particular management and scientific research; and (iv)non-formal means of transmitting knowledge.

    Article 15 invites states to '… endeavour to ensure the widest possible participation of communities, groups and, where appropriate, individuals that create, maintain and transmit such heritage, and to involve them actively in its management.'
29. Paris Agreement, Article 7, para 5.
30. The United Nations Guiding Principles on Business and Human Rights provides a voluntary framework for businesses.
31. Ley del Derecho a la Consulta Previa a los Pueblos Indigenas u Originarios, reconocido en el Convenio 169 de la Organizacion Internacional del Trabajo (OIT).
32. Ibid, article 15.
33. See note 6.
34. International Finance Corporation, Performance Standard, para. 12. The same paragraph notes that consent may be considered granted even if some individuals or groups may not agree. In practice, many development banks apply the IFC Performance Standards as conditions of lending.
35. European Bank for Reconstruction and Development, Performance Requirement 7 on indigenous peoples, May 2014, para 29.
36. See for example the report of the EGM on indigenous peoples: development with culture and development, January 2010, E/C.19/2010/14
37. The concept of 'buen vivir' as a fundamental objective of the state has been incorporated into the Constitutions of Ecuador and Bolivia.
38. E/CN.4/Sub.2/1983/21/Add.8 paras 627–8.
39. The American Declaration on the Rights of Indigenous Peoples includes issues that were not taken up by the UNDRIP, such as the rights of indigenous peoples in voluntary isolation. The Inter-American Court of Human Rights and the African Commission and Court on Human and Peoples Rights have adopted decisions that greatly advance understanding of indigenous peoples' rights.
40. Bolivia, for example, has incorporated the UNDRIP into its legislation.

Disclosure statement

No potential conflict of interest was reported by the author.

The UNDRIP and the legal significance of the right of indigenous peoples to self-determination: a human rights approach with a multidimensional perspective

Dorothée Cambou

ABSTRACT

Ten years have passed since the adoption of the UN Declaration on the Rights of Indigenous Peoples (UNDRIP) and the recognition of the right of indigenous peoples to self-determination. The declaration provides the first universal instrument to recognise and elaborate on the content of the right to self-determination for indigenous peoples. Yet, the adoption of the declaration has not solved all controversies and the implementation of the right to self-determination remains a contentious issue in practice. In this regard, the purpose of this article is to describe and analyse the legal significance of the right of indigenous peoples to self-determination as enshrined in the UNDRIP. Since the declaration emphasises the principle of territorial integrity of sovereign states, this analysis essentially focuses on the examination of what it means to claim self-determination beyond any claims for independence. In this analysis, the study argues that self-determination is based on a democratic model of self-determination that is grounded in human rights law and which calls both for the autonomy and the participation of indigenous peoples in decision-making processes that affect them. This model of self-determination is also multidimensional is so far as it includes a political, a resource and external dimensions. Ultimately, this study evidences that beyond the question of its implementation, the UNDRIP opens the pathway to significantly bolster the democratic understanding of self-determination in a manner that contributes to developing modern international law on the question of self-determination and strengten the human rights of indigenous peoples.

1. Introduction

In 2007, the UN general Assembly adopted the landmark UN Declaration on the Rights of Indigenous Peoples (UNDRIP).[1] This declaration recognises the right of indigenous peoples to self-determination, by virtue of which they can freely determine their political status and freely pursue their economic, social and cultural development. The significance of this document for indigenous peoples and, more broadly, for the development of human rights cannot be underestimated. In effect, the declaration provides the first universal instrument to recognise and elaborate the content of the right to self-determination for indigenous peoples. It is also the first instrument to recognise the right of self-determination for peoples other than peoples territorially organised as states and colonies. Considering the contentious nature of recognising the right of self-determination for a segment of the population of a particular state, the recognition of the right of indigenous peoples to self-determination therefore constitutes a remarkable innovation under international law.

Yet, the adoption of the declaration has not solved all controversies and the implementation of the right to self-determination remains a contentious issue in practice. Ten years after the adoption of UNDRIP, there is still a lack of understanding as to what is really meant by the right of indigenous peoples to self-determination. For indigenous peoples, self-determination implies their right to control their own destiny and to maintain their distinct identity and livelihoods. This also includes their right to manage their traditional land and natural resources. Concurrently, many states remain suspicious of recognising the right of indigenous peoples to self-determination. In particular, they fear that the recognition of self-determination will jeopardise the political unity and territorial integrity of the state as well as challenge its sovereignty over natural resources, even though indigenous claims do not necessarily imply the need for sovereign statehood. In this regard, the question arises as to how the UNDRIP manages and accommodates these conflicting and paradoxical positions.

To answer this question, this study takes a human rights approach to the development of the law of self-determination and a multidimensional conceptual perspective to describe the content of the right in relation to indigenous peoples. From a doctrinal standpoint, this approach is linked to the development of self-determination as a basis for democratic governance,[2] but also goes beyond that in so far as it does not confine self-determination within the political governance of sovereign states. In this regard, this study challenges to some extent the internal/external dichotomy, as it has been well posited by Casesse,[3] instead supporting a relational and human rights perspective, as posited by Young or Anaya in their writing.[4] On this basis, the objective of this study is therefore also to explain the significance of indigenous self-determination consistently with human rights law while questioning the limits of the orthodox interpretation of self-determination under international law.

For the purpose of this analysis, the argument is divided into two main parts. The first section focuses on recognition of the right of indigenous peoples to self-determination and situates the right within the contemporary development of international law on self-determination. Then, the second section examines the content of the right of indigenous peoples to self-determination while taking a multidimensional conceptual perspective to explain the significance of the right and examine more particularly its political, resource and external dimensions.

2. The right of indigenous peoples to self-determination: a human rights approach

In 2007, the UN General Assembly adopted the UNDRIP by a significant margin of 143 states being in favour of the declaration, 12 abstentions and four negative votes. Under Article 3, the declaration unambiguously stipulates that indigenous peoples, treated as a group of peoples rather than individual citizens, have the collective right to exercise the right to self-determination. While Article 3 does not stipulate any limitation for its exercise, the right of indigenous peoples to self-determination is however not absolute. According to Article 46 of the declaration, self-determination should be exercised in respect to the territorial integrity or political unity of sovereign and independent states. Thus, the UNDRIP does not recognise the right of indigenous peoples to create new states, thereby dissociating the right of indigenous peoples from an end-state approach, as asserted during the decolonisation period.

Yet, the UNDRIP should not be interpreted as preventing indigenous peoples' claim to secession. According to Scheinin and Åhren, such an approach would otherwise be discriminatory.[5] In their own words: 'why should Indigenous peoples, populations and groups not be entitled to pursue a quest for secession or far reaching autonomy within the state when this avenue is open to other peoples, communities and groups?'[6] Although it is questionable whether any peoples are entitled to secession under international law,[7] it is indeed arguable that in the absence of further developments at the international level on this topic, it would be problematic to prevent all indigenous peoples from claiming the right to secession. Furthermore, it must also be stressed that indigenous peoples, who fall under the scope of international law on decolonisation, are still entitled to claim independence. This is, for instance, the case of self-governing territories such as Greenland or New Caledonia. However, it must equally be emphasised that the right to self-determination by indigenous peoples is not necessarily fulfilled by decolonisation of the broader territory in which they live alongside others.[8] Self-determination has many aspects beyond statehood and the formal independent status of any territory.[9] In this regard, for the purpose of the UNDRIP the relevance of the right of indigenous peoples to self-determination, while not preventing indigenous peoples' claim for statehood, is situated elsewhere.

Pursuant to the drafting process and the provisions of the UNDRIP, the right of indigenous peoples to self-determination is grounded in human rights law. In accordance with Article 1 of the UN Human Rights Covenants, which equally proclaims the right of all peoples to self-determination, the right of indigenous peoples to self-determination is also more specifically connected with the regime of human rights law on self-determination. In fact, with the adoption of Article 1 of the UN Covenants, it became increasingly clear that self-determination was not only a right for colonised peoples, but also a right belonging to 'all peoples'. In this context, the Human Rights Committee (HRC), charged with providing authoritative interpretations of the norms contained in the International Covenant on Civil and Political Rights (ICCPR), has interpreted Article 1 as the right of peoples to choose the form of their constitution or government.[10] Contrary to the colonial variant of self-determination, this latter form of self-determination must be exercised within the confines of existing states. International doctrine has labelled this interpretation of the right as 'internal self-determination'.[11] However, one caveat with respect to internal self-determination lies in its focus on individual rights and the fact that it was originally not intended to give rights at the level of only some groups residing in one state. Accordingly, the right for indigenous peoples contrasts with the post-colonial approach of self-determination in so far as it recognises and protects the collective identity of indigenous peoples as a polity, as opposed to merely protecting the right of indigenous peoples as individual citizens.

Yet, the rights of indigenous peoples remain closely intertwined with the human rights corpus on self-determination. More simply, as explained by Quane, the right of indigenous peoples to self-determination goes beyond the minimalist concept of internal self-determination, which has been expanded to include an internal right for a group living within a particular state.[12] In other words, it is possible to interpret the right of indigenous peoples to self-determination 'as a development of the existing right to internal self-determination, one that can help make it more responsive to the needs and interests of indigenous groups'.[13] As such, the right of indigenous peoples serves to complement and substantiate the right of 'all' peoples to self-determination as proclaimed under Article 1 of the UN Human Rights Covenants. This is also the position argued by Anaya, former special rapporteur on the rights of indigenous peoples, who explained in a similar respect that the UNDRIP 'recognizes that indigenous peoples have the same right of self-determination enjoyed by other peoples .... premised on the conception of a universal right of self-determination and, on that premise, it affirms the extension of that universal right to indigenous peoples'.[14] From this perspective, the right of indigenous peoples to self-determination therefore constitutes a novelty under international law, but this novelty remains grounded within the contemporary regime of human rights law concerning the right of self-determination.

Although such an understanding of self-determination does not provide the right for indigenous peoples to 'full' self-determination in the traditional sense of the term, it does have several important merits. First, it is in line with indigenous peoples' claims, who 'themselves have almost uniformly denied aspirations to independent statehood in demanding self-determination'.[15] Second, it is also in compliance with the negotiation process surrounding the adoption of the declaration, during which time the human rights model of self-determination detracted from the decolonisation model and the historic sovereignty arguments of indigenous peoples as a basis for self-determination.[16] Such a conceptualisation of self-determination, introduced by Anaya and supported by Asian, African and Southern American delegations, does not limit self-determination to a state-end approach; rather, it is premised on the right of appeal to the universal right of equality between peoples.[17] Finally, this approach is not only consistent with internal self-determination, as enshrined under Article 1 of the UN Human Rights Covenants, but has also been endorsed by human right bodies when they recognised the application of Article 1 of the UN Covenants to the situation of indigenous peoples.[18]

Arguably, this conception of self-determination also provides a fuller right of self-determination than could be achieved through independent statehood. As explained by Anaya,

> such a notion, that full self-determination necessarily means a right to choose independent statehood, ultimately rests on a narrow state-centered vision of humanity and the world, ... (which) is blind to the contemporary realities of (...) a world in which the formal boundaries of statehood do not altogether determine the ordering of communities and authority.[19]

Hence, while such an interpretation of the right of indigenous peoples to self-determination challenges to some extent traditional typologies, it also constitutes a valuable enlargement of the human right norm, one that is more concordant with the contemporary social realities of indigenous peoples and society at large.

3. A multidimensional model of self-determination

While the right of indigenous peoples to self-determination should be understood consistently with the right to self-determination as enshrined under human rights law, its implementation nevertheless requires important transformations, even for the governance of democratic states. Those transformations are multidimensional. They include changes that are linked with the political, resource and external dimensions of the right to self-determination. The following analysis examines each of these dimensions and explores the relationship between the right of indigenous peoples to self-determination and the human rights corpus of self-determination.

3.1. The political dimension of the right of indigenous peoples to self-determination

In accordance with the UNDRIP, the political aspect of the right of indigenous peoples to self-determination is based on two main pillars: the right of indigenous peoples to autonomy and the right to participate in the decision-making process of the state. This interpretation stems from Articles 4 and 5 of the UNDRIP, which respectively state:

> Indigenous peoples, in exercising their right to self-determination, have the right to autonomy or self-government in matters relating to their internal and local affairs, as well as ways and means for financing their autonomous functions.
>
> Indigenous peoples have the right to maintain and strengthen their distinct political, legal, economic, social and cultural institutions, while retaining their right to participate fully, if they so choose, in the political, economic, social and cultural life of the State.

From this perspective, the right of indigenous peoples to self-determination is based on a dual aspect: 'on the one hand, autonomous governance and, on the other, participatory engagement'.[20] As further explained by Anaya, this dual aspect reflects the position that indigenous peoples are distinct units but yet joined with and connected to larger political and social structures, such as the state and the global community itself.[21] Accordingly, the right to self-determination first entails the obligation for states to recognise indigenous representative institutions.[22] In this respect, Article 31 of the UNDRIP indicates that indigenous peoples should be free to establish their own institution, to determine, maintain and develop their structures in accordance with their own procedure and in compliance with human rights law.[23] However, as underlined by the former Rapporteur, Erica Daes,

> [t]he true test of self-determination is not whether Indigenous Peoples have their own institutions of self-determination, legislative authorities, laws, police, or judges. The true test of self-determination is whether Indigenous peoples themselves actually feel that they have choices about their way of life.[24]

In accordance with Article 4 of the UNDRIP, the right of indigenous peoples to self-determination requires that indigenous peoples autonomously govern their own internal and local affairs. In this regard, Wheatley also explains that autonomy in political affairs implies 'the exercise of government functions by state institutions under the control of indigenous peoples'.[25] This is also in accordance with the view of Scheinin and Åhren, who indicate that the right of indigenous peoples to self-determination 'requires a transfer of jurisdiction from state to political bodies to indigenous peoples' representative institutions'.[26] In effect, this position is significant because it 'shifts decision making power in some instances from the states to the indigenous peoples', providing therefore public authority in some areas to indigenous representative institutions.[27] In this regard, Scheinin and Åhren are also right to underline that self-determination 'must conceptually go beyond that of the right to consultation', [28] though consultation is still an elemental aspect of indigenous self-determination.[29]

In practice, the tension in implementing indigenous self-determination lies in the defining of indigenous prerogatives and in the balancing of rights and duties between states and indigenous institutions, especially regarding the scope of indigenous self-government. Although the UNDRIP leaves a wide margin of interpretation as to the scope of the right to autonomy, it is generally agreed that 'the content of indigenous affairs is broad and should not be restricted to cultural affairs only'.[30] According to the *travaux preparatoires* of the UNDRIP, it also includes 'culture, religion, education, information, media, health, housing, employment, social welfare, economic activities, land and resources management, environment and entry by non-members, as well as ways and means for financing these autonomous functions'.[31] While the absence of consensus about the content of autonomy has prevented the adoption of a strict definition during the drafting process of the declaration, the absence of such a definition also provides a degree of flexibility, which guarantees that 'the right can be adjusted to the particular circumstances of each case'.[32] There is indeed no one-size fits all model of autonomy for indigenous peoples, with each people requiring its own governance structure designed in accordance with its own needs and interests. However, Scheinin and Åhren are correct to underline that 'in the absence of clearer instructions, there are fairly few signs of such jurisdiction having been transferred from states to indigenous peoples during the more than ten years that have passed since the adoption of the UNDRIP', [33] and this in spite of the fact that the status of the principle of autonomy is widely 'confirmed by state practice and by the evidence of the requisite opinio juris'.[34]

Besides the right to autonomy in internal and local matters, indigenous peoples also have the right to participate as a collective unit in the decision-making process affecting them. From this perspective, it means that while indigenous peoples have complete autonomy in some instances, in other cases they also have the right to full participation.[35] As explained by Wheatley, beyond the sphere of self-governance arrangements, the right to self-determination finds 'expression in the participation and/or consultation in the rule-making of the State', which guarantees indigenous peoples the 'ability to influence the law- and decision-making processes'.[36] This understanding is grounded in a relational model of self-determination, which takes into account the interdependence of peoples and the embeddedness of their relationships rather than their supposed independence from one another.[37] This model 'emphasizes the importance of self-government and the need for modes of shared decision making capable of governing the complex interdependence characteristic of state-indigenous relationships today'.[38] In effect, this conceptualisation is also exemplified in several provisions of the UNDRIP, such as Article 18, which states that 'indigenous peoples have the right to participate in decision-making in matters which would affect their rights, through representatives chosen by themselves'. It is additionally supported by Article 19, which stipulates the duty of the state to consult and cooperate with indigenous peoples based on the principle of Free, Prior and Informed Consent (FPIC). Hence, whereas the right of indigenous peoples to self-determination goes beyond consultation, a lack of adequate consultation undoubtedly undermines the ability of indigenous peoples to exercise their right to self-determination.

While such an approach to self-determination approach is in compliance with the view that indigenous peoples are distinct but connected polities, this interpretation also stands in contrast with the original interpretation of the right of participation, which has traditionally been considered as an individual right of each citizen. This position was reflected in the Miqmak case, when the HRC concluded in 1991 that Article 25 of the Covenant could 'not be understood as meaning that any directly affected group (of indigenous peoples), large or small, has the unconditional right to choose the modalities of participation in the conduct of public affairs'.[39] In this regard, the HRC did not provide any specification about the right of indigenous peoples to participation or self-government, leaving the process or modalities of participation entirely to the discretion of the state parties.[40] As rightly argued by Quane, the formulation of the UNDRIP provisions are therefore 'generally groundbreaking' because they suggest that 'new structures or modalities of participation are required by virtue of international human rights standards, rather than as is the current position being dependent on the discretion of the State concerned'.[41]

Although the UNDRIP does not impose any particular procedure to ensure the collective participation of indigenous peoples, it puts the obligation on the respective state to guarantee that this right is effectively guaranteed. In this regard, Wheathey is correct to indicate that for participation to be substantially effective, indigenous peoples must have 'the capacity to influence the outcomes of decision-making processes'.[42] In this regard, the right of indigenous peoples to self-determination goes against a minimalist and instrumentalist conception of the duty to consult, but is concordant with a human rights approach to consultation, one which provides the 'means of building trust that can lead to agreed-upon outcomes for the implementation of projects that are both beneficial to indigenous peoples and to the society at large'.[43]Thus, beyond mere autonomy, the right to self-determination for indigenous peoples also requires states to consult and include them as equal political entities in the governance process affecting them.

3.2. The resource dimension of the right of indigenous peoples to self-determination

Besides the political dimension, the right of indigenous peoples to self-determination also includes a resource component that lies in the rights of indigenous peoples to freely dispose of their natural wealth and resources. However, the definition of this dimension of self-determination remains controversial. Traditionally, the rights to control land and natural resources has been interpreted under international law as an aspect of the principle of permanent sovereignty over natural resources (PSNR).[44] In this respect, states have often opposed the recognition of indigenous rights to land and natural resources out of fear that those rights could impair their sovereignty over such lands and natural resources. By contrast, indigenous peoples have continuously emphasised the fact that land and natural resources' rights were crucial elements of their right to self-determination.

In the light of this controversy, Erica Daes was appointed by the Economic and Social Council during the drafting process of the UNDRIP to conduct a 'study on indigenous peoples' permanent sovereignty over natural resources'.[45] Based on the comments made by governments and on the data received from indigenous representatives and NGOs, the rapporteur argues that the principle of PSNR applies to indigenous peoples, short of economic independence. In her words, PSNR for indigenous peoples 'does not mean the supreme authority of an independent State', and 'use of the term in relation to indigenous peoples does not place them on the same level as States or place them in conflict with State sovereignty'.[46] Instead, what PSNR for indigenous peoples involves is 'governmental control and authority over the resources in the exercise of self-determination'.[47] It is 'a collective right by virtue of which States are obligated to respect, protect, and promote the governmental and property interests of indigenous peoples (as collectivities) in their natural resources'.[48] Hence, with respect to indigenous peoples, Daes argues that PSNR does not confer upon them absolute sovereignty over their traditional land and resources, but nevertheless implies their right to exercise self-determination in relation with their traditional lands and resources.[49]

From this standpoint, it is therefore more adequate to speak about the right of indigenous peoples to self-determination over their lands and resources rather than their right to PSNR. Such an approach is also in better compliance with the shift of emphasis from a decolonisation approach to a human rights approach to the right of self-determination, which occurred during the adoption process of the UNDRIP.[50] It is also supported by the HRC, which has confirmed in several concluding observations the application of Article 1.2 to the situation of indigenous peoples.[51] However, such a position is also novel under international law. Never before has a piece of human rights law required a state to recognise the distinct interests of one segment of its population. Traditionally, the right to economic self-determination had been recognised as a right of non-self-governing territories and, more recently, as a right of the population of the state to freely dispose of its natural wealth and resources.[52] Even the intra-state application of the right did not concern the differential application of the rights to one particular segment of the population. As a result, the assertion of the right of indigenous peoples to self-determination over their natural resources not only expands the reach of the democratic understanding of self-determination beyond its political realm. It also challenges the orthodox understanding of economic self-determination by providing specific entitlement for indigenous peoples over their lands and resources within the state in which they live.

Although the rights of indigenous peoples remain contested and the UNDRIP does not wholly clarify relevant international law, the legal implications of the resource dimension of the right of indigenous peoples to self-determination are outlined to some extent under several provisions. At the outset, the right of indigenous peoples to govern and manage land and resources necessarily includes the right to control their traditional land and resources as a basis for maintaining and developing their livelihoods. As underscored by Wheatley, 'indeed, control over traditional lands is the key feature of indigenous peoples' autonomy, conceived as an element of self-determination'.[53] Accordingly, Article 26 of the UNDRIP indicates that indigenous peoples' rights to land and resources include the right of indigenous peoples 'to own, use, develop and control the lands, territories and resources that they possess by reason of traditional ownership or other traditional occupation' and the correlative duty for the state to recognise and protect these lands, territories and resources.[54] Although some ambiguity remains as to the content of these rights, the adoption of the declaration has been instrumental in confirming that states must take action in recognising indigenous rights to land and resources at the domestic level. Furthermore, since the adoption of the declaration, an increasing body of human rights law has underlined the duty of states concerning the rights of indigenous peoples to land, while stressing the obligation of governments to demarcate indigenous lands,[55] to recognise their systems of land tenure,[56] or to 'strengthen legislative and administrative measures in order to guarantee the rights of indigenous peoples to their land and to freely dispose of their natural wealth and resources'.[57] As already mentioned, several recommendations have also emphasised the rights of indigenous peoples to lands and resources under the scope of the right to self-determination, as enshrined under Article 1 of the Human rights Covenants.[58] Hence, this development not only expands and clarifies the content of indigenous peoples' rights to land and natural resources, but also confirms that indigenous peoples have the rights to land and natural resources consistent with the human right of self-determination.

Given the important jurisdictional interdependences in the governance of indigenous lands and natural resources, the right of indigenous peoples to manage their lands and natural resources also entails their right to participate in decision-making processes affecting them, which extends their authority beyond self-government arrangements. From the participatory lens, the resource aspect of the right of indigenous peoples to self-determination includes more specifically the right of indigenous peoples to participate in the development of the resources located in their territories, including subsoil resources such as oil and gas. This interpretation is derived from Article 32 of the UNDRIP, which stipulates in the following, often quoted, paragraph:

> indigenous peoples have the right to determine and develop priorities and strategies for the development or use of their lands or territories and other resources and that states have the duty to consult and cooperate in good faith with the indigenous peoples concerned (...) in order to obtain their free and informed consent prior to the approval of any project affecting their lands or territories and other resources.

The principle of FPIC, which is at the heart of Article 32, is also a cornerstone of the resource aspect of the right of indigenous peoples to self-determination. FPIC implies that it is not sufficient for the state to consult with indigenous peoples when a decision will affect their traditional territories. In addition, the principle requires that states fully engage with the concerned indigenous communities with the requirement to seek consent. Although the implementation of FPIC is still a controversial issue under international law, there is a growing corpus of decisions demonstrating the importance of the principle for the protection of indigenous peoples' rights to land and resources. An important number of recommendations on state reports by the HRC and CESR have, for instance, emphasised that states should 'ensure that prior consultations are held with a view to obtaining their free, prior and informed consent regarding decisions that affect them',[59] and that the free, prior and informed consent of the indigenous peoples concerned should be obtained before granting licences to private companies. Additionally, the Expert Mechanism on the Rights of Indigenous Peoples has also stressed the importance of FPIC for the exercise of the right of indigenous peoples to self-determination, while at the same time emphasising that

> States should also recognise that the right to self-determination of indigenous peoples constitutes a duty for States to obtain indigenous peoples' free, prior and informed consent, not

merely to be involved in decision-making processes, but a right to determine their outcomes.[60]

Thus, the regimes of consultation based on FPIC underlie an instrumental principle to operationalise self-determination in the context of developing traditional indigenous lands and territories.[61] This approach is based on a relational model of self-determination where 'regimes of consultation play a crucial role in ensuring that indigenous peoples are provided with a meaningful opportunity to influence, and in some case to veto government policies that impact their rights and interests'.[62]

Although the role of FPIC and the duty to obtain consent remains disputed, it is increasingly agreed that projects significantly jeopardising indigenous livelihoods require their approval. For instance, actual consent, as opposed to consultation, is required by the UNDRIP in the case of relocation (Art. 10) as well as storage and disposal of hazardous materials on indigenous lands (Art. 29). In similar respects, both the HRC and the Inter-American Court of Human Rights have indicated that consultation is not sufficient in cases of large-scale development projects undertaken on traditional indigenous lands and territories that significantly affect their livelihoods.[63] Instead, FPIC is also required prior to initiating such projects, which indicates that the principle includes a qualified right to veto.[64] As such, the human rights application of FPIC utilises a 'sliding scale approach to participatory rights', one which recognises that the 'level of effective participation is essentially a function of the nature and content of the rights and activities in question'.[65] This also means that the degree of participation of indigenous peoples and their right to object to a particular project will vary in accordance with the impact of the measure on their rights. The ramifications of FPIC are significant for the development of international law. This is especially the case since the application of the principle conflicts with 'the ideas of democracy and political equality of citizens', which emphasise 'that no individual or group within the society should be provided with a veto over legislation with majority support'.[66] By contrast, the principle of FPIC corroborates the idea that the exercise of the right of indigenous peoples to self-determination requires the collective protection of their distinct livelihoods, even when it is in conflict with the societal interests supported by the rest of the population. Hence, the application of FPIC supports a pluralist conception of democratic governance that finds application with the exercise of the right of indigenous peoples to self-determination without challenging the sovereignty of independent states.

3.3. The international dimension of the right of indigenous peoples to self-determination

The livelihoods of indigenous peoples are not inescapably confined to the territories of sovereign states. In this regard, it appears logical to include an external or international dimension to the right of indigenous peoples to self-determination.[67] However, as far as this dimension of self-determination is concerned, it does not necessarily entail the right to secession for indigenous peoples. Instead, what this dimension of self-determination includes is the right of indigenous peoples to protect their collective integrity while participating in and influencing development processes in accordance with their own viewpoints. Given overlapping interests among indigenous and other communities and 'the extension of political power and political activities across the boundaries of the modern-states',[68] self-determination need not only apply within the state, but should be extended to other governance spheres of society as well.[69] As also eloquently explained by Anaya,

> any model of self-determination that does not take into account the larger context of multiple patterns of human association and interdependency is at best incomplete (and is more likely distorted) ... appropriately understood, therefore, self-determination concerns human beings in regard to the constitution and functioning of all levels and forms of government under which they live.[70]

This approach is also grounded in a relational model of self-determination that speaks both about local autonomy and the need to govern the complex interdependent relationship between indigenous peoples and non-indigenous groups at the national, transnational and international levels.[71] Furthermore, this understanding is also in agreement with the principle of global democracy, 'where the demos is not limited to a conception of a people resident in a given territory (although it applies there) but pertains to all institutional contexts of decision-making'.[72] Thus, from this perspective self-determination is not a mere appendage of territorial sovereignty, but benefits individuals and groups in regard to all forms of governance processes under which they live.

From a legal standpoint, the right to self-determination in its international dimension is still incompletely enshrined under current international legal instruments. Nevertheless, several provisions of the UNDRIP allude to this dimension in relation to the rights of indigenous peoples. Article 36, for instance, stipulates that indigenous peoples, in particular those divided by international borders, have the right to maintain and develop contacts, relations and cooperation (...) with their own members as well as other peoples across borders. As explained by Wheatley, this provision is 'aimed at avoiding the deleterious consequences that the establishment of State boundaries has on the life of indigenous people belonging to the same cultural community that are divided by international borders'.[73] In this regard, States are required to facilitate the contacts between indigenous peoples across borders through recognising their right to maintain and develop cross-border contacts with other peoples. An example of the application of such rights is the institutional arrangement developed by the Sami people across the borders of Finland, Norway, Russia and Sweden.[74] Despite the borders that separate them, the Sami people are involved in different institutional arrangements, more specifically the Sami Parliamentary Council, which allows for their transnational institutional representation.[75] Although these arrangements are still far from making self-determination concrete for the Sami as a transnational people, this experience epitomises the idea of a model of self-determination exercised through autonomous representation, with the possible transfer of jurisdiction of public authority in some domains from states to indigenous peoples at the transnational level.[76]

Besides, the rights of indigenous peoples also includes an international participatory aspect that provides them with the right to representation and participation in decision-making processes at the international level. As indicated by Murphy, while local autonomy is the most obvious route to indigenous empowerment, 'indigenous representatives may also need an effective ... voice in select transnational institutions such as United Nations forums'.[77]Although the right is not clearly stated by the UNDRIP, it is nonetheless supported by several provisions in the declaration. For example, Article 18 states that indigenous peoples have the right to participate in decision-making in matters which would affect their rights. An expansive interpretation of this provision provides a basis for applying the right of indigenous peoples to participate not only at the state level, but also at the international level, in governance process affecting them. This interpretation, which is in fact supported by the *travaux préparatoires of the UNDRIP*,[78] is also concordant with Article 41 of the declaration, which enjoins the organs and specialised agencies of the United Nations to establish ways and means for ensuring the participation of indigenous peoples on issues affecting them. In effect, the latter provision has given rise to the development of a UN inquiry about the means to enable indigenous peoples' effective participation in relevant meetings of United Nations bodies on issues affecting them through their representative institutions.[79] In 2017, the UN general Assembly adopted a draft resolution proposing participation and modalities arrangements for the participation of indigenous representatives that would allow for their engagement in decision-making processes, without challenging the primacy of the states in the conduct of international affairs at the UN level.[80] While discussions on the issue are still ongoing, this development is certainly noteworthy in so far as it supports the idea that indigenous peoples have the right to distinct representation and effective participation in the international decision-making processes affecting them. On that account, even though this right remains in practice inadequately recognised and implemented, as indicated by Special Rapporteur Claire Charters, 'it appears to be a clear consensus that Indigenous peoples have the right to participation at the UN level, consistently with the right to self-determination'.[81]

4. Conclusion

The UNDRIP is a remarkable international legal instrument actualising a universal framework of minimum standards for the survival, dignity, well-being and rights of the world's indigenous peoples. One of the most important aspects of the declaration is the recognition of the right of indigenous peoples to self-determination. With the adoption of the UNDRIP, this analysis demonstrates that international law has taken a new step in the re-conceptualisation of self-determination. Although this development could have serious ramifications well beyond the case of indigenous peoples, the declaration nonetheless limits the recognition of self-determination to indigenous peoples in so far as it does not recognise their right to independent statehood. In this regard, the rights of indigenous peoples to self-determination, as enshrined under the UNDRIP, must be implemented in accordance with the principle of territorial integrity and political unity of sovereign states. However, this fact alone should not eclipse the true relevance of the UNDRIP. In contrast with an orthodox understanding of self-determination, this analysis also argues that the significance of the UNDRIP lies beyond the question of self-determination exercised in its sovereign form. This understanding, which is in compliance with most indigenous claims that do not foresee the need for sovereign statehood to exercise full self-determination, is based on a human rights approach to the right to self-determination.

From a human rights perspective, the right to self-determination is embedded in democratic governance. However, because the principle of democratic governance based on the equality of citizens does not support the collective right of indigenous peoples, this analysis has also provided evidence of the fact that the right of indigenous peoples to self-determination challenges to some extent the traditional conceptualisation of 'internal self-determination' by requiring changes in order to protect the distinct identity of indigenous peoples. For this purpose, the UNDRIP contributes to forging a more substantive democratic conception of self-determination where diverse collective units with different identities can equally participate in the governing institutions under which they live. In this regard, the UNDRIP, while going beyond standards that have been ascertained under human rights law, still relies on them to inform an interpretation of the democratic understanding of self-determination. Hence, the right of indigenous peoples to self-determination represents a novelty under international law, but at the same time remains a constitutive part of the human rights corpus of law that underlies the right for all peoples to self-determination.

Ten years after the adoption of the declaration, and the reaffirmed support for the instrument, limited progress has nevertheless been evident with respect to the implementation of self-determination.[82] This lack of progress does not, however, undermine the legal significance of the UNDRIP, which establishes a solid basis for implementing the necessary changes.[83] As described in this analysis, the changes required by the recognition of indigenous self-determination in accordance with the UNDRIP are multidimensional. At the outset, indigenous self-determination requires recognition of the distinct political identity of indigenous peoples and their right to control their local and internal affairs. However, the right to self-determination is not merely an instrument for indigenous peoples to maintain their distinct identity and livelihoods. From a human rights perspective, self-determination also implies their equal participation as a separate collective unit in the decision-making processes that affect them to allow their self-determined development. Accordingly, indigenous peoples have the right to govern their own affairs at the local level while retaining their right to participate in the decision-making processes that affect them. Although the UNDRIP leaves a wide margin of appreciation as to how to operationalise this right in practice, the declaration ultimately requires that states adopt new modalities for allowing indigenous peoples to control their internal and local affairs and to effectively participate in the governance processes that affect them.

Additionally, this study argues that the right of indigenous peoples to self-determination goes beyond political rights and includes a resource dimension. This dimension of the right of indigenous peoples to self-determination requires both the recognition of the rights of indigenous people to govern their land and resources at the local level and the duty of the state to consult with indigenous representatives in order to obtain their FPIC before undertaking development projects that may affect them. In this context, this study also puts emphasis on the principle of FPIC, which requires the right for indigenous peoples to be able to effectively influence the outcome of decision-making processes affecting them, as opposed to merely being consulted. Whereas the implication of the principle remains contested, the importance of FPIC is primordial for the exercise of self-determination in so far as it provides indigenous peoples with the possibility to determine how their land and resources are developed. Although the principle does not provide an absolute veto right to indigenous peoples, FPIC provides a contextual framework of negotiation to ascertain indigenous needs and interests on par with those of the rest of society, also granting them a right to oppose development projects in cases where such projects would have a significant impact on their rights.

Finally, the present analysis also suggests that the exercise of the right of indigenous peoples to self-determination is not confined to state borders. Given the interdependency of indigenous peoples' livelihoods with transnational and global events, the right of indigenous peoples to self-determination must also apply at the international and transnational levels. With respect to the principle of territorial integrity, the application of the right to self-determination in this context does not necessarily entail independent statehood. Rather, self-determination requires the ability for indigenous peoples to establish and develop their influence in decision-making processes affecting them across and beyond states boundaries. Although this interpretation of the right to indigenous self-determination permeates and challenges the traditional internal/external conception of the right, it is nevertheless more in tune with contemporary developments and the global arrangements of society, which transcend states boundaries. Furthermore, this interpretation remains rooted in a democratic understanding of self-determination to the extent that it does not seek to challenge the primacy of democratic states in the conduct of state affairs, but purports instead to ascertain a more diverse and inclusive governance of society. Thus, although much progress still needs to occur in order to actualise such a model of self-determination, this approach to self-determination is novel but consistent with the modern development of international law. Currently, it is therefore wherein lies the legal significance of the right of indigenous peoples to self-determination as enshrined by the UNDRIP, as a right capable of fostering democratic unity, but through diversity.

Notes

1. UN General Assembly, Resolution 61/295. United Nations Declaration on the Rights of Indigenous Peoples (hereinafter, the UNDRIP), 2007.
2. Thomas M. Franck, 'The Emerging Right to Democratic Governance', *American Journal of International Law* 86, no. 1 (1992): 46–91.
3. Antonio Cassese, *Self-Determination of Peoples: A Legal Reappraisal* (Cambridge: Cambridge University Press, 1995).
4. See, in particular, Iris Marion Young, 'Two Concepts of Self-Determination', in *Ethnicity, Nationalism, and Minority Rights*, ed. Stephen May, Tariq Modood, and Judith Squires (Cambridge: Cambridge University Press, 2004); James Anaya, 'The Right of Indigenous Peoples to Self-Determination in the Post-Declaration Era', in *Making the Declaration Work: The United Nations Declaration on the Rights of Indigenous Peoples*, ed. Claire Charters and Rodolfo Stavenhagen (Copenhagen: IWGIA, 2009), 184–99.
5. Martin Scheinin and Mattias Åhren, 'Relationship to Human Rights, and Related International Instruments', in *The UN Declaration on the Rights of Indigenous Peoples: A Commentary*, ed. Jessie Hohmann, Marc Weller, Oxford Commentaries on International Law (Oxford, New York: Oxford University Press, 2017), 72.
6. Scheinin and Åhren, 'Relationship to Human Rights, and Related International Instruments', 72.
7. On the doctrine of remedial session, see, e.g. Lee C. Buchheit, *Secession: The Legitimacy of Self-Determination*, 2nd ed. (New Haven, Conn: Yale University Press, 1978). See also the icj Kosovo Case, Accordance with International Law of the Unilateral Declaration of Independence in Respect of Kosovo, Advisory Opinion, i.c.j. Reports 2010, para. 82 and Reference Re secession of Quebec, 2 scr 217, 1998, Supreme Court of Canada, para. 134.
8. See, e.g. Report of the Special Rapporteur on the rights of indigenous and peoples, James Anaya, 'The Situation of Kanak People in New Caledonia, France UN Doc.A/HRC/18/35/Add.6', 2011, para. 14–7.

9. Report of the Special Rapporteur on the rights of indigenous and peoples, James Anaya, para.16.
10. See HRC, General Comment No. 25: Article 25 UN Doc. CCPR/C/21/Rev.1/Add.7, 1996, para 2.
11. See for instance Cassese, *Self-Determination of Peoples*; Allan Rosas, 'Internal Self-Determination', in *Modern Law of Self-Determination Modern Law of Self-Determination*, ed. Christian Tomuschat (Dordrecht: Marinus Nijhoff Publishers, 1993), 225–52.
12. Helen Quane, 'The UN Declaration on the Rights of Indigenous Peoples: New Directions for Self-Determination and Participatory Rights?', in *Reflections on the UN Declaration on the Rights of Indigenous Peoples*, ed. Stephen Allen and Alexandra Xanthaki (Oxford: Hart Publishing, 2011), 262.
13. Quane, 'The UN Declaration on the Rights of Indigenous Peoples', 262.
14. Anaya, 'The Right of Indigenous Peoples to Self-Determination in the Post-Declaration Era', 185.
15. Ibid.
16. Andrew K. Erueti, 'The Politics of International Indigenous Rights', *University of Toronto Law Journal* 67, no. 4 (2017): 584.
17. Erueti, 'The Politics of International Indigenous Rights', 583.
18. See, e.g. HRC, Concluding Observation: Norway, UN Doc CCPR/C/79/Add/112 (1999), para. 10; Concluding Observation: Canada, UN Doc. CCPR/C/103/Add.5 (1999).
19. James Anaya, 'A Contemporary Definition of the International Norm of Self-Determination', *Transnational Law & Contemporary Problems* 31 (1993): 143.
20. Anaya, 'The Right of Indigenous Peoples to Self-Determination in the Post-Declaration Era', 193.
21. Ibid.
22. UNDRIP, Articles 33, 34, 35.
23. UNDRIP, Articles 33–4.
24. Erica-Irene A. Daes, 'Striving for Self-Determination for Indigenous Peoples', in *First International Conference on the Right to Self-Determination & the United States*, ed. Y.N. Kly and D. Kly (Geneva, 2001), 58.
25. Steven Wheatley in International Law Association, 'The Hague Conference (2010) Rights of Indigenous Peoples, Interim Report' (London: International Law Association, 2010), 13.
26. Scheinin and Åhren, 'Relationship to Human Rights, and Related International Instruments', 67.
27. Ibid.
28. Ibid.
29. See, e.g. Michael A. Murphy, 'Representing Indigenous Self-Determination', *The University of Toronto Law Journal* 58, no. 2 (2008): 200.
30. Daes, 'Striving for Self-Determination for Indigenous Peoples', 58.
31. Draft Declaration on the Rights of Indigenous Peoples, UN Doc. E/CN.4/2005/WG.15/2 (2005), article 31.
32. Natalia Loukacheva, 'On Autonomy and Law', *Working Paper Series, Institute on Globalization and the Human Condition* 5, no. 3 (2005): 3.
33. Scheinin and Åhren, 'Relationship to Human Rights, and Related International Instruments', 67.
34. International Law Association, 'The Hague Conference (2010) Rights of Indigenous Peoples, Interim Report', 16.
35. See also Scheinin and Åhren, 'Relationship to Human Rights, and Related International Instruments', 67.
36. International Law Association, 'The Hague Conference (2010) Rights of Indigenous Peoples, Interim Report', 12.
37. Iris Marion Young, *Global Challenges: War, Self Determination and Responsibility for Justice* (Cambridge: Polity, 2007), 50–1.
38. Murphy, 'Representing Indigenous Self-Determination', 185.

39. HRC, Marshall et al. v. Canada Communication No. 205/19864, UN Doc CCPR/C/43/D/205/1986, (1991), para. 5.5.
40. Ibid., para.5.4.
41. Quane, 'The UN Declaration on the Rights of Indigenous Peoples', 273.
42. International Law Association, 'The Hague Conference (2010) Rights of Indigenous Peoples, Interim Report', 14.
43. James Anaya and Sergio Puig, 'Mitigating State Sovereignty: The Duty to Consult with Indigenous Peoples', *University of Toronto Law Journal* 67, no. 4 (2017): 462.
44. For a general overview, see Nico Schrijver, *Sovereignty over Natural Resources: Balancing Rights and Duties* (Cambridge: Cambridge University Press, 1997).
45. Daes, 'Indigenous Peoples' Permanent Sovereignty over Natural Resources', UN Doc. E/CN.4/Sub.2/2004/30 (2004).
46. Ibid., para 18.
47. Ibid.
48. Ibid., para 40.
49. UNDRIP, Article 26.
50. Erueti, 'The Politics of International Indigenous Rights'.
51. HRC, Concluding Observation: Canada, UN Doc. CCPR/C/79/Add.105 (1999), para.8; Concluding Observation: Australia, UN Doc. A/55/40, vol. I (2000), para. 506- 507; Concluding Observation: Sweden, UN Doc. CCPR/CO/74/SWE (2002), para.15; Concluding Observation: Mexico, UN Doc. CCPR/C/MEX/CO/5 (2010), para. 22;
52. Alice Farmer, 'Towards a Meaningful Rebirth of Economic Self-Determination: Human Rights Realization in Resource-Rich Countries', *New York University Journal of International Law and Politics New York University Journal of International Law and Politics* 39, no. 2 (2006): 417–73; Emeka Duruigbo, 'Permanent Sovereignty and Peoples' Ownership of Natural Resources in International Law', *George Washington International Law Review* 38, no. 1 (2006): 33–100.
53. International Law Association, 'The Hague Conference (2010) Rights of Indigenous Peoples, Interim Report', 13.
54. UNDRIP, Article 26.
55. HRC, UN Doc. CCPR/C/VEN/CO/4 (2015).
56. CESR, UN Doc E/C.12/GUY/CO/2-4 (2015).
57. CESR, UN Doc E/C.12/AGO/CO/4-5 (2016).
58. See HRC supra note 51 and CESCR, Concluding Observation: Finland, UN Doc. E/C.12/FIN/CO/6 (2014), para.9 (a); CESCR, Concluding Observation: Paraguay, UN Doc. E/C.12/PRY/CO/4 (2015), para.6.
59. HRC, UN Doc CCPR/C/THA/CO/2 (2017).
60. EMRIP, 'Final Study on Indigenous Peoples and the Right to Participate in Decision Making', para. 21–2.
61. Jérémie Gilbert, 'The Right to Freely Dispose of Natural Resources: Utopia or Forgotten Right?', *Netherlands Quarterly of Human Rights* 31, no. 3 (2013): 328.
62. Murphy, 'Representing Indigenous Self-Determination', 200.
63. HRC, Poma Poma v. Peru, Communication 1457/2006 of 27 March 2009, UN Doc. CCPR/C/95/D/1457/2006 (2009), para. 7.6; Inter-American Court of Human rights, Saramaka People v. Suriname, Judgment of 28 November 2007, IACtHR Series C, No. 172, para.134.
64. Ibid.
65. G. Pentassuglia, *Minority Groups and Judicial Discourse in International Law: A Comparative Perspective* (Leiden: Martinus Nijhoff Publishers, 2009), 113. + Barelli FPIC p 14
66. International Law Association, 'The Hague Conference (2010) Rights of Indigenous Peoples, Interim Report', 14.
67. For a general overview, see Dorothée Cambou, 'Enhancing the Participation of Indigenous Peoples at the Intergovernmental Level to Strengthen Self-Determination: Lessons from the Arctic', *Nordic Journal of International Law*, no. 87 (2018): 1–30.

68. David Goldblatt et al., *Global Transformations: Politics, Economics, Culture*, 1st ed. (Cambridge: Polity Press, 1999), 49.
69. Goldblatt et al., *Global Transformations*, 212.
70. Anaya, 'A Contemporary Definition of the International Norm of Self-Determination', 143.
71. Young, 'Two Concepts of Self-Determination'; Murphy, 'Representing Indigenous Self-Determination'.
72. Carol C. Gould, *Interactive Democracy: The Social Roots of Global Justice* (Cambridge University Press, 2014), 232.
73. International Law Association, 'The Hague Conference (2010) Rights of Indigenous Peoples, Interim Report', 15.
74. Cambou, 'Enhancing the Participation of Indigenous Peoples at the Intergovernmental Level to Strengthen Self-Determination'.
75. Ibid., 21–8.
76. See 2005 Draft Nordic Sami Convention, Article 20.
77. Murphy, 'Representing Indigenous Self-Determination', 200.
78. Originally, the draft UNDRIP stipulated that 'indigenous peoples have the right to participate fully, if they so choose, at all levels of decision-making in matters which may affect their rights'. Draft Declaration on the Rights of Indigenous Peoples, UN Doc. e/cn.4/Sub.2/1994/2/ Add.1 (1994), Article 19.
79. Draft Resolution by the General Assembly on enabling the participation of indigenous peoples 'representative institutions in meetings of relevant United Nations bodies on issues affecting them (2017), https://www.un.org/development/desa/indigenouspeoples/wp-content/uploads/sites/19/2016/02/CLEAN-FINAL-ZERO-DRAFT-21-APRIL-2017-RESOLUTION-ON-IP-PARTICIPATION.pdf (accessed September 1, 2018).
80. Ibid., para. OP6.
81. Claire Charters, speaking at UN General Assembly, Informal consultations, 71st Session, UN Web TV, 14 December 2016.
82. UN Doc. A/72/186, para 86.
83. Ibid., para 25.

Disclosure statement

No potential conflict of interest was reported by the author.

ORCID

Dorothée Cambou http://orcid.org/0000-0003-2772-0641

Implementation of the UNDRIP around the world: achievements and future perspectives. The outcome of the work of the ILA Committee on the Implementation of the Rights of Indigenous Peoples

Federico Lenzerini

ABSTRACT

The ILA Committee on the Implementation of the Rights of Indigenous Peoples has the purpose of ascertaining the level of implementation of the main legal standards enshrined in the UNDRIP. The Committee's work has so far been based on case studies assessing the degree of implementation of international legal rules concerning the rights of indigenous peoples in specific countries or regions of the world. At the time of this writing, the partial results of the work of the Committee evidence a global reality in the context of which the existence and binding character in principle of international legal standards concerning the rights of indigenous peoples are generally accepted and recognised by States, especially at the level of the legislature and the judiciary. On the other hand, however, in many countries the effective degree of practical implementation and effective realisation of the rights of indigenous peoples is still rather unsatisfactory. This is a crucial aspect, as the phase of implementation is decisive in order to ensure effectiveness of human rights – including indigenous peoples' rights. It is therefore imperative that the level of effective implementation of the international legal standards concerning indigenous peoples' rights is increased in many areas of the world.

1. Introduction

The ILA Committee on the Implementation of the Rights of Indigenous Peoples is composed by over thirty academic experts and activists in the field of indigenous peoples' rights, coming from all regions of the world.[1] The Committee began its activity in 2013 and, so far, its work has been based on case studies developed with the purpose of assessing the level of implementation of international legal rules concerning the rights of indigenous peoples – especially those enshrined in the 2007 *United nations Declaration on the Rights of Indigenous Peoples* (UNDRIP) – in specific countries or regions of the world. At the moment, about 20 studies have been completed and about other 25 are ongoing, covering all different areas of the globe.[2] At least an equivalent number of other case-studies is planned to be completed before the expiration of the Committee's mandate in 2020.

The Committee was conceived to guarantee continuity with the work of a previous ILA Committee, operating from 2006 to 2012, i.e. the Committee on the Rights of Indigenous Peoples. At least in the intentions, the relationship between the two committees is to be seen in terms not only of continuity, but also of complementarity. In fact, while the previous Committee had the task of defining the existing international legal standards on indigenous peoples' rights, as developed after the adoption of the UNDRIP and subsequent practice, the mission of the Committee on the Implementation of the Rights of Indigenous Peoples is to ascertain whether and to which extent those standards are actually implemented and realised in the real world, i.e. within the territories where indigenous peoples live. It follows that the basis of reference of the work of the Committee on the Implementation of the Rights of Indigenous Peoples is represented by the conclusions drawn by the Committee on the Rights of Indigenous Peoples at the end of its activity.

The said conclusions are summarised in ILA Resolution No. 5/2012.[3] The most significant (and, during some of the meetings held by the Committee throughout the years of its existence, also the most controversial) aspect of this resolution is probably represented by the fact that it recognises the existence of certain indigenous peoples' rights under *customary international law*. This conclusion was the result of a very meticulous research on relevant State practice and *opinio juris* at both international and national level. The accuracy of such a research was authoritatively 'certified' by an ICSID Arbitral Tribunal, which in 2011 noted that 'a recent study by a committee of several international law experts assembled under the auspices of the International Law Association, after an exhaustive survey of relevant state and international practice, found a wide range of customary international law norms concerning indigenous peoples'.[4] Quite obviously, the Committee did not conclude that *all* rights provided for by the UNDRIP have now risen to the status of rules of customary international law. On the contrary, only a very few of them – which are the most fundamental and indispensable to preserve the cultural identity and physical integrity of indigenous communities – may be considered as having reached the said status. These rules – limiting our assessment to the rights of *collective* character – are the right of indigenous peoples to self-determination, their right to autonomy or self-government, their rights to their traditional lands, territories and resources, as well as their right to reparation and redress for wrongs they have suffered.[5]

2. Epistemology of the rights of indigenous peoples under customary international law

As just mentioned, in the context of the work of the ILA Committee on the Rights of Indigenous Peoples the validity of the argument supporting the existence of rules of customary international law guaranteeing the said indigenous peoples' rights was the object of a lengthy and controversial discussion, mostly based on the question whether pertinent State practice and *opinio juris* were sufficient to support such an argument. In this respect, main resistances were based on the circumstance that breaches – even blatant violations – of the rights in point take place in many countries on a daily basis. According to some scholars (including some members of the Committee on the Rights of Indigenous

Peoples), the existence of such violations would preclude that the said rules of customary international law would actually come into existence.

In reality, it is well known that, for a rule of customary international law to exist, a uniform practice is not necessary. As emphasised by the International Court of Justice in the case of *Military and Paramilitary Activities in and against Nicaragua* – considered as a prominent authority in the field,

> [i]t is not to be expected that in the practice of States the application of [a] rule [of customary international law] [must be] perfect, in the sense that States [refrain], with complete consistency, from [applying derogations to the rule concerned] [...] [F]or a rule to be established as customary, the corresponding practice must [not] be in absolute rigorous conformity with the rule. In order to deduce the existence of customary rules, [...] it [is] sufficient that the conduct of States should, in general, be consistent with such rules, and that instances of State conduct inconsistent with a given rule *should generally have been treated as breaches of that rule* [...] If a State acts in a way *prima facie* incompatible with a recognized rule, but defends its conduct by appealing to *exceptions* or *justifications* [...], then whether or not the State's conduct is in fact justifiable on that basis, the significance of that attitude is to confirm rather than to weaken the rule.[6]

In other words, it is not necessary to have an undeviating practice for a rule of customary international law to exist. In some circumstances, it seems that the discussion concerning the existence of indigenous peoples' rights under customary international law is based on a sort of epistemological misunderstanding, as this issue is sometimes seen as a black or white exercise. The reluctance to recognise the existence of such rights under customary international is indeed determined by the inaccurate belief that their recognition would imply an obligation for States to ensure the realisation of the rights in point *in all circumstances* – with no exception possible – irrespective of the implications, of whatever kind, arising from their operation. This would mean that all other values, even those which are fundamental for the national society of the State concerned, should be *always* and *peremptorily* sacrificed in the altar of indigenous peoples' rights. Obviously, this is not the real consequence arising from the affirmation of the fundamental rights of indigenous peoples as rules of customary international law.

In this respect, the reference to 'exceptions or justifications' in the *Nicaragua Case* is particularly significant. Affirming that a rule has attained the status of customary international law does not mean that it encumbers States with a peremptory burden to always and fully comply with such a rule, with no exception or derogation possible. This kind of dynamics would only exist with regard to the very limited circle of rules of *jus cogens*. Obligations imposed by 'ordinary' rules of customary international law, differently, may be the object of derogation as well as of comparative evaluation with other legal rules protecting goods or values of equivalent or higher importance. In this respect, the operation consisting in determining which, among two or more conflicting goods or values, is to be considered as prevailing in a concrete situation – as well as the similar operation of drawing a balance between them, when possible – is to be carried out on a case-by-case basis.

This approach is supported, among others – with specific regard to indigenous peoples' land rights – by the Inter-American Court of Human Rights (IACtHR), in the well-known case of the *Yakye Axa Indigenous Community v. Paraguay*.[7] The Court, in particular, in assessing the problem of the possible conflict between indigenous peoples' collective land rights and other competing property rights over the same lands, did not conclude that the former always prevail over the latter. On the contrary, the IACtHR emphasised the necessity of evaluating the specific situation on a case-by-case basis, based on the principle of proportionality, although the judges also underlined the necessity of paying due consideration to the impact that deprivation of traditional lands of indigenous peoples might have on their right to survival as organised peoples and for the reproduction of their culture, for their own development, as well as for carrying out their life aspirations. It follows that '[d]isregarding the ancestral right of the members of the indigenous communities to their territories could affect other basic rights, such as the right to cultural identity and to the very survival of the indigenous communities and their members'.[8] However, this does not necessarily mean 'that every time there is a conflict between the territorial interests of private individuals or of the State and those of the members of the indigenous communities, the latter must prevail over the former'.[9] Consistently, it may be possible that 'States are unable, for concrete and justified reasons, to adopt measures to return the traditional territory and communal resources to indigenous populations',[10] although, when this happens, the indigenous communities concerned are entitled to compensation, which 'must be guided primarily by the meaning of the land for them'.[11]

It is almost inevitable that an analysis of this kind is conditioned by the academic, social, political and ethical formation and/or inclinations of the legal operator(s) entrusted with it. When it is considered under the perspective of indigenous peoples, in most cases the ponderation of the interests at stake will result in the recognition of the rights of those peoples as prevailing over competing interests. But things may be seen under different perspectives, and it is certainly understandable that certain collective interests compelling the national society – e.g. social and economic development, fight against hunger and starvation, etc. – are considered by the national government as paramount values, which are definitely entitled to strongly compete with indigenous peoples' rights when it is not possible to simultaneously realise all interests involved in a concrete case. Ideally, the legal operator concerned should consider such interests objectively, in light of the circumstances of the specific case, and without any favour or bias – even within her/his irrational sphere – for any of them. As a consequence, even taking a sympathetic stance toward the rights of indigenous peoples (as this writer is used to do), it is not possible – and might even be unfair – to exclude a priori that in some situations such rights should leave way to competing interests which, in light of the circumstances of the specific case, deserve to be considered as predominant.

In conclusion, recognising the existence of indigenous peoples' rights under customary international law does not mean depriving governments of any kind of control over all concrete situations in which such rights are involved within their territories. On the contrary, exceptions and derogations are possible, when they are required by the circumstances of a situation in which a competing interest – also protected by law – objectively and strictly deserves to be considered as predominant in the instant case. This is exactly the approach taken by the ILA Committee on the Rights of Indigenous Peoples in considering the issue in point. Using this perspective, the work of such a Committee has disclosed the existence of an amount of State practice and *opinio juris* sufficient to support the existence of the rules of customary international law listed at the end of the previous section, i.e. the rights of indigenous peoples to self-determination, to autonomy or self-government, to their traditional lands, territories and resources, as well as to reparation and redress for wrongs they have suffered.

3. The propulsive force of the UNDRIP in advancing the rights of indigenous peoples under international law

As specified in section 1, *not* all rights contemplated by the UNDRIP can be considered as having reached the status of rules of customary international law. In addition, it is very hard to establish whether any or all of the few indigenous peoples' rights which have actually reached such a status actually rose to the rank of provisions of general international law *before* or *after* the adoption of the Declaration. In any event, it is indisputable that in the past ten years the UNDRIP and its use in the practice have performed a propulsive role – if not in determining – in crystallizing the process leading such rights to be recognised as rules of customary international law.

It is manifest that in principle the UNDRIP – as a declaration of principles – cannot in itself produce binding obligations for States. As specified by the Office of Legal Affairs of the United Nations in 1962, 'in United Nations practice, a "declaration [of principles]" is a solemn instrument resorted to only in very rare cases relating to matters of major and lasting importance where maximum compliance is expected'.[12] Even higher compliance is expected when a declaration is directly linked to the Charter of the United Nations and its text aims at giving concrete execution to one or more provisions of the latter. This is actually the case of the UNDRIP, as evidenced by its first preambular paragraph, stating that the UN General Assembly adopted the Declaration in so far it was '[g]uided by the purposes and principles of the Charter of the United Nations, and good faith in the fulfilment of the obligations assumed by States in accordance with the Charter'. The use in this sentence of the word *obligations* shows that, although the UNDRIP in itself is not binding, respect for its provisions represents an essential prerequisite to ensure compliance by States with compulsory rules established by the UN Charter. It follows that, beyond its technical characterisation, the UNDRIP is something more than a mere hortatory instrument.

Obviously, the conclusion just reached may be approved in terms of legal logics, but, for being transposed into the practical reality of international law, it necessitates that a declaration like the UNDRIP is characterised by a satisfactory degree of *effective* compliance by States, disclosing the existence of the elements of practice and *opinio juris* necessary for a rule of customary international law to exist. This is the usual process through which provisions included in declarations of principles develop into rules of customary international law, or even of *jus cogens*, as happened with some of the provisions included in the *Universal Declaration of Human Rights* of 1948. As previously explained and reiterated, such a process has actually been finalised with regard to the rules of the UNDRIP concerning self-determination, autonomy or self-government, land rights, as well as reparation and redress for wrongs suffered by indigenous peoples (although, again, it is hard to establish the extent to which the UNDRIP has contributed to the accomplishment of the said process, as other documents and legal developments have also played a role in this respect[13]). However, during the first ten years from its adoption, the role played by the UNDRIP has not been limited to contributing to the formation and/or crystallization of those few rules as principles of customary international law. Indeed, it has also been generally acknowledged as the instrument of reference to define State obligations existing in the field of indigenous peoples' rights, if not worldwide certainly very extensively. In addition to the fact that the UNDRIP is explicitly mentioned in the text of important international treaties concluded after its adoption,[14] this is clearly shown by the use made of the Declaration by international human rights monitoring bodies, as well as by domestic courts and other State organs.

For example, according to the UN Committee on Economic, Social and Cultural Rights, 'all indigenous peoples [...] have the right to the full enjoyment, as a collective or as individuals, of all human rights and fundamental freedoms as recognized in the [...] United Nations Declaration on the Rights of Indigenous Peoples'.[15] To a similar extent, the UN Committee on the Rights of the Child considers the UNDRIP as 'important guidance on the rights of indigenous peoples, including specific reference to the rights of indigenous children in a number of areas',[16] urging States parties to the 1989 *Convention on the Rights of the Child*[17] (i.e. all countries of the world, with the only exception of the United States of America)[18] 'to adopt a rights-based approach to indigenous children based on the Convention and other relevant international standards, such as [...] the United Nations Declaration on the Rights of Indigenous Peoples'.[19]

At the regional level, the evolutionary jurisprudence of the IACtHR in the field of indigenous peoples' rights is well known. In the context of this jurisprudence, the Court has extensively referred to the UNDRIP, the provisions of which are considered among 'the relevant international standards'[20] defining the rights of indigenous peoples to be respected by Latin American States, apparently at the same level of ILO Convention No. 169,[21] even for the countries which have ratified the latter. Since 2007, the IACtHR has referred to the UNDRIP in delineating the rights of indigenous peoples translating into obligations of States towards them, including, among others, the right to development and use of lands, territories and resources (Articles 29 and 32 UNDRIP),[22] the right to participate in decisions regarding measures affecting them (Articles 18, 19, 30(2), 32(2) and 38 UNDRIP),[23] the right to cultural identity (Articles 3, 4, 5,18, 19, 20, 23, 32, 33 and 34 UNDRIP),[24] the right not to be subjected to any form of discrimination (Preamble, fifth paragraph, and Articles 2 and 15 UNDRIP),[25] the right to reparation and redress,[26] as well as, obviously, land rights (Articles 25 and 26 UNDRIP).[27]

Still in Latin America, in 2015 the Caribbean Court of Justice (CCJ), ruling on land rights of the Maya community in Belize, found that '[i]t is beyond dispute that international law recognizes and protects the rights of indigenous peoples',[28] and, expressly referring to the UNDRIP, stressed that, while it is not binding in itself, it is 'relevant to the interpretation of the Constitution of Belize which in its preamble explicitly recognizes that state policies must protect the culture and identity of its indigenous peoples but also must promote respect for international law and treaty obligations'.[29]

An equivalent approach is followed by African human rights institutions. In particular, the African Commission on Human and Peoples' Rights has recognised the authority of UNDRIP in defining the legal nature of indigenous peoples' land rights, and in establishing international obligations for African States towards those peoples, who, by virtue of the ownership of their traditional lands, 'can engage with the state and third parties as active stakeholders rather than as passive beneficiaries'.[30] The position of the Commission has been confirmed by the African Court on Human and Peoples' Rights in May 2017, when the Court affirmed that the provisions of the *African Charter on Human and*

Peoples' Rights (ACHPR)[31] pertinent to indigenous peoples 'must be interpreted in light of the applicable principles especially by the United Nations', considering these principles as defined by the UNDRIP.[32]

Last but not least, the legal significance of the UNDRIP has been recognised, although to an heterogeneous extent, by domestic courts and, in some cases, political bodies of several States. For instance, in Bolivia, on 7 November 2007, Law No. 3760[33] was enacted, which attributed binding force to the whole UNDRIP as law of the country. On 30 December 2010, the Parliament of the Republic of Congo adopted a Law for the Promotion and Protection of Indigenous Populations, which was heavily inspired by the UNDRIP and substantially reproduces most of the articles of the Declaration, although in some cases they have been contextualised to better respond to the specific needs of Congolese indigenous communities.[34] More countries – including Ecuador, El Salvador and Kenya – have revised their constitutions after the adoption of the UNDRIP, through incorporating in them standards of protection established by articles of the latter, while discussions on similar constitutional reforms are ongoing in other States, e.g. Australia, Chile, Guatemala and Nepal.[35]

In Belize, in 2007 the Chief Justice of the Supreme Court held that the UNDRIP embodies 'general principles of international law relating to indigenous peoples and their lands and resources, [and] is of such force that the defendants, representing the Government of Belize, will not disregard it'. The same judge also added that '[t]he United Nations, its bodies and specialized agencies including at the country level, and states, are enjoined to promote respect for and full application of the Declaration's provision and to follow up its effectiveness'.[36] Later, in 2014, the Supreme Court held that the government of Belize has an obligation under the UNDRIP 'to respect the rights of the Indigenous Maya Peoples to their lands, territories and resources which they have traditionally owned, occupied or otherwise used or acquired'.[37] Also in other countries, including Colombia and Mexico, supreme and constitutional courts have referred to the UNDRIP as a source of law in their jurisprudence concerning indigenous peoples' rights.[38]

In Chile, in 2010, the Court of Appeal of Valdivia ruled that a bond exists between indigenous communities and the environment which surrounds them, basing on Article 25 UNDRIP (recognising the right of indigenous peoples 'to maintain and strengthen their distinctive spiritual relationship with their traditionally owned or otherwise occupied and used lands, territories, waters and coastal seas and other resources and to uphold their responsibilities to future generations in this regard').[39]

In 2016, the Canadian Human Rights Tribunal affirmed that, '[a]lthough [the UNDRIP] is, at the time being, a declaration and not a treaty or a covenant, and is not legally binding except to the extent that some of its provisions reflect customary international law',[40] it is certainly to be included among the 'international legal instruments [which] reinforce the need for due attention to be paid [by Canada] to the unique situation and needs of [First Nations] children'.[41] These children must therefore

> be provided [with] child and family services of comparable quality and accessibility as those provided to all Canadians off-reserve, including that they be sufficiently funded to meet the real needs of First Nations children and families and do not perpetuate historical disadvantage.[42]

In Japan the UNDRIP played a 'certain influence' on the official recognition of the Ainu people by the government as an indigenous people on 6 June 2008.[43] One year later, the Advisory Council for Future Ainu Policy, entrusted by the Chief Cabinet Secretary with the task of suggesting principles and measures for future Ainu policies, declared that, 'although it is not legally binding, the [UNDRIP] should be fully respected as a general international guideline for indigenous policies'.[44] Furthermore, the UNDRIP has been taken as a parameter of reference in the context of one of the forest certification schemes recently developed in the country, resulting in a requirement for organizstions holding or applying for certification to 'recognize and uphold the rights, customs and culture of Indigenous Peoples as defined in the United Nations Declaration on the Rights of Indigenous Peoples (2007) and ILO Convention 169 (1989)'.[45]

Even in Russia, one of the few countries which in 2007 did not vote in favour of the adoption of the UNDRIP (it actually abstained from voting), domestic courts, although not mentioning the Declaration explicitly, in many cases have ruled consistently with the standards established by the latter with regard to indigenous peoples' hunting and fishing rights.[46] And, despite the fact that in 2013 the Russian Federation declared that it had no intention to approve or endorse the UNDRIP, this statement was grounded on the fact that – according to what was stated by the Russian government – it already complied with the standards defined by the Declaration.[47] It is evident that this position discloses the acceptance by the Russian Federation – at least at an official level – that such standards are actually to be complied with.

Furthermore, independent national human rights institutions in several countries, such as Indonesia, Malaysia, Tanzania, Namibia and Australia, are using the UNDRIP as main reference in monitoring the realization of the rights of indigenous peoples at the national level.[48]

The analysis just provided – with no pretence of exhaustiveness – clearly shows that in its first ten years of existence the UNDRIP has played an impact within the international community which has gone much further than that usually determined by an 'ordinary' UN declaration. Evidence shows that the UNDRIP, just like a rolling river, is progressively overwhelming the formal resistances opposed by some States to its own authority especially in the first years after its adoption, and it is elevating as the international legal framework of reference in order to define the rules to be complied with by States in the context of indigenous peoples' rights, irrespective of whether or not they are parties to whatever treaty providing (explicitly or implicitly) for such rights.

4. The results of the work of the ILA Committee on the Implementation of the Rights of Indigenous Peoples and future perspectives

The partial results of the work of the ILA Committee on the Implementation of the Rights of Indigenous Peoples evidence a global reality in the context of which the existence and binding character in principle of international legal standards concerning the rights of indigenous peoples are generally accepted and recognised by States, especially at the level of the legislature and the judiciary. This is further corroborated by the fact that, when violations of such standards take place, in most cases they are generally treated either as 'breaches' or as *exceptions* validated by the State authorities concerned in the form of *justifications* grounded on the necessity to satisfy important competing values.

This confirms that the relevant standards are actually considered as legal obligations by (the high majority of States composing) the international community, even beyond their (limited) status of rules proclaimed by international conventions. On the other hand, however, in many countries the effective degree of practical implementation and effective realisation of the rights of indigenous peoples, especially on the executive and administrative levels, is still rather unsatisfactory. Obviously, political statements (as those referred to in the previous section) alone are not enough to guarantee effective compliance with human rights rules, which need to be actually realised in the real life of people. Also, sometimes States declare that exceptions to the application of indigenous peoples' rights are grounded on supposed 'fundamental' values of the national society which in reality are not so fundamental, or, worse yet, are used to conceal totally different interests and purposes, which in some cases are not properly commendable. In effect, the level of implementation of indigenous peoples' rights in the different countries of the world is not uniform, and, while it is not common that such rights are totally disregarded (although, unfortunately, cases of blatant violations still occur), it is also not very usual that they are realised to an extent which is fully in line with the levels of protection established by the UNDRIP. The degree of effective implementation of indigenous peoples' rights, therefore, in many cases does not entirely fulfill the standards – in terms of '*quality*' and *effectiveness* – established by the 2007 Declaration. This is a crucial aspect, as the phase of implementation is decisive in order to ensure effectiveness of human rights – including indigenous peoples' rights – i.e. to guarantee that they are actually and fully enjoyed by the individuals and communities concerned. While the actual existence of violations – as previously explained – does not prevent an international legal rule from existing and producing binding effects for States, it is nevertheless imperative that the level of effective implementation of the international legal standards concerning indigenous peoples' rights – particularly those enshrined by the UNDRIP – is increased in many areas of the world. This is the imperative to comply with in terms of future perspectives, an imperative for the realisation of which the active involvement of all relevant components is essential. Among these components, scholars and academics (by whom the ILA Committee on the Implementation of the Rights of Indigenous Peoples is predominantly composed) must continue to monitor the situation and contribute to make the results of their studies and the information they collect available to the public opinion around the world, so as to push governments and international institutions to intensify their action in the field and make it more effective.

5. Conclusion

When the UNDRIP was adopted, on 13 September 2007, by the UN General Assembly, after about 22 years of intense negotiations, it immediately set high expectations, including among indigenous persons and activists. As recently declared by Perry Bellegarde, National Chief of the Assembly of First Nations of Canada, '[t]he adoption of the UN declaration is a milestone in the history of advancing the rights of Indigenous peoples [...] around the world'.[49] However, the same indigenous leader contextually added that, '[n]ow that we have this commitment, we must work [...] to realize those rights'.[50] It is the same old story: rights which exist only on paper may be beautiful to read and attractive, but they are not actual rights, because they obviously lack of effectiveness. With regard to the UNDRIP specifically, if one thinks about the dynamics of human history, ten years are less than a wink of an eye. This notwithstanding – as ascertained, among others, by the ILA Committee on the Implementation of the Rights of Indigenous Peoples, and described in the previous pages – during such an extremely limited span of time very significant steps have been accomplished in many areas of the world to ensure effective realisation of the rights established by the Declaration. However, yet they are obviously not enough, and the struggle has just started.

Notes

1. For the full list of members of the Committee see http://www.ila-hq.org/index.php/committees (accessed 30 November 2017).
2. Most case studies are also available at <http://www.ila-hq.org/index.php/committees>. The decision of whether or not they should be uploaded on the Committee's webpage is left to their respective authors.
3. Also available at <http://www.ila-hq.org/index.php/committees>.
4. See *Grand River Enterprises Six Nations, LTD., et Al. v. United States of America*, Award of 12 January 2011, available at <https://www.italaw.com/sites/default/files/case-documents/ita0384.pdf> (accessed 30 November 2017), para. 210.
5. See, respectively, paragraphs 4, 5, 7 and 10 of the Resolution.
6. See *Case concerning Military and Paramilitary Activities in and against Nicaragua (Nicaragua v. USA)*, Judgment of 27 June 1986, *I.C.J. Reports* 1986, p. 14, para. 186 (emphasis added).
7. See *Case of the Yakye Axa Indigenous Community v. Paraguay*, Series C No. 125, Judgment of 17 June 2005 (Merits, Reparations and Costs).
8. See *Case of the Yakye Axa Indigenous Community v. Paraguay*, para. 147.
9. See *Case of the Yakye Axa Indigenous Community v. Paraguay*, para. 149.
10. See *Case of the Yakye Axa Indigenous Community v. Paraguay*, para. 149.
11. See *Case of the Yakye Axa Indigenous Community v. Paraguay*, para. 149.
12. See Economic and Social Council, Report of the Commission on Human Rights (E/3616/Rev. l), 18th Session, 19 March–14 April 1962, para. 105.
13. See Federico Lenzerini, 'Rights of Indigenous Peoples under Customary International Law', in International Law Association, *The Hague Conference (2010), Rights Of Indigenous Peoples, Interim Report*, http://www.ila-hq.org/index.php/committees, p. 43 ff.; 'Rights of Indigenous Peoples under Customary International Law', in International Law Association, *Sofia Conference (2012), Rights Of Indigenous Peoples, Final Report*, ibid., p. 28 f.
14. In particular, the UNDRIP is 'noted' in the twenty-sixth recital of the Preamble of the 2010 *Nagoya Protocol on Access to Genetic Resources and the Fair and Equitable Sharing of Benefits Arising from Their Utilization to the Convention on Biological Diversity*, available at <https://www.cbd.int/abs/doc/protocol/nagoya-protocol-en.pdf> (accessed 16 January 2018).
15. See General Comment No. 21, 'Right of everyone to take part in cultural life (art. 15, para. 1 (a), of the International Covenant on Economic, Social and Cultural Rights)', UN Doc. E/C.12/GC/21, 21 December 2009, para. 7.
16. See General Comment No. 11 (2009), 'Indigenous children and their rights under the Convention', UN Doc. CRC/C/GC/11, January 2009, para. 10.
17. 1577 *UNTS* 3.
18. See <https://treaties.un.org/pages/ViewDetails.aspx?src=IND&mtdsg_no=IV-11&chapter=4&lang=en> (accessed 26 January 2018).
19. See General Comment No. 11, para. 82.
20. See, *inter alia*, *Case of the Kichwa Indigenous People of Sarayaku v. Ecuador*, Series C No. 245, Judgment of 27 June 2012 (Merits and reparations), para. 166 and footnote 217.
21. *ILO Convention (No. 169) concerning Indigenous and Tribal People in Independent Countries*, 27 June 1989, 1650 *UNTS* 383.

22. See *Case of the Saramaka People v. Suriname*, Series C No. 172, Judgment of 28 November 2007 (Preliminary Objections, Merits, Reparations, and Costs), paras. 131 and 138; *Comunidad Garífuna Triunfo De La Cruz Y Sus Miembros Vs. Honduras*, Series C No. 305, Judgment of 8 October 2015 (Merits, Reparations, and Costs), para. 171; *Case of the Kaliña and Lokono Peoples v. Suriname*, Series C No. 309, Judgment of 25 November 2015 (Merits, Reparations and Costs), para. 296 (footnote 335).
23. See *Case of the Kichwa Indigenous People of Sarayaku v. Ecuador*, Series C No. 245, Judgment of 27 June 2012 (Merits and Reparations), paras. 160, 166, 180 and 187; *Case of the Kaliña and Lokono Peoples v. Suriname*, paras. 196 and 202.
24. See *Case of the Kichwa Indigenous People of Sarayaku v. Ecuador*, para. 215.
25. *Case of Norín Catrimán et Al. (Leaders, Members and Activist of the Mapuche Indigenous People) v. Chile*, Series C No. 279, Judgment of 29 May 2014, para. 203; *Caso Miembros de la Aldea Chichupac y Comunidades Vecinas del Municipio de Rabinal vs. Guatemala*, Series C No. 328, Judgment of 30 November 2016 (Preliminary Objections, Merits, Reparations, and Costs), para. 319 (footnote 369).
26. See *Case of the Kaliña and Lokono Peoples v. Suriname*, paras. 221 and 251 (footnote 298)
27. See *Caso de los Pueblos Indígenas Kuna de Madungandí y Emberá de Bayano y Sus Miembros vs. Panamá*, Series C No. 284, Judgment of 14 October 2014 (Preliminary Objections, Merits, Reparations, and Costs), para. 118; *Comunidad Garífuna Triunfo De La Cruz Y Sus Miembros Vs. Honduras*, paras. 103 and 136; *Case of the Kaliña and Lokono Peoples v. Suriname*, paras. 139 (footnote 178) and 180.
28. See CCJ Appeal No BZCV2014/002, BZ Civil Appeal No. 27 of 2010, *The Maya Leaders Alliance v. The Attorney General of Belize*, 30 October 2015, [2015] *CCJ* 15 (AJ), para. 53.
29. See *The Maya Leaders Alliance v. The Attorney General of Belize*, para. 54.
30. See *Centre for Minority Rights Development (Kenya) and Minority Rights Group (on behalf of Endorois Welfare Council) v. Kenya*, Communication No. 276/03, 25 November 2009, available at <http://www.achpr.org/files/sessions/46th/comunications/276.03/achpr46_276_03_eng.pdf> (accessed 15 January 2018), para. 204.
31. 21 *ILM* 58 (1982).
32. See Application No. 006/2012, *African Commission on Human and Peoples' Rights v. Republic of Kenya*, Judgment of 26 May 2017, available at <http://en.african-court.org/images/Cases/Judgment/Application%20006-2012%20-%20African%20Commission%20on%20Human%20and%20Peoples%E2%80%99%20Rights%20v.%20the%20Republic%20of%20Kenya..pdf> (accessed 15 December 2017), paras. 125–126.
33. Available in Spanish at <https://www.lexivox.org/norms/BO-L-3760.xhtml> (accessed 16 January 2018).
34. See 'Protecting indigenous peoples rights in Africa: The Congolese 2011 Law', available at <http://www1.chr.up.ac.za/chr_old/indigenous/documents/Congo%20Brazz/Legislation/Comment%20on%20the%20Congolese%20legislation%20on%20Indigenous%20Peoples.doc> (accessed 17 January 2018).
35. See 'Statement of Ms. Victoria Tauli-Corpuz', United Nations Special Rapporteur on the Rights of Indigenous Peoples, to the Expert Mechanism on the Rights of Indigenous Peoples, Tenth Session, 12 July 2017, Tenth Anniversary of the United Nations Declaration on the Rights of Indigenous Peoples, available at <http://unsr.vtaulicorpuz.org/site/index.php/statements/190-emrip-undrip> (accessed 17 January 2018).
36. See Claims 171 and 172 of 2007, *Aurelio Cal et al v. Attorney General of Belize*, 18 October 2007, available at <http://www.law2.arizona.edu/depts/iplp/outreach/maya_belize/documents/ClaimsNos171and172of2007.pdf> (accessed 16 January 2018), para. 132
37. See Claim No. 394 of 2013, *Sarstoon Temash Institute for Indigenous Management et. Al. v. The Attorney General of Belize et Al.*, 3 April 2014, available at <https://www.elaw.org/system/files/bz.claim394of2013.satiim.pdf> (accessed 16 January 2018), para. 19.
38. See 'Statement of Ms. Victoria Tauli-Corpuz', note 35 above.
39. See Court of Appeal of Valdivia, *Decision/Rol No. 243-2010*, 4 August 2010, Considerando No.4, described by Alexandra Tomaselli and Rainer Hofmann, 'Case study. Land and

water rights in Chile', prepared for the ILA Committee on the Implementation of the Rights of Indigenous Peoples, available at <http://www.ila-hq.org/index.php/committees> (accessed 16 January 2017), p. 9.

40. See *First Nations Child and Family Caring Society of Canada et al. v. Attorney General of Canada (Representing the Minister of Indian and Northern Affairs Canada)*, 26 January 2016, 2016 *CHRT* 2, available at <https://fncaringsociety.com/sites/default/files/2016%20CHRT%20Ruling%20on%20FN%20child%20welfare%20case.pdf> (accessed 15 January 2018), para. 452.
41. See *First Nations Child and Family Caring Society of Canada et al. v. Attorney General of Canada (Representing the Minister of Indian and Northern Affairs Canada)*, para. 453.
42. See *First Nations Child and Family Caring Society of Canada et al. v. Attorney General of Canada (Representing the Minister of Indian and Northern Affairs Canada)*, para. 455.
43. See Takanobu Kiriyama and Yuko Osakada, 'The Ainu in Japan – The Ainu and International Law', Report prepared for the ILA Committee on the Implementation of the Rights of Indigenous Peoples, Revised version submitted on 14 November 2017, available at <http://www.ila-hq.org/index.php/committees> (accessed 15 January 2017), p. 5.
44. See Kiriyama and Osakada, 'The Ainu in Japan – The Ainu and International Law', p. 5.
45. For more details see Kiriyama and Osakada, 'The Ainu in Japan – The Ainu and International Law', 6–8.
46. See Federica Prina and Alexandra Tomaselli, 'Land and fishing rights of indigenous peoples in Russia', Report prepared for the ILA Committee on the Implementation of the Rights of Indigenous Peoples, p. 22, http://www.ila-hq.org/index.php/committees (accessed January 16, 2017).
47. See Prina and Tomaselli, 'Land and fishing rights of indigenous peoples in Russia', 20–21.
48. See 'Statement of Ms. Victoria Tauli-Corpuz', note 35 above.
49. See 'Indigenous leaders at UN headquarters to discuss landmark rights declaration', cbcnews, 24 April 2017, available at <http://www.cbc.ca/news/indigenous/undrip-one-year-since-implementing-1.4083450> (accessed 26 January 2018).
50. See 'Indigenous leaders at UN headquarters to discuss landmark rights declaration'.

Disclosure statement

No potential conflict of interest was reported by the author.

The World Bank's new Environmental and Social Framework: some progress but many gaps regarding the rights of indigenous peoples

Corinne Lewis and Carl Söderbergh

ABSTRACT
In October 2018, the World Bank began applying its new Environmental and Social Framework to all new Bank investment project financing. However, the final version of the Framework contains a number of weaknesses that could have significant impacts on the rights of indigenous peoples affected by a Bank-financed project. A fundamental problem is the Bank's lack of an express obligation to respect human rights and promote borrowers' respect for human rights. Other weaknesses of the Framework include: the terminology of 'Sub-Saharan African Historically Underserved Traditional Local Communities'; the applicability and determination of free, prior and informed consent; and the limitation on borrowers' need to compensate or offset residual impacts on indigenous communities only when 'technically and financially feasible'. The article draws upon the authors' close knowledge of the World Bank drafting process, and is intended to raise awareness about the insufficient protection afforded by the Framework to indigenous peoples and to encourage further advocacy to ensure that other international financial institutions do not replicate these deficiencies. The article demonstrates how the Bank's handling of these issues reflects the deeper underlying tensions between governments' desire to exploit land traditionally held and used by indigenous peoples and the rights of those communities.

I. Introduction

The World Bank, an international financial institution that provides investment project financing, in the form of loans by the International Bank for Reconstruction and Development (IBRD) and credit/grant and guarantee financing by the International Development Association (IDA) to middle and low-income governments for physical and social infrastructure projects, undertook a four-year process to update the environmental and social standards and produce a new set of standards compiled into a framework ('ESSs' or 'Framework') that apply to such financing.[1] The ESSs, adopted by the Bank in August 2016, provide standards with which Borrowers must comply throughout a project, and obligations of the Bank. These include among others, carrying out due diligence and monitoring the environmental and social performance of a project.[2] The ESSs, therefore, establish the obligations borrowers, as well as the Bank, have toward communities impacted by Bank-funded projects, including indigenous communities.

In providing financing for projects, the Bank asserts that it aims to: 'ensure that the people and the environment are protected from potential adverse impacts. [The Bank does] this through policies that identify, avoid, and minimize harm to people and the environment'.[3] Moreover, the Bank's objective of its environmental and social policies is to 'prevent and mitigate undue harm to people and their environment in the development process'.[4] In practice, however, Bank-financed projects have had significant and severe negative impacts on indigenous communities, including on their cultures and livelihoods as well as their ability to use and reside on the lands that they have traditionally inhabited, as the World Bank Inspection Panel documented in its 2016 report on 'Indigenous Peoples' in the second of its Emerging Lessons Series.[5]

The World Bank's ESSs update its former six environmental and two social policies, termed 'safeguard policies'. The two social policies covered indigenous peoples and involuntary resettlement.[6] The indigenous peoples policy, however, referred to free, prior and informed *consultation* of indigenous peoples rather than 'consent'. In addition, the safeguard policies did not address labour, health, safety and security issues, and community impacts. The International Finance Corporation (IFC), also a member of the World Bank Group, but which lends to private entities, had already replaced the Bank's safeguard policies relating to environmental and social issues in 2006 and then updated these policies in 2012.[7] Thus, the World Bank's policies were out of date. While they had been periodically revised, this had been done, as the Bank stated, 'always in a piecemeal fashion'.[8]

In recognition of the importance of the environmental and social safeguard policies and their need to be updated,[9] the Bank undertook an extensive drafting and consultation process that aimed for wide participation by concerned stakeholders. Before the Bank even issued a first draft of the Framework, it held consultations from October 2012 to March 2014, online and face-to-face, which involved over 2000 stakeholders in more than 40 countries from all regions of the world,[10] including indigenous peoples' representatives.[11] In addition, consultations and written inputs were sought by the Bank and provided by a range of stakeholders on each of the two drafts.[12]

The authors participated in this four-year process through the provision of written comments and engagement in consultations. Throughout, the authors were keenly aware of the numerous recent scandals in which indigenous peoples and other marginalised communities were harmed by World Bank-funded projects. For instance, the Sengwer people in Kenya were repeatedly evicted from their traditional lands, not appropriately consulted, and were harmed by the official designation as 'vulnerable and marginalized groups' rather than 'indigenous peoples' in connection with the Kenyan Natural Resource Management Project in Kenya funded by the Bank.[13]

The new Framework, comprised of 10 environmental and social standards, covers cultural heritage and indigenous peoples, the conduct of environmental and social impact assessments, land acquisition and involuntary resettlement, and stakeholder engagement, among other topics. The final version of the Framework was approved by the World Bank's Board of Executive Directors on 4 August 2016 and as of 1 October 2018 applies to all new Bank investment project financing. Yet, many civil society organisations and others remain extremely concerned about the Bank's commitment to fully ensuring respect for the rights of indigenous peoples in Bank-funded projects.

In order to understand the strengths and weaknesses of the Framework regarding the protection of the rights of indigenous peoples, this article considers the main issues of contention during the process in order to highlight concerns about the resulting ESSs. Therefore, this article first turns to a fundamental issue of interest during the consultations, namely the Bank's failure to express a commitment to uphold international human rights and to cite international human rights instruments in the Framework. This is followed by consideration of a number of significant issues during the consultations that have left indigenous peoples' rights inadequately protected in the finalised version of the Framework.

II. Issues that underpin the World Bank's approach

A. Human rights

1. Lack of general commitment to respect human rights

The issue of human rights, flagged by stakeholders in the very first stage of the consultation process,[14] would prove to be a sensitive one. The Bank was clearly reluctant to articulate an express commitment to promote respect for human rights, despite its status as a specialised agency of the United Nations. It also shied away from requiring its borrowers, which are States already bound by international treaties and customary international law, to respect human rights. Civil society as well as some Member State representatives fought hard to strengthen the wording on human rights in the Framework, but the final result is hardly satisfactory.

The first draft of the Framework signalled the Bank's disinclination to embrace human rights: 'the Bank's operations are *supportive* of human rights and *will encourage* respect for them in a manner consistent with the Bank's Articles of Agreement'.[15] Thus, the Bank's operations, not the Bank itself, would 'encourage respect' for human rights, but only, according to the draft, 'in a manner consistent with the Bank's Articles of Agreement'. In referring to its Articles of Agreement, the Bank was referring to its 'nonpolitical mandate',[16] which the Bank has historically interpreted as an obstacle to embracing human rights.[17]

In a letter to the Bank, 28 UN Special Procedures mandate holders strongly rejected the Bank's conservative interpretation of its mandate, stating:

> the Bank's Articles of Agreement should be interpreted in the context of today's international legal order, rather than that of the mid-1940s. The Bank and its Member States are bound by both the Articles of Agreement, and by international human rights law.[18]

The wording in the first draft was also strongly criticised by civil society organisations.[19] However, the reference to the Bank's Articles of Agreement would remain in the text.

The Bank did appear to try to respond to the heavy criticism on the human rights wording. It added wording to the 2nd draft, stating that the Bank 'shares the aspirations of the Universal Declaration of Human Rights (UDHR) and helps its clients fulfill those aspirations', but 'such approach' was to be carried out by the Bank 'in a manner consistent with its Articles of Agreement'.[20] Consequently, this new wording subordinated the

UDHR to the Bank's Articles of Agreement and suggested that the Bank had misread the UDHR's authoritative status in international law.

In the final version, the Bank took the positive step of eliminating the subordination of the UDHR to the Bank's Articles of Agreement. Yet, the text once again provided that the Bank's operations, not the Bank, supports human rights: 'the World Bank's activities support the realization of human rights expressed in the Universal Declaration of Human Rights'.[21] Therefore, the Bank makes no explicit commitment to respect the UDHR and fails to pledge to avoid causing or contributing to violations of human rights by borrowers.

The final version also fails to express the intention or obligation of the Bank to actively promote borrowers' respect for human rights. Instead, the wording provides:

> Through the projects it finances, and in a manner consistent with its Articles of Agreement, the World Bank seeks to avoid adverse impacts and will continue to support its member countries as they strive to progressively achieve their human rights commitments.[22]

Yet, the Bank's avoidance of adverse impacts is noncommittal and its expression of 'support' to borrowers is vague. Also, the Bank seems to have again misunderstood human rights in referring to States' progressive achievement. Although some human rights commitments (i.e. economic, social and cultural rights) can be met progressively, other rights should be immediately realised.

As a result, the Bank never expressed a commitment to respect human rights. Instead, the Bank adopted 'a risk-based approach', which the Bank articulated as one of the five key elements of its investment lending reform and modernisation launched in 2009.[23] This risk-based approach continues to be a hallmark of its work today[24] and suggests that the Bank is more oriented toward enabling financing rather than protecting the human rights of persons affected by the projects it funds.

As a UN specialised agency, the Bank's risk-based approach to investment lending, which lending is intended to 'promote poverty reduction and sustainable development',[25] starkly contrasts with the human-rights based approach of the United Nations family of institutions to development cooperation, policies, programming and technical assistance.[26] Human rights are 'one of the core purposes' of the UN system and constitute one of the three main pillars of the organisation, together with development and peace and security; these three pillars are interlinked and mutually reinforcing.[27]

However, despite UN and international consensus on the integral nature of human rights in sustainable development, the international law obligations of the Bank and its Member States, and the UN Guiding Principles on Business and Human Rights, the World Bank adopted a Framework that fails to commit the Bank to respect human rights or to ensure that borrowers do not use the Bank's investment financing in a manner that causes significant violations of indigenous peoples' rights. While this result might in large part be explained by the Bank's internal management culture, the opposition of China, which has become more dominant as a World Bank shareholder, to human rights requirements on borrowing governments also may have contributed.[28]

2. Lack of specific references to human rights

From the very first draft of the Framework, the general reluctance of the Bank to commit to respect and promote human rights was coupled with the Bank's unwillingness to expressly articulate the link between the human rights principles, which underpin the rights of persons affected by projects financed by the Bank, and the international legal instruments that articulate those rights. The Bank failed to include references to key international human rights texts, such as those of the International Bill of Human Rights, or relevant instruments containing the rights of indigenous peoples. The Bank maintained this position throughout the drafting process.

Thus, despite the fact that the substance of the standard on indigenous peoples, ESS7, should be based on indigenous peoples' rights, there is only one reference to human rights in the text of the standard. This reference is found in one of ESS7's objectives: '[t]o ensure that the development process fosters full respect for the *human rights*, dignity, aspirations, identity, culture, and natural resource-based livelihoods of Indigenous Peoples'.[29] As with the general human rights language mentioned above, this objective is vague. It refers, not to the borrower's need to respect the rights of indigenous peoples, but rather to 'the development process' fostering respect for human rights.

One positive development in the Framework can be seen when contrasted with the Bank's prior operational safeguards; specifically, the Framework introduces the principle of non-discrimination. The Vision statement of the Framework provides that the ESSs will 'enhance non-discrimination',[30] and in the standard concerning the borrower's environmental and social assessment, ESS1, the assessment is to:

> take into account all relevant environmental and social risks and impacts of the project, including: ... risks that project impacts *fall disproportionately* on individuals and groups who, because of their particular circumstances, may be disadvantaged or vulnerable, [and] any *prejudice or discrimination* toward individuals or groups in providing access to development resources and project benefits, particularly in the case of those who may be disadvantaged or vulnerable.[31]

The principle of non-discrimination is also to be respected by borrowers when carrying out meaningful consultation.[32] Yet, there is no reference to the international human rights instruments that underpin this principle.

Other human rights principles are mentioned in the Framework, but again, without references to specific human rights instruments that enshrine the principles. The Framework includes the principle of free, prior and informed consent (FPIC), but without a reference to the UN Declaration on the Rights of Indigenous Peoples. Also, the grievance mechanism 'is expected to address concerns promptly and effectively, in a transparent manner'[33] and the definition of 'forced eviction' provides that it shall be 'conducted in a manner consistent with basic principles of due process (including provision of adequate advance notice, meaningful opportunities to lodge grievances and appeals, and avoidance of the use of unnecessary, disproportionate or excessive force)'.[34] Consequently, these principles float within the text detached from the international standards that provide parameters and content to them, thereby creating a risk that borrowers will apply their own lower national law standards instead of the applicable international human rights law standards.

3. Resulting contradictions

The Bank's incorporation of the principle of non-discrimination, indigenous peoples' right to FPIC, and references to other principles such as 'transparency [and] participation',[35] clearly indicate that human rights form the foundation for many of the borrower's obligations under the Framework. Yet, the Bank evidences a conceptual contradiction in assiduously avoiding any mention of specific human rights instruments throughout the text. In fact, the Framework makes only one general reference to international human rights instruments; the borrower, in carrying out an environmental and social impact assessment, takes into account 'obligations of the country directly applicable to the project under *relevant international treaties and agreements*'.[36] This meagre reference to international human rights instruments is not even particularly strong since the wording allows a discretionary determination by the borrower as to what are the 'international treaties and agreements' that are '*relevant*'.

The Bank also creates several practical contradictions by avoiding an explicit acknowledgement of its own responsibility to respect human rights, and consistent with this obligation, its responsibility to encourage, promote and require respect for human rights by its borrowers. First, governmental borrowers obtaining investment project financing from the Bank will likely contract with private entities to carry out the ground, infrastructure and other works on a project. These private entities are expected to comply with international human rights principles, consistent with the UN Guiding Principles on Business and Human Rights. These Guiding Principles encourage States to 'promote respect for human rights' through their commercial transactions with businesses.[37] Yet, the Bank fails to hold these very same governmental borrowers responsible for respecting human rights.

In addition, the World Bank's failure to reference international human rights standards, and to require governmental borrowers to respect the human rights of persons affected by their projects, implicitly results in the World Bank Group holding private entities to a higher standard than States. While the IFC recognises that its private entity borrowers have the responsibility to respect human rights,[38] the Bank shuns away from reminding governmental borrowers of their human rights obligations and holding them responsible for respecting human rights in the projects they undertake with funding from the Bank, under the Framework. A question then arises: will this disparity create an incentive for a shift of borrowing for development projects among World Bank Group entities, specifically, from the IFC to the IBRD and the IDA, and thus, from private entities to governmental borrowers, as the private entities seek to avoid the explicit human rights obligations under the IFC Performance Standards?

III. The ESSs and specific indigenous peoples' rights

Indigenous peoples' issues figured prominently throughout the consultation process on the Framework as civil society organisations advocated for standards that demonstrated greater compliance with international human rights norms. Among the most significant issues, related to the protection of indigenous peoples' rights, were: definition of indigenous peoples, FPIC, and opt-outs of protections for indigenous peoples in the Framework.

A. Designation/recognition of indigenous peoples

The Framework, as noted above, provides obligations and actions that the borrower must take with respect to indigenous peoples which may be affected by the borrower's development project. The determination of who qualifies as 'indigenous peoples' then becomes critical as a prerequisite for the application of the provisions of the Framework, and in particular, those in the standard on indigenous peoples, ESS7. The terminology for the designation of indigenous peoples was an unexpected but worrying concern during the drafting and consultation process, along with a number of issues concerning the designation and recognition of indigenous peoples.

1. New terminology – 'Indigenous Peoples/Sub-Saharan African Historically Underserved Traditional Local Communities'

A surprising development, during the consultations and drafting process, was the World Bank's modification of the title of the indigenous peoples standard, ESS7, as well as all references to 'indigenous peoples' throughout this standard. Specifically, the phrase 'Sub-Saharan African Historically Underserved Traditional Local Communities' was added alongside 'Indigenous Peoples' throughout ESS7, thereby creating the unwieldy term 'Indigenous Peoples/Sub-Saharan African Historically Underserved Traditional Local Communities'. The Bank inserted this change into the finalised version of the Framework, without input or feedback from indigenous peoples or civil society, which seemed particularly incongruent with the World Bank's approach of transparency and consultation.

The modification appears to be, in large part, a result of the World Bank's high-level dialogue on ESS7 in Addis Ababa in February 2016, before the issuance of the final version of the Framework. The meeting was attended by representatives from the Governments of the Democratic Republic of Congo, Ethiopia, Kenya, Tanzania, Sudan and South Sudan, and also by representatives from the UN Office of the High Commissioner for Human Rights, as well as the former and current Special Rapporteurs on the rights of indigenous peoples.[39] According to the Bank, at the meeting there was 'broad acceptance that, while the term Indigenous Peoples is a widely accepted concept in international law, it presents implementation challenges in Africa'.[40] The Bank therefore appears to have compromised with a number of African governments that 'reject the use of the term "Indigenous peoples" in their countries', according to Amnesty International.[41] While the proposed alternative wording was 'Indigenous Peoples and Historically Underserved Traditional Local Communities', in the end the Bank added an additional phrase: 'Sub-Saharan African'.[42]

As a result, the phrase 'Sub-Saharan African Historically Underserved Traditional Local Communities' was introduced into the final version of the Framework absent consultation and agreement by indigenous peoples consistent with their right to determine and express their identity.[43] As the Bank's own Inspection Panel has suggested in a report based on cases brought to the panel relating to indigenous peoples' issues, 'consideration needs to be given to the terms preferred by project-affected [indigenous peoples] through effective consultation with them'.[44] The text of ESS7 indicates that the term was introduced: 'in recognition of the different terminology which may be used to refer to Indigenous Peoples in the national context'.[45] However, the Bank failed to ensure that indigenous peoples' views on this new wording, including how it affects the expression of their identity, were obtained and reflected in the final terminology.

Proper terminology is essential, since recognition as 'indigenous peoples' permits the application of rights and relevant international standards. The phrase 'Sub-Saharan

African Historically Underserved Traditional Local Communities' does not exist in international law, nor is it underpinned by any international instrument in the same way as the term 'Indigenous Peoples'. Thus, the concern is that the former term may result in a delinkage between indigenous peoples and their rights. For instance, how should the principle of self-identification, which is key to the understanding of indigenous peoples' rights be applied? Essentially, the introduction of this phrase risks undermining standards specifically relating to indigenous peoples.

There are a number of other problems with the inserted wording. The phrase is over inclusive. 'Historically Underserved Traditional Local' can encompass communities belonging to majorities, which may be underserved because of remote geographic locations or past marginalisation. Such communities may then have important development needs that should be addressed, but these would be different from the structural discrimination and other challenges that continue to affect indigenous peoples and other marginalised groups. Thus, it might not be appropriate to treat 'historically underserved traditional local communities' and 'indigenous communities' in the same manner.

At the same time, the new phrase is limiting. Specifically, it is unclear why the geographic specificity of 'Sub-Saharan African' has been introduced, particularly given that there are presumably 'Historically Underserved Traditional Local' communities in the Sahara region and North Africa as well as in other regions of the world. Moreover, while the 'Introduction' to ESS7 lists nine various terms used by different countries, the World Bank has only selected one of these, 'Sub-Saharan African Historically Underserved Traditional Local Communities', to use alongside the international law term 'Indigenous Peoples'.[46]

2. The phrase 'disadvantaged or vulnerable'

A challenge that arose during the initial stages was the disempowering terminology 'disadvantaged or vulnerable' that encompassed indigenous peoples. The conception of disadvantage is paternalistic and many marginalised communities feel that the word 'vulnerable' is reductive and marginalising. The phrase 'disadvantaged or vulnerable' also depicts affected persons as passive in the face of human rights abuses, as opposed to characterising them as active rights-owning individuals.

In the final version, the Bank replaced 'disadvantaged', in the phrase 'disadvantaged or vulnerable' in ESS7 on indigenous peoples, with 'marginalized'. Nevertheless, it left 'disadvantaged or vulnerable' in other standards of the Framework where such references cover indigenous peoples. For example, under the terms of the Framework, the Bank, in conducting its due diligence on a project, and the Borrower in carrying out the environmental and social assessment, are to consider social risks and impacts that 'fall disproportionately on individuals or groups who … may be *disadvantaged or vulnerable*'.[47] The Bank also left the term 'vulnerable' throughout the Framework and failed to mention intersectionality of marginalised groups, including those facing exclusion by other members of their own marginalised groups as well as those who are discriminated against by majorities.

Additionally, there were scattered and inconsistent references to the specific categories of persons who could be considered 'disadvantaged or vulnerable', in the first draft; in the second draft, these references became more comprehensive and inclusive, but were still not consistent across the whole draft.[48] In the final version, the Bank deleted most, but not all, references to specific categories of persons considered 'disadvantaged or vulnerable',[49] and instead, issued a Directive binding on its staff: *Addressing Risks and Impacts on Disadvantaged or Vulnerable Individuals or Groups*,[50] which gives examples of individuals or groups of 'disadvantaged or vulnerable' rather than providing a comprehensive list. This incomplete listing fails to mention language, descent (as in caste), political or other opinion or even migration status.

In the absence of a reference or list of specific categories of persons in the Framework, it will be incumbent upon Bank staff to apprise borrowers of potential categories of persons in connection with the borrower's environmental and social assessment.[51] The Bank will need to ensure that in advising borrowers of relevant categories of persons, it includes not only those mentioned in the Directive, but also others. As a result, there is a risk that the Bank, and thus, the borrower, will overlook particular categories of marginalised persons in evaluating the project's risks and impacts.

A final concern relates to the Bank's grouping of all categories of marginalised persons together as 'disadvantaged and vulnerable'. In doing so, the World Bank failed to note, in the Framework, the diverse needs of such groups of persons, and the particular international standards that apply to them. As mentioned above in discussing the Bank's approach to human rights in the Framework (Section II.A.2), the final Framework fails to mention any applicable international human rights instruments, including the UN Declaration on the Rights of Indigenous Peoples.

3. Process used to recognise indigenous peoples

Another concern related to the recognition of indigenous peoples under the Framework arises as a result of the ability of the Bank to use the borrower's national processes, rather than the provisions in the standard of the Framework on indigenous peoples, ESS7, to identify indigenous peoples. Specifically, ESS7 provides that during the project screening phase, the Bank 'may follow the Borrower's national processes' for the 'identification of indigenous peoples where these processes meet the requirements of ESS7'.[52] The application of Borrower's national processes to identify indigenous peoples was already part of the previous operational policy on indigenous peoples,[53] and it was not surprising that this was maintained in the Framework since the Bank has articulated, as one of its main goals, the strengthening of borrowers' national systems.[54] Therefore, as the Bank has stated, the Framework 'places greater emphasis on the use of Borrower frameworks'.[55] Fortunately, following concerns raised about this provision during the consultations, the Bank added a footnote that requires the Bank to consult the indigenous peoples concerned. The Bank seemed to wish to keep some balance and therefore also added that the Bank will consult the borrower.[56]

From a practical standpoint, the Bank's selection of the borrower's process of identification of indigenous peoples would seem to involve two aspects that require thorough evaluation by the Bank. The Bank should: (i) evaluate the provisions of the borrower's laws and regulations to determine whether they provide for identification of indigenous peoples consistent with ESS7 and (ii) determine whether the practice of the borrowing country complies with these standards.

However, with respect to the first aspect, there is no provision in ESS7 that specifies what the requirements of ESS7 are that the national processes must meet. In this connection, although ESS7 provides for 'self-identification', it is not clear how the Bank will handle the situation where national processes do not acknowledge this principle and/or where the national processes would not recognise the community. Additionally, ESS7 does not specify whether the Bank will evaluate the borrower's actual practices. This evaluation would require a rather delicate, but comprehensive, inquiry into the actual practices of the borrower.

Thus, given concerns about: the new terminology; past deficiencies in the Bank's identification of indigenous peoples, as highlighted by an Inspection Panel report;[57] and the disparity between the standards of ESS7 and borrowers' processes and standards,[58] there is still a significant risk that the Bank's use of the borrower's identification processes for indigenous peoples could result in exclusion of certain indigenous communities.

4. Indigenous peoples not in the project area

ESS7 consistently uses 'the project area' to define its scope of application to indigenous peoples;[59] yet, while some indigenous peoples impacted by a Bank-financed project actually reside or customarily use land within the planned project area, there may be indigenous peoples living outside the area that are also affected and who should therefore be included in the coverage of ESS7. Of particular concern is the fact that ESS7, and particularly FPIC, do not appear to apply to indigenous communities adjacent to project areas or *downstream*, despite the fact that they could be equally or even more seriously affected, and even though the Framework acknowledges that negative impacts can occur through 'transboundary and global risks and impacts, such as impacts from effluents and emissions'.[60]

Another group of persons who are not residing in the project area are indigenous peoples with a 'collective attachment to' the area.[61] These people may have been displaced or had to migrate, but still remain strongly attached to their ancestral lands. The Bank has carried over the idea of 'collective attachment' from its former operational policy on indigenous peoples.[62] Unfortunately, the Bank also continues to limit the application of 'collective attachment' by requiring the loss of such collective attachment to have occurred during the lifetime of members of the community or group.[63] Another narrowing of the application of 'collective attachment' occurs as a result of the requirement that there must have been not just physical presence on land and territories, but also 'economic ties', including for sacred sites.[64] Finally, a further limitation is contained in a footnote to ESS7 and provides that ESS7 does not generally apply to 'individuals or small groups migrating to urban areas in search of economic opportunity'.[65] This is frankly unjust since groups migrate for a complex range of reasons, and the search for economic opportunity may well be induced by the discrimination faced back home.

B. Free, prior and informed consent

1. Situations in which FPIC applies

The recognition of the right of indigenous peoples to FPIC, in the first draft of the Framework, signalled a significant improvement over the language in the former safeguard policy on indigenous peoples. The former safeguard provided for 'free, prior and informed consultation',[66] which thereby permitted projects to proceed where the community had merely been consulted, but had not provided 'consent'. Thus, it was no surprise that FPIC was one of the issues that stakeholders asked the Bank, during the initial consultations, to address and incorporate into the new Framework.[67] However, some governments did not wish to see FPIC incorporated and preferred the previous standard of 'free prior and informed consultation'.[68] Consequently, while the Bank provided for the FPIC of indigenous peoples in the indigenous peoples standard, ESS7, it limited the right in a manner inconsistent with indigenous peoples' rights.

From the very first draft of the Framework, the Bank evidenced its reluctance to fully support FPIC by including the statement that there is 'no universally accepted definition' of FPIC.[69] This statement would remain in the final version, thereby weakening the import of FPIC throughout ESS7.[70]

The Bank also refused to move from its initial position, contained in the first draft of the Framework, of only allowing FPIC to apply in three situations: (a) adverse impacts on indigenous peoples' land and resources; (b) relocation of such communities; and (c) where there are significant impacts on their cultural heritage.[71] As a result, the circumstances for the application of FPIC ended up being overly circumscribed, compared with UN Declaration on the Rights of Indigenous Peoples, which provides that FPIC should apply to 'any project affecting their lands or territories and other resources',[72] and other international norms and support.[73] Essentially, the Framework fails to incorporate the obligation that the FPIC of indigenous peoples should be obtained whenever there are impacts on any indigenous peoples' rights.

Instead of broadening the situations in which FPIC applies, in subsequent versions of the Framework, the World Bank narrowed the applicability by incorporating additional restrictive terms. The final wording on situations when FPIC applies provides:

> the Borrower will obtain the FPIC of the affected Indigenous Peoples when the project will:
>
> (a) have **adverse** impacts on land and natural resources **subject to traditional ownership or under customary use or occupation**;
>
> (b) cause relocation of Indigenous Peoples ... from land and natural resources **subject to traditional ownership or under customary use or occupation**; or
>
> (c) have **significant** impacts on Indigenous Peoples ... cultural heritage **that is material to the identity and/or cultural, ceremonial, or spiritual aspects of the affected Indigenous Peoples ... Communities' lives**. (Emphasis added)[74]

In the first draft, the borrower was given responsibility for making several determinations without input by indigenous peoples and without their FPIC. Under both (a) and (b), the borrower is required to determine whether the land and natural resources are 'subject to traditional ownership or under customary use or occupation'; under (c), the borrower has to determine whether the 'impacts' on 'cultural heritage' will be 'significant'.[75]

Instead of addressing requests of civil society that the borrower be required to obtain indigenous peoples' input and their FPIC in making such determinations, the Bank added more qualifying terms, which require additional assessments by the borrower, to the final version, and thus, without comment or input from civil society on these additions. Specifically, in (a) an additional determination as to whether the 'impacts' are 'adverse' was added. The effect is to exclude impacts that the borrower considers to be positive contributions to development, even when affected indigenous communities do not agree. Also, in the case of (c), wording was added so that the borrower now determines whether the cultural heritage 'is material to the identity and/or cultural, ceremonial, or spiritual aspects of the affected Indigenous Peoples ... '.

In addition, the draft Framework attempted to strengthen legal recognition of the traditional land ownership or customary usage rights of indigenous peoples, but ultimately, the final wording resulted in another denial of indigenous peoples' right to FPIC. The first draft provided for the borrower to prepare 'a plan for legal recognition of [indigenous peoples'] perpetual or long-term renewable custodial or use rights' where the project would have 'significant impacts on land that is traditionally owned or under customary use or occupation by Indigenous Peoples'.[76] However, when the second draft elaborated the objective of such plan as 'full legal recognition of existing customary land tenure systems of Indigenous Peoples' or 'conversion of customary usage rights to communal and/or individual ownership rights',[77] it failed to provide for FPIC, let alone consultation with indigenous peoples, when a conversion to individual ownership rights was intended.

Following consultations on the second draft of the Framework,[78] the Bank included a footnote in the final version that obliges the borrower to conduct an 'assessment of the impacts of such conversion on the communities and their livelihoods' and to consult the indigenous peoples concerned prior to the borrower's determination that such conversion to individual ownership is an objective.[79] Despite this additional requirement, if the borrower views the conversion to individual ownership rights as not rising to the level of an 'adverse impact' under the FPIC provision,[80] the FPIC of the indigenous community is not assured. Thus, given that individual titling processes have repeatedly led to a weakening of customary land tenure and ultimately the displacement of communities, the failure to provide for indigenous peoples' right to FPIC in such situations may lead to violations of this right as well as other rights.

2. Definition of 'consent'

The Bank also weakened the designation of what constitutes 'consent' of FPIC in its final version with the insertion of the following:

> consent refers to the *collective support* of affected Indigenous Peoples ... for the project activities that affect them, reached through a culturally appropriate process. It may exist even if some individuals or groups object to such project activities ... .[81]

In particular, the term 'collective support' was criticised by 'indigenous peoples' organisations for not being sufficiently rigorous and for not 'ensuring respect for the results of affected indigenous peoples' independent and collective decision-making processes'.[82]

The Bank's use of the term 'collective support' to define consent seems to have resulted from the High-Level Dialogue it held with some African governments in Addis Ababa in February 2016. Governments preferred to specify that the outcome of the FPIC process should be defined consistently with the previous operational policy on indigenous people as 'broad community support'.[83] Consequently, while the World Bank states in the Framework that there is no 'universally accepted definition' of FPIC, at the same time it diminishes FPIC's consensual nature and leaves the determination of whether there is 'consent' to the borrower.[84]

C. Opt-outs

Three important opt-outs were included in the first draft of the Framework that would allow governmental borrowers to set aside the application of certain provisions of the

Framework relevant to indigenous peoples. In the case of two of the opt-outs, the provisions of the indigenous peoples standard, ESS7, would not be applied, and in the third, the borrower would not be obligated to compensate indigenous peoples for residual impacts.

1. Opt-out of ESS7 and application of ESS5 for indigenous peoples who hold individual legal title

One of the crucial opt-out clauses was initially placed in a footnote to ESS7 and stated:

> Where indigenous peoples individually hold legal title, or where relevant national law recognizes customary rights for individuals, the requirements of ESS5 [Land acquisition, restrictions on land use and involuntary resettlement] will apply, rather than the requirements under [ESS7].[85]

The effect of this opt-out is that when land is held individually, rather than collectively, or when customary rights of individuals are recognised under national law, the borrower's obligation under ESS7, to obtain the FPIC of the indigenous peoples to any relocation, is not applicable. This clause seemed to be a prelude to land-grabbing. The opt-out also resulted in a determination without the involvement of the indigenous community, which was particularly objectionable given that the opt-out was being done at the request of a borrowing government. The drafters, during a meeting with civil society representatives (including one of the article's authors) in London in January 2015, admitted that the formulation was flawed and rewrote the provision.[86] The phrase 'rather than' was replaced by 'in addition to',[87] and thus, the requirements of ESS5 apply in addition to those of ESS7 in the case of indigenous peoples holding individual legal titles or where national law recognises customary legal titles for individuals.

2. Opt-out of application of ESS7 in its entirety

Another opt-out provision in the first draft proved to be far more contentious. The draft provided that a borrower could request the Bank's agreement to the borrower opting out of applying ESS7, relating to indigenous peoples, where the borrower was concerned about 'ethnic tension or civil strife', or where the borrower's national constitution contained provisions on the identification of culturally distinct groups that were inconsistent with those in ESS7.[88] Practically, this meant that customary land rights and other indigenous peoples' rights, including FPIC, which are not covered by the other ESSs, might be ignored when the alternative approach was taken.

The language was also deeply stigmatising through its association of indigenous peoples with 'tension' and 'strife'. Moreover, there was concern that this 'alternative approach' would be taken without proper indigenous community involvement or FPIC. The UN Special Procedures mandate holders, in their letter to the World Bank, clearly noted the discordance of the opt-out with the UN Declaration on the Rights of Indigenous Peoples stating: it 'appears incompatible with the fundamental purpose of the Declaration, which seeks to redress the wrongful denial of the existence of indigenous peoples and their right to self-determination'.[89]

Following a great deal of criticism, from civil society in particular, the 'alternative approach' was removed in the second draft. However, the issue was not completely settled. The World Bank's 'Issues for Phase 3 Consultations' paper raised the possibility that a waiver could be reintroduced into the final version.[90] Therefore, civil society had to continue to vigorously argue against the possibility of the reinsertion of a provision setting aside ESS7. It is likely that the World Bank managed to secure agreement on the deletion of this opt-out, especially with African member States, in exchange for the inclusion of modified terminology for 'indigenous peoples', and the reference to 'consent' as meaning 'collective support' as discussed above in Sections III.A.1 and III.B.2, respectively.

3. Opt-out of compensation or offset for residual impacts

A final opt-out, included in the first draft and strongly opposed by civil society, remains in the Framework and was actually strengthened by the Bank, despite opposition. This opt-out concerns what is termed the 'mitigation hierarchy'. The 'mitigation hierarchy' establishes a framework for a borrower's response to adverse impacts of the project on persons, including indigenous peoples. The hierarchy favours avoidance of impacts over minimisation or reduction of the impacts; any remaining impacts are to be compensated or offset 'whenever technically and financially feasible'.[91] In other words, compensation or other measures to address remaining human rights impacts are dependent on whether the borrower finds them to be technically and financially feasible. However, this 'technical and financial feasibility' standard has no bearing on the determination of whether a project should be financed by the Bank.

The determination by the Borrower as to what is a 'significant remedial impact' also abrogates the indigenous community's right to FPIC. Consequently, where the borrower is responsible for severe violations of indigenous peoples' rights, which are due to the scale, scope and/or irremediable character of such violations,[92] the borrower is not held accountable, by even the Bank, despite the borrower's human rights obligations.

The Bank appeared to try to offset concerns that the determination of 'technical and financial feasibility' would be made by the borrower too late in the project process to allow the ramifications of such feasibility to be considered by the Bank and opposed by project-affected persons; it added a footnote that requires the borrower to take several steps. The borrower is to 'make reasonable efforts to incorporate the costs of compensating and/or offsetting for the significant residual impacts as part of project costs'.[93] Additionally, the borrower is to provide in its environmental and social assessment 'the significance of such residual impacts, the long-term effect of these on the environment and project-affected people, and the extent to which they are considered reasonable in the context of the project', as well as the reasons for the determination that it is 'not technically or financially feasible to compensate or offset for such residual impacts'.[94]

However, the incorporation of the costs for offsetting residual impacts, into the overall project costs, is not a requirement; the borrower must only use 'reasonable efforts'. The requirement that the borrower provide additional information in its environmental and social assessment should assist the Bank in determining whether a project's residual impacts outweigh the benefits of the project. The Bank reviews the borrower's environmental and social assessment, and can request additional information and provide guidance to the borrower, in connection with its oversight role.[95]

Yet, the Bank has been criticised for insufficient supervision and monitoring,[96] and there is no provision in the Framework that provides that where there are severe impacts on indigenous peoples that the Bank will cancel a project. In addition, there are several determinations required by the borrower in providing such additional information in its environmental and social assessment, such as: the evaluation of the 'significance of such residual impacts'; 'the long-term effect' of residual impacts on indigenous peoples; and the reasons why it would not be 'technically or financially feasible to compensate or offset for such residual impacts'.[97] These determinations remain within the borrower's control and for which indigenous peoples will neither provide input nor have the possibility to exercise their FPIC in violation of their rights.

D. Additional areas of concern

Although it is not possible within this article to undertake an exhaustive treatment of other issues related to indigenous peoples that remain of concern in the finalised Framework, two additional areas merit attention because of their importance.

1. Ensuring appropriate consultation and engagement of indigenous peoples

In the first draft of the Framework, the Bank did not seem to take an approach that appropriately engaged indigenous peoples affected by a project, since they would not be fully consulted or engaged in plans or decisions, by both the Bank and the Borrower, that affected them. Some of these gaps were resolved in the subsequent draft and the final version of the Framework.[98] However, the final version still contains numerous areas where indigenous peoples' right to participate in decision-making, a right expressed in more than 20 provisions of the UN Declaration on the Rights of Indigenous Peoples, is effectively denied.[99] Specifically, with respect to the Bank, the final version of the Framework fails to provide for indigenous peoples' input into the Bank's due diligence of a project.[100]

The borrower has a general obligation to 'undertake an engagement process with affected Indigenous Peoples', which includes 'meaningful consultation';[101] however, this obligation is limited by a rather vague qualification: '[t]he scope and scale of consultation ... will be proportionate to the scope and scale of potential project risks and impacts as they may affect Indigenous Peoples ... '.[102] Also, there is no guidance in the Framework as to how a consultation will be conducted 'proportionately'.

In addition, there are a number of places in the Framework where the obligation of the borrower to carry out meaningful consultation with indigenous peoples is not given concrete expression. This creates gaps in the full respect of indigenous peoples' right to consultation and to participation in decision-making processes that affect them. For example, while the borrower is to 'assess the nature and degree of the expected direct and indirect economic, social, cultural (including cultural heritage) and environmental impacts on Indigenous Peoples', it does so without any reference to input or consultation with affected indigenous communities.[103]

Moreover, the borrower, which has primary responsibility for monitoring the 'environmental and social performance of the project' that is, its own performance, is to engage indigenous peoples, and other stakeholders, '[w]here appropriate and as set out in the [Environmental and Social Commitment Plan]'.[104] Yet, the phrase 'where appropriate' is vague and the determination of when it is 'appropriate' to consult indigenous peoples seems to be left to the borrower. Also, the borrower designs the grievance mechanism without input from the communities for whose use it is intended.[105] Finally, the

Framework also fails to explicitly mention any obligation of the borrower to consult indigenous peoples in the design of the consultation processes.[106]

Compounding these difficulties is the fact that the obligation of the borrower to engage indigenous communities is articulated as involving 'Indigenous Peoples ... Communities' representative bodies and organizations (e.g. councils of elders or village councils, or chieftains) and, where appropriate' other community members.[107] However, from an indigenous peoples' rights perspective, the determination of participation by the indigenous community should be made by the community itself in accordance with its own practices and customs.

2. Cultural heritage and risk of total loss of culture

The standard on cultural heritage, ESS8, expanded the scope of cultural heritage, relative to the Bank's previous operational policies.[108] 'Cultural heritage' now includes not just tangible cultural heritage, but also *intangible* cultural heritage. At the same time, however, the Bank limited the latter to 'intangible cultural heritage only if a physical component of a project will have a material impact on such cultural heritage'.[109] This reference to a 'physical component' narrows the application of the protection of cultural heritage inappropriately since the presence of a project can have other quite well documented consequences that affect the intangible culture of indigenous communities, even without specific physical components, for instance simply through the presence of a large number of non-indigenous project staff bringing with them their own cultural norms and practices.

Despite repeated comments on the various drafts of the Framework, the final version of the Framework still does not adequately protect against the risk of the total loss of culture. Specifically, the Framework provides compensatory remedies that are formulated in purely economic terms. It does not recognise that for certain cultures removal from their lands intrinsically linked to their traditional livelihoods would essentially mean the end of the cultures within a couple of generations (e.g. pastoralists, fisherpeoples, forest-dwellers).[110]

IV. Conclusion

After a two-year process, the Bank created an environmental and social Framework applicable to its investment financing that is significantly more coherent and cohesive than its prior set of operational standards. Despite the gaps in the Bank's approach as outlined above, one positive step forward has been its move from the previous outdated 'free, prior and informed consultation' standard to FPIC. However, the final version of the Framework contains a number of weaknesses that could have significant impacts on the rights of indigenous peoples affected by a Bank-financed project.

A fundamental problem with the Framework is the Bank's lack of an express obligation to respect human rights and to promote respect for human rights by borrowers receiving investment financing from the Bank, which leads to an overall weakening effect on the rights of indigenous peoples in Bank-financed projects. The Bank's risk-management, rather than human rights-based approach, to the risks and impacts of projects on the rights of indigenous peoples, and its failure to reference specific human rights instruments in the Framework, further compound concerns that the Bank will not always act to ensure that borrowers respect the human rights of impacted indigenous communities. Further, the absence of an emphasis on the rights of affected indigenous peoples sends the wrong message to borrowers about the approach and treatment of impacted indigenous communities.

The Bank's treatment of a number of issues during the consultation and drafting process amplifies concerns about the Bank's commitment to protect indigenous communities impacted by projects it funds. The new terminology, 'Indigenous Peoples/Sub-Saharan African Historically Underserved Traditional Local Communities', introduced in the final version of the Framework, without input from indigenous communities, alongside the Bank's use of the borrower's identification processes for indigenous peoples, could result in exclusion of certain indigenous communities. In addition, the borrower's exclusion of indigenous persons who live or use lands outside the defined 'project area', but who are affected by a project, and the Framework's limitations on the term 'collective attachment', may result in the exclusion of indigenous peoples from the coverage and protections, including FPIC, contained in the Framework.

The resulting Framework also fails to ensure full respect for indigenous peoples' right to exercise their FPIC consistent with international law standards, including the UN Declaration on the Rights of Indigenous Peoples. In addition, the Framework's provisions offer a borrower the possibility of opting out of remedying remaining adverse impacts on the rights of indigenous peoples where the borrower finds that it is not 'technically or financially feasible' to do so. Thus, indigenous communities could be left with severe violations of their rights that threaten not only the livelihood, culture, and health and well-being of their members, but also the very survival of their communities. Finally, the Framework does not fully ensure the right of indigenous peoples to be consulted and participate in decisions that affect them nor protect against their total loss of culture.

The failure of the Bank to wholly protect the rights of indigenous peoples throughout the Framework reflects the tension between the Bank's desire to move forward with investment projects versus international obligations of the Bank and its borrowers to ensure the full protection of the rights of affected persons, in particular indigenous peoples. This tension is particularly acute at a time when the outside pressures on indigenous lands have become ever more intense. At the time of writing, the Bank was drafting Guidance Notes for borrowers on the implementation of the Framework.[111] They will not be mandatory, however, which means that indigenous peoples' representatives, civil society organisations and academics will need to refer back to the Framework to ensure that it is being implemented. Activists will need to draw on the Framework, despite its gaps and limitations, while reminding the Bank and borrowers of their international obligations. Consequently, civil society organisations and others will need to maintain even greater vigilance to ensure that indigenous peoples' rights are fully respected by both the borrower and the Bank.

Notes

1. The ESSs do not apply to the World Bank's Development Policy Financing or Program for Results. According to the World Bank, '[o]ver the last three years, investment operations have accounted for 82 percent of the Bank's projects and 66% of financial commitments'. World Bank, 'The World Bank's Safeguard Policies Proposed Review and Update: Approach

Paper' (October 2012), 6, http://siteresources.worldbank.org/EXTSAFEPOL/Resources/584434-1306431390058/SafeguardsReviewApproachPaper.pdf.
2. World Bank, 'Environmental and Social Framework' (2017), http://documents.worldbank.org/curated/en/383011492423734099/pdf/114278-WP-REVISED-PUBLIC-Environmental-and-Social-Framework-Dec18-2017.pdf.
3. World Bank, 'Environmental and Social Policies for Projects', https://www.worldbank.org/en/projects-operations/environmental-and-social-policies.
4. World Bank Group, *The World Bank Group A to Z 2015* 150 (World Bank Group, 2014).
5. See World Bank Inspection Panel, 'Indigenous Peoples', Emerging Lessons Series No. 2 (October 2016), http://documents.worldbank.org/curated/en/447361478156710826/Inspection-Panel-Indigenous-peoples.
6. World Bank, 'The World Bank Operational Manual, OP 4.10 Indigenous Peoples' (July 2005), https://policies.worldbank.org/sites/ppf3/PPFDocuments/090224b0822f89d5.pdf and World Bank, 'The World Bank Operational Manual, OP 4.12 Involuntary Resettlement' (December 2001), https://policies.worldbank.org/sites/ppf3/PPFDocuments/090224b0822f89db.pdf.
7. International Finance Corporation, 'Former Environmental and Social Safeguards and Support Materials', http://www.ifc.org/wps/wcm/connect/topics_ext_content/ifc_external_corporate_site/sustainability-at-ifc/policies-standards/safeguards-pre2006#safeguard.

   The Multilateral Investment Guarantee Agency (MIGA) also adopted new policies in 2007; consequently, the World Bank's 'current safeguards framework has led to the exclusion from scrutiny of some project-induced risks already included in IFC/MIGA Performance Standards … '. See World Bank Independent Evaluation Group, 'Safeguards and Sustainability Policies in a Changing World: An Independent Evaluation of World Bank Group Experience' (2010), xiv, 102, http://siteresources.worldbank.org/EXTSAFANDSUS/Resources/Safeguards_eval.pdf.
8. See World Bank Independent Evaluation Group, 'Safeguards and Sustainability Policies', 101.
9. The World Bank decided to update its safeguard policies for investment financing due to a combination of factors, which included greater awareness and import of environmental and social issues and increasing use of sustainability frameworks by the international and development finance community. World Bank, 'Approach Paper', 4–7.
10. World Bank, 'Review and Update of the World Bank Environmental and Social Safeguard Policies: Plan for Consultations with External Stakeholders for Phase 2 of the Policy Review and Update', https://consultations.worldbank.org/Data/hub/files/consultation-template/review-and-update-world-bank-safeguard-policies/en/phases/safeguards_review_consultation_plan_august_2014_2.pdf.
11. For an overview of the consultations held with indigenous peoples, see World Bank, 'World Bank Safeguard Policies Review and Update: Dialogue with Indigenous Peoples October 2013–March 2014 Summary', https://consultations.worldbank.org/Data/hub/files/consultation-template/review-and-update-world-bank-safeguard-policies/en/materials/final_summary_dialogue_with_ip_october_2013-march_2014.pdf.
12. World Bank, 'Review and Update of the World Bank Environmental and Social Safeguard Policies'.
13. World Bank Inspection Panel, 'Indigenous Peoples', 29. Sadly, the crisis facing the Sengwer continues, despite the fact that the European Union has taken over from the World Bank. Jonathan Watts, 'Kenya Forest Death: Activists Blame EU for Ignoring Human Rights Warnings', *The Guardian*, January 19, 2018, https://www.theguardian.com/environment/2018/jan/19/kenya-forest-death-activists-blame-eu-for-ignoring-human-rights-warnings.
14. World Bank, 'Approach Paper', 11.
15. World Bank, 'Environmental and Social Framework, First Draft for Consultation' (July 2014), 5, http://www.worldbank.org/content/dam/Worldbank/Event/ECA/central-asia/environmental-and-social-standard-framework-en.pdf.
16. The Bank 'shall not interfere in the political affairs of any member … . Only economic considerations shall be relevant to their decisions … '. World Bank, 'IBRD Articles of Agreement'

(2012), Article IV, Section 10. Also see World Bank, 'IDA Articles of Agreement' (1960), Article V, Section 6.

17. UN Special Procedures Mandate Holders of the UN Human Rights Council to Jim Yong Kim, President, World Bank, December 12, 2014, 4, http://consultations.worldbank.org/Data/hub/files/un_special_procedures_comments_on_the_draft_environmental_and_social_framework.pdf. Footnote 18 in the letter also states that 'The World Bank has however often treated the Articles of Agreements as a self-contained regime that is isolated from its surrounding legal environment'.
18. UN Special Procedures Mandate Holders to Jim Yong Kim at 4.
19. World Bank, 'Review and Update of the World Bank's Environmental and Social Safeguard Policies: Phase 2: Feedback Summary' (January 2015), 10, https://consultations.worldbank.org/Data/hub/files/consultation-template/review-and-update-world-bank-safeguard-policies/en/meetings/final_feedback_summary_london_csos_20_jan_2015.pdf. During the discussions in Brussels, which the authors attended, Bank representatives expressed concern about taking on the role of supervision or as an enforcer of the human rights obligations of borrower States.
20. World Bank, Environmental and Social Framework, Second Draft for Consultation (July 2015), 5, http://consultations.worldbank.org/Data/hub/files/consultation-template/review-and-update-world-bank-safeguard-policies/en/phases/clean_second_draft_es_framework_final_draft_for_consultation_july_1_2015.pdf. This second draft also provides that: 'To help ensure development effectiveness, the World Bank intends to maintain, in a manner consistent with its Articles of Agreement, the promotion of such approach in the design and implementation of the development projects that it supports'.
21. World Bank, 'Environmental and Social Framework', 1.
22. Ibid., 1.
23. World Bank, 'Investment Lending Reform: Modernizing and Consolidating Operational Policies and Procedures' (October 2012), 1, http://documents.worldbank.org/curated/en/777241468331877549/Investment-lending-reform-modernizing-and-consolidating-operational-policies-and-procedures. The other four elements mentioned in the document are: (i) 'enhancing implementation support'; (ii) 'consolidating and rationalizing the menu of financing options support'; (iii) 'providing a better enabling environment'; and (iv) 'Modernizing the IL policy framework, consolidating the policy, embedding these IL reforms, and taking advantage of the enhanced enabling environment'.
24. See World Bank, 'Annual Report 2017' (September 2017), 13, http://documents.worldbank.org/curated/en/143021506909711004/World-Bank-Annual-Report-2017.
25. World Bank, 'Bank Policy: Investment Project Financing' (November 2017), 3, https://policies.worldbank.org/sites/ppf3/PPFDocuments/Forms/DispPage.aspx?docid=2675&ver=current.
26. See 2003 UN Common Understanding adopted by the UN Development Group, 'The Human Rights Based Approach to Development Cooperation: Towards a Common Understanding Among UN Agencies' (2003), https://undg.org/document/the-human-rights-based-approach-to-development-cooperation-towards-a-common-understanding-among-un-agencies/.
27. UN Development Group, 'UNDG Guidance Note on Human Rights for RCS and UNCTS', https://undg.org/human-rights/undg-guidance-note-on-human-rights/about-the-undg-guidance-note-on-human-rights-for-rcs-and-uncts/. Also see United Nations, 'Human Rights Up Front: A Summary for Staff', http://www.un.org/News/dh/pdf/english/2016/Human-Rights-up-Front.pdf. Also see 2030 Agenda for Sustainable Development, unanimously endorsed by 193 States in 2015, which aims to foster sustainable development and to end poverty and hunger and is 'grounded in the Universal Declaration of Human Rights'. UN General Assembly, 'Transforming our World: The 2030 Agenda for Sustainable Development', A/RES/70/1 (October 21, 2015), http://www.un.org/ga/search/view_doc.asp?symbol=A/RES/70/1&Lang=E.

28. Human Rights Watch, 'World Bank: Human Rights All but Absent in New Policy' (July 2016), https://www.hrw.org/news/2016/07/21/world-bank-human-rights-all-absent-new-policy.
29. World Bank, 'Environmental and Social Framework', 76.
30. Ibid., ix (Vision, para. 4).
31. Ibid., 19–20 (ESS1 para. 28(b)(ii) and (iii)). Nondiscrimination provisions are also contained in ESS2 concerning Labor and Working Conditions.
32. Ibid., 98, 100 (ESS10, para. 7 and 22(g)).
33. Ibid., 100 (ESS10, para. 27(a)).
34. Ibid., 104.
35. For example, see Ibid., ix (Overview, para. 4) and 1–2 (Vision, para. 3).
36. Ibid., 100 (ESS1, para. 26.)
37. UN Office of the High Commissioner for Human Rights, 'Guiding Principles on Business and Human Rights', UN Doc. HR/PUB/11/104 (2011), 8 (Principle 6), http://www.ohchr.org/Documents/Publications/GuidingPrinciplesBusinessHR_EN.pdf. Admittedly, there is a dearth of governments that include human rights stipulations in their requirement for awarding procurement contracts to private entities and those that do, according to a study in 2016, only address selected human rights issues such as human trafficking, child labour or reference specific human rights instruments such as ILO labour standards. See Danish Institute for Human Rights, International Corporate Accountability Roundtable, Harrison Institute of Public Law, 'Public Procurement and Human Rights: A Survey of Twenty Jurisdictions' (July 2016), 9–10, http://www.hrprocurementlab.org/wp-content/uploads/2016/06/Public-Procurement-and-Human-Rights-A-Survey-of-Twenty-Jurisdictions-Final.pdf.
38. International Finance Corporation, 'IFC Performance Standards on Environmental and Social Sustainability' (2012), 6, https://www.ifc.org/wps/wcm/connect/topics_ext_content/ifc_external_corporate_site/sustainability-at-ifc/publications/publications_handbook_pps.
39. James Anaya was the UN Special Rapporteur on the rights of indigenous peoples from 2008 to 2014 and Victoria Tauli-Corpuz currently serves in this post. World Bank, 'Review and Update of the World Bank's Environmental and Social Safeguard Policies, Phase 3, High-Level Dialogue on Environmental and Social Standard 7, Participant List', https://consultations.worldbank.org/Data/hub/files/consultation-template/review-and-update-world-bank-safeguard-policies/en/meetings/high_level_dialogue_on_ess7_addis_ababa_ethiopia_feb_11-12_16_participant_list.pdf.
40. World Bank, 'High-Level Dialogue on the Proposed ESS 7 on Indigenous Peoples', 1, https://consultations.worldbank.org/Data/hub/files/consultation-template/review-and-update-world-bank-safeguard-policies/en/meetings/final_summary_-_high-level_dialogue_on_ess_7.pdf.
41. Amnesty International, 'World Bank: Draft environment and social safeguards fail to uphold rights of Indigenous Peoples', public statement (August 2, 2016), https://www.amnesty.org/en/documents/ior30/4599/2016/en/.
42. World Bank, 'High-Level Dialogue on the Proposed ESS 7 on Indigenous Peoples', 2.
43. UN General Assembly, 'United Nations Declaration on the Rights of Indigenous Peoples', A/RES/61/295 2 (Article 8) (2007), http://www.un.org/esa/socdev/unpfii/documents/DRIPS_en.pdf.
44. World Bank Inspection Panel, 'Indigenous Peoples', 7.
45. World Bank, 'Environmental and Social Framework', 76 (ESS7, para. 6).
46. Ibid., 76 (ESS7, para. 6).
47. Ibid., 4 (para. 4(b)), 19 (ESS1, para. 28(b)).
48. As an example, in the second draft, Annex 1 to ESS1, para. 7(g) included 'migrant or internally displaced status', but these groups were not included in the list in the policy section or in ESS1. See World Bank, 'Environmental and Social Framework: Second Draft'. However, on a positive note, the Bank did include 'forest dwellers, hunter-gatherers, pastoralists or other nomadic groups' in the coverage of ESS7. See World Bank, 'Environmental and Social Framework', 77 (ESS7, para. 9).

49. See for example, World Bank, 'Environmental and Social Framework', 1 (Vision, para. 3) which mentions 'women, children, persons with disabilities, youth and minorities'.
50. World Bank, 'Bank Directive: Addressing Risks and Impacts on Disadvantaged or Vulnerable Individuals or Groups' (August 2016), 1, https://policies.worldbank.org/sites/ppf3/PPF Documents/e5562765a5534ea0b7877e1e775f29d5.pdf.
51. The Bank Directive notes that:

    The task team reviews the terms of reference for the environmental and social assessment to verify that ... the terms of reference (a) identifies (or requires the identification of) groups or individuals affected by the project that may be disadvantaged or vulnerable; and (b) requires an assessment of project risks and impacts, and identification of differentiated mitigation measures, as they pertain to the disadvantaged or vulnerable individuals or groups that are identified.

    World Bank, 'Bank Directive: Addressing Risks and Impacts on Disadvantaged or Vulnerable Individuals or Groups', 2 (Section III, point 3).
52. World Bank, 'Environmental and Social Framework', 10 (Policy, para. 54) and 77 (ESS7, para. 10).
53. See footnote 7 defining 'Collective attachment' in World Bank, 'OP 4.10 Indigenous Peoples'.
54. World Bank, 'World Bank Board Approves New Environmental and Social Framework', press release (August 4, 2016), http://www.worldbank.org/en/news/press-release/2016/08/04/world-bank-board-approves-new-environmental-and-social-framework.
55. Ibid.
56. World Bank, 'Environmental and Social Framework', 77 (ESS7, para. 10, footnote 8).
57. World Bank Inspection Panel, 'Indigenous Peoples', 5–7.
58. For example, the Independent Evaluation Group of the World Bank noted that 'The social safeguard policies were found to have irreconcilable differences with national laws in UCS pilot countries. Not a single pilot country was found equivalent to the World Bank on social safeguards ... '. World Bank Independent Evaluation Group, 'Safeguards and Sustainability Policies', 86.
59. World Bank, 'Environmental and Social Framework', 76–77 (ESS7, paras. 7, 9 and 10).
60. Ibid., 4 (Policy, para. 4(a)(iii)); 19 (ESS 1, para. 35).
61. Ibid., 10 (Policy, para. 54); 76 (ESS7, para. 7).
62. Ibid., 77 (ESS7, para 9).
63. See World Bank, 'OP 4.10 Indigenous Peoples', para. 4, footnote 8. Also see World Bank, 'Environmental and Social Framework', 77 (ESS7, para. 9).
64. World Bank, 'Environmental and Social Framework', 77 (ESS7, para. 8, footnote 6).
65. Ibid., 77 (ESS7, para. 9, footnote 7).
66. World Bank, 'OP 4.10 Indigenous Peoples', para. 1.
67. World Bank, 'Approach Paper', 11.
68. See for example, the following comments from stakeholders, most likely governments, during the second phase of the Bank's consultations:

    We are not comfortable with this provision (FPIC). Domestic laws of acquisition and protection of such communities already provide for adequate safeguards including consent before acquisition can take place in certain cases. The Bank thus needs to rely on such domestic laws/guidelines where the domestic laws and rules etc. take care of such issues.

    Also, 'Our government perceives the switch from consultation to consent ... to be a step back in the safeguard policies'. World Bank, 'World Bank Safeguard Policies Review and Update: Summary of Phase 2 Consultations and Bank Management Responses' 48 (on file with authors).
69. World Bank, 'Environmental and Social Framework, First Draft', 17 (Policy, para. 45) 75 (ESS7, para. 5).
70. Ibid., 10 (Policy, para. 55) and 80 (ESS7, para. 25).

71. Ibid., 78 (ESS7, para. 19).
72. UN General Assembly, 'United Nations Declaration on the rights of Indigenous Peoples', 2 (Article 32, para. 2).
73. The recognition of the right of indigenous peoples to exercise their FPIC in connection with development projects that impact a range of rights, including the right to life, health, self-determination, development, and culture, among others, can be seen from the following: Kichwa Indigenous People of Sarayaku v. Ecuador, Judgment (Merits and Reparations), Inter-American Court of Human Rights (June 27, 2012) 33 (para. 127); Saramaka People v. Suriname, Judgment (Interpretation of the Judgment on Preliminary Objections, Merits, Reparations and Costs), Inter-American Court of Human Rights (August 12, 2008) 6 (para.17) and Judgment (Preliminary Objections, Merits, Reparations, and Costs), Inter-American Court of Human Rights (November 28, 2007), 26, 40–41 (paras. 86, 133–137). African Court on Human and Peoples' Rights, African Commission on Human and Peoples' Rights v. Republic of Kenya, Judgment (May 26, 2017), 11–12 (para. 43, E, iii). African Commission on Human and Peoples' Rights Case 276 / 2003 – *Centre for Minority Rights Development (Kenya) and Minority Rights Group International on behalf of Endorois Welfare Council v Kenya* (2009) para. 291; Poma Poma v. Peru, UN Human Rights Committee, Comm. 1457/2006, UN Doc. CCPR/C/95/D/1457/2006 (March 27, 2009) para. 7.6; UN Committee on Economic, Social and Cultural Rights, 'General Comment No. 21, Right of eight of everyone to take part in cultural life' (2009), 9 (para. 37); U.N. Committee on the Elimination of Racial Discrimination, General Recommendation 23 on the rights of indigenous peoples (1997), 1 (para. 4d).

    In addition, see compilation UN REDD Programme, 'Legal Companion to the UN-REDD Programme Guidelines on Free, Prior and Informed Consent (FPIC): International Law and Jurisprudence Affirming the Requirement of FPIC' (January 2013) https://www.uncclearn.org/sites/default/files/inventory/un-redd05.pdf and see the 'Report of the Special Rapporteur on the rights of indigenous peoples' that states: 'Where the rights implicated are essential to the survival of indigenous groups and foreseen impacts on the rights are significant, indigenous consent to those impacts is required, beyond simply being an objective of consultations'. UN Human Rights Council, 'Report of the Special Rapporteur on the rights of Indigenous Peoples', A/HCR/21/47, para. 85 (2012), http://www.ohchr.org/Documents/HRBodies/HRCouncil/RegularSession/Session21/A-HRC-21-47_en.pdf.

    Also, the UN Global Compact Business Reference Guide on UNDRIP articulates the current standard in stating that 'FPIC should be obtained whenever there is an impact on indigenous peoples' substantive rights (including rights to land, territories and resources, and rights to cultural, economic and political self-determination)'. UN Global Compact, 'The Business Reference Guide to the UN Declaration on the Rights of Indigenous Peoples' (2013) 45.

    Furthermore, the 2014 Outcome Document of the World Conference on Indigenous Peoples states:

    > We recognize commitments made by States, with regard to the United Nations Declaration on the Rights of Indigenous Peoples, to consult and cooperate in good faith with the indigenous peoples concerned through their own representative institutions in order to obtain their free and informed consent prior to the approval of any project affecting their lands or territories and other resources.

    UN General Assembly, 'Outcome Document of the High-level Plenary Meeting of the General Assembly Known as the World Conference on Indigenous Peoples', A/RES/69/2, para. 20 (2014), http://www.refworld.org/docid/543f7a114.html.
74. World Bank, 'Environmental and Social Framework', 79–80 (ESS7, para. 24).
75. World Bank, 'Environmental and Social Framework, First Draft', 78 (ESS7, para. 19).
76. World Bank, 'Environmental and Social Framework', 79 (ESS7, para. 23).
77. World Bank, 'Environmental and Social Framework, Second Draft', 107 (ESS7, para. 21).

78. World Bank, 'Summary of Phase 3 Consultations and Bank Management Responses' 50 (Issue 65), https://consultations.worldbank.org/Data/hub/files/consultation-template/review-and-update-world-bank-safeguard-policies/en/materials/summary_of_phase_3_consultations_and_bank_management_reponses_final_for_public_disclosure_post_board_august_4.pdf.
79. World Bank, 'Environmental and Social Framework', 81 (ESS7, para. 29, footnote 17).
80. Ibid., 79 (ESS7, para. 24(a)).
81. Ibid., 80 (ESS7, para. 26).
82. See Coalition for Human Rights in Development, 'World Bank Leaves Holes in Safety Net', press release (August 8, 2016) quoting Prabiindra Shakya with Asia Indigenous Peoples Pact, http://rightsindevelopment.org/?page_id=6115.
83. World Bank, 'High-Level Dialogue on the Proposed ESS 7 on Indigenous Peoples', 1.
84. It should be noted that 'When the FPIC of the affected Indigenous Peoples ... cannot be ascertained by the Bank, the aspects of the project relevant to those affected Indigenous Peoples ... for which the FPIC cannot be ascertained will not be processed further'. World Bank, 'Environmental and Social Framework', 80 (ESS7, para. 27).
85. World Bank, 'Environmental and Social Framework, First Draft', 81 (ESS7, para. 25, footnote 14).
86. Carl Söderbergh attended the London meeting and assisted World Bank staff in the reformulation of the wording of the footnote.
87. World Bank, 'Environmental and Social Framework', 82 (ESS7, para. 31, footnote 20).
88. World Bank, 'Environmental and Social Framework, First Draft', 27 (ESS1, para. 28) and 76 (ESS7, para. 9).
89. UN Special Procedures Mandate Holders of the UN Human Rights Council to Jim Yong Kim, President, World Bank, December 12, 2014, 15.
90. See World Bank, 'Issues for Phase 3 Consultations: CODE Introduction' (August 2015), 3 (on file with authors).
91. World Bank, 'Environmental and Social Framework, First Draft', 26 (ESS1, para. 25). Also see page 81 (ESS7, para. 28) in this first draft. Footnotes in ESS1 defined 'technical and financial feasibility'.

    > Technical feasibility is based on whether the proposed measures and actions can be implemented with commercially available skills, equipment, and materials, taking into consideration prevailing local factors such as climate, geography, demography, infrastructure, security, governance, capacity, and operational reliability. (See page 26 (ESS1, para. 25, footnote 21))
    > Financial feasibility is based on relevant financial considerations, including relative magnitude of the incremental cost of adopting such measures and actions compared to the project's investment, operating, and maintenance costs, and on whether this incremental cost could make the project nonviable for the Borrower. (See page 27 (ESS1, para. 25, footnote 22))

    These definitions remain unchanged in the final version. World Bank, 'Environmental and Social Framework', 16 (ESS1, footnotes 2 and 3).
92. See UN Office of the High Commissioner for Human Rights, 'The Corporate Responsibility to Respect Human Rights: An Interpretive Guide' (2012), 19, http://www.ohchr.org/Documents/Issues/Business/RtRInterpretativeGuide.pdf.
93. World Bank, 'Environmental and Social Framework', 19 (ESS1, para. 27(d), footnote 26).
94. Ibid., 19 (ESS1, para. 27(d), footnote 26).
95. Ibid., 7 (Policy, para. 32).
96. See World Bank Independent Evaluation Group, 'Safeguards and Sustainability Policies', xvii.
97. World Bank, 'Environmental and Social Framework', 19 (ESS1, para. 27(d), footnote 26).
98. For example, originally there was no obligation for the Bank to consult indigenous peoples in connection with the Bank's assessment of the Borrower's environmental and social framework and its determination of whether to allow the use of such framework. World Bank, 'Environmental and Social Framework, First Draft', 13 (Policy, paras. 23–26). Also, the

Borrower was not required to consult indigenous peoples in connection with consideration of 'feasible alternative project designs to avoid or minimize land acquisition or restrictions on land use ... '. See page 59 (ESS5, para. 7). The final version now provides for consultation in both situations. See World Bank, 'Environmental and Social Framework', 7 (Policy, para. 26) and 56 (ESS5, para. 17).

99. See in particular articles 18 and 19, in the UN Declaration on the Rights of Indigenous Peoples, that are integrally linked to an indigenous community's right to self-determination, a right explicitly expressed in article 3 of the Declaration. UN General Assembly, 'United Nations Declaration on the rights of Indigenous Peoples'.
100. World Bank, 'Environmental and Social Framework', 7 (Policy, para. 31).
101. Ibid., 79 (ESS7, para. 23).
102. Ibid., 77 (ESS7, para. 11).
103. Ibid., 77–78 (ESS7, para. 12). The absence of a reference to consultation with indigenous peoples in this paragraph is particularly striking when contrasted with the subsequent paragraph 13, which provides that the 'Borrower's proposed measures and actions will be developed in consultation' with indigenous peoples.
104. Ibid., 22 (ESS1, para. 45).
105. Ibid., 100 (ESS10, para. 26).
106. This can be contrasted, *inter alia*, with the UN Global Compact, *The Business Reference Guide to the UN Declaration on the Rights of Indigenous Peoples* (2013) which includes extensive advice on meaningful consultation.
107. World Bank, 'Environmental and Social Framework', 79 (ESS7, para. 23(a)).
108. World Bank, 'The World Bank Operational Manual, OP 4.11 Physical Cultural Resources' (July 2006), 1 http://web.worldbank.org/archive/website01541/WEB/0__-1678.HTM.
109. World Bank, 'Environmental and Social Framework', 86 (ESS8, para. 7).
110. Ibid., 58 (ESS5, paras. 26 and 27).
111. Editor's note: These were issued by the World Bank in June 2018.

Disclosure statement

No potential conflict of interest was reported by the authors.

Implementing free prior and informed consent: the United Nations Declaration on the Rights of Indigenous Peoples (2007), the challenges of REDD+ and the case for the precautionary principle

Malayna Raftopoulos and Damien Short

ABSTRACT

Over 21 years after the United Nations Declaration on the Rights of Indigenous Peoples (September 2007 – hereafter UNDRIP) was passed, it is useful to examine the functionality and utility of a core principle it contains- the notion of Free Prior and Informed Consent (FPIC) with respect to the twin challenges of environmental destruction and a key 'mitigation' policy: REDD+. While UNDRIP, and to a lesser extent, the International Labour Organisation Convention No. 169 (ILO 169) has strengthened the legal status of FPIC, its application has proved to be extremely difficult. This article argues that when considering the potential harm of environmental and REDD+ climate change policies there needs to be a greater emphasis placed on the 'precautionary principle' when applying FPIC. Demonstrating why precaution needs to be taken in order to ensure human rights, this article argues that increasing the prominence of the precautionary principle within FPIC can impact significantly on the protection of biodiversity as well as the way in which environmental harm, laws and regulations are understood in relation to their social and cultural impact and shape future responses to the climate change crisis.

Introduction

The mechanism Reducing Emissions from Deforestation, Forest Degradation and as well as Conservation, Sustainable Management of Forests and Enhancement of Forest Carbon Stocks (REDD+) has emerged as the key pillar of the international climate change regime. Widespread concern about climate-induced ecological collapse has led to a 'seismic shift' in the role of forests in socio-economic development and an increased interest in tackling the drivers of deforestation and degradation.[1] With deforestation and forest degradation accounting for between 12 and 18 percent of annual 'greenhouse gas' (GHG) emissions, developing strategies to reduce and stabilise atmospheric concentrations of GHG has become of global importance.[2] Recognising the financial value of stored carbon, REDD + is a broad framework that sets out to create a system that provides forest users with economic incentives to reduce net emissions of greenhouse gases through enhanced forest management and improved forest carbon stocks. REDD+ has become the 'world's largest experiment in Payments for Ecosystem Services (PES)', designed to create a multi-level system that transfers economic resources from carbon offset buyers to sellers.[3] Proponents of REDD+ argue that the scheme has the potential to generate co-benefits such as poverty alleviation, biodiversity conservation, financial incentives, technical assistance and facilitated technology transfer.[4] However, REDD+ has also faced strong opposition due to concerns over its impact on the protection of human rights, the potential loss of forest people's territories to large-scale commercial forest operations, the restriction of access and use of natural resources by these communities, the lack of equitable benefit-sharing of REDD+ activities, and the exclusion of forest communities from the design and implementation of REDD+ policies.[5] Furthermore, there are fears that it could slow or reverse improvements to forest governance at a national level by creating incentives for governments and commercial interests to deny or ignore forest dwellers access and control over forest resources.[6]

As REDD+ proposals and projects continue to gather momentum there is general consensus among observers that its success will depend on whether indigenous people and local communities' interests are integrated into policy deliberations and decision-making processes and if their rights, including their right to give or withhold FPIC as well as respect for customary land rights, are recognised. Although the legal status of FPIC has been strengthened through the adoption of the UNDRIP in 2007 and the ILO Convention No. 169 and has gained prominence in recent years as the world confronts multiple crises including climate change, its application has proved to be extremely difficult. Nonetheless, widely used against those economic sectors that exploit land and resources, FPIC has become an important mechanism for protecting indigenous rights and natural resources, as well as an instrument to ensure responsible development in indigenous territories. This article argues that when considering the potential harm of environmental and climate change policies such as REDD+, there needs to be a greater emphasis placed on the 'precautionary principle' when applying FPIC. The principle can be invoked to justify cautious decision making where there is the distinct possibility of harm from an action, and/or where there is a lack of extensive scientific knowledge on the issue. In essence, the principle invokes the social responsibility to protect publics from exposure to harm, often when scientific investigation has found a plausible, sometimes tentative, risk. Once applied, the precautionary approach should only be relaxed once further scientific findings emerge that provide sound evidence that no harm will result. The article demonstrates why precaution needs to be taken to guarantee human rights, environmental rights and, in particular, indigenous rights given that the majority of the world's forests are located on indigenous land and territories.[7] Increasing the prominence of the precautionary principle within FPIC can impact significantly on the protection of biodiversity as well as the way in which environmental harm, laws and regulations are understood in relation to their social and cultural impact and shape future responses to the climate change crisis.

UNDRIP, ILO 169 and the legal framework of FPIC

Recent developments regarding the human rights of indigenous peoples such as UNDRIP and ILO 169, which are compatible and mutually reinforcing, are particularly relevant to

REDD+. Both IL0 169 and UNDRIP provide the legal framework for FPIC. According to the UN Development Group Guidelines on Indigenous Peoples' Issues, 'free' should imply no coercion, intimidation or manipulation and 'prior' should imply that consent has been sought sufficiently in advance to the authorisation or the beginning of activities and time requirements for indigenous consultation processes to occur have been respected. 'Informed' should imply that the information provided covers (at a minimum) the nature, size, pace reversibility and scope of the proposed project or activity, the reason (s) or purpose and duration of the proposed project or activity, the areas that would be affected, those who are likely to be involved, the procedures the project or activity may entail and 'a preliminary assessment of the likely economic, social, cultural and environmental impact, including potential risks and fair and equitable benefit sharing in a context that respects the precautionary principle'.[8]

The ILO 169 convention, signed in 1989, was the first international instrument to recognise the importance of self-identification of indigenous and tribal peoples. Moreover, it is the only 'international instrument concerning the rights of indigenous peoples that produces legally binding obligations (when ratified) and is still open for ratification'.[9] ILO 169 has played a critical role in the construction and promotion of indigenous rights, however, it has also become an important mechanism for protecting nature and the environment and is widely used against those economic sectors that exploit land and resources such as mining and forestry. ILO 169 covers a broad range of issues pertaining to indigenous peoples' rights and well-being, reflecting the historical discrimination experienced by these group, with the concept of land, territory, consultation and participation found at the core of the Convention. Article 14 acknowledges the rights of ownership and possession of land which has been traditionally occupied or used by indigenous peoples for their subsistence and traditional activities. Loss of territory and ancestral lands, which forms the basis of most economies and livelihood strategies of indigenous peoples, would threaten their very survival. Recognising the special relationship that exists between indigenous peoples' and land, Article 13 stipulates that governments shall respect the special importance for the cultures and spiritual values of their relationship with their lands and territories.

Article 6 and 7 of the ILO Convention establish appropriate and effective mechanisms for the consultation and participation of indigenous and tribal peoples regarding issues that affect and concern them. Article 6 states that indigenous peoples have the right to be consulted and to freely participate at all levels of decision-making regarding any policies and programmes that may affect them. These consultations shall be carried out in good faith and in appropriate circumstance. Furthermore, Article 7 recognises that indigenous peoples' have the right to control their own economic, social and cultural development and also develop their own institutions and initiatives. However, as Barelli comments 'in order to appreciate the significance of this provisions in relation to FPIC one has to read it in combination to with Article 15'.[10] Article 15 recognises that indigenous peoples' rights to the natural resources pertaining to their lands, including their right to use, manage and conserve these resources, shall be specially safeguarded. However, acknowledging that in many cases the state owns mineral or sub-surface resources and other resources, Article 15 also pertains that in such as cases, governments shall consult indigenous peoples. The consultation process shall ascertain if and to what extent the interests of indigenous communities would be prejudiced before undertaking or allowing the exploration or exploitation of any resources pertaining to their lands. It further stipulates that indigenous peoples have the right to share in the benefits generated from these activities.

Also of importance in the context of REDD+ is Article 16, which states that indigenous peoples shall not be removed from the lands which they occupy and where relocation is considered necessary as an exceptional measure, it can only take place with their free and prior informed consent. However, what is considered an 'exceptional measure' is not defined and there is no functional clarity as to what constitutes 'consent', although it is generally understood to mean collective decision-making.[11] it does not give indigenous communities the 'unqualified right to veto'.[12] When consent cannot be obtained, relocation can only take place following appropriate procedures established by national laws and regulations. Furthermore, whenever possible indigenous peoples should have the rights to return to their ancestral lands once the reasons for relocation cease to exist. The main objective of ILO 169 is to ensure that indigenous peoples' can effectively participate at all levels of decision-making in political, legislative and administrative processes and bodies with regards to decision that directly affect them. However, while ILO 169 imposes significant requirements on states it does not require them to legally obtain consent before implementing any development project on their land. ILO 169 takes a pragmatic approach to FPIC, empowering indigenous peoples without going as far as granting them a veto power.[13]

Adopted by the UN General Assembly in 2007, UNDRIP 'represents the culmination of a complex legal and political process that led to the affirmation of a number of key rights and principles related to indigenous people'.[14] However, unlike ILO 169, it is often suggested that UNDRIP does not carry legally binding obligations and is considered by many to simply be an instrument of soft law, providing the international community with a common framework for the realisation of indigenous rights. However, it's status in international law is subtler than that, as Davis writes: 'the Declaration exists in an amorphous in-between state of constituting both a "nonbinding", influential and aspirational statement of soft law but equally an instrument that reflects already binding rules of customary international law'.[15]

UNDRIP focuses on the critical elements of self-determination for indigenous peoples and the parameters to achieve this. The Declaration acknowledges that indigenous peoples have the right to freely pursue their economic, social and cultural development, which cannot be realised unless their practices, customs, priorities and institutions are fully acknowledged (Articles 3 and 4). Similar to ILO 169, UNDRIP recognises the special relationship that exists between indigenous peoples and their land. This is recognised in Article 25 of the Declaration which states that indigenous peoples have the right to maintain and strengthen their distinctive spiritual relationship with their lands. Of equal importance to indigenous peoples right to land is Article 26 which asserts that they have the right to the land and resources which they have traditionally owned, occupied or used. Moreover, indigenous peoples have the right to own, use, develop and control their lands and resources by reason of traditional ownership. Article 26 also affirms that indigenous peoples have the right to lands, territories and resources which they have traditionally owned or occupied and the right to own, use, develop and control the lands, territories and resources that they possess. Furthermore, the state should give legal recognition and protection of these lands, territories and resources.

The key elements of UNDRIP, as with ILO 169, focus on consultation and participation. The Declaration establishes that the purpose of consultation is to achieve FPIC and is laid out in a number of Articles. In accordance to Article 18 and 19, indigenous peoples have the right to participate in decision-making whenever the matter at hand affects their rights. Furthermore, states shall consult and cooperate with indigenous peoples through their own representative institutions to obtain their FPIC before adopting and implementing any legislative or administrative measure that would affect them. Article 32, states that

> Indigenous peoples have the right to determine and develop priorities and strategies for the development or use of their lands or territories and other resources ... (and) ... States shall consult and cooperate in good faith with the indigenous peoples concerned through their own representative institutions in order to obtain their free and informed consent prior to the approval of any project affecting their lands or territories and other resources, particularly in connection with the development, utilization or exploitation of mineral, water or other resources.[16]

Also, important in relation to REDD+ is Article 10 which states that no indigenous peoples shall be forcibly removed from their lands or territories and no relocation should take place without the FPIC of those involved or before an agreement on just and fair compensation.[17] Furthermore, wherever possible, indigenous peoples should have the option to return.

The Convention on Biological Diversity (CBD) which was opened for signature at the Earth Summit held in Rio de Janeiro in 1992, also pertains to the principle of FPIC. Regarded as a key international treaty in relation to sustainable development, the CBD has become one of the most widely accepted multilateral environmental agreements. Imposing legal obligations on its parties, the Convention sets out three main objectives: the conservation of biodiversity, the sustainable use of its components and the fair and equitable sharing of the benefits that arise from the use of resources. In setting out the framework for the Convention's third objective, Article 15 states that 'access to genetic resources shall be subject to prior informed consent of the Contracting Party (states) providing such resources, unless otherwise determined by that party'.[18] Emphasis is also placed on the importance of tradition knowledge and practices, with Article 8(j) requesting that each state respect, preserve and maintain indigenous and local knowledge, innovations and practices and promote their wider application with the approval and involvement of the holders.

Developing REDD+

It was during COP11 in 2005, that the 'Coalition for Rainforest Nations' via the Papua New Guinea government and the government of Costa Rica called upon the UNFCCC and the Kyoto Protocol to take note of present rates of deforestation within developing nations, acknowledge the resulting carbon emissions, and open up a dialogue to discuss options for reducing emissions from deforestation in developing countries. Included as an official negotiation item in the Bali Action Plan, the principle of providing financial support for addressing reduced emissions from deforestation and forest degradation was formally introduced onto the international climate agenda in 2007.[19] Since Bali, REDD+ has emerged through a number of successive agreements under the guidance of the UNFCCC. Concerns about the impact of REDD+ on forest-dependent communities led to the introduction of safeguards built upon a human rights and consultative normative framework.[20] Addressed in the Cancun Agreements of 2010, the UNFCCC adopted seven non-mandatory safeguards for REDD+ activities into Annex 1. The safeguards agreed by the parties concluded that REDD+ projects should complement or be consistent with relevant national forest programmes and international protections. REDD+ initiatives must respect domestic legislation and sovereignty and also fully respect the knowledge and rights of indigenous peoples and members of the local community, taking into account international and national obligations such as UNDRIP and ILO 169. Furthermore, the safeguards mandate the full and effective participation of relevant stakeholders, in particular indigenous peoples and local communities. The remaining safeguards ensure that REDD+ actions are consistent with the conservation of natural forests and biodiversity, address the risks of reversals and reduce displacement of emissions. However, these safeguards present the minimum requirements established by the UNFCCC framework, rather than defining the acceptable and unacceptable performances of REDD+ initiatives.

At COP19 in 2013, the Warsaw Framework for REDD+ was adopted and largely concluded the negotiations on REDD+. Building on the Cancun Agreement on REDD+, the Warsaw Framework included seven decisions and provided clarity on a number of key issues related to the implementation of REDD+. These included decisions on national forest monitoring systems, REDD+ finance, summary on information on safeguards, forests reference emission levels, measuring, reporting and verification forest-related emissions (MRV), coordination of support for the implementation of REDD+ activities, and the drivers of deforestation and forest degradation. Most recently at COP21 held in Paris in 2015, parties explicitly recognised the role forests have in offsetting human actions. Three REDD+ decisions were adopted alongside the Paris Outcome relating to safeguards, alternative policy approaches, such as joint mitigation and adaptation (JMA) for the integral and sustainable management of forests and non-carbon benefits, marking the end of the negotiations on REDD+ methodological issues and guidance.[21] Underlying the REDD+ framework is a strong global partnership based on a commitment by developing countries to embark on low-carbon climate resilient development and on developed countries providing significant funding as an incentive for reduced forest-based carbon emissions.[22] Working outside of the UNFCCC, new international programmes have been created by multilateral bodies such as the World Bank's Forest Carbon Programme (FCPF), the UN-REDD Programme and the World Bank's Forest Investment Programme (FIP) to fund or provide technical assistance.

The precautionary principle and REDD+

The 'precautionary principle' is highly relevant to REDD+ given that it deals with the conservation and sustainable use of forests. Moreover, the indigenous peoples and forest-dependent communities that inhabit those forests are especially vulnerable to policies such as REDD+ because of their reliance on natural resources and ecosystems. As Howell observes, 'what was originally perceived as a straight forward project with technocratic solutions has turned into a highly complex "society" project'.[23] Instead of viewing forests as complex eco-systems that support wide varieties of life and biological processes, the REDD+ framework has redefined the role of forests as carbon sinks. In doing so, policy makers have ignored the intrinsic link that exists between people and their environment, placing forests outside of society.[24] Concerns regarding the consequences of REDD+ initiatives on forest-dependent and indigenous communities have forced aside this 'assumed and unquestioned conceptual division between nature and society' as environmental and human rights non-governmental organisations (NGOs) question the impact of REDD+ on local communities.[25] In recent years REDD+ has faced increasing criticism from forest communities and indigenous peoples who argue that it has 'brought an onslaught of global and extractive economy measures directly to their doorstep, often resulting in ghastly negative environmental consequences for their territories and livelihoods'.[26]

Emerging in the mid 1970s from the former West Germany, the precautionary principle has become widely accepted as the guiding principle of environmental policy and decision-making. It marks a shift in policy thinking from one of post-damage control to pre-damage control in order to protect humans and the environment from the damage and harm caused by human actions.[27] Based on the three core elements of potential harm, scientific uncertainty and precautionary action, the World Commission on the Ethics of Scientific Knowledge and Technology characterised the precautionary principle as a strategy to deal with human activities that 'may lead to morally unacceptable harm that is scientifically plausible but uncertain'.[28] In accordance to this working definition, morally unacceptable harm refers to harm caused to both humans and the environment. This includes harm that threatens human life or health, is serious and effectively irreversible, and that is equitable to present or future generations or imposed without sufficient consideration of the human rights of those affected.[29] Focusing on the 'philosophical and spiritual relationship between humankind and the environment which sustains our physical existence', the precautionary principle has come to play a significant role in current environmental law and policy.[30] As O'Riordian and Jordan comment, 'the precautionary principle has much efficacy because it captures an underlying misgiving over the growing technicalities of environmental management at the expense of ethics, environmental rights in the face of vulnerability, and the facilitative manipulation of cost–benefit analysis'.[31] Moreover, it challenges 'many of the unstated assumptions' with regards to the manner in which the environment is used and valued by society.[32]

The precautionary principle has increasingly been incorporated into a number of international treaties and declarations related to sustainable development and environmental protection, reflecting the rise in political interest and global consciousness in protecting the environment. Most notably, the precautionary principle was incorporated in the 1992 Rio Declaration under Principle 15, where it stated that 'where there are threats of serious or irreversible damage, lack of scientific certainty shall not be used as a reason for postponing cost-effective measures to prevent environmental degradation'.[33] Similar language was also used in the preamble to the Convention on Biological Diversity and in the 1992 Framework Convention on Climate Change which also emphasised that

> Parties should take precautionary measures to anticipate, prevent or minimise the cause of climate change and mitigate its adverse effects. Where there are threats of serious or irreversible damage, lack of full scientific certainty should not be used as a reason for postponing such measures.[34]

Whilst the precautionary principle remains only a guiding principle and is not yet legally binding in international and national law, its increasing inclusion in international declarations has resulted in it receiving broad international recognition.

FPIC and REDD+ in practice

While FPIC is not a new concept and has previously been applied to other development activities occurring on indigenous territories such as natural resource extraction, particularly in relation to oil and gas,[35] it has only recently been applied to REDD+ and has highlighted the lack of respect for the principles and practice of FPIC across the forest sector.[36] FPIC has become a key component of effective stakeholder engagement and consultation, but its interpretation and application remains a challenge for those developing countries entering into REDD+. As Pham et al. note,

> there is so far no common understanding on how to integrate all parts of FPIC: the elements of *free, prior* and *informed consent*; the links between processes and outcomes; and the requirement that FPIC is employed at certain points in time during a REDD+ activity,[37]

consequently there is often a gap between international norms and practice on a national level. Furthermore, it has been argued that in many countries FPIC remains a politically sensitive issue, with governments 'reluctant to recognise the collective right of indigenous peoples to self-determination out of fear that it could threaten state sovereignty and lead to an escalation in claims for independence by indigenous peoples'.[38]

In the context of REDD+, FPIC is addressed indirectly though the text on safeguards, added during into Annex 1 of the Cancun Agreements, which notes that the General Assembly has adopted UNDRIP. The application of FPIC is a means to meet the Cancun Agreements requirement that REDD+ partner countries promote and support 'respect for the knowledge and rights of indigenous peoples and members of local communities' and ensure 'the full and effective participation of relevant stakeholders, *inter alia*, indigenous peoples and local communities'[39] (UN-REDD, 2012: 7). In discussing the application of FPIC to REDD+, Carodenuto and Fobissie explain that '"Free" means that there must be no coercion, intimidation or manipulation and if a community does say "no", there must be no repercussions' (2015: 158). '"Prior" means that consent must be sought and obtained before engaging in any activity on community land and that enough time must be given for communities to appreciate the impacts of the proposed activities' (ibid). '"Informed" means there has been a complete disclosure of all information related to the plans for REDD+ in a language and medium that is comprehensible and easily accessible by the affected communities' (Ibid.). '"Consent" means that the relevant communities have the choices to accept or refuse the project at hand' (ibid.). However, while there remains little clarity over what constitutes 'consent', it is generally agreed that consent is not a one-time process but rather a recurring process whereby the various stages of the project require continual affirmation and consent. Consent should be sought to discuss the proposed REDD+ project, to participate in developing a detailed plan of the project and also to implement the project in question.[40] (Anderson, 2011). In making a prima facie case for increasing the prominence of the precautionary principle within FPIC, it is necessary to examine each aspect of FPIC in turn in order to understand how it is practiced on the ground within REDD+ projects.

'Free'

Ensuring that indigenous peoples' and local communities' voices are heard in the development of REDD+ projects remains a challenge on both the national and international level. As Brown, Seymour, and Peskett note, 'although REDD may also provide an opportunity for further progress in reformist legislation, special attention to safeguards is needed to ensure that the interests of national elites and international commercial interests do not override the rights of forest communities'.[41] Community members, regardless of gender, age or standing, must be able to make a decision on their involvement in REDD+ projects free from coercion, bias, conditions, bribery or rewards. In their study of the TFCG/Mjumita REDD+ project in Lindi, Tanzania, Scheba and Rakotonarivo reported that REDD+ project staff had used the issue of rain water, whereby it was 'emphasised to villagers that protecting trees could "drag and pull in clouds" and therefore attract rain' to create a sense of urgency for farmers who were reliant on rain-fed agriculture in order to sell the project.[42] Furthermore, false expectations over future carbon income and other development benefits such as tenure security, agricultural improvements and increased production were raised among the villagers and played a substantial role in incentivising the community to approve the project.[43] Leggett and Lovell also reported that in the case the April-Salomei project in Papua New Guinea, communities were promised millions of Kina within the year and the project would provide 'everlasting' benefits, so much so that landowners could abandon their subsistence garden once the project had begun.[44] Moreover, landowners reported that there was a degree of borderline coercion by the project organisers who ignored or dismissed negative opinions and questions in order to ensure that a positive view of the project was presented.[45] In those instance where communities have rejected REDD+ projects such as the Matsés, a Panoan speaking indigenous people whose ancestral territory lies in lowland jungle between the Javari and Galvez rivers in the frontier region between Peru and Brazil, indigenous leaders have faced legal actions and criminalisation by the developers.[46] Other opponents of REDD+ reported increased persecution and violence by pro-REDD advocates. One such example was the executive director of the Rainforest Resource and Development Centre (RRDC) in Cross River State, Nigeria, Odey Oyama, who was repeatedly harassed and intimidated by state security agents and eventually forced to flee his home.[47]

'Prior'

Meaningful participation in REDD+ has become a key issue for indigenous peoples. As Osborne et al., note, 'as indigenous areas are among the most forested and biodiverse, scholars and policy makers agree that indigenous peoples represent key stakeholders in the development and expansion of conservation-based activities under REDD+'.[48] In order for indigenous peoples to be able to fully participate in REDD+ projects, they must be given enough time – as established by the right-holders – to understand, access, and analyse information on the proposed activity. They must also be provided with information before activities can be initiated, at the beginning or initiation of an activity, process or phase of implementation, including conceptualisation, design, proposal, information, execution, and following evaluation. Although indigenous communities should be engaged both during the conceptualisation and development phases of projects, opponents of REDD+ have argued that 'meaningful local participation in the design and implementation of REDD+ has been negligible'.[49] A report produced by the Forest Peoples Programme on REDD+ projects in Peru showed that consultations were not being planned as prior processes but rather incorporated later only after the project had started or ratified. Moreover, 'consultations' had become about 'reaching an agreement to conduct technical studies of carbon stocks with a view to developing offset credits'.[50] Consequently, communities were 'entirely unaware of the nature of such markets and are being pressured into signing up to carbon offsetting projects without a full understanding of the commercial, climatic, ethical or social implications of these deals'.[51]

There is also a lack of consultation with any civil society or potentially critical observers such as in the case of Maderacre project in the Madre de Dios region of Peru. In this instance there was no consultation with the Federation of the Native Peoples of the River Madre de Dios and its Tributaries (FENAMAD), the regional indigenous peoples' organisation, regarding the issue of isolated peoples who inhabit and transit one of the concessions.[52] Friends of the Earth reported that in Indonesia's Ulu Masen project in in Aceh province, community consultation and involvement in the design and implementation of the REDD+ had been overlooked in order to expedite the project.[53] Furthermore, they criticised REDD+ projects for their lack of transparency, reporting instances of closed meetings and the issuing of invitations so late that the relevant stakeholders have been unable to make travel arrangements in time (Hall, 2012). In instances when consultations have taken places, residents have complained that the consultation periods were too short lasting as little as one hour as in the case of the Amerindian community of Chenapou in Guyana. The inadequate length of the consultations prevented residents from engaging in the topic, actively participating and having their opinions heard.[54]

'Informed'

As REDD+ proposals and projects continue to gather momentum there is general consensus among observers that its success will depend on whether indigenous and forest-based communities' interests are integrated into decision-making processes and if their rights are recognised. Given the potential impacts of REDD+ on indigenous peoples' and livelihoods, informing indigenous communities of both the positive and negative aspects in a balanced manner and providing them with full access to information about proposed projects is vital to ensuring their human rights are respected and preventing them from being side-lined in as projects are developed. In order to move ahead with REDD+ projects, communities must be able to fully understand the potential impact of the proposed project in an appropriate language and culturally appropriate format with sufficient time for it to be understood and be able to obtain more information if requested. The community should also receive updates of proposed project as it evolves and be kept fully informed. However, increasing evidence demonstrates the lack of effective actions to ensure the participation of indigenous peoples and local communities in the planning and implementation of REDD+ schemes. A study carried out by the Forest Peoples Programme in 2013 on the conditions of the implementation of the Takamanda National Park project in Cameroon, showed that residents from two enclave villages – Obonyi I and Obonyi III – had neither been informed nor consulted on the implementation of REDD+ projects.[55] Participation by local people was found to be severely limited, with the highest governance structure of the park, the Park Management Committee, having only two representatives from park villages and no clear selection process in place. Locals voiced concern that, without clear selection criteria, community representatives would be handpicked, motivated by per diems or sitting allowances, and not accountable to the communities. In case of the April-Salomei project in Papua New Guinea, there was also a considerable lack of community awareness and knowledge of REDD+. Among the community there was a commonly held belief that 'the project would generate money "*moni bilong skai*" (money from the sky) or for nothing, that without any work'.[56] Furthermore, despite low levels of literacy in either language, project questionnaires were distributed in English and Tok Pisin.[57] Confusion over the meaning of REDD+ and carbon and minimal awareness of climate change policies at a community level was reported by several studies and remains a consistent problem.[58] While some have equated this to the limited experience and understanding of the concept of REDD+ by NGOs and government officials operating in the field,[59] organisations like the Forest Peoples Programme have criticised project developers for providing partial and biased information to communities on the basis that it was 'necessary' to explain things in more simple terms during the early stages of the project. Moreover, few practitioners presented any of the potential risks such as market uncertainty and the restricted use of resources to communities.[60] There have also been complaints that additional information, including project costs and assumptions of carbon values, documentation of community consultations and approvals and baseline studies of community resource use, has only made available to the validator and to the general public.[61]

'Consent'

As Anderson argues, 'part of the motivation for ensuring FPIC is respected as a requirement for REDD+ mechanisms is to give rights holders the power to veto REDD+ activities or policies on the basis of "unreasonable claims"'.[62] Although consent in the context of FPIC is not sought from every individual, it is required from the affected group and is based on collective considerations in accordance with their own customs and traditions. In order to ensure that the specific interest of the groups directly affected by REDD+ projects are met, consent is required to be solicited over specific periods of time and for distinct stages or phases of the project in question. Stakeholders should also agree on how often verification should occur and who will carry out the verification of consent.[63] However, recent studies have shown that a number of issues have risen with regards to the issue of consent, in particular, the intimidation of community members, the lack of consent verification processes, the subordination of communities wishes and interests by governments in the name of 'national interest' and forgery. In the case of the Takamanda National Park project in Cameroon, villagers felt that they had been intimidated into signing the paperwork to create the national park by government and park officials who claimed that the land belonged to the government and that the communities had encroached onto the reserve. The lack of verification processes is a recurring problem, with some communities not being able to vote on whether or not to implement REDD + and others simply being asked if they wanted their forests to be conserved or not, with a yes being taken as consent for the REDD+ project to go ahead.[64] In 2012, Vía Campesina declared its opposition to REDD+ activities taking place in the Lacandón jungle in

Chiapas, Mexico. In 2010 the government of the Mexican state of Chiapas signed an agreement under the Governors' Climate and Forest Task Force to sell carbon permits from REDD+ projects in the Lacandon jungle to the California state government, led by Arnold Schwarzenegger, to offset their emissions, without any semblance of free, prior, and informed consent, imposing the project on farming and indigenous communities.[65] In some instances, such as the case of April-Salomei project in Papua New Guinea, signatures have even been forged.[66] Scheba and Rakotonarivo also highlighted how social inequalities along the lines of gender, age and income group also play a role in the discussion and voting on REDD+ projects, noting that 'while women are generally present in public discussions, we observed that they often find themselves in a situation of passive participation where listening and accepting the majority consent dominates'.[67]

The precautionary principle and REDD+

Within the context of REDD+, FPIC is particularly challenging because of the developing nature, scope, and scale of the programme. Pham et al. argues that applying FPIC to REDD+ is difficult for a number of reasons. Firstly, there is a lack of understanding of how FPIC is adopted in different political and social contexts as well as the institutional arrangements required to implement FPIC. Secondly, there is a lack of experience in implementing FPIC in the context of REDD+, with relatively few initiatives having been undertaken so far. Thirdly, the procedural norms of FPIC have yielded unexpected and ambiguous result and lastly, there is a 'subjective understanding of the terms and requirements of FPIC, influenced by both cultural interpretations and political interests'.[68] Respecting the right to FPIC cannot be reduced to a bureaucratic 'tick-box exercise' and should not be viewed as a linear process. Rather it should be viewed as an ongoing process that involves forest-dependent and indigenous communities and guarantees them the right to FPIC at every stage of the REDD+ process through the continual monitoring, maintenance, and reaffirmation of the various stages of a REDD+. Moreover, interaction with forest-dependent and indigenous communities should not be focused on the negotiation of financial compensation given that the price, regulation and market stability of carbon credits are still unknown and carbon credits are not yet tangible or widely understood.[69] The implementation of a robust and verifiable process to implement a continual process of obtaining FPIC would undoubtedly require a significant investment in people, time, communication materials and strategies, training and skills development, community institution building, independent verification, and technical and legal advice to build up the capacity of communities to clearly understand the implications of REDD+ at each stage, resolve conflicts that arise and make an informed decision on the project in question.[70] The significant investment needed to implement FPIC has resulted in some project proponents failing to seek consultation and participation from those communities involved in REDD+ activities and have taken at face value claims by government and non-government organisation (NGO) stakeholders to 'represent' indigenous peoples and local communities.[71] However, despite the difficulties associated with implementing and applying FPIC, it has become a cornerstone of many indigenous groups' demands in view of the adverse social impacts of REDD+.

Given the increasingly complex nature of REDD+ and its interconnection with indigenous and forest-dependent communities and ecosystems, it has become increasingly clear that it is necessary to adapt precautionary approach to implementing REDD+ projects. An approach that advocates taking precautionary decisions, with the aim of protecting those communities most vulnerable to the impacts of REDD+ and achieving sustainable development, is vital given the long-term threat climate change poses to both the environment and human beings. While it is widely acknowledged that climate change can cause serious and irreversible damage, the threat and risk of mitigations strategies, such as REDD+, are yet to fully understood. Therefore, the precautionary principle is necessary in order to:

- Clearly identify the risks associated with REDD+;
- Develop effective policies and measures to prevent such risks and protect both forest-dependent communities and biodiversity in areas affected by REDD+ projects;
- Advance our understanding of the relationship between ecosystem and forest-dependent communities and the long-term implications of REDD+ of this relationship;
- Employ methodologies capable of analysing and assessing the impact of REDD+ such as a Human Rights Impact Assessment as advocated by Raftopoulos and Short (2016);[72]
- Allow for the development of alternative forest and climate change initiatives that do not threaten the protection of forests and consider the social, cultural, economic and political context of indigenous communities and 're-prioritisation of policy responses to climate change away from one focused solely on carbon accounting and toward one that considers more fully principles of equity, fairness, and the impact on the most vulnerable' (Hunter, 2009: 334–5);
- Curtail or restrict powerful commercial interests who are seeking to benefit from REDD + at the expense of local communities;
- Increase the level of transparency of decision-making processes by explicitly characterising and examining the uncertainties, gaps in information, ethics and values associated with REDD+ projects.

Conclusion

We have discussed how the legal status of FPIC has been fortified, and codified, through the adoption of the UNDRIP and the ILO 169, but that its application has proved to be extremely challenging. Even so, it has been widely used against the economic and extractive interests that exploit land and resources. Indeed, FPIC has undoubtedly become an important mechanism for protecting indigenous rights and natural resources, as well becoming a viable instrument to ensure responsible, if not always sustainable, development in indigenous territories. We have shown that the policies associated with the REDD+ mechanism have been particularly problematic. REDD+ emerged as the key pillar of the international climate change regime; but as we have discussed, while proponents of REDD+ argue that the scheme has the potential to generate benefits such as poverty alleviation, biodiversity conservation, financial incentives, technical assistance and facilitated technology transfer, REDD+ has also faced strong opposition due to concerns over its impact on the protection of human rights, the potential loss of forest people's territories and access to natural resources, large-scale commercial forest operations, the lack of equitable benefit-sharing, and perhaps most importantly, exclusion of forest communities from the design and implementation of REDD+ policies. Thus, we argued that a key challenge for the international community will be to ensure that REDD+, in addition to delivering emissions reductions as well as the promised co-benefits, protects human rights and biodiversity. We have also discussed how, indigenous peoples have increasingly adopted a human-rights based approach to address their concerns over REDD+ initiatives taking place in their territories, which has has largely focused on securing land rights and control over resources through the principle of FPIC.

This paper argued that when considering the potential harms of policies such as REDD +, the precautionary principle is a useful way of more effectively implementing FPIC principles. We showed why precaution is necessary to guarantee basic human, environmental and indigenous peoples' rights standards in this context. Furthermore, we argued that increasing the prominence of the precautionary principle within FPIC can significantly improve the protection of vitally important biodiversity, as well as improving the way in which we understand how best to respond to environmental law and regulatory breaches that produce harms as these must be understood in relation to their social and cultural impact so as to shape future responses to the climate change crisis.

Notes

1. William D. Sunderlin and Stibniati Atmadja, 'Is REDD+ an Idea Whose Time Has Come or Gone?', in *Realising REDD+: National Strategy and Policy Options*, ed. Arild Angelsen (Bogor Barat: CIFOR, 2009), 45–57.
2. Matthew Leggett and Heather Lovell, 'Community Perceptions of REDD+: A Case Study from Papua New Guinea', *Climate Policy* 12, no. 1 (2012): 115–34.
3. Esteve Corbera, 'Problematizing REDD+ as an Experiment in Payments for Ecosystem Services', *Current Opinion in Environmental Sustainability* 4 (2012): 612–9, 612.
4. Stefano Pagiola, Agustin Arcenas and Gunars Platais, 'Can Payments for Environmental Services Help Reduce Poverty? An Exploration of the Issues and the Evidence to Date from Latin America', *World Development* 33, no. 2 (2005): 237–53; Oscar Venter et al., 'Harnessing Carbon Payments to Protect Biodiversity', *Science* 326, no. 5958 (2009): 1368.
5. David J. Kelly, 'The Case for Social Safeguards in a Post-2012 Agreement on REDD', *Law Environment and Development Journal* 6, no. 1 (2010): 63–80; Annalisa Savaresi, 'REDD+ and Human Rights: Addressing Synergies between International Regimes', *Ecology and Society* 18, no. 3 (2013): 5–13; Malayna Raftopoulos, 'REDD+ and Human Rights: Addressing the Urgent Need for a Full Community-Based Human Rights Impact Assessment', *International Journal of Human Rights* 20, no. 4 (2016): 509–30; Roberto Espinoza Llanos and Conrad Feather, *The Reality of REDD+ in Peru: Between Theory and Practice* (Lima: Forest Peoples Programme', 2011), http://www.forestpeoples.org/sites/fpp/files/publication/2011/11/reality-redd-perubetween-theory-and-practice-website-english-low.res.pdf.
6. David Brown, Frances Seymour, and Leo Peskett, 'How Do We Achieve REDD Co-benefits and Avoid Doing Harm?', in *Moving Ahead with REDD: Issues, Options and Implications*, ed. Arild Angelsen et al., (Bogor Barat: CIFOR, 2008), 107–19, 113.
7. Sophie Chao, *FOREST PEOPLES: Numbers across the World* (2012), http://www.forestpeoples.org/sites/fpp/files/publication/2012/05/forest-peoples-numbers-across-world-final_0.pdf.
8. UNDG, *United Nations Development Group Guidelines on Indigenous Issues* (Geneva: United Nations, 2008), 1–53, 28, http://www.ohchr.org/Documents/Issues/IPeoples/UNDGGuidelines.pdf.
9. Mauro Barelli, 'Free, Prior and Informed Consent in the Aftermath of the UN Declaration on the Rights of Indigenous Rights: Developments and Challenges Ahead', *International Journal of Human Rights* 16, no.1 (2012): 1–24, 9.
10. Ibid., 10.

11. Thuy Thu Pham et al., 'Adapting Free, Prior and Informed Consent (FPIC) to Local Contexts in REDD+: Lessons from Three Experiments in Vietnam', *Forests* 6 (2015): 2405–23, 2407.
12. Barelli, 'Free, Prior and Informed Consent', 21.
13. Ibid., 11.
14. Ibid., 17.
15. Megan Davis, 'To Bind or Not to Bind: The United Nations Declaration on the Rights of Indigenous Peoples Five Years On', *Australian International Law Journal* (2012): 19, http://www.austlii.edu.au/au/journals/AUIntLawJl/2012/3.pdf.
16. The *United Nations Declaration on the Rights of Indigenous Peoples* (13 September 2007) A/RES/61/295, http://www.un.org/en/genocideprevention/documents/atrocity-crimes/Doc.18_declaration%20rights%20indigenous%20peoples.pdf.
17. Ibid.
18. The Convention on Biological Diversity (1992), https://www.cbd.int/convention/text/default.shtml.
19. Anthony Hall, *Forests and Climate Change: The Social Dimensions of REDD in Latin America* (Cheltenham, UK: Edward Elgar Publishing Ltd, 2013).
20. Kathleen Birrell, Lee Godden, and Maureen Tehan, 'Climate Change and REDD+: Property as a Prism for Conceiving Indigenous Peoples' Engagement', *Journal of Human Rights and the Environment* 3, no. 2 (2012): 196–216.
21. UNFCCC, *Technical Resource Series 3: Towards a Common Understanding of REDD+ under the UNFCCC* (Geneva: UN-REDD Programme Secretariat, 2011), http://www.unredd.net/documents/redd-papers-and-publications-90/un-redd publications-1191/technical-resources-series/15901-towards-a-common understanding-of-redd-under-the-unfccc.html.
22. Hall, *Forests and Climate Change.*
23. Signe Howell, 'Divide and Rule: Nature and Society in a Global Forest Programme', in *Anthropology and Nature*, ed. Kirsten Hastrup (New York: Routledge, 2015), 147–65, 147.
24. Ibid.
25. Ibid., 147.
26. Pablo Reed, 'REDD+ and the Indigenous Question: A Case Study from Ecuador', *Forests* no. 2, (2011): 525–49, 525.
27. COMEST, *The Precautionary Principle* (Paris: UNESCO, 2005), 1–52, 7, http://unesdoc.unesco.org/images/0013/001395/139578e.pdf.
28. Ibid., 14.
29. Ibid.
30. James Cameron and Julie Abouchar, 'The Precautionary Principle: A Fundamental Principle of Law and Policy for the Protection of the Global Environment', *Boston College International and Comparative Law Review* 14, no. 1 (1991): 1–27, 2.
31. Timothy O'Riordan and Andrew Jordan, 'The Precautionary Principle in Contemporary Environmental Politics', *Environmental Values* 4, no. 3 (1995): 191–212, 192.
32. Ibid.
33. UN, *Convention on Biological Diversity* (Geneva: United Nations, 1992), 1–30, 3, https://www.cbd.int/doc/legal/cbd-en.pdf.
34. UNFCCC, *The United Nations Framework for Climate Change* (Geneva: United Nations, 1992), 1–25, 4, https://unfccc.int/resource/docs/convkp/conveng.pdf.
35. John, R. Owen and Deanna Kemp, 'Free Prior and Informed Consent', Social Complexity and the Mining Industry: Establishing a Knowledge Base', *Resources Policy* 41 (2014): 91–100; Kathryn Thomlinson, 'Indigenous Rights and Extractive Resource Projects: Negotiations over the Policy and Implementation of FPIC', *The International Journal of Human Rights* (2017), doi:10.1080/13642987.2017.1314648.
36. Patrick Anderson, *Free, Prior, and Informed Consent in REDD+: Principles and Approaches for Policy and Project Development* (Bangkok: RECOFTC and GIZ, 2011), 1–90, 8. http://redd.unfccc.int/uploads/2_74_redd_20130710_recoftc_free_2C_prior_2C_and_informed_consent_in_reddplus.pdf.
37. Pham et al., 'Adapting Free, Prior and Informed Consent (FPIC)', 2407.

38. Ibid., 2409.
39. UN-REDD, *FPIC for REDD+ in the Asia Pacific Region: Lessons Learned, Challenges and Recommendations* (2012), 1–39, 7, http://www.vietnamredd.org/Upload/Download/File/FINAL_FPIC_for_REDD_in_the_Asia_Pacific_region_-_Lessons_learned,_challenges_and_recommendations_(August_2012)_5036_4324.pdf.
40. Anderson, 'Free, Prior, and Informed Consent in REDD+'.
41. Brown, Seymour and Peskett, 'How Do We Achieve REDD Co-benefits and Avoid Doing Harm?', 112.
42. Andreas Schebaa and O. Sarobidy Rakotonarivo, 'Territorialising REDD+: Conflicts Over Market-Based Forest Conservation in Lindi, Tanzania', *Land Use Policy* 57 (2016): 625–37, 629.
43. Ibid.
44. Leggett and Lovell, 'Community Perceptions of REDD+', 125.
45. Ibid.
46. Espinoza Llanos and Feather, 'The Reality of REDD+ in Peru', 43.
47. No REDD in Africa Network, Nigeria: Persecution and Criminalization of Activists, http://www.no-redd-africa.org/index.php/16-redd-players/84-the-worst-redd-type-projectsinafricacontinent-grab-for-carbon-colonialism.
48. Tracey Osborne, Laurel Bellante and Nicolena von Hedemann, *Indigenous Peoples and REDD+: A Critical Perspective* (Cusco: IPCCA, 2014), 1–94, 34, https://pdfs.semanticscholar.org/38cf/f57cf41aff8700ec3d7b72dd2af39dbd4b11.pdf.
49. Osborne et al., 'Indigenous Peoples and REDD+', 36.
50. Ibid., 51.
51. Ibid.
52. Ibid., 53.
53. Ronnie Hall, ed., *REDD: The Realities in Black and White* (Amsterdam: Friends of the Earth, 2012), 1–28, 16, http://www.foei.org/wp-content/uploads/2014/01/REDD-ingles-final-17-11.pdf.
54. Sam Airey and Torsten Krause, '"Georgetown Ain't Got a Tree. We Got the Trees"—Amerindian Power & Participation in Guyana's Low Carbon Development Strategy', *Forests* 8, no. 51 (2017): 1–24, 9.
55. Samuel Nnah Ndobe and Klaus Mantzel, *Deforestation, REDD and Takamanda National Park in Cameroon - A Case Study* (UK: Forest Peoples Programme, 2014), 4–43, https://www.forestpeoples.org/sites/fpp/files/private/publication/2014/07/cameroon-final.pdf.
56. Leggett and Lovell, 'Community Perceptions of REDD+', 125.
57. Ibid.
58. Rodriguez-Ward and Pilar Paredes del Aguila, 'Valuation of Environmental Services in the Managed Forests of Seven Indigenous Communities in Ucayali, Peru', in *REDD+ on the Ground: A Case Book of Subnational Initiatives across the Globe*, ed. Erin O'Sills (Bogor Indonesia: CIFOR, 2014), 166–87, 181; Cut Augusta Mindry Anandi et al., 'Ulu Masen REDD+ Initiative, Aceh, Indonesia', in *REDD+ on the Ground: A Case Book of Subnational Initiatives across the Globe*, ed. Erin O'Sills (Bogor Indonesia: CIFOR, 2014), 380–400, 394.
59. Cut Augusta Mindry Anandi et al., 'Ulu Masen REDD+ Initiative', 394; Signe Howell, 'No RIGHTS–No REDD': Some Implications of a Turn Towards Co-Benefits, *Forum for Development Studies*, 41, no. 2 (2014), 253–72.
60. Espinoza Llanos and Feather, 'The Reality of REDD+ in Peru', 50–1.
61. Ibid., 53.
62. Anderson, 'Free, Prior, and Informed Consent in REDD+', 17.
63. Ibid.
64. Mucahid Mustafa Bayrak and Lawal Mohammed Marafa, 'Ten Years of REDD+: A Critical Review of the Impact of REDD+ on Forest-Dependent Communities', *Sustainability* 8 (2016): 2–22, 7.

65. Chris Lang, 'Vía Campesina Declares its Opposition to REDD in the Lacandón Jungle', 21 September 2012, https://redd-monitor.org/2012/09/21/via-campesina-declares-its-opposition-to-redd-in-the-lacandon-jungle/.
66. Leggett and Lovell, 'Community Perceptions of REDD+', 125.
67. Schebaa and Rakotonarivo, 'Territorialising REDD+', 629.
68. Pham et al., 'Adapting Free, Prior and Informed Consent (FPIC)', 2408.
69. Anderson, 'Free, Prior, and Informed Consent in REDD+', 8.
70. Ibid., 26.
71. Ibid., 8.
72. Malayna Raftopoulos and Damien Short, 'A New Benchmark for Green Criminology: The Case for Community-Based Human Rights Impact Assessment of REDD+', in *Greening Criminology in the 21st century: Contemporary Debates and Future Directions in the Study of Environmental Harm* ed. Matthew Hall et al., (London and New York: Routledge, 2017), 165–82.

Disclosure statement

No potential conflict of interest was reported by the authors.

Towards new development paradigms: the United Nations Declaration on the Rights of Indigenous Peoples as a tool to support self-determined development

Jérémie Gilbert and Corinne Lennox

ABSTRACT
Since the adoption of the UN Declaration on the Rights of Indigenous Peoples, indigenous peoples' agency and ideas of development have become more central to wider development processes. This change finds its roots in the concept of 'self-determined development' (SDD), which has been fortified by the adoption of UNDRIP. SDD is built around key norms of UNDRIP, such as the rights of self-determination, free, prior and informed consent, the links between cultural rights and development and rights pertaining to land and natural resources. The normative shift towards SDD is surveyed in this article by looking at three topics: the jurisprudence of regional human rights courts on case law concerning development on indigenous peoples' land; the advocacy of indigenous peoples around the indicators of the Sustainable Development Goals; and the adoption of community bio-cultural protocols by indigenous peoples to regulate development of their land, natural resources and cultural heritage. In each example, UNDRIP has influenced positive changes in law and policy concerning indigenous peoples' views on development.

Introduction: moving beyond mainstream development 'aggression'

Mainstream development modalities have had a weak understanding of how to address structural causes of inequality. This is particularly true for groups whose cultural identity is seen as a barrier to mainstream development policy, whose cultural identity is completely invisible and ignored in development policy planning and implementation or whose exclusion serves the interests of economic exploitation. Development, as typically understood by the dominant actors of the state, is enacted for the public good and measured by a narrow indicator of economic growth. Factors like poverty reduction, health, education and even the environment matter more in this narrative than in the past, but the central push remains growth oriented and rests on the outdated assumption that increased productively and technological progress will yield better social outcomes for all.[1] In such contexts, development is imposed by state authorities on the local populations who do not get much say in the decision-making process leading to these so-called development projects. This approach to development, which is based on a very state-centric vision, reposes on what Nader referred to as the 'theory of lack' under which less 'developed' segments of the society are seen as 'lacking proper development', which then needs to be imposed on them.[2]

These kinds of approaches have not served indigenous peoples well. From the very beginning of colonial expansion on indigenous territories, the rights of indigenous peoples in development have mattered little to the 'developers'. The concept of 'development aggression'[3] has been used to describe and challenge top down economic development policies having a negative impact on indigenous communities. This is especially accurate when it comes to large-scale developmental projects taking place on indigenous peoples' territories. In many countries, large-scale natural resource development projects constitute a central element of national development policies, especially in countries rich in natural resources that have centred their developmental polices around natural resources exploitation.[4] In practice, for many local and indigenous communities living in the vicinity of the concerned natural resources, these type of projects often become synonymous with forced displacement, land dispossession and environmental degradation. Even peripheral attempts at recognising the rights of indigenous peoples, for example through land titling, have been viewed more as facilitative of neoliberal economic interests, such as legal land acquisition, than as commitments to indigenous peoples' self-determination.[5]

The turn towards human development in the early 1990s helped to shift the focus more towards social well-being but the approach was largely one-size-fits-all, lacking due regard for how structures of discrimination, colonialism and cultural difference might result in differential inclusion in development policy benefits. A reluctance in many states to measure impact of development with ethnically disaggregated data has long obscured the nature of inequality and the harms – or ineffectiveness – of mainstream development policies. Even the Millennium Development Goals, agreed in 2000 and hailed as new era for development, aimed for only a portion of the population to benefit (e.g. reduce hunger by half, reduce maternal mortality by three-quarters), and did not account for how groups like indigenous peoples might be left behind.[6] Few states fully accounted for indigenous peoples in their periodic MDGs reports and indigenous peoples were rarely, if ever, engaged in full participation of the elaboration of MDGs planning despite experiencing inequalities on key MDGs targets such as extreme poverty, maternal and child mortality, access to education and clean water and sanitation.[7] Indigenous peoples' leadership in securing Goal 7 on 'ensuring environmental sustainability', was largely ignored. The MDGs paid no attention to restitution for historical injustices that are often the root cause of contemporary development failures and 'aggression'.

Since the adoption of the UN Declaration on the Rights of Indigenous Peoples in 2007, there have been some important changes in the landscape of development policy and practice. Significantly, indigenous peoples' agency and ideas of development have become more central to these processes. This change finds its roots in the concept of 'self-determined development' (SDD), which we believe has been fortified by the adoption of UNDRIP. To analyse the impact that the UNDRIP has had in supporting the emergence of a right to SDD, we will first outline the meaning of SDD and then review how it has been manifested at different levels, from international legal jurisprudence, to global development indicators, and in local initiatives. To analyse how the right to SDD has been integrated into international legal jurisprudence, the article shows how regional human rights courts have engaged with the right to SDD, and the role of UNDRIP in supporting this. Next, the article examines how the UNDRIP is supporting the implementation of the Sustainable Development Goals (SDG). We argue that the norms of SDD are evident in new approaches to data collection under the SDGs. Finally, at the community and local level, we will provide some examples of community protocols on development, which demonstrate how principles of UNDRIP are being realised through these tools for the management of biological diversity and natural resources. We hope this survey of practice at both international and local levels will highlight the utility of UNDRIP in shaping new approaches to development and, crucially, giving substance to the emerging norm of self-determined development for indigenous peoples.

Development in UNDRIP: from development and identity to self-determined development

Self-determined development has emerged as a potential way to support indigenous peoples' own vision and approaches to development. Historically, there have been many calls by indigenous peoples for the adoption of an approach to development which is more supportive of their own visions and cultures. For example, in 1981 a Declaration on Ethnodevelopment was adopted under the auspices of UNESCO. The Declaration proclaimed that 'ethno-development is an alienable right of Indian groups' and affirming their 'inalienable right' to consolidate their cultural identity and to 'exercise … self-determination'.[8] However, it was not until the adoption of the UNDRIP that the concepts of the right to self-determination, participation and cultural development were formally adopted in a universal instrument recognising indigenous peoples' own approaches to development.

The central place accorded to indigenous peoples' right to development is evident from the preamble of the declaration, which includes seven references to it. The preamble notes that 'control by indigenous peoples over developments affecting them and their lands, territories and resources will enable them to maintain and strengthen their institutions, cultures and traditions, and to promote their development in accordance with their aspirations and needs'. The declaration puts a lot of emphasis on self-determination, identity and culture, recognising that identity and culture embody indigenous peoples' relationship with their lands and resources, the maintenance and development of distinctive institutions, their continuation and revival of their customs, practices, judicial systems and traditional knowledge. These rights are elaborated in the context of participation and ownership rights. The declaration also addresses other important aspects of identity and culture in the context of development. These include the right to develop manifestations of indigenous cultures (Art. 11), the right to develop and teach spiritual and religious traditions (Art. 12), the right to develop oral traditions, philosophies and languages (Art. 13), and the right to control and develop their cultural heritage, traditional knowledge and traditional cultural expressions (Art. 31). The right of indigenous peoples to determine and formulate their developmental priorities and strategies regarding their lands or territories and other resources is articulated in Article 32(1) of the UNDRIP. Article 32(2) then links this to the obligation of states to 'consult and cooperate' with indigenous peoples in order to obtain free, prior and informed consent (FPIC) in the context of development projects affecting these lands or resources. Whilst the concept of self-determined development is not in itself proclaimed in the UNDRIP, more than half of out of the 46 operational articles concern the expression of indigenous peoples' right to self-determined development.

The term self-determined development has emerged as part of an advocacy effort led by indigenous peoples to support the vision inscribed within the UNDRIP.[9] Also referred to as development with culture and identity,[10] the term is used to advocate for the respect of indigenous peoples' own perspectives and approaches to development and to assert a new meaning of the right to development. As stated by indigenous leader Victoria Tauli-Corpuz:

> Self-determined development for indigenous peoples is not a grand paradigmatic, generic alternative to mainstream development. It is simply part of our assertion of our right of self-determination and to remain as diverse and distinct cultures and communities. It captures the essence of our struggles since colonization to define our own development within the framework of our inherent rights and in consonance with the relationship we have with nature.[11]

There have been some debates amongst indigenous peoples' representatives over whether the term 'development' itself should be avoided; however, the agreement is that SDD represents a useful advocacy tool to support indigenous peoples' own vision of sustainable and locally based process of development.[12] The concept reflects and tries to integrate localised visions of what development means, including, for example, concepts such as *sumak kawsay* among the Quichua, *suma qamaña* by the Aymara, *laman laka* for the Miskitu, *gawis ay biag* for the Kankana-ey Igorot, and *vivir buen/buen vivir* in Spanish. The concept of SDD represents an important vision of the meaning of the right to development, which has often been approached from a top-down perspective, with indigenous peoples as passive recipients (and often victims of harms caused by development interventions). The very concept of development is relational and creates hierarchies and to that extent possible domination notably *vis à vis* indigenous peoples who are seen as passive targets to receive 'development'. Self-determined development challenges such passivity by putting indigenous peoples at the heart of the process of development in respecting their own visions and understandings of development. As analysed by Carling and Lasimbang, for many indigenous communities across the globe development is understood as 'the growth and progress of an indigenous community in their originality or within the context of their ethnic identity in a holistic way'.[13]

Legally, the concept is located within the rights to self-determination, development and participation. As stated by Tauli-Corpuz:

> The UNDRIP established the basic concepts and principles of self-determined development. It established that we have the right of self-determination, which is a foundational right. It not only recognizes our right to our lands, territories and resources but also our cultural rights and right to development.[14]

She analysed in detail how important the concept of self-determined development is as it allows the junction between the right to culture and the right to development, highlighting the inherent indivisibility of culture and development, something that was lacking in previous instruments. The concept of self-determined development is also visible in other norms proclaimed in indigenous peoples' specific instruments such as the ILO Convention 169 Concerning Indigenous and Tribal Peoples, which in its article 7.1 states:

> The peoples concerned shall have the right to decide their own priorities for the process of development as it affects their lives, beliefs, and institutions and spiritual well-being and the lands they occupy or otherwise use and to exercise control, to the extent possible, over their own economic, social and cultural development.

Likewise, in the American Declaration on the Rights of Indigenous Peoples (2016), article XXIV states: 'Indigenous peoples have the right to be actively involved in developing and determining development programmes affecting them and, as far as possible, to administer such programmes through their own institutions ...' (para. 3).

Indigenous peoples have used their presence in global governance institutions to push for some recognition of the norm of SDD in international policy on development. Many international development agencies, financial institutions and key donors have adopted some recognition of the rights of indigenous peoples in the development process. The World Bank was one of the first to do so, drafting an internal safeguarding policy.[15] Some good use has been made of the World Bank Inspection Panel to assert claims to SDD when such internal policies have failed.[16] The United Nations Development Programme (UNDP) was also an early adopter of specific policies on indigenous peoples: its Social and Environmental Standards (SES) aim at ensuring that

> UNDP Projects that may impact indigenous peoples are designed in a spirit of partnership with them, with their full and effective participation, with the objective of securing their free, prior, and informed consent (FPIC) where their rights, lands, resources, territories, traditional livelihoods may be affected.[17]

The International Finance Corporation has adopted a particular Performance Standard (No. 7) on indigenous peoples, which requires clients to obtain the FPIC of affected indigenous communities in the context of projects that: have impacts on their lands and natural resources; imply relocation; or have implications for critical cultural heritage.[18] Two major regional development banks, the Inter-American Development Bank and the Asian Development Bank, also have policies on indigenous peoples.[19]

These policies mark an important emerging recognition of SDD but as institutions governed and funded by states, there has been a limit to what international development agencies, donors and financial institutions can do when faced with state resistance to indigenous peoples' rights. Although the World Bank, for example, has replaced its early policy with a new suite of environmental and social standards, including protection for indigenous peoples' rights, advocates argue that this has not evolved to fully recognise SDD.[20] SDD is a norm pushing against dominant paradigms of state sovereignty and often, losing. One ally in this fight has been regional human rights courts, which have issued some key judgements that use existing international human rights law and UNDRIP to reach decisions that have shaped SDD norms for national contexts.

Self-determined development and litigation

Although there is little adjudication and jurisprudence on the right to development, several cases concerning indigenous peoples' rights in the context of developmental projects taking place on their territories have supported the emergence of jurisprudence linking human rights law and SDD. The case concerning the Endorois community in Kenya that was examined by the African Commission on Human and Peoples' Rights put into perspective the connections between participation, development and human rights law.[21] The case concerned a pastoralist community who saw its access to their ancestral land and natural resources greatly limited following the establishment of a nature reserve, mining, and tourism on their ancestral territory. This combination of mining, tourism and nature conservation led to the loss of access to important natural resources and land with great cultural and spiritual significance for the community. After years of frustrations for not getting any remedies and recognition of their fundamental rights at the national level, the Endorois sought remedies with the African Commission, which highlighted the need to recognise the fundamental rights to land and natural resources of the community. In its examination of the case, the African Commission specifically looked at the issue of development as the government had put forward the argument that the forced displacement of the community was justified to support the economic development of the country. Arguing that the loss of land and natural resources for the community was an inevitable price to pay for development, the government stated 'the task of communities within a participatory democracy is to contribute to the well-being of society at large and not only to care selfishly for one's own community at the risk of others'.[22] On the other hand, the Endorois and their supportive advocates had put forward the fact that such imposed development had resulted in their loss of access to essential natural resources and a negative impact on their cultural rights, which significantly violated their rights as enshrined in the African Charter on Human and Peoples' Rights. Linking self-determination and development, they highlighted that they had 'suffered a loss of well-being through the limitations on their choice and capacities, including effective and meaningful participation in projects that will affect them'.[23]

Hence, the African Commission had to examine two competing claims over development, the governmental perspective that displacement and loss of access to natural resources for the community was part of the inevitable process of development, and the claim from the community that their forced displacement and loss of land and natural resources were inherently violating their fundamental rights. It is worth noting that the argumentation put forward by the government of Kenya is not unusual or isolated. When it comes to development and exploitation of natural resources governments often put forward the argument that they cannot stop such large-scale developments that will bring significant wealth to the whole country to protect just a few 'marginalised' local indigenous communities.[24] To address these claims concerning the meaning of development, the Commission concentrated on two principal issues: (1) to what extent was the community consulted prior to the establishment of the wildlife reserve on their lands and (2) whether this development provided benefits to the concerned community. The Commission highlighted that in the context of a developmental project taking place on indigenous territories, governments have to put in place three safeguards to ensure the rights of indigenous peoples. First, the government has to ensure the effective participation of the members of the community in conformity with their customs and traditions, regarding any development, investment, exploration or extraction plan that will take place on their lands. Second, there should be a guarantee that the concerned community will receive a reasonable benefit from any such plan within their territory. Third, the government should ensure that no concession will be issued unless and until independent and technically capable entities perform a prior environmental and social impact assessment.[25]

In this case, the Commission highlighted that the government 'did not obtain the prior, informed consent of all the Endorois before designating their land as a Game Reserve and commencing their eviction'.[26] The Commission concluded that there was a clear violation of the right to development since 'no effective participation was allowed for the Endorois, nor has there been any reasonable benefit enjoyed by the community'.[27] Crucially, the Commission stated that the

> result of development should be empowerment of the Endorois community. It is not sufficient for the Kenyan Authorities merely to give food aid to the Endorois. The capabilities and choices of the Endorois must improve in order for the right to development to be realised.[28]

Whilst there is no direct mention of SDD, the Commission noted that the peoples concerned 'have not been accommodated by dominating development paradigms and in many cases they are being victimised by mainstream development policies and thinking and their basic human rights violated'.[29]

This approach was echoed in the 2017 African Court ruling concerning the Ogiek community, which examined similar dynamics concerning the meaning of development. In this case the African Court highlighted that Article 22 of the Charter (on the right to development) should be read in light of Article 23 of the UNDRIP.[30] The court found that the authorities had violated the right to development of the concerned communities as 'the evictions have adversely impacted on their economic, social and cultural development. They have also not been actively involved in developing and determining health, housing and other economic and social programmes affecting them'.[31]

There are very strong echoes to this approach linking development and direct participation and benefit for indigenous peoples in the extensive jurisprudence of the Inter-American Court of Human Rights. In the case of Saramaka, the Court established several connections between the right to property and indigenous peoples' rights to self-determined development. Pertinently, the court highlighted that the right to property is inseparable from other fundamental human rights, including common Article 1 of the International Covenant on Civil and Political Rights and the International Covenant on Economic, Social and Cultural Rights (the right to self- determination), Articles 4 and 5 of the American Convention on Human Rights (the right to life and the right to physical, moral and mental integrity), Articles 6 and 15 of the ILO Convention 169 (right to prior consultation) and Article 32 of UNDRIP (right to give or withhold consent). The court highlighted that the government has a duty to actively consult with the community according to their customs and traditions and such consultations must be in good faith, through culturally appropriate procedures and with the objective of reaching an agreement.[32] This progressive interpretation of Article 21 of the American Convention (right to property) is notably based on its connection to indigenous peoples' rights to freely determine their own social, cultural and economic development as expressed in article 32 of UNDRIP.[33] The court made similar comments in the case of the Sarayaku, referring to the UNDRIP and to several soft-law instruments related to cultural identity and development when interpreting the provisions of the American Convention.[34] The court also made a direct connection between the right to self-determination and development in the case of the Kaliña and Lokono peoples.[35] The court stated that this approach supports

> an interpretation of Article 21 of the American Convention that requires recognition of the right of the members of indigenous and tribal peoples to freely determine and enjoy their own social, cultural and economic development, which includes the right to enjoy their particular spiritual relationship with the territory they have traditionally used and occupied.[36]

Overall, through their support in the jurisprudence to indigenous peoples' right to SDD, even though SDD is not specifically expressed, the court has made direct connection between development and self-determination, land rights, cultural rights and participation.

It is against this backdrop of developing case law that the Sustainable Development Goals have emerged as a key opportunity for indigenous peoples to push beyond the limitations of current global policy and national failings to forge a better framework for SDD. The next section will critically examine the role of the indigenous movement in seeking to shape the new SDGs through the SDD lens.

The sustainable development goals: a framework for self-determined development?

The Sustainable Development Goals (SDGs) were agreed by UN Member States in 2015 and are embedded in *Transforming our world: the 2030 Agenda for Sustainable Development* (Agenda 2030).[37] They include many themes that directly affect indigenous peoples, and indigenous peoples are named in a small number of the Goals, including six specific references to indigenous peoples in committing to double the agricultural output of indigenous small-scale farmers (target 2.3 and indicators 2.3, 2.3.2) and to ensure equal access to education for indigenous children (target 4.5 and indicators 4.5, 4.5.1). The Agenda 2030 political declaration also calls for the empowerment of, *inter alia*, indigenous peoples (para 23) and for the follow-up and review process to include, *inter alia*, indigenous peoples' participation (para 79).

This represents an improvement on the MDGs, agreed in 2000, prior to the adoption of UNDRIP, which did not expressly name indigenous peoples among its eight goals or 21 targets. This shift is largely attributable to the indigenous movement, which was highly engaged in the global consultation process for drafting the new SDGs, benefiting also from the operational input and mobilisation capacities of the UN Permanent Forum on Indigenous Issues (PFII). The fact that the SDGs bring together both social and environmental rights has created an even greater imperative for indigenous self-determined development in realising the Goals. Importantly, unlike the MDGs, the SDGs apply also to the Global North states, providing a platform for dialogue and action on achieving SDD for indigenous peoples across the globe.

Agenda 2030 does not currently conform to indigenous peoples' understanding of SDD. At a global level, the indigenous movement has repeatedly emphasised that many core norms of indigenous peoples' rights are missing from Agenda 2030, including the right to self-determination and collective rights. The fact that indigenous peoples are singled out in several paragraphs of the Agenda 2030 is no substitute for a bottom-up reconceptualization of international and national development aims in line with core norms of UNDRIP. From this perspective, advocacy by indigenous peoples in the drafting of the SDGs has fallen short of their aims. With the Agenda 2030 now agreed, indigenous peoples have moved on to focus on key aspects of the SDGs that intersect with core UNDRIP provisions. Among the priority areas of focus are: SDGs impacting on land rights, traditional knowledge and biocultural rights, and rights in education; the need for appropriately disaggregated data; and calls for participation of indigenous peoples at all levels of SDG implementation and follow-up.

We will give attention here to the topic of disaggregated data because there is good evidence that a SDD approach is being advanced in this area. The SDGs have foreseen a 'data revolution' that is required to furnish Agenda 2030 with global and reliable statistics that would measure progress, including through disaggregated data.[38] This is one entry point where SDD can be transformative, both in terms of what new statistics measure as 'development' but also in terms of participation in the process of data collection and governance over decisions pertaining to the data.

Well before the SDGs took their final shape, the UN Permanent Forum on Indigenous Issues (PFII) was engaged in reviewing UN capacity on data collection concerning indigenous peoples, starting from its first session. In 2004, an expert meeting was convened under the auspices of the PFII to develop modalities for 'Data Collection and Disaggregation for Indigenous Peoples'.[39] A number of core principles were established through that dialogue, including many that constitute self-determined development, such as: all data collection should follow the principles of FPIC; the principle of self-identification should be paramount in determining the subjects/categories of data collection; participation of indigenous peoples in the collection process is essential; and moreover, 'data collection must respond to the priorities and aims of the indigenous communities themselves'.[40] The workshop acknowledged that data collection was not without its challenges, both in terms of capacity and method, but it was agreed that the paucity of data available on indigenous peoples needed to be addressed. Importantly, the workshop made a distinction between quantitative and qualitative data, the former conventionally focused on comparing the impact of mainstream development on different populations, and the latter used more to assess different experiences of development and to understand why certain outcomes are unequal. For self-determined development, these qualitative measurements are important for asserting counter-narratives of development 'progress', and to measure, 'to what extent indigenous peoples perceive that their rights are being implemented – for example, whether their views have been reflected in a development plan'.[41] In contrast, conventional data collection has had a 'strong focus on indigenous disadvantage, including comparisons with the non-Indigenous population, and a focus on governments' information needs'.[42]

In line with this challenge, and further to the aim of SDD, a second workshop was convened in 2006 under the PFII on the topic of 'Indigenous Peoples and Indicators of Well-Being',[43] which further emphasised the particular world views of development for indigenous peoples. Among the conference aims was to find 'a space between statistical reporting requirements of governments and representation of indigenous peoples' perceptions and understanding of well-being'.[44] The recommendations included a call that 'The United Nations should identify and adopt appropriate indicators of indigenous identity, lands, ways of living, and indigenous rights to, and perspectives on, development and well-being'.[45] This work continued with several subsequent workshops on data collection during the MDG period and culminated with a recommendation in the outcome document of the World Conference on Indigenous Peoples, in which UN Member States committed 'to working with indigenous peoples to disaggregate data, as appropriate, or conduct surveys and to utilizing holistic indicators of indigenous peoples' well-being to address the situation and needs of indigenous peoples'.[46]

With the onset of the SDGs, the PFII saw an opportunity to take these aims further by establishing within the new development modalities an approach to development that would recognise the self-determination of indigenous peoples. Data was a key strand of this work. The Indigenous Peoples Major Group[47] submitted a Position Paper on Proposed SDG Indicators in 2015.[48] The report argued that the MDGs had done little to improve data collection on indigenous peoples and that the proposed indicators for the SDGs continued to make indigenous peoples and their rights invisible. The report asserted that 'An adequate monitoring framework must reflect the two fundamental principles of indigenous peoples' rights: the right to self-determination and equality'.[49] The rights elaborated in UNDRIP were argued to be central to the targets and indicators, alongside wider human rights standards. On UNDRIP, the report notes that for some targets, UNDRIP is

> the sole human rights instrument that provides specific guidance on conservation and sustainable use of the environment, terrestrial and water-related ecosystems, and biodiversity, including disposable of hazardous materials (Goals 6 and 15), traditional knowledge and intellectual property, (Goals 2 and 15), and traditional occupations, such as pastoralism (Goals 2 and 8).[50]

In this way, UNDRIP was being offered as a tool not just for indigenous peoples but as a general standard for wider human rights protection under Agenda 2030.

There are presently several avenues being pursued at the international and national levels to secure self-determined development in and through data collection. The first is a recommendation under the PFII to establish a global 'indigenous sustainability and well-being' index, which is still at a nascent stage.[51] The second is the Indigenous Navigator, a tool adapted for the SDGs' existing indicators. A third is focused on influencing SDG indicators where data collection methods are still being negotiated – the indicator 1.4.2 on land will be discussed here briefly. The fourth is at the national level, where ad hoc work continues to improve reporting in the Voluntary National Reviews, which will be surveyed below.

Indigenous navigator

The Indigenous Navigator is 'a framework and set of tools for and by indigenous peoples to systematically monitor the level of recognition and implementation of their rights'.[52] It was designed to enable full participation of indigenous peoples in data collection, having a strong emphasis on enabling community-based monitoring. It is a tool also to encourage national statistical offices and other stakeholders to collect data on indigenous peoples in a manner consistent with UNDRIP and SDD principles. It provides various resources, such as questionnaires, indicators and a country ranking, that indigenous peoples can use to monitor compliance with UNDRIP, the SDGs and the outcome document of the World Conference on Indigenous Peoples. One of the resource books helps indigenous peoples to align Indigenous Navigator indicators with those in the SDGs, with a view to conducting their own SDG progress assessments.[53]

The tool manifests as SDD in several ways. First, it advances a set of indicators that were designed by indigenous peoples. This means that indigenous peoples have established their own benchmarks for measuring the implementation of UNDRIP and the SDGs and in accordance with their own ideas of development. Second, the data collection is led and conducted by indigenous peoples themselves, giving them autonomy over the process. Third, indigenous peoples have sovereignty over the data they have collected. This gives them the power to decide how it is used, including in holding states to account on their failure to fulfil the provisions of UNDRIP. Although the Indigenous Navigator is still emerging from its pilot phase, it marks a genuine attempt to make data collection *by* and *for* indigenous peoples rather than merely *about* indigenous peoples and thus represents a vital step towards 'indigenous data sovereignty'.[54]

Land rights indicator 1.4.2

There is one particular SDG indicator where indigenous peoples are facing genuine challenges to their sovereignty. This is indicator 1.4.2 on land rights, namely 'Proportion of total adult population with secure tenure rights to land, with legally recognized documentation and who perceive their rights to land as secure, by sex and by type of tenure'. The concern is that land tenure will be measured on the basis of individual title rather than collective or communal title. Prioritising or imposing individual title would not be consistent with UNDRIP and could undermine indigenous peoples' land rights claims. It is striking that this indicator never explicitly mentioned indigenous peoples, despite four other indicators doing so. The indicator 1.4.2 was originally classified as 'Tier III', meaning that it lacked conceptual clarity on the methodology and there was no universal practice of collecting this kind of data. In order to be part of the routine data collection under the SDGs (i.e. to become a Tier I indicator), both of these points needed to be addressed.[55] Indigenous peoples have tried to influence this process, with the PFII calling for legally recognised customary collective land rights as part of the SDGs indicators on land.[56] Indigenous peoples secured a key victory when the latest round of negotiations on the indicator adopted an 'approved methodology [that] gives equal value for legally documented tenure rights and perception of tenure security'.[57] This provides stronger grounds for indigenous peoples' customary law claims to territory being recognised. To move the indicator to Tier I status by 2019 will require further capacity-building of national statistics offices and local communities to gather data on land tenure. Tools like the Indigenous Navigator can help ensure indigenous peoples land rights are fully documented by indigenous communities themselves. It is an important step towards indigenous SDD on land rights, which the SDGs could potentially enable.

Voluntary national reviews

The Agenda 2030 sets out some guiding principles for the Voluntary National Review (VNR) reports on SDG progress. This includes an overarching emphasis on 'national ownership'.[58] Although the idea of national ownership is not problematised and assumes sovereignty only of the state, there are calls for the reviews to 'draw on contributions from indigenous peoples, civil society, the private sector and other stakeholders, in line with national circumstances, policies and priorities'.[59] Moreover, the call for disaggregated data is repeated, including the provision of data disaggregated by, inter alia, ethnicity, geographic location and 'other characteristics relevant in national contexts'.[60] The reports are also supposed to give attention to respect for human rights and have a particular focus on the poorest and most marginalised. Finally, the reports should be open to 'the development of new methodologies'.[61]

All of these principles set the stage for the VNR being a useful vehicle for documenting and advancing SDD in the achievement of the SDGs. A review of existing VNRs shows this potential has not been met by states in their reporting process to date. There are 162 state reports in the VNR database submitted over the years 2016–2018. A keyword search in the database of the term 'indigenous' or 'tribal' yielded 16 VNRs with relevant mentions.[62] This is surprising given that indigenous peoples feature among the named groups in the targets and indicators. There is very little disaggregated data on indigenous peoples in the reports, with only Nepal and Malaysia providing any quantitative data;[63] recall that the SDGs include targets for ethnically disaggregated data and indigenous peoples have repeatedly called for an 'indigenous identifier' in official statistics.[64] Perhaps the strongest example of SDD in the VNRs comes from the note in Denmark's report, that 'the Action Plan does not include Greenland and the Faroe Islands as most of the elements fall within the jurisdiction of Greenland and the Faroe Islands', a reflection of self-government for the peoples of those territories.[65] Five other VNRs make note of official consultation processes with indigenous peoples: for example, Chile indicates that the National Indigenous Council was consulted and Norway cites the role of the Sami Parliament.[66] In terms of SDD norms, only the report of Canada mentions UNDRIP, self-determination and free, prior and informed consent explicitly.[67] Malaysia gives priority to 'empowering indigenous and local communities to have the right to give or withhold consent to proposed projects that may affect their lands'.[68] Notably, two of the VNRs[69] discuss indigenous peoples in relation to private corporations in mining. In the example from Botswana, a diamond mining company pledges that its guiding principles for sustainable development include: responding to the needs of indigenous people; free and informed consultation; respecting cultural integrity; stakeholder dialogue; partnership with stakeholders; and non-infringement of community rights.[70] Private corporations bear no direct responsibility for implementing the SDGs in Agenda 2030, an omission that was heavily criticised by civil society groups.

The Indigenous Navigator holds out the possibility that alternative VNRs prepared by indigenous peoples could provide more accountability in the SDGs process. However, it remains the case that indigenous peoples do not determine most SDGs policies at the national level, despite their influence in global processes. The governance of development remains in the control of central government and is still rarely devolved in any meaningful way. Bio-cultural community protocols offer one possible way forward to design management of a key aspect of the SDGs: natural resources. The origins and potential of these agreements for self-determined development will be considered below.

Self-determined development and community bio-protocols

Over the last decade, several indigenous communities across the globe have adopted their own 'biocultural community protocols', or community protocols.[71] These community protocols are tools created to support indigenous peoples and community rights, in particular with regard to natural resources, biodiversity and traditional knowledge.[72] Community protocols are relatively new instruments that have emerged under biodiversity law. Legally these protocols are rooted within the Convention on Biological Diversity (CBD) which recognises the traditional knowledge, innovations and practices of local and indigenous peoples and communities over natural resources. Article 8(j) of the CBD invites states to enact national legislation to preserve, protect, maintain, and promote the wider application of indigenous peoples' traditional knowledge relevant to the conservation and sustainable use of biodiversity, provided that such use takes place with the approval and involvement of the holders of such knowledge. Article 8(j) also encourages equitable sharing of benefits arising from the utilisation of such knowledge, innovations and practices. The operationalisation of these principles was put into action with the adoption of the 2010 Nagoya Protocol on Access to Genetic Resources and Benefit Sharing, which notably supports the establishment of community bio-cultural protocols. Its article 12(1) stipulates that states '... shall in accordance with domestic law take into consideration indigenous and local communities' customary laws, community protocols and procedures, as applicable, with respect to traditional knowledge associated with genetic resources'. Article 13(3)(a) determines that public authorities should support the development of 'community protocols in relation to access to traditional knowledge associated with genetic resources and the fair and equitable sharing of benefits arising out of the utilisation of such knowledge'.

It is worth noting that the UNDRIP has played an important role to support the emergence of these protocols. The concept has emerged during the negotiations of the Nagoya Protocol and the several meetings of the Ad Hoc Open-Ended Working Group on Access and Benefit-Sharing (ABS) that took place during the years 2007–2009.[73] In this context, UNDRIP was an important tool for indigenous peoples' representatives, NGOs and advocates of indigenous rights to push for the recognition of the direct participation of indigenous peoples in the ABS process.[74] The reference to UNDRIP, and especially its article 31, supported the advocacy effort to recognise the right of indigenous peoples to grant access to their traditional knowledge and genetic resources subject to their free, prior and informed consent.[75] More specifically, the preamble of the Nagoya protocol specifically refers to UNDRIP as a source of interpretation for the Nagoya protocol. The adoption of the Nagoya Protocol has resulted in a significant increase of adoption of community bio-cultural protocols by indigenous peoples and local communities across the globe. Nonetheless, many community protocols have been adopted outside the strict remits of the Nagoya Protocol, and also are not limited to genetic resources and issues of benefit-sharing. These protocols usually determine the conditions of access to and use of natural resources and associated traditional knowledge and use of natural resources contained on indigenous territories.

Although many of these protocols have emerged under the banner of biodiversity and traditional knowledge, in practice they have taken on a much larger life as they are not usually limited to genetic resources but are often used by the concerned communities as a way to record and affirm their relation to natural resources.[76] For many communities, these protocols have become important tools to affirm their fundamental rights over their land and natural resources. They have become a vehicle to determine and express their traditions, management practices and overall customary practices in relation to their land and natural resources. More generally, the development of these protocols has acted as a catalyst for many communities to propose new approaches to the way development should be undertaken in reflecting on the community's development priorities and aspirations.[77] These protocols also play an important part in supporting a much more direct and participatory role for indigenous peoples in development plans regarding the use of natural resources located on their territories. Importantly, these protocols are based on a process of self-determination, with communities undertaking an internal process of consultation and decision-making in which the community itself decides on the use of their land and natural resources including options for self-determined development.

The self-determined aspect of these protocols is quintessential as they are developed and adopted by indigenous peoples themselves, and as such they contain rules for entering into mutually agreed terms regarding the use of the natural resources located on their territories. Hence, they become a basis for negotiations with public authorities but also private entities with regard to social, economic and development aspects that may affect their territories.[78] Crucially most of the existing community protocols refer to the right to free, prior and informed consent (FPIC) as the key condition for accessing not only genetic resources but also more generally land and natural resources. In a global context where many governments and private companies investing in land are meant to engage in FPIC processes but often claim that there is no guidance on how to conduct FPIC, these protocols offer a significant framework to support these negotiations. From this perspective, these protocols integrate and embrace the fundamental human rights of indigenous peoples over their land and natural resources. Whilst there might not be any specific direct formal connection between human rights law and bio-cultural protocols in treaty law, the fact that these protocols are a direct expression of indigenous peoples' right to self-determination over the use of their natural resources and their right to development make them a very important avenue to support the implementation of the UNDRIP.

The situation of the Ogiek community in Kenya provides a good illustration of these dynamics. The Ogiek, a traditionally hunter-gatherer community, have adopted a bio-cultural community protocol in 2015.[79] As noted earlier, the Ogiek have also been at the heart of legal battle that has lasted for more than 20 years regarding their right to land and natural resources. That battle culminated with the 2017 ruling of the African Court of Human and Peoples' Rights which recognised their fundamental rights to land and natural resources. In parallel to their engagement in litigation, the Ogiek have developed their own bio-cultural protocol. The protocol is defined as 'a tool to safeguard our community's rights as well as traditional knowledge and resources by providing clear terms and conditions to regulate access to our assets as well as sharing benefits that accrue from any development of these assets'.[80] The protocol was elaborated through a participatory process that involved community consultations. It establishes a very detailed and long-term proposal for the management, development and administration of their land and natural resources. The protocol also explains the system of governance and decision making of the community, as well as mechanisms for dispute resolution and land allocation. Every proposal in the Ogiek protocol is based on national and international legal norms to support their argumentation. This makes the protocol a very solid foundation to support a rights-based approach to development, as well as a proper self-determined process of development. The Ogiek have highlighted that their plans for development are not only valuable to them, but also for the whole country and the global environment. As they say: 'We are holders of this valuable knowledge which can make an important contribution to sustainable social and economic development'.[81] Importantly, the Ogiek have made a link between their self-determined plan for development and the overall governmental and international polices for development highlighting how their plans could support larger developmental strategies without harming their community.

The Ogiek protocol is only an illustration of the rich and deep engagement of indigenous communities with bio-cultural protocols as many other communities have adopted similar protocols across the globe. These protocols offer some solid foundation to support the implementation of the UNDRIP, and notably the self-determined development aspect of the declaration. They represent a very valuable avenue to support and enhance indigenous peoples' self-determined development. The issue which arises relates to their implementation and respect by external actors operating on indigenous territories, including public authorities but also private corporations and investors. The formalistic legal nature of these protocols is complex due to the voluntary nature of the protocols. From a positivist and formal legal perspective, bio-cultural protocols are 'only' voluntary and self-defined agreements. Nonetheless, this argumentation could be challenged as legally speaking these protocols are part of international biodiversity law for being the operationalisation of the Nagoya Protocol. Moreover, by entrenching these protocols within the UNDRIP and other international human rights laws, these protocols acquire a more formal legal nature by integrating universal, adopted norms. As such they are entrenched in positivist legal norms and therefore become an instrument for their implementation. There is still a long way to go until the formal recognition of the legal value of these protocols by public authorities and legal institutions at the national level is secured. As noted by Ruiz:

> The question of whether they would stand up in court is very difficult to determine, but it could be strongly argued that inasmuch as they are already legally recognised at the international level, they could be considered by courts or in administrative procedures (…).[82]

In many ways, this is the next battle: indigenous peoples and supportive organisations have started to gather up strategies to ensure that these protocols become an essential element to support indigenous peoples' rights. This includes using them in all their external engagements with external actors, using them for their advocacy strategies, and using them as evidence in legal processes and for policy planning.[83] The use of the community protocol by the Ogiek as a tool to support the implementation of the ruling the African Court might offer some new development on the legal role that could be played by these bio-cultural protocols. It also makes a direct connection between human rights law and the bio-cultural protocol. At the time of writing, there is still no progress on the implementation of the judgment, but the protocol could prove to be a key tool to support future implementation.[84]

It is also worth highlighting that the emergence of the bio-cultural protocols is part of the larger development of a global jurisprudence on biocultural rights. Biocultural rights emerge from the junction between the fields of environmental, cultural and human rights law.[85] As noted by Bavikatte:

> The term 'biocultural rights' denotes a community's long established right, in accordance with its customary laws, to steward its lands, waters and resources. Such rights are being increasingly recognized in international environmental law. Biocultural rights are not simply claims to property, in the typical market sense of property being a universally commensurable, commodifiable and alienable resource; rather, as will be apparent from the discussion offered here, biocultural rights are collective rights of communities to carry out traditional stewardship roles vis-à-vis Nature, as conceived of by indigenous ontologies.

Bio-cultural protocols are the clear operationalisation of such rights which are based on concerns for the environmental, development and human rights law. As such they represent a unique platform to challenge the legal fragmentation that has been taking place under international law where norms concerning cultural heritage, environmental protection, development and human rights have been divided between specific legal frameworks. For indigenous peoples the approach based on bio-cultural principles is a way to re-establish a more cohesive means to manage and protect their cultural heritage, traditions and natural resources. In terms of human rights law, this approach grounded on a bio-cultural framework offers a very positive and self-determined way to support the implementation of the norms on self-determination, development, cultural rights and land and natural resources management, including in the UNDRIP. Importantly, bio-cultural protocols are also a clear operationalisation of the right to FPIC and SDD.

Conclusion

This survey of data collection in the SDGs, regional jurisprudence and community protocols demonstrates several ways in which self-determined development is evolving as a norm within international and national development policy and through case law. This takes place against an ongoing struggle in national and local contexts to challenge prevailing development norms of the state and private sector that undermine indigenous peoples' right to self-determination. The adoption of UNDRIP did not radically transform existing structures of inequality, colonialism or capitalism, but its negotiation and adoption has certainly influenced the way development can be conceptualised at all levels. Indigenous peoples have used their hard-won space in global governance to shape new development modalities agreed since 2007, principal among these being the SDGs. They have framed their claims within the norms of UNDRIP and sought to translate these norms into tangible policy commitments. UNDRIP has been a tool, alongside international human rights law, to assert claims regarding development aggression and its effects before the courts. The opportunity to articulate a community protocol to protect biocultural diversity, traditional knowledge and natural resources has provided a means to safeguard not only an indigenous view of self-determined development but also to protect environmental and cultural diversity for the benefit of all.

It has sometimes been a case of two steps forward, one step back in norm emergence on SDD. Cases have been won but implementation has been poor. Community protocols are increasingly being developed but are still often not seen as binding on outside development actors. The SDGs have firm commitments to indigenous peoples, but state National Voluntary Reviews show a lack of concrete and meaningful leadership of indigenous peoples in local SDGs activities. Nevertheless, UNDRIP remains a firm basis for advancing claims for SDD in these areas and as UNDRIP becomes more mainstreamed into development processes, the potential for indigenous peoples' views of development to prevail are improved.

Notes

1. See Wolfgang Sachs, *The Development Dictionary: A Guide to Knowledge as Power* (Johannesburg: Witwatersrand University Press, 1993).
2. Nadia Nader, 'Promise or Plunder? A Past and Future Look at Law and Development', *Global Jurist* 7, no. 2 (2007). See also Balakrishnan Rajagopal, *International Law from Below: Development, Social Movements and Third World Resistance* (Cambridge University Press, 2003).
3. Cathal Doyle and Jérémie Gilbert, 'Indigenous Peoples and Globalization: From "Development Aggression" to "Self-Determined Development"', *European Yearbook on Minority Issues* 8 (January 2011).
4. See Michael T. Klare, *The Race for What's Left: The Global Scramble for the World's Last Resources* (Picador, 2012); Leif Wenar, *Blood Oil: Tyrants, Violence, and the Rules that Run the World* (OUP, 2016).
5. Charles Hale, 'Neoliberal Multiculturalism: The Remaking of Cultural Rights and Racial Dominance in Central America', *Political and Legal Anthropology Review* 28, no. 1 (2009): 10–28.
6. Corinne Lennox, 'Minority and Indigenous Women and the Millennium Development Goals', in *State of the World's Minorities and Indigenous Peoples 2011* (London: Minority Rights Group International, 2011), 21–31; Permanent Forum on Indigenous Issues, *Report on the fifth session (15–26 May 2006); Special Theme, The Millennium Development Goals and Indigenous Peoples: Re-defining the Millennium Development Goals*, UN Doc. E/C.19/2006/11.
7. See, for example, Kelley Laird, *MDGs Reports and Indigenous Peoples: A Desk Review*, Secretariat of the UN Permanent Forum on Indigenous Issues (2006); Christopher Foley, *MDGs Reports, CCAs and UNDAFs and Indigenous Peoples: A Desk Review 2010* (Secretariat of the UN Permanent Forum on Indigenous Issues, 2010).
8. See also the Rio+20 Indigenous Peoples International Declaration on Self-Determination and Sustainable Development, adopted 19 June 2012, Rio de Janeiro; https://www.iitc.org/wp-content/uploads/2013/07/Rio-20-Indigenous-Peoples'-International-Declaration-on-Sustainable-Development-and-Self-Determination-9-June-2012-Rio-de-Janeiro.pdf.
9. Permanent Forum on Indigenous Issues, 'Consultation Workshop and Dialogue on Indigenous Peoples' Self-Determined Development or Development with Identity', 14–17 March 2008, Tivoli, 11–18 April 2008, UN Doc. E/C.19/2008/CRP.11.
10. International Expert Meeting on the UN Permanent Forum's theme for 2010, the theme was 'Indigenous Peoples' Development with Culture and Identity: Articles 3 and 32 of the UN Declaration on the Rights of Indigenous Peoples'.
11. Victoria Tauli-Corpuz, 'Indigenous Peoples' Self-Determined Development: Challenges and Trajectories', in *Towards an Alternative Development Paradigm Indigenous People's Self-Determined Development*, eds. Victoria Tauli-Corpuz, Leah Enkiwe-Abayao, and Raymond de Chavez (Tebtebba Foundation, 2010), 4.
12. See Victoria Tauli-Corpuz, Leah Enkiwe-Abayao, and Raymond de Chavez, eds., *Towards an Alternative Development Paradigm Indigenous People's Self-Determined Development* (Tebtebba Foundation, 2010).
13. See Processes Towards the Development of an Indigenous Peoples' Self-Determined Development Paradigm, in Victoria Tauli-Corpuz, Leah Enkiwe-Abayao, and Raymond de Chavez (eds.), *Towards an Alternative Development Paradigm Indigenous People's Self-Determined Development* (Tebtebba Foundation, 2010).
14. Victoria Tauli-Corpuz, 'Indigenous Peoples' Self-Determined Development', 3.
15. World Bank, OP 4.10 – Indigenous Peoples, July 2005.
16. World Bank, *Inspection Panel: Indigenous Peoples*. Emerging Lessons; no. 2 (Washington, DC: World Bank Group, 2016), http://documents.worldbank.org/curated/en/447361478156710826/Inspection-Panel-Indigenous-peoples.

17. See Standard 6: Indigenous Peoples. UNDP, *UNDP Social and Environmental Standards* (UNDP, 2014), http://www.undp.org/content/dam/undp/library/corporate/Social-and-Environmental-Policies-and-Procedures/UNDPs-Social-and-Environmental-Standards-ENGLISH.pdf. See also the preceding *United Nations Development Group Guidelines on Indigenous Peoples* (adopted in 2008) https://www.ohchr.org/Documents/Issues/IPeoples/UNDGGuidelines.pdf.
18. International Finance Corporation, Performance Standard 7: Indigenous Peoples, 1 January 2012.
19. Inter-American Development Bank, *Operational Policy on Indigenous Peoples and Strategy for Indigenous Development* (Washington, DC: IADB, 2008); Asian Development Bank, *The Bank's Policy on Indigenous Peoples* (April 1998); Asian Development Bank, *Safeguard Policy Statement* (June 2009). The African Development Group Bank includes some recognition of indigenous peoples in its safeguard policies but does not have a dedicated policy on indigenous peoples. See African Development Group Bank, *African Development Bank Group's Integrated Safeguards System – Policy Statement and Operational Safeguards* (AFDB, 2013).
20. These were adopted by the World Bank in 2016 and come into force in 2018. See Corinne Lewis and Carl Soderbergh, 'The World Bank's New Environmental and Social Framework: Some Progress but Many Gaps Regarding the Rights of Indigenous Peoples', *International Journal of Human Rights*, this volume.
21. African Commission on Human and Peoples' Rights, *Centre for Minority Rights Development (Kenya) and Minority Rights Group International on Behalf of Endorois Welfare Council v Kenya*, Communication 276/2003 (2010).
22. Id., para. 270.
23. Id., para. 129.
24. See Mario Blaser, Harvey A. Feit, and Glenn McRae, eds., *In the Way of Development: Indigenous Peoples, Life Projects and Globalization* (Zed Books and the International Development Research Centre, 2004).
25. Endorois Case, para. 227.
26. Id., para. 290.
27. Id., para. 228.
28. Id. para. 238.
29. Id. para. 148.
30. Ogiek, para. 209. Article 23 states: 'Indigenous peoples have the right to determine and develop priorities and strategies for exercising their right to development. In particular, indigenous peoples have the right to be actively involved in developing and determining health, housing and other economic and social programmes affecting them and, as far as possible, to administer such programmes through their own institutions'.
31. Ogiek, para. 210.
32. Inter-American Court of Human Rights, *Case of the Saramaka People v Suriname* Inter-Am. Ct. H.R., (Ser. C) No. 172 (2007).
33. Ibid, See para. 131 where the court refers to Art. 32 United Nations Declaration on the Rights of Indigenous Peoples.
34. *Kichwa Indigenous People of Sarayaku v. Ecuador*, Judgment, Inter-Am. Ct. H.R. (ser. C) No. 4 (27 June 2012), see para. 214–216.
35. Ibid, para. 121.
36. Ibid, para. 124.
37. UN General Assembly, *Resolution 70/1, Transforming our world: the 2030 Agenda for Sustainable Development*, UN Doc. A/RES/70/1 (21 October 2015).
38. See target 17.18 and para 74 (g) of Agenda 2030.
39. Permanent Forum on Indigenous Issues, *Report of the Workshop on Data Collection and Disaggregation for Indigenous Peoples*, UN Doc. E/C.19/2004/2 (10 February 2004).
40. Ibid, para 33 (4).

41. Meghan Davis, 'Data and the United Nations Declaration on the Rights of Indigenous Peoples', in *Indigenous Data Sovereignty: Toward an Agenda*, eds. Tahu Kukutai and John Taylor (ANU Press, 2015), 36.
42. Richard Maddena, Per Axelsson, Tahu Kukutai, Kalinda Griffiths, Christina Storm Mienna, Ngaire Brown, Clare Coleman, and Ian Ring, 'Statistics on Indigenous Peoples: International Effort Needed', *Statistical Journal of the IAOS*, 32 (2016): 39.
43. Permanent Forum on Indigenous Issues, *Report of the Meeting on Indigenous Peoples and Indicators of Well-Being*, UN Doc. E/C.19/2006/CRP.3 (20 April 2006).
44. Ibid, para 10.
45. Ibid, para 33.
46. UN General Assembly, *Resolution 69/2, Outcome Document of the High Level Plenary Meeting of the General Assembly known as the World Conference on Indigenous Peoples*, UN Doc. A/RES/69/2 (25 September 2014): para 10.
47. The Indigenous Peoples Major Group is one of the nine recognised Major Groups that can officially participate in the SDG processes at the global level. It is coordinated by the Tebtebba Foundation and the International Indian Treaty Council. See Indigenous Peoples Major Group at https://www.indigenouspeoples-sdg.org/index.php/english/.
48. Indigenous Peoples Major Group, *Indigenous Peoples Major Group Position Paper on Proposed SDG Indicators* (2015), https://www.iwgia.org/en/resources/publications/306-briefings/3203-indigenous-peoples-major-group-position-paper-on-proposed-sdg-indicators.
49. Ibid., 3.
50. Ibid., 8.
51. This idea emerged initially in the series of PFII workshops on data collection (see *supra* note 42). The 2016 PFII Expert Group Meeting on Indigenous Peoples and the 2030 Agenda recommended that the plan be taken forward. PFII, *Meeting Report of the Expert Group Meeting on Indigenous Peoples and the 2030 Agenda*, UN Doc. E/C.19/2016/2 (16 February 2016): paras 34 and 39 (i).
52. See Indigenous Navigator, http://nav.indigenousnavigator.com/index.php/en/.
53. Indigenous Navigator, *Leaving No One Behind!: Integration of Global SDG Indicators in the Indigenous Navigator Monitoring Framework* (n.d.), http://nav.indigenousnavigator.com/images/Documents/Tools/Navigator_IntegrationSDGIndicators.pdf.
54. Tahu Kukutai and John Taylor, eds., *Indigenous Data Sovereignty: Toward an Agenda* (ANU Press, 2016).
55. This became a Tier II indicator in November 2017 and there is a commitment to move it to Tier I by the end of 2019. See Everlyne Nairesiae, *IAEG-SDGs Upgrade Indicator 1.4.2 to Tier II Status* (Land Links, 2017), https://land-links.org/2017/11/iaeg-sdgs-upgrade-indicator-1-4-2-tier-ii-status/.
56. See, for example, a report of the 2018 session of the PFII: ECOSOC, *Update on Indigenous Peoples and the 2030 Agenda for Sustainable Development; Note by the Secretariat*, UN Doc. E/C.19/2018/2 (1 February 2018): para 24 (d); also see paras 9 and 21 for discussion on land indicators.
57. Nairesiae, supra note 55.
58. Agenda 2030, para 74 (a). See also, Department of Economic and Social Affairs, United Nations, *Handbook for the Preparation of Voluntary National Reviews: The 2018 Edition* (Department of Economic and Social Affairs, n.d.).
59. Agenda 2030, para 79.
60. Agenda 2030, para 74 (g).
61. Agenda 2030, para 74 (f).
62. Search made on 20 September 2018. The following VNRs include at least one mention of indigenous peoples: Botswana, Canada, Chile, Denmark, Estonia, Finland, Germany, Indonesia, Japan, Malaysia, Nepal, Norway, the Philippines, Sweden and Uganda. The Bangladesh VNR mentions tribal communities. See Sustainable Development Knowledge Platform, *Voluntary National Reviews Database*, https://sustainabledevelopment.un.org/vnrs/.

63. Government of Malaysia, *Malaysia Sustainable Development Goals Voluntary National Review 2017; High Level Political Forum* (Economic Planning Unit, 20017), https://sustainabledevelopment.un.org/content/documents/16397BOTSWANA_VNR.pdf; Government of Nepal National Planning Commission, *National Review of Sustainable Development Goals* (2017), https://sustainabledevelopment.un.org/content/documents/16513Nepal.pdf.
64. Permanent Forum on Indigenous Issues, *Substantive Inputs to the High-Level Political Forum; Thematic Review of the 2030 Agenda for Sustainable Development* (Secretariat of the Permanent Forum on Indigenous Issues, 2016), 3, https://sustainabledevelopment.un.org/content/documents/10314Permanent%20Forum%20on%20Indigenous%20Issues%20(PFII).pdf.
65. Danish Government, *Report for the Voluntary National Review; Denmark's Implementation of the 2030 Agenda for Sustainable Development* (Ministry of Finance, 2017), 17.
66. Government of Chile, *Chile Agenda 2030 Objetivos de Desarrollo Sostenible; Informe National Voluntario* (2017), 2, https://sustainabledevelopment.un.org/content/documents/15776Chile.pdf; Norway, *Initial Steps Towards the Implementation of the 2030 Agenda: Voluntary National Review Presented at the High-Level Political Forum on Sustainable Development* (2016), 2, https://sustainabledevelopment.un.org/content/documents/10692NORWAY%20HLPF%20REPORT%20-%20full%20version.pdf. See also the reports of: Government of the People's Republic of Bangladesh, *Eradicating Poverty and Promoting Prosperity in a Changing World; Voluntary National Review 2017* (2017), 6, https://sustainabledevelopment.un.org/content/documents/15826Bangladesh.pdf; Government of Canada, *Canada's Implementation of the 2030 Agenda for Sustainable Development; Voluntary National Review* (Global Affairs Canada, 2018), 3, https://sustainabledevelopment.un.org/content/documents/20312Canada_ENGLISH_18122_Canadas_Voluntary_National_ReviewENv7.pdf; Finland Prime Minister's Office, *National Report on the Implementation of the 2030 Agenda for Sustainable Development Finland* (2016), 13 and 35, https://sustainabledevelopment.un.org/content/documents/10611Finland_VNR.pdf.
67. Government of Canada, *Canada's Implementation of the 2030 Agenda for Sustainable Development; Voluntary National Review* (Global Affairs Canada, 2018), 11–13, https://sustainabledevelopment.un.org/content/documents/20312Canada_ENGLISH_18122_Canadas_Voluntary_National_ReviewENv7.pdf.
68. Government of Malaysia, *Malaysia Sustainable Development Goals Voluntary National Review 2017; High Level Political Forum* (Economic Planning Unit, 20017), 36, https://sustainabledevelopment.un.org/content/documents/16397BOTSWANA_VNR.pdf.
69. See also Sweden, *Sweden and the 2030 Agenda; Report to the UN High Level Political Forum 2017 on Sustainable Development* (2017), 59, https://sustainabledevelopment.un.org/content/documents/16033Sweden.pdf.
70. Republic of Botswana, *Botswana Voluntary National Review on Sustainable Development Goals 2017*, Figure Four: Sustainability Guiding Principles, https://sustainabledevelopment.un.org/content/documents/16397BOTSWANA_VNR.pdf.
71. See http://www.community-protocols.org. For analysis, see Holly Shrumm and Harry Jonas, eds., *Biocultural Community Protocols: A Toolkit for Community Facilitators* (Natural Justice: Cape Town, 2012).
72. See Kabir Bavikatte and Harry Jonas, eds., *Bio-Cultural Community Protocols: A Community Approach to Ensuring the Integrity of Environmental Law and Policy* (Nairobi: United Nations Environment Program, 2009).
73. See Maria Yolanda Teran, 'The Nagoya Protocol and Indigenous Peoples', *The International Indigenous Policy Journal* 7, no. 2 (2016).
74. However, see Kimberly R. Marion Suiseeya, 'Negotiating the Nagoya Protocol: Indigenous Demands for Justice', *Global Environmental Politics* 14, no. 3 (2014): 102–24.
75. For analysis, see Kabir Bavikatte and Daniel F. Robinson, 'Towards a People's History of the Law: Biocultural Jurisprudence and the Nagoya Protocol on Access and Benefit Sharing', *Law, Environment and Development Journal* 7, no. 1 (2011).

76. See Kabir Bavikatte, Sanjay, Daniel Robinson, and Maria Julia Oliva, 'Biocultural Community Protocols: Dialogues on the Space Within', *IK: Other Ways of Knowing* 1, no. 2 (2015): 1–31.
77. See Louisa Parks, 'Challenging Power from the Bottom Up? Community Protocols, Benefit-Sharing, and the Challenge of Dominant Discourses', *Geoforum* 88 (2018): 87–95.
78. Harry Jonas, Kabir Bavikatte, and Holly Shrumm, 'Community Protocols and Access and Benefit Sharing', *Asian Biotechnology and Development Review* 12, no. 3 (2010): 49–76.
79. Ogiek Bio-Cultural Community Protocol (BCP), Ogiek Peoples' Development Program (2015), https://www.ogiekpeoples.org/images/downloads/Ogiek-Bio-Cultural-Protocol.pdf
80. Ibid.
81. Ibid.
82. Manuel Ruiz, *Possibilities and Limitations for a Biocultural Protocol(s) in Countries in the Andes and Amazon Basin* (Deutsche Gesellschaft für Internationale Zusammenarbeit, 2012), 22.
83. See *Community Protocols Toolbox, Developing and Using Community Protocols: Booklet 3* (Natural Justice & e Heinrich Böll Stiftun, 2016), https://za.boell.org/sites/default/files/booklet-3.pdf.
84. For updates on implementation and follow up to the judgment, see https://www.ogiekpeoples.org.
85. See Kabir Sanjay Bavikatte, *Stewarding the Earth: Rethinking Property and the Emergence of Biocultural Rights* (Delhi: Oxford University Press, 2014); Giulia Sajeva, 'Rights with Limits: Biocultural Rights–Between Self-Determination and Conservation of the Environment', *Journal of Human Rights and the Environment* 6, no. 1 (2015): 30–54.

Acknowledgement

The authors would like to thank Marcus Erridge (University of Coimbra) and Fumiya Nagai (University of British Colombia) for their research assistance.

Disclosure statement

No potential conflict of interest was reported by the authors.

Creating a space for indigenous rights: the Universal Periodic Review as a mechanism for promoting the rights of indigenous peoples

Noelle Higgins

ABSTRACT
In 2006, the Human Rights Council created a new method of overseeing the implementation of universal human rights standards, including the rights of indigenous peoples, in the form of the Universal Periodic Review (UPR). The UPR is a peer-review mechanism which requires States to report on their human rights practices in a variety of fields every 4-5 years and encourages other States to discuss, and make recommendations on, these reports. Since the UPR was created, every member state of the United Nations (UN) had been reviewed twice, and some have been reviewed 3 times. The paper analyses the first two cycles of the UPR to identify the ways in which indigenous peoples can play a role in the process, and also to query how the rights of indigenous peoples have been raised as part of this mechanism. The article will conclude with a number of recommendations as to how indigenous groups can engage with the UPR process to their benefit in the future.

Introduction

Created in 2006, the Universal Periodic Review (UPR) has as its aim an examination of the human rights practices and policies of all UN member states every 4 to 5 years. Its scope is universal, and thus includes themes that may not otherwise be reported on in other facets of the UN human rights framework, which is particularly important in the context of issues which are not specifically the subject of a core UN human rights treaty, such as the rights of indigenous peoples. The UPR has also opened up significant opportunities for the participation of non-governmental organisations (NGOs) and civil society groups in the state review process. This development provides an important avenue for the involvement of groups representing indigenous peoples within the UN human rights framework, and for the voices of indigenous peoples to be better heard within the organisation. This article explores the opportunities provided by the UPR to those who seek to promote and protect the rights of indigenous peoples. The first section sets out the how the UPR procedure operates. The next section then assesses how the UPR provides opportunities for NGOs representing indigenous peoples to advocate on behalf of the groups they represent. The third section discusses some of the recent practice relating to indigenous peoples during the UPR process by highlighting some recommendations made by states on this issue throughout both of the completed cycles of the review.[1] While there will be a disparity in the way in which different states engage with the UPR process, Australia was chosen as a lens through which to view the UPR mechanism in the context of indigenous peoples, as the government has provided informative updates on the implementation of UPR recommendations and there has been significant commitment by NGOs representing indigenous peoples in the process to date. The analysis of Australia's engagement with the process has been based on its state, NGO and UN reports submitted as part of the UPR process. Based on the analysis of the UPR and state practice to date, the Conclusion of the article provides some thoughts on the effectiveness of the UPR as a tool for promoting the rights of indigenous peoples, as well as recommendations as to how the full potential of the process can be harnessed for the benefit of indigenous peoples in the future.

The UPR mechanism

The UN created the Human Rights Council in 2006[2] in response to many years of harsh criticism of the Human Rights Commission,[3] and in an attempt to rebuild the institution's reputation as a protector and promoter of human rights.[4] The Human Rights Council was mandated to

> undertake a universal periodic review (UPR), based on objective and reliable information, of the fulfilment by each State of its human rights obligations and commitments in a manner which ensures universality of coverage and equal treatment with respect to all States.[5]

After much discussion and negotiation,[6] the UPR mechanism was established through the adoption by the Human Rights Council of its 'institution-building package' in 2007, with the main objective of monitoring and improving human rights practices of all states, as well as measuring positive developments within states in the field of human rights, and facilitating the sharing of best practices between states.[7]

Because the aim of the UPR is the assessment of the 'fulfilment by each State of its human rights obligations and commitments',[8] the Universal Declaration of Human Rights (UDHR) serves as a basis for the review, in addition to any other human rights instruments which have been ratified by the state under review, as well as applicable international humanitarian law, and any other commitments or pledges concerning human rights issues made by it.[9] The UDHR does not contain any provisions which deal specifically with indigenous peoples, but Article 27(1), (which provides: 'Everyone has the right freely to participate in the cultural life of the community, to enjoy the arts and to share in scientific advancement and its benefits'[10]), is relevant in reviewing how states deal with the rights of indigenous peoples. Other provisions of international human rights instruments, including the International Covenant on Civil and Political Rights (particularly Article 27),[11] the International Labour Organisation (ILO) Convention No. 169,[12] and other core human rights treaties,[13] can also be used as benchmarks against which to gauge how states protect and promote the rights of indigenous peoples. Furthermore, the United Nations Declaration on the Rights of Indigenous Peoples (UNDRIP),[14] which was adopted in 2007, the year when the UPR was established, has been referred to throughout the UPR process as a framework which should inform state action with regard to indigenous peoples.

There are a number of different phases in the UPR process: Preparation, Interaction, Consideration, Adoption, and Implementation.[15]

Preparation phase

The first phase involves information gathering, whereby 3 reports on states' human rights policies and practices are complied. The first is completed by the state under review, the second consists of a summary of reports from other stakeholders including NGOs which deal with the rights of indigenous peoples, which is collated by the Office of the High Commissioner for Human Rights, and the third is based on information from independent human rights experts, human rights treaty bodies and other UN entities. In the context of indigenous peoples, this report could include state reports submitted to UN treaty body mechanisms, for example, reports to the Human Rights Committee, as well as information gathered through Special Procedure mechanisms, such as the Special Rapporteur on the Rights of Indigenous Peoples, in addition to other UN machinery such as the Expert Mechanism on the Rights of Indigenous Peoples.

Interaction phase

The interaction phase of the UPR takes places during a UPR Working Group session, when each state under review provides an oral report on their human rights policies and practices. Reviews are conducted by the UPR Working Group, i.e. the 47 members of the Human Rights Council. This is also named the 'interactive dialogue' phase of the review process, as representatives of any UN member state can ask questions and make comments and recommendations on the state under review's report and the other stakeholder information provided. While this is an important tool for facilitating discussion, tight time constrains apply and states under review are given a total of 70 min for presentation and discussion, and other states have a combined total of 140 min to make recommendations. These time limitations have resulted in 'many States not being able to speak at all, and diplomats lining up in the pre-dawn darkness to register to speak.'[16] Sweeney and Saito state that the limited time allowances led to 'a negative trend was established of "friendly States" filling the speakers' list to compliment the State under review.'[17] However, it should be noted that states which do not have a chance to speak during the interactive dialogue stage can submit their comments on the UPR's extranet.[18]

Consideration and adoption phases

Following the interactive dialogue session, the state under review can consider the recommendations made to it concerning its human rights policies and practices and can decide which ones it will support. A report is then completed by a 'Troika', i.e. three members of the Human Rights Council tasked with the role of preparing an 'Outcome Report', with the assistance of the Office of the High Commissioner for Human Rights. This provides a summary of the dialogue, and includes questions, comments and recommendations made to the state under review. No sooner than 48 h after the interactive dialogue session there is a further 30 min discussion on the adoption of the Outcome Report. During this time, the state under review may make preliminary comments on recommendations, stating whether it 'supports' or 'notes' recommendations. According to Resolution 5/1, the state under review cannot 'reject' recommendations but it can provide comments on recommendations which it notes, explaining why it does not support them. All of the recommendations made are included in the final Plenary Session Report of the Human Rights Council and the Outcome Report is adopted by the UPR Working Group. The state under review presents its response in an addendum to the Working Group, which is officially adopted at the Human Rights Council during a plenary session 3–4 months after the review in the Working Group.

Implementation phase

Focus then moves to the implementation of the UPR recommendations domestically. Unfortunately, while states can support numerous recommendations during the interactive phase, how these recommendations are implemented is not always clear because there is no official follow up mechanism within the UPR framework. States can choose to undergo a mid-term review, in order to report on how they have been implementing recommendations after 2 years. Up to 30 July 2018, 71 states had submitted UPR mid-term reports. 55 states submitted reports in relation to recommendations put forward during the first cycle of the UPR, 34 submitted reports in respect of Cycle 2 and 18 states submitted mid-term reports in relation to recommendations put forward during both cycles.[19] Other stakeholders, including civil society and non-governmental organisations can also submit mid-term reports, commenting on the progress of state implementation of UPR recommendations.[20]

The Human Rights Council noted that Cycle 2 reports should particularly focus on implementation of Cycle 1 recommendations, and this focus on implementation will continue during future cycles. There have been numerous criticisms of the UPR because of the lack of consequences of non-implementation. Therefore, tracking of recommendations through to the implementation stage is very important. While some states take recommendations seriously and amend their domestic policies and practices in line with recommendations, other states take a more lax approach to the review process. States can defer any action on recommendations until just before their next review which can result in superficial and non-consultative changes in policy and legislation rather than a systemic change to the human rights environment. UPRInfo has attempted to address some of these problems by creating the Follow-up Programme in 2011 which encourages all UPR stakeholders to more actively participate in the follow-up to the UPR recommendations.[21] It also developed the Implementation of the Recommendation Index in order to categorise the level of implementation for the UPR recommendations.

Cycle 1 of the UPR process began in 2008 and ended in 2011. 48 states were reviewed each year in different sessions of the Human Rights Council. The process was fine-tuned before the beginning of Cycle 2 in May 2012 which was completed in 2016, with some minor changes being made to the modalities, including an increase in the time dedicated to each state's review before the Human Rights Council and the subsequent extension of the timeframe of Cycle 2 from 4 to 4 and a half years.[22] Cycle 3 is currently ongoing, beginning in 2017, and ending in 2021. Over Cycle 1 and Cycle 2, a total of 57,686 recommendations were made and, while all 193 members of the UN were reviewed, almost all states also engaged in the UPR process by making recommendations to other states on a variety of issues, with only 22 states failing to make any recommendations at all.[23]

The UPR architecture and indigenous peoples

This article seeks to identify how indigenous peoples can utilise the UPR to its fullest potential in order to improve how states promote and protect their rights. In this context, it is important to note that the process does provide a space for the discussion of issues concerning indigenous peoples, in addition to opportunities for NGOs representing indigenous peoples to have a voice. This section provides a discussion of how indigenous peoples can contribute to the UPR process at each phase in order to benefit from this tool. According to Joshua Cooper, 'these five phases amount to a 24-month campaign that educates, engages, and empowers Indigenous Peoples to connect issues at the grassroots level with global governmental responsibility based on recommendations drafted in their own communities and countries.'[24]

Preparation phase

It is important that indigenous peoples harness the potential of the UPR for their benefit by engaging in it to the fullest extent possible at each phase. With regard to the preparation phase, the UN provides guidance to states as to the format of their reports, including guidance on 'thematic clustering'.[25] The guidance note includes 'examples to States in the way in which the information provided in the national report may be thematically organized.'[26] There are divided into 5 areas, i.e. (a) 'cross cutting issues', (b) 'civil and political rights', (c) 'economic, social and cultural rights', (d) 'rights of specific persons or groups' and (e) 'specific regions or territories.' Of particular importance to the current discussion is the fact that under section (d) 'minorities and indigenous peoples' are specifically mentioned as groups on which states should provide information as part of their review. This is very significant given the fact that under the current UN core human rights treaty framework, there are no other specific reporting requirements on indigenous peoples.[27] Under the UN treaty monitoring system, the rights of indigenous peoples are scantily protected and, while states are required to submit periodic reports under the nine core treaties which form part this system, none of these instruments deal significantly with the rights of indigenous issues.[28] However, states have an opportunity to report on the rights of indigenous peoples under a number of provisions which form part of the treaty monitoring system, e.g. Article 27 of the International Covenant on Civil and Political Rights,[29] various provisions of the International Covenant on Social, Economic and Cultural Rights,[30] and the International Convention on the Elimination of All Forms of Racial Discrimination,[31] the Convention on the Rights of the Child,[32] and the Convention on the Rights of People with Disabilities,[33] and some state reports to these treaty bodies include references to indigenous peoples.[34] In this context, it is noted that Article 27 of the ICCPR has been used effectively in a number of cases concerning the rights of indigenous peoples and the Human Rights Committee has built up significant jurisprudence on this topic.[35] Furthermore, a number of treaty monitoring bodies have developed indigenous rights through their analyses in General Comments.[36] However, the treaty body monitoring mechanism can result in a fractured understanding of the rights of indigenous peoples. Certain states where indigenous peoples live may choose not to include indigenous issues in their reports, as there may be conflict between the group and the state. In addition, not every state with indigenous peoples has ratified the relevant UN treaties which would provide an outlet for the reporting on such groups. Therefore, it has been impossible to date to ascertain a universal picture of the rights of indigenous peoples. However, because the UPR applies to all member states of the United Nations and the reporting guidance includes a subsection on the rights of indigenous peoples, at the most basic level, additional information on the state of indigenous peoples globally can be distilled from this process. On a more advanced level, states can receive recommendations on indigenous peoples which can lead to an amendment of domestic policies and practices with regard to indigenous rights.

It is clear then that the UPR framework expects a discussion on indigenous rights when states in which indigenous peoples live are undergoing a review. However, in order to make the most of this discussion, NGOs representing indigenous peoples must prepare well to optimise the impact of the process. The preparation phase begins 18 months prior to a review and during the lead up to the review, it is vital that stakeholders, such as NGOs, educate the community about the work of the UPR, in order to encourage research and recording of state violations of the rights of indigenous peoples. It is an opportunity for stakeholders to hold consultations and write submissions which will contribute to the final Stakeholder report for the UPR. An interesting example of recording of state violations of the rights of indigenous peoples in the context of the UPR is the Testify Campaign co-ordinated by WITNESS and the US Human Rights Network, which collected video testimony from people across the United States, who shared their stories of human rights abuse during the preparation phase for America's review.[37]

It is important during the Preparation Phase that NGOs work together in order to share resources and knowledge in writing a submission to the UPR, and thus to increase impact. It is also key that when writing submissions (both for NGOs and states) that recommendations are written in a straight-forward and actionable way, as this will facilitate implementation. UPRInfo refer to these as SMART (specific, measurable, achievable, relevant, and time-bound) indicators. In this context UNDRIP should be used as a framework for recommendations, and its provisions referred to in recommendations for action.

It is essential that NGOs work with the government throughout the Preparation Phase to ensure that there is an open dialogue on priority issues for indigenous peoples. According to UPRInfo, 'the UPR has been successful in providing a platform for unprecedented dialogue between CSOs and governments', because '[g]overnments frequently appreciate that civil society is willing to seek compromises and solutions to common issues rather than embarking on naming and shaming campaigns.'[38]

Interaction phase

During the Interaction Phase at Geneva, groups representing the rights of indigenous peoples can advocate effectively on behalf of indigenous peoples. In order to encourage effective engagement of NGOs, including those representing indigenous peoples, with the Interaction Phase, UPRInfo established UPR 'Pre-sessions' in 2012, at the start of the second UPR cycle. These meetings are open to a variety of stakeholders, including states, civil society organisations, national human rights institutions, academics, media, and UN bodies. UPRInfo invites the state under review to attend its own pre-session, and the majority of such states do attend. The Pre-sessions have a 'dual aim'; first, they provide civil society with an international platform to directly advocate to state delegations prior to the UPR session, and second, to allow diplomatic delegations to access information on states' human rights practices and policies.[39] Instead of relying solely on the large number of UPR written submissions, the Pre-sessions provide states with the opportunity to hear directly from grass roots organisations about the human rights situation on the ground. According to UPRInfo, 'the ultimate aim of the Pre-sessions is to ensure that the recommendations that will be made at the Review are specific and well-targeted.'[40] These Pre-sessions take place in Geneva one month before the actual UPR Session and each one is country-specific, mirroring the actual UPR process. At the Pre-sessions, selected civil society organisations and national human rights institutions present on human rights issues which are important in the state under review, and then make a number of recommendations, which they would like the recommending states to make at the UPR. Given time restraints, not all civil society organisations can take part.[41]

In addition to the Pre-sessions, UPR Info also organises UPR training session the day before the Pre-sessions begin. The training sessions helps to prepare NGOs for their participation in the UPR process and to educate them as to how to employ advocacy strategies at the various stages of the UPR process. Groups representing indigenous peoples should take an active part in these UPRInfo initiatives, to focus attention on their priorities and to be well prepared for the UPR process.

NGOs representing indigenous peoples must also distil the priorities included in stakeholder reports to produce a succinct advocacy sheet which will facilitate a dialogue with diplomatic missions who are participating in the review in Geneva. Another way to highlight their priorities is to organise a Side Event, which focuses on the challenges facing indigenous peoples.

Consideration and adoption phases

Side Events can also be organised during the Consideration Phase, 'to allow impacted individuals to share stories with member states that can transform into real recommendations for change.'[42] A useful way to illustrate the importance of the UPR to indigenous communities is to organise a viewing of the state's review, which is broadcast live online, in local centres. This engages local communities and can encourage an interest in ensuring implementation of recommendations.

Once the review has been completed but before the report has been adopted, NGOs representing indigenous peoples can distribute the results of the Review and maintain pressure on states going forward into the implementation phase. During the Adoption phase, there are a small number of opportunities to make a 2 min intervention before the Human Rights Council in Geneva. NGOs representing indigenous peoples can take part in this or they can prepare a video to be shown instead of travelling to Switzerland. These sessions during the Adoption Phase are also webcast and so domestic screenings can also be organised in indigenous communities.

Implementation phase

UPRInfo states that '[o]nce the state under review accepts a recommendation, the real work begins to build a culture of human rights by changing conditions through the realization of rights reflected in the recommendations.'[43] The level of implementation of recommendations varies hugely between states. This can depend on the subject-matter of the recommendation, the action called for, and indeed, the nature of the state.[44] Consistent pressure by advocacy groups and the tracking of implementation of recommendations is necessary in order to make the UPR a successful tool for the promotion of the rights of indigenous peoples. Some organisations have produced templates which help track the implementation of recommendations, and accurately record the progress states have made. For example, Kenyan civil society stakeholders developed a document outlining how the recommendations received by the Kenyan government should be implemented.[45] In addition, The Working Group on Human Rights in India and the UN (WGHR) developed a table incorporating information regarding the UPR recommendations, as well as possible actions on the recommendations, indicators that could help to monitor implementation, and also the government department or ministry responsible for the implementation. This document also includes a column that indicates the type of measures that have been taken by the state, thus helping to keep track of the progress made to date.[46] Indigenous communities should be encouraged to prepare a similar template for recommendations pertaining to them.

UPRInfo also suggests that NGOs should '[w]hen possible, work with the government to ensure that implementation of recommendations is effective and sustainable.'[47] Non-governmental organisations need to work with governments in order to implement recommendations if possible, by reminding them of their obligations, and informing the public of states' promises.[48] Thus, representatives of indigenous should use the UPR as a framework for dialogue with state agencies.

Indigenous peoples and the UPR: practice to date

During both of the UPR cycles which have been completed to date, the rights of indigenous peoples have been regularly included in state reports, in the reports of stakeholders, and in recommendations made to states under review. This issue has been discussed during the interactive dialogue stage of the UPR and the recommendations made have led to states undertaking to change their policies and practices in respect of indigenous peoples.

UPRInfo, a non-governmental organisation which monitors the UPR process, has identified a total of 56 different 'issues' which have been raised in recommendations made to states under review as part of the UPR mechanism. The top 5 issues raised in the recommendations over the first two cycles were: 1. International instruments (12,714); 2. Women's rights (10,718); 3. Rights of the Child (10,112); 4. Torture and other Cruel, Inhumane and Degrading Treatment (4,529) and 5. Justice (4,336).[49] The issue of indigenous peoples came in 34th position, with a total of 999 recommendations being made over the two cycles, which amounted to 1.73% of the total recommendations made.[50] It should be noted that the issue of minority rights comes in 10th position with 2,621 recommendations, amounting to 4.54% of the total recommendations made over the two cycles, and some of recommendations made in respect of minority rights may also have an impact on the rights of indigenous peoples. In Cycle 1, the issue of indigenous peoples was in 33rd position, with 389 recommendations, amounting to 1.82% of the total. The issue remained in 33rd position in Cycle 2, however while the number of recommendations rose to 610, this amounted to a decrease in percentage share of total recommendations made at 1.68%. This shows that while states are engaging more with the UPR process over time, and while more recommendations concerning indigenous peoples are being made, that unfortunately, overall, the importance of this issue has not increased from Cycle 1 to Cycle 2. Indeed, the fall in importance as expressed in percentage share of overall recommendations made is worrying, as the situation of indigenous peoples remains precarious in many states the world over and the topic needs additional attention at the UN. With fewer than 2% of all recommendations focusing on the rights of indigenous peoples, and that percentage falling between Cycle 1 and Cycle 2, it is clear that the UPR could be much better used as a tool to highlight the issue of indigenous rights going forward.

The first cycle of the UPR ran from 2008-2011. During this cycle 389 recommendations were made in respect of indigenous peoples.[51] 81 states made recommendations with regard to indigenous peoples and 55 states received recommendations on this topic.[52] The states which made and received the most recommendations on indigenous peoples are as follows:[53]

Top 5 Receiving States	Top 5 Recommending States
1. Australia (39)	1. Norway (38)
2. Chile (30)	2. Mexico (30)
3. Canada (29)	3. Bolivia (26)
4. Mexico (22)	4. Denmark (15)
5. Paraguay (20)	5. Austria (15)

During the second cycle of the UPR, running from 2012-2016, the number of recommendations in respect of indigenous peoples increased to 610.[54] The number of states making recommendations on this issue rose to 121 and 78 states received recommendations on this topic.[55] The states which made and received the most recommendations on indigenous peoples during this cycle are as follows:[56]

Top 5 Receiving States	Top 5 Recommending States
1. Canada (62)	1. Mexico (28)
2. Australia (59)	2. Norway (26)
3. New Zealand (33)	3. Bolivia (23)
4. Costa Rica (29)	4. Peru (17)
5. Chile (29)	5. Uzbekistan (13)

One of the main issues which was raised in the UPR recommendations on indigenous peoples was the implementation of UNDRIP.[57] UNDRIP provides a common frame of reference for all states, and a standard to which all states should aspire. For example, during Cycle 1, Denmark recommended that Australia take further steps to ensure the implementation of UNDRIP, and Ghana recommended that Australia '[e]nsure effective implementation of the Declaration on the Rights of Indigenous Peoples, including in the Northern Territory, and provide adequate support to the National Congress of Australia's First Peoples to enable it to address the needs of indigenous people'. In a similar vein, Mexico recommended to Belize that it '[r]edouble its efforts in favor of the respect of the rights of indigenous peoples, in line with the provisions of the United Nations Declaration on the Rights of Indigenous Peoples' and Pakistan recommended that Canada support and fully implement UNDRIP. During Cycle 2, Denmark recommended that the Russian Federation '[o]fficially endorse the United Nations Declaration on the Rights of Indigenous Peoples, and fully implement all relevant national laws and regulations' and Bolivia recommended to the United States that it '[i]mplement the United Nations Declaration on the Rights of Indigenous Peoples.'[58]

However, while UNDRIP was referred to throughout the UPR process, a more direct and exact referencing to specific provisions of this instrument may have resulted in more specific action by states under review. While a number of issues that are covered in UNDRIP are raised in UPR recommendations, they are not always linked back to UNDRIP. For example, a number of recommendations focused on the question of indigenous lands, (an issue which is dealt with in Articles 8, 10, 25, 26, 27, 28, 29, 30, 32), including Slovenia's recommendation to Belize to protect Mayan customary property rights in accordance with Mayan customary laws and land tenure practices in consultation with affected Mayan people in Cycle 1.[59] In Cycle 2, Suriname accepted Canada's recommendation that it respect and ensure the rights of indigenous peoples related to the preservation of their land, culture and resources,[60] but these recommendations did not specifically refer to the UNDRIP framework.

In addition, cultural sensitivity is another theme which can be identified in the recommendations concerning indigenous peoples, particularly, training as regards the culture and language of indigenous peoples for state officials (issues which are dealt with in Articles 8, 11, 13, 14, 15, 16, 31 of UNDRIP). For example, in Cycle 1 Austria recommended to Australia that it enhance the contacts and communication between Aboriginal and Torres Strait Islander communities and law enforcement officials and enhance the training of those officials with respect to cultural specificities of these communities.[61] During Cycle 2, the Republic of Congo accepted a recommendation made by Sweden that it take additional steps for civic education and promote human rights awareness and ensure access to justice for indigenous groups.[62] Again, the UNDRIP framework is not specifically mentioned.

Along with UNDRIP, another international legal instrument which featured a lot in the UPR recommendations regarding indigenous peoples is ILO Convention No. 169.[63] However, as with UNDRIP, this Convention was referred to in a general way rather than there being a focus on specific provisions. For example, during Cycle 1, Bolivia recommended to Australia that it '[r]atify ILO Convention No. 169 and incorporate it into its national norms',[64] which was accepted by Australia. Mexico recommended to both Botswana and the Cameroon that they consider the ratification of this Convention, which was noted, rather than accepted in both cases.[65] During Cycle 2, numerous other recommendations were made concerning the ratification of ILO Conventions, including a recommendation made by Uzbekistan to Sweden that it consider ratification of the ILO convention on indigenous peoples,[66] which was accepted.

While each state will approach the UPR in its way, given the flexibility that is inherent in the mechanism, it is interesting to analyse how one state dealt with the process over the two cycles, to question how indigenous peoples played a role in it, and how the state dealt with recommendations regarding indigenous peoples. The state chosen for this analysis here is Australia. When UNDRIP was adopted in September 2007, Australia was among only four countries to vote against its adoption, along with New Zealand, the United States and Canada. However, following a changes of government, Australia changed its position and made a statement in support of the instrument on 3 April 2009, with the then Minister for Families, Community Services and Indigenous Services, Jenny Macklin, stating that UNDRIP 'Australia takes another important step in re-setting the relationship between Indigenous and non-Indigenous Australians and moving forward towards a new future'.[67] Thus, Australia accepted it as a framework for better recognising and protecting the rights of Aboriginal and Torres Strait Islander Australians. The UPR can now facilitate a discussion of how Australia has addressed the rights of indigenous peoples which are protected in UNDRIP.

Cycle 1

The state report highlighted some planned and recently implemented initiatives with regard to indigenous Australians, including the planned recognition of Aboriginal and Torres Strait Islander peoples in the Constitution and the establishment of an Expert Panel on this recognition,[68] the National Congress of Australia's First Peoples.[69] A full section of the report is dedicated to 'Indigenous Australians', and a number of challenges facing indigenous peoples in Australia are mentioned, including disadvantages in education, employment, and health. The report refers to UNDRIP, stating that Australia gave its support to the instrument in April 2009, 'reaffirming the entitlement of Australia's Indigenous peoples to all human rights and fundamental freedoms,'[70] but it does not refer to specific provisions of the instrument.

The stakeholder report on Cycle 1 of the UPR contained a summary of the 14 submissions from 97 groups in total, illustrating that Australian NGOs felt that the UPR was an important process with which to engage. One of the joint submissions was prepared by NGOs working on the issue of indigenous rights, i.e. the Joint Submission submitted by the Aboriginal and Torres Strait Islander Legal Services of Australia (ATSILS) composed of: Aboriginal and Torres Strait Islander Legal Service (Qld) Ltd; Aboriginal Legal Rights Movement Inc; Aboriginal Legal Service (NSW/ACT); Aboriginal Legal Service of Western Australia (Inc.), Perth (Australia); Central Australian Aboriginal Legal Aid Service; North Australian Aboriginal Justice Agency; and Victorian Aboriginal Legal Service Co-operative Limited, Fitzroy, Victoria (Australia). The information provided in this report was much more detailed with regard to specific issues of concern facing indigenous peoples that the state report, including the establishment of a reparation scheme,[71] and the principle of free, prior and informed consent of Aboriginal and Torres Strait Islander peoples in the development of policy that directly affect these communities.[72] The report included recommendations from organisations[73] that the government 'develop a framework to implement and raise awareness about' UNDRIP 'in consultation with Aboriginal and Torres Strait Islander peoples'.[74] In a similar vein, OceaniaHR recommended that 'Australia should immediately create and coordinate a national implementation strategy plan to achieve the human rights of Aboriginal and Torres Strait Islanders recognized in the UNDRIP'.[75]

The UN report on Australia for Cycle 1 of the UPR[76] recalls that the Special Rapporteur on the Rights of Indigenous Peoples particularly noted the many instances of commitment made by the Australian government to reconcile with indigenous peoples, including its support for UNDRIP and the fact that he recommended that the Commonwealth and state governments should review all legislation, policies, and programmes that affect Aboriginal and Torres Strait Islanders, in light of the Declaration on the Rights of Indigenous Peoples,[77] thus placing UNDRP at the centre of the discussion on indigenous peoples in Australia. It also references recommendation from other UN institutions in respect of indigenous Australians, including concerns about the serious limitations of the current Native Title Act framework which raised by Committee on the Elimination of All Forms of Racial Discrimination, the Human Rights Committee and the Committee on Economic, Social and Cultural Rights.[78]

During Cycle 1, 51 states made 162 recommendations to Australia. 144 recommendations were supported. Of these 162 recommendations, 39 related to indigenous peoples. This was the most common subject that was raised in recommendations. A number of these recommendations focused on the implementation of UNDRRIP, e.g. Denmark recommended that Australia 'take further steps to ensure the implementation of the Declaration on the Rights of Indigenous Peoples', Norway recommended that Australia 'fully implement the Racial Discrimination Act and the revision of federal laws to be compatible with the United Nations Declaration on the Rights of Indigenous Peoples', Bolivia recommended that Australia 'revise its Constitution, legislation, public policies and programmes for the full implementation of the United Nations Declaration of the Rights of Indigenous Peoples', Ghana recommended that Australia 'ensure effective implementation of the Declaration on the Rights of Indigenous People, including in the Northern Territory, and provide adequate support to the National Congress of Australia's First Peoples to enable it to address the needs of indigenous people', Hungary recommended that Australia 'develop a detailed framework to implement and raise awareness about the Declaration in consultation with indigenous peoples', and Guatemala recommended that Australia

> launch a constitutional reform process to better recognize and protect the rights of the Aboriginals and Torres Strait Islanders which would include a framework covering the principles and objectives of the United Nations Declaration on the Rights of Indigenous Peoples and would take into account the opinions and contributions of indigenous peoples.[79]

Other issues were raised in the recommendations on indigenous peoples, including recommendations that Australia ratify ILO Convention No 169 (Bolivia and Norway), land rights (United Kingdom and Thailand), and education rights (Malaysia, Thailand, and Iran).[80]

However, while Australia supported all of these recommendations, apart from 1 (the recommendation by Slovenia that it establish a National Compensation Tribunal for indigenous Australia impacted by the state's assimilation policy), there was a gap in respect of implemented the recommendations. The Joint NGO Report on Australia's Human Rights Record provides an update on Australia's progress towards implementing Universal Periodic Review Cycle 1 recommendations.[81] The Report notes that there had not been much progress made with regard to implementing the recommendations which had been made by the United Nations Special Rapporteur on the Rights of Indigenous Peoples following his 2009 visit, and significantly, the report also concludes that 'there has been limited incorporation of the Declaration on the Rights of Indigenous Peoples ... into public policy or legislation.'[82] This report also states that there is a 'need for a formal commitment to the development of a national implementation strategy for' UNDRIP.[83] However, it does set out some initiatives which the Australian government has taken in respect of indigenous peoples following on from the UPR, including some activity with regard to the operation of the native title system and the reinstatement of the Racial Discrimination Act 1975 in the Northern Territory.[84] The Australian government has also taken a number of steps towards constitutional recognition of Aboriginal and Torres Strait Islander people,[85] e.g. in 2010 Australia appointed an Expert Panel on Constitutional Recognition of Indigenous Australians to provide advice on the best way to provide recognition for Aboriginal and Torres Strait Islander peoples in the Constitution. Some of these moves reflect the rights enshrined in UNDRIP provisions, while others may have a more general aim, e.g. the purpose of consolidating anti-discrimination laws into one act was not specifically to ensure compatibility with UNDRIP, but this was one of the consequences.[86]

Mid-term report

Australia supported almost 95 per cent of the recommendations made during Cycle 1, and subsequently committed to using these recommendations to inform the development of the government's National Human Rights Action Plan.[87] As part of its mid-term report to the Human Rights Council, Australia submitted the Action Plan; a document setting out 'Highlights regarding progress on Australia's National Human Rights Action Plan 2012'; and a 1 page explanatory note on the Action Plan. This latter document includes a number of important developments to be noted by the Human Rights Council, including the adoption of the Aboriginal and Torres Strait Islanders Peoples Recognition Act, which came into effect on 28 March 2013, and is identified as a first step towards constitutional recognition of Australia's first peoples.[88]

In the Action Plan, all of the UPR recommendations supported or partly supported by Australia during the UPR are tracked to specific legal and policy changes made / to be made in response to the recommendations, in addition to the agency leading the initiative and a timeline for implementation of the changes. Issues concerning indigenous Australians are referred to throughout the plan and there is also a discrete section entitled 'Aboriginal and Torres Strait Islander peoples'. This section states that '[c]urrent data shows a significant gap in these critical areas between Aboriginal and Torres Strait Islander and non-Indigenous populations',[89] and sets out specific measures which are designed to 'close the gap' in addressing the disadvantages faced by indigenous Australians. This is a very useful document, to keep the government on track and to facilitate co-operation with NGOs working on the issues set out in the plan.

Cycle 2

Australia's state report for Cycle 2 highlights that the government has recognised the importance of working with NGOs throughout the UPR process. Paragraph 10 states that

> As with Australia's response to its first review, this national report was developed following consultations across the Australian Government, and state and territory governments. The

> views of peak non-government organisations (NGOs) on a draft version of the report were sought at, and following, the Australian Government's annual NGO forum on human rights. The Australian Attorney-General, Senator the Hon George Brandis QC, also subsequently met with peak NGOs to discuss the report and has committed to engaging with the NGO sector throughout the process. Following Australia's second UPR the Government intends to once again engage with NGOs and the AHRC in relation to recommendations it receives.[90]

This illustrates an excellent opportunity for groups representing indigenous Australians to engage with government on their priority issues.

As requested by the Human Rights Council, the report focuses on how the government implemented recommendations to the state from Cycle 1. The state report thus tracks the recommendations made in Cycle 1 and notes progress made in relation to these recommendations. The first issue which the 2nd state report focuses on is giving constitutional recognition to indigenous Australians (Recommendations 103-105 and 107 from Cycle 1). Constitutional recognition had not been granted by the time of the 2nd review, but the government states that it 'is strongly committed to holding a referendum to recognise Indigenous Australians in the Constitution.'[91]

The rights of indigenous Australians is also dealt within the report's section on Equality and Non-discrimination. The reports highlights that the government has an agenda for reform in the rights of indigenous Australians in the areas of: ensuring children go to school; getting adults into work; making sure communities are safer to live in and that the rule of law is applied; and achieving constitutional recognition for Aboriginal and Torres Strait Islander peoples.[92] These issues echo provisions of UNDRIP, although the report does specifically identify the relevant provisions (Article 14 (education); Article 3, Article 5 (economic development); Article 1 (rule of law). However, the report reiterates that: 'Australia continues to support the United Nations Declaration on the Rights of Indigenous Peoples as a set of important guiding principles for the Government's engagement with Indigenous Australians.'[93]

The report deals with indigenous peoples under other sections of the report, e.g. 'Justice and the Rule of Law'

> The Australian Government will continue to directly fund Indigenous legal assistance providers in line with the Government's Indigenous affairs priorities and ongoing commitment to improving law and justice outcomes for Indigenous Australians. The Government will invest $358 million over five years in legal assistance services to Indigenous Australians),[94]

'Social Security' ('the Australian Government provides a range of payments and services to Australians, including retirees, the unemployed, families, carers, parents, persons with disabilities, students, and Indigenous people'),[95]

While the state report records progress it has made in the field of indigenous rights it does not say that initiatives in respect of indigenous peoples are set up specifically as a result of the UPR process, nor, predictably, does it identify the areas in which it has not made progress and which recommendations it has failed to implement, e.g. no mention is made of the non-ratification of ILO Convention No. 169.

The stakeholder report[96] for the second cycle included a summary of 22 stakeholders' submissions. 16 groups made individual submissions, and 5 joint submissions were made by numerous NGOs. One joint submission was made which summarised submissions made by 190 NGOs working on a variety of issues, including groups focusing on the rights of indigenous Australians. 14 submissions referred to indigenous related issues,[97] and one section of the report is entitled 'Indigenous peoples', although issues facing indigenous Australians are also picked up in other parts of the report. The section on 'Indigenous peoples' relays some of the progress made by the government since the previous UPR cycle (e.g. the adoption of the World Conference of Indigenous Peoples Outcome Document),[98] but also highlights the lack of implementation of some of the UPR recommendations. One of the submissions raised the issue that Australia was impeding the right to self-determination of indigenous peoples 'by continuing to impose forced integration on its peoples'.[99] However, the report does not refer to UNDRIP in this context. It does, however, refer to the Declaration in regard to the strict requirement of the Native Title Act 1993 (Cth) of continuous connection to the land since colonisation and states that it was incompatible with UNDRIP. The report also records that the Australian Human Rights Commission recommends that the government develop, in partnership with indigenous Australians, a National Strategy to give effect to UNDRIP.

The UN report[100] summarises the interactions of a number of UN institutions with the Australian government. In the context of indigenous Australians, this focused on the Committee on the Rights of the Child, which noted 'inadequate consultation and participation of Aboriginal and Torres Strait Islander persons in the policy formulation, decision-making and implementation processes of programmes affecting them'.[101] The Committee was also concerned at the large numbers of indigenous children being separated from their homes and communities and placed into care that, where the preservation of their cultural and linguistic identity was not facilitated. It recommended that Australia review its progress in implementing the recommendations in the report 'Bringing them home: national inquiry into the separation of Aboriginal and Torres Strait Islander children from their families'.[102]

The report also reiterates the Committee on the Elimination of Racial Discrimination's statement on the need to guarantee the free, prior and informed consent of the communities concerned.[103] The report also refers to the Special Rapporteur on the Rights of Indigenous Peoples and his comments that the government should maintain ongoing consultations with Aboriginal peoples concerning the implementation of the Stronger Futures legislation.[104]

The section concerning indigenous peoples does not refer to UNDRIP, but the instrument is referred to in the section on 'Constitutional and Legislative Framework', where it notes that in June 2015, the United Nations High Commissioner for Human Rights welcomed proposals to introduce a reference to the United Nations Declaration on the Rights of Indigenous Peoples in the Human Rights (Parliamentary Scrutiny) Act.

Cycle 2 saw an increase in recommendations made to Australia in respect of indigenous peoples to 59. 15 of these recommendations were noted, but all of the rest were accepted. UNDRIP again was the focus of a number of recommendations made to Australia in respect of indigenous peoples. Senegal recommended that Australia 'adhere to' UNDRP, Estonia recommended that Australia to 'develop in partnership with Aboriginal and Torres Strait Islander peoples a National Strategy to give effect to the United Nations Declaration on the Rights of Indigenous Peoples, and to facilitate the constitutional recognition of Aboriginal Australians', and Hungary once again recommended that Australia 'develop, in partnership with indigenous communities, a national strategy to implement the United Nations Declaration on the Rights of Indigenous Peoples'.[105] Other issues which were raised include, once again, the ratification of ILO Convention No. 169 (Chile), and constitutional recognition of indigenous Australians (Georgia, Sri Lanka, Republic of Korea and Estonia).[106]

A number of states raised concerns in relation to Australia's treatment of indigenous peoples, including high-levels of discrimination against Aboriginal and Torres Strait Islander peoples (Japan), disproportionately high rates of indigenous incarceration (Norway), however, as before, there was a lack of reference to specific provisions of UNDRIP. In response to the UPR Cycle 2 recommendations, Australia reaffirmed its commitment to improving the situation of indigenous Australians, including implementing its Indigenous Strategy 2015-2019. However, a number of major problems continue to exist, including in the areas of discrimination, health, life expectancy, education justice etc.[107]

The case study of Australia illustrates that the UPR can be beneficial to indigenous peoples by opening and / or maintaining a dialogue between the government on indigenous rights and priorities, by facilitating discussion and collaboration between NGOs working on indigenous issues, and by concerting pressure on the Australian government to constantly improve. Australia is to be commended for its mid-term report to the UN Human Rights Council on Cycle 1 recommendations and its Action Plan, which clearly tracks UPR recommendations. This is an excellent initiative and provides a framework for consistent improvement in the field of the rights of indigenous peoples. However, despite this, Australia was slow in implementing some Cycle 1 recommendations and others had not been addressed by the time of writing the mid-term report or the Cycle 2 report. In addition, Australia has not submitted a mid-term report in respect of Cycle 2 of the UPR, and so it is difficult to make conclusions on the actual impact of the UPR in this state. What is clear is that is that lobbying on the part of indigenous rights groups in respect of the UPR recommendations is needed in order to maintain pressure on the government to fulfil its UPR promises.

Conclusion

At the outset, there were high hopes for the success of the UPR process and it was heralded by UN officials as a very positive addition to the UN human rights monitoring framework, with former Secretary General Ban Ki moon stating in 2007 that the UPR had 'great potential to promote and protect human rights in the darkest corners of the world.'[108] Now that 2 cycles have been completed, some observations can be made in respect of the process's effectiveness. To date, there has been a certain amount of ambivalence towards the process from non-governmental groups and academics alike. One of the main criticisms levelled at the process is that states are 'soft' with their recommendations to neighbouring and / or friendly states, with Abebe commenting that '[t]here are ominous signs that the problem of regional block voting, which had seriously afflicted the former Commission, remains a formidable challenge to the Council's decision making process.'[109] This situation led UN Watch to report in 2009 that the UPR facilitated a 'mutual praise society',[110] rather than acting as a strong accountability tool. Unfortunately, if this is the case, it is doubtful if a genuine appraisal of the rights of indigenous peoples can be encouraged by this process.

However, other reviews of the UPR have highlighted positive aspects of this review process. For example, Frazier states that 'the UPR has been effective in promoting human rights in the short term. It has helped to highlight serious human rights violations and has done so in a public forum that allows debate to occur on the best way to address those problems. The UPR has also helped to give countries specific guidance, and individualized, achievable goals to meet in progressing respect for human rights; goals which many countries have met or are in the process of meeting.'[111]

While a number of commentaries adopted a 'wait and see' approach,[112] as time has passed commentaries have generally been more positive towards the UPR,[113] as observers have had the opportunity to evaluate the implementation of UPR recommendations,[114] which show that states have, to a significant extent, seriously considered recommendations made to them by other states during the UPR process and have amended some of their policies and practices accordingly.[115] Recommendations made as part of the UPR process have influenced domestic practice through amendment of domestic laws, ratification of international instruments and changes in governmental policies in a number of states. However, states have taken different approaches to recording how they have implemented the recommendations which they have accepted as part of the UPR process. Unfortunately, the mid-term assessment is currently optional, and thus some states may delay reviewing the UPR recommendations which they accepted until close to their second review. What would be very help in this context is first, making the mid-term review a requirement of the UPR process, and second, the adoption of an implementation template, applicable to all states, whereby all states would be require to 'map' their actions, in terms of adoption of legislation, policy changes, institution building, in response to their accepted UPR accepted recommendations. This would allow for a clearer analysis of improvement (or otherwise) in states' human rights practices. Some states have adopted a very clear tracking approach,[116] e.g. Kenya has prepared an 'Implementation Matrix', which illustrates the domestic measures taken as a result of the recommendations made.[117] Another effective model is used in Paraguay, known as SIMORE,[118] which is coordinated by the Ministry of Foreign Affairs and the Ministry of Justice. Groups representing indigenous peoples should also track UPR recommendations which relate to indigenous rights, to ensure that UPR commitments are not forgotten or pushed aside. In addition, UNDRIP provisions should be explicitly referred to when recommendations concerning the rights of indigenous peoples are made (both by states and NGOs), to highlight the importance of this instrument as an expression of indigenous rights and to ensure consistency across the board.

One of the most positive aspects the UPR process is that it provides a space for civil society and non-governmental organisations to participate in the review. A central issue with regard to the current framework seeking to promote and protect the rights of indigenous peoples is its state-centric nature. This means that the voice of indigenous peoples can be difficult to heard, as they can generally only participate indirectly in the system, via state representatives.[119] If there is a confrontational relationship between states and an indigenous group, it is difficult for the rights of that group to be raised before the UN system. However, with the UPR, indigenous groups can organise and advocate on their own behaves and contribute to the stakeholder report. Unfortunately, Universal Rights Group has commented that 'these crucial "shadow" reports are not fulfilling that function.'[120] Therefore, additional work is needed to prepare stakeholders to contribute in a more effective way to these reports. One option for indigenous groups is to take advantage of the tools and training sessions offered by UPRInfo, described above, in order to be well prepared for the UPR process and optimise its benefits. Given the nature of the UPR, which facilitates interactive dialogue and lesson learning between groups, indigenous groups can learn from one another and share advice. The UPRInfo Pre-sessions are an opening to learn lessons from each other and to strengthen advocacy on behalf of indigenous peoples.

According to Indigenous World in 2011, the UPR process was a 'limited success'.[121] More encouragingly, in 2014 Joshua Cooper characterised the UPR as 'a potent process for the realization of human rights in indigenous homelands.'[122] He also stated that:

> The ultimate aspiration of the Universal Periodic Review is the improvement of human rights in every country with significant consequences for people around the globe. If Indigenous Peoples participate in each phase, there will be a rigorous review and the results will be substantive. It can become a regular measure of how states are implementing the rights enshrined in the Declaration, and it can be the catalyst for the conversation with a country's leadership to ensure the Declaration is beyond paper, building better lives for Indigenous Peoples.'

If groups representing indigenous peoples embrace the opportunities provided by the UPR process to engage in stakeholder reports, to track recommendations to implementation and to maintain pressure on states to fulfil UPR commitments, the UPR can indeed be a powerful tool for improving their rights worldwide in the future.[123]

Notes

1. The NGO UPRInfo provides excellent online tools, which facilitate searches for keywords raised and recommendations made during the UPR.
2. UNGA Res 60/251, 15 March 2006. With regard to the history and functions of the Human Rights Council, see P.J. Flood, 'The U.N. Human Rights Council: Is its Mandate Well-Designed?', *ILSA Journal of International and Comparative Law* 15 (2008–2009): 472–84 and J. Matiya, 'Repositioning the International Human Rights Protection System: The UN Human Rights Council', *Commonwealth Law Bulletin* 36, no. 2 (2010): 313–24.
3. See H. Boekle, 'Western States, the UN Commission on Human Rights and the "1235" Procedure: The Question of Bias Revisited', *Netherlands Quarterly of Human Rights* 13 (1995): 367–402 and T. Franck, 'Of Gnats and Camels: Is there a Double Standard in the United Nations?', *American Journal of International Law* 78 (1984): 811–34. For a discussion of the transition from the Human Rights Commission to the Human Rights Council, see P.G. Lauren, 'To Preserve and Build on its Achievements and to Redress its Shortcomings: The Journey from the Commission on Human Rights to the Human Rights Council', *Human Rights Quarterly* 29 (2007): 307–45.
4. The Human Rights Council replaced the Human Rights Commission by virtue of UN General Assembly Resolution 60/251 (2006). See generally, B. Ramcharan, The UN Human Rights Council (UK: Routledge, 2011); M. Bossuyt, 'The Human Rights Council: A First Appraisal', *Netherlands Quarterly of Human Rights* 24, no. 4 (2006): 551–5 and N. Schrijver, 'The UN Human Rights Council: A New "Society of the Committed" or Just Old Wine in New Bottles?', *Leiden Journal of International Law* 20, no. 4 (2007): 809–23.
5. UNGA Res 60/251, 15 March 2006. For a discussion of the UPR see P.J. Flood, 'The U.N. Human Rights Council: Is its Mandate well-designed?', *ILSA Journal of International and Comparative Law* 15 (2008–2009): 472–84 and E. McMahon and M. Ascherio, 'A Step Ahead in Promoting Human Rights? The Universal Periodic Review of the UN Human Rights Council', *Global Governance* 18 (2012): 231–48.
6. Different States had varying views on the format they hoped the UPR would take. See Human Rights Peer Review, Draft Concept and Opinions Paper, prepared by Canada, 29 April 2005,

at para. 9, www.humanrightsvoices.org/assets/attachments/documents/human_rights_peer_review_canada.pdf (accessed February, 2018).

7. UN Human Rights Council, 'Institution-building of the United Nations Human Rights Council', HRC Res 5/1 UN GAOR, 5th Sess., 9th mtg., (2007) 1 UN Doc A/HRC/5/1.
8. UN Human Rights Council, 'Institution-building of the United Nations Human Rights Council', HRC Res 5/1 UN GAOR, 5th Sess., 9th mtg., (2007) 1 UN Doc A/HRC/5/1.
9. Human Rights Council Resolution 5/1, annex at 1.A.1.
10. Universal Declaration of Human Rights, proclaimed by the United Nations General Assembly in Paris on 10 December 1948 (General Assembly resolution 217 A).
11. International Covenant on Civil and Political Rights, adopted by General Assembly resolution 2200A (XXI), 16 December 1966.
12. ILO Convention No. 169, Convention concerning Indigenous and Tribal Peoples in Independent Countries 1989.
13. For example, some regional instruments protect indigenous peoples' rights, including the African Charter on Human and Peoples' Rights (adopted 27 June 1981) OAU Doc CAB/LEG/67/3 rev. 5, 21 ILM 58 (1982).
14. United Nations Declaration of the Rights of Indigenous Peoples, adopted by General Assembly resolution 61/295, 2007.
15. See: J. Cooper, 'Universal Periodic Review: A Potent Process for the Realization of Human Rights in Indigenous Homelands', Cultural Survival Quarterly Magazine 38(2) (2014), https://www.culturalsurvival.org/publications/cultural-survival-quarterly/universal-periodic-review-potent-process-realization-human (accessed July, 2018).
16. E. McMahon, 'Herding Cats and Sheep: Assessing State and Regional Behavior in the Universal Periodic Review Mechanism of the United Nations Human Rights Council', www.upr-info.org/IMG/pdf/McMahon_Herding_Cats_and_Sheeps_July_2010.pdf, 12 (accessed February, 2018).
17. G. Sweeney and Y. Saito, 'An NGO Assessment of the New Mechanisms of the UN Human Rights Council', *Human Rights Law Review* 9, no. 2 (2009): 203–23, 210.
18. The UPR Extranet is http://www.ohchr.org/EN/HRBodies/UPR/Pages/UPRRegistration.aspx (accessed July, 2018).
19. See United Nations Human Rights Council, 'UPR Mid-term Reports', http://www.ohchr.org/EN/HRBodies/UPR/Pages/UPRImplementation.aspx. These mid-term reports are http://www.ohchr.org/EN/HRBodies/UPR/Pages/UPRImplementation.aspx (accessed July, 2018).
20. See United Nations Human Rights Council, 'UPR NGOs Mid-term Reports', http://www.ohchr.org/EN/HRBodies/UPR/Pages/UPR-NGOs-Mid-term-reports.aspx (accessed July, 2018).
21. UPRInfo, 'Follow-up Programme', https://www.upr-info.org/followup/ (accessed July, 2018).
22. See resolution 16/21, 15 March 2011 and decision 17/119.
23. https://www.upr-info.org/database/statistics (accessed July, 2018).
24. J. Cooper, 'Universal Periodic Review: A Potent Process for the Realization of Human Rights in Indigenous Homelands', Cultural Survival Quarterly Magazine 38(2) (2014), https://www.culturalsurvival.org/publications/cultural-survival-quarterly/universal-periodic-review-potent-process-realization-human (accessed July, 2018).
25. See United Nations Office of the High Commissioner on Human Rights, '3rd Cycle Universal Periodic Review National Report – Guidance Note', www.ohchr.org/Documents/... /3rdCycle_GuidanceNotePreparationReports_EN.docx (accessed July, 2018).
26. See United Nations Office of the High Commissioner on Human Rights, '3rd Cycle Universal Periodic Review National Report – Guidance Note', www.ohchr.org/Documents/... /3rdCycle_GuidanceNotePreparationReports_EN.docx (accessed July, 2018).
27. Under Article 22 of the ILO Constitution, each Member State must provide periodic reports to the International Labour Office on ratified conventions, setting out the measures taken to implement the provisions of those Conventions it has ratified.
28. See B. Saul, *Indigenous Peoples and Human Rights* (London: Hart Publishing, 2016) and B. Saul, 'Introduction: Indigenous Peoples and Human Rights – Institutions and Influences',

Sydney Law School, Legal Studies Research Paper No. 16/39, May 2016, https://ssrn.com/abstract=2778903 (accessed February, 2018).

29. This provision states that '[i]n those States in which ethnic, religious or linguistic minorities exist, persons belonging to such minorities shall not be denied the right, in community with the other members of their group, to enjoy their own culture, to profess and practise their own religion, or to use their own language'. Article 27 International Covenant on Civil and Political Rights, adopted by General Assembly resolution 2200A (XXI), 16 December 1966.
30. International Covenant on Economic, Social and Cultural Rights, adopted by General Assembly resolution 2200A (XXI), 16 December 1966. While no provisions of this instrument specifically refer to indigenous peoples, numerous of its provisions are of relevance to indigenous peoples, including Article 15(1), which states: 'The States Parties to the present Covenant recognize the right of everyone: (a) To take part in cultural life ... '
31. International Convention on the Elimination of All Forms of Racial Discrimination, adopted General Assembly resolution 2106 (XX) of 21 December 1965. As with the International Covenant on Economic, Social and Cultural Rights, no provisions of this instrument explicitly deal with indigenous peoples. However, a number of provisions are relevant to this group, including Article 2(1), which states: 'States Parties condemn racial discrimination and undertake to pursue by all appropriate means and without delay a policy of eliminating racial discrimination in all its forms and promoting understanding among all races'.
32. Convention on the Rights of the Child, adopted by General Assembly resolution 44/25 of 20 November 1989. Articles 17, 29 and 30 specifically mention indigenous peoples. Article 30 states: 'In those States in which ethnic, religious or linguistic minorities or persons of indigenous origin exist, a child belonging to such a minority or who is indigenous shall not be denied the right, in community with other members of his or her group, to enjoy his or her own culture, to profess and practise his or her own religion, or to use his or her own language'.
33. See Preamble, Convention on the Rights of People with Disabilities, adopted by General Assembly resolution A/RES/61/106 of 13 December 2006.
34. For example, the 6th state report from New Zealand on the ICCPR to the Human Rights Committee contains numerous references to the Māori population and discusses various topics, including education, incarceration rates, equality, language, political representation, amongst others. CCPR/C/NZL/6, 24 July 2015.
35. See B. Saul, *Indigenous Peoples and Human Rights* (Hart Publishing, London, 2016) and A. Xanthaki, 'Indigenous Rights in International Law over the Last 10 Years and Future Developments: Reflections on a Decade of International Law', *Melbourne Journal of International Law* 10 (2009): 27–37.
36. This can be seen from the work of the Committee on Economic, Social and Cultural Rights, which, in General Comment No 14, recognised the rights of indigenous peoples to control their own health services and to have medical care delivered in a manner which is culturally appropriate. CESCR, General Comment No 14: The Right to the Highest Attainable Standard of Health (Article 12 of the International Covenant on Economic, Social and Cultural Rights), 22"d sess, Agenda Item 3, UN Doc E/C. 12/2000/4 (11 August 2000). See A. Xanthaki, 'Indigenous Rights in International Law over the Last 10 Years and Future Developments: Reflections on a Decade of International Law', *Melbourne Journal of International Law* 10 (2009): 27–37, 28.
37. https://witness.org/portfolio_page/monitoring-human-rights-united-states/ (accessed July, 2018).
38. UPRInfo, 'The Butterfly Effect', (UPRInfo Geneva, 2016), iv.
39. https://www.upr-info.org/en/upr-process/pre-sessions (accessed July, 2018).
40. Ibid.
41. Priority is given on the following bases: Grassroots and national CSOs; National coalitions; CSOs that have submitted a report to the UPR and are committed to engaging in the process, in particular in the implementation phase; A broad representation of the various human

rights issues representing the concerns of the local population. In particular, a balance is sought amongst civil and political rights, and economic, social and cultural rights; and ensuring a gender perspective for each Pre-sessions; where possible, gender parity amongst panellists is also sought.

42. J. Cooper, 'Universal Periodic Review: A Potent Process for the Realization of Human Rights in Indigenous Homelands', *Cultural Survival Quarterly Magazine* 38(2) (2014), https://www.culturalsurvival.org/publications/cultural-survival-quarterly/universal-periodic-review-potent-process-realization-0 (accessed July, 2018).
43. Ibid.
44. See S. Gujadhur and M. Limon for Universal Rights Groups, 'Towards the Third Cycle of the UPR: Stick or Twist' (2016), https://www.universal-rights.org/wp-content/uploads/2016/07/URG_UPR_stick_or_twist.pdf (accessed July, 2018), p. 5.
45. See: From commitments to actions: the stakeholder's outcomes charter on the UPR of Kenya', http://s.upr-info.org/kenyacharter (accessed July, 2018).
46. See: WGHR Press Release, Comprehensive review of India's human rights record at the UN Human Rights Council: Glaring Omissions, Some Progress, September 21, 2012, http://www.wghr.org/pdf/WGHR%20UPR%20press%20release%20 21.09.2012.pdf (accessed July, 2018).
47. UPRInfo, 'Beyond Promises', https://www.upr-info.org/sites/default/files/general-document/pdf/2014_beyond_promises.pdf (accessed July, 2018), p. 8.
48. UPRInfo, 'Beyond Promises', https://www.upr-info.org/sites/default/files/general-document/pdf/2014_beyond_promises.pdf (accessed July, 2018), p. 64.
49. https://www.upr-info.org/database/statistics (accessed July, 2018).
50. Ibid.
51. Ibid.
52. Ibid.
53. Ibid.
54. Ibid.
55. Ibid.
56. Ibid.
57. United Nations Declaration of the Rights of Indigenous Peoples, adopted by General Assembly resolution 61/295, 2007.
58. https://www.upr-info.org/database/index.php?&limit=0&f_SUR=All&f_SMR=All&order=&orderDir=ASC&orderP=true&f_Issue=26&searchReco=&resultMax=100&response=&action_type=&session=&SuRRgrp=&SuROrg=&SMRRgrp=&SMROrg=&pledges=RecoOnly (accessed July, 2018).
59. Ibid.
60. Ibid.
61. Ibid.
62. Ibid.
63. ILO Convention No. 169, Convention concerning Indigenous and Tribal Peoples in Independent Countries 1989.
64. https://www.upr-info.org/database/index.php?&limit=0&f_SUR=All&f_SMR=All&order=&orderDir=ASC&orderP=true&f_Issue=26&searchReco=&resultMax=100&response=&action_type=&session=&SuRRgrp=&SuROrg=&SMRRgrp=&SMROrg=&pledges=RecoOnly (accessed July, 2018).
65. Ibid.
66. Ibid.
67. Reconciliation Australia, 'The United Nations Declaration on the Rights of Indigenous Peoples (UNDRIP)', p. 1, https://www.reconciliation.org.au/wp-content/uploads/2017/11/Reconciliation-Australia-United-Nations-Declaration-on-the-Rights-of-Indigenous-Peoples-UNDRIP.pdf (accessed July, 2018).
68. National report submitted in accordance with paragraph 15 (a) of the annex to Human Rights Council resolution 5/1, Australia, A/HRC/WG.6/10/AUS/1, 5 November 2010, para. 14.

69. Ibid, para. 35.
70. Ibid, para. 59.
71. Summary prepared by the Office of the High Commissioner for Human Rights in accordance with paragraph 15 (c) of the annex to Human Rights Council resolution 5/1, Australia, A/HRC/WG.6/10/AUS/3, 11 November 2011, para. 52.
72. Ibid, para. 56.
73. Joint Submission submitted by the Aboriginal and Torres Strait Islander Legal Services of Australia (ATSILS) composed of: Aboriginal and Torres Strait Islander Legal Service (Qld) Ltd; Aboriginal Legal Rights Movement Inc; Aboriginal Legal Service (NSW/ACT); Aboriginal Legal Service of Western Australia (Inc.), Perth (Australia); Central Australian Aboriginal Legal Aid Service; North Australian Aboriginal Justice Agency; and Victorian Aboriginal Legal Service Co-operative Limited, Fitzroy, Victoria (Australia).
74. Summary prepared by the Office of the High Commissioner for Human Rights in accordance with paragraph 15 (c) of the annex to Human Rights Council resolution 5/1, Australia, A/HRC/WG.6/10/AUS/3, 11 November 2011, para. 55.
75. Ibid.
76. Compilation prepared by the Office of the High Commissioner for Human Rights in accordance with paragraph 15 (b) of the annex to Human Rights Council resolution 5/1, Australia, A/HRC/WG.6/10/AUS/2, 15 November 2010.
77. Ibid, para. 41.
78. Ibid, para. 43.
79. See UPRInfo, 'Database of Recommendations', https://www.upr-info.org/database/index.php?&limit=0&f_SUR=9&f_SMR=All&order=&orderDir=ASC&orderP=true&f_Issue=26&searchReco=&resultMax=100&response=&action_type=&session=1-2-3-4-5-6-7-8-9-10-11-12&SuRRgrp=&SuROrg=&SMRRgrp=&SMROrg=&pledges=RecoOnly (accessed July, 2018).
80. Ibid.
81. (2014). http://www.naclc.org.au/resources/Joint_NGO_Report_on_Australia_s_Human_Rights_Record_Final.pdf (accessed July, 2018).
82. Ibid, p. 2.
83. Ibid.
84. Ibid.
85. Ibid, p. 3.
86. Ibid, p. 13.
87. Australia's National Action Plan (2012), https://lib.ohchr.org/HRBodies/UPR/Documents/Session10/AU/ImplementationAustralia_1.pdf (accessed July, 2018).
88. These 3 documents are available on the website of the Human Rights Council, at: https://www.ohchr.org/en/hrbodies/upr/pages/uprimplementation.aspx (accessed July, 2018).
89. Australia's National Action Plan (2012), https://lib.ohchr.org/HRBodies/UPR/Documents/Session10/AU/ImplementationAustralia_1.pdf (accessed July, 2018), p. 24.
90. National report submitted in accordance with paragraph 5 of the annex to Human Rights Council resolution 16/21, Australia, A/HRC/WG.6/23/AUS/1, 7 August 2015.
91. Ibid, para. 13.
92. Ibid, para. 40.
93. Ibid, para. 39.
94. Ibid, para. 115.
95. Ibid, para. 116.
96. Summary prepared by the Office of the United Nations High Commissioner for Human Rights in accordance with paragraph 15 (c) of the annex to Human Rights Council resolution 5/1 and paragraph 5 of the annex to Council resolution 16/21, Australia, A/HRC/WG.6/23/AUS/3, 10 August 2015.
97. Ibid, para. 66.
98. Ibid, para. 67.
99. Ibid, para. 66.

100. Compilation prepared by the Office of the United Nations High Commissioner for Human Rights in accordance with paragraph 15 (b) of the annex to Human Rights Council resolution 5/1 and paragraph 5 of the annex to Council resolution 16/21, Australia, A/HRC/WG.6/23/AUS/2, 31 August 2015.
101. Ibid, para. 60.
102. Commonwealth of Australia, 'Brining them Home. Report of the National Inquiry into the Separation of Aboriginal and Torres Strait Islander Children from Their Families' (1997), https://www.humanrights.gov.au/sites/default/files/content/pdf/social_justice/bringing_them_home_report.pdf (accessed: July, 2018).
103. Compilation prepared by the Office of the United Nations High Commissioner for Human Rights in accordance with paragraph 15 (b) of the annex to Human Rights Council resolution 5/1 and paragraph 5 of the annex to Council resolution 16/21, Australia, A/HRC/WG.6/23/AUS/2, 31 August 2015, para. 60.
104. Ibid, para. 61.
105. UPRInfo, 'Database of Recommendations', https://www.upr-info.org/database/index.php?&limit=0&f_SUR=9&f_SMR=All&order=&orderDir=ASC&orderP=true&f_Issue=26&searchReco=&resultMax=100&response=&action_type=&session=1-2-3-4-5-6-7-8-9-10-11-12&SuRRgrp=&SuROrg=&SMRRgrp=&SMROrg=&pledges=RecoOnly (accessed July, 2018).
106. Ibid.
107. Reconciliation Australia, 'The United Nations Declaration on the Rights of Indigenous Peoples', https://www.reconciliation.org.au/wp-content/uploads/2017/11/Reconciliation-Australia-United-Nations-Declaration-on-the-Rights-of-Indigenous-Peoples-UNDRIP.pdf (accessed July, 2018).
108. Address to the 4th session of the UN Human Rights Council by UN Secretary-General, Ban Ki-moon, www.un.org/apps/news/story.asp?NewsID=21834#.UYD0q6JayPc (accessed July, 2018).
109. A.M. Abebe, 'Of Shaming and Bargaining: African States and the Universal Periodic Review of the United Nations Human Rights Council', *Human Rights Law Review* 9, no. 1 (2009): 1–35, 19.
110. UN Watch, Mutual Praise Society. Country scorecard and evaluation of the Universal Periodic Review system of the UN Human Rights Council. Presented at the United Nations Human Rights Council, February 6, 2009.
111. D. Frazier, 'Evaluating the Implementation of UPR Recommendations: A Quantitative Analysis of the Implementation Efforts of Nine UN Member States', https://www.upr-info.org/sites/default/files/general-document/pdf/-david_frazier_paper_upr_implementation_2011-2.pdf (accessed February, 2018).
112. See, for example, R. Brett, A Curate's Egg, Quaker United Nations Office August 2009, http://www.quno.org/sites/default/files/resources/A%20Curate%27s%20Egg.pdf (accessed July, 2018).
113. See, for example, Human Rights Watch, Curing the Selectivity Syndrome. The 2011 Review of the Human Rights Council, https://www.hrw.org/sites/default/files/reports/hrc0610webwcover.pdf (accessed July, 2018) and E. McMahon, The Universal Periodic Review: A Work in Progress. An Evaluation of the First Cycle of the New UPR Mechanism of the United Nations Human Rights Council, 2012, http://library.fes.de/pdf-files/bueros/genf/09297.pdf (accessed July, 2018).
114. See, for example, UPRInfo, Universal Periodic Review; On the Road to Implementation, (2012), www.upr-info.org (accessed July, 2018). A number of studies have reviewed the UPR from the perspective of children's rights. See, for example, Children's Rights Information Network, Status of Children's Rights in the UPR, (November, 2010), www.crin.org/resources/infoDetail.asp?ID=22015&flag=report#vv (accessed February, 2018), J. Jolley, An Academic Study of the Universal Periodic Review (UPR) from the Perspective of Children's Rights, (2012), https://resourcecentre.savethechildren.net/sites/default/files/documents/6982.pdf (accessed July, 2018), and N. Higgins, 'Advancing the Rights of

Minorities and Indigenous Peoples: Getting UN Attention via the Universal Periodic Review', *Netherlands Quarterly of Human Rights* 34 (2014): 379–407. Other reviews have concentrated on the experience of specific States of the UPR, see, for example, E. Dewhurst, and N. Higgins, 'Ireland and the Universal Periodic Review: A Two way Process', *Socio-Legal Studies Review* 1 (2012): 140–51.

115. See E. McMahon, The Universal Periodic Review: A Work in Progress. An Evaluation of the First Cycle of the New UPR Mechanism of the United Nations Human Rights Council, 2012, http://library.fes.de/pdf-files/bueros/genf/09297.pdf (accessed February, 2018).
116. See H. Fridlund, 'A butterfly effect-steps to improve UPR implementation', OpenGlobalRights, January 2017, https://www.openglobalrights.org/butterfly-effect-steps-to-improve-upr-implementation/ (accessed July, 2018).
117. Office of the Attorney General and Department of Justice, 'Universal Periodic Review, 2nd Cycle Implementation Matrix 2015–2019', https://www.upr-info.org/sites/default/files/general-document/pdf/kenya_2nd_cycle_final_matrix_2016.pdf (accessed July, 2018).
118. See https://www.youtube.com/watch?v=5R-spwu0YXc (accessed July, 2018).
119. However, it is a very positive move that indigenous peoples are establishing a voice in certain UN organs, by means of UN General Assembly Resolution 71/321 (2017), Enhancing the Participation of Indigenous Peoples' Representatives and Institutions in Meetings of Relevant United Nations Bodies on Issues Affecting Them.
120. S. Gujadhur and M. Limon for Universal Rights Groups, Towards the Third Cycle of the UPR: Stick or Twist (2016), https://www.universal-rights.org/wp-content/uploads/2016/07/URG_UPR_stick_or_twist.pdf (accessed July, 2018), p. 4.
121. IWIGA, The Indigenous World 2011, IWIGA, Copenhagen (2011), 515.
122. J. Cooper, 'Universal Periodic Review: A Potent Process for the Realization of Human Rights in Indigenous Homelands', *Cultural Survival Quarterly Magazine* 38(2) (2014), https://www.culturalsurvival.org/publications/cultural-survival-quarterly/universal-periodic-review-potent-process-realization-0 (accessed July, 2018).
123. Reconciliation Australia, 'The United Nations Declaration on the Rights of Indigenous Peoples (UNDRIP)', https://www.reconciliation.org.au/wp-content/uploads/2017/11/Reconciliation-Australia-United-Nations-Declaration-on-the-Rights-of-Indigenous-Peoples-UNDRIP.pdf (accessed July, 2018).

Disclosure statement

No potential conflict of interest was reported by the author.

Looking back to move forward: the status of environmental rights under the UN Declaration on the Rights of Indigenous Peoples

Adriana Giunta

ABSTRACT

The 2007 UN Declaration on the Rights of Indigenous Peoples (UNDRIP) was adopted after contentious negotiations. When compared with the 1994 UN Draft Declaration on the Rights of Indigenous Peoples (Draft Declaration), article 29 of UNDRIP falls short on the definition of environment, its management and accountability for environmental violations. Therefore, the article analyses whether article 29 lacks effective environmental-rights protection, and what imprint the Draft Declaration has on UNDRIP? This article further examines the development of international law on business and human rights, sustainable development, climate change, and trade law after 2007. The consequence of ignoring this development is having tragic outcomes on indigenous peoples' environmental rights upon which they depend for their subsistence, culture and development rights. Looking at indigenous peoples' environmental rights through the Draft Declaration, therefore, will help to understand both the challenges faced by UNDRIP and gives the opportunity to discuss a potential free-standing environmental right under the Convention on the Rights of Indigenous Peoples, which would be the natural progression from the UNDRIP. Such a right could eliminate conflicts with indigenous peoples' rights to development and culture. Also, it could bring coherence and integration between indigenous peoples' rights and international law developed after 2007.

On 13 September 2007, the General Assembly adopted the UN Declaration on the Rights of Indigenous Peoples (UNDRIP) by a recorded vote of 143 in favour, 4 against (Australia, Canada, New Zealand and the United States) and 11 abstentions (Azerbaijan, Bangladesh, Bhutan, Burundi, Colombia, Georgia, Kenya, Nigeria, Russia Federation, Samoa and Ukraine).[1] Interestingly, all four countries that voted against the UNDRIP have now endorsed it.[2] Thus, the UNDRIP is unquestionably the most comprehensive international instrument on the rights of indigenous peoples. Its progress in legal thought rests on the recognition of indigenous peoples as distinctive peoples entitled to existing or inherent collective and individual rights. Particularly, the UNDRIP recognises indigenous peoples as holders of the collective right to the conservation and protection of the environment, the right to self-determination and the right to development. These distinctive rights are interrelated and interdependent and important for the well-being and survival of indigenous peoples, who share a deep relationship with their natural environment. Yet, because of this deep relationship, they face constant threats.

According to Tauli-Corpuz the biggest threats to indigenous peoples are the extractive industry, conservation projects and climate change.[3] Equally, Anaya assesses that the impact of extractive industries operating within or near indigenous territories is becoming the greatest challenge to the exercise of the rights of indigenous peoples. This is because States, whose economies are significantly based on the extractive industry, are often involved in development that infringes on the lives and rights of indigenous peoples rather than ensuring their protection.[4]

In legal terms, land and natural resources rights can deal with conservation projects affecting indigenous peoples, but how can those rights protect indigenous peoples from serious environmental-climate change degradation?[5] How can land and natural resources rights, for instance, protect the Arctic indigenous peoples (whose livelihood, health and survival depend on ice) when the ice is melting as a consequence of climate change?[6] The status and limits of current understanding of this issue are exposed by Durkalec, Furgal, Skinner, Sheldon and Ford: for Inuit and Alaska Natives, who are undergoing rapid sea-ice climatic and socioeconomic change, already constraining food access is linked with implications for nutrition and cultural well-being.[7]

I believe that the insufficient debate on the importance of indigenous peoples' environmental rights gives limited opportunities to indigenous peoples to effectively protect also their subsistence rights, culture, land and natural resources from the threat posed to them by environmental-climate change degradation, to which the extractive industry is a contributor. In fact, the issues presented by Tauli-Corpuz and Anaya are further frustrated by focusing the debate on indigenous peoples' land, natural resources and cultural rights rather than their environmental rights. Therefore, this article aims to start a debate about the need to update UNDRIP into a Convention on the Right of Indigenous Peoples (the Convention) recognising a free-standing environmental right.

De jure the UNDRIP has already influenced important decisions,[8] but *de facto* how effective are these decisions in guaranteeing indigenous' environmental and subsistence rights protection, which will ultimately guarantee their physical survival? In order to answer these questions, this article concerns only the collective 'right to the conservation and protection of the environment' contained in article 29 of the UNDRIP[9] and compares it with the relevant articles from the UN Draft Declaration on the Rights of Indigenous Peoples (Draft Declaration)[10] from which article 29 was negotiated. This comparison may appear irrelevant to some readers, considering that the Draft Declaration is a legal document updated into the UNDRIP. However, the aim is to be able to hold the relationship between the Draft Declaration and the UNDRIP as a constructive basis for a unifying understanding of indigenous peoples' environmental rights.

Can the Draft Declaration shed light on the protection of environmental rights and still have an impact on clarifying what environmental rights protection should embody for indigenous peoples? The Draft Declaration has the potential to shed light: first, on the definition of the environment, its management and accountability for violations of indigenous peoples' environmental rights, which are missed in the UNDRIP; and second, on issues of integration and coherence between international law and the UNDRIP, which will be presented later in this article and, again, are missed in the UNDRIP. Thus, I also examine the development of international law affecting indigenous peoples' environmental rights, since the adoption of the UNDRIP in 2007.

Such development should be integrated with the UNDRIP. Particularly, in the area of business and human rights, sustainable development, climate change, and trade law. Special attention will be given to the conflict between corporate responsibility and indigenous peoples' environmental rights, economic development and environmental and social sustainable development and, trade law and indigenous' environmental rights using international and domestic jurisprudence. The consequence of ignoring these developments, which could have partly found protection in the Draft Declaration, is having tragic outcomes on indigenous peoples' environmental rights upon which they depend for their subsistence, land and natural resources, development and culture rights protection.

This integration should not be limited to the development of international law, such as UN Guiding Principles on Business and Human Rights (Guiding Principles),[11] the Paris Agreement,[12] and the Sustainable Development Goals (SDGs),[13] but it should also include studies and new research in the area of environmental rights and climate change. In this regard, the 2014 report published by the International Bar Association 'Achieving Justice and Human Rights in an Era of Climate Disruption'[14] and the submission of the 'Global Pact for the Environment' (Global Pact),[15] by President Macron to the UN Security Council, are particularly relevant. Both are calling on States to recognise a free-standing international right to environment or right to an ecologically sound environment.[16]

Following the celebration of the 10th anniversary of the adoption of the UNDRIP, the article's goal is to provide an overview of the achievements and challenges faced by indigenous peoples over their environmental rights. It aims to establish that looking at indigenous peoples' environmental rights through the lens of the Draft Declaration will help to understand both the challenges faced by the UNDRIP and give the opportunity to discuss a potential Convention. Such a discussion could open new venues for indigenous peoples' environmental-rights protection. The article finds that a Convention could eliminate conflicts between environmental rights and other rights, such as the right to culture and the right to development. Such a Convention could also bring coherence and integration between indigenous peoples' environmental rights and international environmental law, climate change law and trade law.

Looking back at the 2007 UNDRIP through the lens of the 1994 draft declaration

Since 2007 studies have shown that environmental-climate change degradation are a real threat to human lives,[17] international law, human rights[18] and, that indigenous peoples lives will be affected more severely than other individuals around the world.[19] Fitzmaurice, Manley-Casimir and Bowman, voiced their concerns that indigenous peoples are more affected by environmental damage due to their reliance on resources drawn directly from their lands[20] and by climate change because it is causing lack of access to traditional subsistence resources.[21]

Indeed, indigenous peoples' environmental rights should be their most protected rights in order to guarantee their subsistence rights and, ultimately, their survival. Hence, the article's first goal is to provide an interpretation of article 29 of the UNDRIP that clarifies the meaning of indigenous peoples' right to the conservation and protection of the environment. The second goal is to look at articles 26, 28 and 31 of the Draft Declaration to fully understand what is needed to effectively protect indigenous peoples' environmental rights, especially considering new developments of international law since 2007.

Article 29 of the UNDRIP

It is submitted in article 29 that

> indigenous peoples have the right to the conservation and protection of the environment [...]. States shall establish and implement assistance programmes for indigenous peoples for such conservation and protection, without discrimination. States shall take effective measures to ensure that no storage or disposal of hazardous materials shall take place in the lands or territories of indigenous peoples without their free, prior and informed consent. States shall also take effective measures to ensure, as needed, that programmes for monitoring, maintaining and restoring the health of indigenous peoples, as developed and implemented by the peoples affected by such materials, are duly implemented.

When analysing the content of article 29, it can be identified that indigenous peoples have the right not only to have their environment preserved but also to have it safeguarded from possible damage by the State, which shall implement assistance and take effective measures to monitor, maintain and restore the health of indigenous peoples. From the wording in article 29, it seems that is the responsibility of the State to control the environment of indigenous peoples rather than being controlled by themselves. Furthermore, the term 'environment' is not defined in article 29. If we look at the Cambridge dictionary, 'environment' is defined as the air, water, land in or on which people, animals, and plants live.[22] Clearly, such definition supports indigenous peoples' worldview, as being part of their environment, but leaves out the subsoil natural resources.

However, several questions arise: what about ice, beaches and sea where actually many indigenous peoples live? Would those be considered part of their environment and land? What about flora and fauna? I have previously argued the need for environmental protection of flora, fauna and water – all elements essential to the fulfilment, for instance, of global food security and for the protection of the right to food and human security.[23] Undoubtedly, the right to global food security cannot be achieved if the natural environment is not legally protected for its own sake.[24] In fact, without first the protecting the flora, fauna and water, the protection and fulfilment of all subsistence rights, including dignity and right to life itself cannot be guaranteed. This is true for both human being and the natural environment.[25] Meaningful protection of environmental rights must include the protection of the natural environment. Instead, the focus in article 29 seems to be on the environment as an abstract entity, rather than an entity with its own needs to be protected.

Moreover, article 29 recognises indigenous peoples' right to the conservation and protection of the environment, but what about the right to own, control and develop their environment? Thus, who holds the decision-making power regarding indigenous peoples' environmental rights? From article 29 wording it appears that such decision-making stays within the State. Who then have the right to development and management of indigenous peoples' environment and natural resources?

Who will be accountable for any environmental harm to indigenous peoples' environment given that States shall take measures to ensure that no-storage or hazardous material shall be disposed of in their land without their consent? For instance, article 29 does not contain references to Non-State Actors or business corporates. What about environmental harm caused by business corporate? And what about environmental harm caused by climate change? Who will be responsible for restoring or 'cleaning up' indigenous peoples' environment in case of environmental-climate change degradation? Article 29 does not contain references to climate change or the restoration of the environment.

Again, the focus in article 29 is on restoring the health of indigenous peoples and not on what happens when it is assessed that the environment of a certain indigenous group is damaged and cannot be restored. In the environmental rights' landmark case of *Ogoni v. Nigeria,* the Ogoni peoples are still waiting for proper compensation and 'clean up' of their severely damaged environment by Shell Corporation during their oil extraction activities between the 1950s and 1990s.[26] Neither Nigeria nor Shell have taken responsibility for the destruction of the environment of the Ogoni peoples or even redressed the environmental rights' violation findings by the African Commission since 2003.[27]

Metcalf, Glazebrook and Heinämäki argue that an environmental right should be recognised to protect indigenous peoples' environment and way of life, in order to guarantee their survival.[28] I emphasise that respect for indigenous peoples' way of life further contributes to the protection of their environmental rights. Glazebrook observes that the development of 'such a right would provide a focus on the rights of indigenous peoples and recognise the importance of the environment for such peoples, culturally, spiritually and economically, and it would empower participants to participate in decisions affecting their environment'.[29] I will further argue that the recognition of such right is in itself essential to protect indigenous peoples' way of life and physical survival, as explained in the coming sections.

From the analysis above, however, it appears that article 29 falls short on the definition of the environment, its management and accountability for violations of indigenous peoples' environmental rights. How then, can indigenous peoples' environmental rights be protected if such legal limitations continue to persist? My view is that articles 26, 28 and 31 of the Draft Declaration – which recognise the importance of the environment of such peoples and, it empowers them to have control and take decisions affecting their environment – are of paramount importance because they contain provisions that clarify indigenous peoples' environmental rights.

Article 26 of the Draft declaration

If we examine the corresponding article 26 of the Draft Declaration,

> indigenous peoples have the right to own, develop, control and use the lands and territories, including the total environment of the lands, air, waters, coastal seas, sea-ice, flora and fauna and other resources [...]. This includes the right to the full recognition of their laws, traditions and customs, land-tenure systems and institutions for the development and management of resources, and the right to effective measures by States to prevent any interference with, alienation of or encroachment upon these rights.

By comparing and contrasting the UNDRIP with the Draft Declaration is clear that the UNDRIP lacks effective protection of indigenous environmental rights. In fact, article 26 of the Draft Declaration provided indigenous peoples with the '*right to own, develop, control and use the total environment*'. It also supplies a definition of the 'environment', as '*the total environment of the lands, air, waters, coastal seas, sea-ice, flora and fauna and other resources*'. From the definition provided in article 26, it is apparent that soil and subsoil natural resources are part of indigenous peoples' environmental rights. Such a definition of the 'environment' would also support Metcalf, Glazebrook and Heinämäki's arguments that environmental rights should be recognised to protect indigenous peoples' environment and way of life. It would further support my argument that protection for their environmental rights would protect not only their way of life but also guarantee their survival; and vice-versa, respect for indigenous peoples' way of life further contributes to the protection of their environmental rights.

These statements are fully supported by paragraph 2 of article 26 which provides full recognition of indigenous' law, institutions and customs which guarantee respect for indigenous' deep relationship with their environment and way of life, as well as indigenous peoples' environmental rights protection against States, business corporate or individuals who interferes with their rights. Moreover, Metcalf affirms that recognition of indigenous peoples' environmental rights would add another layer to the currently State-based process of establishing international solutions to environmental problems.[30]

Therefore, article 26 of the Draft Declaration is important in clarifying the definition of environment, its management and accountability for violation of indigenous peoples' environmental rights. Correctly, Heinämäki observed that under article 26 indigenous peoples could argue that States are in fact obliged to their best to slow climate change because this environmental problem interferes with indigenous' environmental rights.[31] I emphasise that article 26 is very important because it gives indigenous peoples the legal tools to fight States or business corporate for causing environmental damage not only within indigenous territories but also near indigenous land or even as a result of climate change.

This claim is supported by the ongoing legal proceeding before the New Zealand Waitangi Tribunal submitted by the Mataatua District Māori Council against the New Zealand Crown concerning indigenous rights and climate change obligations under the Waitangi Act 1975.[32] Interestingly, this is not the only New Zealand judgment that was issued recently. *Thompson* has recently won a legal proceeding against the Minister for Climate Change Issues for failing to consider the Intergovernmental Panel on Climate Change (IPCC) report[33] and not doing enough to stop climate change.[34]

This is a promising development showing the leading position lawyers can play in interpreting and shaping the global response to concrete climate change solutions. It is striking, though that such proceedings[35] as having already been made, have been made domestically, rather than through a regional or international legal regime. Given that the issues involved in those climate-change litigations include the broader concern of human rights, should not indigenous peoples' environmental rights be legally binding under international law? This would provide a practical global solution to the global responsibility toward indigenous peoples' environmental and subsistence rights protection against environmental-climate change degradation.

Article 28 of the Draft declaration

It can be argued that article 28 supports an ecocentric-anthropocentric approach to environmental-rights protection. In fact, article 28 recognises that indigenous peoples have a '*right to the conservation, restoration and protection of the total environment as well as to assistance for this purpose from States and through international cooperation*'. A similar ecocentric-anthropocentric approach can already be found under international law. Likewise, Principle 7 of the Rio Declaration establishes that 'States shall cooperate in a spirit of global partnership to conserve, protect and restore the health and integrity of the Earth's ecosystem'.

This means that the protection of environmental rights should be aimed not only at humans but also at the natural environment itself[36] in order to guarantee the integrity of the Earth's ecosystem or of the total environment. Hence, article 28 appears to recognise indigenous peoples as guardians of their environment. Article 28 at first adopts an anthropocentric approach while it recognises the right to indigenous peoples, but then it embraces an ecocentric approach when it recognises the *conservation, restoration and protection of the total environment as well as to assistance for this purpose from States and through international cooperation.* Such ecocentric-anthropocentric approach to environmental rights protection would respect indigenous peoples' ecological worldview and way of life. It will further provide a legal framework that will protect the total environment – land, air, waters, coastal seas, sea ice, flora, fauna, and other resources – for its own sake. Furthermore, it could be argued that indigenous peoples could claim *locus standi* on behalf of their environment in case of environmental degradation before a court of law.

Thus, article 28 could guarantee an ecocentric-anthropocentric approach to indigenous peoples' environmental rights protection and put pressure on States to take responsibility for environmental-climate change degradation and deliver climate-change justice.[37] According to Heinämäki, article 28 offers a further active role to indigenous participation in environmental management on all level of decision-making to protect their own environment, and therefore, receive assistance from States and through international co-operation, all in all, to be able to protect their environment.[38]

Additionally, article 28 recognises indigenous peoples' right to assistance for the purpose of restoration of their total environment from States and through international cooperation. I believe this aspect of article 28 is interesting because it can open new frontiers regarding the interpretation of States' responsibility and the international community's obligations in relation to climate change and natural disasters. This would help to assist and/or restore indigenous peoples' environments, as well as assist States whose territories are disappearing. Arguably, article 28 of the Draft Declaration could support a claim from indigenous peoples from the Pacific Ocean, the Indian Ocean and the Caribbean islands (which are disappearing because of climate change raising sea level)[39] to seek redress from the international community in the form of relocation.

Article 31 of the Draft Declaration

Article 31 states that

> indigenous peoples, as a specific form of exercising their right to self-determination, have the right to autonomy or self-government in matters relating to their internal and local affairs,

including [...] economic activities, land and resources management, environment and entry by non-members [...].

Article 31 directly links indigenous peoples environmental rights to their right to self-determination and right to development, as it recognises indigenous peoples' right to self-government in matters including economic activities, land and resources management and environment.

There is not a correspondent right in the UNDRIP. However, as Xanthaki pointed out, the UNDRIP's inclusion of the right to self-determination finally confirms the most important claim made by indigenous peoples worldwide.[40] According to Otto, the right to self-determination can, therefore, be reconfigured to engender a novel conception of indigenous sovereignty.[41] I will add that the right to self-determination is necessary to indigenous peoples in order to protect their environmental rights and adopt their own environmental policies for their present and future generations' survival. Article 31 further provides indigenous peoples with effective environmental-right protection because it offers a link between their right to soil and subsoil resources with their right to sustainable development, as part of their right to self-governance in economic activities.

Concluding observations

Articles 26, 28 and 31 of the Draft Declaration appear to be able to address concrete global solutions against environmental-climate change degradation. Those solutions appear capable of protecting indigenous peoples' environmental rights, guaranteeing their survival and achieving climate-change justice. Additionally, there is no doubt that under the Draft Declaration indigenous peoples have a strong environmental right, including the right to soil and subsoil resources as part of their environmental rights. Furthermore, the Draft Declaration could support an ecocentric-anthropocentric environmental right in respect with indigenous peoples' ecological worldview, as being part of their environment.

By contrast article 29 of the UNDRIP – where were eliminated the words 'own', 'develop', 'control', 'use' 'total environment of the lands', 'air', 'waters', 'coastal seas', 'sea-ice', 'flora', 'fauna and other resources' and 'restoration' if it read alone, it is not clear what is: the 'environment' of indigenous peoples, including their ecological worldview; their decision-making powers; development and management of their environment; and leaves out any responsibility to restore indigenous peoples' environment in case of environmental harm even within indigenous territories, let alone as a consequence of climate change.

While article 29 of the UNDRIP appears to miss the opportunity to clarify indigenous peoples' environmental rights, the Draft Declaration elucidates the scope of indigenous peoples' environmental rights, especially in many areas that are crucial to their survival. Following the above arguments, it is clear to me that the UNDRIP needs to be updated because indigenous peoples' environmental rights should aim to tackle the environmental-climate change degradation discussed above, as well as it should integrate the new development of international law that will be discussed below.

UNDRIP at 10: new developments of international law and lack of integration with UNDRIP

When the UNDRIP was drafted, climate change, the extractive industry and international trade were not taken into consideration as possible causes of serious violations against indigenous peoples' environmental rights. However, we will see that these three areas represent some of the biggest concerns for indigenous peoples' environmental rights. Since the adoption of the UNDRIP in 2007, there have been several developments in international law, as well as concerns over the challenges faced by the current national, regional and international legal regimes to address environmental-climate change degradation.

In order to understand those issues, is important to give a brief introduction on the status of environmental rights under international law in general. Given that a free-standing general environmental right is still not recognised under international law, few UN organisations have addressed the issue of whether a free-standing environmental right should be recognised. It may appear irrelevant to some readers to address the lack of a free-standing international environmental right. However, this issue is interdependent with the lack of effective implementation of indigenous peoples' environmental rights.

UN efforts to develop a free-standing environmental right to tackle climate change

After the Rio Conference and the adoption of the UN Framework Convention on Climate Change (UNCCC) in the 1990s,[42] academics restarted a debate[43] on whether a right to environment is necessary under international law.[44] However, until 2007 there was no literature on the need to adopt concrete solutions against climate change[45] or literature on the 'gap between the aspirations of human rights and the legal norms intended to back them up',[46] including the impact of climate change on indigenous peoples.[47]

In 2004, the UN former *Sub-Commission* on the Promotion and Protection of Human Rights appointed the member of the Working Group on Indigenous Populations, Françoise Hampson, to conduct a study on the human rights situation of indigenous peoples in States or territories threatened with extinction by climate change.[48] Five years later, the Office of the High Commissioner on Human Rights (OHCHR) notes: how the multiplicity of causes for environmental degradation and the difficulty to attribute responsibility to any one State is problematic; and how 'human rights litigation is not well-suited to promote precautionary measures based on risk assessments, unless such risks pose an imminent threat to the human rights of specific individuals'.[49]

Furthermore, the 2011 OHCHR Report recognises that many forms of environmental damage are transnational in character and that the extraterritorial application of human rights law in this context remains unsettled,[50] it advises that 'further guidance is needed to inform options for further development of the law in this area'.[51] The OHCHR reports highlight why it is important to recognise a legally binding environmental right, under international law. In 2011, the UNHRC attempted to codify and develop a free-standing right to environment,[52] but lack of consensus has made this task rather challenging.

The recent call for a free-standing environmental right under international law

Following raising concerns over climate change, the International Bar Association (IBA), which represents the voice of the global legal profession, launched the Task Force on Climate Change Justice and Human Rights (Task Force) to assess the challenges to current national, regional and international legal regimes on climate change, with a focus on their justice implications and deficiencies, and to make recommendations.[53] This is the most compelling study of existing international law, including environmental law, human rights, climate change, trade law and States responsibilities, as well as regional and domestic legal frameworks relevant to climate change.

The Task Force report recognises that climate change disproportionately affects vulnerable peoples, such as indigenous peoples, who have less ability to prevent, adapt or otherwise respond to climate change[54] and called for the 'clarification of human rights obligations relating to climate change'.[55] The Task Force notes that in addition to the human rights to life, health and subsistence everyone depends upon, indigenous community-based rights – such as environmental and cultural rights – are particularly at risk due to climate change.[56] The Task Force concludes that just as international law is inadequate to tackle climate change so too are regional and national law ineffective in securing climate-change justice.[57] Thus, the IBA Task Force addresses the need to develop a free-standing right to environment.[58]

In 2017, President Macron submitted to the UN Security Council the Global Pact calling States to recognise the: 'right to an ecologically sound environment asserting that' every State or international institution, every person, natural or legal, public or private, has the duty to take care of the environment;[59] to contribute to the conservation, protection and restoration of the integrity of the Earth's ecosystem;[60] and calling State Parties to integrate environmental protection into sustainable development in order to promote the fight against climate change, the protection of oceans and the maintenance of biodiversity.[61]

It is ground-breaking for a body like the IBA to be recommending the recognition of a new anthropocentric 'right to a safe, clean, healthy and sustainable environment' because the legal tools available to lawyers are inadequate to protect existing human rights from climate change. It is unprecedented for a Head of States calling to other Heads of States to take joint responsibility to protect the environment from climate change. Indeed, it is extraordinary of Macron to be calling the international community to recognise a free-standing ecological sound environment right having an ecocentric and anthropocentric approach. In 2018, the former UN Special Rapporteur on Human Rights and the Environment, John Knox affirmed that 'the time has come for the United Nations to formally recognize the [...] human right to a healthy environment'.[62]

This is a new development on the discourse for a free-standing environmental right under international law, which is of paramount importance for indigenous peoples' environmental rights implementation and protection of their way of life. Justice Glazebrook argues that a legally binding environmental right must include the environment for its own sake, embrace communities, consider inter-generational equity and stress responsibilities (of States, businesses, communities and individuals) because the focus on rights rather than responsibilities is inappropriate in the environmental area.[63]

I agree with Justice Glazebrook and President Macron that such a right should have a focus on duty toward the protection of the environment for its own sake, in order to protect the global environment and global environmental rights. Indeed, I argued elsewhere that an ecocentric-anthropocentric legally-binding environmental right under international law can open new frontiers to tackle climate change, especially its impact on subsistence rights and human security.[64] Equally, I argue that an ecocentric-anthropocentric environmental right would protect indigenous peoples' environmental rights and ecological worldview because they are part of their environment.

In support of my argument, I will recall Gilbert's witness expert opinion in the *Kaliña and Lokono* landmark case before the ICHR:

> the indigenous peoples are part of the natural protection; there is no need to expel the indigenous peoples in the name of protecting nature. [...] Regarding their legitimacy, the protection of nature is legitimate, but based on [what has been said,] the indigenous peoples are part of the protection of nature, so there is no legitimate reason to eliminate these peoples who have been part of such resources.[65]

I emphasise, thus, that an ecocentric-anthropocentric free-standing indigenous peoples' environmental right is necessary because indigenous peoples are part of the natural protection, in order to preserve not only their ecological survival but also their physical and cultural survival. Therefore, UNDRIP and indigenous peoples' environmental-rights protection debate should also be updated to the recent debate to recognise a free-standing international environmental right in general (having an ecocentric-anthropocentric approach) because its interdependence is negatively affecting the implementation of indigenous peoples' environmental rights. Article 28 of the Draft Declaration could be of help in drafting an ecocentric-anthropocentric free-standing indigenous peoples' environmental right.

UNDRIP and lack of effective implementation of the UN Guiding Principles on Business and Human Rights

Whilst, article 29 of the UNDRIP makes explicit reference to States responsibility to *take effective measures to ensure that no storage or disposal of hazardous materials take place in the lands or territories of indigenous peoples and their health is restored* – there is no specific reference in the UNDRIP to Non-State Actors, corporate business or extractive industry activities destroying or threatening indigenous peoples' environment.

In 1989, Sands noted that

> Non-State Actors (corporate business, non-governmental organisations, people and so on) are not recognised as legal persons, and thus have not standing to protect the environment on the international plane. However, Non-State Actors or business corporate exist in a quasi-feudal state in which the sovereign (the State) is vested with all rights and powers.[66]

This issue has continued to persist. Given that indigenous peoples' territories are often rich in natural resources, they are most affected by corporate extractive industry's environmental damage. In 2009, the UN State of the World's Indigenous Peoples confirmed how large-scale extractive projects destroy forests, and consequently threaten indigenous peoples' survival because, for indigenous peoples, forests are means of subsistence, medicine plants and the ability to practice their customs.[67]

With such a degree of serious violations, the Guiding Principles were adopted in 2011 establishing that: States' international human rights law obligations require that they *respect*, *protect* and *fulfil* the human rights of individuals within their territory and/ or jurisdiction.[68] This includes the duty to protect against human rights abuse by third parties, including business corporate, and to provide remedies to victims.[69] Eight years since the adoption of the Guiding Principles and indigenous peoples are still victims of devastating environmental abuses.[70]

Thus, there is a gap existing between the theoretical responsibility of States to respect human rights placed upon corporations under the Guiding Principles, and the real-world practice in which 'corporate businesses are not directly bound under international human rights law because their regulation rests with the States'.[71] Hence, it appears that consent has still not been reached on what legal obligations those corporate business have toward citizens or indigenous peoples' environmental rights.

Another issue linked with corporate business violations, but not included in the UNDRIP, is the type of remedy available,[72] which might not be always appropriate. Particularly, where the maximum amount of compensation does not cover the cost of litigation because the barriers to effective remedy are also created by the lack of resources indigenous peoples have in commencing and maintaining litigation over several years, including the costs associated with gathering evidence, let alone in a foreign court.[73] By creating or allowing these obstacles and barriers to remain, States fail in their duty to protect indigenous peoples' environmental and subsistence rights violated by Non-State Actors and ensure access to effective remedy through the judicial process.

Shelton confirms that at present, remedies for human rights violations are not particularly coherent.[74] Glazebrook asserts that when developing new remedies relating to human rights and the environment, there will be the opportunity to ensure that they are complementary rather than inconsistent with or duplicative of existing environmental remedies and that the latter are, at the same time, strengthened[75] especially, with regard to victims of environmental degradation. However, the Guiding Principles are still lacking integration with international law and the UNDRIP.

My examination of articles 26, 31 and 28 of the Draft Declaration could eliminate the issue concerning environmental rights violation by Non-State Actors and the lack of remedies available to indigenous peoples. In fact, article 26 recognises indigenous peoples' right to effective measures by States to prevent any interference with these rights. Furthermore, article 31 recognises indigenous peoples' right to autonomy and self-government in economic activities, resources management and their environmental right.

And finally, article 28 recognises the right to assistance from states and through the international cooperation, which would support indigenous peoples' protection of their own environment, as well as claims to seek redress from their own States or through the international community. Thus, my arguments further point to the need to update the UNDRIP because it does not contain provisions on Non-State Actors or business corporate or effective access to remedy to victims of environmental-climate change degradation.

Conflicts between indigenous peoples' environmental rights, sustainable development and climate change law

The importance of article 3 of the UNDRIP and the recent adoption of the SDGs are interrelated with the adoption of the Paris Agreement. The UN adopted the SDGs following the end of the Millennium Development Goals. The SDGs also aim to address the threat posed by environmental-climate change degradation. Climate change threat calls for the widest possible international cooperation aimed at accelerating the reduction of global greenhouse gas emissions to hold the increase in global average temperature below 2 degrees Celsius, or 1.5 degrees Celsius above pre-industrial levels and, addressing adaptation to the adverse impacts of climate change.

Similar objectives are contained in the Paris Agreement adopted in 2016. Whilst, the SDGs call

> for further effective measures to remove the obstacles to the full realization of the right of self-determination of peoples living under colonial and foreign occupation, which continue to adversely affect their economic and social development as well as their environment,[76]

there is no specific reference, however, to indigenous peoples. Nevertheless, the adoption of the SDGs are important to indigenous peoples' right to development because such a right is interdependent with their right to self-determination and their environmental right.

Similarly, article 3 of the UNDRIP recognises that '*indigenous peoples have the right to self-determination. By virtue of that right they freely determine their political status and freely pursue their economic, social and cultural development*'. However, article 3 of the UNDRIP refers to cultural development rather than to environmental development, which is one of the three pillars of sustainable development under international law[77] and is re-affirmed in the SDGs. Therefore, article 3 of the UNDRIP should be integrated with the definition of sustainable development under international law.

Yet, the focus of the SDGs appears to be on economic development rather than environmental and social development. Currently, there is a conflict between indigenous peoples' environmental-rights protection and economic development because economic development is given priority over environmental and social development. I argued elsewhere that to achieve effective sustainable development, it is necessary that the three pillars of sustainable development should be – at its core – first, environmental sustainable development, second social sustainable development and third economic sustainable development, rather than economic first, social second and environmental sustainable development last.[78] Many indigenous peoples share this hierarchy and it is in respect with their ecological worldview.[79]

Good environmental practice that provides strong sustainable development – based on environmental, social and economic sustainable development – has demonstrated to bring more wealth, equality and non-discrimination and less environmental damage than a weak sustainable development based on the economic, social and environmental development hierarchy.[80] The hierarchy I suggest has proved to eliminate conflicts between the protection of environmental rights and sustainable development,[81] as the priority is to protect the environment in order to sustain social and economic development.

It also raises the question of whether indigenous peoples' environmental rights protection should trump other rights, which at times may compromise the right to economic development in order to achieve sustainable development. An affirmative answer to this question would be justified based on the findings by the Intergovernmental Panel on Climate Change (ICCP) that 'some of the worst impacts on sustainable development are expected to be felt among indigenous people, [...], and people and ecosystems in the Arctic and Small Island Developing States'.[82]

Climate change is one of the main causes of environmental disasters and indirectly it contributes to basic human rights violations. Not prioritising environmental-rights protection under international law in general and under indigenous peoples' *lex specialis*, it will compromise international human rights law protection, including the right to development for indigenous and non-indigenous peoples. Therefore, I argue that States shall grant a reasonable degree of sovereignty to indigenous peoples in order to pursue their own right to sustainable development. This would also allow them to choose their own policies on sustainable development, management of their environment, and recognition of their laws on accountability for environmental harm, as recognised for instance, in articles 26 and 31 of the Draft Declaration.

Regarding climate change, the Paris Agreement holds the increase in global average temperature below 2 degrees Celsius or 1.5 degrees Celsius above pre-industrial levels. The reference to environmental-climate change degradation and human rights obligations in the Paris Agreement is a welcome integration. Yet, the significance of this step depends on whether human rights obligations will form part of the Paris Agreement's implementations guidelines promoting climate actions, originally, to be adopted at the Conference of the Parties (COP24) in Katowice in December 2018.[83] This issue is increasingly concerning all indigenous peoples, especially the Inuit, Alaskan Native and Sami peoples.

The Paris Agreement's climate actions implementations will be effective only if it integrates environmental-climate change degradation solutions with human rights obligations, especially indigenous peoples' environmental and subsistence rights obligations. The 2018 ICCP Special Report on the Impacts of Global Warming of 1.5°C above Pre-industrial Levels (SR1.5) warns that the consequences of 1°C of global warming through more extreme weather, rising sea levels and diminishing Arctic sea-ice, among other changes, will adversely affect livestock and crop production, especially livelihoods and poverty, on indigenous groups, rural communities and marginalised people.[84]

Furthermore, it must be seen whether the target to hold the temperature below 2°C or 1.5°C is achievable. Until the top GHG emitters (Brazil, China and India, which rank among the top ten GHG emitters) do not take on binding emission reduction commitments, climate change law is constrained in its ability to tackle climate change,[85] resulting in all human rights violations, especially indigenous peoples' environmental right on which their survival depends.

Whilst article 29 of the UNDRIP is inadequate to tackle climate change, I argue above how article 28 of the Draft Declaration could help to tackle climate change and to assist and/or restore indigenous peoples' environment, including supporting claims from indigenous peoples whose islands are disappearing because of climate change. Therefore, this analysis further supports my argument that the UNDRIP need to be updated following the development of international law on sustainable development and climate change law.

Lack of expertise, coherence and integration between UNDRIP and domestic, regional and international law relating to the environment

Concerns in support for the effectiveness of indigenous peoples' environmental rights is further highlighted by Sand and by the 2009 OHCRH report analysis on the impact of scientific evidence and risk assessment submitted but not used by the international courts due to limited resources and limited expertise on the threshold of environmental damage.[86] It is problematic for an international court to deal with such issues, as well as for regional and national courts. This issue is particularly illustrated in the *Nunatukavut Community Council* case where the court found that: first, the 'UNDRIP cannot be used to displace Canadian jurisprudence or laws regarding the duty to consult [...]';[87] and second, that

> the environmental assessment process is already a long and arduous one, both for proponents and opponents of a project. To turn the reviewing Court into an "academy of science" [...] would be both inefficient and contrary to the scheme of the Act.[88] Therefore, the case was dismissed.

According to Glazebrook, current human rights bodies lack expertise relating to the environment.[89] Lack of expertise in environmental risks assessment and integration within international law is another issue affecting indigenous peoples' environmental rights. In the landmark case of the *Kaliña and Lokono,* the ICHR sought the expert opinion of the Special Rapporteur Tauli-Corpuz. Tauli-Corpuz indicated to the Court that: 'international environmental law and international human rights law should not be considered separate, but rather interrelated and complementary bodies of law'.[90] Particularly, Tauli-Corpuz recalled

> the Convention on Biological Diversity (CBD) to incorporate respect for rights and obligations into their decision on protected areas in relation to indigenous peoples. [...] This permits the application of the whole range of the State's human rights obligations as defined by the American Convention on Human Rights (American Convention) and established in the UNDRIP.[91]

Hence, the Court followed Tauli-Corpuz's opinion and determined that environmental impact assessments under article 14 of the CBD and Principle 17 of the Rio Declaration help to evaluate the possible damage or impact that a development or investment project may have on the property and community in question. And the Court reiterated that

> when considering development plans within the territories of indigenous and tribal peoples, the State should, within reason, share the benefits of the project in question, as appropriate. This concept is inherent in the right to compensation recognized in Article 21(2) of the American Convention, which refers not only to total deprivation of a property title by means of expropriation by the State, but also includes the deprivation of the normal use and enjoyment of that property.[92]

Indeed, this is a landmark case for integrating human rights law and environmental law and for referring directly to article 29 of the UNDRIP, especially given past rejections of the relevance of UNDRIP and of the environmental impact assessment on indigenous environmental rights. However, there are few issues with the Court's analysis of the notion of benefits-sharing and compensation. In fact, the benefits-sharing obligations found under the CBD should not be confused with the compensation scheme sometimes paid by States or Corporate Businesses, for instance, under article 21(2) of the American Convention.[93]

If we examine article 1 of the CBD, it states that 'the objectives of this Convention are the conservation of biological diversity, the sustainable use of its components and the fair and equitable sharing of the benefits arising out of the utilization of genetic resources [...]'. Thus, article 8(j) of the CBD establishes that 'indigenous and local communities embodying traditional lifestyles relevant for the conservation and sustainable use of biological diversity and encourage the equitable sharing of the benefits arising from the utilization of such knowledge innovations and practices'. Whilst article 21(2) of the American Convention states that 'no one shall be deprived of his right to property except upon payment of just compensation, for reasons of public utility or social interest'.

It is surprising that ICHR interpreted article 21(2) of the American Convention to embody the concept of benefits-sharing when its actual content regards compensation for expropriation of property. Clearly, the objective of the CBD is the conservation of biological diversity, its sustainable use and a fair and equitable sharing of the benefits arising out of the utilisation of genetic resources and indigenous peoples' knowledge of genetic resources, nothing to do with the right to property and compensation.

It is concerning that the ICHR lacked the expertise to understand the important distinction between biological diversity's benefits-sharing and right to property' compensation. Such confusion means a huge financial loss for indigenous peoples, violation of their environmental right, as well as violation of their right to development. In practice, States have been given the green light by the ICHR to violate indigenous peoples' rights and to appropriate their knowledge of genetic resources without a fair and equitable benefits-sharing. Instead, paying a very paltry sum in the form of compensation.

Such an interpretation of 'compensation/benefits-sharing' can also lead to confusion when evaluating the environmental risks assessment for the possible damages a new investment or development project may have on indigenous peoples' environmental rights. This issue is of grave concern. Yet, it could be eliminated interpreting correctly the CBD and the American Convention and, adopting article 26 of the Draft Declaration recognising to indigenous peoples the right to own, develop, control and use their land and total environment, as analysed above. This examination demonstrates again the need to update the UNDRIP.

Conflicts and lack of integration between indigenous peoples' environmental rights and international trade law

On the tenth anniversary of the UNDRIP is not surprising that Tauli-Corpuz stated that there has been limited progress in the actual implementation of the UNDRIP.[94] Tauli-Corpuz's report on the impact of international investment and free trade on indigenous peoples' rights, discusses the systemic impact of these regimes on the direct violations that indigenous peoples' environmental rights, self-determination and the right to development face.[95] It is relevant to clarify that investment agreements are intended to provide investors with rights that protect investors against expropriation and unfair or discriminatory conduct by States hosting investment project.

In recent years, there has been a major trend to adopt the 'fair and equitable treatment clauses' and 'non-discriminatory treatment clauses' on investor-State dispute settlement.

According to the Task Force, international trade law can inadvertently work against the development of pro-environment and pro-climate justice policies under the current international system.[96] In fact, the protection of indigenous peoples' rights, the environment and actions to tackle climate change have all led to trade lawsuit. I will only discuss the *Silver Mining* lawsuit,[97] which highlights all those concerns, including conflicts and lack of coherence and integration between the UNDRIP and trade law.[98]

In 2013, Silver Mining initiated a lawsuit against Bolivia and is seeking of US$ 307.2 million, plus compounded pre- and post-award interest for the alleged expropriation of 10 mining concessions and violations of 'fair and equitable treatment clause'.[99] Bolivia responded that it had acted in the public interest and had been justified in reverting ownership to the State in accordance with the principles of proportionality and necessity: 'to avoid security concerns arising out of indigenous peoples' opposition to the project, as the project violates rights recognized in the UNDRIP and bilateral investment treaty had no applicable law clause, because there should be "systemic interpretation" in accordance with article 31 (3) (c) of the Vienna Convention, including human rights obligations towards indigenous peoples under national and international law'.[100]

Silver Mining is not disputing that a systemic interpretation of the Treaty is called for under international law. However, it contends that Bolivia has not satisfactorily established why the Tribunal should give primacy to the rights of indigenous over the clear terms of the Treaty,[101] and much less demonstrated the scope and content of indigenous people's rights under the UNDRIP and the Guiding Principles which are non-binding instruments; while the ILO Convention 169, the Inter-American Commission on Human Rights and the jurisprudence of the ICHR are not binding on the United Kingdom.[102]

This case summarises the struggle the UNDRIP, the Guiding Principles and indigenous peoples' environmental rights are facing at the international, regional and domestic level against conflicts and lack of integration with trade law. In fact, it appears to be no integration and coherence between human rights law and trade law. Whilst article 29 of the UNDRIP is not legally binding,[103] I emphasise that the 'systemic interpretation of international, regional and domestic human rights law cannot be dismissed in favour of international trade law against pro-indigenous, pro-environment or/and climate change laws and policies under current international, regional and domestic regimes'.

Given that international human rights law, environmental law and trade law play significant roles in governing the behaviour of host States in relation to indigenous peoples, the environment and climate change, it is imperative that there is coherence within these areas of international law. Such lack of coherence could be eliminated updating the UNDRIP with provision like the one contained in article 26 of the Draft Declaration recognising indigenous peoples the right to own, develop, control and use their land and total environment, in addition to and the right to effective measures to be taken by States to prevent any interference with these rights, as analysed above.

In fact, article 26 could provide integration and coherence between international law and indigenous peoples' environmental rights. Therefore, the legal tools contained in the Draft Declaration could guarantee a practical solution to indigenous peoples' environmental-rights protection because their environmental rights would be elevated to the same spectrum as trade law. This cannot be achieved under the UNDRIP unless it is updated.

Concluding observations

The development of international law after the adoption of the UNDRIP in 2007 appears to suggest that UNDRIP is already obsolete and it needs to be updated. This is because there are conflicts between indigenous peoples' environmental rights and sustainable development, climate change, trade law, as well as lack of expertise, coherence and integration between international environmental law and human rights.

Furthermore, the lack of a free-standing international environmental right is interdepending with the lack of effective implementation of indigenous peoples' environmental rights. The recent call by the IBA Task Force, President Macron and the former UN Special Rapporteur Knox for a free-standing international environmental right is an important new development of paramount importance for indigenous peoples' environmental rights. The consequence of ignoring these developments is having tragic outcomes on indigenous peoples' rights and survival.

Moving forward with the UNDRIP: a potential convention on the rights of indigenous peoples?

This article has examined whether the weakened final form that emerged from the Draft Declaration fails to guarantee effective environmental-rights protection to indigenous peoples. Much of emphasis has been placed on political implementation of the UNDRIP, but as stated by Tauli-Corpuz, there remains an implementation gap between legal recognition of the UNDRIP and concrete action.[104] This article proves that the issue is deeper than a lack of implementation of article 29 of the UNDRIP.

Progress has been made since the adoption of the UNDRIP, but article 29 should be legally binding, otherwise, it is not clear how the UNDRIP can be effectively implemented to protect indigenous peoples' environmental rights. The UNDRIP, as it stands, lacks capacity to deal with climate change, the extractive industry and trade deal situations, as well as Non-State Actors' obligation because it does not contain references to any of those concerns.

The UNDRIP should be updated to the new realities discussed in this article because this would eliminate gross violations against indigenous peoples' environmental rights, protect their subsistence rights and right to development, as it would guarantee the survival of their present and future generations. That would appear to suggest that indigenous peoples or an official UN body need to be given the authority to make a comprehensive proposal for a global legal or practical solution to protect indigenous peoples' environmental rights, which I suggest in the form of a Convention.

Indeed, a Convention would eliminate any conflict on the definition of the environment, its management and accountability for environmental rights violations and, would elevate indigenous peoples' environmental rights to the same spectrum than other areas of international law eliminating any inconsistency within. Therefore, the Convention should define 'the environment', its management, accountability for violation against indigenous peoples' environmental rights, as well, it should be updated to deal with climate change, Non-State Actors, especially the extractive industry, trade deal situations and redress for environmental-climate change degradation.

It is important to understand and clarify what the environment is for indigenous peoples, as they consider themselves an integral part of their environment, but not part of an environment with Genetically Modified Organisms. My argument for the recognition of a legally binding indigenous peoples' environmental right is based on the need to further protect their subsistence rights, as part of their environmental-rights protection rather than part of their cultural rights.

From a socio-anthropological perspective, for instance, the Sami peoples' ecological worldview, based on reindeer herding through which these peoples relate to reindeer inhabiting their environment, is associated with their environmental rights because it provides their community with clothes, shelter, food and livelihood, which are all essential for their subsistence rights protection.[105] The case of Inuit, Alaskan Native and Sami peoples dependence on ice for food, shelter and clothing raises the question: how they can physically survive if/when the Arctic ice is melting because the Arctic atmosphere is warming twice as quickly as in the rest of the world?[106]

Indigenous peoples' dependence on ice or forests for food, shelter, and clothing should not have linked their subsistence rights with their culture but with their environmental rights, under international law. As explained in my introduction, this issue is further frustrated by looking at indigenous peoples' environment and way of life through culture, land and natural resources protection, rather than under their right to the conservation and protection of the environment recognised in article 29 of the UNDRIP. However, in this article, I demonstrate that article 29 is ineffective, as it stands. Thus, it requires new approaches to achieve effective implementation and, climate-change justice.

The UNDRIP has also to be updated to include recent developments of international law, which are not contained in the UNDRIP and this omission is negatively affecting indigenous peoples' environmental rights. The lack of coherence, expertise and integration between international law will inevitably cause violations of indigenous peoples' environmental rights. And indigenous peoples' environmental-rights violations will inevitably cause violations of their subsistence rights, their right to development, and right to self-determination because these rights are all intertwined.

The impact of the recognition of a legally binding indigenous peoples' environmental right would help, not only in protecting their subsistence rights, but also it would eliminate conflict with their cultural rights because indigenous peoples right to own, use and control their environment in order to hunt or fish is part of their subsistence needs, rather than cultural needs. This could also provide a better balance between their environmental rights and their duty to protect species in extinction because global climate change may possibly become a real threat to those species. This means that climate change might increase the pressure for indigenous peoples, as well as for the international community to prioritise environmental sustainability to save these species from extinction[107] and leave a similar amount of resources to future generations.

A positive outcome of the Convention would further eliminate conflicts between indigenous peoples' environmental rights and their right to development, as sustainable development can be achieved only if environmental and social development are protected before economic development. Finally, it would give environmental concerns a greater weight when competing with other rights, as well as it would elevate environmental concerns to the same spectrum than another area of international law.

Conclusion

Looking at indigenous peoples' environmental rights through the lens of the Draft Declaration, it helps to understand both the challenges faced by the UNDRIP and give the opportunity to discuss a potential free-standing environmental right under the potential Convention on the Rights of Indigenous Peoples, which would be the natural progression from the UNDRIP. The time is right to start a discussion on a potential Convention to enable indigenous peoples to protect their environmental rights and ultimately guarantee their survival because we have a global responsibility toward them. Therefore, the article's conclusions seek to start a debate on the need to update UNDRIP and whether a legally binding Convention is feasible. The situation is urgent, at least in the case of indigenous peoples.

Notes

1. See Resolution 61/295.
2. For a discussion on the change of position by Australia, Canada, New Zealand and the United States see Sheryl Lightfoot, *Global Indigenous Politics: A Subtle Revolution* (Abingdon, UK and New York, US: Rouledge, 2016).
3. Victoria Tauli-Corpuz, 'Indigenous Peoples Are the Best Guardians of the World', interview by David Hill, *The Guardian*, August 9, 2017, https://www.theguardian.com/environment/andes-to-the-amazon/2017/aug/09/indigenous-peoples-are-the-best-guardians-of-the-worlds-biodiversity (accessed January 4, 2019)
4. James Anaya, 'Extractive Industries Operating within or near Indigenous Territories', UN Special Rapporteur's Report, no. A/HRC/18/35, 11 July 2011.
5. The article does not enquire into the causes of environmental-climate change degradation, but take them as a fact.
6. Sheila Watt-Cloutier, *The Right to Be Cold: One Woman's Story of Protecting Her Culture, the Arctic and the Whole Planet* (Canada: Penguin Press, 2015); also Sheila Watt-Cloutier, 'Petition to the Inter American Commission on Human Rights Seeking Relief from Violations Resulting from Global Warming Caused by Acts and Omissions of the United States', (2005), 7, 13, 33. http://www.ciel.org/Publications/ICC_Petition_7Dec05.pdf (accessed January 4, 2019); Rachel Baird, 'The Impact of Climate Change on Minorities and Indigenous Peoples', *Minority Rights Group International* (2008).
7. Agata Durkalec, *Chris* Furgal, *Mark W* Skinner, *and Tom* Sheldon, 'Climate Change Influences on Environment as a Determinant of Indigenous Health: Relationships to Place, Sea Ice, and Health in an Inuit Community', *Social Science and Medicine* (2015): 136–7; James D. Ford, 'Indigenous Health and Climate Change', *American Journal of Public Health* 102, no. 7 (2012): 1260–66.
8. For instance, Inter-American Court of Human Rights (ICHR), *'Garífuna Community of "Triunfo de la Cruz" and Its Members v. Honduras'*, Series C, No. 305 (2015); also *'Garífuna de Punta Piedra Community v. Honduras'*, Series C, No. 304 (2015).
9. This article does not enquire into the right to participation, free, prior and informed consent.
10. See Chap. XVI. E/CN.4/Sub.2/1994/56.
11. Guiding Principles on Business and Human Rights, UN Doc. A/HRC/17/31 [thereafter Guiding Principles], 21 Mar. 2011.
12. UN Climate Change Paris Agreement [thereafter Paris Agreement], 4 November 2016.
13. Sustainable Development Goals 2015–2030, UN General Assembly no. A/RES/70/1, 25 September 2015.
14. IBA Climate Change Justice and Human Rights Task Force Report, *Achieving Justice and Human Rights in an Era of Climate Disruption* (London: IBA, 2014).
15. Emmanuel Macron, President of the French Republic, *Global Pact for the Environment* (presented to the United Nations General Assembly, September 2017).

16. See also John Knox, 'Human Rights Obligations Relating to the Enjoyment of a Safe, Clean, Healthy and Sustainable Environment', UN Special Rapporteur's Report, no. A/73/188, 19 July 2018.
17. See latest report of the Intergovernmental Panel on Climate Change, "Global Warming of 1.5°C, an IPCC Special Report on the Impacts of Global Warming of 1.5°C Above Pre-industrial Levels and Related Global Greenhouse Gas Emission Pathways, in the Context of Strengthening the Global Response to the Threat of Climate Change, Sustainable Development, and Efforts to Eradicate Poverty," (2018), [thereafter IPCC SR1.5]. http://www.ipcc.ch/report/sr15/ (accessed January 4, 2019).
18. Timo Koivurova, 'International Legal Avenues to Address the Plight of Victims of Climate Change: Problems and Prospects', *JELL* 22, no. 2 (2007): 267–99; Stephen Humphreys, *Human Rights and Climate Change* (Cambridge: University Press, 2009); Sébastien Duyck, Sébastien Jodoin and Alyssa Johl, *Routledge Handbook of Human Rights and Climate Governance* (Routledge International Handbooks, 2018).
19. IBA, *Achieving Justice*, 43; Briefing Paper No 117, *Climate Wrongs and Human Rights*, (Oxfam Int'l, September 2008), 7.
20. Kirsten Manley-Casimir, 'Reconciliation, Indigenous Peoples Rights and Offshore Oil and Gas Development in the Canadian Arctic', *Review of European Community and International Law* 20 (2011): 32; Also Laura Bowman, 'Sealing the Deal: Environmental and Indigenous Justice and Mining in Nunavut', *Review of European Community and International Law* 20 (2011): 19.
21. Malgosia Fitzmaurice, 'Tensions Between States and Indigenous People over Natural Resources in Light of the 1989 ILO Convention No. 169 Concerning Indigenous and Tribal Peoples in Independent Countries and the 2007 UN Declaration on the Rights of Indigenous Peoples Including Relevant National Legislation and Case-law', *The Yearbook of Polar Law* 3 (2012): 234–5.
22. https://dictionary.cambridge.org/dictionary/english/environment#dataset-cald4 (accessed January 4, 2019).
23. Adriana Giunta, 'Can an Ecocentric Approach Open New Frontiers for a Legally Binding International Environmental Right? A Study of Norway's Environmental Constitutional Right', in *New Frontiers in Global Environmental Constitutionalism*, eds. Erin Daly, Louis Kotze, James May, and Caiphas Soyapi (Nairobi: United Nations Environment Programme, 2017), 63. https://www.unenvironment.org/resources/publications/new-frontiers-environmental-constitutionalism (accessed January 4, 2019); See also Adriana Giunta, review of *Achieving Justice and Human Rights in an Era of Climate Disruption* by International Bar Association Climate Change Justice and Human Rights Task Force, *Journal of Human Rights and the Environment* 7, no. 1, (March 2016).
24. Giunta, 'Achieving.'
25. Giunta, 'Can an Ecocentric', 77.
26. *The Social and Economic Rights Action for Economic and Social Rights v. Nigeria* Communication No. 276 (2003) [thereafter *Ogoni v. Nigeria*].
27. Environmental Rights Action, Amnesty International, and Friends of the Earth Europe, 'Nigerian and International Civil Society Call for Clean-up of Oil Pollution in the Niger Delta to Finally Begin', Index no. AFR 44/6411/2017, 2 June 2017; also see UNEP, 'Environmental Assessment in Ogoniland', 4 August 2011, http://postconflict.unep.ch/publications/OEA/UNEP_OEA.pdf (accessed January 4, 2019).
28. Susan Glazebrook, 'Human Rights and the Environment', Human Rights and Environment Report (2), Presented at the Conference '*Strategies for the Future: Protecting Rights in the Pacific*', (Samoa, 27–29 April 2008): 54; Cherie Metcalf, 'Indigenous Rights and the Environment: Evolving International Law', *Ottawa Law Review* 35 (2003–2004); Leena Heinämäki, 'Environmental Rights Protecting the Way of Life of Arctic Indigenous Peoples: ILO Convention No. 169 and UN Draft Declaration on Indigenous Peoples', in *Arctic Governance*, eds. Timo Koivurova, Tanja Joona and Reija. Shnoro, (Juridica Lapponica 29, University of Lapland, 2004), 231–59.

29. Glazebrook, 'Human Rights', 30–1.
30. Metcalf, 'Indigenous Rights', 134.
31. Heinämäki, 'Environmental Rights', 255.
32. *Mataatua District Māori Council v. The New Zealand Crown*, New Zealand Waitangi Tribunal, 4 July 2017. http://blogs2.law.columbia.edu/climate-change-litigation/wp-content/uploads/sites/16/non-us-case-documents/2017/20170704_WAI-2607_application-1.pdf (accessed January 4, 2019).
33. IPCC Fifth Assessment Report (AR5), 2014.
34. See *Thomson v. Minister for Climate Change Issues*, High Court of New Zealand, CIV 2015-485-919 [2017] NZHC 733, judgement 2 November 2017; See also Magallanes Catherine Iorns, 'Maori Cultural Rights in Aotearoa New Zealand: Protecting the Cosmology that Protects the Environment', *Widener Law Review* 21, no. :2 (2015): 273–327.
35. See 'Case of Thomson;' See also Urgenda Foundation v The State of the Netherlands (Ministry of Infrastructure and the Environment), Case number 200.178.245/01, 9 October 2018 [thereafter the Urgenda 2018 case] and Case number: C/09/456689/HA ZA 13-1396, Judgment of 24 June 2015 [thereafter Urgenda 2015 case]; Juliana v. Unite States, 217 F.Supp.3d 1224, 1233 (D. Or.2016).
36. Giunta, 'Can an Ecocentric', 65.
37. IBA, *Achieving Justice.*
38. Heinämäki, 'Environmental Rights', 255–6.
39. See Françoise Hampson, 'The Human Rights Situation of Indigenous Peoples in States and Territories Threatened with Extinction for Environmental Reasons', UN Commission on Human Rights Working Group on Indigenous Populations, E/CN.4/Sub.2/AC.4/2004/CRP.1, 13 July 2004; Françoise Hampson, 'The Human Rights Situation', E/CN.4/Sub.2/2005/28, 16 June 2005; Françoise Hampson, 'The Human Rights Situation', E/CN.4/Sub.2/AC.4/2006/CRP.2, 30 June 2006.
40. Alexandra Xanthaki, *Indigenous Rights and United Nations Standards* (New York: Cambridge University Press, 2007).
41. Dianne Otto, 'A Question of Law or Politics? Indigenous Claims to Sovereignty', *Syracuse J.Int'L L. & Com.* 21, 65, 85 (1995): 93.
42. United Nations Conference on Environment and Development (UNCED), Rio de Janeiro, 3–14 June 1992.
43. The debate on environmental rights started in the 1970s following the adoption of the Stockholm Declaration.
44. For a discussion see: Alan E. Boyle and Michael R. Anderson, *Human Rights Approaches to Environmental Protection* (Oxford: Clarendon Press, 1996); Alan Boyle, 'Human Rights or Environmental Rights? A Reassessment', *Fordham University Law School,* March 2, 2007; Alan Boyle, 'Human Rights and the Environment: Where Next?', *EJIL* 23, no. 3 (2012): 642.
45. Koivurova, 'International'; also *Hari M.* Osofsky and *William C.* Burns, *Adjudicating Climate Change: State, National, and International Approaches* (Cambridge University Press, 2009).
46. Humphreys, *Human Rights,* 317.
47. Randall S. Abate and Elizabeth Kronk Warner, *Climate Change and Indigenous Peoples. The Search for Legal Remedies* (Cheltenham Edward Elgar, 2013).
48. Hampson, 'The Human Rights Situation', 2004; Hampson, 'The Human Rights Situation', 2005; Hampson, 'The Human Rights Situation', 2006.
49. UN HRC, Report of the OHCHR on the Relationship Between Climate Change and Human Rights, UN Doc. A/HRC/10/61 [hereafter OHCHR 2009], 15 Jan. 2009, para. 70.
50. OHCHR, Analytical Study on the Relationship Between Human Rights and the Environment, UN Doc. A/HRC/19/34 [hereafter OHCHR 2011], 16 Dec. 2011, para. 64–73.
51. OHCHR 2011, Analytical Study, para. 64-73.
52. UN Human Rights Council (UN HRC) res. 16/11, 'Human Rights and the Environment', 24 Mar. 2011; UNHRC res. 19/12, 'Human Rights and the Environment', 20 Mar. 2012.
53. IBA, *Achieving Justice.*
54. IBA, *Achieving Justice,* 43.

55. IBA, *Achieving Justice*, 117.
56. IBA, *Achieving Justice*, 43 [Emphasis added].
57. IBA, *Achieving Justice*, 62.
58. IBA, *Achieving Justice*, 119.
59. Article 1 of the Global Pact.
60. Article 2 of the Global Pact.
61. Article 3 of the Global Pact.
62. Knox, 'Human Rights', 13.
63. Glazebrook, 'Human Rights', 28.
64. Giunta, 'Can an Ecocentric', 63.
65. *Kaliña and Lokono Peoples v. Suriname*, Merits, reparations and costs, Series C, No. 309 (2015): para 175.
66. Philippe Sands, 'The Environment, Community and International Law', *Harv. Int'l LJ* 30 (1989): 393, 398.
67. Department of Economic and Social Affairs (Division for Social Policy and Development, Secretariat of the Permanent Forum on Indigenous Issues), ST/ESA/328, UN (2009), 89.
68. Guiding Principles, paras 73–4.
69. Guiding Principles, paras 73–4.
70. Environmental Rights Action, Amnesty International, and Friends of the Earth Europe, "Nigerian and International".
71. IBA, *Achieving Justice*, 68.
72. Amnesty International, Injustice Incorporated: Corporate Abuses and the Human Right to Remedy (Amnesty International Ltd, 2014).
73. International Corporate Accountability Roundtable (ICAR), CORE, and the European Coalition for Corporate Justice (ECCJ), *The Third Pillar: Access to Judicial Remedies for Human Rights Violations by Transnational Business*, eds. Gwynne Skinner, Robert McCorquodale, Olivier De Schutter, and Andie Lambe (December 2013); See also Amnesty International, *Injustice Incorporated.*
74. Dinah. Shelton, *Remedies in International Human Rights Law*, 2nd ed. (Oxford University Press, 2006).
75. Glazebrook, 'Human Rights', 29.
76. SDGs 32.
77. The Rio Declaration on Environment and Development, UN DOC.A/CONF/151/4 (1992).
78. Giunta, 'Can an Ecocentric', 75.
79. See Tauli-Corpuz, 'Indigenous Peoples'; However, the Greenlandic peoples' worldview, perhaps, represent an exception to the principle of sustainable development contained in the Rio declaration, as they are focusing on achieving economic development before environmental and social development – see Bent Ole Gram Mortensen, 'Mining and Pollution: Arctic Environmental Law in Greenland and the Mining Industry', *The Yearbook of Polar Law* IV (2012): 673–88.
80. Giunta, 'Can an Ecocentric', 75–6.
81. Giunta, 'Can an Ecocentric', 75–7.
82. IPCC SR1.5, 2018, Chapter 5, 4.
83. Sébastien Duyck, Erika Lennon, Wolfgang Obergassel and Annalisa Savaresi, 'Human Rights and the Paris Agreement's Implementation Guidelines: Opportunities to Develop a Rights-Based Approach', *Carbon and Climate Law Review* 12, no. 3 (2018): 191–202.
84. IPCC SR1.5, Chapter 3, 166.
85. IBA, *Achieving Justice,* 63.
86. Philippe Sands, 'Water and International Law: Science and Evidence in International Litigation', *ELM* 20, (2010). http://www.ukela.org/content/doclib/190.pdf (accessed January 4, 2019); also OHCHR 2009, para 70.
87. *Nunatukavut Community Council Inc v Canada (Attorney General),* FC 981 (August 18, 2015): para 104.
88. 'Case of the *Nunatukavut Community*': para 303

89. Glazebrook, 'Human Rights', 28; see also IBA, *Achieving Justice.*
90. ICHR, 'Cases of the *Kaliña and Lokono*': para 174
91. ICHR, 'Cases of the *Kaliña and Lokono*': para 174.
92. 'Cases of the *Kaliña and Lokono*; para 227. Similar argument was adopted in other cases: see ICHR, 'Cases of the *Garífuna "Triunfo de la Cruz"*, the *Garífuna de Punta Piedra*'.
93. See Jérémie Gilbert, *Indigenous Peoples' Land Rights under International Law: From Victims to Actors*, 2nd ed. (Online: Brill Publishers, 2016), 280.
94. Victoria Tauli-Corpuz, 'Implementation of the United Nation Declaration on the Rights of Indigenous Peoples', UN Special Rapporteur's Report, no. A/72/186, 21 July 2017.
95. Victoria Tauli-Corpuz, 'The Impact of International Investment and Free Trade on the Human Rights of Indigenous Peoples', UN Special Rapporteur's Report, no. A/70/301, 7 August 2015.
96. IBA, *Achieving Justice*, 75–6.
97. *South American Silver Limited v. Bolivia*, UNCITRAL, PCA Case No. 2013-15.
98. For a more complete analysis on the issue see: Victoria Tauli-Corpuz, 'Promotion and Protection of all Human Rights, Civil, Political, Economic, Social and Cultural Rights, Including the Right to Development', UN Special Rapporteur's Report, no. A/HRC/33/42, 11 August 2016.
99. 'Case of *South American Silver*': para 106.
100. Tauli-Corpuz, 'The Impact', 11.
101. 'Case of *South American Silver*': para 238.
102. 'Case of *South American Silver*': paras 245–9.
103. Although, the ILA perceives that to an extent UNDRIP codified customary international law (CIL), the poor debate on the importance of indigenous peoples' environmental rights, makes difficult to argue that article 29 has achieved CIL status - see ILA Committee on the Rights of Indigenous Peoples, Report *'Implementation of the Rights of Indigenous Peoples'*, (Johannesburg Conference, 2016).
104. Tauli-Corpuz, 'Implementation.'
105. Elina Helandre-Renvall, 'Relationship between Sami Reindeer Herders, Land, and Reindeer', in *Routledge Handbook of Human-Animal Studies*, eds. Garry Marvin and Susan McHugh (New York: Routledge, 2014).
106. Baird, 'The Impact', 4.
107. Leena Heinämäki, 'Protecting the Rights of Indigenous Peoples – Promoting the Sustainability of the Global Environment?', *International Community Law Review* 11, no. 1 (2009): 3–68; Malgosia Fitzmaurice, *Whaling and International Law* (Cambridge University Press, 2015).

Acknowledgements

The author would like to thank Professor Timo Koivurova, Director of the Arctic Centre at the University of Lapland for his helpful comments and the anonymous reviewers for their comments on the previous version of this article. The faults, however, remain the author's. She also would like to thank Aino Berg for proofreading this article and Dr Karin Altenberg, Royal Literary Fund Fellow for editing the article.

Disclosure statement

No potential conflict of interest was reported by the author.

ORCID

Adriana Giunta http://orcid.org/0000-0002-2749-5184

Treaty making and the UN Declaration on the Rights of Indigenous Peoples: lessons from emerging negotiations in Australia

Harry Hobbs

ABSTRACT

No treaties between Aboriginal and Torres Strait Islander peoples and the Australian state have ever been recognised. In recent months, however, several states and territories have committed to entering treaty negotiations with the First Nations whose lands they claim. Negotiations are in their preliminary stages and it remains to be seen what eventuates, but these developments are promising. Nonetheless, many challenges exist. In this paper, I explore the initial developments in Victoria, and assess whether and how the United Nations Declaration on the Rights of Indigenous People has influenced the debate thus far. This analysis reveals lessons for all Indigenous peoples seeking to enter treaty negotiations with states across the globe.

Introduction

The United Nations *Declaration on the Rights of Indigenous Peoples* (the 'UNDRIP') is 'the most comprehensive and progressive of international instruments dealing with Indigenous peoples' rights'.[1] Recognised as a 'milestone in the re-empowerment of the world's aboriginal groups',[2] the Declaration was welcomed as representing 'the beginning of a new phase in the debate on Indigenous rights'.[3] Reflecting this epochal shift, debate has since moved from identification to implementation. In this vein, the Expert Mechanism on the Rights of Indigenous Peoples (EMRIP) has recently surveyed the UNDRIP's impact, examining its application by UN treaty bodies, the Human Rights Council's Universal Periodic Review procedure, regional human rights bodies, domestic courts, and UN agencies. The review reveals that the UNDRIP informs the work of a variety of actors in international and domestic spheres and has influenced legislative and constitutional drafting as well as judicial interpretation, across the globe.[4] While the report makes clear that there is much to be done, it also demonstrates that – ten years after its adoption – the Declaration is increasingly valuable as a political and legal instrument to protect and promote the rights of Indigenous peoples.

Australia has a complicated relationship with the UNDRIP. It was – along with Canada, Aotearoa/New Zealand and the United States – one of only four states to vote against the

Declaration in September 2007. While this decision may owe more to Australia's distinctive approach to settler-state constitutionalism, rather than any objection to international standard-setting on Indigenous rights per se,[5] the decision was greeted by many Aboriginal and Torres Strait Islander people with regret.[6] All four states have since endorsed the UNDRIP, but Australia's reversal remains qualified by the same objections it expressed in 2007.[7] Nonetheless, despite these qualifications, Australia maintains that it is committed to the norms and principles of the Declaration. In 2013, for instance, it informed the UN Permanent Forum on Indigenous Issues that it is working with the Australian Human Rights Commission and the National Congress of Australia's First Peoples to 'increase awareness of, and encourage dialogue about, the Declaration in policy development, program implementation and service delivery as a way to embed the Declaration in how business is done'.[8] This is positive, but Australia's reluctance to wholeheartedly endorse the Declaration augurs challenges.

Australia also has a complicated relationship with the Aboriginal and Torres Strait Islander peoples whose land it claims. In contrast to the situation in Canada, Aotearoa/New Zealand and the United States, no treaty between Aboriginal and Torres Strait Islander peoples and the Australian state has ever been recognised, leaving both the constitutive legitimacy of the state, and its exercise of authority over First Nations people, open to question. The absence of treaties is reproduced in a politico-legal framework that neither constitutionally protects Indigenous rights nor provides for specific mechanisms to promote Indigenous interests in the processes of Australian government. Consequently, Aboriginal and Torres Strait Islander peoples have long fought for recognition of their unique status as prior self-governing nations whose sovereignty has never been ceded, calling for a reconstituted politico-legal structure that empowers them 'to take *a rightful place* in [their] country'.[9] This struggle has been ongoing for generations but has re-emerged in recent years as part of a decade-long national discussion over 'recognising' Aboriginal and Torres Strait Islander people in the Australian Constitution.[10] In 2016, this debate was reinvigorated as several Australian states and territories – Victoria, South Australia, and the Northern Territory – committed to undertake treaty negotiations with First Nations whose traditional lands fall within their boundaries.[11]

This article ties these two complex issues together by exploring the relevance and salience of the UNDRIP to modern treaty negotiations in Australia and across the globe, through a detailed examination of the preliminary stages conducted thus far in Victoria. This issue is important, because Indigenous peoples must negotiate treaties and other legal arrangements with states to safeguard their interests and embed their aspirations and values in legal forms. The Declaration establishes a 'framework that states can adopt to underpin their relationship with Indigenous peoples and … guide them in the development of domestic law and policy'.[12] The procedural and substantive rights recognised in the Declaration should therefore inform consultation and negotiation between First Nations and the state. Does this occur in practice, and if not, what consequences might flow?

In exploring this issue, I divide the article into three substantive parts. Part I identifies two key themes relevant to treaty-making that underlie the UNDRIP – self-determination and participation – in order to articulate a standard against which negotiations can be assessed. In Part II, I take an empirical look at the initial stages of treaty negotiations in Victoria, examining whether the Declaration has informed this process. Focus on Victoria is appropriate because although many scholars have analysed modern treaty processes in Canada, no one has yet studied the unprecedented emerging negotiations in Australia. Furthermore, while Canada has recently committed to fully implementing the UNDRIP,[13] Australia's relationship to the Declaration remains strained; criticism exists over Canada's approach, but Australia's engagement with the UNDRIP is more common globally and may present particular challenges in negotiations moving forward.

In a final Part III, I draw on the Victorian material, as well as experiences of modern negotiations in Canada, to identify several lessons for all treaty processes. The UNDRIP is a positive and productive instrument that has the potential to invigorate and strengthen Indigenous advocacy as well as inform the content of any treaty. In the absence of legally enforceable provisions or standards, however, asymmetrical power relations and non-legal forces may negatively impact negotiations. Nonetheless, the Declaration enjoys considerable moral and political force and there is significant value for Indigenous peoples in framing their aspirations in its language. Employing the Declaration in this way may increase pressure on state actors, and enhance the prospect that negotiations lead to a renewed relationship built on mutual trust and respect.

Articulating a treaty-making standard

As the preeminent instrument on Indigenous rights, the UN Declaration recognises a swathe of procedural and substantive entitlements relevant to protecting and promoting the position of Indigenous peoples. Explicit reference to treaties is minimal, however. Only Article 37 expressly refers to treaties, guaranteeing that Indigenous peoples are entitled to their 'recognition, observance and enforcement', though, several preambular paragraphs do consider the value of such agreements as affirming key rights and obligations and representing 'the basis for a strengthened partnership'. Nevertheless, despite relatively little overt reference, two key themes that underlie the process, purpose, and content of treaties reverberate through the operative clauses of the Declaration: self-determination and participation. It is these values that inhere within the Declaration that create a framework for Indigenous dialogue and political advocacy with states.[14] This part briefly highlights how these principles connect to, and strengthen treaty-making, by establishing a working standard against which negotiations can be assessed.

The Declaration acknowledges that over hundreds of years, many forms of agreements have been concluded between Indigenous peoples and states. Although it considers – correctly – that all such arrangements should be respected,[15] it does not consider what elements are necessary for an agreement to constitute a treaty. Recent Australian scholarship, informed by the UNDRIP and other developments internationally, argues that treaties are a distinct form of agreement that must satisfy three criteria.[16] First, a treaty recognises Indigenous peoples as a polity, distinctive from other citizens of the state, based on their status as prior self-governing communities. Second, a treaty is reached by a fair process of negotiation conducted in good faith and in a manner respectful of each participant's standing as a polity. Third, a treaty recognises or establishes concrete outcomes, including some form of decision-making and control that amounts to at least a limited form of self-government. The principles that underpin the Declaration are helpful in elucidating these criteria.

A polity is a political community differentiated from and different to other citizens of the state. This first condition therefore requires states to acknowledge and accept that

Indigenous peoples are not merely an ethnic or cultural minority group, but a distinct society whose relationship to the state must be mediated in a dialogic fashion. The Declaration recognises and affirms this understanding by emphasising the multiple nested or overlapping nationalities that Indigenous peoples may have.[17] For example, the UNDRIP confirms that Indigenous peoples have the right 'to a nationality',[18] as well as the right to 'belong to an Indigenous community or nation' determined in accordance with the 'traditions and customs of the community or nation concerned'.[19] Recognition of Indigenous peoples as a polity clearly entails commitment to Indigenous self-constitution and self-determination.

Participation is most clearly evidenced in the second condition; a treaty must be reached by way of a fair process of negotiation. Although the Declaration affirms this right, it does not clearly articulate a practical standard, indicating simply that states must undertake 'effective consultation'[20] or 'consult[] and cooperat[e]'[21] with Indigenous peoples. UN mechanisms and international human rights jurisprudence have, however, elaborated on these provisions, suggesting that consultation should be 'undertaken in good faith' through culturally appropriate procedures and with representatives freely chosen by Indigenous peoples through their own representative structures. Indigenous representatives should be afforded sufficient time and information to reach a decision, and the process should entail 'no coercion, intimidation or manipulation'.[22] This requires a fair, independent, impartial and transparent mechanism to facilitate consultation and alleviate power imbalances.[23] In other words, any fair process of negotiation will safeguard Indigenous rights and mitigate inequities,[24] respecting Indigenous peoples' authority as self-determining communities.[25]

Reflective of Indigenous nations' status as self-determining polities who freely participate in negotiations, a treaty must also recognise or establish some form of decision-making and control amounting to at least a limited form of self-government. Self-determination has been identified as the 'the heart and soul' of the UNDRIP, constituting the 'river in which all other rights swim'.[26] Indeed, the Declaration upholds the 'evolving right of democratic governance at international law',[27] confirming that self-rule is the 'oldest aspect of democratic entitlement'[28] entailing a right to determine one's political destiny 'in a democratic fashion'.[29] References to self-government and participation in decision-making are replete throughout the instrument. Under Article 3, self-determination is conceived as a right of Indigenous peoples to 'freely determine their political status and freely pursue their economic, social and cultural development'. Although broadly framed and suggestive of an expansive understanding of sovereignty, this right is conditioned by Article 46(1), which protects the territorial integrity of existing states, and Article 4, which qualifies the right to self-determination to the 'right to autonomy or self-government' in relation to 'internal and local affairs'.

Some Indigenous scholars and activists have critiqued this elaboration of self-determination,[30] contending that it will 'inevitably reinstate colonial law'.[31] This formulation may be 'an inherently pragmatic decision',[32] but it reflects a strong, majority current of Indigenous thinking. Throughout negotiations, Indigenous peoples involved in the drafting frequently asserted that they 'have no interest in secession' but desire greater autonomy and decision-making authority in order to 'finally become part of' the state.[33] As Megan Davis has explained, the UNDRIP's underlying values of self-determination, 'participation, engagement and consultation',[34] are based on the 'assumption of interdependence between states and Indigenous peoples'.[35] Such interdependence is, however, grounded on the pre-existing sovereignty of Indigenous nations,[36] who enjoy the right to maintain their distinct institutions,[37] and exercise real governmental authority over certain matters, rather than a relationship between the state and undifferentiated citizens.

As this brief survey demonstrates, the UNDRIP makes only occasional explicit reference to treaty-making, but its underlying themes support and articulate a working standard against which treaties can be assessed. Treaties should accurately recognise Indigenous peoples' status, negotiations should be conducted in a fair and respectful manner, and they should enable some form of self-government to be exercised. However, obligatory statements as to what is 'required' by the UNDRIP may be misleading. As a General Assembly Declaration, the instrument is, at least formally, legally non-binding. Is this a relevant standard to assess treaty negotiations?

Notwithstanding its formal status, the Declaration has always enjoyed a distinctive character. Adopted with overwhelming majority support, some scholars have suggested it carries particular authority.[38] Others have argued, and some courts have accepted, that while the Declaration is a soft-law instrument, many of its provisions, including those on self-determination, political participation and consultation – themes that inhere in treaty-making – reflect hard law norms.[39] Certainly, in UN practice, Declarations are considered 'formal and solemn' instruments, restricted to 'rare occasions when principles of great and lasting importance are being enunciated' and as such, there is 'a strong expectation that members of the international community will abide by' them.[40] The subsequent use and endorsement of the Declaration by a range of international and domestic actors as expounded by the EMRIP adds further credence to its legal authority.[41] In any case, however, as Amy Maguire has argued, in practice, what may be more important than whether a rule is hard or soft law is whether it is effective in changing state behaviour.[42] Australia and Canada, two states engaged in modern treaty processes have endorsed the UNDRIP. Is the Declaration influencing their negotiations? The following Part takes an empirical look at the preliminary negotiations in Victoria – the first in Australia.

Treaty-making in Australia

No treaties were ever signed between representatives of the British Crown or colonial governments and the Aboriginal and Torres Strait Islander peoples of the continent. Treaty has therefore always been a key aspiration of Aboriginal and Torres Strait Islander peoples, though the Australian state has often equivocated. In 1979, the National Aboriginal Conference, a nationally elected Indigenous body advising government, passed a resolution calling for a 'Makarrata', a Yolŋu word meaning 'a coming together after a struggle'.[43] Several years later, in 1983, the Senate Standing Committee on Constitutional and Legal Affairs delivered a report on the concept of a treaty, recommending constitutional change in order to implement a 'compact'.[44] Five years later, in 1988, Prime Minister Bob Hawke promised to negotiate a treaty to respect and recognise Indigenous sovereignty within three years.[45] The treaty did not eventuate, and was quietly shelved. Calls for treaty by the Council for Aboriginal Reconciliation and the Aboriginal and Torres Strait Commission in the new millennium also fell on deaf ears.[46] Despite these setbacks, Aboriginal and Torres Strait Islander calls for treaty have never abated. Most recently, in the 2017 Uluru Statement from the Heart, around 250 Aboriginal and Torres Strait Islander delegates from across Australia called for the establishment of a Makarrata Commission to 'supervise a process of agreement-making between governments and First Nations'.[47]

The Federal government dismissed the recommendations arising from the Uluru Statement, but several state and territory governments have responded to these demands. Over the last two years, Victoria,[48] the Northern Territory,[49] and South Australia,[50] officially committed to enter treaty negotiations with Aboriginal peoples. Reflecting the political nature of these agreements, however, the situation is complex and subject to change; in June 2018, for instance, a newly elected South Australian government formally abandoned their treaty process.[51] Despite this step backwards, political leaders in several other states and territories have indicated that they may soon commence negotiations. The Queensland Labor government adopted treaty as part of their policy platform in 2016, and is currently considering how talks might be conducted.[52] Similarly, the New South Wales Labor opposition has promised to hold treaty talks with Aboriginal nations within the state if they win the next election, due in 2019.[53] The Tasmanian Labor Opposition made a similar promise, though it failed to secure election in 2018.[54]

Reflective of the shift in national debate, treaty is not simply the province of Labor governments and parties. In Western Australia, the conservative Liberal government signed the largest and most-comprehensive agreement to settle Aboriginal interests in land in Australian history with the Noongar people in 2015.[55] The agreement involves 30,000 Noongar people and covers around 200,000 km^2. The total value of the package is about $1.3 billion, and includes agreement on rights, obligations, and opportunities relating to land, resources, governance, finance, and cultural heritage. In exchange for this package, the Noongar people have agreed to surrender all current and future claims relating to historical and contemporary dispossession. Although this agreement was conducted under the framework of the *Native Title Act 1993* (Cth) rather than a specific treaty process, its size and scope reveal that it is Australia's first de facto, if not de jure, treaty.[56] This fact was recognised at the time by Deputy Western Australia Opposition Leader Roger Cook, who explained in Parliament that, 'by its very nature, the Noongar agreement is in fact a classic treaty'.[57] However, notwithstanding the significance of the Noongar Settlement and the emerging negotiations in the Northern Territory, this Part will only explore the Victorian process, as it is being conducted under an explicit treaty process and is the most advanced.

Preliminary negotiations in Victoria

In June 2018, the Victorian Parliament passed Australia's first treaty bill. The *Advancing the Treaty Process with Aboriginal Victorians Act 2018* ('*Treaty Act*') creates a legislative basis for negotiating a treaty with Aboriginal people in the state. Under the Act, the government must recognise an Aboriginal-designed representative body empowered to determine a treaty negotiation framework and administer a self-determination fund to support Aboriginal Victorians in treaty negotiations. The Act is the culmination of a two-year process of preliminary negotiations initially catalysed by concern that the national debate on 'recognising' Indigenous peoples in the Australian *Constitution* would fail to deliver meaningful reform.

The process began in February 2016, when the Victorian government convened a meeting with representatives of Victorian Aboriginal communities to understand what self-determination might mean for their communities. At this meeting, Aboriginal representatives affirmed their support for a treaty.[58] These views were reiterated at the first ever state wide Aboriginal Victoria Forum held on 26–27 May 2016, where 500 participants unanimously agreed to advance self-determination and a treaty by establishing an Aboriginal representative body.[59] The state government responded positively to these demands, establishing an Aboriginal Treaty Working Group to consult with Aboriginal Victorians over the design of an appropriate body to represent them in treaty negotiations, and to advise the Minister for Aboriginal Affairs on progress towards a treaty and 'the broader self-determination agenda'.[60] The Working Group is composed entirely of Aboriginal people with a balance between male and female representatives. It is not clan-based but is comprised of representatives of Victorian Aboriginal community organisations and members appointed in their individual capacity by the Minister for Aboriginal Affairs.[61]

Consultations were organised by the management consulting company EY to provide structural independence from government. Initial consultations took place at ten locations across Victoria in the second-half of 2016. Participants were asked what representation meant to them and discussed design principles as well as potential roles and functions of a putative Aboriginal representative body.[62] A further six consultations were held in March 2017 to refine the structure and framework of the body. Community members considered who should be eligible to vote and stand for election, as well as how the electorate should be divided.[63] In an effort to 'allow the community to drive the next steps in the Treaty process',[64] this latter round of consultations included a series of 'Treaty Circles'. These community-run conversations were coordinated and supervised by self-nominated individuals who held discussions in their local area, with the aim of 'ensuring maximum participation by as many members of the Victorian Aboriginal community as possible'.[65] An online 'Message Stick' was created to allow those unable to attend a community consultation or Treaty Circle to have their say as well. Approximately 7,500 Aboriginal Victorians were consulted or engaged directly through this process.[66]

The results of these consultations were presented to an Aboriginal Victoria Forum at the end of April 2017. At this meeting, the state government committed to provide $28.5 million to progress the treaty process in the 2017/18 budget.[67] This funding included provision for an Aboriginal Community Assembly to discuss and provide further advice to the Working Group on the design of a representative body, and a Victorian Treaty Advancement Commission (VTAC) to operationalise the outcomes of the Community Assembly. The VTAC has broad responsibilities; it is empowered to guide establishment of the representative body, maintain momentum for treaty, consult with Aboriginal Victorians, provide research and advice on the process, and keep all Victorians informed.[68] Once the representative body is established, the VTAC is to be abolished.

All Aboriginal Victorians aged over 18 years were eligible to apply for membership of the Aboriginal Community Assembly. Three Aboriginal Victorians reviewed the applications, and 33 people were eventually selected with the aim of ensuring accurate demographic representation in the Assembly.[69] In November and December 2017, 31 of these members 'from across Victoria with a diversity and wealth of cultural knowledge, expertise and experience' met over six days to deliberate and provide their advice.[70] That same month, Jill Gallagher, a Gunditjmara woman from Western Victoria, was appointed the Victorian Treaty Advancement Commissioner.[71]

The June 2018 Act constitutes the next steps in this process. The design of the Representative Body is still being considered. Once it has been constituted and recognised by the state government, these two entities will work together to establish a treaty negotiation framework. That framework must accord with several guiding principles set out in the Act: self-determination and empowerment; fairness and equality; partnership and good faith; mutual benefit and sustainability; and, transparency and accountability.[72] The representative body will not negotiate for Aboriginal Victorians but simply assist in developing an appropriate framework. In the meantime, Aboriginal Victorians will need to organise their negotiating position, decide what Treaty means to them, and what form a treaty or treaties should take. The final step will involve negotiations between Aboriginal Victorians and the state. This stage could take many years.

Is the Declaration informing negotiations?

In acknowledging Indigenous peoplehood and recognising mechanisms for democratic self-rule, treaties are consistent with the UNDRIP's vision and endorsement of a pluralised account of the state, where sovereignties are dispersed among multiple polities.[73] It is, however, too early to say whether the treaty process in Victoria, let alone the Northern Territory and elsewhere, will be successful. It is also unclear whether state and territory governments are interested in recognising Indigenous self-governance or other rights enshrined in the UNDRIP; simply calling an agreement a 'treaty' will not make it so. This section explores the extent to which the Declaration is being used as a framework to guide preliminary negotiations in Victoria.

In answering this question, it is important to begin with a note of caution; this section is based only on publicly available material. I do not have access to internal government policy briefs, cabinet documents, legal advice, or other such material. Equally, I am not privy to information held by Aboriginal groups engaging in the preliminary stages of treaty negotiation. This carries a risk that I may miss critical themes or principles underlying and giving force to practices of negotiation as well as the substantive terms that may be agreed in the future. Nonetheless, assessing the public record of the initial stages of negotiations is valuable. While debate over the legal status of the Declaration is important, its real value lies in its political force. As Claire Charters has argued, articulating aspirations in the language of the Declaration 'can contribute to state internalisation of its norms',[74] intensifying its political, if not legal salience. Use of the Declaration in private fora or confidential memoranda necessarily has a more limited impact.

The Victorian government has often made clear its commitment to the UNDRIP, but a close analysis reveals some areas of potential tension going forward. First, the *Treaty Act* specifically refers to the Declaration in its preamble, noting that the State 'recognises the importance of the treaty process proceeding in a manner that is consistent with' the Declaration. This reference was, however, absent in the initial Bill presented to Parliament,[75] and the government rejected a proposed amendment to insert an operative clause requiring consistency.[76] Consequently, the Declaration's norms and values remain aspirational rather than obligatory and there is no mechanism to enforce compliance with its standards. This could give rise to complications in the future, as the preamble to the *Treaty Act* may provide a window on the government's future negotiating position. Indeed, despite the historical absence of any treaty or act ever legitimating British colonisation, the *Treaty Act* merely acknowledges that 'Victorian traditional owners *maintain* that their sovereignty has never been ceded'.[77] Will recognition of sovereignty be a sticking point? Second, the UNDRIP also does not appear to be playing a key role within the public service, who provide advice to government and will undertake many essential functions once treaty negotiations commence. In fact, the Declaration is cited only once on the Victorian government's *Aboriginal Victoria* departmental website – under heritage protection rather than the treaty process.[78]

Third, a search of the Victorian Parliamentary Hansard reveals similarly patchy executive consideration of the Declaration within the legislature. Although the Bill was introduced into Parliament on 7 March 2018, the first reference on the floor was not made until almost three weeks later – and not by a member of the government. Rather, reference was made by Gunnai and Gunditjmara woman Lidia Thorpe,[79] the first Aboriginal woman elected to the Parliament and a member of the Greens Party. While the Declaration has been mentioned more frequently since this date, only six government members have specifically cited the Declaration,[80] and often only in response to its invocation by non-government members. The government's limited engagement with the UNDRIP mirrors the Parliament's approach before the Bill's introduction. Prior to this date, the Declaration had only been referred to three times in the 58th Parliament, all of which were made in 2015, before treaty discussions commenced. Intriguingly, only one of these three references was made to the *Declaration on the Rights of Indigenous Peoples*,[81] with the other two referring to the Declaration *of* the Rights of Indigenous Peoples,[82] suggesting an imperfect awareness of the instrument.

Formal government engagement with the Declaration may be inconsistent but it is clear that the principles, norms, and values underling the instrument are playing a role. In March 2015, Premier Daniel Andrews declared that his government's approach to Aboriginal affairs would be guided by the principle of self-determination.[83] Narelle Hutchins, the Minister for Aboriginal Affairs, has frequently echoed this statement and explicitly connected it to the Declaration, acknowledging that 'self-determination is one of the over-arching principles of the *Declaration on the Rights of Indigenous Peoples*'.[84] In the 2017–18 budget the government allocated $68.2 million to improving Indigenous self-determination, including by supporting the treaty process and, 'looking at ways within government we can embed self-determination for decision-making ... for Aboriginal Victorians'.[85] In the 2018–19 budget, a further $9 million was committed to the establishment of the Aboriginal Representative Body.[86] The government's commitment to Indigenous self-determination extends beyond the treaty process. For instance, important amendments to the *Traditional Owner Settlement Act 2010* (Vic), developed in close consultation with Indigenous people,[87] make it easier for traditional owners to exercise their rights to Crown land and natural resources for cultural, social, and economic purposes.[88]

The values and standards underlying the Declaration are identifiable in the processes undertaken so far. Consistent with articles 3 and 4 of the UNDRIP, treaty was initiated entirely by Aboriginal people. Aboriginal Victorians first instigated the push towards a treaty by rejecting the state-sponsored national constitutional recognition process. Rather than ignore this call, or seek to confine it, the government met these aspirations by providing adequate resources for Aboriginal people to conduct consultations across the state on the design of a representative body. When those consultations revealed broader feelings of disempowerment and alienation from political and governmental processes,[89] the government acknowledged that the body could be more than just an entity that negotiates a Treaty but may be capable of playing a longer-term role as a representative voice for the Aboriginal community in the political, economic, social, and cultural life of the State, including perhaps by participating in devising legislative or administrative measures that affect them. At the same time, the government has batted away questions about the content of any treaty, correctly noting that that is an issue for negotiation, after the establishment of a representative body. Reflecting this commitment, the government has made it clear that it envisages the treaty process as meeting obligations under the UNDRIP. In the *Treaty Act*'s Second Reading Speech, Narelle Hutchins explained that the government firmly believes that 'all stages of the treaty process' must be guided by Aboriginal self-determination, and that the state perceives itself acting in 'partnership with Aboriginal Victorians'.[90] Special Minister of State, Gavin Jennings echoed these comments, noting that the guiding principles set out in the Act 'are more than aspirational'; they 'crystallise' the government's commitment and 'draw on' the Declaration.[91]

These comments are positive, and it is important to note that the government has demonstrated a commitment to the UNDRIP by amending its Treaty legislation to incorporate the instrument. However, the government's more limited broader engagement with the Declaration suggests challenges going forward. Scarce references in Parliament, across the public service, and within the executive, potentially signal that the document itself is not contributing to debate. In the absence of an enforceable standard, it remains to be seen how far Victoria's rhetorical or political commitment to the UNDRIP and Indigenous self-determination extends once negotiations commence.

Engagement with the Declaration may be inconsistent, but the values that underpin it are clearly playing a role in the Victorian government's approach to treaty. Significantly, Aboriginal approaches have adopted a similar position; the UNDRIP is not always explicitly publicly employed, but the instrument is driving their demands. For example, while Jill Gallagher has noted that the Declaration is a 'central principle of the Working Group',[92] it does not appear in any public records of their meetings. Similarly, although some participants in community consultations and members of the Working Group have expressed their views in the language of the Declaration, including Lidia Thorpe who resigned from her position on the Working Group when she felt her cultural integrity was being compromised,[93] the Declaration itself is absent in official reports of the community consultations. This may reflect limited awareness of the UNDRIP, suggesting that it has not permeated within the community. Considering the values and principles expressed at these community consultations, however, it may be more likely that the limited public use of the Declaration is a pragmatic calculation by Aboriginal people to not articulate their claims through this instrument, believing either that it will have little salience with state officials, or that it will spark anxiety within the non-Indigenous community. This pragmatic calculation may be working. Despite some concerns, the process so far has been largely positive. Even if Indigenous people and leaders are not publicly articulating their claims through the Declaration, they are speaking in the language of its values, standards, and principles. Even more importantly, the state has proved receptive to these calls. Should this strategy continue once negotiations commence?

Treaties and the value of the Declaration

The norms and values underlying the UNDRIP are driving the push towards treaty in Victoria, but in the public sphere, government and Aboriginal invocations of the instrument itself are largely sporadic. Is this a problem? While the preliminary stages of treaty negotiations may be resolved in the absence of the Declaration, this could prove dangerous when negotiations commence. Although the Victorian government assures us it is committed to its values and principles, without more clearly grounding that commitment in clear and enforceable standards and obligations concerning process and outcomes, negotiations may flounder. Even a principled but inchoate understanding of the terms of the Declaration may mean that agreements conducted under the guise of treaty negotiations fail to result in meaningful reform. This Part draws back from the specific Victorian process to identify several challenges that may arise in all modern treaty negotiations conducted in the shadow of the UNDRIP.

First, in the absence of explicit legislative endorsement of the UNDRIP, either by the Victorian government or other relevant state, there is a risk that both the negotiations and content of any treaty may not satisfy the minimum standards recognised in the Declaration. The experience in Canada, where modern treaties have been negotiated since 1973, suggests that the negotiation stage will be the most difficult, and it is easy to imagine that a state's much vaunted political commitment to Indigenous self-determination may be discarded or at least downgraded during the tumult of negotiation, as it is here where a rhetorical promise to an amorphous concept must be concretised into specific terms. How will state's respond if, for instance, Aboriginal Victorians insist on powers of self-government consistent with First Nations in Canada, or concomitant to the guarantees in the Declaration, including the right to convene their own law-making bodies?

It is critical to remember that the UNDRIP constitutes the 'minimum standards for the survival, dignity and well-being of the Indigenous peoples of the world';[94] the rights expressed therein are not bargaining chips. Without the Declaration acting as an enforceable framework to guide state approaches and policies, there is a real danger that substantive Indigenous rights may not be realised. In Australia, concerns along these lines had been raised even before the South Australian process was abruptly dismantled. In announcing the South Australian government's commitment to treaty in 2016, the Minister for Aboriginal Affairs and Reconciliation characterised Indigenous self-governance and autonomy only in terms of 'cultural authority'.[95] While maintaining cultural authority is a critical component of Indigenous peoples' aspirations, it does not entail the entirety of their self-governance rights. This risk is particularly pronounced where support for the treaty process is divided along partisan lines. Indeed, the failure to expressly ground treaty negotiations in the UNDRIP in South Australia, may have contributed to the new government's rejection of the process. Similar concerns exist in Victoria, where the Opposition voted against the Treaty bill. Although the Victorian government secured re-election in late 2018, displacing the most significant immediate challenge, longer-term challenges cannot be ignored.

Second, the absence of UNDRIP in public debate may exacerbate First Nations' unequal bargaining position. Notwithstanding the Victorian government's positive steps in resourcing community consultations on the design of an Aboriginal Representative Body as well as the body itself, the negotiation stage will be very challenging for Indigenous peoples as they will face a significant disparity in bargaining power. In Australia, this is intensified by the absence of common law fiduciary duties imposed on the Crown in their dealings with Indigenous peoples,[96] which means that there are little constitutional limits preventing the state from undertaking 'sharp dealings'[97] in their relationship with Indigenous peoples. The UNDRIP can be helpful here. Julie Jai, a former negotiator for the Yukon government, has argued that First Nations in Canada have been able to enhance their negotiating power by using the Declaration as an external standard of legitimacy,[98] holding the state accountable to its standards, articulated in Part II above. Without suggesting that contemporary negotiations in Canada always reach this benchmark, it is clear that agreements reached prior to 2007 were often characterised by considerable political and economic pressure levied on Indigenous nations.[99] Nonetheless, without explicit endorsement by the state, and without First Nations publicly pressuring government, Indigenous peoples may not be able to use the Declaration in this way, placing Indigenous negotiators in a worse position than they might otherwise be.

The UNDRIP may be useful in articulating and pressuring government to stick to a minimum standard in negotiations, but the experience in Canada suggests that conducting debate in the language of the Declaration does not resolve all challenges. Following the election of Justin Trudeau, the federal government committed to legislation that would align government action and policies with the UNDRIP as well as ensure 'rigorous, full and meaningful' implementation of all treaties.[100] Several provincial governments, including British Columbia, have followed suit.[101] These governments often expressly link standards and obligations set out in the Declaration to Canada's historic treaties as well as the modern treaty process. For instance, in 2016, Carolyn Bennett the Minister for Indigenous and Northern Affairs, declared that the Declaration 'reflects the spirit and intent of our treaties', and explained that the state conceives 'modern treaties and self-government agreements as the ultimate expression of free, prior and informed consent among partners'.[102] Similarly, the British Columbia Treaty Commission has argued that the treaty process in the province is consistent with key principles of the UNDRIP, which 'breathe[s] life into negotiations',[103] while the Ministry of Indigenous Relations and Reconciliation seeks to 'transform the treaty process so it respects … the UNDRIP'.[104]

The modern treaty process in Canada provides a 'clear pathway' to forms of self-government arrangements,[105] but invocations of the Declaration in the context of these negotiations has garnered considerable criticism. As many have argued, the 'setting in which treaties … have been negotiated (since 1973) is not one of cooperative agreement, but a context of asymmetrical power relations'[106] that coerces First Nations into a process that fails to satisfy UNDRIP's procedural and substantive guarantees. In particular, extreme resource disparities as well as powerful non-Indigenous non-government actors, such as the extractive and pastoral industries, challenge the ability of negotiations to remain free and fair. The boundaries of modern treaty negotiations in Canada are thus policed by the state, with concerns frequently raised over both the 'narrowness of what governments have been willing to discuss'[107] and the grounding of those negotiations within the context of Canadian law.[108] Drawing these threads together, James Tully contends that the provincial and federal governments consider themselves 'entering into negotiations with "minorities" within Canada', presupposing a 'relationship of subordination and some form of subjection to the Crown', 'foreclos[ing] precisely what the negotiations should be about'.[109] Similar challenges have impacted on negotiations in Australia, most seriously in leading to amendments in 1998 that substantially weakened the *Native Title Act 1993* (Cth).

The Canadian experience reveals that express government commitment to the Declaration, rising even to a public *intention* to legislate, does not resolve strains over the process and outcomes of negotiations but shifts debate towards what the UNDRIP requires. Nonetheless, Indigenous peoples should insist that all treaty negotiations remain under the aegis of the Declaration. Structuring negotiations in this way maintains the focus on Indigenous *rights* (notwithstanding dispute over the content of those rights) rather than on lesser agreements, such as contracts or service delivery arrangements. This is particularly important in countries like Australia where governments have historically preferred to minimise the Indigenous rights agenda in favour of a focus on 'practical' reconciliation.[110] This preference remains strong. In announcing that the South Australian government would abandon the treaty process, for example, newly-elected Premier Stephen Marshall declared that state-based treaties are 'expensive gestures' and committed to reforms aimed at delivering 'practical' outcomes.[111]

Finally, treaties between Indigenous peoples and the state are distinct from legal contracts. Treaties are 'constitutional accords' that 'articulate basic terms and conditions of social co-existence' and 'establish the constitutional parameters of state power'.[112] Indigenous nations enter into treaties 'as keepers of a certain place',[113] and their settlement constitutes 'a form of political recognition and a measure of the consensual distribution of powers'.[114] In this sense, a treaty is intended to ground an ongoing relationship between Indigenous peoples and the state. In states where dominant conceptions of identity and citizenship operate to deny Indigenous normative distinctiveness,[115] the UNDRIP can help to articulate justifications for both that distinct status and the necessity of a treaty relationship to reconcile the coexisting sovereignty of multiple political communities that share the land.[116] At their highest, the treaty relationship is a symbol of equal partnership, based on 'mutual recognition, mutual respect, sharing, and mutual responsibility'.[117] Without the UNDRIP framing negotiations, the nation-to-nation relationship that a treaty embeds may be dropped or otherwise lose prominence, leaving reconciliation precariously placed. This risk is particularly acute where, for constitutional reasons, negotiations are conducted by a subnational entity rather than the federal government itself.

Conclusion

Aboriginal and Torres Strait Islander peoples' agitation for structural reform of Australia's political and legal system long predates the signing of the UNDRIP in 2007. Nonetheless, the Declaration has the potential to revitalise and strengthen Indigenous advocacy for meaningful reform by acting as a framework to underpin and guide development of law and policy in Australia.[118] The absence of explicit legislative endorsement of the UNDRIP by the Victorian government, and its muted public invocations by Aboriginal Victorians, is therefore concerning. Writing in the aftermath of the General Assembly's adoption of the Declaration, Megan Davis argued that in order to shift the ground in public debate in Australia, Aboriginal and Torres Strait Islander people 'need[] to be strategic about adopting a new direction in advocacy for self-determination as underpinned by the UNDRIP'.[119] Davis considered that this new direction should be built on the moral and educative value of the Declaration.[120] Preliminary steps towards treaty in Victoria and elsewhere suggest that some Australian governments are interested in pursuing a new direction. Whether that interest is real largely depends upon whether state actors have internalised the instrument's norms and values. If they have, then treaty negotiations should result in meaningful substantive reform. If they have not, then negotiations may falter.

Developments in Australia have lessons for all modern treaty negotiations. A state's rhetorical commitment to the Declaration or ritual public incantation of its terms will not automatically lead to meaningful reform. In the absence of enforceable standards holding the state to account, asymmetrical power relations will affect the process and outcomes of any negotiation. To challenge this, Indigenous peoples could publicly use the UNDRIP and seek to embed its values within state actors. Critically, norm internationalisation will not occur if those advocating for structural reform fail to articulate their aspirations in the language of the Declaration. In the words of Claire Charters, Indigenous peoples should 'use it' rather than 'lose it'.[121]

Notes

1. Claire Charters, 'Indigenous Peoples and International Law and Policy', in *Indigenous Peoples and the Law*, eds. Benjamin J. Richardson, Shin Imai and Kent McNeil (Hart Publishing, 2009), 161, 175.
2. James Anaya and Siegfried Wiessner, 'The UN Declaration on the Rights of Indigenous Peoples: Towards Re-Empowerment', *Jurist*, October 3, 2007. http://www.jurist.org/forum/2007/10/un-declaration-on-rights-of-indigenous.php.
3. Stephen Allen and Alexandra Xanthaki, 'Introduction', in *Reflections on the UN Declaration on the Rights of Indigenous Peoples*, eds. Stephen Allen and Alexandra Xanthaki (Hart, 2011), 1, 7.
4. Expert Mechanism on the Rights of Indigenous Peoples, *Ten Years of the Implementation of the United Nations Declaration on the Rights of Indigenous Peoples: Good Practices and Lessons Learned—2007–2017*, UN Doc A/HRC/EMRIP/2017/CRP.2 (10–14 July 2017) 3, [4].
5. Kirsty Gover, 'Settler-State Political Theory, "CANZUS" and the UN *Declaration on the Rights of Indigenous Peoples*', *European Journal of International Law* 26 (2015): 345.
6. 'Australia Refuses to Sign UN Declaration on Indigenous Rights', *ABC Lateline*, September 14, 2007.
7. Jenny Macklin, 'Statement on the United Nations Declaration on the Rights of Indigenous Peoples' (Official Statement, 3 April 2009). Of course, from a purely doctrinal perspective, issuing a qualification to a General Assembly Declaration is unnecessary as they are formally non-binding. As such, it is likely that the qualification was intended to serve a rhetorical purpose.
8. Mandy Doherty and Jenny Bedford, 'Implementation of the Declaration of the Rights of Indigenous Peoples' (speech on behalf of the Australian government and Australian human rights commission to the permanent forum on indigenous issues, New York, May 22, 2013).
9. *Uluru Statement from the Heart*, cited in Referendum Council, *Final Report of the Referendum Council* (June 2017) i.
10. See generally George Williams and Megan Davis, *Everything You Need to Know about the Referendum to Recognise Indigenous Australians* (NewSouth Publishing, 2015).
11. For more information on these developments see Harry Hobbs and George Williams, 'Treaty Making in the Australian Federation', *Melbourne University Law Review* (forthcoming).
12. Megan Davis, 'Indigenous Struggles in Standard-Setting: The United Nations *Declaration on the Rights of Indigenous Peoples*', *Melbourne Journal of International Law* 9 (2008): 439, 465.

13. Carolyn Bennett, 'Speaking Notes' (address delivered to the UN permanent forum on indigenous issues, 16th Session, New York, May 10, 2016). Speech available at: 'Fully Adopting UNDRIP: Minister Bennett's Speech at the United Nations', *Northern Public Affairs*, May 11, 2016 http://www.northernpublicaffairs.ca/index/fully-adopting-undrip-minister-bennetts-speech/.
14. Megan Davis, 'The United Nations Declaration on the Rights of Indigenous Peoples', *Indigenous Law Bulletin* 6, no. 30 (2007): 6, 6.
15. Willem van Genugten and Federico Lenzerini, 'Legal Implementation and International Cooperation and Assistance: Articles 37–42', in *The UN Declaration on the Rights of Indigenous Peoples: A Commentary*, eds. Jessie Hohmann and Marc Weller (Oxford University Press, 2018), 539, 572.
16. Harry Hobbs and George Williams, 'The Noongar Settlement: Australia's First Treaty', *Sydney Law Review* 40 (2018): 1. See further Michael Mansell, *Treaty and Statehood: Aboriginal Self-Determination* (Federation Press, 2016) 99–102; Sean Brennan et al., *Treaty* (Federation Press, 2005) 3–11.
17. Michael Keating, *Plurinational Democracy: Stateless Nations in a Post-Sovereignty Era* (Oxford University Press, 2001), 27.
18. UNDRIP art 6.
19. UNDRIP art 9. See also UNDRIP art 33.
20. UNDRIP art 30(2).
21. UNDRIP arts 15(2), 17(2), 19, 32(2), 36(2), 38.
22. Permanent Forum on Indigenous Issues, 'Report of the International Workshop on Methodologies regarding Free, Prior and Informed Consent and Indigenous Peoples', UN Doc E/C.19/2005/3 (New York, January 17–19, 2005), 12 [46]–[47].
23. UNDRIP art 27.
24. James Anaya and Sergio Puig, 'Mitigating State Sovereignty: The Duty to Consult with Indigenous Peoples', *University of Toronto Law Journal* 67 (2017): 435. See also Patrick Macklem, *The Sovereignty of Human Rights* (Oxford University Press, 2015).
25. UN Commission on Human Rights, Sub-Commission on the Promotion and Protection of Human Rights Working Group on Indigenous Populations, *Preliminary Working Paper on the Principle of Free, Prior and Informed Consent of Indigenous Peoples, Submitted by Antoanella-Iulia Motoc and the Tebtebba Foundation*, 22nd sess, Agenda Item 5, UN Doc E/CN.4/Sub.2/AC.4/2004/4 (8 July 2004) [13].
26. Michael Dodson, cited in Craig Scott, 'Indigenous Self-Determination and Decolonisation of the International Imagination: A Plea', *Human Rights Quarterly* 18 (1996): 814, 814. See also Brenda Gunn, 'Self-Determination and Indigenous Women: Increasing Legitimacy through Inclusion', *Canadian Journal of Women and the Law* 26 (2014): 241, 260.
27. Davis, 'Indigenous Struggles in Standard-Setting', 459.
28. Thomas Franck, 'The Emerging Right to Democratic Governance', *American Journal of International Law* 86 (1992): 46, 52.
29. Ibid.
30. See for e.g. (2011) 20(3) *Griffith Law Review* 'Special Issue: The 2007 Declaration on the Rights of Indigenous Peoples: Indigenous Survival – Where to from Here?'
31. Irene Watson, *Aboriginal Peoples, Colonialism and International Law: Raw Law* (Routledge, 2015) 2.
32. Megan Davis, 'To Bind or not to Bind: The United Nations *Declaration on the Rights of Indigenous Peoples* Five Years On', *Australian International Law Journal* 3 (2012): 17, 47.
33. Ted Moses, Cree Leader, cited in Ronald Niezen, *The Origins of Indigenism: Human Rights and the Politics of Identity* (University of California Press, 2003) 156.
34. Davis, 'Indigenous Struggles in Standard-Setting', 470.
35. Roderic Pitty and Shannara Smith, 'The Indigenous Challenge to Westphalian Sovereignty', *Australian Journal of Political Science* 46 (2011): 121, 128.
36. UNDRIP art 9.
37. UNDRIP art 5.

38. Clive Baldwin and Cynthia Morel, 'Using the United Nations Declaration on the Rights of Indigenous Peoples in Litigation', in *Reflections on the UN Declaration on the Rights of Indigenous Peoples*, eds. Stephen Allen and Alexandra Xanthaki *Reflections on the UN Declaration on the Rights of Indigenous Peoples* (Hart, 2011), 121, 123–4.
39. See for example Javaid Rehman, 'Between the Devil and the Deep Blue Sea: Indigenous Peoples as Pawns in the US "War on Terror" and the Jihad of Osama Bin Laden', in *Reflections on the UN Declaration on the Rights of Indigenous Peoples*, eds. Stephen Allen and Alexandra Xanthaki (Hart, 2011), 561. See also James Anaya, *Promotion and Protection of all Human Rights, Civil, Political, Economic, Social and Cultural Rights, including the Right to Development*, UN Doc A/HRC/12/34 (July 15, 2009) 12–15 [38]–[42].
40. Commission on Human Rights, *Report of the Eighteenth Session*, UN ESCOR, 34th sess, Supp No 8,UN Doc E/CN.4/832/Rev.1 (March 19–April 14, 1962) 15 [105].
41. Mattias Åhrén, *Indigenous Peoples' Status in the International Legal System* (Oxford University Press, 2016), 105.
42. Amy Maguire, 'The UN Declaration on the Rights of Indigenous Peoples and Self-Determination in Australia: Using a Human Rights Approach to Promote Accountability', *New Zealand Yearbook of International Law* 12 (2014): 105, 112.
43. See Julie Fenley, 'The National Aboriginal Conference and the Makarrata: Sovereignty and Treaty Discussions, 1979–1981', *Australian Historical Studies* 42 (2011): 372.
44. Senate Standing Committee on Legal and Constitutional Affairs, Parliament of Australia, *Two Hundred Years Later…* (1981), Recommendation 1.
45. 'Barunga Festival', *Land Rights News* 2 (1988): 22–7.
46. Council for Aboriginal Reconciliation, *Reconciliation: Australia's Challenge* (Final Report of the Council for Aboriginal Reconciliation, 2000), 106, Recommendation 6; Hannah McGlade, ed., *Treaty: Let's Get it Right!* (Australian Institute of Aboriginal and Torres Strait Islander Studies, 2003).
47. Referendum Council, *Final Report of the Referendum Council*, i. The *Uluru Statement* also called for a national representative Indigenous body empowered to advise Parliament on laws that affect Indigenous peoples, as well as a process of local and regional truth-telling.
48. *Advancing the Treaty Process with Aboriginal Victorians Act 2018* (Vic).
49. *The Barunga Agreement* (June 8, 2018), 13.
50. Kyam Maher MLC, 'Treaty Speech' (Parliament House, Adelaide, December 14, 2016), https://statedevelopment.sa.gov.au/upload/aboriginal-affairs/treaty-speech.pdf?t=1504335059137; Dr Roger Thomas, *Treaty Talk: Summary of Engagements and Next Steps* (Office of the Treaty Commissioner, July 2017).
51. Michael Owen, 'Aboriginal People Failed by "Expensive Gesture" Treaties', *The Australian*, June 11, 2018, https://www.theaustralian.com.au/national-affairs/indigenous/aboriginal-people-failed-by-expensive-gesture-treaties/news-story/84b000a2f0b81c82801d93cc9a45cb3c.
52. Stephen Fitzpatrick and Michael McKenna, 'Queensland Considers Treaty Talks as Federal Bids Stall', *The Australian*, July 17, 2018, https://www.theaustralian.com.au/national-affairs/indigenous/queensland-considers-treaty-talks-as-federal-bids-stall/news-story/1431f48699d2085e65631efcb9e55a02.
53. Calla Wahlquist, 'NSW Labor Plans to Sign Treaty Recognising Indigenous Ownership', *Guardian Australia*, January 25, 2018, https://www.theguardian.com/australia-news/2018/jan/25/nsw-labor-plans-to-sign-treaty-recognising-indigenous-ownership.
54. Matthew Denholm, 'Tasmanian Labor promises Aboriginal Treaty Talks', *The Australian*, June 1, 2017, http://www.theaustralian.com.au/national-affairs/indigenous/tasmanian-labor-promises-aboriginal-treaty-talks/news-story/a5352d573913ce86794ff641a37806bc. See further Hobbs and Williams, 'Treaty Making in the Australian Federation'.
55. Gian De Poloni, 'WA Premier Signs $1.3 Billion Noongar Native Title Settlement', *ABC News*, June 8, 2015, http://www.abc.net.au/news/2015-06-08/premier-signs-noongar-native-title-settlement/6530434.
56. Hobbs and Williams, 'The Noongar Settlement'.

57. Western Australia, *Parliamentary Debates*, Legislative Assembly, November 19, 2015, 8688.
58. Hamish Fitzsimons, 'Victorian Government to Begin Talks With First Nations on Australia's First Indigenous Treaty', *ABC News*, February 26, 2016, http://www.abc.net.au/news/2016-02-26/victoria-to-begin-talks-for-first-indigenous-treaty/7202492.
59. Aboriginal Victoria, *Summary of the Aboriginal Victoria Forum, May 26–27, 2016, Melbourne* (2016) 1.
60. Aboriginal Victoria, *Aboriginal Treaty Interim Working Group, Terms of Reference* (2017).
61. Ibid., TOR 4.
62. Aboriginal Treaty Interim Working Group, *Aboriginal Community Consultations on the Design of a Representative Body* (December 2016).
63. Aboriginal Treaty Interim Working Group, *Aboriginal Community Consultations on the Design of a Representative Body—Phase 2* (June 2017) 9.
64. Aboriginal Treaty Interim Working Group, *Treaty Circle Facilitators Handbook* (2017), 27.
65. Ibid.
66. Aboriginal Treaty Interim Working Group, *Aboriginal Community Consultations on the Design of a Representative Body—Phase 2*, 6.
67. NITV Staff Writer, 'Victorian Government Commits $28.5M for Treaty Discussions, Amid Confusion and Criticism', *NITV News*, May 2, 2017, http://www.sbs.com.au/nitv/nitv-news/article/2017/05/01/victorian-government-commits-285m-treaty-discussions-amid-confusion-and-criticism.
68. Aboriginal Victoria, 'Victorian Treaty Advancement Commission', https://www.vic.gov.au/aboriginalvictoria/treaty/victorian-treaty-advancement-commission.html.
69. *Aboriginal Community Assembly Information Handbook: Continuing on the Journey towards Treaty* (2017) 15.
70. Aboriginal Community Assembly, *Final Statement and Recommendations to the Aboriginal Treaty Working Group* (December 2017), 3.
71. Reconciliation Victoria, 'Jill Gallagher Named Victorian Treaty Advancement Commissioner', http://www.reconciliationvic.org.au/news/jill-gallagher-named-victorian-treaty-advancement-commissioner.php.
72. *Advancing the Treaty Process with Aboriginal Victorians Act 2018* (Vic), ss 21–5.
73. Will Kymlicka, 'Beyond the Indigenous/Minority Dichotomy?', in *Reflections on the UN Declaration on the Rights of Indigenous Peoples*, eds. Stephen Allen and Alexandra Xanthaki, (Hart, 2011), 183, 188. See UNDRIP arts 6, 8(1)–(2), 9, 33, 36(1).
74. Claire Charters, 'Use It or Lose It: The Value of Using the Declaration on the Rights of Indigenous Peoples in Māori Legal and Political Claims', in *International Indigenous Rights in Aotearoa New Zealand*, ed. Andrew Erueti (Victoria University of Wellington Press, 2017), 137, 151.
75. Advancing the Treaty Process with Aboriginal Victorians 2018 Bill (introduced 7 March 2018).
76. Greens Amendments, item 24, proposed insertion of Clause E after Clause 21; Victoria, *Parliamentary Debates*, Legislative Assembly, June 7, 2018 (clause defeated); Victoria, *Parliamentary Debates*, Legislative Council, June 21, 2018, 2924 (clause negatived).
77. *Advancing the Treaty Process with Aboriginal Victorians 2018 Act* (Vic), preamble (emphasis added).
78. Aboriginal Victoria, *Working with Aboriginal Intangible Heritage*, https://www.vic.gov.au/aboriginalvictoria/heritage/aboriginal-intangible-heritage-in-victoria/working-with-aboriginal-intangible-heritage.html (accessed July 19, 2018).
79. Victoria, *Parliamentary Debates*, Legislative Assembly, March 27, 2018, 806–7.
80. Victoria, *Parliamentary Debates*, Legislative Assembly, March 28, 2018, 871 (Narelle Hutchins, Minister for Aboriginal Affairs), June 5, 2018, 1723 (Lily D'Ambrosio), 1738 (Sonya Kilkenny), 1741 (Steve Dimopoulos), June 7, 2018, 1923–4 (Richard Wynne, Narelle Hutchins); Legislative Council, June 21, 2018, 2915, 2925 (Gavin Jennings). No members of the Opposition have cited the UNDRIP. Accurate as of January 14, 2019.
81. Victoria, *Parliamentary Debates*, Legislative Assembly, November 26, 2015, 5132 (Narelle Hutchins).

82. Victoria, *Parliamentary Debates*, Legislative Assembly, October 8, 2015, 3668 (Anthony Carbines); Victoria, *Parliamentary Debates*, Legislative Assembly, October 20, 2015, 3805 (Heidi Victoria; opposition member).
83. Daniel Andrews, 'Closing the Gap – Premier's Speech', March 19, 2015.
84. Victoria, *Parliamentary Debates*, Legislative Assembly, November 26, 2015, 5132 (Narelle Hutchins, Minister for Aboriginal Affairs).
85. Victoria, *Parliamentary Debates*, Legislative Assembly, June 22, 2017, 2061 (Narelle Hutchins, Minister for Aboriginal Affairs).
86. Victoria, *Victorian Budget 18/19: Getting Things Done – Overview* (2018), 40.
87. Victoria, *Parliamentary Debates*, Legislative Council, November 8, 2016, 5851 (Mr Herbert).
88. *Traditional Owner Settlement Amendment Act 2016* (Vic); Victoria, *Parliamentary Debates*, Legislative Council, November 8, 2016, 5837 (Gayle Tierney).
89. Aboriginal Treaty Interim Working Group, *Aboriginal Community Consultations on the Design of a Representative Body—Phase 2*, 6.
90. Victoria, *Parliamentary Debates*, Legislative Assembly, March 28, 2018, 870.
91. Victoria, *Parliamentary Debates*, Legislative Council, June 8, 2018, 2571 (Gavin Jennings).
92. Jill Gallagher, 'The Treaty Process in Victoria' (address to the public law conference, *The Frontiers of Public Law*, University of Melbourne, 13 July 2018).
93. Rachel Hocking, 'Where is Treaty at in Victoria', *NITV News*, April 17, 2017 http://www.sbs.com.au/nitv/nitv-news/article/2017/04/17/where-treaty-victoria. Thorpe became the first Aboriginal woman elected to the Victorian Parliament after a by-election in November 2017.
94. UNDRIP art 43.
95. Kyam Maher MLC, 'Treaty Speech' (Parliament House, Adelaide, December 14, 2016) https://statedevelopment.sa.gov.au/upload/aboriginal-affairs/treaty-speech.pdf?t=1504335059137.
96. Kirsty Gover, 'The Honour of the Crowns: State–Indigenous Fiduciary Relationships and Australian Exceptionalism', *Sydney Law Review* 38 (2016): 339.
97. *R v Badger* [1996] 1 SCR 771, 794 [41] (La Forest, L'Heureux-Dubé, Gonthier, Cory and Iacobucci JJ).
98. Julie Jai, 'Bargains Made in Bad Times: How Principles from Modern Treaties can Reinvigorate Historic Treaties', in *The Right Relationship: Reimagining the Implementation of Historical Treaties*, eds. John Borrows and Michael Coyle (University of Toronto Press, 2017), 105, 117.
99. For example, for criticism of the 1975 James Bay and Northern Quebec Agreement see: Paul Rynard, '"Welcome In, But Check Your Rights at the Door", The James Bay and Nisga'a Agreements in Canada', *Canadian Journal of Political Science* 33 (2000): 211, 217.
100. Canada, *Parliamentary Debates*, House of Commons, Vol 148, no. 264, February 14, 2018, 17219 (Justin Trudeau); Bill C-262 (2016).
101. John Horgen, 'Statement from Premier John Horgan on the 10th Anniversary of the UN Declaration on the Rights of Indigenous Peoples' (Media Release, 13 September 2017).
102. Bennett,'Speaking Notes'.
103. British Columbia Treaty Commission, *Annual Report 2016* (2017), 1.
104. British Columbia Ministry of Indigenous Relations and Reconciliation, *2018/19–2020/21 Service Plan* (2018), 6.
105. Blaine Favel and Ken Coates, *Understanding UNDRIP* (McDonald-Laurier, 2016), 10.
106. Jason Tockman, 'Eliding Consent in Extractivist States: Bolivia, Canada, and the UN Declaration on the Rights of Indigenous Peoples', *The International Journal of Human Rights* 22 (2018): 325, 338.
107. Ravi de Costa, 'History, Democracy, and Treaty Negotiations in British Columbia', in *The Power of Promises: Rethinking Indian Treaties in the Pacific Northwest*, ed. Alexandra Harmon (University of Washington Press, 2008), 297, 305.
108. Taiaiake Alfred, 'Deconstructing the British Columbia Treaty Process', *Balayi: Culture, Law and Colonialism* 3 (2001): 37, 39–43.
109. James Tully, 'Reconsidering the B.C. Treaty Process', in *Speaking Truth to Power: A Treaty Forum* (British Columbia Treaty Commission, 2000), 3, 8.

110. John Borrows, 'Practical Recolonisation?', *UNSW Law Journal* 28 (2005): 614.
111. Michael Owen, 'Aboriginal People Failed by "Expensive Gesture" Treaties', *The Australian*, June 11, 2018, https://www.theaustralian.com.au/national-affairs/indigenous/aboriginal-people-failed-by-expensive-gesture-treaties/news-story/84b000a2f0b81c82801d93cc9a45cb3c.
112. Patrick Macklem, 'The Constitutional Identity of Indigenous Peoples in Canada: Status Groups or Federal Actors?' (working paper, https://papers.ssrn.com/sol3/papers.cfm?abstract_id=2956605), 12. To be published in Andrew Arato, Jean Cohen and Astrid von Busekist, eds., *Forms of Pluralism and Democratic Constitutionalism* (Columbia University Press, 2018).
113. James [Sakej] Henderson, 'Interpreting Sui Generis Treaties', *Alberta Law Review* 37 (1997): 46, 46.
114. Russel Lawrence Barsh and James Youngblood Henderson, *The Road: Indian Tribes and Political Liberty* (University of California Press, 1980), 270. See further James Youngblood Henderson, 'Empowering Treaty Federalism', *Saskatchewan Law Review* 58 (1994): 241, 323.
115. Harry Hobbs, 'Constitutional Recognition and Reform: Developing an Inclusive Australian Citizenship through Treaty', *Australian Journal of Political Science* 52 (2018): 176.
116. British Columbia Treaty Commission, *Annual Report 2016*, 17: 'It leads to the recognition of Nation-to-Nation relationships, a recognition that shapes the negotiations and leads to constitutionally entrenched treaties.'
117. Paul Patton, 'The "Lessons of History"', in *Empire by Treaty: Negotiating European Expansion 1600–1900*, ed. Saliha Belmessous (OUP, 2014), 243, 250.
118. Davis, 'Indigenous Struggles in Standard-Setting', 465.
119. Megan Davis, 'Indigenous Rights and the Constitution: Making the Case for Constitutional Reform', *Indigenous Law Bulletin* 7, no. 6 (2008): 6, 8.
120. Davis, 'Indigenous Struggles in Standard-Setting', 468.
121. Charters,'Use It or Lose It'. See also Michael Dodson, quoted in Australian Human Rights Commission, *The Community Guide to the UN Declaration on the Rights of Indigenous Peoples* (2010), 65.

Acknowledgements

Thanks to Stephen Young, Gabrielle Appleby, participants at the 10th Anniversary of the UN Declaration on the Rights of Indigenous Peoples: Conference to Review Progress and Challenges, University of London, 20 October 2017, and the anonymous reviewer for helpful comments on earlier drafts.

Disclosure statement

No potential conflict of interest was reported by the author.

ORCID

Harry Hobbs http://orcid.org/0000-0001-9903-6908

The self divided: the problems of contradictory claims to Indigenous peoples' self-determination in Australia

Stephen M. Young

ABSTRACT
When the United Nations General Assembly endorsed the *United Nations Declaration on the Rights of Indigenous Peoples* ('*UNDRIP*') in 2007, many extolled it for recognising Indigenous peoples' right of self-determination. Although there is some consensus that all peoples have self-determination, as a legal claim it has routinely inspired criticism that it will lead to contradictory claims, interpretations, and further political contestation. Ten years after *UNDRIP*'s endorsement, some Indigenous claims of self-determination in Australia are contradictory. While contradictory claims may not be inherently problematic, in the context explored in this article, there are problematic effects. This article examines how contradictory self-determination claims arose in response to Australia's recent *Native Title Amendment (Indigenous Land Use Agreements) Act 2017* (Cth) ('*2017 Amendments*'), which amended and weakened the *Native Title Act 1993* (Cth) *('NTA')*. It also evaluates the consequences of those contradictory claims and argues for renewed critical assessment of who legitimately determines the self who claims self-determination.

Introduction

In 2007 the UN General Assembly endorsed the *UNDRIP*.[1] It recognised Indigenous peoples' self-determination,[2] which other international instruments had not previously done.[3] With international recognition that Indigenous peoples have self-determination, in theory, international law no longer regulated those individuals and communities as minorities of State populations[4] – a classification many resisted.[5] Since then, scholars, advocates and Indigenous peoples have constructed an immense body of scholarship on self-determination with a particular focus on Indigenous peoples' self-determination.[6] In some ways, the amount of scholarship on Indigenous peoples and self-determination reflects longstanding historical concerns about the concept. For instance, when Woodrow Wilson proposed 'self-determination' in a draft League of Nations charter, his delegation and fellow allies dismissed it.[7] Wilson's Secretary of State Robert Lansing said that self-determination was, 'loaded with dynamite . . . . In the end it is bound to be discredited, to be called the dream of an idealist, who failed to realize the danger until too late'.[8] Lansing was critical of Woodrow's 'idealism' because identifying one group as a holder of self-determination would deny it to a competing group.[9] Later, Michla Pomerance would later assert that 'the first and pivotal question is: who is the "self" to whom the right of self-determination attaches?'[10] Questioning the 'self' to whom the right attaches is as pertinent as ever, especially in the Indigenous rights context when claims of self-determination contradict each other.

When *UNDRIP* was endorsed, Canada, Australia, New Zealand and the United States voted against it.[11] They claimed, among other issues, that self-determination was legally unworkable.[12] When those States endorsed *UNDRIP* in 2009 or 2010, they upheld the instrument as aspirational.[13] Today, Indigenous people are claiming self-determination. And one might adopt a view, like James Tully's, that settler-states that have illegitimately asserted sovereignty on colonial and imperial bases have opportunities to legitimate their sovereign claims by recognising Indigenous peoples' equal status as sovereigns and negotiating with them on a 'nation-to-nation' basis.[14] While that would seem to predominantly benefit States, Tully also writes that Indigenous peoples 'struggle within the structure of domination vis-à-vis techniques of government, by exercising their freedom of thought and action with the aim of modifying the system in the short term and transforming it from within in the long term'.[15]

But a careful examination of State legal contexts reveals that identifying the 'self' to whom self-determination attaches remains a pivotal question – especially when self-determination claims contradict one another. The problem is not that self-determination is legally unworkable, as those settler-states originally maintained. Problems arise, as Patrick Macklem writes, because '[a] community is not an indigenous people in international law until a State or group of State recognizes it as such'.[16] Although Indigenous peoples can self-identify, Macklem's point is that State actors must recognise a community as Indigenous peoples to uphold and enforce international law's human rights for them. And if, as evaluated here, self-determination ostensibly provides groups or communities with the power to determine their selves, that power is undermined to the extent States play a role in recognising, determining, or constructing which self has self-determination. I agree with Tully that when Indigenous peoples assert self-determination, settler-states have an opportunity to legitimate its sovereign claims by recognising Indigenous peoples' equal status as sovereigns and negotiating with them on a 'nation-to-nation' basis.[17] But where a State plays a role in recognising the self, those who struggle within the structure of domination vis-à-vis techniques of government, are also discursively modified and transformed through exercises of their freedom of thought to be recognisable as a Nation.[18]

When contradictory self-determination claims arise, theorising 'who are Indigenous peoples',[19] or 'what is self-determination',[20] cannot answer how States choose to recognise a community as a Nation or as Indigenous people with self-determination. Asking those questions belies Wilson's idealism in expropriating legal subjects and objects from existing legal contexts and fails to address Pomerance's 'first and pivotal question'. As argued here, who the State recognises cannot be apprehended by retrospectively reading who 'wins' and 'loses' cases or claims. Instead, this article builds upon Judith Butler's acknowledgement that 'the law produces and then conceals the notion of "a subject before the law" in order to invoke that discursive formation as a naturalized foundational premise that subsequently legitimates that law's own regulatory hegemony'.[21] As such, this article makes a methodological intervention based upon Butler's notion of performativity to problematise how State laws are involved in producing the subjects it recognises, which legitimates the State's own regulatory and colonial hegemony. I argue that States recognise those Indigenous peoples who performatively replicate the exclusionary domain of a Nation, which the State then includes within its regulatory domain as a subject.[22] The State does so to legitimate its own assertions of sovereignty as well as the nation-hood and self-determination claims of those it recognises, which are those claimants who work alongside and do not attempt to undermine or question the State. One effect is a modification and transformation of the particular social, political economic relationships between the State and the claimant it recognises, which maintains as it reproduces the structural social, political and economic colonial status quo.[23] Another effect is that the State's validation of that performative also creates a domain of 'abject' beings.[24] Butler explains that entrance of 'a subject before the law' into an exclusionary domain also produces 'abject beings, those who are not yet "subjects" but who form the constitutive outside to the domain of the subject'.[25] As we will see, those who claim self-determination which the State does not recognise, and despite their self-identify as a people or a nation, are treated as minorities. The contradictory claims of self-determination that arose in response Australia's recent *2017 Amendments* of the *NTA* reveal how the State recognises those Indigenous people who construct themselves in ways that mirror the exclusionary domain of a Nation by themselves contributing to the production of their own abject beings, National minorities.

Because this article examines and problematises the role of the State in producing who is identified as having self-determination, Section 1 provides a succinct history of the construction of the Australian Nation, Australia's Native Title regime, and the human rights criticism that arose of it in 1998. Section 2 examines the case law that led to the *2017 Amendments* and excavates how the *NTA* produced legal struggles which gave rise to contradictory self-determination claims. Section 3 then discusses and analyses how State actors identify, select, or side with those self-determination claimants that support and reproduce the exclusionary domains of State legality and some consequences.

A brief history of *NTA*, 1998 human rights criticism, and the *Bygrave* standard

This section provides a succinct history of the construction of the Australian Nation, its native title regime, and the human rights criticism that arose of it in 1998. It reveals how the colonies asserted that it was 'people', became a Nation, included Aboriginal and Torres Strait Islanders in its definition of 'people', and recognised native title, while continuously maintaining an exclusionary domain. It then begins to examine how and when international human rights of Indigenous people were used to critique Australia's native title.

The people identified today as Aboriginal and Torres Strait Islander peoples have, according to the Western archaeological discipline, inhabited what is known as Australia anywhere from 50,000 to 60,000 years ago.[26] Colonists landed and established a penal colony in 1788 that they named New South Wales. It became a formal colony in 1823,[27] with additional settlements forming throughout the nineteenth century. In the late nineteenth century, the colonies asserted that they were a 'people' and become a Federated Commonwealth – a Nation – which the British Parliament and then Queen Victoria assented to in 1901.[28] The Commonwealth's understanding of 'the people' excluded Aboriginal and Torres Strait Islanders,[29] which reveals the Australian Nation's exclusionary domain at that time. It become more overtly inclusive when, in 1967, the Australian people voted to amend the Constitution to include Aboriginal and Torres Strait Islander peoples in the census and allow the Commonwealth to create laws for them. Even if Aboriginal and Torres Strait Islanders became recognisable citizens of the State, the State did not yet recognise a 'native' title to property.

In 1992, *Mabo v Queensland (No. 2)* ('*Mabo*') found that native title and Crown sovereignty co-existed, but only where the Crown had not exhibited a 'clear and plain intention' to extinguish native title.[30] Regarding extinguishment, Irene Watson charges that it is a 'power of colonialism' the State has 'assumed to determine that First Nations Peoples' title to land no longer exists'.[31] In comparison, Watson argues that 'the philosophical and jurisprudential frameworks that underpin First Nations laws do not enable the extinguishment of law to occur'.[32] Essentially, the application of common law produced a new type of subject, a native title claimant that had extinguishable title, and then concealed the notion of the subject before law, by stating that had always been the case.[33] The abject domain then contained, as an example, First Nation laws that do not enable the extinguishment of their law.

In the year after *Mabo*, Parliament passed the *NTA*. Damien Short explains that 'commercial interests lobbied the government to ensure that when [native title] rights were institutionalized via legislation, they would pose no threat to commercial interests and maintain existing inequalities'.[34] Commercial interests were able to do so by transforming a right claim that posed a 'minor problem for an enormously affluent industrial lobby' into a 'national crisis'.[35] The result was that one of the *NTA*'s objectives was to 'establish ways in which future dealings affecting native title may proceed and to set standards for those dealings'.[36] To provide that objective with legal effect, the *NTA* created a Future Dealings process called the Right to Negotiate (RTN). It sought to facilitate development projects by validly extinguishing native title rights that conflict with those proposed land uses. As initially created, the RTN is a structured negotiation process facilitated by the National Native Title Tribunal (NNTT). It enables grantees (developers) to petition the NNTT or Minister to decide whether the development may proceed.[37] Under that process, the members of the registered native title claimant (RNTC) can agree to an RTN, which may extinguish native title rights. Where RNTC members do not agree, then so long as six months of negotiation have taken place and the developer exhibits good faith, the NNTT or Minister must determine that the 'doing of the act' may be done or not.[38] The RTN has and continues to override native title claimants' objections and may extinguish native title where the grantee may do the act[39] – which Watson identified, above, as the 'power of colonialism'. Essentially, the Australian legal system's identification of native title rights produces those claimants, who the RNTC represents, and their extinguishable rights.

The 1997 *Wik Peoples v Queensland* case held that pastoral leases were not granted under the common law so that pastoral leases and native title could exist over the same lands.[40] In response, Parliament passed the *Native Title Amendment Act 1998* (Cth) ('*1998 Amendments*'). The *1998 Amendments* were another legislative reaction to a judicial opinion that, borrowing from Short, 'would pose no threat to commercial interests and maintain existing inequalities'.[41] It also added a second Future Dealings process called Indigenous Land Use Agreements (ILUAs). ILUAs sought to 'facilitate the negotiation of voluntary but binding agreements as an alternative to more formal native title machinery' outside of the NNTT's structuring.[42] However, for the NNTT to register an ILUA, members of the RNTC need to approve it. Who or what comprises the RNTC, how the law produces its subjects, and how subjects produce themselves to be identifiable within the settler-state are the central issues explored below.

Adding the ILUAs process increased flexibility and efficiency of the *NTA*, but the *1998 Amendments* drew significant criticism.[43] Importantly, the United Nation Committee for the Elimination of Racial Discrimination (CERD) criticised the *1998 Amendments* as inconsistent with the *International Convention on the Elimination of All Forms of Racial Discrimination* and Australia's *Racial Discrimination Act*.[44] CERD noted that the 'provisions ... replace the right to negotiate with the lesser right to be consulted and to object to the land use', and criticised Australia's narrowing of what native title claims would be considered valid.[45] It also noted that the *1998 Amendments* were inconsistent with its General Recommendations XXI and XXIII, which require States to recognise Indigenous self-determination and ensure that 'no decisions directly relating to [Indigenous] rights and interests are taken without their informed consent'.[46] The Expert Mechanism on the Rights of Indigenous Peoples notes that free, prior and informed consent (FPIC) 'needs to be understood in the context of indigenous peoples' right to self-determination because it is an integral element of that right'.[47] *UNDRIP* recognises both FPIC and self-determination.[48] Parliament never amended the *NTA* to address CERD's criticisms.

CERD's criticisms of the *NTA* are significant for at least two reasons. First, CERD's criticisms may act as a yardstick for measuring the *NTA* against international human rights law. And, second, to the extent CERD's criticism is treated as yardstick – some sort of objective standard for measurement – it treats the subject of those rights claims, Indigenous peoples, as an idealised or abstract subject. The subject is 'idealised' or 'abstract' in the sense that CERD treats all Aboriginal and Torres Strait Islanders as a singular or collective 'Indigenous peoples' – a singular self with international legal subjectivity – that opposes the *1998 Amendments* for not upholding its self-determination and FPIC. As explored below, when Aboriginal communities claim self-determination and FPIC, they do not always act as a singular or collective self nor are those claims always against legislative amendment.

Although there are cases after 1998 that alter and narrow the *NTA*,[49] the next case described here, which also reveals how the law discursively produces its subjects, is from 2010. In 2010, a Federal Court evaluated the composition of the RNTC – those who can agree to an ILUA – in *QGC Pty Ltd v Bygrave (No 2)* ('*Bygrave*').[50] In *Bygrave*, a natural gas company sought to enter into an ILUA with the Iman peoples. The company obtained eight of nine signatures of the Iman listed as the RNTC members. The ninth named RNTC member refused to sign, and hence the NNTT refused to give notice for the ILUA's registration, effectively prohibiting it from being registered.[51] A question in *Bygrave* was whether the RNTC was a 'collective entity' or comprised of all individuals members of the RNTC.[52] Justice Reeves found that the RNTC was not a legal person, so it was neither a collective entity nor all the named individuals. Instead, Reeves held that the RNTC was one or more persons named in the RNTC acting in a representative capacity, so the ILUA was registerable despite one member withholding their signature.[53] In short, Justice Reeves interpreted and shaped the RNTC to represent a majority interest, which made registering ILUAs more flexible and economically efficient by weakening the ILUA registration standard.

Experts estimate that between 2010 and 2017, industry members entered into around 120 ILUAs with Aboriginal and Torres Strait Islander RNTCs under the *Bygrave* standard.[54] In early 2017, a Full Federal Court decided *McGlade v Native Title Registrar* ('*McGlade*'),[55] which overturned *Bygrave* and held that all RNTC members must agree to an ILUA to be registrable. Commonwealth Parliament then proposed and eventually passed the *2017 Amendments* in response *McGlade*, which reinstituted the *Bygrave* standard. The contradictory claims of self-determination, which are the primary focus this article, arose in response to the proposed *2017 Amendments*. The following section analyses the cases leading to the *2017 Amendments* for how they produce contradictory self-determination claims.

The contradictory claims of self-determination

The next two sub-sections examine and evaluate how self-determination claims arose in two contexts, the Noongar's and the Wangan and Jagalingou's. Regardless of whether the self-determination claimants support or oppose the *2017 Amendments*, claiming it expresses individual and community interests. However, the claims arose out of problems the *NTA* produced, which has implications for understanding how the State plays a role in determining who has self-determination.

Noongar claims to self-determination

The *McGlade* case involved Noongar communities in southwest Australia. It sought to resolve controversies that arose in two cases that were read together, *Bennell v Western Australia* ('*Bennell*'); *Bodney v State of Western Australia* ('*Bodney*').[56] In those cases, a Federal court interrogated who legally comprises the Noongar to resolve the contradictory six native title claims that the petitioners presented. In *Bennell*, 80 applicants acting on behalf of all Noongar – and positioning itself as the Noongar Nation – brought one native title claim to cover the entirety of south-west Western Australia. That claim arose from the South West Aboriginal Land and Sea Council's (SWALSC's) efforts to aggregate all outstanding native title claims into a single claim for the entirety of Noongar country.[57] In *Bodney*, petitioners presented the other five native title claims. They asserted native title claims to Perth and the surrounding urban areas, which were territories the *Bennell* petitioners also claimed. As such, the *Bodney* and *Bennell* native title claims conflicted: if the *Bennell* claimants proved their claims, it would be detrimental to the *Bodney* claims, and vice versa. The *Bennell* claimants asserted that the Noongar peoples and, hence, the Noongar Nation observed their own laws and customs when settlers formed Western Australia in 1829 as they do today.[58] On the other hand, the *Bodney* petitioners asserted there were multiple groups with distinct interests. They sought to preserve their interests against the *Bennell* petitioner. The Australian Commonwealth, the State of Western Australia, local government, and industry groups also asserted there were multiple groups with distinct issues because the *Bennell* petitioner's far larger claims could presumably undermine Western Australia's and Perth's colonial legitimacy and some commercial interests.

Presiding over the cases, Justice Wilcox, noted that the Noongar had several dialects, but found that

> a striking feature of the evidence of the Aboriginal witnesses was that none of them treated their local name as a sufficient, or even primary, statement of their identity. Each of them strongly asserted they were "Noongar", although a Noongar associated with a particular local group.[59]

In constituting the Noongar as a singular people, Wilcox upheld the *Bennell* claims to the detriment of the *Bodney* claims (as well as government and industry interests).[60] Wilcox did not determine the precise nature of the native title rights, whether native title rights existed, were extinguished, or if the Noongar were entitled to compensation.[61] The Aboriginal and Torres Strait Islander Social Justice Commission hailed *Bennell* as the 'first decision that native title existed over a capital city in Australia'.[62] Despite praise for the ruling, and because Wilcox had not determined those outstanding issues, many believed that the urban expansion of Perth extinguished most if not all of the native title rights in and around that capital city, which both the *Bodney* and *Bennell* petitioners claimed.[63] Shortly afterwards, the Full Federal Court overturned Wilcox's ruling in *Bodney v Bennell*.[64] It found that Justice Wilcox erred in treating Noongar land as a whole because, at that stage of analysis, the Noongar Nation petitioners had not proven continued observance of traditional laws and customs to all of that land since 1829.

Rather than pursue additional rounds of litigation, the Noongar Nation began negotiating a settlement with Western Australia.[65] The ability of the SWALSC to constitute itself as the Noongar Nation and pursue negotiations with Western Australia starts to reveal how State actors validate the identity on those who performatively replicate the State's exclusionary domain. That is, even if *Bodney v Bennell* overturned the ruling favouring the *Bennell* petitioners, SWALSC/Noongar Nation's negotiations with Western Australia excluded the interests of the *Bodney* petitioners. The Noongar Nation reproduced the exclusionary domain of the State and the *Bodney* petitioners thus constituted the abject domain by becoming the presumptive 'minorities' of the Noongar Nation.

Western Australia and the Noongar Nations reached an Agreement-in-Principle in October 2014. The Noongar then met, and a majority voted to approve the Agreement-in-Principle as six separate ILUAs. However, there was internal opposition. Herbert Kenneth Bropho, a co-petitioner in *Bodney v Bennell* (who supported the *Bodney* claims) told reporters that the SWALSC 'was picking and choosing the family members that were allowed in the meeting, they had a bus load of people going to the meeting who was the "yes" vote'.[66] Despite those concerns, the agreement received acclaim from politicians[67] and academics[68] – and for a good reason. It is the most comprehensive native title settlement, with some calling it Australia's 'First Treaty'.[69] It recognises the Noongar's laws, cultures and self-government, transfers 320,000 hectares of Crown land to be held in Trust for their benefit, and provides a compensatory package of $1.3 billion (AUD) for the 'loss, surrender, diminution, impairment and other effects' of any native title rights.[70] It was a good deal for both negotiating parties. The Noongar Nation received land, compensation, and recognition from Western Australia as a legitimate Nation. In turn, Western Australia maintained legal security and commercial stability by resolving all potential native title claims in the southwest, which could otherwise have questioned the legitimacy of its colonial acquisition of title. Problematically, the settlement overrode the *Bodney* petitioners' interests and traded their native title claims as well as all potential claims in Western Australia's southwest for land elsewhere. In an attempt to preserve those interests and argue that their laws were not extinguishable, the *Bodney* petitioners challenged the settlement before it went into effect.

To provide the settlement with legal effect, Western Australia passed legislation that allowed it to enter into the agreement and abide by those terms.[71] The final hurdle was registration of the six ILUAs. And this is where the *Bygrave* and *McGlade* cases become a central feature to evaluating the contradictory self-determination claims. Under *Bygrave*, the six ILUAs were registerable because a 'majority' had voted 'yes' – even though others disputed the validity of the settlement and the formation of that majority. Some RNTC members would not sign the ILUAs, choosing instead to support the *Bodney* petitioners. They challenged the ILUA registrations in *McGlade*. There, the Full Federal Court overturned *Bygrave*, holding that all RNTC members must sign an ILUA for it to be registerable by the NNTT.[72] In essence, it reinstituted the *1998 Amendments* standard so the six ILUAs that comprised the settlement were no longer registerable. While *McGlade* re-legitimated the *NTA* and the Court as the judicial arbiter of native title, it also threatened to undermine the efforts and interests of the negotiators, which includes the Noongar Nation's land, compensation and recognition as a Nation as well as Western Australia's interests in securing commercial and legal stability.

In response to *McGlade*, the Commonwealth sought to legislatively amend the *NTA* and re-institute a standard for ILUA registration that was relatively consistent with *Bygrave*. Commonwealth Attorney-General George Brandis released an Explanatory Memorandum which declared that the *2017 Amendments* were necessary because '[t]he *McGlade* decision created uncertainty in the native title sector regarding the status of areas ILUAs'.[73] Brandis's concerns were that *McGlade* called into question the validity the roughly 120 ILUAs registered between 2010 and 2017 and all outstanding but not yet registered ILUAs, including the six Noongar/Western Australia ILUAs.[74] In opposition to that view, as examined below, others claimed that Brandis's invocation of 'uncertainty' was an attempt to 'manufacture' a 'crisis' to support industry interests.[75] That claim mirrors Short's view that commercial interests were able to lobby for the *NTA* legislation by transforming a right claim that posed a 'minor problem for an enormously affluent industrial lobby' into a 'national crisis'.[76] Undoubtedly, the *2017 Amendments* would maintain and legitimate the Commonwealth's and Western Australia's legal authority and commercial interests. But because one of the reasons for passing the *2017 Amendments* was to support the Noongar Nation's settlement with Western Australia, Brandis also justified the legislation as consistent with Indigenous peoples' rights to self-determination as recognised in *UNDRIP* and elsewhere.[77] That is not necessarily inaccurate, so long as the Noongar Nation is the Indigenous people that matter for international human rights purposes. But the Noongar Nation were not the only Aboriginal claimants asserting self-determination as Indigenous peoples. Various Aboriginal communities and others submitted comments to the Senate before Parliament passed the *2017 Amendments*, many of whom cited self-determination in support or opposition.

Some Aboriginal Land Councils feared that *McGlade* cast doubt on their ILUAs and supported passing the *2017 Amendments*.[78] Likewise, SWALSC members and their supporters – those who constituted the Noongar Nation – claimed that the *2017 Amendments* supported their self-determination.[79] They saw the *2017 Amendments* as providing them with the opportunity to obtain a settlement for land rights that the Crown would have extinguished either before the *NTA* came into effect in 1993,[80] or under contemporary *NTA* processes.[81] Glen Kelly, a SWALSC member, the lead negotiator for the Noongar Nation Negotiation Team, and writing on behalf of the NNTT, noted that the *McGlade* opinion disempowered native title claimants by providing holdouts with a veto over the majority, which would be inconsistent with 'the principle of self determination and in contravention of article 3, 18, 21.1, 23, and 32.1 of the [*UNDRIP*]'.[82]

On the other hand, some Noongar claimed that the *2017 Amendments* 'crushes the Human Rights of the Noongar people' and is 'in complete disregard for the [*UNDRIP*]'.[83] Other Aboriginal groups supported this view, seeing the 'proposed amendment [as] a direct violation of our Human Right, our right to self-determining [sic] and is in direct violation of our own First Nation Law and decision-making'.[84] The Cape York Land Council argued that if Parliament passed the *2017 Amendments*, it would deprive the *McGlade* litigants of their self-determination.[85] The successful *McGlade* petitioners asserted that there were around 20,000 eligible Noongar voters and that only 1578 voted to approve the ILUAs.[86] They essentially argued that the SWALSC/Noongar Nation's negotiation with Western Australia represented a politically mobilised minority rather than a majority of Noongar. Similarly, Albert Corunna, a self-identifying 'Nyoongar Elder' of the Swan River people asserted that SWALSC did not represent them and that the *2017 Amendments* 'will allow outsiders – who have not demonstrated their connection and are not prepared to give evidence in court – to sign away our property rights'.[87]

Because the *2017 Amendments* altered the *NTA*, which is Commonwealth law, the effects would impact all potential native title claimants.

Wangan and Jagalingou claims to self-determination

In July 2014, an energy company from India, Adani, received environmental approval to develop a coal deposit in Central Queensland. As planned, the mine would be on some native title land claimed by the Wangan and Jagalingou. After Adani's negotiations with the Wangan and Jagalingou failed to obtain an ILUA, it sought approval through an RTN process.[88] In response, Adrian Burragubba submitted an 'unsolicited letter' to the NNTT reviewing Adani's RTN application.[89] In the letter, Burragubba explained that the Traditional Owners Family Representative Council ('Family Council') was a central governing body of an 'indivisible whole'. He claimed the Family Council broadly represented the

> heart of our rights as an Indigenous People, and the issue of obtaining our free, prior and informed consent for matters affecting our traditional territories, upon which we uphold all of our spiritual, cultural, family and social, environmental and economic values, rights and interests.[90]

He asserted that the Wangan and Jagalingou Elders had self-determination, the ability to decide for themselves, and would continue to reject the project.[91] Ultimately, the NNTT found that the leases could be granted as it was likely that the mine would have a net positive economic impact which would be in the public interest.[92] Burragubba then appealed that decision to the Federal Court, claiming that Adani had overinflated its economic benefits.[93] The Federal Court denied the appeal in August 2016,[94] which Burragubba then appealed to the Full Federal Court in September 2016. While litigation continued through the Courts, Adani continued to pursue an ILUA, which the Family Council opposed.

While Adani continued to pursue an ILUA, in late 2015 Adani's owner Gautam Adani held a private meeting with Australia's Prime Minister, Malcolm Turnbull in an attempt to expedite the mine development. Adani asked Turnbull to introduce a law prohibiting activists from seeking further judicial review of the mine.[95] He explained that multiple rounds of legal challenges were making the project uncertain and no 'lenders will be willing to finance it'.[96] Again, industry members sought to use legislation to secure their commercial interests against otherwise legitimate legal challenges. The State did not adopt legislation specifically to help Adani, but the Noongar conflicts would present an opportunity to amend the *NTA*.

In March 2016, a Wangan and Jagalingou claim group met and rejected an ILUA.[97] Media outlets then reported that the Wangan and Jagalingou had sought to finalise a deal, but it fell through because 'anti-coal activists [were] funding Adani opponents within the indigenous group'.[98] It quoted Irene White, a Wangan and Jagalingou member listed on the RNTC, who said,

> last year, there was majority support in a vote of the native title applicants to go ahead with the negotiations .... And then last month, this public notice appears from another greenie, an Aboriginal woman from Victoria, to stop the agreement.[99]

White continued,

> [w]e have been saying this all along, and that it is about a future for our people. Why shouldn't our kids get the opportunity to get a job, earn a living, buy a car and save up for a house just like any other Australians?[100]

In the following month, April 2016, it was reported that seven of twelve RNTC members, a majority, agreed to an ILUA.[101] Murrawah Johnson, a Family Council spokesperson, objected and accused Adani of bussing 'in a large number of people, including non-members of our claim group who have no connection to the country' to vote on the ILUA.[102] Burragubba claimed, '[w]e are disadvantaged by the law and denied our international rights of self determination and free, prior informed consent. We are required to participate in the native title regime against a backdrop of financial disadvantage and discrimination'.[103]

Under the *Bygrave* standard, which was in effect in April 2016, the ILUA was registerable even though Burragubba and other RNTC members had not signed it. As such, *McGlade* supported the Family Council's interests because the NNTT could not register the Adani ILUA without all RNTC member signatures. Because the *2017 Amendments* sought to return the ILUA registration process to the *Bygrave* standard, it threatened to undermine the Family Council's interests and would allow Adani to register the ILUA and develop the mine.

Before Parliament passed the *2017 Amendments*, the Family Council submitted comments to the Senate. They claimed that the legislation was against their self-determination and that they had not given their FPIC.[104] The Family Council published a press release that decried the 'Adani Amendment' as 'a con on the public and part of a manufactured crisis'.[105] As mentioned above, that accusation mirrors Short's analysis that industry lobbying efforts were able to pass the 1993 *NTA* legislation by transforming a judicial articulation of native title rights into a 'national crisis'.[106] The Family Council then appealed to Special Rapporteur Victoria Tauli-Corpuz, asserting that, '[t]his system does not respect indigenous peoples' right to free, prior and informed consent, including our right to give or withhold our consent to a proposed destructive project, like a mine, on our traditional lands'.[107]

On the other hand, the lawyer for the Wangan and Jagalingou native title claim group submitted a comment to Parliament that the 'majority' partially supported the *2017 Amendments.*[108]

Law's productive domain and the contradictory claims

This section analyses the way in which State law produces contradictory self-determination claims and what that means for Indigenous peoples' human rights. In examining the Noongar or the Wangan and Jagalingou struggles, it is too hasty to conclude that any group's claim of self-determination is the 'right', 'correct' or 'proper' one. Each assertion of self-determination expresses claimants' self-determination and self-interests. Each claimant is a legitimate actor with legitimate interests and various ways of self-identifying. And, yet, the self-determination claims arose from legal struggles and problems produced by the *NTA*, which shape and structure the claimants' immediate interests and, hence, their self-determination claims.

Those who claimed self-determination in support of the *2017 Amendments* did so to protect their interests, which – to some degree – State law and the *NTA* produced. Kelly saw the negotiations as a 'Nation to Nation dialogue', which he explained as:

> a chance for us, as Noongars, to come to terms with today's world and the undeniable fact that history cannot be undone, to secure recognition and rights to traditional lands and secure a footing in today's world which can be used to advance our people and our culture in a way that works today ... [109]

Resignation to the 'terms of today's world', what others have been excoriated for calling 'the tides of history',[110] to the *NTA* and its maintenance of the 'power of colonialism', shape as it produces a willingness to compromise with the State through state-sanctioned legal processes. Kelly lamented how the creation and expansion of Perth and the surrounding areas extinguished the Noongar peoples' native title claims to much of that land.[111] But, as a negotiator, he saw an opportunity to trade that presumably foregone conclusion for official recognition, economic gain, and land elsewhere. That is an immense and pragmatic achievement. The rationale underlying Kelly's views is reflected in Wangan and Jagalingou member Irene White's question, 'Why shouldn't our kids get the opportunity to get a job, earn a living, buy a car and save up for a house just like any other Australians?'[112] Like Kelly, White saw the ILUA with Adani as an opportunity to gain 'a future for our people' by negotiating over rights that they believe the State would otherwise extinguished.[113] Both sought to use available State-based legal processes to achieve some gains rather than pursue costly and expensive litigation only to find that the State extinguished their rights.

On the other hand, those who did not want to compromise with the State or enter into an ILUA held interests that were shaped by their opposition to the *NTA*. The Noongar who opposed the *2017 Amendments* viewed the settlement as eroding any future claims, and their legitimacy to question the State, by blunting opposition to the illegitimate and exclusionary practices of the State.[114] Likewise, Burragubba claimed the *2017 Amendments* were 'con on the public' and railed against being 'required to participate' in the *NTA*.[115] The Family Council and the *McGlade* and *Bodney* petitioners invoked self-determination against the *2017 Amendments* to preserve their oppositional positionality. Where they engaged in *NTA* litigation, it was to protect and establish their claims against others who believed that their rights were extinguished or extinguishable.

Whether one supported or opposed the *2017 Amendments*, the various communities' interests were produced by State laws which the communities attempted to bolster by claiming self-determination. When the contradictory claim arose, State actors could side with those who were willing to negotiate and comprise, which does several things. As a settler-state, Australia was able to legitimate its own assertions of sovereignty by recognising some Indigenous peoples' self-determination claims and negotiating with them on a 'nation-to-nation' basis.[116] When it passed the *2017 Amendments*, the State also legitimated the self-determination of the Noongar Nation, which has at least three other interrelated effects.

First, the State was able to adopt legislation that weakened the *NTA* but upheld that legislation as consistent with Indigenous peoples' human rights. As discussed above, CERD criticised the *1998 Amendments* for creating an ILUA process that weakened the substantive rights contained in the *NTA* and violating Indigenous peoples' self-determination and FPIC.[117] In 2010, *Bygrave* weakened the *NTA* standard for ILUA registration by making it easier to form and register agreements, which, in many cases, extinguishes native title rights. The *2017 Amendments* adopted a similar standard to *Bygrave*, which demonstrates a legislative weakening of the *NTA*. After the *2017 Amendments*, the *NTA* is 'weaker' than the *NTA* after the *1998 Amendments* in the sense that it increases economic flexibility and possibility of extinguishment, which maintains what Watson identifies as the 'power of colonialism'. However, it may benefit the 'majority'. But who constitutes the majority and, furthermore, what processes determine who constitutes the majority are problematised below. The State asserted that these actions were consistent with Indigenous peoples' self-determination, which some Aboriginal groups supported. This leads to the second effect.

Second, there might be a reduction in the legal-political salience of Indigenous peoples' human rights claims. For instance, if one views CERD's criticisms of the *1998 Amendments* as a yardstick for measuring Indigenous peoples' human rights, a weaker post-*2017 Amendments NTA* would be even less consistent with Australia's human rights obligations than it was after the *1998 Amendments*. But the *2017 Amendments* have not received the same criticism as the *1998 Amendments*. The Special Rapporteur on the Rights of Indigenous peoples Victoria Tauli-Corpuz commented that she was concerned about Australia's passing the *2017 Amendments* in a 'rushed through' manner, but also emphasised, 'that the principle of free, informed and prior consent does not require the consent of all'.[118] By commenting on the legislative process, and choosing not to address self-determination as a substantive issue, Tauli-Corpuz seemed to suggest that the *McGlade* standard is more burdensome than the international human right of FPIC – and that may very well be.[119] But when compared to CERD's criticisms of the *1998 Amendments*, Tauli-Corpuz's unwillingness to take a more robust stand against the

2017 Amendments, might reveal the legal-political diminution of Indigenous peoples' human rights.

The problem with that view, of course, is that there is not an idealised, abstract or singular Indigenous peoples subject, as CERD's criticism presupposes. Instead, there are communities, groups, individuals, peoples and nations who have competing and contradictory approaches to State law who can invoke self-determination to support their interests. And in appreciating that, Tauli-Corpuz's unwillingness to adopt a more critical stance towards the *2017 Amendments* could be viewed as a strategic and sophisticated way of upholding the self-determination claims of the Noongar Nation as well as the putative majority of the Wangan and Jagalingou. And because there were contradictory self-determination claims, Tauli-Corpuz may also have – whether wittingly or not – legitimated State and industry interests too. And this relates to the third insight.

Third, and potentially most problematic, the State's ability to choose from among contradictory positions implicitly relied on State laws and processes to produce majority and minority positions, which the State could then legitimately uphold as constitutive of the majority interests. Questioning which group constitutes a majority returns us, in international law, to Pomerance's 'first and pivotal question': 'who is the "self" to whom the right of self-determination attaches?'[120] One could believe that State law merely clarifies or discovers who is or is not the minority. But that belief does not reveal how the Noongar Nation positioned and constructed itself to negotiate with the State or how others excluded as minorities. It further presupposes that majorities and minorities had been previously and firmly constructed or delineated and that the State was always going to negotiate with the Noongar Nation. That is untenable to believe. *Bennell v Western Australia* ('*Bennell*'); *Bodney v State of Western Australia* ('*Bodney*') demonstrates that the Australian Commonwealth, the State of Western Australia, and local government initially opposed the native title claims of the Noongar Nation when those judicial claims could have undermined State legitimacy and commercial interests. State legal processes do not merely clarify or discover who is or is not a minority. Instead, State legal processes structure, create and produce what it recognises as the majority positions.[121] As the following explains, when the State legitimated those who sought to compromise with the State by using State laws and processes, the State re-established its own legitimacy as a sovereign by legitimating the self-identity of those it recognised. The State constructed those who did not wish to compromise, those who maintained positions that were more oppositional to the State and its processes, as minorities. Consider how this happened.

When the government of Western Australia chose to negotiate with the Noongar Nation Negotiation Team, it excluded the *Bodney* or *McGlade* petitioners and their interests, who then became identifiable as minorities of the Noongar Nation. In choosing to negotiate, the State validated a delineation between majority and minority positions which had been pre-constructed by State law. The SWALSC-qua-Noongar Nation is a land council corporation registered according to Western Australia's law,[122] where the *Bodney* or *McGlade* petitioners are not. The SWALSC formed itself into the Noongar Nation

> to come to terms with today's world and … secure recognition and rights to traditional lands and secure a footing in today's world which can be used to advance our people and our culture in a way that works today.[123]

Stephen Cornell reads the events retrospectively – where the State had already legitimated the majority – to explain that 'the Noongar Nation has used the native title process and land claims to assert the nationhood of a dispersed Indigenous population, taking a host of disparate claims and consolidating them under the umbrella of a Noongar Nation'.[124] Although not inaccurate, it depends on as it presumes the legitimacy of the State and the Nation over the other more oppositional claims. For instance, Cornell's assertion belies a reading that some Noongars, I assume, would dispute. He re-signifies those who may self-identify as Indigenous people, including the *McGlade* and *Bodney* petitioners,[125] as members of an 'Indigenous population' who brought 'disparate claims' to be managed and properly represented by the majority-Nation. That retrospective reading upholds the self-determination of the Noongar Nation but negates or overlooks that the so-called minorities are self-identifying people attempting to express their self-determination. Of course, those who formed themselves into the Noongar Nation performatively upheld themselves as a Nation to express their self-determination. That means, even if the Noongars had sovereignty, self-determination, and identified as a Nation before being recognised by the State, it is the State's recognition that confers legitimacy on that determined self as those Indigenous peoples with self-determination. And in further submitting to and using the native title processes, they include themselves within the exclusionary domain of the State and reproduce that exclusionary domain by upholding itself as *the* Noongar Nation.

Regarding the constitution of the majority and minority of the Wangan and Jagalingou, Justice Reeves (the same judge in *Bygrave*) previously compared how individuals constituted the Family Council to how many had voted for the April 2016 ILUA to find that the Family Council represents a 'minority' interest of the Wangan and Jagalingou.[126] When the State passed the *2017 Amendments*, it validated the claims and interests of the majorities, which State laws produced by delineating them from the minority positions of the abject domain. In the Noongar and Wangan and Jagalingou contexts, those who use State process or conform to State laws were identified by the State as the majorities.

In both scenarios, the newly formed 'minorities' actively disputed who the majorities were and that the formation of a 'majority' was legitimate. The *McGlade* petitioners stated that they were not minorities of the Noongar Nation.[127] They accused SWALSC of bussing in select members to approve the ILUAs,[128] which was a numerical minority of eligible voters[129] and reflected an interest of 'outsiders'.[130] Similarly, the Family Council maintained that Adani bussed in 'a "rent-a-crowd" of persons who had never previously identified as Wangan and Jagalingou people' to approve the April 2016 ILUA.[131] The Family Council maintains that almost seventy-five per cent of those who approved the April 2016 ILUA are not 'true and valid Wangan and Jagalingou people'.[132] By casting doubt on the representation and identification of the others, they attempted to performatively construct themselves as true, self-determining Indigenous peoples.

Wither self-determination?

The Australian State's settlement with and recognition of the Noongar Nation is remarkable. The settlement is likely a positive development for the Noongar Nation, but not all Noongar peoples and perhaps not the majority. While the struggle for self-determination continues, it is not a struggle that can be apprehended by considering who 'wins' claims.

As argued here, understanding how States come to recognise a community as Indigenous peoples involves excavating the productive and formative aspects of State law and legal practice. In the situations explored in this article, State legal processes constructed and delineated the majority who has a self from the minority who belong to the abject domain. When the majority subjected itself to legal processes to compromise with the State, which State actors supported by negotiating with them and then passing the *2017 Amendments*, it appears the State has upheld the majority of Indigenous peoples' self-determination. But before the State did that, it was not clear if there was majority position. And after the State has done so, it is not clear whose majority was upheld.

The passage of the *2017 Amendments* may benefit the most number of individuals who might be Australians, Noongars, or Indigenous peoples. Its passage will ensure flexibility and economic gain by preserving low barriers to ILUA registration.[133] Although self-determination was invoked, and the Noongar Nation has achieved recognition from the State, the State also re-legitimated its assertions of sovereignty and 'that law's own regulatory hegemony',[134] while weakening the native title regime. When the State validated the Noongar Nation's self-determination and included them within its exclusionary domain, it also legitimated the Noongar Nation's 'taking host of [the] disparate claims' to 'consolidate them' and its 'dispersed Indigenous population'.[135] While potentially beneficial, there are two outstanding questions. First, where States confer recognition on internally colonised Nations while simultaneously maintaining the political-economic legitimacy of industry and the State, what prevents States from consolidating the disparate and divided claims of its Indigenous peoples and Nations as members of the States' population? And, second, what is the expense for the newly constructed 'minorities' of the abject domain? Contrary to Lansing's view, self-determination is not 'loaded with dynamite', but maybe it should be 'discredited'.[136]

Notes

1. *Declaration on the Rights of Indigenous Peoples*, GA Res 61/295, UN GAOR, 61st sess, UN Doc A/RES/47/1 (13 September 2007) [hereinafter *UNDRIP*].
2. *UNDRIP* art 3.
3. *See e.g.* Convention No. 169 Concerning Indigenous and Tribal Peoples in Independent Counties, International Labour Organization, 27 June 1989, 28 I.L.M. 1382; Howard R Berman, 'The International Labour Organization and Indigenous Peoples: Revision of ILO Convention No. 107 at the 75th Session of the International Labour Conference, 1988', *International Commission of Jurists* 47 (1988): 53.
4. Convention (No. 107) Concerning the Protection and Integration of Indigenous and Other Tribal and Semi-Tribal Populations in Independent Countries, June 26, 1957, International Labour Conference, 328 U.N.T.S. 247 (entered into force June 2, 1959).
5. *See e.g.* Damien Short, 'The Social Construction of Indigenous "Native Title" Land Rights in Australia', *Current Sociology* 55, no. 6 (2007): 870.
6. *See e.g.* James Anaya, 'The Rights of Indigenous Peoples to Self-Determination in the Post-Declaration Era', in *Making the Declaration Work: The United Nations Declaration on the Rights of Indigenous Peoples*, eds. Claire Charters and Rodolfo Stavenhagen (Copenhagen: International Work Group for Indigenous Affairs, 2009), 184; Mario Barelli, 'Shaping Indigenous Self Determination: Promising or Unsatisfactory Solutions?', *International Community Law Review* 13, no. 4 (2011): 413; Alexandra Xanthaki, 'The Right to Self-Determination: Meaning and Scope', in *Minorities, Peoples and Self-Determination*, eds. Nazila Ghanea and Alexandra Xanthaki (Boston: Martinus Nijhoff Publishers, 2005), 15–34; Joshua Castellino,

'Conceptual Difficulties and the Right to Indigenous Self-Determination', in *Minorities, Peoples and Self-Determination*, ibid., 55–74; Catherine J. Iorns, 'Indigenous Peoples and Self Determination: Challenging State Sovereignty', *Case Western Reserve Journal of International Law* 24 (1992): 199; Karen Knop, *Diversity and Self-Determination in International Law* (Cambridge: Cambridge University Press, 2002); Nathaniel Berman, 'Sovereignty in Abeyance: Self-Determination and International Law', *Wisconsin Journal of International Law* 7 (1988): 51.

7. Thomas D. Musgrave, *Self-Determination and National Minorities* (Oxford: Clarendon Press, 1997), 30.
8. Ibid., *quoting* Robert Lansing, 'Self-Determination', *Saturday Evening Post*, April 9, 1921, 101.
9. Michla Pomerance, *Self-Determination in Law and Practice* (London: Martinus Nijhoff Publishers, 1982), 4; W. Ofuatey-Kodjoe, *The Principle of Self-Determination in International Law* (Ann Arbor: Nellen Publishing Company, Inc., 1977), 2–8; Musgrave, above note 7, 31.
10. Pomerance, above note 9, 2.
11. UN Doc A/61/PV.107, 11–15.
12. Ibid.
13. Australia, Statement on the United Nations Declaration on the Rights of Indigenous Peoples, April 3, 2009, http://www.un.org/esa/socdev/unpfii/documents/Australia_official_statement_endorsement_UNDRIP.pdf; Australian Human Rights Commission, 'Questions and Answers on the UN Declaration on the Rights of Indigenous Peoples (2009)', *Australian Human Rights Commission*, April 2, 2009, https://www.humanrights.gov.au/publications/questions-and-answers-un-declaration-rights-indigenous-peoples-2009; New Zealand, House of Representatives, Ministerial Statements – UN Declaration on the Rights of Indigenous Peoples – Government Support, April 20, 2010, Hansard, vol. 662, 10029, https://www.parliament.nz/en/pb/hansard-debates/rhr/document/49HansD_20100420_00000071/ministerial-statements-un-declaration-on-the-rights-of; Canada, Statement of Support on the United Nations Declaration on the Rights of Indigenous Peoples, November 12, 2010, http://www.aadnc-aandc.gc.ca/eng/1309374239861/1309374546142; United States, Remarks by the President at the White House Tribal Nations Conference, December 16, 2010, https://obamawhitehouse.archives.gov/the-press-office/2010/12/16/remarks-president-white-house-tribal-nations-conference.
14. James Tully, 'The Struggles of Indigenous Peoples for and of Freedom', in *Public Philosophy in a New Key* (Cambridge University Press, 2008), 279–80.
15. Tully, above note 14, 276.
16. Patrick Macklem, *The Sovereignty of Human Rights* (Oxford University Press, 2015), 158.
17. Tully, above note 14, 279–80.
18. Ibid., 276.
19. *See e.g.* Patrick Thornberry, *Indigenous Peoples and Human Rights* (Manchester: Manchester University Press, 2002), Ch 2; Ben Saul, 'Identifying "Indigenous" Peoples in International Law', Sydney Law School, Legal Studies Research Paper No. 16.40 (2016); Benedict Kingsbury, '"Indigenous Peoples" in International Law: A Constructivist Approach to the Asian Controversy', *American Journal of International Law* 92 (1998): 414.
20. Note, above note 11.
21. Judith Butler, *Gender Trouble: Feminism and the Subversion of Identity* (Routledge, 1993), 2.
22. The nation-to-nation relationship may be, as Tully forecasted, a type of 'treaty federalism'. Tully, above note 14, 279–80.
23. *See* Short, above note 5, 859.
24. Butler, *Bodies that Matter: On the Discursive Limits of "Sex"* (Routledge, 1993), 3.
25. Ibid.
26. Richard G. Roberts et al., 'The Human Colonisation of Australia: Optical Dates of 53,000 and 60,000 Years Bracket Human Arrival at Deaf Adder Gorge, Northern Territory', *Quarternary Science Reviews* 13 (1994): 575.
27. *New South Wales Act 1823 (UK).*

28. *Commonwealth of Australia Constitution Act 1900* (Imp).
29. Elisa Arcioni, 'Excluding Indigenous Australians from "the People": A Reconsideration of Sections 25 and 127 of the *Constitution*' (2012) 40 *Federal Law Review* 287, 292.
30. (1992) 175 CLR 1, [75].
31. Irene Watson, *Aboriginal Peoples, Colonialism and International Law: Raw Law* (New York: Routledge, 2015), 42.
32. Ibid., 40.
33. *See* Butler, above note 24, 3.
34. Short, above note 5, 860.
35. Ibid., 861–62.
36. *NTA* Pt 1, s (3)(b).
37. *NTA* ss 28(f), 25(3), 29, 35, 38.
38. *NTA* s 36.
39. There are three cases where the RTN process has not overridden native title claimants concerns. *Western Desert Lands Aboriginal Corporation (Jamukurnu-Yapalikunu)/Western Australia/Holocene Pty Ltd* [2009] NNTTA 49 (27 May 2009); *Weld Range Metals Limited/ Western Australia/Simpson* [2011] NNTTA 172; *Seven Star Investments Group Pty Ltd/ Western Australia/Freddie* [2011] NNTTA 5.
40. (1996) 187 CLR 1.
41. Short, above note 5, 860.
42. John Howard, 'Amended *Wik* 10-Point Plan', Prime Minister of Australia, News Release, May 8, 1997; *cf* National Indigenous Working Group, 'Critique of the 10 Point Plan', *Indigenous Law Bulletin* 4, no. 3 (1997): 10.
43. *See* Katharine Gelber, 'Human Rights Treaties in Australia – Empty Words?', *Australian Review of Public Affairs*, April 12, 2001, http://www.australianreview.net/digest/2001/04/gelber.html; Greg Marks, 'Australia, the Committee on the Elimination of All Forms of Racial Discrimination and Indigenous Rights', *Indigenous Law Bulletin* 6, no. 7 (2004): 11; *also* Richard Bartlett, 'A Return to Dispossession and Discrimination: The Ten Point Plan', *University of Western Australia Law Review* 27 (1997): 50.
44. Australia's *Racial Discrimination Act 1975* (Cth) gave domestic effect to its ratification of the International *Convention on the Elimination of All Forms of Racial Discrimination.*
45. Committee on the Elimination of Racial Discrimination, Decision 2 (54) on Australia – Concluding Observations/Comments, March 18, 1999, 6, UN Doc CERD/C/54/MISC.40/rev.2, para 13.
46. Ibid., [87], *citing* Committee on the Elimination of Racial Discrimination, General Recommendation XXI – Right to self-determination, 48th sess, 1996, UN Doc: A/45/18, para 7–9; and Committee on the Elimination of Racial Discrimination, General Recommendation XXIII concerning Indigenous Peoples, August 18, 1997, UN Doc CERD/C/51/Misc.13/Rev.4.
47. Human Rights Council, *Final Report of the Study on Indigenous Peoples and the Right to Participate in Decision-Making: Report of the Expert Mechanism on the Right of Indigenous Peoples*, UN DOC A/HRC/18/42 Annex ¶ 20 (Aug. 17, 2011).
48. *UNDRIP* arts 3, 18, 21(1), 23, and 32(1).
49. *See* Christopher Tomlins, '"Be Operational, or Disappear": Thoughts on a Present Discontent', *Annual Review of Law and Social Sciences* 12 (2016): 1, 10–12.
50. [2010] 189 FCR 412.
51. *See NTA*, s 24CD(1).
52. *Bygrave*, above note 50, [56].
53. Ibid., [85].
54. The Senate, Legal and Constitutional Affairs Legislation Committee, Native Title Amendment (Indigenous Land Use Agreements) Bill 2017, 10, *citing* Ms Livermore, Proof Committee Hansard, March 13, 2017, 2.
55. [2017] FCAFC 10.
56. (2006) 230 ALR 603.

57. Harry Hobbs and George Williams, 'The Noongar Settlement: Australia's First Treaty', *Sydney Law Review* 40 (2018): (forthcoming, 26).
58. *See also* South West Aboriginal Land and Sea Council, John Host and Chris Own, *"It's Still In My Heart, This Is My Country" The Single Noongar Claim History* (University of Western Australia Press, 2009).
59. (2006) 230 ALR 603, paras. 445–446.
60. Ibid., Introductory Statement of Justice Wilcox, paras. 872–76.
61. Aboriginal and Torres Strait Islander Social Justice Commission, *Native title Report 2007* (Human Rights and Equal Opportunity Commission, 2008), 149.
62. Ibid., 146.
63. *See* Glen Kelly and Stuart Bradfield, 'Winning Native Title, or Winning out of Native Title? The Noongar Native Title Settlement', *Indigenous Law Bulletin* 9, no. 2 (2012): 14; *generally* Richard Bartlett, 'An Obsession with Traditional Laws and Customs Creates Difficulty Establishing Native Title Claims in the South: *Yorta*', *Western Australia Law Review* 31 (2003): 35–46.
64. [2008] FCAFC 63.
65. Hobbs and Williams, above note 57, 26.
66. Kathryn Diss, 'Claimants Ink $1.3 Billion Western Australia Noongar Native Title Deal', *ABC News*, March 30, 2015, http://www.abc.net.au/news/2015-03-30/south-west-noongar-native-title-deal-inked/6357746.
67. *See* Michael Mccagh, 'Native Title in the Southwest: The Noongar Recognition Bill', *Indigenous Law Bulletin* 18, no. 8 (2015): 26; Department of Premier and Cabinet, 'Noongars Vote to Accept Historic Offer', News Release, March 30, 2015, https://www.mediastatements.wa.gov.au/Pages/Barnett/2015/03/Noongars-vote-to-accept-historic-offer.aspx.
68. Shireen Morris, 'Lessons from New Zealand: Towards a Better Working Relationship Between Indigenous Peoples and the State', *Australian Indigenous Law Review* 18 (2015): 79–80; Hobbs and Williams, above note 57, 31.
69. Hobbs and Williams, above note 57.
70. *Land Administration (South West Native Title Settlement) Act 2016* (WA) Preamble; *Noongar (Koorah, Nitja, Boordahwan) (Past, Present, Future) Recognition Act 2016* (WA).
71. Ibid.
72. *McGlade*, above note 55, paras 234–247, 490–495. Native title claimants can remove an RNTC member according to *NTA* s 66B. There are problems with s 66B, including procedural burdens as well as the sensitive matter of uttering the names of deceased peoples.
73. Explanatory Memorandum, Native Title Amendment (Indigenous Land Use Agreements) Bill 2017 (Cth), [11] [hereinafter EM]. There are three types of ILUAs, one of which is area ILUAs. *See NTA* Subdiv C of Div 3 Pt 2. I use 'area ILUAs' and 'ILUAs' synonymously throughout.
74. EM, above note 73, [2]; The *Amendment Act* s 24CD(2)(a), states that if a person(s) have been nominated or determined under subsection 251A(2) they may sign an ILUA. If no person(s) have been nominated or determined under subsection 251A(2), then a majority of the RNTC is sufficient to register an ILUA. Section 251A(2) allows a native title claim group to nominate one person who comprise the RNTC to be a party to the agreement or specify a process for determining which person(s) who comprise the RNTC it to be a party/parties.
75. Burragubba and Johnson, below note 104.
76. Short, above note 5, 861–62.
77. EM, Statement of Compatibility with Human Rights, above note 73, paras. 9–21. Other submissions also upheld the *Amendment* as consistent with self-determination, *UNDRIP* and Indigenous peoples' rights.
78. Rodney Carter (Group Chief Executive Officer of the Dja Wurrung Clans Aboriginal Corporation) Submission No 13 to *Amendment Bill 2017*, March 2, 2017; Yawuru Native Title Holders Aboriginal Corporation, Submission No 42 to *Amendment Bill 2017*, 3.

79. Glen Colbung, Submission No 7 to Senate Legal and Constitutional Affairs Committee, *Native Title Amendment (Indigenous Land Use Agreements) Bill 2017* [hereinafter *Amendment Bill 2017*], March 2, 2017, 3; David Collard, Submission No 11 to *Amendment Bill 2017*, March 2, 2017, 2–3; Stuart Bradfield, Submission No 46 to *Amendment Bill 2017*, March 3, 2017, 2–3.
80. Suzanne Kelly, Submission No 10 to *Amendment Bill 2017*, March 2, 2017, 2.
81. Kelly and Bradfield, above note 63, 15.
82. Glen Kelly, Submission No 9 to *Amendment Bill 2017*, March 2, 2017, 2.
83. Name Withheld, Submission No to *Amendment Bill 2017*, 2.
84. Ghillar, Michael Anderson, Convenor of Sovereign Union of First Nations and Peoples in Australia, Submission No 36 to *Amendment Bill 2017*, March 3, 2017, 1; *also*, National Congress of Australia's First Peoples, Submission No 57 to *Amendment Bill 2017*, March 2017, 5–6.
85. Richie Ah Mat, Gerhard Pearson and Noel Pearson, Submission No 14 to *Amendment Bill 2017*, March 3, 2017, [13].
86. Mervyn Eads, Margaret Culbong, Mingli McGlade, and Naomi Smit, Submission No 24 to *Amendment Bill 2017*, 1.
87. Albert Corunna, Submission No 5 to *Amendment Bill 2017*, 1–2.
88. *Adani Mining Pty Ltd and Another v Adrian Burragubba, Patrick Malone and Irene White on behalf of the Wangan and Jagalingou People* [2015] NNTTA 16, April 8, 2015, paras. 14, 20 [hereinafter *Adani v Burragubba*].
89. Ibid., [29].
90. Ibid; *also*, Wangan and Jagalingou, 'EXPLAINER: Representation of W&J', *Wangan & Jagalingou Family Council*, August 21, 2015, http://wanganjagalingou.com.au/representation/.
91. *See* Carl Jackson, 'Wangan and Jagalingou People Take on Coal Giant Adani', *Redflag*, April 12, 2015, http://redflag.org.au/article/wangan-and-jagalingou-people-take-coal-giant-adani; 'Traditional Owners Reject Adani's Huge Carmichael Coal Mine in Queensland's Galilee Basin', *Green Left Weekly*, March 28, 2015, https://www.greenleft.org.au/node/58640.
92. *Adani v Burragubba*, above note 88.
93. *Burragubba v State of Queensland* [2016] FCA 984, August 19, 2016.
94. Ibid.
95. Lisa Cox, 'Gautam Adani Makes Special Request to Malcolm Turnbull over $15b Deal', *Canberra Times* (online), December 9, 2015, http://www.canberratimes.com.au/business/mining-and-resources/adani-demanded-certainty-from-turnbull-20151208-gliuk8.html.
96. 'Adani Group Seeks Uncontestable Nod from Australia for Its Mega Projects', *The Economic Times* (online), December 8, 2015 http://articles.economictimes.indiatimes.com/2015-12-08/news/68865561_1_gautam-adani-galilee-basin-adani-group.
97. Joshua Robertson, 'Traditional Owners Vote to Sack Representatives Who Received Benefits from Adani', *The Guardian*, March 21, 2016, https://www.theguardian.com/environment/2016/mar/21/adani-mine-traditional-owners-vote-to-sack-representatives-who-received-benefits-from-adani. In *Burragubba on behalf of the Wangan and Jagalingou People v State of Queensland* [2017] FCA 373, April 11, 2017, paras. 33–38, Justice Reeves found that the meeting 'was to address concerns held by a minority of the members of the existing W& J Application and those members of the W&J claim group who held the same concerns, relating to the ILUA negotiations with Adani'.
98. Michael McKenna, 'Greens Bankroll Indigenous Rebels Opposed to Carmichael Mine', *The Australian*, March 12, 2016, http://www.theaustralian.com.au/national-affairs/indigenous/greens-bankroll-indigenous-rebels-opposed-to-carmichael-mine/news-story/001f2f4514e07829a5318f88cc444587.
99. Ibid.
100. Ibid.
101. 'Acrimony and Legal Threat as Indigenous Groups Approves Adani Mine', *The Guardian*, April 16, 2016, https://www.theguardian.com/australia-news/2016/apr/17/wangan-and-jagalingou-indigenous-group-approves-adani-carmichael-mine.

102. Wangan Jagalingou, 'Traditional Owners' Rejection of Carmichael Stands, Despite Adani Bank Rolling Bogus "Land Use Agreement"', *Wangan & Jagalingou Family Council*, April 16, 2016, http://wanganjagalingou.com.au/traditional-owners-rejection-of-carmichael-stands-despite-adani-bank-rolling-bogus-land-use-agreement/.
103. Ibid.
104. Adrian Burragubba and Murrawah Johnson, Submission No 17 to *Amendment Bill 2017*, 7 March 2017, 4 *annex* Martin Wagner, *Australia's Ongoing Violation of the Rights of the Wangan & Jagalingou People to Be Adequately Consulted in Good Faith about the Development of the* Native Title Amendment (Indigenous Land Use Agreements) Bill 2017 (Cth) *and its impacts on the Wangan & Jagalingou*, 1 March 2017, 5–11; Helen Szoke, Oxfam Australia, Submission No 43 to *Amendment Bill 2017*, 1. It seems unlikely that submitting comments to the Senate and testifying satisfies FPIC. I do not analyse that issue here.
105. Wangan Jagalingou, 'Traditional Owners Condemn Brandis' "Adani Amendment" to Native Title Act as a Con on the Public', *Wangan & Jagalingou Family Council*, February 13, 2017, http://wanganjagalingou.com.au/traditional-owners-condemn-brandis-adani-amendment-to-native-title-act-as-a-con-on-the-public/.
106. Short, above note 5, 861–62.
107. Adrian Burragubba and Murrawah Johnson, 'Update on the Situation of the Wangan and Jagalingou People's Opposition to the Proposed Carmichael Coal Mine and Comments on Australia's Response to the Special Rapporteur's Letter Dated 1 April 2016', *Wangan & Jagalingou Family Council*, March 8, 2017, http://wanganjagalingou.com.au/wp-content/uploads/2017/03/Wangan-Jagalingou-reply-submission-to-SR-indigenous-peoples-17-03-10.pdf, 1,2, 7.
108. Philip Hunter, HWL Ebsworth Lawyers, Submission No 23 to *Amendment Bill 2017*, paras. 7–19.
109. Kelly and Bradfield, above note 63, 15.
110. *See* Ann Genovese, 'Turning the Tides of History', *Griffith Review* (2003–2004).
111. Kelly and Bradfield, above note 63, 14.
112. McKenna, above note 98.
113. Ibid.
114. Eads, Culbong, McGlade and Smit, above note 85, 1; Burragubba and Johnson, above note 107, 7.
115. Wangan and Jagalingou, above notes 102 and 105.
116. Ibid., 279–80.
117. Notes, above note 43, 45.
118. 'End of Mission Statement by United Nations Special Rapporteur on the rights of indigenous peoples, Victoria Tauli-Corpuz on her visit to Australia', April 3, 2017, http://unsr.vtaulicorpuz.org/site/index.php/statements/181-end-statement-australia.
119. *UNDRIP* arts 11, 18, 21(1), 23, and 32(1).
120. Pomerance, above note 9, 2.
121. Butler, above note 24, 3.
122. South West Aboriginal Land & Sea Council, *Aboriginal Corporation Rule Book*, December 24, 2014, s 1.1(b); *Corporations (Aboriginal and Torres Strait Islander) Act 2006 (Cth).*
123. Kelly and Bradfield, above note 63, 15.
124. Stephen Cornell, 'Processes of Native Nationhood: The Indigenous Politics of Self-Government', *International Indigenous Policy Journal* 6, no. 4 (2015): 10.
125. Corunna, above note 87, 1.
126. *See Burragubba on behalf of the Wangan and Jagalingou People v State of Queensland* [2017] FCA 373, April 22, 2017, paras. 37–38.
127. Corunna, above note 87; Eads, Culbog, McGlade and Smit, above note 86.
128. Diss, above note 66.
129. Eads, Culbong, McGlade and Smit, above note 85, 1.
130. Corunna, above note 87, 2.
131. Wangan Jagalingou, above note 102, 3–4.

132. Wangan and Jagalingou, *Facebook.com*, November 28, 2017, https://www.facebook.com/WanganandJagalingou/videos/1944744928874008/?hc_ref=ARRnfZddHt9kapkuxJZmo31YrcC_LY-3XUvVuoY8mGaJ7tM8ZPg70huWYvb8D7yLug8&fref=nf.
133. *See* Short, above note 5, 859.
134. Butler, above note 21, 2.
135. Cornell, above note 124, 10.
136. Musgrave, above note 7, *citing* Lansing, above note 8.

Acknowledgements

The author would like to thank the editors and special editors of the International Journal of Human Rights, as well as the anonymous referee, Harry Hobbs and Ben Golder for comments on earlier drafts of this paper.

Disclosure statement

No potential conflict of interest was reported by the author.

ORCID

Stephen M. Young http://orcid.org/0000-0002-3472-3093

Indigenous rights and the legal politics of Canadian coloniality: what is happening to free, prior and informed consent in Canada?

Jeremy Patzer

ABSTRACT

The Supreme Court of Canada has been reshaping Aboriginal law for decades, but characterisations of these changes as purely beneficial to Indigenous groups overlook the inclination of Canadian courts to eschew categorical frameworks of legal obligation toward Indigenous peoples. Past legal principles for defending Indigenous interests have been dismissed or deemphasised in favour of more flexible doctrines. The SCC has structured a Crown-Indigenous relationship that envisions governments and third party interests operating in a self-interested, but jurisprudentially regulated, fashion. This jurisprudential ethics of interrelation, however, holds in reserve the potential for infringing Indigenous rights and title without Indigenous consent. With this framework established as the standard for reconciliatory legal-politics in Canada, stronger conceptualisations of free, prior and informed consent – particularly the ability to withhold and withdraw consent – are susceptible to being cast as unreasonable and disproportionate, as embodied in the spectre of the 'Indigenous veto'. The UNDRIP and its controversial, indeterminate principle of consent are thus being moulded to a 'Canadian definition' which shows little sign of surpassing those obligations already imposed upon governments by the courts, and which raises larger questions about how the declaration is absorbed into the legal-political contexts of individual states.

At the passage of the United Nations Declaration on the Rights of Indigenous Peoples (UNDRIP) at the United Nations General Assembly on 13 September 2007, Canada was accompanied by only three other states – the United States, Australia, and New Zealand – in voting against the declaration. As Sheryl Lightfoot explains, with only minor variations in their lists of grievances with the declaration, the four largest settler states in the Anglosphere complained about – among other things – the declaration's 'incompatibility with their domestic laws and their commitment to the equality of all of their citizens. All four of them objected to the declaration's provisions on self-determination as well as land and resources rights'.[1]

If, at that moment, Canada displayed a certain amount of resolve in objecting to a rights declaration that 144 member states were backing, the years that followed would reveal a striking amount of equivocality. Though nothing had changed in the declaration itself, all four states announced reversals of their positions from 2009 to 2010. Even after that reversal, pronouncements from federal ministers have ranged from celebratory declarations of its full embrace to defensive assertions that its adoption into Canadian law – as called for by some proponents – is 'unworkable' and a 'distraction'.[2] This equivocality is reflective of the unwieldy politics of extolling the virtues of reconciliation with Indigenous peoples while simultaneously seeking to limit the scope of reconciliatory change. Claims suggesting the declaration's incompatibility with domestic law also signal that this equivocality is, to some extent, rooted in and shaped by Canadian jurisprudence.

My objective is to give a deeper context to the current controversy surrounding the declaration and the concept of free, prior and informed consent (FPIC) in Canada. My contention is that an examination of some of the significant doctrinal changes in Aboriginal law since the late twentieth century is required in order to do this. Past legal principles for defending Indigenous interests have been either dismissed or deemphasised in favour of more *flexible* doctrines such as justified infringement and the duty to consult. The Supreme Court of Canada (SCC) has structured a Crown-Indigenous relationship that envisions Canadian governments and third party interests operating in a self-interested, but jurisprudentially regulated, fashion. This jurisprudential ethics of interrelation, however, holds in reserve the potential, albeit rare, for assertions of raw, instrumental coloniality – the disregard of the Indigenous possession and use of land. With this framework established as the standard for reconciliatory legal-politics in Canada, stronger conceptualisations of FPIC – notably those maintaining the ability of Indigenous peoples to withhold or withdraw consent – are susceptible to being discursively cast as inflexible, unreasonable, and disproportionate, as embodied in the menacing spectre of the 'Indigenous veto'.[3] Although the principle of FPIC is proving both indeterminate and controversial, indications are that it is nevertheless more robust than contemporary doctrines created by the SCC, and, indeed, that Canadian politics is capitalising on FPIC's equivocality, ensuring that its interpretation does nothing to transcend the obligations already imposed upon it by Canadian courts.

Canada and the declaration

International instruments centring on a concern for Indigenous peoples, including their place in processes of national development, have existed for well over a century, although it is only in relatively recent history that these have begun to move away from Eurocentric, paternalistic and assimilationist approaches.[4] The effects on Indigenous peoples from resource extraction and development projects has garnered particular attention in recent years, both prior to and after the adoption of the UNDRIP. In 2003, special rapporteur Rodolfo Stavenhagen reported to what was then the United Nations Commission on Human Rights that 'Indigenous peoples are said to bear disproportionately the costs of resource-intensive and resource-extractive industries, large dams and other infrastructure projects, logging and plantations, bio-prospecting, industrial fishing and farming, and also eco-tourism and imposed conservation projects'.[5] In 2011, his successor, James Anaya, delivered a report to the Human Rights Council on extractive industries operating within or near Indigenous territories:

> Extractive industry activities generate effects that often infringe upon indigenous peoples' rights; public agencies and private business enterprises involved in the extraction or development of natural resources, in both developing and developed countries, have contributed to these effects. Notably, some Governments have attempted to mitigate the negative effects of extractive operations, yet human rights continue to be violated as a result of an increasing demand for resources and energy. The Special Rapporteur considers the ever-expanding operations of extractive industries to be a pressing issue for indigenous peoples on a global scale.[6]

The fact that the 'negative effects' noted by Anaya span both developed and developing countries is telling. It is this global scale of the risk to Indigenous peoples that makes bedfellows of otherwise distinct countries. Jason Tockman thus offers a comparative analysis of UNDRIP implementation between Canada and Bolivia, two countries that are distinct in many ways but which, when it comes to Indigenous rights, demonstrate analytically suitable similarities. Aside from the parallels of their colonial histories, Tockman notes that both economies 'are significantly based on natural resource extraction on or under Indigenous land', thus labelling both as *extractivist.* 'Countries whose economies are significantly based on natural resource extraction', Tockman argues, 'experience particular political dynamics and patterns of development that often infringe on the lives and rights of indigenous peoples'.[7]

Indeed, anxieties around potential ramifications for natural resource development likely formed a large undercurrent to Canada's concerns over the UNDRIP. John McNee, Canada's permanent representative to the United Nations during its passage, had the task of explaining Canada's opposition to the declaration on the day of the vote. Pertaining to the content of the declaration, Sheryl Lightfoot recounts that Canada objected to its provisions on land and resources as well as the provisions emphasising free, prior, and informed consent from Indigenous peoples in a number of matters concerning them. Canada specifically expressed concern 'that the declaration's provisions enabled the "establishment of a complete veto power over legislative and administrative action for a particular group"'[8] – namely, Indigenous peoples who so often find their traditional lands and activities on the fault lines of conflict concerning natural resource extraction and development.

In the declaration, Article 26 states that 'Indigenous peoples have the right to the lands, territories and resources which they have traditionally owned, occupied or otherwise used or acquired', and that 'states shall give legal recognition and protection to these lands, territories and resources'. Some articles mention free, prior and informed consent within the context of its breach, such as calling for redress for having committed certain wrongs without the consent of the Indigenous peoples concerned. This includes having taken, without consent, Indigenous cultural, intellectual, religious or spiritual property (Article 11), having taken Indigenous lands, territories or resources (Article 28), and having approved any project affecting Indigenous lands, territories or resources (Article 32). Other clauses emphasise the ongoing need to pursue free, prior and informed consent *prior* to certain measures, events or potentialities, such as prior to the relocation of Indigenous peoples from their lands or territories (Article 10), prior to the adoption of legislative or administrative measures that may affect Indigenous peoples (Article 19), prior to the storage or disposal of hazardous waste on Indigenous lands (Article 29), and, again, prior to projects affecting Indigenous lands, territories or other resources (Article 32). Evidently, the declaration is an instrument that seeks to be simultaneously corrective of sins of the past and representative of the way forward for states to respect the rights of Indigenous peoples. The declaration and the principle of free, prior and informed consent have thus become a heated source of debate concerning the rights of Indigenous peoples in Canada. Nevertheless, the principle of FPIC follows as a relatively recent interloper amongst an extant series of common law doctrinal concepts that have figured prominently in the reconciliatory legal-politics of Canada as a settler state.

Juriprudence, reconciliation and crown obligations

To put centuries of history and decades of case law into a few paragraphs, there are several types of dispute, rooted in the colonial dispossession of Indigenous peoples, that Canadian courts have proved willing to legally problematise since the late twentieth century, and which have thus held a certain moral-legal sway over the country. The modern legal question of Aboriginal title developed largely because of a profound contradiction in the settlement and creation of Canada. Notably, the Crown struck treaties to obtain Indigenous territory for European settlement – instruments that therefore by their very nature suggest the recognition of the Indigenous possession of land – but it did so with only some Indigenous groups and not with others. With the 1973 *Calder* case, the Supreme Court of Canada signalled its readiness to recognise an ongoing title of some sort for Indigenous groups able to prove that their original title was not legitimately extinguished by treaty or otherwise – a change of significant consequence for vast swaths of Canada.[9] In essence, Aboriginal title gained a certain *inherence* – its recognition was now rooted in the prior occupation of Indigenous peoples, and no longer dependent on legislation or proclamation from the colonising sovereign. For those Indigenous groups who *did* sign treaties with the Crown – be they land cession treaties or merely treaties of peace and friendship – the higher courts also began to signal in the late 1960s their willingness to hold governments to the terms of those historical agreements.[10] Lastly, recognition of that prior occupation of Indigenous peoples also brought the courts to affirm that rights to more discrete practices and activities could exist, beyond what may or may not be enumerated in treaties. Since the late twentieth century, then, Canadian courts have been dealing with a burgeoning number of disputes concerning Aboriginal title, treaty rights, and Aboriginal rights, respectively.

In addition to the installation of inherence for Aboriginal rights and title, and the courts' development of the modern principles of treaty interpretation, section 35 of the *Constitution Act, 1982* has also played a pivotal role in the evolution of Indigenous rights in Canada – but with the unintended consequence of putting the courts in the lead in their development. Section 35 states, in all vagueness and brevity, that 'the existing aboriginal and treaty rights of the aboriginal peoples of Canada are hereby recognized and affirmed', and that 'In this Act, "aboriginal peoples of Canada" includes the Indian, Inuit and Métis peoples of Canada'.[11] With this, Aboriginal title, Aboriginal rights, and treaty rights gained the robustness of constitutional protection. Yet, it is notable that the act does nothing to define or delimit the nature of those rights and title. Rather, the act stipulated that a series of constitutional conferences involving the federal government, the provinces, and Indigenous representatives were to take place in the years following its enactment. Negotiations at these conferences failed, leaving a blank slate of undefined Indigenous rights – all constitutionally protected – as a source of uncontrolled eventuality for the settler state.

The fact that an idiosyncrasy of Canadian political history threw the interpretation of section 35 into the laps of judges explains why the courts have become so pivotal to Indigenous rights in Canada. This is not to overlook, of course, the fact that the courts played a lead role in instigating positive change for treaty rights and Aboriginal title in the 1960s and 1970s. However, as generators and managers of Indigenous rights in the context of an extractivist settler state, it is my contention that the higher courts in Canada are also quietly but studiously attuned to a need to incorporate into the jurisprudence principles and rationalities that pace, manage, and delimit those rights in a controlled fashion. It is to several significant examples in Canadian case law that I now turn.

Curtailing the fiduciary duty

At base, a fiduciary relationship is one involving trust, in which one party has discretionary control over the interests of another – and thus an ethical expectation to act for the benefit and interest of the beneficiary arises. A version of this concept arose in Canadian Aboriginal law precisely because of the paternalistic and controlling nature of Canada's *Indian Act*.

The traditional territory of the Musqueam is located on the lower mainland of British Columbia, coinciding greatly with what is now Vancouver – a city that presently has some of the highest property values in the world. In the 1950s, the Indian agent in charge of the Indian Affairs branch in Vancouver – a Mr. Anfield – had a keen appreciation for the potential value of any surplus land within the Musqueam band's small reserve. He described it as 'undoubtedly the most potentially valuable 400 acres in metropolitan Vancouver today'.[12] The band agreed in principle with the idea of leasing out surplus land for the benefit of their people, and thus authorised and paid for an appraisal of 162 acres of their land. The Indian agent had significant agency in managing the situation for the Musqueam, however. The band technically had to surrender the land in question to the Crown so that the Crown could lease it out on their behalf, and, after hearing the Musqueam's desired terms for any possible lease agreement, Anfield pursued negotiations with a neighbouring golf course. The band did not receive a copy of the appraisal, nor did Anfield apprise them of the fact that he had agreed to much less favourable terms without their consent. In fact, the band did not receive a copy of the lease until 1970, twelve years after the agreement was put in place. The band's response was to file a suit against the Crown for breach of trust.

The case of *Guerin v. The Queen* eventually climbed to the Supreme Court of Canada, with the SCC rendering its decision in 1984. The Court determined that the inalienable nature of reserve land – the fact that the Musqueam had no choice but to surrender the land to the Crown and to rely on the latter to make the necessary arrangements on their behalf – was a 'source of distinct fiduciary obligation owed by the Crown to the Indians'.[13] The establishment of this category of Crown obligation toward Indigenous peoples was no small act on the part of the SCC. It marked another significant late twentieth century precedent that helped to extricate Canada from an era of policy, legislation, and legal positivist jurisprudence that had been highly unsympathetic to the plight of Indigenous Canadians. The SCC essentially created a Canadian common law principle that the Crown, when assuming discretionary control over First Nations' interests, is to act in the best interests of those First Nations, and that the relationship is trust-like rather than adversarial.

In 1990, the SCC entertained a fishing rights dispute in the case of *R. v. Sparrow*, and its decision states clearly that one of its guiding precedents is that of *Guerin* and the fiduciary duty. It is notable, however, that the substance of the two cases is distinct – from the Crown's discretionary management of reserve land on behalf of a First Nation on the one hand, to a dispute concerning the length of net permissible under the band's fishing licence. Because of its application to the *Sparrow* case, legal scholars and Indigenous advocates took notice of the seeming expansion of the fiduciary duty. John Borrows and Leonard Rotman argued 'the Crown's fiduciary obligations to Aboriginal peoples extended beyond the surrender of Aboriginal lands to Crown-Native relations more generally and that those obligations were constitutionally entrenched in section 35(1) of the *Constitution Act, 1982*'.[14] They go on to posit that, 'since fiduciary law does not require the existence of a legally recognizable property interest, there is no doctrinal difficulty in having hunting, trapping or fishing rights be the subject of a Crown fiduciary obligation to an Aboriginal group'. As such, Borrows and Rotman suggest that the fiduciary principle developed in Canadian Aboriginal law would be 'capable of applying to a wider range of claims against the Crown than trust law'.[15]

Not surprisingly, the Crown faced a wave of litigation from Indigenous groups over the ensuing years, alleging breaches of its fiduciary duty in relation to a variety of substantively distinct circumstances and conflicts. The SCC listed some examples of these in its 2002 decision for *Wewaykum Indian Band v. Canada*, and used that case to temper the litigious exuberance of Indigenous claimants.[16] The *Wewaykum* judgment challenged the idea of the fiduciary duty 'as a source of plenary Crown liability covering all aspects of the Crown-Indian band relationship', stating that 'this overshoots the mark. The fiduciary duty imposed on the Crown does not exist at large but in relation to specific Indian interests'.[17] The Court asserted that the fiduciary duty applies only to situations where the Crown's role brings it to assume *discretionary control* over *specific* Aboriginal interests.

The evolution of the fiduciary duty speaks to the nature of the Crown-Indigenous relationship that the SCC has sought to structure in contemporary case law. An initial, probative move to correct and compensate for the infamies of history was to cast the relationship between the Crown and Indigenous peoples as trust-like and fiduciary in nature. Two decades later, the *Wewaykum* case signalled a re-evaluation on the part of the SCC and a reluctance to hold the Crown to such a broad, categorical form of obligation toward Indigenous peoples. According to the assessment of Jamie Dickson, the SCC decisions for *Wewaykum* and then *Haida Nation v. British Columbia (Minister of Forests)*[18] were the final nails in the coffin for the fiduciary duty, which was to be eclipsed by the principle of the honour of the Crown.[19] The move away from a Crown-Indigenous relationship 'where one party's interests are uniquely at the mercy of the other',[20] taken together with other contemporary doctrinal precepts developed by the SCC, suggests that the Court wishes to structure a new relationship between the Crown and Indigenous peoples. It is one in which the state is still open to pursuing its own interests, rather than being held exclusively and categorically to the interests of Indigenous peoples, within the confines of certain jurisprudential guidelines rooted in juridical notions of honourable conduct.

Expanding infringement

Canada has had generations of case law asserting that it is within the exclusive sphere of power of the federal government to legislate in regards to Indigenous peoples. This had its origins in the *Constitution Act, 1867* – previously known as the *British North America Act, 1867*, the very act that created Canada. The act delineated the division of powers between the federal and provincial governments for the new dominion, and amongst the heads of power accorded to the federal government was 'Indians, and Lands reserved for the Indians'.[21] With the *Constitution Act, 1982* came the added constitutional protection of Indigenous rights, and the provision that 'any law that is inconsistent with the provisions of the Constitution is, to the extent of the inconsistency, of no force or effect'.[22] It is clear, however, that by 1990 the Supreme Court of Canada had the controlled management of these reconciliatory legal-politics in mind just as much as 'the promise' of section 35 of the 1982 act. Simultaneous to the creation of inherent common law Aboriginal rights in the *Sparrow* decision, then, the Court introduced the concept of infringement of these constitutionally protected rights, justifiable in cases of compelling public interest. The SCC has significantly promulgated infringement, through a test of justification first set out in *Sparrow*, within a relatively short amount of time.

While it was in 1973 that the SCC created the possibility of the common law recognition of an inherent Aboriginal title for groups that had not signed land cession treaties, it was not until the decision for *Delgamuukw v. British Columbia* in 1997 that the Court finally offered a definition of that title.[23] Nevertheless, alongside the judicial creation of an Indigenous right that was unparalleled in Canadian legal history – a form of exclusive title over land – the last resort pressure-release valve of infringement was preserved for Aboriginal title as well. In fact, for the higher-stakes question entertained in *Delgamuukw*, the Supreme Court of Canada made a point of exploring the possibilities for infringement even further, giving specific hypothetical mention to a laundry list of objectives that could justify the further dispossession of Indigenous peoples of their land:

> ... the range of legislative objectives that can justify the infringement of aboriginal title is fairly broad ... In my opinion, the development of agriculture, forestry, mining, and hydroelectric power, the general economic development of the interior of British Columbia, protection of the environment or endangered species, the building of infrastructure and the settlement of foreign populations to support those aims, are the kinds of objectives that are consistent with this purpose and, in principle, can justify the infringement of aboriginal title.[24]

To post-1982 Aboriginal law in Canada, the concept of infringement has been rare in use yet essential in its existence – so much so that the SCC quickly extended it over Aboriginal rights, Aboriginal title, and treaty rights. This relatively rapid change came with some growing pains, as it created inadvertent contradictions with decades of already established case law. Namely, the SCC presented the *Sparrow* test for justifying infringement as a measure for both the federal *and* provincial interference with rights, contradicting a founding constitutional act which maintained that 'Indians, and Lands reserved for the Indians' were the exclusive head of power of the federal government,[25] as well as decades of case law that employed a doctrine called *interjurisdictional immunity* to sort out jurisdictional disputes between the federal government and provinces.[26] Nigel Bankes and Jennifer Koshan have thus asked, 'just what is left, if anything, at the core of s.91(24)'?[27] In other words, what does it mean to have a founding constitutional act that enumerates Indigenous peoples and their lands as the sole jurisdiction of the federal government, when the highest court has propagated the power to infringe Indigenous rights and title to all the provinces and territories as well? Bankes and Koshan argue that the SCC has chosen 'calibration and uncertainty at the expense of a bright line and certainty' in its confounding of the division of powers.[28] I agree, but I argue that 'calibration and uncertainty' is actually a comforting form of security for the settler state. It is the preservation of discretion and it is reassurance for the SCC of the ability to manage this most challenging and high stakes body of jurisprudence.

From injunctive relief to the duty to consult

The recognition of common law Aboriginal title in the 1973 *Calder* case cast a new light on those vast regions of Canada that had been settled by Europeans without the benefit of land surrender treaties. Shortly after the decision, the federal government launched the earliest iteration of the comprehensive claims process, also known as land claims or the modern treaty process. The vast majority of the province of British Columbia was in the situation of having been settled without treaty, and many British Columbia First Nations had been insisting on their claims to their traditional lands since settlement began in the nineteenth century. Modern treaties are much more complex than their eighteenth and nineteenth century forebears, however, and the unfortunate situation for Indigenous peoples in unceded regions of Canada is that the comprehensive claims process is long, slow, complicated, and expensive.

A particular issue symptomatic of this began to arise in the 1980s, especially in British Columbia: what legal recourse could Indigenous peoples take to protect their land from extractive industries and outside development during the long wait to finalise their claim to their own land? Two Nuu-chah-nulth bands on the west coast of Vancouver Island, the Clayoquot and the Ahousaht, were locked in disputes with MacMillan Bloedel because the company had government-issued 'tree farm licences' on their territory and was attempting to conduct logging operations. The Nuu-Chah-Nulth Tribal Council had already initiated their land claim, the federal government had accepted that land claim for negotiation, but the perspective of the provincial government and the forestry company was that, until the claim was formally negotiated and finalised, the province held legal title to the land and the Indigenous inhabitants had no legal right to be accommodated. Protestors blocked MacMillan Bloedel workers from accessing the area of their tree forest licence. MacMillan Bloedel, with the support of the Attorney General of British Columbia as intervenor, sought a restraining order against the protestors and anyone else who might try to stop their logging activities. The two bands went before the courts seeking a declaration that their Aboriginal title was unextinguished, as well as an interlocutory injunction against MacMillan Bloedel in order to prevent the company from logging or trespassing on their land.

Judge Gibbs of the British Columbia Supreme Court heard the injunction requests. From reading Gibbs's decision, one gets the impression that he saw granting the Nuu-

Chah-Nulth request as equivalent to opening the floodgates of economic disaster for the province. His decision states that granting an injunction

> would represent, and be interpreted as, some recognition, even though only pending trial, of an overriding aboriginal title. It would be looked upon as a precedent and would spawn a rash of similar applications throughout the province. I do not regard that as being in any sense an exaggerated expectation.[29]

Gibbs goes on to express his worry that the potential flood of other requests from Indigenous groups in the province would not necessarily be restricted to the logging and forestry industry:

> ... similar challenges could be made to any resource or wild life harvesting authorized by the provincial Crown in the land claim areas. It is the prospect of the havoc which wholesale challenges would create in the financial, business and public activities in this province which has led me to conclude that it is urgent and imperative that I reach a decision based upon the relative strength of each party's case and grant one or other of the applications.[30]

Gibbs's lead up to his decision leaves little room for surprise when he ultimately finds that 'relative strength' residing in MacMillan Bloedel's case and rules in the company's favour. However, in an exceptional turn of events, the British Columbia Court of Appeal heard an appeal from the Nuu-chah-nulth. Reflecting on the larger issues that had been ignored for so long and that the *Calder* decision had begun to address, Justice Seaton wrote:

> There is a problem about tenure that has not been attended to in the past. We are being asked to ignore the problem as others have ignored it. I am not willing to do that.
>
> I test my conclusion by asking this question: If the Indians wished to do something that had the effect of making the area unusable by MacMillan Bloedel, would we let them, or would we preserve the forest in its present state? I think that we would preserve the forest. I think we should do that for either party.[31]

Nigel Bankes suggests that the courts began looking to alternatives to interlocutory injunctions in part because it 'can be an expensive and time-consuming process and there is no guarantee of success given the applicable standards for obtaining interlocutory relief'.[32] The SCC has also found the practice of seeking interlocutory injunctions wanting, for a variety of reasons. Its decision for the 2004 *Haida Nation* case mentions, amongst other things, that injunctions are meant to be a short-term stopgap remedy, and land claims negotiations can take years. The *Haida Nation* decision also suggests that 'the balance of convenience test tips the scales in favour of protecting jobs and government revenues, with the result that Aboriginal interests tend to "lose" outright pending a final determination of the issue'.[33] While such claims may be true, there is also an unfortunate element of casuistry to them. The highest court in Canada, which has demonstrated its willingness to engage in sweeping doctrinal creativity for the past forty years, casts itself as powerless but to hold as immutable those jurisprudential elements that would favour revenues over the recognition of Indigenous peoples' prior occupation of land. This leaves the Court to play the pragmatic yet sympathetic arbiter by finding a solution *other than* the injunction. With the volatile combination of large-scale natural resource projects and unresolved land claims, it is likely that the most critical factor for the SCC's disdain of injunctions was their categorical nature. One choice offers the threat of negative economic consequences for non-Indigenous interests, while the other offers the travesty of allowing the outside exploitation of land whose original owners still occupy it.

Thus, when the Haida Nation of British Columbia faced a similar problem with Weyerhaeuser in 2004, the Supreme Court of Canada was spurred into another flurry of doctrinal productivity. The Haida had actually argued a breach of fiduciary duty on the part of the Crown, since this case did have at stake the Haida's interest in their own land, and the Crown in right of the province, in having the option to grant or not grant forestry licences, had been exercising a discretionary control over that interest. As I have argued above, however, the SCC has grown uncomfortable with the inflexible obligation imposed by the fiduciary duty. Therefore, for an Indigenous people who had occupied a group of islands to the exclusion of all others since time immemorial, the SCC problematised the use of the fiduciary duty with the assertion that 'Aboriginal rights and title have been asserted but have not been defined or proven'.[34] In effect, even though their case for title was admittedly strong, the fiduciary duty requires that the Crown assume discretionary control over a *specific* interest. Pending the completion of land claims negotiations, the SCC found that 'the Aboriginal interest in question is insufficiently specific for the honour of the Crown to mandate that the Crown act in the Aboriginal group's best interest, as a fiduciary'.[35] Thus, with the *Haida Nation* decision, the SCC expounded the new doctrine of the duty to consult. The SCC now casts the duty to consult – and whatever remains of the fiduciary duty – as enforceable Crown obligations flowing from the larger umbrella principle of the honour of the Crown. The duty to consult, for its part, 'arises when the Crown has knowledge, real or constructive, of the potential existence of the Aboriginal right or title and contemplates conduct that might adversely affect it'.[36]

The scope or content of the duty to consult varies along a scale and 'is proportionate to a preliminary assessment of the strength of the case supporting the existence of the right or title, and to the seriousness of the potentially adverse effect upon the right or title claimed'.[37] As with so much in contemporary Aboriginal law, though, there is a profound ambivalence to the duty to consult. Similar to other Crown obligations rooted in the honour of the Crown, such as the fiduciary duty, it amounts to a contemporary jurisprudential ethics that imposes certain fundamental guidelines on the relationship between the settler state and Indigenous peoples. As such, it likely represents a much more positive state of affairs for Indigenous groups in Canada than what was available prior to 1982. Still, there are reasons for circumspection. The SCC states in *Haida Nation* that 'the commitment is to a meaningful process of consultation' and *perhaps* accommodation, but 'there is no duty to agree'.[38] Thus, the duty to consult is essentially coterminous with the concept of infringement in that it can provide for the potential override of Aboriginal rights and title.

Parallel with infringement as well, the duty to consult has also benefited from a rapid expansion. Although the original basis for its creation was the 'unspecific' nature of 'unproven' rights and title, the SCC's decision for the 2005 case of *Mikisew Cree Nation v. Canada* used the duty to consult framework to assess the First Nation's challenge of a proposed road project through their hunting territory.[39] As a Treaty 8 First Nation, there is nothing unspecific about the Mikisew Cree's treaty rights. The nineteenth century treaty that outlines their hunting rights, however, has a clause stipulating that tracts of land will be 'taken up from time to time for settlement, mining, lumbering, trading or other purposes'.[40] The SCC's ruling specifically precludes scrutinising an act of taking up hunting grounds for development as an infringement of treaty rights necessitating a *Sparrow* justification – unless *no* meaningful right to hunt remains over the *entirety* of the group's traditional territory.[41] Consultation has thus become a required process prior to undertaking activity which may adversely affect any rights or title, be those rights established or yet to be established.

Obligations and equivocality

The Supreme Court of Canada thus holds that the honour of the Crown obliges the Crown to a meaningful process of consultation with Indigenous groups when it contemplates conduct that might adversely affect their rights or title. While this *may* result in forms of accommodation, ultimately there is no absolute obligation to arrive at agreement.[42] Although the Supreme Court of Canada has not addressed the UNDRIP or the issue of FPIC directly, it has stated in multiple decisions – before and after the adoption of the declaration – that Indigenous peoples do not have a generalised 'veto' over final Crown decisions.[43] The SCC had briefly mentioned in the 1997 *Delgamuukw* case – the first to outline a definition of modern Aboriginal title – the possibility of full consent being *required* in some cases of the infringement of Aboriginal title.[44] Perhaps it is a case of the stakes of reconciliation becoming clearer to the Court, but subsequent decisions from the SCC give a narrower, less forceful context of applicability for this passing remark. The unanimous decision for *Haida Nation* from 2004 asserts that 'the Aboriginal "consent" spoken of in *Delgamuukw* is appropriate only in cases of established rights, and then by no means in every case. Rather, what is required is a process of balancing interests, of give and take'.[45] The Court's unanimous 2014 decision for *Tsilhqot'in Nation v. British Columbia* then presents justified infringement of Aboriginal title as an alternative to consent, so long as that infringement is supported by a compelling and substantial public purpose and it passes the Court's test for justification.[46] In this sense, no Aboriginal right or title is sufficiently absolute that its impairment does not have the potential to be considered under the doctrine of justified infringement. Stated otherwise, the only situation in which one can claim that consent to infringe rights or title is *required* in Canadian Aboriginal law is in those situations where the courts determine that the infringement in question is not justifiable under the test first set out in *Sparrow*.

The UNDRIP and its principle of free, prior and informed consent do share important commonalities with contemporary Canadian Aboriginal law. Both the declaration and the Supreme Court of Canada envision good faith consultation as essential to legitimating projects and development activities that may affect Indigenous rights or title. Both also avoid an absolutist approach to Indigenous rights. While the jurisprudence on consultation and infringement examined above makes it abundantly clear that Canadian law continuously weighs Indigenous rights against other interests, Sasha Boutilier argues that the analogous role of the final article in the declaration is often overlooked.[47] Article 46(1) asserts that nothing in the declaration should be 'construed as authorizing or encouraging any action which would dismember or impair, totally or in part, the territorial integrity or political unity of sovereign and independent States'. Article 46(2) states that rights set forth in the declaration may be subject to limitations 'solely for the purpose of securing due recognition and respect for the rights and freedoms of others and for meeting the just and most compelling requirements of a democratic society'. Thus, according to Paul Joffe, Indigenous rights embodied in the declaration 'are relative in nature, not absolute. Article 46 makes clear that the rights in this instrument are balanced with the rights of others'.[48] Just what the limitations on the rights in the declaration are, and where the balance with non-Indigenous interests lies, is not clear. Indeed, the declaration and its principle of FPIC are not immune to equivocality and indeterminacy. Nor are debate and disagreement concerning the true meaning of FPIC unique to Canada.

Some voices have promoted robust notions of FPIC. The UN Expert Mechanism on the Rights of Indigenous Peoples has asserted that 'the duty of the State to obtain Indigenous peoples' free, prior and informed consent entitles Indigenous peoples to effectively determine the outcome of decision-making that affects them, not merely a right to be involved in such processes'.[49] A manual on FPIC put out by the UN Food and Agriculture Organisation, in conjunction with a number of humanitarian organisations, outlines a similarly strong view of FPIC. It states that FPIC, as recognised in the UNDRIP, allows Indigenous peoples 'to give or withhold consent to a project that may affect them or their territories. Once they have given their consent, they can withdraw it at any stage'. It goes on to state that 'the FPIC process does not guarantee consent as a result'.[50] Marco Odello states that, even beyond the UNDRIP, the UN Committee for the Elimination of Racial Discrimination (CERD), in its interpretation of Article 5(c) of the *1965* International Convention on the Elimination of All Forms of Racial Discrimination,

> has underlined that states' obligations include respect for indigenous peoples' right to effective participation through their own representatives in state bodies and structures, including in constitutional reform processes, and has affirmed that decisions directly relating to indigenous peoples' rights shall be taken only with 'their informed consent'.[51]

On the other hand, Mauro Barelli points out that potential interpretations of FPIC were an active point of contention in the negotiations for the declaration. In outlining the evolution of Article 32 – pertaining to projects affecting Indigenous lands and resources – Barelli observes that a prior wording of the article described Indigenous peoples' '*right to require that States obtain their free and informed consent prior to the approval of any project*'.[52] The final version of the declaration, on the other hand, apparently responded to various states' concerns by establishing that states 'shall consult and cooperate in good faith with the indigenous peoples concerned through their own representative institutions *in order to obtain* their free and informed consent prior to the approval of any project'.[53] According to Barelli's interpretation, if FPIC was meant to recognise irrefutably a general right to veto, the original version of the article would have been preserved.[54] Nevertheless, even Barelli's examination of FPIC, along with his ultimate argument that the jurisprudence of the Inter-American Court of Human Rights (IACtHR) should be considered instructive in our interpretation of it, suggests that *some circumstances* should require the consent of Indigenous groups – namely, large-scale projects that will have a major impact on the lands and lives of Indigenous peoples.[55]

In a 2009 report, James Anaya, as special rapporteur to the UNHCR, suggests that the declaration 'should not be regarded as according indigenous peoples a general "veto power" over decisions that may affect them'.[56] However, similar to Barelli, Anaya makes the distinction that certain circumstances do merit a requirement for consent. Anaya's report specifically interprets the wording for Article 10 (relocation of Indigenous peoples from their traditional lands) and Article 29 (storage or disposal of toxic wastes in Indigenous lands) as obliging states to obtain prior consent. He then turns to the jurisprudence of the IACtHR as well. Taking inspiration from that court's decision concerning the Saramaka people of Suriname, Anaya also argues that large-scale projects with high impact should require this heightened level of obligation.[57]

At first glance, the attention to scale and impact draws a parallel with Canadian case law, since the duty to consult operates on a spectrum that becomes more onerous on the Crown as the potential for adverse effects on Indigenous rights and title increases. However, one can infer from the SCC case law that there may be an essential, underlying contrast as well. In *Delgamuukw*, the very objectives that the SCC has listed as potential justifications for the unilateral infringement of Aboriginal title tend toward precisely those of greater scale and impact: 'the development of agriculture, forestry, mining, and hydroelectric power, the general economic development of the interior of British Columbia ... the building of infrastructure and the settlement of foreign populations to support those aims ... '.[58] In essence, the very way in which the Court has entertained justifying the violation of the Indigenous possession and use of land suggests that the large-scale and high impact nature of some projects, while demanding a more onerous process of consultation, does not necessarily bring with it a *requirement* for consent. Rather, it could merit the opposite: a stark, forcible disregard for Indigenous rights and title due to a heightened, 'high stakes' sense of importance for the interests of the extractivist settler state.

Briefly, there are other differences of note between Canadian law and the declaration. The SCC has indicated circumstances that are at or approach a *de minimis* threshold in the duty to consult and infringement case law, thereby triggering little or no obligation from the Crown. For the duty to consult where the potential for infringement is minor, 'the only duty on the Crown may be to give notice, disclose information, and discuss any issues raised in response to the notice'.[59] The Court has deemed some forms of infringement of Aboriginal rights minor enough as to not amount to infringement in the legal sense. What the SCC has termed 'insignificant interference' therefore does not trigger a test for justification.[60] Lastly, Article 19 of the UNDRIP also calls for consultation in order to obtain the free, prior and informed consent of Indigenous peoples prior to implementing *legislative measures* that may affect them. The Canadian Federal Court of Appeal has come out against the idea of importing the duty to consult to the legislative process, however, arguing that it 'offends the separation of powers doctrine and the principle of parliamentary privilege'.[61] A final determination on this issue is yet to come from the SCC.

Despite the uncertainty and disagreement concerning FPIC and the declaration, then, Sasha Boutilier's suggestion that the declaration likely represents a higher standard of Indigenous rights recognition than Canadian law seems founded.[62] How these two frameworks of obligation will be reconciled is a critical question, particularly in a country whose current administration has sought to distinguish itself, on almost all counts, as the youthful and progressive contrast to the politics of the former Conservative government.[63] Current indications are that FPIC is actively being mined for its indeterminacy and equivocality in order to mould it into conformity with Canada's legal and political landscapes – notably the low tolerance for bogeymen such as an 'Indigenous veto'.

In effect, even with the 2010 announcement of Canada's support of the declaration, the prior Conservative administration referred to the declaration as 'an aspirational document' and stated that, after learning from the experiences of other countries, the government was 'confident that Canada can interpret the principles expressed in the Declaration *in a manner that is consistent with our Constitution and legal framework*'.[64] Since then, under Trudeau's Liberal government, efforts have revolved around accentuating and idealising *process* and *relationship* with Indigenous peoples rather than the unilateral and mutually opposing menaces of vetoes and rights infringement. In 2017, after clarifying that the federal government was retracting all objections to the declaration, Carolyn Bennett – Minister of what was then called Indigenous and Northern Affairs – was interviewed by a national daily:

> Dr. Bennett said 'free, prior and informed consent' merely means there is a commitment to developing policies in conjunction with Indigenous people on matters that will affect them.
>
> 'This is about making decisions together' from the inception, the minister said. 'It means not putting some fully baked project in front of people and getting them to vote yes or no'.[65]

With a series of similarly idealised explanations of FPIC-as-process having come from the prime minister and several ministers, Jason Tockman suggests that 'the prime minister seems to grasp the *process* of obtaining consent, but not the *outcome*'.[66] Conveniently, this models a conceptualisation of FPIC that integrates a court-mandated duty to consult with no absolute obligation to find agreement.

In early 2018, the Trudeau government released a policy document outlining ten principles respecting the federal government's relationship with Indigenous peoples. With a subtle adaptation of the language used in the declaration itself, the sixth principle states that the 'Government of Canada recognizes that meaningful engagement with Indigenous peoples *aims to secure* their free, prior, and informed consent when Canada proposes to take actions which impact them and their rights, including their lands, territories and resources'.[67] The specific wording chosen is no doubt intended to reflect not only Canada's past characterisations of the declaration as an *aspirational* document, but also to attribute even more of a processual character to the UNDRIP's principle of consent. Dwight Newman, a legal scholar specialising in the duty to consult, criticised the government's lack of transparency in quietly changing the wording and argues that the words in the declaration and the government's principles may look similar to the average reader, but the differences 'matter immensely to lawyers, bureaucrats and Indigenous communities'.[68]

For Sheryl Lightfoot, the shift in position on UNDRIP presented by the four major states of the Anglosphere – namely Canada, Australia, New Zealand and the United States – was all the more enigmatic because 'their commitments, qualifications and exclusions related to Indigenous rights remained remarkably consistent whether they were opposing or supporting the declaration'.[69] Indeed, if nothing significant has changed in the declaration, in Canadian law, or in Canadian policy toward Indigenous peoples, then it is likely that those reversals reflect a change in how the terms of the declaration themselves are interpreted and recognised. This is why, according to Lightfoot, analysis of international human rights instruments requires something more than the simple binary of commitment and non-commitment, or endorsement and non-endorsement. Her concept of *selective endorsement* illustrates the fact that states such as Canada strategically 'write down international norms so that those rewritten norms align with state interests as well as the legal and institutional status quo, all the while securing their standing in the community of states that support the norms'.[70]

In effect, indications are that the jurisprudential contours drawn by Canadian courts fall short of the more robust conceptualisations of FPIC, and, conversely, that Canadian politics will see to it that the interpretation of FPIC does not exceed the obligations already imposed upon it by contemporary Aboriginal law doctrines. As stated by the minister of Natural Resources Jim Carr – and as intimated by the Canadian government's begrudging endorsement of the declaration as well as its ten principles respecting the federal government's relationship with Indigenous peoples – 'the government is in the process of providing a Canadian definition of the declaration'.[71]

Reconciling consent

Punditry in Canada has a tendency to portray the work of the contemporary courts as purely beneficial to Indigenous groups. The inherence of rights and title, the sympathetic view of treaty promises, and the constitutionalisation of these changes all represent positive changes for the Indigenous peoples of Canada. Nevertheless, such generalisations overlook a profound ambivalence that Canadian Aboriginal law holds for Indigenous claimants. The other areas of doctrinal change that I have highlighted – the move away from the fiduciary duty, from the doctrine of interjurisdictional immunity, and from the use of injunctive relief – represent moves toward a greater manageability of the stakes of reconciliation. Compared with an earlier era, contemporary courts wield greater discretion to discipline the sometimes-imperious attitudes of settler state governments and prod them toward acknowledging the rights and interests of Indigenous peoples. These modern jurisprudential changes, however, also allow the courts, when they feel the need is compelling, to place limits on reconciliation and to exercise legal governance over the decolonising aspirations of Indigenous peoples.

It is worthwhile pointing out that, thus far, the use of the doctrine of infringement of Aboriginal rights or title in Canadian courts is relatively rare.[72] What is important to the legal-politics of Canada as an extractivist settler state, however, is that, when competing interests reach a fevered pitch, the legal-constitutional capacity for obviating Indigenous rights *is* there. It is my contention that this fundamental concern underlies both the case law and the politics of Canada as a settler state. This dynamic is thus representative of the legal-political environment into which the United Nations Declaration on the Rights of Indigenous Peoples is being absorbed in Canada. In effect, given the demonstrably indeterminate nature of the principle of FPIC within the declaration, the question of what consequences the legal-political discourses of various countries will have on the declaration (and its principle of FPIC) should be asked just as much as the inverse.

Since Canada's switch to endorsing the declaration, voices from both sides of the divide – governments concerned about natural resource development on the one hand and advocates for Indigenous rights on the other – have demonstrated a desire to avoid the contentious and polemical debates around vetoes or hard necessities of Indigenous consent. They often do this through emphasising process over outcome. Despite his 2009 UNHCR report that some circumstances could *require* consent, special rapporteur James Anaya, during a controversial visit to Canada in 2013, stated that

> the declaration doesn't say indigenous people have a right to withhold consent. It says states shall consult with indigenous peoples with the objective of achieving their consent. The sense there is that the parties come together and work hard and resolve to arrive at a consensual arrangement and that is the norm. That has to be what the debate has to be about. Not, "Who has a veto?" That is a very, very narrow and misguided way of looking at it.[73]

Prime Minister Trudeau, when pressed in 2016 on the question of whether the rights in the declaration amount to a power of veto for Indigenous groups, responded with a more philosophical comment about community support and social licence. 'What I've heard from business communities', he said, 'is they've recognized that ignoring community voices, trying to run roughshod across environmental concerns, has resulted in not getting ... pipelines and projects built that people wanted'.[74]

To be sure, processes of consultation, negotiation, and accommodation of Indigenous interests are critically important in all national colonial contexts. The difficulty with the absorption of the UNDRIP in various national settings – especially in the context of equivocal notions of FPIC – is that differing meanings and intentions can underlie the same desire to emphasise process over outcome. While Indigenous advocates may accentuate process over outcome in order to avoid the polemics of the Indigenous veto, government interests may do the same in order to gloss over fundamentally differing interpretations of their obligations to Indigenous peoples.[75] Jennifer Henderson and Pauline Wakeham, in their examination of the trope of 'healing' within the context of calls for reconciliation in Canada, suggest something similar. 'The iteration of the trope of healing might mean different things in different contexts of utterance', they argue, which 'might produce a certain reconciliation effect' – but those notions of healing can carry within them hegemonic deployments which depoliticise the work of reconciliation just as much as they can carry calls for decolonisation.[76] In the case of the UNDRIP and its principle of free, prior and informed consent, Indigenous leaders who seek to refocus the debate away from polemical questions about an Indigenous veto might find unexpected bedfellows with endorsing governments, but contemporary legal-political history in Canada suggests that they have reason to be circumspect.

Notes

1. Sheryl Lightfoot, 'Selective Endorsement without Intent to Implement: Indigenous Rights and the Anglosphere', *International Journal of Human Rights* 16, no. 1 (2012): 103.
2. For the former, see 'Government Supports Indigenous Declaration without Reservation: Wilson-Raybould', 20 July 2016, https://www.cbc.ca/news/indigenous/government-supports-undrip-without-reservation-1.3687315 (accessed August 3, 2018). For the latter, see 'Justice Minister Jody Wilson-Raybould Says Adopting UNDRIP into Canadian Law "Unworkable"', 12 July 2016, http://aptnnews.ca/2016/07/12/justice-minister-jody-wilson-raybould-says-adopting-undrip-into-canadian-law-unworkable/ (accessed August 3, 2018).
3. In Canada, the politics of Indigenous rights and (de)colonisation are so intimately infused with the work of the courts that I have the inclination to use the term *legal-politics*.
4. See Evan Fox-Decent and Ian Dahlman, 'Sovereignty as Trusteeship and Indigenous Peoples', *Theoretical Inquiries in Law* 16, no. 2 (2015): 518–20.
5. Rodolfo Stavenhagen, 'Human Rights and Indigenous Issues', Report of the Special Rapporteur on the Situation of Human Rights and Fundamental Freedoms of Indigenous People, no. E/CN.4/2003/90, 21 January 2003: Executive Summary.

6. James Anaya, 'Extractive Industries Operating Within or Near Indigenous Territories', UN Special Rapporteur's Report, no. A/HRC/18/35, 11 July 2011: 26.
7. Jason Tockman, 'Eliding Consent in Extractivist States: Bolivia, Canada, and the UN Declaration on the Rights of Indigenous Peoples', *International Journal of Human Rights* 22, no. 3 (2018): 342n1.
8. Lightfoot, 'Selective Endorsement', 112. Lightfoot also recounts that Canada's dissatisfaction was deep enough to go beyond the content of the declaration, with McNee expressing that the process had been neither open, nor inclusive, nor transparent. Canada also asserted that the declaration was aspirational, non-binding, of no legal effect in Canada, and not representative of customary international law.
9. *Calder v. British Columbia (Attorney General)*, [1973] SCR 313. As I will discuss below, this marked the advent of the modern comprehensive land claims process.
10. This begun mainly with *White and Bob*, one of the few key precedents in modern Aboriginal law not to come from the SCC. *R. v. White and Bob*, [1964] 50 DLR (2d) 613 (BCCA), aff'd [1965] 52 D.L.R. (2d) 481 (SCC).
11. *Constitution Act, 1982*, s. 35, being Schedule B to the *Canada Act 1982* (U.K.), 1982, c. 11. In Canada, the umbrella terms 'Indigenous' and 'Aboriginal' therefore encompass the three categories of Indian, Inuit and Métis. Though replaced by terms such as 'First Nations' in common parlance years ago, the antiquated term 'Indian' lives on in Canada in legal and constitutional usage.
12. Cited in *Guerin v. The Queen* [1984] 2 SCR 335 at 342. The quote is from a report Mr. Anfield submitted to the Indian Commissioner for British Columbia in 1955.
13. Ibid., 376.
14. John Borrows and Leonard Rotman, *Aboriginal Legal Issues: Cases, Materials & Commentary*, 4th ed. (Markham: LexisNexis), 466.
15. Ibid., 463.
16. *Wewaykum Indian Band v. Canada*, 2002 SCC 79, [2002] 4 SCR 245.
17. Ibid., 81.
18. *Haida Nation v. British Columbia (Minister of Forests)*, 2004 SCC 73, [2004] 3 SCR 511 [*Haida Nation*].
19. Jamie Dickson, *The Honour and Dishonour of the Crown: Making Sense of Aboriginal Law in Canada* (Saskatoon: Purich, 2015). Dickson counts himself among those critical of the Court's concept of the fiduciary duty in Aboriginal law and thus offers a comprehensive outline and critique of this Crown obligation.
20. Ibid., 9.
21. *Constitution Act, 1867* (U.K.), 30 & 31 Vict., c. 3, s. 91, reprinted in R.S.C. 1985, App. II, No. 5. The SCC has since interpreted the term 'Indians' in nineteenth century constitutional parlance as applying to all categories of Indigenous peoples in Canada: status and non-status Indian (according to the *Indian Act*), Inuit, and Métis.
22. *Constitution Act, 1982*, s. 52, being Schedule B to the *Canada Act 1982* (U.K.), 1982, c. 11.
23. *Delgamuukw v. British Columbia*, [1997] 3 SCR 1010 [*Delgamuukw*].
24. Ibid., 165.
25. *Constitution Act, 1867* (U.K.), 30 & 31 Vict., c. 3, s. 91, reprinted in R.S.C. 1985, App. II, No. 5.
26. For more on the confusion and contradictions this created, see Kerry Wilkins, '*R. v. Morris*: A Shot in the Dark and Its Repercussions', *Indigenous Law Journal* 7, no. 1 (2008): 12; Kerry Wilkins, 'Dancing in the Dark: Of Provinces and Section 35 Rights After 2010', *Supreme Court Law Review* 54 (2011): 533.
27. Nigel Bankes and Jennifer Koshan, 'The Uncertain Status of the Doctrine of Interjurisdictional Immunity on Reserve Lands', *ABlawg: The University of Calgary Faculty of Law Blog*, October 28, 2014, http://ablawg.ca/2014/10/28/the-uncertain-status-of-the-doctrine-of-interjurisdictional-immunity-on-reserve-lands/.
28. Ibid.
29. *MacMillan Bloedel v Mullin*, [1985] 2 WWR 722; [1985] 2 CNLR 26 at para. 27 (BCSC).

30. Ibid.
31. *MacMillan Bloedel Ltd. v. Mullin*, [1985] 61 BCLR 145; [1985] 2 CNLR 58 at para. 78–79 (BCCA).
32. Nigel Bankes, 'The Implications of the *Tsilhqot'in (William)* and *Grassy Narrows (Keewatin)* Decisions of the Supreme Court of Canada for the Natural Resources Industries', *Journal of Energy & Natural Resources Law* 33, no. 3 (2015): 194–5.
33. *Haida Nation*, 14.
34. Ibid., 18.
35. Ibid.
36. Ibid., 35.
37. Ibid., 39.
38. Ibid., 42.
39. *Mikisew Cree Nation v. Canada (Minister of Canadian Heritage)*, 2005 SCC 69, [2005] 3 SCR 388.
40. Ibid., 2.
41. Ibid., 48.
42. *Haida Nation*, 42.
43. *Haida Nation*, 48; *Chippewa of the Thames v. Enbridge*, 2017 SCC 41, [2017] 1 SCR 1099 at para. 59.
44. *Delgamuukw*, 168.
45. *Haida Nation*, 48.
46. *Tsilhqot'in Nation v. British Columbia*, 2014 SCC 44, [2014] 2 SCR 257 at para. 76–77.
47. Sasha Boutilier, 'Free, Prior, and Informed Consent and Reconciliation in Canada: Proposals to Implement Articles 19 and 32 of the UN Declaration on the Rights of Indigenous Peoples', *Western Journal of Legal Studies* 7, no. 1 (2017): 4.
48. Paul Joffe, 'Canada's Opposition to the UN Declaration: Legitimate Concerns or Ideological Bias?', in *Realizing the UN Declaration on the Rights of Indigenous Peoples: Triumph, Hope, and Action*, eds. Jackie Hartley, Paul Joffe and Jennifer Preston (Saskatoon: Purich, 2010), 80.
49. United Nations Expert Mechanism on the Rights of Indigenous Peoples, 'Final Study on Indigenous Peoples and the Right to Participate in Decision-making', no. A/HRC/EMRIP/2011/2, 26 May 2011, 20.
50. UN FAO, *Free, Prior and Informed Consent: An Indigenous Peoples' Right and a Good Practice for Local Communities* (Rome: FAO, 2016), 3.
51. Marco Odello, 'Indigenous Peoples' Rights and Cultural Identity in the Inter-American Context', *International Journal of Human Rights* 16, no. 1 (2012): 39.
52. Mauro Barelli, 'Free, Prior and Informed Consent in the Aftermath of the UN Declaration on the Rights of Indigenous Peoples: Developments and Challenges Ahead', *International Journal of Human Rights* 16, no. 1 (2012): 10. Emphasis is Barelli's.
53. Ibid., 11. Emphasis is Barelli's.
54. Ibid., 11.
55. Ibid., 14.
56. James Anaya, 'Promotion and Protection of All Human Rights, Civil, Political, Economic, Social and Cultural Rights, Including the Right to Development', Report of the Special Rapporteur on the Situation of Human Rights and Fundamental Freedoms of Indigenous People, no. A/HRC/12/34, 15 July 2009: 46.
57. Ibid., 47.
58. *Delgamuukw*, 165.
59. *Haida Nation*, 43.
60. *R. v.* Côté, [1996] 3 SCR 139 at para. 88; *R. v. Morris*, 2006 SCC 59, [2006] 2 SCR 915 at para. 47–48. The term 'insignificant interference' first appears in *R. v. Morris.*
61. *Canada (Governor General in Council) v. Mikisew Cree First Nation*, 2016 FCA 311, [2017] 3 FCR 298 at para. 3, leave to appeal to SCC granted.
62. Boutilier, 'FPIC and Reconciliation'.

63. In his mandate letter to Carolyn Bennett, Minister of Indigenous and Northern Affairs, Trudeau wrote that 'no relationship is more important to me and to Canada than the one with Indigenous Peoples. It is time for a renewed, nation-to-nation relationship with Indigenous Peoples, based on recognition of rights, respect, co-operation, and partnership.' The first in his list of priorities for the new minister was 'to implement recommendations of the Truth and Reconciliation Commission, starting with the implementation of the *United Nations Declaration on the Rights of Indigenous Peoples*'. Justin Trudeau to Carolyn Bennett, Ottawa, November 15, 2015, in *Mandate Letters*, (Ottawa: Office of the Prime Minister, 2015), https://pm.gc.ca/eng/minister-indigenous-and-northern-affairs-mandate-letter_2015.
64. Indigenous and Northern Affairs Canada, 'Canada's Statement of Support on the UN Declaration on the Rights of Indigenous Peoples', November 12, 2010, https://www.aadnc-aandc.gc.ca/eng/1309374239861/1309374546142 (accessed August 1, 2018). Emphasis mine.
65. Gloria Galloway, 'Ottawa Drops Objections to UN Resolution on Indigenous Consent', *Globe and Mail*, April 24, 2017. Shortly thereafter Carolyn Bennett's portfolio was renamed Crown-Indigenous Relations.
66. Tockman, 'Eliding Consent', 339.
67. Department of Justice, 'Principles Respecting the Government of Canada's Relationship with Indigenous Peoples', July 14, 2017, http://www.justice.gc.ca/eng/csj-sjc/principles-principes.html (accessed August 1, 2018). Emphasis mine.
68. Dwight Newman, 'Ottawa's Sly Change on Consent May Damage Indigenous Relationships', *Globe and Mail*, August 3, 2017.
69. Lightfoot, 'Selective Endorsement', 116.
70. Ibid., 119.
71. APTN National News, 'Ottawa Developing "Canadian Definition" of UNDRIP, says Liberal Minister', April 21, 2016, http://aptnnews.ca/2016/04/21/ottawa-developing-canadian-definition-of-undrip-says-liberal-minister/ (accessed July 20, 2018).
72. In the legislative sphere, the most common occurrence would be the periodic banning of hunting or fishing for all persons – including rights-bearing Indigenous harvesters – in regions where the government deems that population decline of a particular species warrants it.
73. 'UN Envoy Accused of "Publicity Stunt" Promises "Constructive" Advice for Harper Government on Aboriginal Issues', *National Post*, October 7, 2013.
74. Larry Lintz, 'UN Declaration Doesn't Give Canadian First Nations a Veto: Minister', *Vancouver Sun*, June 30, 2016.
75. There is an entire line of analysis to be conducted, beyond the scope of this article, on the varying interpretations of FPIC and how they relate to the notion of veto power. Unsurprisingly, critics of Indigenous claims readily conflate consent with veto, while advocates for Indigenous rights allow for more nuance. According to Paul Joffe, the term veto implies 'complete and arbitrary power, with no balancing of rights' – which the UNDRIP does not provide. From this perspective, the right to withhold consent in a processual, consultative and consensus-seeking relationship does not necessarily constitute veto power. Paul Joffe, 'Veto and Consent – Significant Differences', unpublished paper, March 26, 2016, 1.
76. Jennifer Henderson and Pauline Wakeham, 'Colonial Reckoning, National Reconciliation?: Aboriginal Peoples and the Culture of Redress in Canada', *ESC: English Studies in Canada* 35, no. 1 (2009): 16–17.

Disclosure statement

No potential conflict of interest was reported by the author.

ORCID

Jeremy Patzer http://orcid.org/0000-0002-1462-0097

A critical evaluation of the domestic standards of the right to prior consultation under the UNDRIP: lessons from the Peruvian case

Amelia Alva-Arévalo

ABSTRACT

The adoption of the UNDRIP gave new hope to indigenous peoples in constituting a tool to defend their rights when facing major political and economic powers that impose development projects. The right to prior consultation, foreseen by the UNDRIP, implies an intercultural dialogue between the state and indigenous peoples with the objective to achieve their consent. In addition, it empowers them to demand the fulfilment of other rights and to rule their destinies according to their own criteria and priorities of life. Peru is the first Latin American country that approved a legislation focused on the right to prior consultation. This experience is seen as a successful model by its neighbours. However, after the first years of its application, this legislation has started to be under scrutiny. This article analyses the new Peruvian legislation of prior consultation, its congruence with the UNDRIP and its requirement of free, prior and informed consent through the presentation of an emblematic process of consultation on hydrocarbons.

1. As introduction: rights to prior consultation and consent in the United Nations Declaration on the Rights of Indigenous Peoples

One of the greatest threats that indigenous peoples face are extractive activities that take place in their territories. Governments often implement development programmes and grant concessions in order to extract the wealth of the soil and sub soil, without considering the environmental damages of these activities and neglecting indigenous' ways of life, their conceptions of development and the supply of necessary resources for their subsistence. In nearly all cases, these decisions are made regardless of their opinion or will. Apart from irreparable environmental damage therefore, conflicts or extremely intolerant positions against private investments often emerge. In this context, prior consultation arises as a collective right that allows indigenous peoples to be co-participants in government decisions, creating the possibility to discuss, accept, reject or modify state's legislative or administrative measures that may affect them. In the case of extractive activities, it also allows indigenous peoples, to evaluate environmental impact studies, to establish the conditions for exploration or exploitation or to determine economic benefits.

Article 6 of the Convention concerning Indigenous and Tribal Peoples in Independent Countries (ILO Convention N. 169) establishes that consultations must be conducted in good faith, through the indigenous peoples' representative institutions, according to the circumstances and in order to obtain agreement or consent. Unlike the ILO Convention N. 169, the UNDRIP is more emphatic to protect indigenous peoples' rights by the explicit requirement of consent. Its Article 19, considered as a general principle,[1] states as the sole purpose of the consultation process to obtain the free, prior and informed consent while it removes the term 'agreement'. This article also eliminates the term 'directly', used in the ILO Convention, extending the coverage of this right to indirectly affected people.[2]

Despite the fact that the UNDRIP is soft-law,[3] that is, it does not create any binding legal obligations in domestic legal systems,[4] its application should be considered 'as a political, moral and legal imperative'[5] since it contains current concerns of indigenous peoples and enshrines rights that allow them to be directly involved with the decision-making related to their conservation, survival and full development, contributing in this way to establish a joint relationship with the states. This international legal instrument has expressly determined cases in which it is essential to obtain the free, prior and informed consent of the concerned indigenous peoples: when a measure includes their relocation (Article 10) and when a measure concerns storing or disposing hazardous materials in their territories (Article 29).[6] Additionally, the UNDRIP establishes that consultations must be conducted in order to obtain free and informed consent prior to the approval of projects affecting their lands or territories and other resources, particularly in connection with the development, utilisation or exploitation of mineral, water or other resources (Article 32).

At the same time, pronouncements of human rights institutions show a growing support to the right to consent, notably for special cases. The Inter-American Court of Human Rights is one example. In the judgment of Saramaka people v. Suriname, it held that the state has an obligation to obtain consent when the development plans or large-scale investment have an impact on indigenous territories and lands.[7] According to the Inter-American Commission on Human Rights this interpretation should be regarded as a *heightened safeguard* of essential rights (such as life or cultural identity), which ensures the existence of indigenous peoples.[8] Another example is the UN Expert Mechanism on the Rights of Indigenous Peoples which stated that through the right to consent, indigenous peoples may express their accordance with the measure and, in turn, can set down their conditions. Obtaining consent would give the consultation process more *effective* meaning, involving a negotiation towards mutual agreements by the participants of the process, in contrast to the mere fulfilment of a simple formality.[9]

In the opinion of the former UN Special Rapporteur on the Rights of Indigenous Peoples, James Anaya, the importance of obtaining consent depends on the circumstances and on the indigenous peoples' interest. If a measure or project may directly and considerably impact the lives or territories of indigenous peoples, then a *strong presumption* towards its prohibition will be established in the absence of indigenous consent.[10] Regarding this presumption and under the light of the UNDRIP and the principles enshrined in it, this article aims to criticise the current application of the right to prior consultation and consent in the Peruvian context through the presentation of an emblematic case.

2. The Peruvian case under scrutiny

In 2009, submerged in a growing number of social conflicts, the Peruvian government faced an indigenous mobilisation that had a tragic outcome that shook Peruvian society and politics. This conflict, known as *Baguazo*, constitutes a milestone for the legal implementation of the right to prior consultation.[11] The former UN Special Rapporteur on the Rights of Indigenous Peoples observed that the lack of consultation contributed to the fact that indigenous peoples opted for social protest to defend their rights.[12] The Peruvian Constitutional Tribunal agreed with this position, recognising that the emergence of violence was due to the absence of effort by the state to implement the right to prior consultation.[13]

Considering the requirements of the indigenous leaders, the Peruvian government opened a space for negotiation between representatives of the indigenous organisations and the executive power in order to elaborate a law to regulate the right to prior consultation. This negotiation was the first tangible legislative effort of the Peruvian state to implement this right, an opportunity without precedents in Latin America. As an answer to the crisis, the Law of Prior Consultation[14] attempts to integrate the principal human rights standards, to develop the content, principles and procedures of this right concerning legislative or administrative measures, and to develop plans, programmes and projects at the regional and national level that may improve the rights of indigenous peoples directly.

The first years of application of this law were challenging because of the high expectations of the indigenous organisations on the one hand, and the 'implementation gap' between legislation on indigenous issues and day-to-day reality on the other.[15] To fill the 'implementation gap' each public entity must conform its internal procedures to the Law of Prior Consultation (LPC) and its Regulation (RLPC)[16] but above all to the rights and freedoms recognised by the Peruvian Political Constitution and to the international instruments of human rights such as the United Nation Declaration on the Rights of Indigenous Peoples (UNDRIP).[17] Following Professor Stavenhagen, to implement the right to prior consultation, all national norms have to be made and interpreted in order to promote and protect indigenous peoples' rights and not to limit them.[18]

In the period between September 2011, when the Law of Prior Consultation was enacted, and February 2018, the Peruvian state has organised 36 consultation processes, of which 34 have been concluded; 11 of them approved contracts to explore and exploit hydrocarbons.[19] All consultation processes have agreements with the affected indigenous peoples and are considered 'successful' by the Peruvian government since the consulted measures were approved. Nonetheless, indigenous organisations denounce that prior consultations have been reduced to an informative process, a State's tool to proceed exploring or exploiting natural resources.[20]

The focus of what follows is on the consultation on hydrocarbon activities. There are three reasons for this perspective: (i) the hydrocarbon activity is carried out to a great(er) extent in the Peruvian Amazon region, a region of great biological and cultural diversity which implies a great sensitivity to the frequent environmental damages reported; (ii) socio-environmental conflicts arise mainly around extractive projects[21]; (iii) the first consultation processes were carried out, for the most part, within the hydrocarbon sector, a sector that on adapted its internal standards to the new legislation on prior consultation early.[22]

2.1. Congruency of the Peruvian legal framework on prior consultation (and the free prior and informed consent) with the UNDRIP

In Peru, the debate around the purpose of the prior consultation has been erroneously focused on the right to veto.[23] In fact, this is a pointless discussion since veto power is not expressly recognised by any international instrument. The emphasis is on the principle of good faith to conduct the process of prior consultation in sense that seeks to give the indigenous people all the necessary elements to issue a free and informed decision. However, it must be admitted that this is a rather controversial issue where the recognition of the right to free, prior and informed consent plays a principal role. It even seems that the former UN Rapporteurs on the Rights of Indigenous Peoples have different positions: while Stavenhagen (2003) defended that indigenous peoples have the 'right to say no' to defend their own vision of development[24]; Anaya (2009) stated that consultations do not provide to indigenous peoples a 'veto power', but that they were designed to build dialogue with the objective to achieve 'mutually satisfactory agreement'.[25]

Apart from this controversy, the mistake is to approach the consultation process from a negative perspective, which assumes that indigenous peoples will reject the proposed measure. This position will inevitably lead to the idea of the right to veto. Instead, reflections on the purpose of the consultation should be made on the two possibilities provided for in international law: agreement or consent. This approach should be considered as a general rule. The ILO Committee of Experts on the Application of Conventions and Recommendations has pointed out that Article 6 of the ILO Convention N. 169 provides that consultation has the objective of achieving agreement or consent on the proposed measures and that it allows 'the full expression of the viewpoints of the concerned people, "so that they may be able to affect the outcome and a consensus could be achieved"'.[26] Therefore, on the potential of agreements there seems to be no discussion (what deserves to be analysed independently is the quality of these agreements). However, the ways to achieve consent need more examination.

Although the Peruvian state approved the UNDRIP, the Law of Prior Consultation establishes the ILO Convention No. 169 as the only legal frame of interpretation.[27] This is an important omission, since because of this the Law of Prior Consultation fails to request consent for the special cases foreseen by the UNDRIP. This gap was pointed out by indigenous organisations, who demanded to modify this law, but there is no political will to attempt it so far. Currently, in order to protect the communal property, the Regulation of the Law of Prior Consultation is the only legal instrument that foresees in a free, prior and informed consent, but it does this only in cases of: relocations and disposal of hazardous materials.[28] Once again, the recognition of consent is omitted when a measure seeks to approve large-scale development or investment projects that would have a major impact within indigenous territory. This makes that in such cases, the state has been granted the right to make the final decision. In sum, since the free, prior and informed consent is not required by the Law of Prior Consultation, all legislative or administrative measures will be inevitably approved if an evaluation conducted by the state entity concludes that it does not affect indigenous peoples' collective rights.

The recognition of the right to free, prior and informed consent by the Law of Prior Consultation would have demonstrated the good faith of the state and a genuine desire to protect indigenous peoples' rights facing extractive activities. A common argument of the Peruvian government not to implement consent is to offer extractivism as a development paradigm.[29] This creates mistrust among indigenous peoples through their assumption that the decision is already made before the beginning of the consultation process. Indigenous peoples perceive that the consultation process does not offer them a real possibility to express their consent. At this point, consultation loses its meaning, because in many cases indigenous peoples, instead of discussing the substance of the measure, use this right to obtain something in return, mainly the coverage of basic services, since they believe that in any case the state will impose its own development model. Consequently, consultation is not understood as a right that could allow to protect and ensure their survival.

Nonetheless, the omission of the free, prior and informed consent in the Law of Prior Consultation can still be perfectly corrected by an interpretation that takes into account *all* international human rights standards, which the Fourth Final and Transitory Provision of the Constitution provides.[30] In this regard, it is interesting to take into account the standards developed by the Inter-American Court of Human Rights, which recognises that states may limit or subordinate property rights – private or collective – and allow them to interpret that the extraction of natural resources is of general interest. The Inter-American Court has expressly established that Article 21 of the American Convention of Human Rights cannot prevent the state from issuing any type of concession for the exploration or extraction of natural resources, but that the restriction of property may be possible only if it is legal, necessary, proportional and if its purpose is to achieve a legitimate objective in a democratic society.[31]

In the case of indigenous lands, the Court also notes that the survival of the group and its members must be considered as a 'crucial factor'.[32] Therefore, it establishes three guarantees that must be complied by states before granting licenses and that will help to determine if the survival of indigenous or tribal people is threatened: (i) *The effective participation* of indigenous peoples according to their own uses and customs (ii) the reasonable benefit for indigenous people from the extractive activity, and (iii) The elaboration of a technical and independent environmental and social impact study.[33] The Court recognises that consultation (and its objective) varies according to the nature and content of the rights that are at stake, and therefore the state must ensure, in accord with indigenous traditions and customs, to obtain the free, prior and informed consent when major development or investment plans that may have a profound impact on indigenous property rights are intended.[34] Only then the safeguard of an *effective participation* can be fulfilled.[35]

The Inter-American Court of Human Rights has recognised the relationship of indigenous peoples to their lands as a 'fundamental basis of their cultures, their spiritual life, their integrity and their economic survival'.[36] In fact, the Inter-American Court has clarified that when states seek to apply Article 21 of the American Convention on Human Rights, they also must take into account Articles 1.1 and 29.b. The first enshrines the pro homine principle or the commitment of the state and its public officials at different levels to respect the rights and freedoms recognised by the American Convention,[37] while the second prohibits to interpret the American Convention on Human Rights in detriment of the rights or freedoms recognised in domestic and international law.[38] In this way, legislation that aims to restrict the right to property must take into account the cultural characteristics of indigenous peoples and their spiritual link with their territories.[39]

In addition to these perspectives of the Inter-American Court of Human Rights, two more reasoning can help to defend the right to consent of indigenous peoples, especially when dealing with extractive activities: (i) a correct interpretation of the limits to the rule of the majority and (ii) the exercise of the Right to self-determination.

(i) Decisions that benefit majorities, even if they seek the common good, should be subject to a proportionality test[40] to determine whether the measure involves disproportional sacrifices for minorities that are unacceptable for a democratic society. If the proportionality test concludes that the measure is going to have an impact on the survival of indigenous peoples, the state should refrain from continuing with the measure.[41] In this regard, the Inter-American Court has limited the rule of majority affirming that:

> The bare existence of a democratic regime does not guarantee, per se, the permanent respect of International Law, including International Law of Human Rights, and which has also been considered by the Inter-American Democratic Charter. *The democratic legitimacy of specific facts in a society is limited by the norms of protection of human rights* recognized in international treaties, such as the American Convention, in such a form that the existence of one true democratic regime is determined by both its formal and substantial characteristics, and therefore, particularly in cases of serious violations of non-revocable norms of International Law, *the protection of human rights constitutes a impassable limit to the rule of the majority* (…).[42] (Emphasis added)

In fact, Peruvian legislation includes the proportionality test, but its application is doomed to fail if the entity who defines necessity and proportionality is the same as the one that is interested in carrying out the measure.. This is exactly what the Law of Prior Consultation does: it has delegated to the 'promoter entity'[43] the task to organise the prior consultation process on the measure and to take the final decision at the end of the whole consultation process.[44] This is one of the legal problems that the exercise of the right to consultation in Peru faces, since the person in charge of determining whether the rights of indigenous peoples will be harmed and to what extent, is the promoter entity that, as its name indicates, *promotes* the measure. In consequence, so far eleven consultation processes on oil projects have ended with the approval of the measure. Of course, if indigenous peoples disagree with the final decision taken by the promoter entity, the Law of Prior Consultation allows them to prosecute the state before a court or tribunal, alleging non-compliance with international human rights standards, but the problem with litigation is that indigenous peoples have to demand the fulfilment of their rights in (juridical) spaces that are not their own and are also difficult for them to access due to cultural, linguistic or economic barriers.[45]

(ii) Obtaining consent as a manifestation of the full exercise of the right to self-determination is recognised by the UNDRIP. According to Article 32, indigenous peoples have the right to decide and control their own development, which implies they should give their consent to *all* measures that states plan to implement in their territories, *including those with less impact*. This contrast with the interpretations of Inter-American Court, which establishes the need to obtain consent only in the case of high-impact measures that endanger their survival.[46] It should be mentioned that Article

> 7.1 of the ILO Convention No. 169 had already recognised the right of indigenous peoples to *decide and control* their own [economic, social and cultural] development.

Notwithstanding the importance of the UNDRIP, the Peruvian state still refuses to comply with its provisions, given its soft law character and because no way has been yet how to harmonise the exercise of rights to self-determination, autonomy and self-government of indigenous peoples, enshrined in Articles 3 and 4 of the UNDRIP with the exercise of self-determination of the rest of the population, whose will is attributed to the state. Facing this situation and applying Article 46.2 of the UNDRIP,[47] I wonder if states can limit the right to self-determination using the Inter-American Court's restrictions developed for the right to property. If this limitation is applied, it should be subject to detailed scrutiny.[48] This approach could work if an impartial institution such as, for example, the Ombudsman's Office, that takes a broader perspective on the human rights at stake, is in charge to assess the relevance of the restriction of the right to self-determination. This perspective should also take into account that, due to the multicultural nature of the nation, there are different visions of development that must be respected.

2.2. Exercising the right to consultation and free, prior and informed consent in the Peruvian Amazon

2.2.1. The background

Historically, the Amazon region or 'selva' (jungle) was conceived as faraway from Lima, the economic, political and administrative capital of Peru. One of the factors that brought dynamism in this region was the exploitation of hydrocarbons, an activity that dates back to the late 1930s with the exploitation of the field Aguas Calientes, located in the central jungle.[49] In the early 1970s, another project started in the Amazon with the concession of oil blocks 1-A and 1-B to the Occidental Petroleum Corporation.[50] The exploitation of these oil blocks represented the first 'oil boom' and covered the national demand for decades. The second 'oil boom' started in 2003, the year with the largest number of granted oil concessions. These concessions increased the hydrocarbon activity in the Peruvian Amazon between 2003 and 2009 from 7.1% to 41.2% of its total area. A total of 69.1% of the Peruvian Amazon has been under oil or gas concession at some point between 1970 and 2009. Out of 52 active concessions in 2010, 46 overlapped titled indigenous lands and 17 were superimposed on indigenous reserves.[51] A same pattern emerges in all cases: the expansion of extractive industries in territories of indigenous peoples deepens unequal power relations[52] and creates spaces in which the Peruvian state fails to guarantee the protection of human rights.[53]

In July 2012, shortly after the Regulation on the Law of Prior Consultation was adopted, the Peruvian Ministry of Energy and Mines approved the *Resolución Ministerial* No. 350-2012-MEM/DM. Article 1 of this resolution establishes seven administrative procedures for the consultation process in the hydrocarbon sector,[54] the promoter entity in charge of the consultation, and the time schedule within which consultations must be conducted. In relation to licensing contracts to explore and exploit hydrocarbons, the *Resolución Ministerial* states that the administrative measure to be consulted is the *Decreto Supremo*,[55] which should be done before its emission, and delegates[56] the function to conduct the consultation on these measures to the state company Perupetro S.A.

Regarding hydrocarbon projects, the Peruvian state started in 2013 with separate consultations for thirteen oil block. All of these consultation processes have been concluded with agreements, but of these consultations only the one related to the oil block 192 complied with promulgating the *decreto supremo*.[57] Particularly this case is important, since it constitutes a good example of the difficulties to exercise the right to prior consultation in accord to the UNDRIP. The oil block 192 is located in the Andoas district, Datem del Marañon province, and in the Tigre and Trompeteros districts. It covers territories of indigenous communities of the Quechua, Achuar, Kichwa and Urarina peoples along the basins of the Pastaza, Corrientes, Tigre and Marañon rivers in the department of Loreto (Northern Peru). The hydrocarbon operations began with the concession granted to Occidental Petroleum Corporation in block 1-A (22 June 1971) and in block 1B (3 April 1978). In 2001, the *Cesión de Posición contractual en el contrato de servicios para la explotación de hidrocarburos en el lote 1AB* was signed between Perupetro S.A. and Pluspetrol Perú Corporation S.A.[58]

When the Occidental Petroleum Corporation carried out its operations, environmental regulatory frameworks were non-existent in Peru, causing a devastating environmental pollution.[59] During decades indigenous organisations have reiteratedly denounced that the physical and cultural existence of their communities were at risk because of this extractive activity. They also claimed that a consultation process was not conducted, even though in 2000 the Peruvian state granted the control of the operations to the company Pluspetrol Norte S.A., a date in which the duty to consult was already in force.[60]

2.2.2. Prior consultation on the block 192

Not until August 2012, when the Regulation on the Law of Prior Consultation was recently approved, the government announced a prior consultation process on the continuation of the oil activity in block 192. This process would be the first in the extractive sector under the new legislation on prior consultation and caused considerable expectations as it needed to be ended by August 2015, the ending date of the licence contract with Pluspetrol Norte S.A. However, almost three years after being announced, the consultation did not begin yet because the indigenous organisations of block 192 demanded to the state first to meet the main demands of their communities: compensation for forty years of oil exploitation and use of their lands; compensation for environmental impacts; titling of their lands; remediation of their lands and rivers; and an environmental and social diagnosis.[61]

In November 2012, the Peruvian government had to initiate a direct negotiation with the representatives of the affected indigenous communities. This negotiation reached its greatest achievement after three years, in March 2015, with the *Acta de Lima*,[62] a document that included agreements on sanitation, intercultural development, environmental remediation and land titling. This was the tangible achievement that indigenous peoples needed to accept their participation in the prior consultation process which began in May 2015.

The Peruvian legislation foresees seven stages for the consultation process: (1) identification of the measure that affects the indigenous peoples' collective rights; (2) identification of the indigenous peoples to be consulted; (3) publicity of the measure; (4) information on the measure; (5) internal evaluation within the indigenous institutions and organisations about the measure; (6) dialogue between representatives of the state and indigenous peoples, and (7) the final decision taken by the promoter entity of the measure.[63] Deficiencies of the consultation related to block 192 were evident when, in the dialogue stage, the indigenous leaders requested to discuss the concession contract. This request was rejected by the representatives of the promoter entity because, parallel to the consultation process, the Peruvian state had already launched the bidding rules with, among its annexes, the format of the contract.[64] In addition to this problem, the indigenous representatives complained about not having enough time to deliberate on the percentage of the social fund proposed by the government. Only 0.75% of the controlled oil production was provided to cover environmental development and monitoring projects, whereas the two indigenous organisations most affected by the oil activity, *Federación Indígena Quechua del Pastaza* (FEDIQUEP) and *Federación de Comunidades Nativas del Río Corrientes* (FECONACO), proposed 2.25%.[65]

Obviously, after forty years of suffering the impacts of oil exploitation, the indigenous representatives were interested in discussing issues such as the environmental remediation and monitoring as well as the respect for their ways of life.[66] But the Peruvian state's interest was mainly to tender block 192 as soon as possible. As a result, the consultation process was conducted in only three months,[67] and on the 29th of August 2015 the tender contract was signed for two years with the company Pacific Stratus Energy (PSE). One of the consequences of this questionable consultation is that the contract did not set measures to protect indigenous peoples from oil spills. Two years after the start of the operations of the PSE, these add up to forty.[68]

The case of block 192 shows the limitations of the Peruvian legislation to apply the prior consultation and obtain the free, prior and informed consent according to the UNDRIP, since the decision of the state on the continuation of the oil activity was taken before the beginning of the consultation. Having launched the international public tender for this block in parallel to the prior consultation process affirms this. The 'prior' consultation only legitimised the prior decision of the promoter entity by granting it the power to approve the draft of the Supreme Decree that, in turn, approved the conformation, extension, delimitation and nomenclature of block 192 and the license agreement for the exploitation of hydrocarbons. In this way, there was no possibility for the indigenous communities to modify or reject the measure, despite the fact that their fair claims seeking to protect their survival had not been satisfactorily addressed.

3. Conclusion

Obtaining free, prior and informed consent for all measures is still subject of extensive discussion. Nonetheless, based on the increasing reporting on irreversible environmental, social and cultural damage suffered by indigenous peoples worldwide, human rights standards are reinforcing the idea that consultations must lead to consent when a measure have high impact on the lives of indigenous peoples or endanger their survival. Unfortunately, in practice, the recognition of the right to free, prior and informed consent is not widely accepted by governments and business actors, especially when dealing with the licensing process to explore and exploit natural resources or to execute infrastructure projects since have large economic interests at stake. Governments choose to recognise the right to prior consultation, because this is erroneously conceived as *softer*. The right to prior consultation implies a dialogue between the state and indigenous peoples to harmonise proposals, to gain the consent and to approve agreements therefore it should not be underestimated since can avoid conflict situations or mitigating the unleashed ones.

The rejection to demand the free, prior and informed consent when dealing with extractive activities, puts at risk indigenous peoples' collective rights and evidences that the Peruvian state has forgotten the UNDRIP's basic principles as the right of indigenous peoples to control their lands, territories and resources (Article 26(2)) and to determine and develop priorities and strategies for the development or use their lands or territories and other resources (Article 32(1)). Particularly, the consultation on block 192 illustrates the asymmetrical relationship between the indigenous peoples and the state, with obvious disadvantages for the former as the legal design of the prior consultation establishes that the final decision will be taken by the promoter entity.

Given the decision power of the promoter entity and the pressure of the government to approve the measure, it can be affirmed that in this case the consultation process became a dialogue process to enable the oil concession on behalf of 'national interest'. Indigenous peoples consent was hardly sought, and the discussion about an alternative project of development was not opened. On the contrary, the oil exploitation was shown as the only model that would solve all the requirements of indigenous peoples. This approach of the consultation process could change if the right of indigenous peoples to decide on their own development is respected, and if an impartial entity, other than the promoter, with personnel correctly qualified to weight the effect of the measure on the collective rights, is responsible to conduct prior consultations. Only then, the efforts of the Peruvian state to implement this right could be consistent with international standards, particularly with UNDRIP.

Notes

1. J. Anaya, UN Special Rapporteur on the Rights of Indigenous Peoples, *Annual Report to the Human Rights Council, UN Doc. A/HRC/12/34*, 15 July 2009, ¶ 38.
2. Article 19 establishes that states shall consult and cooperate in good faith with the indigenous peoples concerned through their own representative institutions in order to obtain their free, prior and informed consent before adopting and implementing legislative or administrative measures that may affect them. In other cases, the UNDRIP also invokes the application of the right to consultation before taking measures: to combat prejudice and discrimination and to promote tolerance, understanding and good relations among indigenous peoples and other segments of society (Article 15(2)); to protect indigenous children from exploitation and possible labour jobs that endanger their physical, mental or moral development (Article 17 (2)); to use indigenous lands or territories for military activities (Article 30); to facilitate the exercise and ensure the implementation of the right of indigenous peoples to maintain and develop contacts, relations and cooperation, including activities for spiritual, cultural, policical, economic and social purposes with their ownn members as well as other peoples across borders (Article 36); and to achieve the purposes of the UNDRIP (Article 38).
3. As category of soft law can be mentioned, among others, inter-state conference declarations, UN General Assembly resolutions, codes of conduct, guidelines and the recommendations of international organisations. See: M. Barelli, 'The Role of Soft Law in the International Law System: The Case of the United Nations Declaration on the Rights of Indigenous Peoples', *International and Comparative Law Quarterly* 58, no. 4, (October 2009): 960.
4. M. Davis, 'Indigenous Struggles in Standard-setting: The United Nations Declaration on the Rights of Indigenous Peoples', *Melbourne Journal of International Law* 9 (2008).

5. J. Anaya, UN Special Rapporteur on the Rights of Indigenous Peoples, *Interim Report to the General Assembly,* UN Doc. A/65/264, 9 August 2010, ¶ 85.
6. The right to consent of indigenous peoples has previously recognised by the Convention concerning the protection and integration of indigenous and other tribal and semi-tribal populations in independent countries (ILO Convention N. 107), to protect them from forced removal from their lands and territories (article 12 (1)), and it has been reaffirmed in Article 16 (1) of ILO Convention N. 169.
7. IACtHR (Judgment) *Saramaka people v. Suriname,* 28 November 2007, ¶ 134.
8. ICHR, *Indigenous and tribal peoples' rights over their ancestral lands and natural resources. Norms and jurisprudence of the Inter-American Human Rights System,* Doc. OEA/Ser.L/V/II. / Doc. 56/09, 30 December 2009, ¶ 333.
9. Expert Mechanism on the Rights of Indigenous Peoples. *Study on indigenous peoples and the right to participate in decision-making.* UN Doc. A/HRC/EMRIP/2010/2, ¶ 88.
10. Anaya, James (Annual Report) UN Doc. A/HRC/12/34, 15 July 2009, ¶ 47.
11. The Baguazo refers to the most critical moment of the mobilizations of the indigenous population against the decision of the government to approve, without prior consultation, a package of more than hundred legislative decrees, in order to implement the United States-Peru Trade Promotion Agreement. They demanded to repeal these decrees and to be consulted, but the Executive power warned that any modification would violate the Agreement with the United States. Fruitless talks between the Peruvian government and indigenous representatives led to the escalation of the conflict. The result of these events was 33 deaths – i.e. 23 police officers and 10 civilians, including 5 indigenous persons –, 200 wounded, 83 arrested persons, one missing person, and extensive damage to public and private property. See: International Amnesty, *Peru: Bagua, six months on* (UK, 2009), 12–13; Defensoría del Pueblo, *Actuaciones humanitarias realizadas por la Defensoría del Pueblo con ocasión de los hechos ocurridos el 5 de junio de 2009, en las provincias de Utcubamba y Bagua, región Amazonas, en el contexto del paro amazónico,* Informe de adjuntía N° 006-2009-DP/ADHPD, Lima, 2009, 3, http://www.defensoria.gob.pe/modules/Downloads/informes/varios/2009/informe-adjuntia-006-2009-DP-DHPD.pdf.
12. J. Anaya, UN Special Rapporteur on the Rights of Indigenous Peoples, *Observaciones sobre la situación de los pueblos indígenas de la Amazonia y los sucesos del 5 de junio y días posteriores en las provincias de Bagua y Utcubamba, Perú,* UN Doc. A/HRC/12/34/Add.8, 18 August 2009, ¶ 50.
13. See: Constitutional Tribunal, judgment No. 5427-2009-PC/TC, ¶ 47.
14. Ley No. 29785, Ley del Derecho a la Consulta Previa de los Pueblos Indígenas u originarios, reconocido en el Convenio 169 de la Organización Internacional del Trabajo, published 7 September 2011.
15. In 2006, Rodolfo Stavenhagen, former UN Special Rapporteur on the Rights of Indigenous Peoples, had already warned for the existence of an 'implementation gap' in the context of constitutional reforms concerning indigenous issues. See: R. Stavenhagen, UN Special Rapporteur on the Rights of Indigenous Peoples, UN Doc. E/CN.4/2006/78, 16 February 2006, ¶ 5.
16. Decreto Supremo No. 001-2012-MC, Reglamento de la Ley de Consulta Previa, published 3 April 2012.
17. See: Political Constitution of 1993, Fourth Final and Transitory Provision.
18. R. Stavenhagen, UN Special Rapporteur on the Rights of Indigenous Peoples, UN Doc. E/CN.4/2006/78, 16 February 2006, ¶ 21.
19. Source: Directorate of Prior Consultation of the Ministry of Culture of Peru.
20. CooperAccion, Organizaciones evalúan aplicación de Consulta Previa, http://cooperaccion.org.pe/organizaciones-indigenas-de-15-regiones-del-pais-evaluan-aplicacion-de-consulta-previa/ (accessed February 20, 2018).
21. Two types of conflicts regarding extractive activities have been distinguished: The first involves local people versus transnational corporations concerning the dispute over land and natural resources or environmental pollution. The second involves local populations

confronting local administrations to determine the use of the proceeds obtained from the central government by extractive activities. See: J. Arellano-Yanguas, 'Aggravating the Resource Curse: Decentralization, Mining and Conflict in Peru', *Journal of Development Studies* 47, no. 4 (2011), 617–38.

22. Unlike the mining sector, the implementation of hydrocarbon consultations was promoted by Perupetro and the hydrocarbons business association – Sociedad Peruana de Hidrocarburos – whose former president, Beatriz Merino, expressed her support for the consultation while holding meetings with the leaders of the main indigenous organisations. See: C. Sanborn and A. Paredes, *Country Study: Peru, in: Americas Quarterly, Consulta Previa and Investment* (Spring 2014), 9, http://americasquarterly.org/content/country-study-peru. It should not be forgotten that the involvement of Mrs. Merino in indigenous issues was a hallmark of her management when she was at the head of the Ombudsman's Office during the 2005–2011 period.
23. See: Congress of the Republic, Commission of Constitution and Bylaws' opinion, Article 3, approved 18 May 2010, http://www2.congreso.gob.pe/Sicr/TraDocEstProc/CLProLey2006.nsf; and Congress of the Republic, Congress of the Republic, Second Ordinary Legislature, 9a C Morning Session, Diario de Debates, 19 May 2010, 26, http://www2.congreso.gob.pe/Sicr/TraDocEstProc/CLProLey2006.nsf.
24. See: R. Stavenhagen, UN Special Rapporteur on the Rights of Indigenous Peoples, UN Doc. E/CN.4/2003/90, 21 January 2003, ¶ 66.
25. See: J. Anaya, UN Special Rapporteur on the Rights of Indigenous Peoples, UN Doc. A/HRC/12/34, 15 July 2009, ¶ 48–49.
26. ILO Committee of Experts on the Application of Conventions and Recommendations, Report III (Part 1A), 99th Session, 2010, Geneva, p. 784.
27. See: Law of Prior Consultation, Article 1.
28. See: Regulation, Seventh Supplementary, Transitional and Final Provision.
29. G. Damonte Valencia, 'Estado, gobierno y extractivismo en el Perú', in *El Perú en los inicios del siglo XXI: Cambios y continuidades desde las ciencias sociales*, ed. M. Quero (Mexico D.F.: Universidad Autónoma de México, 2016), 13–28.
30. Political Constitution of Peru 1993, Fourth Final and Transitory Provision 'Rules concerning the rights and freedoms recognised by this Constitution are construed in accordance with the Universal Declaration of Human Rights and the international treaties and agreements regarding those rights that have been ratified by Peru.'
31. IACtHR (Judgment), *Saramaka People v. Surinam*, ¶ 126–127. Similar restrictions on individual rights has been provided by the International Covenant on Civil and Political Rights, Article 19 (3).
32. IACtHR (Judgment) *Saramaka People v. Surinam*, ¶ 128.
33. IACtHR (Judgment) *Saramaka People v. Surinam*, ¶ 129.
34. IACtHR (Judgment) *Saramaka People v. Surinam*, ¶ 137.
35. The 'effective' participation, together, with the recognition of the FPIC, had been already called by the Human Rights Committee: '*participation in the decision-making process must be effective, which requires not mere consultation but the free, prior and informed consent of the members of the community. In addition, the measures must respect the principle of proportionality so as not to endanger the very survival of the community and its members*'. HRC, *Poma Poma v. Peru*, UN Doc. CCPR/C/95/D/1457/2006, *Communication No. 1457/2006*, ¶ 7.6.
36. IACtHR (Judgment) *Mayagna (sumo) Awas Tingni Community v. Nicaragua*, ¶ 149.
37. IACtHR (Judgment) *Mayagna (sumo) Awas Tingni Community v. Nicaragua*, ¶ 154. See also: IACommHR, (Special report) *Indigenous and Tribal Peoples' rights over their ancestral lands and natural resources. Norms and jurisprudence of the Inter-American Human Rights System*, OEA/Ser.L/Vol/II. Doc. 56/09, 30 December 2009, ¶ 10.
38. IACtHR (Judgment) *Mayagna (sumo) Awas Tingni Community v. Nicaragua*, ¶ 147.
39. IACtHR (Judgment) *Yakye Axa Indigenous Community v. Paraguay*, ¶ 51.

40. Article 200 of the Peruvian Political Constitution of Peru enshrined the principle of proportionality: 'When petitions concerning these constitutional rights are filed with regard to restricted or suspended rights, the corresponding jurisdictional body examines the reasonability and proportionality of the restrictive act.'
41. O. Ruiz Chiriboga, 'Sección especial: Pueblos indígenas y la Corte Interamericana de Derechos Humanos. Fondo y reparaciones', in *Convención Americana sobre Derechos Humanos. Comentario*, eds. C. Steiner and P. Uribe (Lima: Fundación Konrad Adenauer, 2014), 947–1026, 993, 1040.
42. IACtHR (Judgment) Gelman v. Uruguay, ¶ 239.
43. The promoter entity has been defined as the entity of the state that is going to issue legislative or administrative measures directly related to the rights of indigenous or native peoples and is at the same time competent to carry out the prior consultation process. See: Law of Prior Consultation, Article 17; and Regulation of the Law of Prior Consultation, Article 3, g.
44. See: Law of Prior Consultation, Article 15.
45. A. Peña Jumpa, 'Barreras de Acceso a la Justicia, y la Justicia Comunal como Alternativa en el Perú', *Revista Derecho y Sociedad*, No. 38 (Lima: Pontificia Universidad Católica de Perú, 2012), 360–8.
46. J. Gilbert and C. Doyle, 'A New Dawn over the Land: Sheeding Light on Collective Ownership and Consent', in *Reflections on the UN Declaration on Indigenous Peoples, Studies in International Law*, eds. S. Allen and A. Xanthaki (Oxford, Vol. 30, 2011), 389–428, 317–9.
47. UNDRIP, Article 46(2) provides:

    In the exercise of the rights enunciated in the present Declaration, human rights and fundamental freedoms of all shall be respected. The exercise of the rights set forth in this Declaration shall be subject only to such limitations as are determined by *law and in accordance with international human rights obligations*. Any such limitations shall be *non-discriminatory* and strictly necessary solely for *the purpose of securing due recognition and respect for the rights and freedoms of others* and for meeting the just and most compelling requirements of a democratic society. (Emphasis added)

48. H. Quane, 'New Directions for Self-Determination and Participatory Rights', in *Reflections on the UN Declaration on Indigenous Peoples, Studies in International Law*, eds. S. Allen and A. Xanthaki (Oxford, Vol. 30, 2011), 280–1.
49. See: Oficina Nacional de Diálogo y Sostenibilidad, *Willanqniki. Proyectos hidrocarburíferos en el Perú. Lecciones aprendidas y retos frente a la conflictividad social*, No. 28 (Lima: Presidencia del Consejo de Ministros, March, 2015), 16.
50. Block 192 is located in Andoas discrict (Marañon basin, Loreto region, Peru). Its operations began with the concession granted to Occidental Petroleum Corporation in block 1-A (22 June 1971). Later, the contract for block 1B was signed (3 April 1978). In 2001, the *Cesión de Posición contractual en el contrato de servicios para la explotación de hidrocarburos en el lote 1AB* was signed between Perupetro S.A. and Pluspetrol Perú Corporation S.A. This contract was approved by *Decreto Supremo* No. 022-2011-EM (24 May 2001). In 2014, Perupetro S.A. approved the creation, extension, demarcation and new nomenclature of Block 192. The area includes Blocks 1-AB and incorporates additional areas, in which exploratory activities can be developed.
51. M. Finer and M. Orta-Martínez, 'A Second Hydrocarbon Boom Threatens the Peruvian Amazon: Trends, Projections, and Policy Implications', *Environmental Research Letters*, No. 5, 2010, UK, 3–7.
52. See: Human Rights Council, *Follow-up report on indigenous peoples and the right to participate in decision-making, with a focus on extractive industries*, UN Doc. A/HRC/21/55, Annex, 16 August 2012, 10, ¶ 29. Also see: A. Bebbington and D. Humphreys Bebbington, *An Andean Avatar: post-neoliberal strategies for promoting extractive industries.* Working Paper, Brooks World Poverty Institute: Manchester University, 2010, 117; C. Rodríguez Garavito, 'Ethnicity.gov: Global Governance, Indigenous Peoples, and the Right to Prior Consultation in Social Minefields', *Indiana Journal of Global Legal Studies* 18, no. 1 (2011), 267.

53. T. Evans, *Human Rights in the Global Political Economy: Critical Processes* (London: Lynne Rienner Publishers, 2010), 90–92.
54. These administrative procedures in hydrocarbons are the concession of transportation of hydrocarbons through pipelines; concession of natural gas distribution by pipeline network; modification of the concession, authorisation of the installation and operation of the pipeline to own and main use; modification or transference of the authorisation of the installation and operation of the pipeline to own and main use; supreme decree that approve the subscription of contracts to explore and exploit oil and gas; and favourable technical report for the installation of refining and hydrocarbon processing plants.
55. A *Decreto Supremo* is a type of norm of general nature that regulates norms with the rank of a law or sectorial or multisectorial functional activity at the national level. They may or may not require the approving vote of the Council of Ministers, as provided by law. They are signed by the President of the Republic and endorsed by one or more Ministers to whose competence they correspond. See: Ley Orgánica del Poder Ejecutivo, Law No. 29158, Article 11.
56. 'Perupetro S.A. is the state company, on behalf of the Peruvian state and it is responsible for promoting, negotiating, underwriting and monitoring contracts for exploration and exploitation of hydrocarbons in Peru'. See: www.perupetro.com.pe.
57. Consultations that count with the final measure are: Area of Regional Conservation *Maijuna-Kichwa*, National Park *Sierra del Divisor*, the regulation of the *Ley Forestal y Fauna Silvestre*, the *Hidrovía Amazónica* Proyect, the block 192, the mining project Aurora, the mining project Toropunto, the mining project Misha, the policy of intercultural health and the regulation of the *Ley de Lenguas*. See: R. O'Diana Rocca and I. Vega Díaz, *¿Cómo va la aplicación de la consulta previa en el Perú?: Avances y retos* (Lima: Centro Amazónico de Antropología y Aplicación Práctica, October 2017), 8, http://www.caaap.org.pe/2017/documentos/Consulta_previa_25_octubre_2017.pdf.
58. This contract was approved by *Decreto Supremo* No. 022-2011-EM (24 May 2001).
59. Just between 2013 and 2014, the Ministry of Environment declared an environmental emergency in the Pastaza, Corrientes, Marañon and Tigre River basins, having found higher rates than allowed of lead, barium, arsenic, aluminium and hydrocarbons in the water and soil. See: Congreso de la República, Grupo de Trabajo sobre la situación indígena y ambiental de las cuencas de los ríos Pastaza, Tigre, Corrientes y Marañon 2012–2013, Lima, Julio 2013, http://observatoriopetrolero.org/wp-content/uploads/2013/11/Informe-4-Cuencas-Comision-de-Pueblos-2013.pdf. See also: James Anaya, UN Special Rapporteur on the Rights of Indigenous Peoples, *La situatión de los derechos de los pueblos indígenas en el Perú, en relación con las industrias extractivas*, UN Doc. A/HRC/27/52/Add.3, 7 May 2014, ¶ 22.
60. ILO Convention N. 169 entered into force in Peru on 2 February 1995.
61. See: consulta.pe, *Comunidades indígenas de Loreto alertan de un conflicto si el Gobierno licita el lote 192*, published 25 February 2015, https://consultape.com/2015/02/25/comunidades-indigenas-de-loreto-alertan-de-un-conflicto-si-el-gobierno-licita-el-lote-192-2/ (accessed 4 February 2018).
62. Oficina Nacional de Diálogo y Sostenibilidad, *Willaqniki. Informe de diferencias, controversias y conflictos sociales*, No. 29 (Lima: Presidencia del Consejo de Ministros, April 2015), http://onds.pcm.gob.pe/wp-content/uploads/2015/04/W29.pdf.
63. See: Law of Prior Consultation, Article 8.
64. A. Leyva, *Consúltame de verdad. Aproximación a un balance de la consulta previa en el Perú en los sectores minero e hidrocarburífero* (Lima: CooperAcción - Acción Solidaria para el Desarrollo & Oxfam America, June 2018), 18.
65. According to the indigenous representatives, the minister of energy and mines imposed a maximum of two hours to accept the government's proposal on the social fund, since at that time she was 'connected with Perupetro S.A. and the contract will be closed'. See: La República, *Lote 192: Consulta Previa en riesgo*, 29 August 2015, http://larepublica.pe/impresa/opinion/699754-lote-192-consulta-previa-en-riesgo.

66. PUINAMUDT, *Achuares y Quechuas del río Corrientes y Pastaza firman acta histórica en etapa de evaluacion interna por consulta del lote 192*, 8 July 2015, http://observatoriopetrolero.org/achuares-y-quechuas-del-rio-corrientes-y-pastaza-firman-acta-historica-en-etapa-de-evaluacion-interna-por-consulta-del-lote-192/.
67. The process began the 14th of May 2015 when Perupetro S.A. invited the indigenous organisations to the preparatory meetings of the process of consultation and ended the 26th of August 2015 with the official communication of the promoter entity that the stages of the consultation process had been complied. See: Dirección General de Asuntos Ambientales y Energéticos, Ministerio de Energía y Minas, *final report of the prior consultation of block 192*, Report N. 797-2015-MEM/DGAAE/DNAE/DGAE/RCO/SED/CIM, 5 October 2015.
68. A. Leyva, *Consúltame de verdad. Aproximación a un balance de la consulta previa en el Perú en los sectores minero e hidrocarburífero* (Lima: CooperAcción - Acción Solidaria para el Desarrollo & Oxfam America, June 2018), 24.

Acknowledgement

I wish to thank Alexander Michiels and Carolina Sánchez for their comments and suggestions. Any remaining errors are mine.

Disclosure statement

No potential conflict of interest was reported by the author.

ORCID

Amelia Alva-Arévalo http://orcid.org/0000-0002-3228-5405

Implementing the rights of indigenous peoples in Japan: implications and challenges of forest certification for the Ainu

Fumiya Nagai

ABSTRACT
After the adoption of the U.N. Declaration on the Rights of Indigenous Peoples (UNDRIP) in 2007, the Government of Japan recognised the Ainu as an indigenous people in 2008, and it began developing the Ainu policy. However, the policy focuses on individual rights and cultural promotion, failing to implement UNDRIP. In this situation, private standards, notably forest certification, are increasingly paid attention to because the mechanism requires forest managers to respect the rights of indigenous peoples outlined in UNDRIP. With this in mind, the study will discuss the implications and challenges of forest certification in relation to the Ainu indigenous rights in Hokkaido, particularly the 2012 revision of Principles and Criteria of Forest Stewardship Council. It will take a close look at newly added requirements on UNDRIP, identification of indigenous peoples, and the right to free, prior and informed consent. Through this analysis, the study will clarify that the revised standard could improve the relationship between the Ainu and forest managers. However, by considering the current situation of the Ainu, the study will also point out the necessity of careful audit process, further effort in working on the Governmental policy and the increase in auditors' familiarities with indigenous rights.

Introduction

Ten years have passed since the U.N. Declaration on the Rights of Indigenous Peoples (UNDRIP) was adopted at the U.N. General Assembly in 2007. Historically, the identity and legal term 'indigenous peoples' have been embodied and elaborated through the U.N. meetings, notably the Working Group on Indigenous Populations (WGIP). One of the most crucial factors that have drawn these peoples to the international arena was 'domestic powerlessness' and the lack of the national recognition.[1] The significant part of their indigenous identity derives from the history of continued colonialism as they 'did not qualify for decolonization' due to the structural flaw of the U.N. decolonisation processes.[2] Although indigenous peoples 'have almost uniformly denied aspirations to independent statehood',[3] they have fought for recognition as 'peoples' who hold the right to self-determination that requires 'the protections and benefits of international law'.[4] In this regard, their rights movement could have been seen as 'an extension of the process of decolonization',[5] and the adoption of UNDRIP was a momentous achievement. As a next step, the implementation of it has been a significant challenge.

Under this international trend, indigenous peoples in Japan are not irrelevant. Particularly, since 1987 when the Ainu people began participating in WGIP meetings, their representatives and supporters have claimed the rights of indigenous peoples by asserting the history of colonialism and human rights violation of their traditional land of Hokkaido, which is located in the northern part of Japan. However, because of the 'myth' that all the Japanese colonies were liberated due to the defeat of the World War II, Japan's colonial rule on Hokkaido has rarely been acknowledged in the Japanese society.[6] Additionally, even after the Government of Japan recognised the Ainu as an indigenous people in 2008, the Governmental policy has avoided directly implementing UNDRIP.

In this situation, however, there has been implicative progress in private standards, particularly forest certification. Notably, the major amendment of Principles and Criteria (P&C) of Forest Stewardship Council (FSC) from Version 4 (V4) to Version 5 (V5) in 2012 is considered significant due to the inclusion of UNDRIP into its normative references.[7] In the context of Hokkaido, FSC Japan has clarified that forest managers in Hokkaido would no longer ignore indigenous rights for the Ainu people. As the new standards started being used quite recently or will be used soon, the conceptual analysis of these recent developments would be important. The purpose of this paper is thus to examine what the new forest certification standards could offer for the Ainu rights with a particular focus on the amended FSC P&C.

After the introduction, the study will contextualise the situation of the Ainu indigenous rights by discussing the colonisation history and the current Governmental policy. Then, it will clarify the situation of forest certification in Japan and analyse the amended FSC standards, particularly considering the newly added requirements. The research was conducted mainly through the exploration of the literature related to the topic in both English and Japanese. It consulted peer-reviewed academic journal articles and primary and secondary sources, including the Governmental policy papers, the records of drafting FSC Japan's national standard, and semi-structured interviews with those who were involved in the revision process. The author has also been involved in NGO activities supporting the U.N. advocacy by indigenous peoples in Japan, including the Ainu, and some of the data were collected through them.

Brief history of Ainu indigenous rights in Japan

Originally, the Ainu people inhabited Hokkaido and the far-eastern region of Russia.[8] According to the latest survey on the Ainu living condition in Hokkaido in 2017, although it involves limited area and population, the number of the Ainu is at least 13,118.[9]

It was soon after the Meiji Restoration in 1868 that the Government of Japan began having direct control over the Ainu traditional land by renaming it Hokkaido.[10] Based on the doctrine of *terra nullius*, the Government dispossessed the Ainu of their land and sovereignty.[11] In this process, although the forest areas that covered most of Hokkaido had a high importance for the Ainu lifestyle, they were regarded as 'obstacles', and deforestation was accelerated for, for instance, agriculture, land privatisation or corporate activities.[12] The Government also enforced the assimilative legislation and policy, notably 'Former Native Protection Act' in 1899, and prohibited or strictly limited many

Ainu cultural manners and customs as 'uncultivated'.[13] According to Richard Siddle, these attempts of assimilation were conducted through the lens of 'race' to 'legitimate and sustain Japanese superiority', and the Ainu were widely perceived as 'dying race'.[14]

Against this, the Ainu have claimed their rights as a distinct ethnic group. For instance, the 'Draft Law concerning the Ainu people' was adopted in the General Assembly of the former Ainu Association of Hokkaido (AAH) in 1984. It claims to overcome various issues that the Ainu have faced.[15] According to Siddle, it 'challenged the official version of Hokkaido history and the narrative of Ainu non-existence', marking 'the clear emergence of Ainu ethnopolitics'.[16] Notoriously, however, in 1986, the Japanese Prime Minister Yasuhiro Nakasone referred Japan as an ethnically 'homogeneous nation'.[17] His statement represented the national non-recognition of and the historical assimilation towards the Ainu, and it became one of the important factors that triggered the Ainu participation in WGIP from 1987.[18] Since then, through the continued participation in the U.N. meetings on indigenous peoples' rights, their self-recognition as a distinctive ethnic group has been shaped into the indigenous identity.

Simultaneously, the domestic situations have been influenced. For example, in 1997, there was a court case over the illegality of dam construction in an Ainu sacred place in Nibutani, Hokkaido. In this decision, considering the 'international trend', the Sapporo District Court acknowledged the indigenousness of the Ainu and their indigenous cultural rights.[19] The decision was recognised as 'epoch-making' because it was the first decision in Japan that acknowledged the Ainu as an indigenous people.[20] Additionally, in the same year, 'Act on the Promotion of Ainu Culture, and Dissemination and Enlightenment of Knowledge about Ainu Tradition, etc.' was enacted with the abolishment of the assimilative Former Native Protection Act. While it focuses only on cultural promotion and does not include indigenous rights, it is considered an important step as it is based on the recognition that the Ainu formerly inhabited Hokkaido and have self-identification as a distinctive ethnic group.[21]

Nonetheless, while the Government of Japan voted in favour when UNDRIP was adopted, it still failed to recognise the Ainu as an indigenous people on the ground that there is no internationally established definition of 'indigenous peoples'.[22] It was 2008 when the tides unexpectedly turned around due to the G8 Summit scheduled in Hokkaido. In this summit, because the political leaders from countries such as the U.S. and Canada that recognise indigenous peoples within their territories planned to participate, the Japanese politicians might have been 'afraid of being criticised over Ainu issues and suffering a sense of shame over its internal affairs'.[23] Thus, on 6 June 2008, the Diet unanimously adopted the 'Resolution Calling for the Recognition of the Ainu People as an Indigenous People', and in response, the Government recognised the Ainu as an indigenous people. However, the Prime Minister Yasuo Fukuda mentioned that it is impossible to say that the concept of 'an indigenous people' in the Diet's resolution is the same concept in the international law,[24] and this attitude is reflected on the following Ainu policy.

Characteristics of current Ainu policy

After the recognition of the Ainu as an indigenous people, the Government of Japan set up the Advisory Council for the Future Ainu Policy (ACFAP) in July 2008 to review 'the history of the Ainu and their indigenousness' and to consider 'new principles and measures for future Ainu policy'.[25] Based on its final report submitted in July 2009, the Council for Ainu Policy Promotion (CAPP) was established within the Cabinet Secretariat in December 2009 to promote the Ainu policy.

Nevertheless, its policy is based on the 'Japan-specific Indigenous Policy' view promoted by Teruki Tsunemoto, who is a constitutional scholar and a member of both ACFAP and CAPP.[26] According to him, the concept of indigenous peoples can be divided into two kinds.[27] One of them is called 'substantive concept of indigenous peoples', which 'refers to ethnic groups that enjoy sovereign status and related rights, such as the right to self-determination and to the land' as outlined in UNDRIP. However, arguing that this concept does not fit in the context of Japan, Tsunemoto introduces the other concept, which is called 'procedural concept of indigenous peoples'. He explains that this 'focuses not directly on the sovereignty or the rights of the ethnic group but on the process by which they were forced into minority status in their own territory'.[28]

Japan-specific Indigenous Policy is based on this latter concept. In this approach, however, Hideaki Uemura points out that the Ainu indigenous rights can be ignored as UNDRIP would not be referred to if it were not feasible within the Japanese legal system.[29] For example, while the ACFAP's report mentions that UNDRIP 'should be fully respected as a general international guideline for indigenous policies', it also argues that the policy 'must comply with the Constitution of Japan'.[30] However, the Constitution is based on individualism and does not expect the existence of minorities or indigenous peoples. In this regard, collective rights that consist of a major part of UNDRIP are not respected. Yoko Tanabe also argues that the Governmental views on UNDRIP 'exemplify Japan's "skewed" indigenous policy model that treats indigenous rights only from the perspectives of cultural diversity and individual rights'.[31]

In this situation, forest certification has attracted the attention as it has taken a different approach to indigenous peoples' rights. Uemura claims that it has acknowledged Ainu indigenous rights based on UNDRIP in the certification process and could be a very practical approach to requiring the protection of indigenous peoples' rights by utilising the economic benefits in the global market.[32]

Forest certification schemes in Japan

Forest certification was developed in the 1990s in response to environmental concerns on forest practices as a voluntary mechanism that guarantees forests are managed in accordance with ecological, economic and social standards. It comes from civil society organisations, and they have developed their own national, regional or global standards and monitoring schemes.[33] It aims to provide 'incentives for sustainable forest management through product differentiation, access to green markets and premium prices' by labelling certified products.[34] It integrates 'sustainability into economic theory' and extends 'the traditional boundaries of the forest economy'.[35]

Currently, three forest certification schemes are used in Japan: FSC, Programme for the Endorsement of Forest Certification (PEFC) and Sustainable Green Ecosystem Council (SGEC). FSC and PEFC are both global forest certification schemes, and SGEC is a domestically developed scheme. FSC was officially born in 1994, when a group of timber users, traders, and representatives of environmental and human rights organisations 'identified the need for a system that could credibly identify well-managed forests as a source of responsibly produced forest products'.[36] PEFC was established in 1999 by national organisations, particularly in European countries, for 'the independent development of national standards'.[37] Different from FSC, PEFC is an umbrella organisation that endorses national standards in each country in line with its international requirements.[38] In Japan, SGEC, which was established as a domestic scheme by Japanese forestry organisations and NGOs in 2003, became a PEFC-endorsed scheme in June 2016 to increase its international credibility.[39]

There are primarily two types of the certification: Forest Management (FM) and Chain of Custody (CoC). FM certification confirms that 'the forest is being managed in a way that preserves the natural ecosystem and benefits the lives of local people and workers, all while ensuring it sustains economically viability',[40] and CoC certification verifies that certified material 'has been identified and separated from non-certified and non-controlled material as it makes its way along the supply chain from A all the way through to B'.[41] FSC P&C needs to be respected for both types of certification. In the certification process, instead of standard operational organisations such as FSC, independent certification bodies accredited by them carry out assessments on site. In the case of FSC certification, the certification consists of 'a brief initial pre-assessment' and 'an in-depth review of forest management processes and their environmental, social, and economic impact'. Depending on the number and scale of non-conformities, auditors would decide if a certificate could be issued or not. While the certificates are valid for five years, there are annual checks on the requirements, and the renewal certification is necessary every five years.[42] Additionally, these certification bodies are also regularly examined to maintain the quality by third organisations.[43]

In the context of the Japanese market, according to Yuki Yamamoto et al., there are premium prices for certified products although its impact might be relatively low[44] in comparison with other countries such as Switzerland and The Netherlands, where about 80% of the consumers recognise FSC-certified products.[45] In fact, the 2008 research on consumers' preference of certified products in Kyoto City identified that there was only 7.2% of the answerers who know about the logo mark of forest certification[46] although the degree of recognition has increased little by little.[47]

According to Oliver Damette and Philippe Delacote, FSC scheme is essentially performance-based (with outcome requirements), and PEFC scheme is system-based (with criteria to design forest management for reaching environmental performance). In this sense, FSC scheme may be 'taken as a lack of flexibility and limit the access to the scheme for less performing forest managers', and PEFC may 'create heterogeneity and inconsistencies in the real quality'.[48] Damette and Delacote also argue that FSC focuses more on environmental and social issues including indigenous rights protection and can be regarded as more independent than PEFC.[49] In fact, in comparison with FSC standard that dedicates one of its 10 Principles to indigenous peoples' rights (Principle 3) since its establishment, PEFC and SGEC standards may be less strict or precise. For example, due to the revision of PEFC requirements in November 2010, similar to the revised FSC P&C, PEFC's standard requires forest managers to recognise 'the established framework of legal, customary and traditional rights' outlined in ILO Convention 169 (C169) and UNDRIP, which 'shall not be infringed upon without the free, prior and informed consent'. It also requires the compliance of 'property, tenure and land-use rights for indigenous people'.[50] However, for instance, the term of 'indigenous people' is used instead of 'indigenous peoples'. In consideration of the battle of 'S' in the process of drafting UNDRIP,[51] PEFC's requirement may be less desirable. SGEC standard is endorsed along it and similar in this regard.[52] Therefore, although SGEC (PEFC Japan) certifies larger forest areas in Hokkaido as they are less strict and easier to obtain,[53] the analysis on FSC standard may be more implicative for indigenous rights protection in a conceptual sense.

Revision process of criteria on indigenous peoples' rights of FSC P&C

First FSC standard approved in 1994 has been revised in 1996, 1999 and 2001, and it was 2008 when FSC started the process of reviewing P&C V4.[54] In the same year, the FSC Board of Directors developed the first draft, and the public consultations were conducted. In the process, Principle 3 on indigenous peoples' rights was one of the important aspects. For example, FSC set up Permanent Indigenous Peoples' Committee (PIPC) as an advisory body to 'strengthen indigenous involvement in FSC' in recognition that '40% of the world's remaining natural forests are officially recognized as Indigenous Peoples' territories'.[55] The mandates also include making 'on-going recommendations to the FSC Board that will strengthen and renew indigenous peoples' engagement in FSC'.[56]

With this overall revision, including Principle 3, the final draft P&C V5 was approved in 2012.[57] It is recognised that FSC 'fundamental law' was revised,[58] and in comparison with P&C V4, it has become more explicit requirements, including criteria on indigenous peoples' rights.[59] Table 1 compares Principle 3 of V4 and V5. The revision aimed to ensure the clarity and precision of language. Although there has also been a concern that it may reduce flexibility and further limit the access for forest managers to FSC certification,[60] after the revised version was approved, International Generic Indicators (IGI) for transferring it into national standards was completed in June 2015.[61] Based on it, FSC Japan also began working on developing the national standard.

After the first draft of the national standard was finished in April 2016, first public consultations and hearings were held, and two field tests were conducted. Indigenous rights protection was also taken as one of the important points in this process, and it was clarified that Principle 3 applies to the Ainu and forest management units in Hokkaido.[62] In fact, one of the field tests was conducted in Biratori, Hokkaido, with a focus on Principle 3.[63] Additionally, to discuss the rights of indigenous peoples, FSC Japan organised the Working Group to provide opinions based on expert knowledge and stakeholders perspectives. It consisted of representatives from AAH, FSC members from each Standard Draft Group of social, environmental and economic chambers, and experts on indigenous peoples' rights.[64] The final draft was submitted to FSC headquarters before the end of 2017, and it was subsequently approved and became effective on 15 February 2019.[65]

Inclusion of UNDRIP into normative references

Through the revision process, the number of the Criteria on Principle 3 has become 6 in V5 from 4 in V4, and the overall requirements are enriched. Notably, as repeatedly saying, UNDRIP has become one of the normative references when considering 'the rights, customs and culture of Indigenous Peoples' in addition to C169. Before the revision, C169 was the only normative reference on indigenous peoples' rights, but it has not been respected enough in Japan because the Government has not ratified it.[66] Nonetheless,

Table 1. Principle 3 of P&C V4 and V5.

Principle 3 (indigenous peoples' rights) of P&C	
Version 4 (V4)	Version 5 (V5)
The legal and customary rights of indigenous peoples to own, use and manage their lands, territories, and resources shall be recognized and respected. 3.1 Indigenous peoples shall control forest management on their lands and territories unless they delegate control with free and informed consent to other agencies. 3.2 Forest management shall not threaten or diminish, either directly or indirectly, the resources or tenure rights of indigenous peoples. 3.3 Sites of special cultural, ecological, economic or religious significance to indigenous peoples shall be clearly identified in cooperation with such peoples, and recognized and protected by forest managers. 3.4 Indigenous peoples shall be compensated for the application of their traditional knowledge regarding the use of forest species or management systems in forest operations. This compensation shall be formally agreed upon with their free and informed consent before forest operations commence.	The Organization shall identify and uphold Indigenous Peoples' legal and customary rights of ownership, use and management of land, territories and resources affected by management activities. 3.1 The Organization shall identify the Indigenous Peoples that exist within the Management Unit or are affected by management activities. The Organization shall then, through engagement with these Indigenous Peoples, identify their rights of tenure, their rights of access to and use of forest resources and ecosystem services, their customary rights and legal rights and obligations, that apply within the Management Unit. The Organization shall also identify areas where these rights are contested. 3.2 The Organization shall recognize and uphold the legal and customary rights of Indigenous Peoples to maintain control over management activities within or related to the Management Unit to the extent necessary to protect their rights, resources and lands and territories. Delegation by Indigenous Peoples of control over management activities to third parties requires Free, Prior and Informed Consent. 3.3 In the event of delegation of control over management activities, a binding agreement between The Organization and the Indigenous Peoples shall be concluded through Free, Prior and Informed Consent. The agreement shall define its duration, provisions for renegotiation, renewal, termination, economic conditions and other terms and conditions. The agreement shall make provision for monitoring by Indigenous Peoples of The Organization's compliance with its terms and conditions. 3.4 The Organization shall recognize and uphold the rights, customs and culture of Indigenous Peoples as defined in the United Nations Declaration on the Rights of Indigenous Peoples (2007) and ILO Convention 169 (1989). 3.5 The Organization, through engagement with Indigenous Peoples, shall identify sites which are of special cultural, ecological, economic, religious or spiritual significance and for which these Indigenous Peoples hold legal or customary rights. These sites shall be recognized by The Organization and their management, and/or protection shall be agreed through engagement with these Indigenous Peoples. 3.6 The Organization shall uphold the right of Indigenous Peoples to protect and utilize their traditional knowledge and shall compensate Indigenous Peoples for the utilization of such knowledge and their intellectual property. A binding agreement as per Criterion 3.3 shall be concluded between The Organization and the Indigenous Peoples for such utilization through Free, Prior and Informed Consent before utilization takes place and shall be consistent with the protection of intellectual property rights.

IGI clarifies that it 'applies also in countries and jurisdictions that have not endorsed the UN Declaration and/or ratified ILO Convention 169'.[67] Regarding UNDRIP, although it is generally regarded as not legally binding in a strict sense,[68] the Government of Japan voted in favour and has recognised the Ainu as an indigenous people in the following year. Thus, in conjunction with C169, FSC Japan clarified that Ainu indigenous rights would no longer be ignored in its certification process in Hokkaido in 2013.[69]

Due to this, some forest managers have already begun negotiating with the Ainu. Most notably, Mitsui and Co. (Mitsui), a general trading company that owns the FSC-certified forest called the Saru Forest in Biratori, Hokkaido, concluded the 'pioneering' agreements with Biratori Ainu Association (BAA) and the municipality of Biratori in 2010. In this forest unit, one of the field tests for the national standard was conducted,[70] and the FSC Japan's Working Group on indigenous rights recognised that the agreements could be one of the model relationships between forest managers and the Ainu.[71] In Hokkaido, making agreements between the Ainu and forest managers is quite progressive by itself, and under the FSC P&C V5, the 'delegation of control over management activities' is recognised with 'a binding agreement' concluded through 'Free, Prior and Informed Consent'.[72] In this regard, Mitsui's agreements could be highly evaluated.

Nonetheless, the contents of the agreements might be less desirable. Similar to the Governmental policy to some extent, they focus on cultural promotion and avoid discussing indigenous peoples' rights to the Forest. For example, the first agreement between Mitsui and BAA was concluded 'under which action is being taken to stimulate the preservation of the culture of the Ainu people'. Similarly, another agreement between Mitsui and the municipality of Biratori was concluded 'under which Mitsui will cooperate in a municipal project to recreate an iwor (traditional Ainu living territory) and will collaborate in measures to stimulate industry'. For this, it is decided to plant trees such as Manchurian elm and supply the lumber for Ainu cultural activities,[73] but indigenous peoples' rights are not discussed.

One of the reasons for this might be because forest certification has developed mainly in the context of environmental sustainability, not of human rights protection. As Kazuhiro Matsui argues, although indigenous rights under FSC P&C have to be considered in conjunction with human rights standards, legal protection of the rights would not be required because the prevalence of forest certification could be prevented.[74] Considering the voluntary and market-driven characteristics and the limited additional value of certified products in Japan, it might also be true that the possibility of the suspension of forest certificates could not cause much pressure to change forest practices. Certifying bodies are unable to bind them as well, and if the audit process is too strict for forest managers, they would not achieve it and avoid obtaining certificates. In the case of the Saru Forest, FSC Japan recognises that the Ainu in the district are future-oriented, not criticising the land exploitation in the past or asking for the rights to the Forest at the moment.[75] However, the contents of Mitsui's agreements imply that the rights protection could be pigeonholed. In this sense, while it is quite implicative to include UNDRIP into the normative references, the limitations for indigenous rights protection through forest certification remain, and it has been faced with a dilemma.

Identification of Ainu

In addition to the inclusion of UNDRIP into normative references, two other Criteria are newly added through the revision, and they are also implicative in the context of the Ainu indigenous rights. One of them is the requirement on identifying indigenous peoples and their rights relevant to certifying forests (Criterion 3.1), and the other Criterion is the requirement on obtaining 'Free, Prior and Informed Consent' (FPIC) for management activities (Criterion 3.3).[76]

However, both Criteria are not completely new. Regarding the identification, it is necessary to know who are stakeholders in certifying forest units. In fact, some forest managers in Hokkaido consulted local governments about the Ainu in the area prior to the amendment of FSC P&C. However, because it was not always the case that local governments are familiar with the situation, the Ainu relevant to certifying forest units were sometimes overlooked.[77]

In response to this situation, the new national standard addresses the procedure of the identification. According to it, the identification would be conducted 'through consultation with the Ainu Association of Hokkaido, Ainu Associations in the district, or Ainu people in the area'. When it is difficult to identify them, the necessity of an inquiry to AAH is noted.[78] Although AAH does not represent all the Ainu population in Hokkaido, it is regarded as holding the most reliable information about distribution of the Ainu because it administers the Ainu people's registration system, which is used for governmental services to the Ainu.[79]

However, one of the factors that make the identification process more difficult might be the lack of sufficient data on the Ainu population and their situations. Although surveys on the Ainu have been carried out in relation to such as their living condition, they involve only limited area and population.[80] The Ainu human rights advocates have also raised this issue, and the Government has received recommendations from international human rights bodies.[81] In relation to this point, Tanabe also points out that the lack of the official definition in the Ainu policy 'makes the status of the Ainu ambiguous'. Nonetheless, the comprehensive data on them have not been collected because, for example, 'it would be controversial to add a question regarding a citizen's ethnicity to a census, which is probably an uncommon concept to most Japanese people'.[82] Behind this, the historical ignorance towards the Ainu and the 'myth' of the ethnic homogeneity seem to remain influential. It should be also noted that many Ainu people hide, or sometimes are unconscious of, their identity to avoid or minimise racial discrimination and social inequality.[83] The survey on Ainu living condition in 2017 indicates that 23.2% of answerers have experienced discrimination based on racial prejudice (59.4%) or unawareness/non-understanding of the Ainu historical and social background (46.3%).[84]

As in WGIP meetings, indigenous participants 'developed a common position and rejected the idea of a formal definition of indigenous peoples that would be adopted by States',[85] it might also be necessary to be cautious in developing an 'official' definition in the context of forest certification. However, the inclusion of Criterion 3.1 is implicative as it might reduce the risk of overlooking the existence and rights of the Ainu related to certifying forest units. Thus, in consideration of the lack of comprehensive data and the potential risk of an undesirable disclosure of their identity, it would be required to carefully identify who are related to each certifying forest unit in each time through, for example, considering the history and current situations of it and the Ainu, interacting with them and following their ways. Their social organisations such as Kotan, which is the Ainu traditional communities for living, would not be negligible either.[86] The careful approach could promote certain aspects of their indigenous rights, and because national forests also receive the forest certification, if private business corporations work on this point, it might be contributable to the governmental policy in a practical sense as well.

Right to free, prior and informed consent

Another requirement newly added is on the right to FPIC for the conclusion of 'a binding agreement' on 'delegation of control over management activities' (Criterion 3.3).[87] The necessity of FPIC is reiterated in Criterion 3.2 and Criterion 3.6 on the utilisation of indigenous traditional knowledge and also in the Criteria 4.2 and 4.8 in Principle 4 on 'Community Relations'.

Similar to Criterion 3.1, this requirement is not completely new either. Since the first version of P&C in 1994, FSC scheme has recognised 'the right to give or withhold consent',[88] and P&C V4 provided the necessity of 'free and informed consent' in the delegation of forest management and use of their traditional knowledge.[89] However, P&C V5 began clearly including the right to FPIC because of the insufficient examples on good practices of respecting FPIC and the reports on 'several conflicts arising from disregarding this right'.[90] The importance of indigenous peoples' involvement is also increasingly emphasised in international environmental documents.[91] PIPC was also set up in consideration of this, and FSC created the guideline for FPIC in 2012.[92]

While FPIC may not be considered as a 'right' per se, it has been treated as such under the FSC scheme. FSC's guideline for FPIC also considers it as a right for local communities including indigenous peoples and as 'a pre-condition for certification' to 'recognize and uphold the rights ... to their resources, lands and territories'.[93] James Anaya argues that FPIC stems from the right to self-determination and ensures 'autonomous governance' and 'participatory engagement',[94] and he also recognises that 'consultation and free, prior and informed consent are best conceptualized as safeguards against measures that may affect indigenous peoples' rights'.[95]

However, whether it contains veto power or not has been one of the controversial aspects. Comparing 'FPIC' and 'engagement', the FSC guideline clarifies that 'a process based on the right to FPIC' includes the right to say 'No', while 'engagement' gives forest managers 'the right to take the final decision'.[96] It thus implies the right to FPIC has veto power, but the idea of it is the exact factor that makes it difficult for the right to FPIC to be accepted.[97] With this in mind, the FSC guideline mentions Anaya's opinion that the right to FPIC 'should not be regarded as according indigenous peoples a general "veto power" ... but rather as establishing consent as the objective of consultations with indigenous peoples'. In other words, FPIC is 'designed to build dialogue' to 'work in good faith towards consensus' and 'a mutually satisfactory agreement' by avoiding 'the imposition of the will of one party over the other'.[98]

In recognition of these points, because indigenous perspectives are respected for the right to FPIC, it is considered as bringing structural changes in the relationship.[99] For example, including Mitsui's agreements, forest certification is often obtained for Corporate Social Responsibility (CSR).[100] However, the concept of CSR has been criticised in terms of its appropriation of the language of human rights because of its emphasis on corporate perspectives.[101] In this sense, the characteristics of the right to FPIC could lead to changes in what CSR or forest certification might offer with more emphasis on indigenous perspectives.[102] This may be also applied to national forests. In this regard, similar to the Criterion

3.1, private business corporations might show practical approaches that could be implicative for the national Ainu policy. Nonetheless, as mentioned already and implied in Mitsui's agreements, there remains room for indigenous rights protection to be pigeonholed. It might not be ignorable that Jennifer Franco points out that FPIC 'can also be deployed by big capital to still do what it wants while making this seem more socially acceptable'.[103]

Additionally, considering the Ainu situation, who the consent should be obtained from also remains unclear. This point is closely related to the issues on identification. While FPIC does not necessarily mean that 'every single member must agree', the process of obtaining FPIC 'will be undertaken through procedures and institutions determined by indigenous peoples themselves'.[104] However, the Ainu people currently do not have any publicly recognised representative or decision-making institutions.[105] In the FSC's field test, concern was also raised on how it should be dealt with if there were different arguments from different Ainu organisations on the same certifying forest management unit because several regions have two or more Ainu organisations.[106] As a related matter, while there are at least nearly 50 regional Ainu associations that hold the group membership of AAH at present,[107] the representativeness of them, including AAH, might also be unclear. In fact, although AAH is the largest Ainu organisation, the number of its members is much less than that of the answerers for the incomprehensive survey on their living condition.[108] Under this situation, in order to prevent the appropriation of FPIC, it might be also important to shun creating exclusive groups for forest certification, unlike the Ainu policy group that involves only limited Ainu representatives.[109] Their social organisations would be important in this context as well. In this sense, as mentioned already, careful consideration of the history and current situations of each certifying forest unit would be significant.

How to improve forest certification process?

Considering the analysis on the revised FSC P&C V5 in relation to Ainu indigenous rights in Hokkaido, one of the important aspects might be legislation and policy of the national Government. For instance, the lack or insufficiency of what the Government should work on in cooperation with the Ainu such as collection of the comprehensive data makes it more difficult to effectively certify Ainu indigenous rights protection for forest certification. In fact, also due to the voluntary characteristics of forest certification, Mitsui's agreements emphasise cultural promotion without rights protection. In this regard, while Uemura asserts that forest certification is separated from issues on how to make the Government implement UNDRIP,[110] working on the national Ainu legislation and policy is closely linked with it.[111]

Moreover, on a practical level, there might be room for improvement. One of the important aspects could be the quality of auditors because they are the ones who inspect forest practices on-site through, for instance, interactions with indigenous peoples and other stakeholders related to certifying forests and decide whether the certificates are given or not.[112] The quality of them could be a quite influential factor on the quality of forest certification including indigenous rights protection.[113]

However, in general, auditors are professional in forestry, and an evaluation team rarely includes experts on indigenous rights, perhaps because of the limited recognition in the

Japanese society given to indigenous peoples' issues. Thus, particularly in the forest areas in Hokkaido, it may be further important to actively include experts on indigenous peoples' rights into an audit team as a technical expert.[114] However, because adding another member to the team increases the cost for the process, it would depend on the balance of the cost and maintenance of the quality as well. Due to this, some human rights activists have begun considering providing programmes for auditors to learn indigenous peoples' rights,[115] while it should be important to avoid that audit processes become too stringent for forest managers to follow. Considering these aspects above, in addition to the efforts on working on the Governmental policy, by increasing the degree of the familiarity of auditors and an audit team with indigenous peoples' rights, it could be one of the key points to find the balanced way for the Ainu rights implementation through forest certification in Hokkaido.

Conclusion

The Ainu people have suffered from the continued colonisation. Because of the Ainu indigenous rights advocacy, the Government of Japan finally recognised the Ainu as an indigenous people in 2008. However, the Governmental Ainu policy has avoided the protection of indigenous rights outlined in UNDRIP, focusing on individual rights and cultural promotion. On the other hand, private standards, notably forest certification, have taken a different approach. Particularly, the recent amendment of FSC P&C could be implicative because it has precisely required forest managers to respect Ainu indigenous rights.

The study has explored the meaning and scope of it, especially taking a close look at newly added requirements on UNDRIP, identification of indigenous peoples, and the right to FPIC. Through the analysis, it was revealed that forest certification could be contributable to the improvement of the relationships between forest managers and the Ainu through, for example, concluding agreements on forest management. However, it was also clarified that the agreements on the FSC-certified forests could be limited to cultural promotion without rights protection because of some challenging aspects such as the lacks of the comprehensive data or representative bodies. Thus, careful consideration of certifying forest units is necessary. Additionally, the Governmental legislation and policy may not be negligible, and in a practical level, increasing the quality of auditors in terms of their familiarity with indigenous rights could be significant.

However, to further deepen this study, it would be quite important to analyse how the new standards are actually applied in the process of forest certification in Hokkaido. FSC Japan's revised national standard will be used soon, and the new standards of other forest certification schemes also started being used quite recently. In this regard, empirical and comparative research on actual utilisation of the new standards would further reveal the possibilities and challenges of the Ainu indigenous rights protection under forest certification in the future.

Notes

1. Alison Brysk, 'Turning Weakness into Strength: The Internationalization of Indian Rights', *Latin American Perspectives* 23, no. 2 (1996): 46.

2. Colin Samson and Carlos Gigoux, *Indigenous Peoples and Colonialism: Global Perspectives*, (Cambridge: Polity Press, 2017), 148.
3. S. James Anaya 'The Right of Indigenous Peoples to Self-Determination in the Post-Declaration Era', in *Making the Declaration Work: The United Nations Declaration on the Rights of Indigenous Peoples*, ed. Claire Charters and Rodolfo Stavenhagen (Copenhagen: IWGIA, 2009), 185.
4. Ronald Niezen, *The Origin of Indigenism: Human Rights and the Politics of Identity* (Berkeley, CA: University of California Press, 2003), 51.
5. Asbjørn Eide, 'The Indigenous Peoples, the Working Group on Indigenous Populations and the Adoption of the UN Declaration on the Rights of Indigenous Peoples', in *Making the Declaration Work: The United Nations Declaration on the Rights of Indigenous Peoples*, ed. Claire Charters and Rodolfo Stavenhagen (Copenhagen: IWGIA, 2009), 40–1.
6. Hideaki Uemura, 'Nihon niokeru Datsushokuminchika no Ronri to Heiwagaku – Sono Kankeisei no Seiri to Mondaiteiki' [Logic of Decolonisation and Peace Studies in Japan – Summarising the Relationship and Setting the Issues], *Peace Studies* 47 (2016): vii.
7. Hideaki Uemura, 'Koe wo Ageta Nihon no Senjuminzoku – Kokusai Rengou deno Undo ga motarashita Seika to Kadai' [Indigenous Peoples in Japan Who Raised their Voice – Outcome and Challenge brought by thei UN Activism], in *Senjumin kara Miru Gendai Sekai – Watashitachi no <Atarimae> ni Idomu*, ed. Naoko Fukayama, Junko Maruyama and Makiko Kimura (Kyoto: Showado, 2018), 62–5.
8. Ainu Association of Hokkaido (AAH), *Ainu Minzoku no Gaisetsu – Hokkaido Ainu Kyokai no Katsudo wo fukume* [Overview of The Ainu People: Including Activities of Ainu Association of Hokkaido], rev ed., 31 March 2017, https://www.ainu-assn.or.jp/public/files/1d05c1dd9ceb9cf70478cd757622d3075a2c94b7.pdf, 1. Hereinafter, the access dates of the URL referred in the paper are all 30 July 2018 if not specified.
9. Hokkaido Government (HG), *Hokkaido Ainu Seikatsu Jittai Chosa Hokokusho* [Report on Ainu Living Condition in Hokkaido] (2018), http://www.pref.hokkaido.lg.jp/ks/ass/H29_ainu_living_conditions_survey.pdf, 3.
10. Advisory Council for Future Ainu Policy (ACFAP), *Final Report*, trans. Comprehensive Ainu Policy Office, 29 July 2009, http://www.kantei.go.jp/jp/singi/ainu/dai10/siryou1_en.pdf, 2–9.
11. Yoko Tanabe, 'The UN Declaration of the Rights of Indigenous Peoples and the Ainu of Japan: Development and Challenge', *Indigenous Policy Journal* 24, no. 4 (2014), 6; Richard Siddle, *Race, Resistance and the Ainu of Japan* (London: Routledge, 1996), 56.
12. Ishii Hiroshi, 'Hokkaido Kaitaku no Rekishi' [History of Hokkaido Development], in *Hokkaido no Shinrin*, ed. Hoppo Shinrin Gakkai (Sapporo: Hokkaido Shimbun Press, 2011), 74–8.
13. ACFAP, *Final Report*, 9.
14. Siddle, *Race, Resistance and*, 76–7.
15. Their claims include the abolishment of assimilative legislation, 'ethnic' and 'economic self-reliance', basic human rights, the elimination of 'racial discrimination', the guarantee of political participation, and rights pertaining to education, language and culture (AAH, *Ainu Minzoku no*, 13–5).
16. Siddle, *Race, Resistance and*, 183–4.
17. Chris Burgess, 'The "Illusion" of Homogeneous Japan and National Character: Discourse as a Tool to Transcend the "Myth" vs. "Reality" Binary', *The Asia-Pacific Journal* 8-9, no. 1 (2010): 1–24.
18. Siddle, *Race, Resistance and*, 185.
19. Yuji Iwasawa, 'Nibutani Dam Saiban no Kokusaihojo no Igi' [The Significance of the Nibutani Dam Case in International Law], *Intercultural Human Rights* 9 (1998): 56–9.
20. Richard Siddle, 'An Epoch-Making Event? The 1997 Ainu Cultural Promotion Act and Its Impact', *Japan Forum* 14, no. 3 (2002): 410–11.
21. Naohiro Nakamura, '"Ainu Seisaku no Arikata ni kansuru Yushikisha Kondankai" Hokokusho ni kansuru Ronko no Hikaku Kento' [Comparative Examination of Analysis on the Final Report of 'Advisory Council of Future Ainu Policy'], *Hokkaido Ethnology* 10 (2014): 69.

22. Hideaki Uemura, '"Senjuminzoku no Kenri nikansuru Kokuren Sengen" Kakutoku heno Nagai Michinori' [A Long Way to Achieving 'the UN Declaration on the Rights of Indigenous Peoples'], *PRIME* 27 (2008): 64.
23. Tanabe, 'The UN Declaration', 12–3.
24. Yasuo Fukuda, *Shugiin Giin Suzuki Muneo kun Teishutsu Ainu Minzoku wo Senjuminzoku tosurukotowo Seifu ni motomeru Kokkaiketsugi wo uketeno Seifu no Torikumi nikansuru Saishitsumon nitaisuru Tobensho* [Answer to the Resubmitted Question by Muneo Suzuki, a Diet's Member, on the Government's Efforts for 'Resolution on Resolution Calling for the Recognition of the Ainu People as an Indigenous People'], 24 June 2008, http://www.shugiin.go.jp/internet/itdb_shitsumon_pdf_t.nsf/html/shitsumon/pdfT/b169549.pdf/$File/b169549.pdf.
25. ACFAP, *Final Report*, 1.
26. Uemura, 'Koe wo Ageta', 59.
27. Teruki Tsunemoto, 'Ainu Minzoku to "Nihongata" Senjuminzoku Seisaku' [The Ainu and 'Japan-specific' Indigenous Policy], *Gakujutsu no Doko* 16, no. 9 (2011): 80.
28. Teruki Tsunemoto, 'Toward Ainu- and Japan-Specific Indigenous Policies', http://jspsusa.org/FORUM2012/presentation/3-3_Tsunemoto.pdf.
29. Uemura, 'Koe wo Ageta', 59.
30. ACFAP, *Final Report*, 21.
31. Tanabe, 'The UN Declaration', 15. The criticisms also range over the lack of repatriation measures (e.g. Kunihiko Yoshida, *Ainu Minzoku no Senju Hosho Mondai – Minpogaku no Kenchi kara* [Ainu Indigenous Reparation Issue: From the Civil Law Perspective], (Sappro: Sappro Jiyu Gakko 'Yu', 2012), 9–11) or the structural exclusiveness and centralisation of the Ainu policy group (e.g. Takeshi Higashimura, 'Ainu Seisaku no Bunseki Wakugumi – Kyosei sareta "Kyosei" no Kozo' [Analytical Framework of the Ainu Policy: Structure of Forced 'Co-existence'], *Forum of International Development Studies* 47, no. 8 (2016): 1–16).
32. Uemura, 'Koe wo Ageta' 64.
33. Christie Overdevest, 'Comparatin Fores Certification Schemens: The Case of Ratcheting Standards in the Forest Sector', *Socio-Economic Review* 8 (2010): 47–6.
34. Sarah Crow and Cecilia Danks, 'Why Certify? Motivations, Outcomes and the Importance of Facilitating Organizations in Certification of Community-Based Forestry Initiatives', *Small-Scale Forestry* 9 (2010): 197.
35. María Gafo Gómez-Zamalloa, Alejandro Caparrós, Alfonso San-Miguel Ayanz, '15 Years of Forest Certification in the European Union. Are We Doing Things Right?', *Forest Systems* 20, no. 1 (2011): 82.
36. Forest Stewardship Council (FSC), 'FSC Celebrates Its 20th Anniversary: 20 Years of Growth With FSC 1994–2014', https://ic.fsc.org/20-years-of-growth/.
37. Programme for the Endorsement of Forest Certification (PEFC), 'History', https://www.pefc.org/about-pefc/who-we-are/history.
38. PEFC, 'International Endorsement', https://www.pefc.org/standards/endorsement-mutual-recognition.
39. Sustainable Green Ecosystem Council (SGEC), 'SGEC Kokusai Ninsho Seido toshiteno Aratana Shuppatsu – PEFC tono Sogo Shonin no Jitsugen' [Fresh Start as SGEC International Certification Mechanism: Mutual Endorsement with PEFC], 3 June 2016, http://sgec-eco.org/swfu/d/ReporterLecture2016_6_3.pdf.
40. FSC, 'Forest Management Certification: Maintaining Forest Ecosystems and Local Communities', https://ic.fsc.org/en/what-is-fsc-certification/forest-management-certification.
41. FSC, 'Chain of Custody Certification: Providing Credentials for Entering Sustainable Markets', https://ic.fsc.org/en/what-is-fsc-certification/chain-of-custodycertification.
42. FSC, 'Forest Management Certification'.
43. FSC, 'Accreditation Program: Ensuring Excellence in Certification?', https://ic.fsc.org/en/what-is-fsc-certification/accreditation-program.
44. Yuki Yamamoto et al., 'Is There a Price Premium for Certified Wood? Empirical Evidence from Log Auction Data in Japan', *Forest Policy and Economics* 38 (2014): 168–72.

45. Forest Stewardship Council Japan (FSCJ), 'FSC Japan – FSC Nihon Kokunai Shinrin Kikaku Dai 1 Soan Kochokai' [Public Hearing on First Draft of FSC Japan National Forest Standard], 22 July 2016, https://jp.fsc.org/preview..a-391.pdf.
46. Kisato Miura and Masaki Shiba, 'Shinrin Ninsho Seido to Ninsho Shohin nitaisuru Shohisha no Ishiki' [Consumers' Understanding of Forest Certification and Certified Products] (2009), https://www.jstage.jst.go.jp/article/jfsc/120/0/120_0_112/_pdf.
47. Forestry Agency, 'Shinrin Ringyo Hakusho' [White Paper on Forest and Forestry] (2016), http://www.rinya.maff.go.jp/j/kikaku/hakusyo/28hakusyo/attach/pdf/zenbun-4.pdf, 78.
48. Oliver Damette and Phillipe Delacote, 'Unsustainable Timber Harvesting, Deforestation and the Role of Certification', *Ecological Economics* 70 (2010): 1215–6.
49. Ibid.
50. PEFC, *Sustainable Forest Management – Requirements* (2010), https://www.pefc.org/images/documents/PEFC_ST_1003_2010_SFM__Requirements_2010_11_26.pdf, 12–3.
51. This battle occurred from 'the question of whether indigenous peoples are the same "peoples" – with an "S" – so prominent in the Charter of the United Nations, ... and who therefore must be recognized as possessing all the rights that flow from that status, including the right to self-determination' (Niezen, *The Origin of*, 160–5).
52. Hideaki Uemura, 'Shinrin Ninsho to Senju Minzoku' [Forest Certification and Indigenous Peoples], 19 November 2016, https://ainupolicy.jimdo.com/%E5%B8%82%E6%B0%91%E4%BC%9A%E8%AD%B0%E3%81%AE%E8%A8%98%E9%8C%B2/%E7%AC%AC%EF%BC%93%E5%9B%9E%E5%B8%82%E6%B0%91%E4%BC%9A%E8%AD%B02016%E5%B9%B411%E6%9C%8819%E6%97%A5/%E4%B8%8A%E6%9D%91%E8%8B%B1%E6%98%8E-%E6%A3%AE%E6%9E%97%E8%AA%8D%E8%A8%BC%E3%81%A8%E5%85%88%E4%BD%8F%E6%B0%91%E6%97%8F/. See also SGEC, *Principles, Indicators and Guidelines for SGEC Forest Management Certification: Requirements for Forest Management Certification* (2016), https://www.pefc.org/images/stories/documents/NGB_Documentation/Japan/Rev_161014_SGEC_doc_No_3_-_FM_principles_indicators_and_guidelines.pdf, 17–8.
53. In January 2018, FSC certifies 50,000 hectares of forest areas in Hokkaido, while SGEC (PEFC Japan) certifies 1,030,000 hectares of them. See HG, *Hokkaidonai no Shinrin Ninsho Shutoku Jokyo* [The Situation of the Forest Certification in Hokkaido], 10 January 2018, http://www.pref.hokkaido.lg.jp/sr/srk/ninnsyousyutokujyoukyou_180110.pdf.
54. FSC, 'The P&C Review Process: A Consistent Review of the Principles & Criteria', https://ic.fsc.org/en/what-is-fsc-certification/principles-criteria/the-revisited-p-and-c/the-review-process.
55. FSC, *Overview for Prioritization of the Approved Motions from the 2011 General Assembly*, 15 July 2011, http://motions.fsc.org/wp-content/uploads/2011/07/FSC_Report_GA-Motion-Passed_English.pdf, 7. In PIPC, an Ainu person, Koichi Kaizawa, was also appointed as a representative member from the Asia-Pacific region in 2016 (FSC Canada, 'NAFA encourages Canadian leadership on Indigenous rights in the forest and welcomes Ainu representation to the Permanent Indigenous Peoples Committee of FSC', 14 June 2016, https://ca.fsc.org/en-ca/newsroom/id/580).
56. FSC, *Overview for Prioritization of the Approved Motions from the 2011 General Assembly*, 15 July 2011, http://motions.fsc.org/wpcontent/uploads/2011/07/FSC_Report_GA-Motion-Passed_English.pdf, 7.
57. Some amendments were also made in 2014, and the latest version (V5-2) for implementation was approved in 2015 while Principle 3 has not changed.
58. Nature Economy and People Connected (NEPCon), 'FSC "fundamental law" revised and approved', 3 April 2012, https://www.nepcon.org/newsroom/fsc-fundamental-law-revised-and-approved.
59. For the overall changes of P&C, see FSC, *FSC Principles & Criteria Review: Summary of Changes between FSC-STD-01-001 Version 4-0 and FSC-STD-01-001 Version 5-0 D4-0*, 20 March 2011, http://ic.fsc.org/download.fsc-std-01-001-v5-0-d4-0-summary-of-changes-english.570.htm.

60. NEPCon, 'FSC Principles & Criteria review: for better or for worse?', 27 June 2011, https://www.nepcon.org/newsroom/fsc-principles-criteria-review-better-or-worse.
61. FSC, *International Generic Indicators (FSC-STD-60-004 V1-0 EN)* (Bonn: FSC International Center, 2015), http://igi.fsc.org/approved-documents.60.htm, 5–6.
62. Uemura, 'Koe wo Ageta', 63.
63. FSCJ, 'Nihon Kokunai Shinrin Kanri Kikaku Sakutei notameno Field Test' [Field Test for Japanese National Forest Management Standard Draft], 9 February 2017, https://jp.fsc.org/jp-jp/news/id/364.
64. FSCJ, 'FSC Nihon Kokunai Shinrin Kikaku Daiichi Soan Kochokai' [Public Hearing on First Draft of FSC Japan National Forest Standard], 22 July 2016, https://jp.fsc.org/preview..a-391.pdf.
65. FSCJ, 'FM Kokunai Kikaku Sakutei' [Establishment of FM Domestic Standards], 16 February 2019, https://jp.fsc.org/jp-jp/4-fsc/4-3/4-3-1-fm.
66. Uemura, 'Shinrin Ninsho to'.
67. FSC, *International Generic Indicators (FSC-STD-60-004 V1-0 EN)* (Bonn: FSC International Center, 2015), 24.
68. Permanent Forum on Indigenous Issues (PFII), *Concept Note, Expert Group Meeting – Dialogue on an Optional Protocol to the United Nations Declaration on the Rights of Indigenous Peoples*, UN Doc. PFII/2015/EGM, 27–29 January 2015, 3. However, whether UNDRIP already reflect customary international law or not has been an important issue. See S. James Anaya and Siegfried Wiessner, 'The UN Declaration on the Rights of Indigenous Peoples: Towards Reempowerment', *Jurist Legal News and Research* (2007), http://www.jurist.org/forum/2007/10/un-declaration-on-rights-of-indigenous.php; and Alexandra Xanthaki, 'Indigenous Rights in International Law over the Last 10 Years and Future Developments', *Melbourne Journal of International Law* 10, no. 1 (2009), http://law.unimelb.edu.au/__data/assets/pdf_file/0009/1686060/Xanthaki.pdf.
69. Uemura, 'Koe wo Ageta', 63.
70. FSCJ, *FSC Nihon Kokunai Shinrin Kanri Kikaku Daiichi Soan (D1-1) Field Test Hokokusho* [Report on Field Test for the First FSC Japan National Standard Draft (D1-1)], 21 October 2016, https://jp.fsc.org/preview.1.a-445.pdf.
71. FSCJ, *Senju Minzoku Working Group Dai 2 kai Meeting Gijiroku* [Minutes of Second Meeting of Working Group on Indigenous Peoples] (working paper, FSC Japan, 2016).
72. FSC, *FSC Principles and Criteria*, Criterion 3.3.
73. Mitsui & Co., *Environment, Social Contribution Activity: Mitsui & Co., Ltd. Sustainability Report 2015*, http://www.mitsui.com/jp/en/sustainability/sustainabilityreport/2015/__icsFiles/afieldfile/2015/09/08/en_csr_2015-07.pdf, 110.
74. Kazuhiro Matsui, 'Shinrin Ninsho Seido niokeru Senju Minzoku no Kenri' [The Indigenous Peoples' Rights on the Forest Certification], *International Public Policy Studies* 9, no. 2 (2005): 287.
75. FSCJ, 'FSC Nihon Kokunai', 15.
76. FSC, *FSC Principles & Criteria Review*, 4–5.
77. Chisato Mishiba (Policy and Standard Coordinator, FSC Japan National Office), interview by the author, 26 July 2017, via Skype.
78. FSCJ, *The Final Draft of the Nation Forest Stewardship Standard*, https://jp.fsc.org/jp-jp/news/id/455, 30–1.
79. FSCJ, 'Senju Minzoku Working Group Dai 4 kai Meeting Gijiroku' [Minutes of Fourth Meeting of Working Group on Indigenous Peoples] (working paper, FSC Japan, 2016).
80. HG, *Hokkaido Ainu Seikatsu*, 3.
81. See Committee on the Elimination of Racial Discrimination, *Concluding Observations on the Combined Seventh to Ninth Periodic Reports of Japan*, UN Doc. CERD/C/JPN/CO/7-9, 26 September 2014, para. 20.
82. Tanabe, 'The UN Declaration', 19.
83. Ibid.
84. HG, *Hokkaido Ainu Seikatsu*, 49.

85. PFII, *The Concept of Indigenous Peoples*, UN Doc. PFII/2004/WS.1/3, 19–21 January 2004, para. 3.
86. Kyoko Kojima and Ainu Museum, eds., *Ainu Bunka no Kiso Chishiki* [Basic Knowledge on Ainu Culture] enl. rev. (Urayasu: Sofukan, 2018), 178–84.
87. FSC, *FSC Principles and Criteria*, Criterion 3.3.
88. FSC, *FSC Guidelines for the Implementation of the Right to Free, Prior and Informed Consent (FPIC)* (Bonn: FSC International Center GmbH, 2012), https://ca.fsc.org/download.fsc-guidelines-for-fpic.177.pdf, 6.
89. FSC, *FSC Principles and Criteria for Forest Stewardship: FSC-STD-01-001 (version 4-0) EN* (Bonn: Forest Stewardship Council, 1996) https://ic.fsc.org/en/what-is-fsc-certification/principles-criteria/the-revisited-p-and-c, Criteria 3.1 and 3.4.
90. FSC, *FSC Guidelines for*, 6.
91. Mauro Barelli, 'Free, Prior and Informed Consent in the Aftermath of the UN Declaration on the Rights of Indigenous Peoples: Developments and Challenges Ahead', *The International Journal of Human Rights* 16, no. 1 (2012): 3–4.
92. Currently, the Working Group has been established to develop the second version of the guideline. (FSC International, 'FSC establishes FPIC Working Group', 20 June 2018, https://ic.fsc.org/en/news-updates/id/2113).
93. FSC, *FSC Guidelines for*, 8.
94. Anaya, 'The Right of', 192–3.
95. Human Rights Council (HRC), *Report of the Special Rapporteur on the Rights of Indigenous Peoples, James Anaya*, UN Doc. A/HRC/21/47, 6 July 2012, para. 80.
96. FSC, *FSC Guidelines for*, 8.
97. Toyah Rodhouse and Frank Vanclay, 'Is Free, Prior and Informed Consent a Form of Corporate Social Responsibility?', *Journal of Cleaner Production* 131 (2016): 791.
98. FSC, *FSC guidelines for*, 11; HRC, *Report of the Special Rapporteur on the Situation of Human Rights and Fundamental Freedoms of Indigenous People, James Anaya*, UN Doc. A/HRC/12/34, 15 July 2009, paras. 46, 49.
99. Amy K. Lehr and Gare A. Smith, *Implementing a Corporate Free, Prior and Informed Consent Policy: Benefits and Challenges* (Boston: Foley Hoag, 2010), http://solutions-network.org/site-fpic/files/2012/09/Implementing-a-Corporate-Free-Prior-Informed-Consent-Foley-Hoag.pdf, 59.
100. Cf. Mitsui & Co., *2017 Mitsui Bussan Sustainability Report*, https://www.mitsui.com/jp/ja/sustainability/sustainabilityreport/2017/__icsFiles/afieldfile/2017/09/08/ja_sustainability_2017-p.pdf, 37, 41.
101. Nicholas Connolly and Manette Kaisershot, 'Corporate Power and Human Rights', *The International Journal of Human Rights* 19, no. 6 (2015): 666.
102. Cf. Rodhouse and Vanclay, 'Is Free, Prior'.
103. Jennifer Franco, *Reclaiming Free Prior and Informed Consent (FPIC) in the Context of Global Land Grabs* (Amsterdam: Transnational Institute for Hands off the Land Alliance, 2014), https://www.tni.org/files/download/reclaiming_fpic_0.pdf.
104. Office of the High Commissioner for Human Rights, *Free, Prior and Informed Consent of Indigenous Peoples*, September 2013, http://www.ohchr.org/Documents/Issues/IPeoples/FreePriorandInformedConsent.pdf.
105. Nakamura, 'Ainu Seisaku no', 69–70.
106. FSCJ, 'FSC Nihon Kokunai', 15.
107. AAH, 'Kakuchiku Ainu Kyokai Ichiran' [List of Ainu Associations of Each Region], https://www.ainu-assn.or.jp/outline/list.html.
108. The number of the Ainu who answered the latest survey on the Ainu living condition was 13,118 in 2017 while the number of the AAH members is around 3,000. See Nakamura, 'Ainu Seisaku no', 75.
109. Higashimura, 'Ainu Seisaku no'.
110. Uemura, 'Koe wo Ageta', 64–5.

111. Other scholars also discuss the roles of the national Governments in the forest certification. See Lukas Giessen et al., 'From Governance to Government: The Strengthened Role of State Bureaucracies in Forest and Agricultural Certification', *Policy and Society* 35 (2016), 71–89.
112. Uemura, 'Shinrin Ninsho to'.
113. Marie-Gabrielle Piketty and Isabel Garcia Drigob, 'Shaping the Implementation of the FSC Standard: The Case of Auditors in Brazil', *Forest Policy and Economics* 90 (2018), 160–6.
114. Mishiba, interview.
115. Uemura, 'Shinrin Ninsho to'.

Disclosure statement

No potential conflict of interest was reported by the author.

The approach to UNDRIP within the African Regional Human Rights System

Lucy Claridge

ABSTRACT
In May 2017, as the United Nations Declaration on the Rights of Indigenous Peoples prepared to celebrate a decade since its formal adoption, the issue of indigenous peoples' rights in Africa fell to be considered for the first time by the continent's highest human rights body, the African Court of Human and Peoples' Rights, in the *Ogiek* case against Kenya. The Court's ruling followed – and to some extent, drew upon – the African Union's 2010 adoption of the African Commission on Human and Peoples' Rights' landmark ruling against Kenya in the *Endorois* case. The first cases to recognise indigenous peoples' rights over and in connection with their ancestral land, both rulings have been widely recognised as significant developments in the advancement of indigenous peoples' rights in Africa. Despite the fact that Kenya is not a signatory to the Declaration, the Court and the Commission specifically drew inspiration from the concept of indigenous peoples as set out within it. This paper will explore the approaches of these two African human rights bodies to the Declaration, providing authoritative analysis from the lead lawyer litigating Africa's foremost indigenous peoples' rights case and drawing on her extensive experience working with the Endorois to seek implementation of their successful ruling, a decade after the Declaration's adoption.

Introduction

During its 42nd session in November 2007, the African Commission on Human and Peoples' Rights welcomed the adoption of the United Nations Declaration on the Rights of Indigenous Peoples (the 'Declaration'), stating that 'with the adoption of the UN Declaration a giant step has been taken towards securing the survival of indigenous peoples and their unique cultures based on their own needs and visions'.[1] It declared itself 'confident that the Declaration will become a very valuable tool and a point of reference for the African Commission's efforts to ensure the promotion and protection of indigenous peoples' rights on the African continent'.[2]

Just over two years later, in February 2010, the opportunity to examine the strength of that statement first arose, as the African Union adopted the African Commission on Human and Peoples' Rights' ('the Commission') landmark ruling against Kenya in the

Endorois case.[3] The first case to recognise indigenous peoples' rights over their ancestral land and also the first case adjudicating upon the right to development, the ruling has been widely recognised as a significant development in the advancement of indigenous peoples' rights in Africa. The Commission drew heavily on the Declaration within its ruling, notably in the context of the Endorois' land rights, but also in relation to their rights to access religious and cultural sites, and the requirement to seek their free prior and informed consent in relation to developments on Endorois lands. In this way, the Commission endorsed its earlier sanctioning of the Declaration as an authoritative source of law within its 2007 Advisory Opinion.[4]

Seven years later – and in the same year that the Declaration celebrated a decade since its adoption – the issue of indigenous peoples' rights in Africa fell to be considered for the first time by the continent's highest human rights body, the African Court of Human and Peoples' Rights ('the Court'). The case challenged the Kenyan Government's eviction of 30,000 indigenous Ogiek from their ancestral homes.[5] In May 2017, the Court firmly embraced and adopted the concept of indigenous peoples' rights, not only in relation to communal property rights over ancestral land, but also in relation to rights to culture and religion, and also their right to freely enjoy their natural resources. Despite the fact that Kenya is not a signatory to the Declaration, the Court specifically drew inspiration from the concept of indigenous peoples as set out in the Declaration, ruling that such people deserve special protection deriving from their vulnerability. The Court also made some very clear rulings in relation to the role of indigenous peoples, and specifically hunter-gatherers, in conservation, stating in no uncertain terms that the preservation of the forest could not justify the lack of recognition of the Ogiek's indigenous or tribal status nor the denial of the rights associated with that status. It also explicitly confirmed that the Ogiek could not be held responsible for the depletion of the Mau Forest nor could the preservation of the forest justify their eviction or the denial of access to their land to exercise their right to culture. Originally lodged with the Commission but referred to the Court on the basis that it evinced serious and mass human rights violations, the case was the only Commission-referred case to have been heard by the Court, and created significant procedural and substantive precedent.

Drawing upon the Commission and Court rulings in the Endorois and Ogiek cases, this paper will examine the extent to which the Declaration has become both a valuable tool and a point of reference for ensuring the promotion and protection of indigenous peoples' rights on the African continent during the first ten years of its existence.

Kenya's Endorois and Ogiek: a shared story of discrimination and dispossession

Endorois are a semi-nomadic indigenous community of approximately 60,000 people who for centuries have earned their livelihoods from herding cattle and goats in the Lake Bogoria area of Kenya's Rift Valley.[6] They have established and practised a sustainable way of life that is entirely interwoven with their ancestral land, occupying and enjoying undisturbed use of the land for more than three hundred years, even under British colonial administration. Endorois have a strong attachment to the area surrounding Lake Bogoria, which is both fertile land providing pasture and medicinal salt licks for their cattle, and central to their religious and cultural practices. The community's historical prayer sites, places for circumcision rituals, and other cultural ceremonies are situated around Lake Bogoria. Endorois believe that the spirits of all their community, no matter where they are buried, live on in Lake Bogoria, and the Mochongoi forest is considered the birthplace of Endorois and the settlement of the first Endorois community.

When Kenya gained independence in 1963, ownership of Endorois land – previously designated as a native land under the management of the Native Lands Trust Board in London – was transferred to the relevant county council, who held the land in trust and for the benefit of the Endorois community.[7] Endorois remained on the land and continued to hold, use and enjoy it. In 1973, however, the Endorois people were dispossessed of their land by the Kenyan government through the creation of the Lake Hannington Game Reserve in the Central Rift Valley – subsequently renamed Lake Bogoria Game Reserve in 1978.

Endorois challenged their eviction with the Kenyan authorities. They were assured that 400 Endorois families would be compensated with plots of fertile land, that the community would receive 25 per cent of the tourist revenue from the Game Reserve and 85 per cent of the employment generated, and that cattle dips and fresh water dams would be constructed. None of these terms was ever implemented: only 170 out of the 400 families were eventually given some money in 1986, years after the agreements were concluded. This money was always understood to be a means of facilitating relocation rather than compensation for Endorois' loss.

The Endorois community eventually challenged their treatment before the Kenyan High Court in 2000. The High Court gave judgment against them in 2002, finding that although Endorois were the former *bona fide* occupants of the land, their customary claim to the land had been extinguished as a result of the designation of the land as a game reserve in 1973 and 1978.[8] It concluded that the money given in 1986 to 170 families for the cost of relocating represented the fulfilment of any duty owed by the authorities towards Endorois for the loss of their ancestral land. The High Court also stated that it could not address the issue of a community's collective right to property, and that it did not believe Kenyan law should address the issue of special protection to a people's land based on historical occupation and cultural rights. The court further viewed the Lake Bogoria reserve as a national resource, finding that a community such as the Endorois was therefore not entitled to any benefits flowing from the land.[9]

Having had no success in the Kenyan courts, the Endorois community – represented by CEMIRIDE and Minority Rights Group International ('MRG') ('the Complainants') – took the matter to the African Commission in 2003. The evolution and ruling in this case is detailed further below.

The Ogiek share a similar history of oppression, discrimination and dispossession. Numbering approximately 30,000,[10] they are some of Africa's last remaining forest dwellers. Traditionally honey-gatherers, the Ogiek survive mainly on wild fruits and roots, game hunting and traditional bee-keeping. The Ogiek have lived since time immemorial in Kenya's Mau Forest, and are friendly to the environment on which they depend. They have a unique way of life well-adapted to the forest. To them, the Mau Forest is a home, school, cultural identity and way of life that gives them pride and destiny. In fact, the term 'Ogiek' literally means 'caretaker of all plants and wild animals'. Unsurprisingly, the survival of the indigenous Mau Forest is therefore inextricably linked with the survival of the Ogiek.

Since independence, and indeed prior to it, the Ogiek have been routinely subjected to arbitrary forced evictions from their ancestral land by the Kenyan Government, without consultation or compensation. The Ogiek's rights over their traditionally owned lands have been systematically denied and ignored. The Government has allocated land to third parties, including political allies, and permitted substantial commercial logging to take place, without sharing any of the benefits with the Ogiek. The eviction of the Ogiek from their ancestral land and the refusal to allow them access to their spiritual home has prevented the Ogiek from practising their traditional cultural and religious practices. The culmination of all these actions has resulted in the Ogiek being prevented from practising their traditional hunter-gatherer way of life, thus threatening their very existence. Over the last 50 years, the Ogiek have consistently raised objections to these evictions with local and national administrations, task forces and commissions and have instituted several rounds of judicial proceedings in the national courts, to no avail.

In October 2009, the Kenyan Government, through the Kenya Forestry Service, issued a 30-day eviction notice to the Ogiek and other settlers of the Mau Forest, demanding that they leave the forest. Concerned that this was a perpetuation of the historical land injustices already suffered, and having failed to resolve these injustices through repeated national litigation and advocacy efforts, the Ogiek decided to lodge a case against their Government before the Commission,[11] with the assistance of MRG, Ogiek Peoples' Development Programme and CEMIRIDE.[12] In November 2009, the Commission, citing the far-reaching implications on the political, social and economic survival of the Ogiek community and the potential irreparable harm if the eviction notice was actioned, issued an Order for Provisional Measures[13] requesting the Kenyan Government to suspend implementation of the eviction notice. The Ogiek were not evicted on that occasion, but their precarious situation continued. In July 2012, following the Kenyan Government's lack of response on the issue, the Commission seized the Court pursuant to Article 5(1)(a) of the Protocol to the African Charter on Human and Peoples' Rights on the Establishment of the African Court of Human and Peoples' Rights[14] on the grounds that the case evinced serious and mass human rights violations.

The African Commission's approach to the declaration prior to *Endorois*

Long before the adoption of the Declaration, the Commission had already taken several bold steps aimed at better protecting the human rights of indigenous communities living in Africa. Among others, it set up the Working Group on Indigenous Populations/Communities ('WGIP') in 2001, which has since then been conducting promotional and protection missions to different countries, undertaking research and publishing reports on the rights of indigenous peoples.[15] In 2003, the Working Group issued the first ever African Union ('AU') report domesticating or 'Africanising' the term 'indigenous peoples', clarifying the concept of indigenous peoples in the African context and setting out the framework of their rights.[16] More specifically, the Commission played an active role in the debate surrounding the adoption of the Declaration, following the AU's last-minute and strong comments in the final phase of the Declaration's adoption process, which nearly derailed the whole twenty-year negotiation process.[17] This included the Assembly of Heads of State and Government of the AU, meeting in January 2007, taking a decision aimed at requesting the deferment of the consideration by the UN

General Assembly of the adoption of the Declaration with a view to opening negotiations for making amendments, in order to take into consideration the fundamental preoccupations of the African countries. The issues it specifically raised were the definition of indigenous populations, self-determination, land ownership and the exploitation of resources, the establishment of distinct political and economic institutions, and the issue of national and territorial integrity.[18]

At its 41st Ordinary Session in May 2007, the Commission deliberated on the issue and underlined the fact that the concept of indigenous populations in the African continent had been the subject of extensive study and debate resulting in the 2003 report.[19] The Commission decided to ask its WGIP to draft an Advisory Opinion on the various concerns expressed by the African States on the Declaration for submission to and discussion with key AU organs concerned with the matter before and during the upcoming AU Summit. The Commission interpreted the protection of the rights of indigenous populations within the context of a strict respect for the inviolability of borders and of the obligation to preserve the territorial integrity of State Parties, in conformity with the principles and values enshrined in the Constitutive Act of the AU, the African Charter on Human and Peoples' Rights (the African Charter) and the UN Charter. The Commission then adopted an 'Advisory Opinion on the United Nations Declaration on the Rights of Indigenous Peoples', in which it stated that the rights enshrined in the Declaration were consistent with the African Charter and the jurisprudence of the Commission.[20] This officially sanctions the Declaration[21] and is thought to have been particularly persuasive on the African group finally adopting the Declaration.

During its 42nd session, the Commission welcomed the adoption of the Declaration, stating that 'with the adoption of the UN Declaration a giant step has been taken towards securing the survival of indigenous peoples and their unique cultures based on their own needs and visions'.[22] It added that the Declaration 'is in line with the position and work of the African Commission on indigenous peoples' rights as expressed in the various reports, resolutions and legal opinion on the subject matter….. [and] is confident that the Declaration will become a very valuable tool and a point of reference for the African Commission's efforts to ensure the promotion and protection of indigenous peoples' rights on the African continent'. An analysis of both the Ogiek and Endorois rulings will now examine the truth of this statement.

The Endorois ruling: Africa's first chance to apply the declaration in jurisprudence

At the outset, it is worth noting that the Declaration was still a draft at the time that the Complainants lodged their merits submissions[23] (2005) – although it had been adopted by the time the Commission deliberated the case. The Commission explicitly recognised that the Constitution of Kenya, though incorporating the principle of non-discrimination and guaranteeing civil and political rights, does not recognise economic, social and cultural rights as such, as well as group rights. It further noted that the rights of indigenous pastoralist and hunter-gatherer communities are not recognised as such in Kenya's constitutional and legal framework, and no policies or governmental institutions deal directly with indigenous issues. It also noted that while Kenya has ratified most international human rights treaties and conventions, it has not ratified ILO Convention No. 169 on

Indigenous and Tribal Peoples in Independent Countries, and it has withheld its approval of the United Nations Declaration on the Rights of Indigenous Peoples of the General Assembly.[24]

The Commission was not however deterred by Kenya's apparent lack of acceptance of indigenous peoples' rights. In an unprecedented ruling confirming the applicability of indigenous peoples' rights within the African human rights system, it explicitly drew on key provisions and principles enshrined within the Declaration.

Firstly, the Commission found that Endorois are a distinct people whose culture, religion and traditional way of life are intimately intertwined with their ancestral lands. As a result, the Commission found that they are entitled to protection of the collective rights articulated in the African Charter.[25]

The Commission then concluded that the Government of Kenya had violated Endorois' rights to cultural and religious freedom in contravention of Article 8 of the African Charter, by forcibly evicting them from their ancestral and sacred lands, including Lake Bogoria, thereby preventing them from maintaining their religious and cultural practices and threatening their way of life.[26] In the view of the Commission, the conservation and economic development goals sought with the creation of the game reserve did not justify the government's infringement of Endorois' cultural and religious rights. Instead, the Commission noted that Endorois' access to Lake Bogoria, the medicinal salt licks and other ancestral and sacred lands would not 'detract' from those goals, nor would it 'pose any harm to the ecosystem of the Game Reserve'.[27] This would appear to draw directly from the Declaration (which, as earlier stated, was in fact still a Draft at the time that merits submissions were lodged), since the merits submissions relied on the draft text which stated that it gives indigenous peoples the right 'to maintain, protect and have access in privacy to their religious and cultural sites ... '.[28].

In relation to the right to property, the African Commission concluded that the government's 'expropriation and the effective denial of ownership of their land' amounted to an infringement, or encroachment, of Endorois' right to property.[29] In declaring that the government 'must grant title' to Endorois to 'guarantee [their] permanent use and enjoyment' of their lands,[30] it drew on the concept of ownership established in Articles 8(2)(b), 10, 25, 26 and 27 of the Declaration, which 'ensures that indigenous peoples can engage with the state and third parties as active stakeholders rather than as passive beneficiaries'.[31] It also relied on Articles 26 and 27 of the Declaration which refers to the term 'occupied or otherwise used', in recognising that indigenous peoples – and therefore the Endorois – have a recognised claim to ownership to ancestral land under international law, even in the absence of official title deeds.[32]

To remedy the government's failure to obtain the consent of Endorois before conducting development activities on their lands, as well as its failure to include Endorois in a share of the benefits of those activities, the Commission recommended, *inter alia,* that the government 'pay adequate compensation to the community for all the loss suffered'.[33] The Commission reached this conclusion by noting the observations within Article 28 of the Declaration, which, states

> Indigenous peoples have the right to restitution of the lands, territories and resources which they have traditionally owned or otherwise occupied or used; and which have been confiscated, occupied, used or damaged without their free and informed consent. Where this is

> not possible, they have the right to just and fair compensation. Unless otherwise freely agreed upon by the peoples concerned, compensation shall take the form of lands, territories and resources equal in quality, size and legal status.[34]

Following – and indeed in spite of – the ruling recognising the Endorois rights over their ancestral land and requiring its restitution, the Government of Kenya took steps to have Lake Bogoria designated as a UNESCO World Heritage Site, without informing or consulting the Endorois. The Commission was quick to act following concerned voiced by the Complainants, issuing a resolution calling upon 'the World Heritage Committee and UNESCO to review and revise current procedures and Operational Guidelines, in consultation and cooperation with the UN Permanent Forum on Indigenous Issues and indigenous peoples, in order to ensure that the implementation of the World Heritage Convention is consistent with the UN Declaration on the Rights of Indigenous Peoples and that indigenous peoples' Rights, and human rights generally, are respected, protected and fulfilled in World Heritage areas'.[35]

Both the *Endorois* ruling and the Commission's ongoing approaches to its implementation clearly demonstrate that the Commission does indeed see the Declaration as an authoritative tool and point of reference for the promotion and protection of indigenous peoples' rights in Africa. What then of the Court's approach?

The Ogiek case: the court confirms the declaration

The African Court has clearly drawn inspiration from the Declaration in reaching its ruling in the Ogiek case, again despite Kenya not having approved the Declaration. This was indeed the intention of the Ogiek's legal representative, who sought to rely on sources of international comparative law within her legal argument, not just to protect the Ogiek's rights, but also to create wider acceptance of indigenous peoples' rights within the Declaration, as echoed by the approach of the WGIP.

Addressing the Ogiek's submissions, the Court dealt first with the claim that the Ogiek are an indigenous people. The Court stated that

> the concept of indigenous population is not defined in the Charter and therefore, there is no universally accepted definition of 'indigenous population' in other international human rights instruments. There have, however, been efforts to define indigenous populations. In this regard, the Court draws inspiration from the work of the Commission through its Working Group on Indigenous Populations/Communities.[36] The Working Group has adopted the following criteria to identify indigenous populations:
>
> 'i. Self-identification;
>
> ii. A special attachment to and use of their traditional land whereby their ancestral land and territory have a fundamental importance for their collective physical and cultural survival as peoples; and
>
> iii. A state of subjugation, marginalisation, dispossession, exclusion, or discrimination because these peoples have different cultures, ways of life or mode of production than the national hegemonic and dominant model'.

The Court considered that it had received significant evidence to affirm the Ogiek's assertion that the Mau Forest is their ancestral home,[37] recognising the link between indigenous populations and nature, land and the natural environment, and that for centuries they had depended on the Mau as a source of livelihood. The Court also found that the Ogiek exhibit all aspects of the second factor, are distinct from other neighbouring tribes, and are identified as distinct by those tribes. Finally, the Court ruled that the Ogiek have suffered continued subjugation and marginalisation, as evidenced by the evictions from their ancestral lands, their forced assimilation and lack of recognition of their status as a tribe. Accordingly, the Court recognised the Ogiek as an indigenous population that is part of the Kenyan population and deserved special protection deriving from their vulnerability.[38]

In relation to the right to property under Article 14, the Court held that this can apply to groups or communities: that it can be individual or collective.[39] It specifically and directly interpreted the right in light of Article 26 of the Declaration, which recognises indigenous peoples' 'right to own, use, develop and control the lands, territories and resources that they possess by reason of traditional ownership'.[40] It stated

> To determine the extent of the rights recognised for indigenous communities in their ancestral lands as in the instant case, the Court holds that Article 14 of the Charter must be interpreted in light of the applicable principles especially by the United Nations … .. It follows in particular from Article 26 (2) of the Declaration that the rights that can be recognised for indigenous peoples/communities on their ancestral lands are variable and do not necessarily entail the right of ownership in its classical meaning, including the right to dispose thereof (abusus). Without excluding the right to property in the traditional sense, this provision places greater emphasis on the rights of possession, occupation, use/utilization of land.[41]

Since the Government had not disputed that the Ogiek have occupied lands in the Mau Forest since time immemorial, the Court ruled that they have the right to occupy, use and enjoy their ancestral lands.[42] It then referenced the Declaration again in finding that the Ogiek have the right to occupy, use and enjoy their ancestral lands.

> In the circumstances, since the Court has already held that the Ogieks (sic)[43] constitute an indigenous community (supra paragraph 112), it holds, on the basis of Article 14 of the Charter read in light of the above-mentioned United Nations Declaration, that they have the right to occupy their ancestral lands, as well as use and enjoy the said lands.[44] Further, although the Court accepted that the right to property under Article 14 can be restricted in the public interest where necessary and proportionate, the degradation of the Mau Forest could neither be attributable to the Ogiek nor did the preservation of the ecosystem justify their eviction.[45] Accordingly, the Court held that by expelling the Ogieks from their ancestral lands against their will, without prior consultation and without respecting the conditions of expulsion in the interest of public need, the Respondent violated their rights to land as defined above and as guaranteed by Article 14 of the Charter read in light of the United Nations Declaration on the Rights of Indigenous Peoples of 2007.[46]

Addressing the Ogiek's arguments under Article 17(2) and (3) of the African Charter, the Court considered it to have a dual dimension: ensuring protection of individuals' participation in the cultural life of their community whilst also obliging the State to promote and protect traditional values of the community. It considered that the right requires respect for and protection of cultural heritage essential to the group's identity, encompassing the group's total way of life: languages, symbols, economic activities rituals and shared values.[47]

> The Court notes that in the context of indigenous populations, the preservation of their culture is of particular importance. Indigenous populations have often been affected by

> economic activities of other dominant groups and large scale developmental programmes. Due to their obvious vulnerability often stemming from their number or traditional way of life, indigenous populations even have, at times, been the subject and easy target of deliberate policies of exclusion, exploitation, forced assimilation, discrimination and other forms of persecution, whereas some have encountered extinction of their cultural distinctiveness and continuity as a distinct group.[48]

In reaching this conclusion, the Court drew on the work of the WGIP,[49] and also referred to Article 8 of the Declaration, which states that 'indigenous peoples and individuals have the right not to be subjected to forced assimilation or destruction of their culture' and States shall provide effective mechanisms to prevent any action that deprives them of 'their integrity as distinct peoples, or of their cultural values or ethnic identities'.[50] The Court also relied on General Comment No 21 of the UN Committee on Economic, Social and Cultural Rights, which has observed that indigenous peoples' cultural life includes the right to lands, territories and resources which they have traditionally owned, occupied and used.[51] This approach recognising the duality of indigenous peoples' rights to participating in cultural, social and political life of society whilst also maintaining their own separate cultural systems is very much in line with the spirit of the Declaration, particularly Articles 11, 12 and 13. It is also particularly refreshing, since during the merits hearing before the Court, the Government had sought to argue that the Ogiek no longer practised their traditional way of life, by reason of the fact that they do not all live in the forest, some have access to education and some possess mobile phones.

The Court considered that it had sufficient evidence demonstrating the Ogiek have their own distinct culture, and the restrictions on access to and evictions from the Mau Forest have greatly affected their ability to preserve their traditions, resulting in a violation of the Ogiek's right to culture.[52] The Court did not consider that the Ogiek's way of life has changed over time to the extent that it has eliminated their cultural distinctiveness and indeed could see that some of these changes were caused by the Government as a result of restrictions on their right to access their land and natural environment.[53] Finally, given the Court had already found that the Government had not adequately proved its claim that the eviction of the Ogiek was for the preservation of the natural ecosystem of the Mau Forest, this could not constitute a legitimate justification for the interference in the Ogiek's exercise of their cultural rights under Article 17 (2) and (3) of the African Charter.[54]

In relation to the right to development under Article 22 of the African Charter, the Court reiterated its view on the definition of 'peoples' as already developed under Article 21 of the African Charter, stating that all populations which comprise a constitutive element of a State are entitled to social, economic and cultural development under Article 22 of the African Charter. Accordingly, the Court found that the Ogiek population has the right under Article 22 to enjoy their right to development.[55] The Court considered that Article 22 should be read in light of Article 23 of the Declaration, which states 'indigenous peoples have the right to be actively involved in developing and determining health, housing and other economic and social programmes affecting them and ... to administer such programmes through their own institutions'. Since the Ogiek have been continuously evicted from the Mau, without being effectively consulted, adversely impacting on their economic, social and cultural development; and since they have not been actively involved in developing and determining programmes affecting them, the Court held that the Government had violated Article 22 of the African Charter.[56]

The Court's approach to the right to life under Article 4 of the African Charter is worth further examination in the context of the Declaration. In the merits submissions, the Ogiek alleged that the continued prohibition of access to the Mau Forest's resources by the Ogiek prevents the sustainability of the Ogiek's traditional hunter-gatherer way of life, and as such violates the Ogiek's right to life under Article 4 of the African Charter.[57] Specifically, they argued that any act which amounts to disrespect for the life and integrity of a person or group of persons, or an arbitrary denial of that right, will result in a violation of Article 4[58] and that, as the first human right, it follows that the right to life under the African Charter, expansively interpreted, can give an effective content to all guaranteed rights – economic, civil, political, social and cultural.[59] The Ogiek stated that, as a civil right, the right to life imposes an obligation on states to refrain from any infringement of this right or to prevent its possible infringement by a third party. As an economic and social right, it entails a positive obligation to ensure an adequate standard of living. This approach, the Ogiek argued, has been confirmed by the African Commission in the *Endorois* decision which, although it did not consider a violation of Article 4 of the Charter, found the following:

> One of the obligations that the State must inescapably undertake as guarantor to protect and ensure the right to life is that of generating minimum living conditions that are compatible with the dignity of the human person and of not creating conditions that hinder or impede it. In this regard, the State has the duty to take positive, concrete measures geared towards fulfilment of the right to a decent life, especially in the case of persons who are vulnerable and at risk, whose care becomes a high priority.[60]

The Ogiek also relied on the approach adopted in Inter-American jurisprudence, which has incorporated aspects of indigenous community's livelihood – including the possibility of access to traditional means of subsistence, to use and enjoyment of the natural resources necessary to obtain clean water and to practice traditional medicine to prevent and cure illnesses – within the right to life and human dignity.[61] And, in fact, these arguments would seem to be echoed by Article 7 (1) of the Declaration, which provides for indigenous individuals' rights to life, physical and mental integrity, liberty and security of person.

However, assessing these arguments, the Court noted that the right to life is a right to be enjoyed irrespective of the group to which he or she belongs. The Court also understood that the violation of economic, social and cultural rights, including through forced evictions, may generally engender conditions unfavourable to a decent life. However, the Court viewed that a deprivation of economic, social and cultural rights may not necessarily result in a violation of the right to life under Article 4 of the African Charter, finding it necessary to make a distinction between the classical meaning of the right to life and the right to decent existence of a group. Concluding that Article 4 relates to the physical right to life, rather than to existence, and that no causal link had been established between the evictions of the Ogiek and the deaths that had occurred subsequent to their evictions, it found there had been no violation of Article 4.[62] Although it is understandable that the Court was reluctant to interpret the right to life in such an expansive way, given the lack of opportunity to determine its approach to the right within earlier jurisprudence, this is arguably an area that can and should be re-investigated in future cases.

Conclusion

The Endorois and Ogiek rulings keenly demonstrate that the Declaration has been repeatedly and continuously relied upon as an authoritative source of law and guidance by both the Commission and the Court in determining the scope of protection for indigenous peoples' rights in Africa. This builds on the Commission's clear approach to prioritising indigenous rights on the continent even before the Declaration was adopted, including the establishment of the WGIP, its 2003 report and its 2007 Advisory Opinion. Both the Court and the Commission have firmly embraced and adopted these concepts of indigenous peoples' rights, not only in relation to communal property rights over ancestral land, but also in relation to rights to culture and religion, and also their right to freely enjoy their natural resources. By specifically drawing inspiration from the concept of indigenous peoples as set out in Declaration, as well as stating that such people deserve special protection deriving from their vulnerability, it sends a clear message to Governments across the continent that indigenous peoples must be recognised and can no longer be routinely discriminated and marginalised. However, the Court's approach to the right to a dignified life could merit further consideration. Of more immediate importance is the need for both the Commission and the Court to value the importance of their approaches and take all appropriate steps to require the Government of Kenya to implement both rulings.

Notes

1. ACHPR Res.121 (XXXII) 07: Resolution on the United Nations Declaration on the Rights of Indigenous Peoples.
2. Ibid.
3. *CEMIRIDE and MRG (on behalf of the Endorois Welfare Council) v Kenya;*, ACHPR AAR Annex (Jun 2009–Nov 2009), Communication 276/03.
4. *Advisory Opinion of ACHPR on UNDRIP* (Banjul: African Commission of Human and Peoples' Rights, 2007).
5. *ACHPR v Kenya,* African Court of Human and Peoples' Rights, Application 006/2012, African Court of Human and Peoples' Rights, May 2017.
6. Endorois have sometimes been classified as a sub-tribe of the Tugen tribe of the Kalenjin group. Under the 1999 census, Endorois were counted as part of the Kalenjin group, made up of the Nandi, Kipsigis, Keiro, Tugen and Marakwet among others.
7. Section 115(2) of the 1963 Kenya Constitution.
8. *CEMIRIDE and MRG (on behalf of the Endorois Welfare Council) v Kenya*; Communication 276/03, para 11.
9. Ibid., para 12.
10. Judgment in *ACHPR v Kenya* (at note iii above) refers to the Ogiek comprising about 20,000 members (at para. 6) but a more accurate number is provided above and as set out in para. 2 of the Applicant's Submissions on the Merits, available here: http://minorityrights.org/wp-content/uploads/2015/03/Final-MRG-merits-submissions-pdf.pdf (accessed 23 January 2018)
11. *CEMIRIDE, Minority Rights Group International & Ogiek Peoples Development Programme (On Behalf Of The Ogiek Community) v Republic Of Kenya,* ACHPR, Communication 381/09.
12. CEMIRIDE and OPDP are both NGOs registered in Kenya; OPDP works specifically to promote and protect Ogiek culture, land, language, environment, and human rights. The Ogiek were represented by the same legal team as the Endorois, who saw the Ogiek's situation

represented a clear opportunity to continue to advocate for the recognition and protection of indigenous peoples' rights both in Kenya and within the African continent, this strengthening the protection offered by the Declaration.

13. http://en.african-court.org/images/Cases/Orders/006-2012-ORDER__of_Provisional_Measures-_African_Union_v._Kenya.pdf, accessed 6 February 2018.
14. Article 5(1(a) states "The following are entitled to submit cases to the Court: (a) the Commission": available at https://au.int/en/treaties/protocol-african-charter-human-and-peoples-rights-establishment-african-court-human-and.

    As one of the first cases to have been referred to the Court under this rule, and the first case in which judgment has been issued following a full hearing on the merits, the case was a pilot for both the Commission and the Court, testing out the process and creating significant procedural precedent.
15. See further http://www.achpr.org/mechanisms/indigenous-populations/about/
16. *Report of the African Commission's Working Group of Experts on Indigenous Populations/Communities* (Banjul: African Commission of Human and Peoples' Rights and Copenhagen: IWGIA, 2005), first adopted by ACHPR in 2003 by ACHPR/Res.65 (XXXIV) and included in the 17th Annual Activity Report of the African Commission later noted and authorised for publication by the 4th Ordinary Session of the AHSG of the AU held in January 2005 in Abuja, Nigeria (Assembly/AU/Dec.56)
17. Albert K Barume, 'Responding to the concerns of the African States', in *Making the Declaration Work: The United Nations Declaration on the Rights of Indigenous Peoples*, ed. C. Charters and R. Stavenhagen (Copenhagen: IWGIA document no 127, 2009): 170–83.
18. *Advisory Opinion of ACHPR on UNDRIP* (Banjul: African Commission of Human and Peoples' Rights, 2007) para 3; see also *Response Note to the Draft Aide Memoire on the African Group on the UN Declaration on the Rights of Indigenous Peoples*, available at https://www.ipacc.org.za/images/reports/human-rights/Response_to_Aide_Memoire_2007.pdf (accessed 6 February 2018)
19. Ibid., para 4.
20. *Advisory Opinion of ACHPR on UNDRIP* (Banjul: African Commission of Human and Peoples' Rights, 2007) para 8. Note that at this point, very little jurisprudence had been delivered by the African Commission on the rights of indigenous peoples, which at that point included simply *The Katangese People Congress vs. Zaire*, Communication 75/92, ACHPR 1995, on the right to self-determination; and *The Social and Economic Rights Action Center and the Center for Economic, and Social Rights v Nigeria*, Communication 155/96, ACHPR 2001, on peoples' and group rights.
21. See, for example, *CEMIRIDE and MRG (on behalf of the Endorois Welfare Council) v Kenya;*, ACHPR AAR Annex (Jun 2009–Nov 2009), Communication 276/03, para. 204.
22. ACHPR Res.121 (XXXII) 07: Resolution on the United Nations Declaration on the Rights of Indigenous Peoples.
23. Merits submissions in full are available here: http://minorityrights.org/wp-content/uploads/2015/03/CEMIRIDE-on-behalf-of-the-Endorois-Community-Communication-276.pdf (accessed 6 February 2018)
24. *CEMIRIDE and MRG (on behalf of the Endorois Welfare Council) v Kenya;*, ACHPR AAR Annex (Jun 2009–Nov 2009), Communication 276/03, para. 155.
25. Ibid., para. 162.
26. Ibid., paras. 173 and 251.
27. Ibid., para. 173.
28. See merits submissions, available at http://minorityrights.org/wp-content/uploads/2015/03/CEMIRIDE-on-behalf-of-the-Endorois-Community-Communication-276.pdf (accessed 6 February 2018), para 155.
29. Ibid., para. 199.
30. Ibid., para. 206.
31. Ibid., para. 204 (see reference to the Declaration in footnote 108)
32. Ibid., para. 207.

33. Ibid., Recommendation 1(c)
34. Ibid., para. 232.
35. ACHPR Res.197 (L) 11: Resolution on the Protection of Indigenous Peoples' Rights in the Context of the World Heritage Convention and the Designation of Lake Bogoria as a World Heritage site.
36. This specifically referenced the African Commission's Advisory Opinion on the UNDRIP – see footnote (iv) above; the Court also stated that it was entitled to draw such inspiration pursuant to Articles 60 and 61 of the Charter (*ACHPR v Kenya*, African Court of Human and Peoples' Rights, Application 006/2012, African Court of Human and Peoples' Rights, May 2017, para 108)
37. *ACHPR v Kenya*, African Court of Human and Peoples' Rights, Application 006/2012, African Court of Human and Peoples' Rights, May 2017, para 109.
38. Ibid., para 112.
39. Ibid., para 123.
40. Ibid., para 126.
41. Ibid., para 127.
42. Ibid., para 128.
43. Ogiek is already plural: Ogiot is the singular term.
44. Ibid., para 128.
45. Ibid., paras 129–30.
46. Ibid., para 131.
47. Ibid., paras 177–9.
48. Ibid.,, paras 180.
49. *Indigenous Peoples in Africa: the Forgotten Peoples?* (Banjul: African Commission of Human and Peoples' Rights and Copenhagen: IWGIA, 2006): 17.
50. *ACHPR v Kenya*, African Court of Human and Peoples' Rights, Application 006/2012, African Court of Human and Peoples' Rights, May 2017, para 181.
51. Ibid.
52. Ibid., para 183.
53. Ibid., paras 184–6.
54. Ibid., paras 187–90.
55. Ibid., para 208.
56. Ibid., paras 209–11.
57. Ibid., para. 147–9.
58. See further *The Social and Economic Rights Action Center and the Center for Economic, and Social Rights v Nigeria*, Communication 155/96, ACHPR 2001, where a violation of Article 4 was found against an indigenous community.
59. An interesting line of jurisprudence has emerged from the Indian Supreme Court in this respect: see, for example, *Mohini Jain v State of Karnataka AIR* (1981) Sup. Ct. 1864 (App 6), as referenced in Nwobike, Justice C, *The African Commission on Human and Peoples' Rights and the Demystification of Second and Third Generation Rights under the African Charter: Social and Economic Rights Action center (SERAC) and the Center for Economic and Social rights (CESR) v Nigeria*, 1 Afr J Legal Stud 2 (2005) 129–46 at 135.
60. *CEMIRIDE and MRG (on behalf of the Endorois Welfare Council) v Kenya*;, ACHPR AAR Annex (Jun 2009–Nov 2009), Communication 276/03para 217.
61. See, for example, I/A Court H.R.,*Yakye Axa Indigenous Community v. Paraguay*. Merits, Reparations and Costs. Judgment of June 17, 2005. Series C No. 125; I/A Court H.R., *Sawhoyamaxa Indigenous Community v. Paraguay*. Merits, Reparations and Costs. Judgment of March 29, 2006. Series C No. 146; I/A Court H.R., *Xákmok Kásek Indigenous Community v Paraguay* Merits, Reparations and Costs. Judgment Merits and reparations. Judgment of August 24, 2010. Series C No. 214.
62. *ACHPR v Kenya*, African Court of Human and Peoples' Rights, Application 006/2012, African Court of Human and Peoples' Rights, May 2017, paras 151–6.

Disclosure statement

No potential conflict of interest was reported by the author.

Indigenous peoples' rights in Morocco: subaltern narratives by Amazigh women

Silvia Gagliardi

ABSTRACT

Morocco's 2011 Constitution affirmed the principle of equality between men and women (art. 19) and officialised the (indigenous) Amazigh language (art. 5) alongside Arabic. However, despite apparent progress in the areas of minority groups' and indigenous peoples' rights and gender equality, Amazigh women's rights continue to be violated both from within and from outside their own communities. While the Moroccan State fails to guarantee, *inter alia*, the Amazigh community's access to language and education rights (as enumerated in arts. 13–14 of UN Declaration on the Rights of Indigenous Peoples [UNDRIP]), this article challenges dominant approaches to the study of Amazigh rights for failing to take into account the lived experiences and counter-narrative of Amazigh women. As such, this article departs from the international human rights-based vindications of Amazigh cultural groups to focus instead on the rights and identity articulation among Amazigh women themselves. This article considers whether local-based remedies might be more effective than trying to graft on larger international approaches when looking at the issue of minority and indigenous women.

1. Introduction

Adopting an inter-sectional approach,[1] this article aims to deconstruct the relationship between feminism, multiculturalism and group rights, discourses and tools so as to understand how the subaltern female Others understand these concepts and describe their identities. It will attempt to do so by: first, engaging with the question of Amazigh identity(-ies) in Morocco; second, analysing the changes brought by Morocco's 2011 Constitution, which, *inter alia*, affirmed the principle of equality between men and women (art. 19) and officialised the Amazigh language (art. 5); third, examining and deconstructing hegemonic discourses on indigenous peoples, minority groups and women's rights; fourth, making space for subaltern narratives of the female Other and exploring local remedies; fifth, drawing conclusions.

In order to engage with the relevant theoretical debates, it is pertinent to deconstruct minority and indigenous peoples' rights discourses and tools, as well as to unpack how they are constructed.[2] As it emerges from ethnographic research undertaken between 2014 and 2017 across Morocco, those rights discourses and frameworks are utilised by a mostly male, urban, educated elite to craft a certain narrative, a 'collective history'[3] and an 'imagined community',[4] to preserve the status quo and current power distribution. While much of the literature on group rights and multiculturalism focuses on the role of the State vis-à-vis minority and indigenous peoples, the emphasis of this article is on dynamics within groups themselves and how individual members articulate and demand rights within their own communities.

To grasp the full scope of this dilemma, it is necessary to take a step back and recall some of the key debates pertaining to group versus individual rights.[5] While it has been argued that minority and indigenous peoples have a collective right to the protection of their group identity and culture, both the definitions of those groups and what constitutes their identities and cultures remain contested. At the same time, some feminist scholars have presented the position of subordination of many minority and indigenous female subjects as a justification for overcoming group rights and focusing on individual rights.[6] This holds especially true when the right of exit cannot be guaranteed for members of illiberal groups.[7] Other feminists have contested the justifiability of eradicating 'oppressive' cultures and 'traditional harmful practices' as they critique this position as a neo-colonial, imperialist attempt to silence or appropriate the voice of the non-Western, non-White, subaltern Other.[8] Gunning has attempted to find a new paradigm to engage with 'culturally sensitive practices' and women's rights in an interconnected, non-arrogant, mutually respectful dialogue between the 'I' and the 'Other'.[9] Other relevant positions on this debate have been informed by post-orientalism, post-structuralism, third world approaches to international law and post-colonial theories and scholarships.[10]

Aware of the 'inaccessible blankness'[11] that the subaltern Other might present to the non-Other external scholar, this article attempts to adopt Gunning's 'world-travelling' methodology[12] to identify ways to support minority and indigenous women's agency without appropriating their voices or essentialising, re-colonising and re-orientalising the study subject. Combining scholarly insights with on-the-ground practical research and original fieldwork, this article hopes to make space for voices that have so far been marginalised or silenced to preserve existing power structures.

2. A short history of the Amazigh identity/ies

Although the Amazigh community constitutes one of Morocco's largest ethno-linguistic groups, comprising 40% to 60% of the indigenous population,[13] they are best categorised as a 'majoritarian minority'.[14] As Castellino and Cavanaugh explain,

> [t]hat political and cultural factors play visible roles in determining minority status is perhaps most clearly illustrated in cases where the relative size of a particular community is not determinant of its status. (…) Minority status is best understood by examining how socio-political groups engage (or are excluded from) various sites of power.[15]

In examining the scholarship on the Amazigh peoples, their identities, their communities, their histories, the movements for their group rights, it is often difficult to unpack and dissect the conflicting narratives. Although there is a common baseline for the Amazigh identity kit, various interest groups have tried to exert hegemonic control over what this set of attributes consists of. Narratives surrounding the Amazigh peoples have often served the interests of various power centres – the Sultanate, the French colonial apparatus, Morocco's armed resistance and nationalists, Amazigh activists, the Monarchy and the academic establishment. Despite attempts by these disparate interest groups to control how Amazigh identity is defined, national group awareness has gradually begun to materialise within this community. Yet, even at the grassroots level, it is possible to find *multiple* Amazigh identities based on shared tribal, dialectal, geographical, gender and class affiliations rather than one *single* group identity. This diversity and history of divisions and confrontations within the different Amazigh communities poses questions relating to the nature of the Amazigh identity in Morocco 'with some writers arguing that it is a constructed identity, while others contend that all identity is constructed, and still others argue the presence of a historical legacy of Amazigh consciousness'.[16]

In order to provide an answer to the main questions raised by this article, one has to first delve into the so-called 'Amazigh question'. [17] This relates to the identification and definition of a pan-national and transnational Amazigh identity as opposed to the multiplicity of localised Amazigh identities. This question has been considered at various critical junctures in Morocco's history: namely, at the time of the Arab-Islamic conquest of North Africa in the late seventh century; in pre-colonial times; during the French Protectorate (1912–1956) in Morocco; at the time of the 1930 Berber Dahir [18] (royal decree); during the struggle for and after Moroccan independence[19]; at the time of the 1980 Algeria-based Berber Spring[20]; and, ultimately, in the aftermath of the 2011 Arab Spring.[21]

Despite the Amazigh elite-driven depiction of a unified group identity, the difficulty in defining the Amazigh people and its core characteristics is complicated by its diversity, extension across national borders, different dialects spoken and tribal affiliations, non-aligned demands and priorities between urban and rural communities etc. To complicate matters further, 'it has been non-Berbers who have written the Berbers into the historical record as a collective. (…) It is only in recent decades that a self-conscious, pan-Berber identity has been asserted from within'.[22]

Whilst Amazigh female combatants are celebrated in Moroccan oral history, their important role in both armed resistance and nationalist struggle was not acknowledged and did not bring a change to their subordinate condition in post-independence Morocco.[23] The inadequacy and unwillingness by power centres and special interest groups to credit Amazigh women (and Moroccan women more generally) for their anti-colonialist and pro-independence efforts was a harbinger of how gender relations would shape up in post-independence Morocco.

Once independence was achieved across North Africa, the ensuing postcolonial states, along with their nation-building projects, side-lined their Amazigh components to favour pan-Arabism and pan-Islamism.[24] What does not transpire from most historical and anthropological accounts of post-colonial Morocco is that it was not simply the Amazigh community, as a whole, to be marginalised from Morocco's collective history and main narratives. Moroccan women, and especially Amazigh female figures, suffered most due to this erasure in the pan-Arabist, pan-nationalist, elitist and male construction of national identity.

Against this backdrop, in their forward-looking strategy, 'Amazigh militants have promulgated a redefinition of Morocco on the basis of its pre-colonial and pre-Islamic Berber heritage, and have sought political change to preserve Berber culture and language as a "human right."'[25] While this strategy might pay political dividends to the elite-driven Amazigh Cultural Movement,[26] it appears unlikely that it will produce a tangible difference in the daily lives of Amazigh women.

3. Hegemonic discourses

3.1. Minority groups' and indigenous peoples' rights

In analysing the narratives of Amazigh cultural groups and movement, it is crucial to differentiate between the movements' agendas and demands to the State on one hand and the needs and concerns of the overall Amazigh population, and specifically women, on the other. Different strategies and priorities seem at play in the Amazigh movement's demands for group rights. In this context, as Castellino and Cavanaugh remarked,

> [w]hilst a push for recognition of language was one common Berberophone goal, another yet unfulfilled demand is for improved socio-economic conditions. This is not to graft on to the mythology of an urban (Arab)–rural (Berber) divide; it is a demographic fact that many of the 'rural poor are Tamazight speakers'. Whether these factors engender a unified and more powerful Amazighophone political consciousness and movement remains to be seen.[27]

In this light, 'what Berberness we might attribute to villagers is mostly a lived and unconscious experience rather than a notable basis of political identity. This does not seem to be the case among the city-based activists'.[28] It should be reiterated here that high levels of poverty and low literacy disproportionately affect Amazighophone areas in the countryside. Hence one cannot discuss Amazigh cultural identity without considering the socio-economic circumstances of rural Amazigh.[29] Alongside a growing self-consciousness of the Amazigh as a constituent group of Moroccan society, there is an increasing discontent within the Amazigh community with the unmatched socio-economic needs of the rural population, largely Amazighophone.[30]

Traditionally, the Amazigh movement leaders have been university-educated urbanites whilst the larger Amazigh community remains rural, illiterate and divided in multiple Amazigh-dialect speaking communities. Amazigh leaders' 'vision of the significance of being Berber [does not necessarily equate] (...) to that of the masses of mostly rural and often illiterate Berber speakers (...)'.[31] Student-led Amazigh organisations are few. Mostly male lawyers and politically active intellectuals lead Amazigh groups.[32] Furthermore, leadership positions are male dominated as 'the structure of the grassroots local organizations and their activities has ensured minimal female participation, as these organizations tend to hold meetings in the evenings, and sometimes in bars, both of which discourage female attendance'.[33] Hence, the Amazigh movement, as such, appears not to be representative of Morocco's Amazigh people in their different needs and priorities.

In the course of this author's ethnographic research conducted across Morocco, it became clear that rural Amazigh did not causally associate challenges in their lived experiences, often characterised by poor socio-economic conditions, with their being Amazigh. This being the case, it was unsurprising to find that, to a large extent, rural Amazigh did not identify with the advocacy terminology often used by urban Amazigh activists, such as 'violations of basic human rights' and 'linguistic and cultural discrimination' against Amazigh people.[34] Interestingly, 'to fight for these "human" rights, Amazigh activists have had to carve themselves as a unique group, a defined subsection of humanity making themselves look like a group with a "shared identity."'[35]

As regards the development of a human rights discourse within the Amazigh movement,

> [m]uch of this discussion is very sophisticated, and conceptions of the unique and specific nature of Berbers - Imazighen as group are infused with the rhetoric and sentiments of nationalism, indigenousness, human rights, resistance movements, subaltern and post-colonial studies, and other cultural self-determination movements.[36]

It is clear from the comparison between urban versus rural Amazigh identities that the urban intelligentsia understood the full potential of the 'international cultural activism'.[37] Whilst urban Amazigh activists stress the importance of language and culture to the recognition of the Amazigh identity,[38] this characterisation does not adequately represent the lived experiences of the majority of Amazigh people. The latter, mostly composed of rural Amazigh, are not deprived of their identity kit (language and culture) to the same extent as the urban Amazigh.[39]

Of pivotal importance is the notion that individuals acknowledge their culture only once they are outside of it; multi-lingual urban Imazighen experience a 'prise de conscience' due to their exposure to other languages, cultures and groups, while rural Amazigh may seem less aware of this group's overall condition within the Moroccan polity due to their cultural, linguistic and geographic isolation.[40] The task of achieving linguistic rights for the Amazigh is made harder by the challenge of envisioning (at least linguistically) a united Amazigh community.[41] Amazigh dialects are quite different from each other and often not understood outside of a specific Amazigh community. The dialect spoken by a given community is an indicator of a local identity rather than a connection to a 'general Berberness'.[42] Furthermore, it was not until 2003 that the Tifinagh (Amazigh) script became codified,[43] while it remains today understood by a minority of Amazigh speakers, mostly stemming from the educated elites.

3.2. Women's rights

In Morocco, women's groups of different political colour and ideology have contributed to various 'movement moments' or 'mobilization conjunctures', which have resulted in the 'feminization of Islamist women and the Islamization of the feminist movement'.[44] As these so-called 'mobilization conjunctures' demonstrate, different movements constantly inform one another and highlight the importance of 'vernacularisation' of their arguments.[45] In this vein, this article concurs with Reilly's argument that, '[e]mancipatory possibilities of human rights-oriented transnational feminisms reside in dialogic, solidarity-building feminist praxis tied to transnational processes of counter-hegemonic (re)interpretation and (re)claiming of human rights from previously excluded positions'.[46]

As it emerges from the author's fieldwork in Morocco, in the struggle to define independently the meaning of women's rights and gender equality, feminist women's groups in Moroccan society have largely been excluding dissenting and marginalised voices both within and outside their circles, including those of indigenous (Amazigh) women.[47] Within the discourse of discrete categories between secular and religious feminisms,[48] for instance, fieldwork conducted among women's groups in Morocco – similarly to the work of other scholars – demonstrated a high level of intolerance by secular feminists towards religious feminists. As observed in a recent ethnographic study in Morocco, the very secular feminists who demonise Islamists for their purported intolerance and disrespect for individual choices or difference,

> [...] seemed to experience no dissonance when they spoke derisively about the hijab or expressed relief at its absence. Not only did they seem to have no trouble reconciling their aversion towards the hijab with their discourse about tolerance and acceptance of difference, they did not seem to think that these discourses needed reconciling.[49]

Proponents of this secular versus religious binary fail to consider the inter-linkages and mutual influences occurring among different women's groups. They also seem unable or unwilling to identify common obstacles and localised strategies. To the contrary, Guessous argues, 'Morocco is unique in the sense that one cannot really speak of Islamic and secular feminisms as discrete categories. All Moroccan feminists, whether liberal or religious, confront patriarchy yet do not put Islam as a religion into question'.[50] As Fatima Mernissi, one of Morocco's leading feminists, argues,[51] Islam and women's rights can be compatible as for both liberal and Islamic feminists, the ultimate goal is to fight patriarchy and, to a large extent, the political manipulation of Islam.[52]

The absence of dialogue and co-operation among different women's groups has allowed the Monarchy to politicise gender issues to its advantage and to the preservation of the status quo.[53] In this context,

> [t]he state manipulation of the liberal rhetoric of gender equality has decreased the spaces for independent organizing by feminist and Islamist women's groups alike. In addition to co-opting both movements, the state is now able to monitor the discourse and activism of these groups while acting as a neutral mediator.[54]

In Morocco, among other post-colonial contexts, women's movements are often driven by urban elites who, by strictly adhering to their differing ideological positions and reference frameworks, fail to foster de facto progress on women's rights and represent the majority of women as well as the diversity of their views.[55] Without overcoming an exclusive, elitist reading of women's rights and gender equality, it is unlikely that any 'solidarity-building feminist praxis'[56] will take root across different women's groups, especially in post-colonial societies. Except through a vernacularisation of women's human rights and gender equality, changes will continue to be perceived as undemocratic and externally imposed.

4. The 2011 constitution

Widely regarded as the culmination of the Arab Spring-influenced protests in Morocco, the 2011 Moroccan constitution responded to some of the key grievances that motivated the 20 February Movement (20FM) to take to the streets in the first place. In the course of 2011, the mainly urban-based 20FM 'led a wave of protests against the widely perceived social ills (...) and raised the political consciousness of the average Moroccan citizen'.[57] Resorting to its habitual political savoir-faire, the monarchy found a way to put an end to the uprisings, regenerate support for its rule through a public referendum and simultaneously concede, at least on paper, crucial changes in the foundation law of the country. Significantly, this article illustrates how elite-driven minority and indigenous human rights demands (including the adoption of human rights-compliant national legislation) often falls short of representing and addressing the needs of the population on the ground.

To begin with, the constitution enshrined the primacy of duly ratified international conventions onto domestic law, albeit with the proviso 'dans le respect de son identité nationale immutable'.[58] The constitution also declared that Morocco's unity is forged by convergence of its components (incl. Arab-Islamic, Amazigh, Saharo-Hassanian etc.) while the pre-eminence is accorded to Islam.[59] More significantly, the constitution officialised the Amazigh language (as 'an' official language) while Arabic remains 'the' official language.[60] Further, the constitution enshrined the principles of non-discrimination[61] and equality between men and women with the proviso 'dans les constantes du Royaume'.[62] Those 'permanent characteristics' are not explicitly mentioned although selected articles mention the 'non-derogable' aspects of Morocco as being: 'Islam, the monarchy, (…) national unity or territorial integrity of the Kingdom'.[63] The 'constantes' are also commonly referred to as 'red lines', including by respondents who participated in this study's ethnographic research: 'Nowadays we can criticise a little bit, without going off limits, without surpassing some red lines that the constitution drew'.[64] As it has been argued,

> The 2011 constitutional text refers, on the one hand, to human rights as they are universally recognized and to identity, Islam and the 'permanent character of the kingdom' (…) on the other. This dual reference makes it difficult to understand and interpret a text that aspires to appeal both to the principles of a liberal democracy and to those that claim to rely on a particular interpretation of 'tradition'.[65]

In addition to the vague and contradictory language of the constitution, while constitutional provisions seem, at least nominally, to recognise Amazigh and women's rights, they ring hollow in the absence of relevant domestic legislation after the promulgation of the new constitution. Furthermore, there is no constitutional recognition of ancestral lands, group or indigenous rights or acknowledgement of different ethnicities. This approach was confirmed by the 2014 census, which contained no ethnicity-based questions, but merely questions on mother tongue and daily spoken languages. In addition to this, it is unconstitutional to form linguistic- and ethnic-based political parties or to bring harm to the permanent characteristics of the Kingdom.[66] It is useful to recall, in this context, that Morocco is not a state party to the ILO Indigenous and Tribal People Convention 1989 (no. 169).[67] The latter, together with the prior Indigenous and Tribal Populations Convention 1957 (no. 107),[68] are 'the only comprehensive internationally binding instruments of the rights of indigenous peoples and of States' obligations towards them'.[69] Tellingly, Morocco was one of the countries that were absent during the voting on the United Nations Declaration on the Rights of Indigenous Peoples (UNDRIP).[70] While the latter is not a legally binding document, it does represent both a 'standard of achievement'[71] and the culmination of decades of work by indigenous peoples' activists for the recognition of indigenous peoples' rights.

Historically, different power-yielding actors in Morocco have categorised the Amazigh as a distinct group (whether as a minority, an indigenous people, a linguistic community etc.) for their own political goals. A prime illustration of this divide-and-rule tactic was the afore-cited 1930 Berber Dahir (decree) enacted during the French Protectorate. Under the purported objective of dividing Berber (Amazigh) from Arab areas for the administration of separate justice, the decree was intended to benefit the French in their separatist colonial policy.[72] More recently, the 2011 constitutional recognition of both Amazigh as 'an' official language and a key element of Morocco's cultural diversity offer an example of the 'co-optation' by the State.[73] In fact, these 'concessions' to the Amazigh elites bear no meaningful impact on the everyday lives of Amazigh women in the absence of organic laws and policies addressing their grievances in terms of access to education, employment and health, including rights to bodily integrity and privacy.[74]

5. Subaltern narratives of the female other

'There are no human rights for the Amazigh in Morocco'.[75]

In an attempt to deconstruct the identity of Amazigh women, what this article suggests is that, perhaps unsurprisingly, Amazigh women's allegiance, first and foremost, is to the country of Morocco, often identified with the monarchy, rather than to their specific group movement and leaders. This reveals that the Amazigh group identity can be partly regarded as an 'imagined community of postcolonial oppositional struggles'[76] that fails to represent the lived experience of non-elite Amazigh women. As W.B. explained,

> [I feel] Moroccan. I cannot say that I am Arab or Amazigh. I am Moroccan. I will be more comfortable if I say that I am a woman, and I get along with French women, Spanish women, to say a human being. But I would say Moroccan, because I am part of the Moroccan culture.[77]

Also, those who expressed attachment or sense of belonging to the Amazigh community often did so due to linguistic ties, albeit at a local, tribal level rather than at a national or supranational one. Significantly, some of the interviewees that most strongly refused the idea of a separate Amazigh ethnic identity stemmed from a higher social class and were also fluent in Arabic. A.A., for instance, argued that,

> Everybody is well integrated. So, in the North, you're either from the mountains (*jbeli*) or the Rifi [*sic*]. It means the same thing, but the only difference is linguistic. So, I have lot of friends and family from both sides, so that is why I don't like differentiating between everybody, but when it comes to rights, I think the *minority here are women* [emphasis added], and the minority here are people who don't live near cities. *It is not about being Amazigh or not Amazigh* [emphasis added].[78]

> S.B. argued similarly,
>
> Participant (P): Yes, it [Amazigh] is only a different linguistic group.
>
> Investigator (I): But is it not an ethnicity of its own?
>
> P: Absolutely not.
>
> I: Is it not a minority?
>
> P: No, we share the same characteristics but we pronounce words differently.[79]

F.A. was also sceptical about a separate Amazigh identity,

> Personally speaking, I would say that it's an abstract idea. Everyone is on their [*sic*] own; people are mainly not gathered. And, that depends on which community of Amazigh you belong to.[80]

Presenting critical views about the Amazigh movement and especially their vindication of a group identity, S.B. affirmed that,

> The cause of activists in the Amazigh field is to recognise their language and culture, to take advantage of the State holidays and to recognise that they were the inhabitants of Morocco before the Arab invasion. But, according to me, if these things are recognised or not, that there is teaching for the Amazigh or not, for me it doesn't change anything because the evolution of the country doesn't depend on this community and culture. (…) So, the Amazigh language remains optional even if I am Amazigh, but I don't think it will have an impact on the country's different levers (…) Amazigh will only remain as folklore maybe, but it doesn't touch the development of the country.[81]

Yet, in contrast, some interviewees with no formal education or formal employment, but who enjoyed a comfortable status, rejected this ethnic classification. As Z.Y. noted, 'We are all Moroccans, the only difference is the language, which is Amazigh'.[82] Other interviewees felt that they belonged to the Amazigh community because their parents or ancestors were Amazigh although the former often did not speak the language or understand the Tifinagh alphabet. In this context, the author asked L.K. if she felt Amazigh even if she did not speak the language. Her answer is telling in deconstructing and understanding her identity: 'Yes, because my mother's family is Amazigh'.[83] Conversely, other interviewees' narrations instantiate the pressure they felt in identifying themselves as part of a certain group or speaking a given language.

> Of course I feel Amazigh, but I don't like saying it. So, if I meet people I'm like: 'I'm from Tetouan.' I don't want to go into details because that is very personal to me. When I meet Amazigh people, I may mention it, because I may understand what they're saying and I don't want them to think that I am spying on them or something, because I understand what they're saying. But I am just Moroccan.[84]

S.I. felt compelled to speak the Amazigh language as a proof of her group identity. 'I am more comfortable with Arabic, but I always tend to speak Amazigh because it's my native language and I *should* [emphasis added] feel comfortable speaking Amazigh as well'.[85] Other interviewees imagined the whole of Morocco as an Amazigh country. Z.W., a high school student, grew up in a neighbouring Arab country before returning home to Morocco in the aftermath of the Arab Spring. In terms of identity, she nullified differences in identity between Amazigh and Moroccan peoples as '[*their identity*] is either Amazigh-Moroccan or Moroccan-Amazigh, because before there were only Amazigh living in Morocco'.[86] As H.B. observed, '[f]irst, we consider that *all* [*emphasis added*] Moroccans are Amazigh but some were Arabised and some of them kept their Amazigh identity'.[87] When the author asked her who she meant by 'we', H.B. explained, 'Yes, "we the Amazigh people" from the Amazigh movement'.[88] N.A. is a high school graduate and intern at a women's local development centre. She expressed her grief over the conditions of Amazigh people in the country signifying the existence of a group identity, as far as she was concerned,

> I am Amazigh, because I live in an Amazigh country, and my family is Amazigh. (…) Especially here in this city, there are no human rights, especially for Amazigh people. (…) I have a lot of Amazigh family and I see how they suffer, they don't have access to health and they don't have access to school. As for the girls, they can't complete their education, because there are no schools where they are, and they cannot go to cities, so they just stay at home.[89]

Others expressed the view that Morocco was more than just Amazigh while still vindicating their own Amazigh identity. 'I feel Moroccan because Morocco is diverse but, in my veins, I am Amazigh'.[90] 'I am a Moroccan Amazigh (…) because my hope here is to live in my country with my rights. (…) Arab people who ignore us want to get rid of our identity'.[91] 'Arab people are educated and they know what to do, but it is not the case for the Amazigh'.[92]

In the context of rights negotiation and contestation, it is useful to evoke Koskenniemi's (2004) analysis of the issue of fragmentation. It is here worth considering whether local-based remedies might be more effective than trying to graft on larger transnational and globalised approaches when looking at the rights vindication by minority and indigenous women. While a localised women's rights contestation is struggling to emerge in various rights areas (including relating to health, employment and education), Morocco's indigenous 'Sulaliyyates Movement' for equal land rights represents a notable exception. The Sulaliyyates are 'tribal' women from Arabophone and Amazighophone communities who demand an equal share to the men, when their land becomes privatised or divided. As Salime points out, 'No women's movement has marked the political debate in Morocco, after the North African uprisings as much as the Sulaliyyates'.[93] In this movement, rural women are increasingly articulating collective rights in opposition to the rest of their (male) community members.[94] Despite their originally inalienable status, collective lands have been increasingly expropriated to allow for their commercialisation, transfer and sale.[95] As Salime explained,

> Although communal land could in the past neither be seized nor sold, it could be transferred from fathers to sons over the age of sixteen. According to hegemonic understanding of *'urf* (customary law), women can only benefit through male relatives. Unmarried women, widows, divorcees — and those with no sons — often face expropriation and become destitute.

Unlike for other women's issues where a rights-based grassroots contestation seems harder to emerge and crucial gaps remain between urban elite-led movements and rural populations, in the case of land rights,

> the language of rights, poverty reduction, and gender equality is instrumental in the Sulaliyyates movement. Trained by the ADFM [*Democratic Association of Moroccan Women*] members, providing with basic legal literacy, the Sulaliyyates specifically use state language to refer to equality and poverty alleviation. This is a rejection of any reference to the Islamic inheritance laws, and instead a use of the secular language of gender justice and equality already sanctioned by Morocco.[96]

Tellingly, in the case of the Sulaliyyates movement, rural women 'fail' to perform the roles and duties assigned to them by their (male) leaders and groups of belonging and have found emancipatory ways to use human rights language, advocacy and training to their advantage. Significantly, the ethnic and linguistic diversity of Sulaliyyates women does not seem to impact negatively the cohesion and strength of this movement. Importantly, as Berriane argued, this emancipation may require bringing together elite and 'rural, dispossessed and mainly illiterate women'.[97] As Berriane explained, this movement

> (...) sheds light on the inequalities and fluid power hierarchies that are constitutive of it. It therefore goes beyond interpretations that read women's grassroots activism as the sole result of international and elite-led gender empowerment projects and norms, highlighting processes of cross-fertilisation and hybridisation instead.[98]

6. Conclusions

There are some key points to emerge from this analysis of the subaltern narratives of rights and equality by Morocco's Amazigh women. The Amazigh community is Morocco is diverse and comprised of both urban and rural components. Throughout Morocco's history, different power brokers have constructed an Amazigh 'imagined community' and 'collective identity' to their own benefit and, tangentially, to the (dis-) advantage of groups and individuals, specifically women. Despite this, it is apparent that an elite-driven Amazigh ethno-linguistic consciousness exists across Morocco today and that a sense of collectivity within the trans-national Amazigh-speaking community in North Africa is growing. However, Amazigh cultural groups and women's rights movements are largely top-down, urban intelligentsia-driven efforts that do not reflect either the full composition or the priorities of Amazigh women. The urban elites' international rights-based activism and selected advocacy language do not appear to be responding to the core needs of the group members they purport to represent. In its current format, it is doubtful whether Morocco's urban-led Amazigh and women's rights movements will be able to reach out and represent in its advocacy and institutions even remote components of these constituencies, including rural women. Against this backdrop, it becomes imperative to promote and focus on current examples of cross-fertilisation among movements and groups; this, in turn, may enable indigenous women to find emancipatory ways to use the rights language and toolkit to their advantage.

Notes

1. Kimberlé Crenshaw, 'Mapping the Margins: Intersectionality, Identity Politics, and Violence against Women of Color', *Stanford Law Review* 43, no. 6 (1991): 1241–99.
2. Joshua Castellino and Kathleen Cavanaugh, *Minority Rights in the Middle East* (Oxford University Press, 2013).
3. Eric Davis, *Memories of State - Politics, History, and Collective Identity in Modern Iraq* (University of California Press, 2005).
4. Benedict Anderson, *Imagined Communities: Reflections on the Origin and Spread of Nationalism* (London: Verso, 1991).
5. Will Kymlicka, ed., *The Rights of Minority Cultures* (Oxford University Press, 1995); Susan Moller Okin, 'Feminism and Multiculturalism: Some Tensions', *Ethics* 108, no. 4 (1998): 661–84; Ayelet Shachar, 'Should Church and State Be Joined at the Altar? Women's Rights and the Multicultural Dilemma', in *Citizenship in Diverse Societies*, eds. Will Kymlicka and Norman Wayne (Oxford University Press, 2000); Ratna Kapur, 'The Tragedy of Victimization Rhetoric: Resurrecting the "Native" Subject in International/Post-Colonial Feminist Legal Politics', *Harvard Human Rights Journal* 15 (2002): 1–37; Valerie Amos and Pratibha Parmar, 'Challenging Imperial Feminism', *Feminist Review*, no. 80 (2005): 44–63.

6. Susan Moller Okin, ed., *Is Multiculturalism Bad for Women?* (Princeton University Press, 1999).
7. Chandran Kukathas, 'Are There Any Cultural Rights?' in *The Rights of Minority Cultures*, ed. Will Kimlicka (Oxford University Press, 1992).
8. Gayatri Chakravorty Spivak, 'Can the Subaltern Speak?' in *Marxism and the Interpretation of Culture*, eds. Cary Nelson and Lawrence Grossberg (Urbana and Chicago: University of Illinois Press, 1988); Kapur, 'The Tragedy of Victimization Rhetoric', 1–37; Ekaterina Yahyaoui Krivenko, 'Rethinking Human Rights and Culture through Female Genital Surgeries', *Human Rights Quarterly* 37, no. 1 (2015): 107–36.
9. Isabelle R. Gunning, 'Arrogant Perception, World-Travelling and Multicultural Feminism: The Case of Female Genital Surgeries', *Columbia Human Rights Law Review* 23 (1992): 189.
10. Edward W. Said, *Orientalism* (Pantheon Books, 1978); Spivak, 'Can the Subaltern Speak?'; Homi K. Bhabha, *The Location of Culture* (London and New York: Routledge, 1994); Bart Moore-Gilbert, *Postcolonial Theory: Contexts, Practices, Politics* (London and New York: Verso, 1997); Anthony Anghie, *Imperialism, Sovereignty and the Making of International Law* (Cambridge: Cambridge University Press, 2004).
11. Spivak, 'Can the Subaltern Speak?'.
12. Gunning, 'Arrogant Perception, World-Travelling and Multicultural Feminism', 189.
13. Morocco has the world's highest proportion of Amazigh-speakers while estimates of their actual number in Morocco vary between 40% and 60%. For more information, see: http://minorityrights.org/country/morocco/ (accessed January 15, 2018). According to a leading Amazigh activist, the latest statistics as posted on official websites estimated exclusively Amazigh-speakers to be 28% of the whole population while this number would rise to 70% if it included Moroccans who speak both Arabic and Amazigh. Official meeting with A.A. during TWIZA Festival, Tangiers, 16 August 2013.
14. Castellino and Cavanaugh, *Minority Rights in the Middle East*, 5.
15. Ibid., 6–7.
16. Ibid., 172.
17. 'It is commonly accepted in the literature on North African history that the indigenous people of this area are the Berbers, or the Imazighen, as they refer to themselves. (…) [*However*] The current number of Imazighen, or rather speakers of one of the Amazigh varieties, has remained a matter of estimates.' Katherine E. Hoffman, 'Berber Language Ideologies, Maintenance, and Contraction: Gendered Variation in the Indigenous Margins of Morocco', *Language & Communication* 26, no. 2 (2006): 144–67.
18. As external and internal agents use respectively the terms 'Berbers' and 'Amazigh' (literally, free man) to refer to this community, the author will follow whatever appellation a given scholar or community member used for the group. Throughout the text, the terms will be thus used interchangeably.
19. Allen Fromherz, 'Between Springs: The Berber Dilemma', *Muslim World* 104, no. 3 (2014): 243.
20. In the spring of that year, the Algerian Government decided to cancel an academic lecture by Mouloud Mammeri, a Kabyle intellectual and important member of Algeria's Berber community. The Government's decision caused mass protests to erupt in Tizi Ouzou and others parts of Algeria, which came to a head between student protesters and riot police on the 20 April 1980. This series of protests 'did not bring immediate results, but it did mark the effective birth of a socio-political movement striving to defend Berber rights.' Raphaël Lefèvre, 'North Africa's "Berber Question"', *The Journal of North African Studies* 21, no. 4 (2016): 546. See also: Bruce Maddy-Weitzman, 'Contested Identities: Berbers, "Berberism" and the State in North Africa', *The Journal of North African Studies* 6, no. 3 (2001): 32.
21. Jane E. Goodman, 'Reinterpreting the Berber Spring: From Rite of Reversal to Site of Convergence', *The Journal of North African Studies* 9, no. 3 (2004): 61.
22. Maddy-Weitzman, 'Contested Identities', 25.

23. Alison Baker, *Voices of Resistance: Oral Histories of Moroccan Women*, Suny Series in Oral & Public History (New York: State of University of New York Press, 1998), 19.
24. Bruce Maddy-Weitzman, 'A Turning Point? The Arab Spring and the Amazigh Movement', *Ethnic and Racial Studies* 38, no. 14 (2015): 2499.
25. Fromherz, 'Between Springs', 241.
26. Lauermann defines the Amazigh Cultural Movement as one of 'Amazigh cultural groups, which operate at the state level.' See: John Lauermann, 'Amazigh Nationalism in the Maghreb', *Geographical Bulletin* 50, no. 1 (2009): 40.
27. Castellino and Cavanaugh, *Minority Rights in the Middle East*, 173.
28. David Crawford, 'Morocco's Invisible Imazighen', *Journal of North African Studies* 7, no. 1 (2002): 59.
29. Moha Ennaji, 'The Berber (Amazigh) Movement in Morocco: Local Activism, the State, and Transnationalism', in *Multiculturalism and Democracy in North Africa: Aftermath of the Arab Spring, Routledge Series in Middle Eastern Politics*, ed. Moha Ennaji (London and New York: Routledge, 2014), 97.
30. Maddy-Weitzman, 'Contested Identities', 28.
31. Crawford, 'Morocco's Invisible Imazighen', 54.
32. David Crawford and Katherine E. Hoffman, 'Essentially Amazigh: Urban Berbers and the Global Village', *The Arab-African and Islamic Worlds: Interdisciplinary Studies* (2000): 119.
33. Hoffman, 'Berber Language Ideologies, Maintenance, and Contraction', 146.
34. Crawford, 'Morocco's Invisible Imazighen', 60–7.
35. Ibid., 67.
36. Crawford and Hoffman, 'Essentially Amazigh', 119.
37. Ibid.
38. Salem Chaker, *Berbères Aujourd'hui* (Paris: L'Harmattan, 1989), 7.
39. Crawford, 'Morocco's Invisible Imazighen', 63.
40. Ibid., 62.
41. Ibid., 65.
42. Crawford and Hoffman, 'Essentially Amazigh', 121.
43. Ahmed Boukous, 'The Planning of Standardizing Amazigh Language: The Moroccan Experience', *IRCAM* (2014): 11.
44. Zakia Salime, *Between Feminism and Islam: Human Rights and Sharia Law in Morocco, vol. 36, Social Movements, Protest, and Contention*, ed. Bert Klandermans (University of Minnesota Press, 2011), XV.
45. Ibid., XVII.
46. Niamh Reilly, 'Doing Transnational Feminism, Transforming Human Rights: The Emancipatory Possibilities Revisited', *Irish Journal of Sociology* 19, no. 2 (2011): 60.
47. An example of this practice was displayed at several international conferences in Morocco in which the author participated during the 2012–2014 biennium, wherein some secular feminists would not agree to discuss women's issues at the same table as Islamic feminists. See also: Zakia Salime, 'Between Feminism and Islam:· Human Rights and Sharia Law in Morocco', vol. 36, *Social Movements, Protest, and Contention*, ed. Bert Klandermans (University of Minnesota Press, 2011).
48. Lila Abu-Lughod, 'Do Muslim Women Really Need Saving? Anthropological Reflections on Cultural Relativism and Its Others', *American Anthropologist* 104, no. 3 (2002).
49. Nadia Guessous, *Genealogies of Feminism: Leftist Feminist Subjectivity in the Wake of the Islamic Revival in Contemporary Morocco* (Columbia University, 2011), 12.
50. Ibid.
51. Fatima Mernissi, *Beyond the Veil: Male-Female Dynamics in a Modern Muslim Society*, Revised 1st Midland Book ed. (John Wiley & Sons, 1987).
52. Fatima Sadiqi, 'The Impact of Islamization on Moroccan Feminisms', *Signs: Journal of Women in Culture & Society* 32, no. 1 (2006): 38.
53. Guessous, *Genealogies of Feminism*.

54. Zakia Salime, 'The War on Terrorism: Appropriation and Subversion by Moroccan Women', *Signs: Journal of Women in Culture & Society* 33, no. 1 (2007): 21.
55. Guessous, *Genealogies of Feminism*; Aura Lounasmaa, *Women and Modernity: The Global and the Local in Moroccan Women's Ngos's Advocacy and Public Awareness Work* (National University of Ireland in Galway, 2013).
56. Reilly, 'Doing Transnational Feminism', 60–76.
57. Sylvia I. Bergh and Daniele Rossi-Doria, 'Plus Ça Change? Observing the Dynamics of Morocco's 'Arab Spring' in the High Atlas', *Mediterranean Politics* 20, no. 2 (2015): 198.
58. Dahir Pertaining to the Promulgation of the Constitution of Morocco (2011), preamble.
59. Ibid.
60. Ibid., art. 5.
61. Ibid., preamble.
62. Ibid., art. 19.
63. Ibid., arts. 6 and 64.
64. Interview with W.B., Marrakech area, 15 May 2017.
65. International Institute for Democracy and Electoral Assistance, 'The 2011 Moroccan Constitution: A Critical Analysis' (2012), 17.
66. Dahir Pertaining to the Promulgation of the Constitution of Morocco (2011), art. 17.
67. ILO Convention Concerning Indigenous and Tribal Peoples (No. 169). 1991 (entered into force).
68. ILO Indigenous and Tribal Populations Convention (No. 107). 1959 (entered into force).
69. Lee Swepston, 'Indigenous Peoples in International Law and Organizations', in *International Law and Indigenous Peoples*, eds. Joshua Castellino and Niamh Walsh (Leiden/Boston: Martinus Nijhoff Publishers, 2005), 55.
70. Irène Bellier and Martin Préaud, 'Emerging Issues in Indigenous Rights: Transformative Effects of the Recognition of Indigenous Peoples', *The International Journal of Human Rights* 16, no. 3 (2012): 486, note 8.
71. See: http://www.un.org/esa/socdev/unpfii/documents/DRIPS_en.pdf, p. 4 (accessed February 5, 2018).
72. See, inter alia: Mounira M. Charrad, *States and Women's Rights: The Making of Postcolonial Tunisia, Algeria, and Morocco* (London: University of California Press, 2001); David M. Hart, 'The Berber Dahir of 1930 in Colonial Morocco: Then and Now (1930–1996)', *The Journal of North African Studies* 2, no. 2 (1997): 11–33; William A. Hoisington, 'Cities in Revolt: The Berber Dahir (1930) and France's Urban Strategy in Morocco', *Journal of Contemporary History* 13, no. 3 (1978): 433–48; Susan G. Miller, *A History of Modern Morocco* (Cambridge University Press, 2013).
73. In the RNGS model, the State responses can be: Dual Response (special group involved in policy process and policy coincides with movement goals); pre-emption (special group is not involved in policy process while policy coincides with movement goals); co-optation (special group is involved in policy process while the policy does not coincide with movement goals); and, no response (special group is not involved in policy process and policy does not coincide with movement goals). See: Melissa Haussman and Birgit Sauer, *Gendering the State in the Age of Globalization: Women's Movements and State Feminism in Postindustrial Democracies* (Plymouth, UK: Rowman and Littlefield Publishers, Inc., 2007), 10.
74. See: UNGA Universal Declaration of Human Rights (Adopted 10 December 1948) Resolution 217 a(Iii) (UDHR); International Covenant on Civil and Political Rights (Adopted 16 December 1966, Entered into Force 23 March 1976) 999 UNTS 171 (ICCPR), art. 9.
75. Interview with F.A., young, homeworking mother, with few years of primary education, originally from the countryside and living in an urban setting, Agadir area, 14 October 2016.
76. Shital V. Gunjate and Udgir Shivaji Mahavidyalaya, 'Postcolonial Feminist Theory: An Overview', (Nanded, 2012), 286.
77. Interview with W.B., university professor and women's rights activist, Marrakech area, 15 May 2017.

78. Interview with A.A., university graduate and job seeker in an urban area but originally from the mountains Middle Atlas area, 26 September 2017.
79. Interview with S.B., Amazigh activist and university graduate working for an NGO, Rabat area, 21 September 2016.
80. Interview with F.A., high school English teacher in rural area, Agadir area, 13 October 2016.
81. Interview with S.B., project manager and PhD graduate, Agadir area, 7 October 2016.
82. Interview with Z.Y., illiterate, homeworking rural mother, Middle Atlas area, 27 September 2016.
83. Interview with L.K., illiterate, homeworking, young mother living in an urban area, Marrakech area, 15 May 2017.
84. Interview with A.A. (afore cited), Middle Atlas area, 26 September 2016.
85. Interview with S.I., university student in her early 20s living in an urban area, Agadir area, 17 October 2016.
86. Interview with Z.W., high school student who grew up in a neighbouring Arab country before returning home to Morocco in the aftermath of the Arab Spring, Rabat area, 22 September 2016.
87. Interview with H.B., primary school French teacher in an urban area Rabat area, 22 September 2016.
88. Ibid.
89. Interview with N.A., high school graduate and intern at a women's local development centre, Middle Atlas area, 27 September 2016.
90. Interview with M.Z., child minder working in a hotel with few years of university education, Middle atlas area, 29 September 2016.
91. Interview with S.B. (afore cited), Rabat area, 21 September 2016.
92. Interview with Z.B., illiterate, homeworking mother living in a rural setting, Ait Baha area, 10 October 2016.
93. See: https://pomeps.org/2016/04/15/women-and-the-right-to-land-in-morocco-the-sulaliyyates-movement/ (accessed November 23, 2017).
94. 'As a legal status, collective land dates back to the time of the French protectorate (1912–56), which issued a royal decree in 1919 to give status to land that belonged neither to individuals nor to the state but was used by communities (Bouderbala 1996). Since then this decree has regulated the property rights of the vaguely defined category of "tribes, fractions, villages or other ethnic groups" (decree of 1919, Article 1) over agricultural or pastoral land that they use as a collective.' Yasmine Berriane, 'Bridging Social Divides: Leadership and the Making of an Alliance for Women's Land-Use Rights in Morocco', *Review of African Political Economy* 43, no. 149 (2016): 351. See also: Negib Bouderbala, Les Terres Collectives du Maroc dans la Première Période du Protectorat (1912–1930), 79 Revue du Monde Musulman et de la Méditerranée (1996).
95. Berriane, 'Bridging Social Divides'.
96. See: https://pomeps.org/2016/04/15/women-and-the-right-to-land-in-morocco-the-sulaliyyates-movement/ (accessed November 23, 2017).
97. Berriane, 'Bridging Social Divides'.
98. Ibid., 352.

Disclosure statement

No potential conflict of interest was reported by the author.

Funding

This work was supported by Irish Research Council [grant number RCS1327].

ORCID

Silvia Gagliardi http://orcid.org/0000-0003-3802-5521

Reflections on indigenous peoples' rights vis-à-vis the law of occupation

Shlomit Stein

ABSTRACT
The article examines the application of the UN Declaration on Indigenous Rights (UNDRIP) beyond the confines of a State entity. Specifically, it explores the potential integration of indigenous housing, land and property protections into an occupation setting – where sovereignty is suspended and the responsibility to protect the population's rights is vested in an external governing power. Can and should indigenous protections be integrated into the law of occupation? What implications would that entail vis-à-vis the limits that the law of occupation imposes on the occupant to introduce new legal obligations into occupied territory? The need to address this theoretical inquiry arises from the dire conditions of indigenous Bedouin in the West Bank, a Palestinian territory occupied by Israel since 1967. Historically and culturally, the West Bank Bedouin have close ties to Bedouin within Israel, the latter acknowledged internationally as indigenous people. Therefore, arguably, the West Bank Bedouin are also entitled to indigenous protections – the relevant difference being that the latter live in occupied territory. The case study of the West Bank Bedouin offers thus a unique opportunity to examine the potential relationship between the law of occupation and the indigenous rights regime as embodied in UNDRIP.

1. Introduction

This article offers a critical reflection on the protection of indigenous peoples' rights in the context of military occupation, assessing the law of occupation vis-à-vis the indigenous peoples rights framework – a relationship which has hitherto received little attention.[1] Specifically, the article focuses on the following tension:

(1) the obligation set out by the law of occupation on the occupant to refrain from changing the legal and political institutions in occupied territory, 'unless absolutely prevented'[2]

versus

(2) the requirement stemming from indigenous peoples' rights to acknowledge the unique status of an indigenous people by incorporating progressive and new legal obligations into the local legal system (thus changing the legal regime in force).

In a strict legal sense, I argue that obligation (1) overrides (2) because it is difficult to persuasively argue that the occupant is legally obliged to incorporate new rights and obligations such as those entailed in the United Nations Declaration on the Rights of Indigenous Peoples (UNDRIP)[3] into occupied territory. On a principled level, however, resolving the formal legal question does not satisfy the basic intuition that indigenous peoples' rights should be protected, regardless of where they reside. In other words: why should the legal status of the territory (within the borders of a sovereign state/under military occupation) be a defining factor for the application of indigenous rights? Could this tension be settled, if not in the strict legal sense as the law stands to date, then perhaps theoretically, in hope of paving a path for future interpretation of the law of occupation that would include protection of indigenous rights? The inquiry is thus into the law as it exists ('lex lata') as well as into potential future developments of the law ('lex ferenda').

Furthermore, even if such a development could be *feasible*, would imposing such obligation on the occupant be *desirable*, i.e. would it enhance the protection of civilians, belonging to an indigenous people, under military occupation? Posed from a different perspective: can indigenous peoples' rights – formulated in dialogue with states and on the assumption that their realisation is subject to a state framework – be transplanted into a non-state setting such as occupation?

This inquiry draws on the dire conditions of indigenous Bedouin in the West Bank (WB), a Palestinian territory occupied by Israel since 1967. Within the WB, the Bedouin and other herding communities are arguably the group most negatively affected by Israeli policies amongst the Palestinians.[4] Some of the Bedouin communities have undergone displacement and are constantly struggling to prevent further displacement brought about by: border changes; establishment of Israeli settlements; closure of areas for military training purposes; lack of formal land title; and lack of adequate planning schemes which render illegal any construction under the existing planning laws and thus in threat of demolition. Historically and culturally, the WB Bedouin have close ties to Bedouin living in the Naqab desert within the borders of Israel, the latter acknowledged by the two recent UN Special Rapporteurs on the Rights of Indigenous Peoples as indigenous people.[5] Therefore, arguably the WB Bedouin are also entitled to such recognition.

Different, however, to the Bedouin in Israel – the majority of which are Israeli citizens – the WB Bedouin live in occupied territory and have therefore a different legal status vis-à-vis Israel. On one hand, as civilians residing in occupied territory, they have a unique set of rights prescribed by the law of occupation. On the other hand, Israel, as the occupant, has not only a set of complementing obligations, but also protected interests which may prevail, in certain circumstances, over its obligations to fully realise the civilian population's rights.

The case of the WB Bedouin provides the opportunity to concretise the theoretical inquiry on the potential integration of indigenous peoples' rights into an occupation context. It shall serve as a case study accompanying the inquiry, yet not be the focus of the article. Therefore, for the present purpose, I shall take their indigenous status as a given. Arguments supporting, as well as negating, the attribution of indigenous status to the WB Bedouin (and to Bedouin at all) are beyond the article's scope.[6]

Section I briefly overviews the WB Bedouin and their legal status. Section II delves into the law of occupation, specifically into provisions concerning housing, land and property rights (HLP), the violations of which are arguably the most destructive for indigenous livelihood and culture. Section III presents HLP protections included in indigenous peoples' rights regime, specifically in UNDRIP and ILO Indigenous and Tribal Peoples Convention, C169 (ILO 169).[7] Section IV confronts the protections discussed in sections II and III, discussing considerations as to the feasibility and desirability of integrating the two legal regimes and questioning whether indigenous peoples' rights add an additional layer of protection for indigenous people living under military occupation. Section V concludes.

2. The WB Bedouin and their legal status - overview

The Bedouin residing in the occupied Palestinian territory (oPt) are a semi-nomadic people who have lived in southern historical Palestine at least since the seventh century and survived mostly by herding camels, sheep and goats. They originate from the Negev/Naqab desert— today part of Israel — from which they were compelled to flee during and following the 1948 Arab-Israeli war. They live primarily in Gaza, Sinai, Jordan and throughout the WB.

Following the 1967 Arab-Israeli war, , the Bedouin communities in the WB came under the effective control of the Israel military. Today, there are some 30,000 Bedouins living in 183 communities in the WB, the overwhelming majority in Area C.[8] The communities are sparsely located. Within each community, the residential clusters – assembled of light building materials, e.g. iron, wood and tin and covered with makeshift cloth and plastic roofs – are spatially divided according to family affiliation. This reflects the significance of personal privacy and the need for open grazing spaces, which are constantly being carved away at for the expansion of Israeli settlements.[9] Another estimated 75,000 live in the Gaza Strip in 18 Bedouin communities, many in access restricted areas adjacent to the border.[10]

The legal status of the WB Bedouin is diverse. Some are 1948 Palestine refugees, registered with UNRWA and entitled to refugee assistance and protection.[11] Following the 1967 Arab-Israeli War many of them were again displaced, this time from their post-1948 habitual site, making them also internally displaced persons (IDPs).[12] Those who live within the municipal boundaries of Jerusalem are Israeli residents or entitled to residency. Though the annexation of East Jerusalem is unlawful under international law,[13] Palestinian residents are granted various rights under domestic Israeli law.[14] Under the law of occupation, a part of International Humanitarian Law, they are 'protected persons',[15] a status conferred to all Palestinians in the WB. Though Israel does not formally acknowledge that the oPt is indeed occupied and that the law of occupation applies de jure, it de facto acknowledges the application of its humanitarian provisions.[16]

3. HLP rights under the law of occupation

3.1. Concurrent application of IHL & IHRL

The modern law of occupation is set out first and foremost in International Humanitarian Law (IHL) instruments, namely, Hague Regulations ('HR'), 4th Geneva Convention ('GC

IV') and Additional Protocols I and II to the Geneva Conventions ('AP').[17] In addition, it is nowadays acknowledged that international human rights laws (IHRL) applies concurrent to IHL in occupied territory,[18] especially in a setting of protracted occupation.[19] While outright contradictions between the content of the two legal regimes is seldom, the interplay between the two regimes is still a subject of lively debate.[20] Moreover, Israel and the US contest that human rights treaties confer extraterritorial obligations and deny that they are obliged to apply IHRL to the administration of occupied territories. Notwithstanding, extraterritorial application of IHRL is widely recognised in situations where states exercise jurisdiction beyond their borders. 'Jurisdiction' is understood broadly,[21] wherever a state exercises de facto control, such as in occupied territory. Specific to the case at hand, Israel is a party to the main human rights instruments. The International Court of Justice has subsequently concluded that the ICCPR and the ICSECR apply in the oPt and has assessed Israel's activities in the oPt under these conventions.[22] Its IHRL obligations towards the occupied Palestinian population is further enhanced due to the length of occupation, spanning over 50 years.

3.2. Specific HLP protections

IHL instruments include numerous provisions that protect real and personal property from attack, destruction,[23] confiscation[24] or requisition.[25] Also specified are the limits on the occupant's use of public property.[26] Exceptions are, nonetheless, allowed where 'such destruction is rendered absolutely necessary by military operations' (GC IV, art.53) or 'unless such destruction or seizure be imperatively demanded by the necessities of war' (HR, art.23).[27] The comparison of military advantages gained by destruction to the damages done is subject to proportionality.[28]

Per private property, while the prohibition on confiscation is absolute and does not allow for exceptions, HR (art.52) permits the occupant to requisition land and supplies for the needs of its army, in return for payment.[29] HR art.52 further prescribes that requisitions 'shall be in proportion to the resources of the country.' GC IV (art.55) adds that requisition must consider the potential harm to the civilian population.[30] Requisition carried out lawfully under HR 52 transfers title to the occupant, in return for compensation.[31]

The prohibition to confiscate private property protects not only against loss of ownership, but also against the owner being prevented from exercising its rights related to the land, such as access.[32] Unlike expropriation which is permitted when carried out according to the local law, for public purposes, and adequately compensated for — compensation does not automatically render confiscation lawful.[33]

Per public land and the use of natural resources, the guiding rationale is that occupation does not transfer ownership. The occupant is regarded as temporary administer, who can make use of public property, but must safeguard the capital value of the properties and administer them according to usufruct rules (HR, art. 55). The occupant must also, as read into the provision by the Israeli High Court of Justice, preserve the property and ensure its continued existence.[34] While the occupant may not sell the property nor strip it off, it may lease, utilise or cultivate the land.[35] The selling of yield harvested from public lands is generally permitted, provided that the fruit consumption by the occupant does not encroach upon the capital. However, the line between acceptable use and unlawful exploitation in cases where capital is non-renewable (e.g. quarrying activities) is fuzzy.[36] The weight ascribed to the interests of the local population has proven to be a double-edged sword in this regard.[37]

The occupant may also take possession of (seize) any movable property, belonging to the state, for use in military operations (HR, art. 53). This act transfers title. Thus, the occupant is on its face allowed to sell the property. However, then the possession is utilised for commercial – not military — purpose and is arguably prohibited.[38]

IHL prohibits to destroy or remove objects indispensable to the survival of the civilian population, regardless of the motive, and specifically if such acts are meant to induce the population to move.[39]

Under the principle that use of force and subsequent occupation of a territory does not transfer sovereignty over the land and its resources, the protection of property embodied in IHL is not linked to title, but rather to its usage to alleviate civilian suffering:

> the Fourth Geneva Convention drew a link between protecting property and preventing suffering, and by and large neglected traditional, perhaps more "Western," concepts of ownership[40] ... IHL is driven by a conception of property that is more instrumental, and values property in direct proportion to its role in assuring the survival of civilians. Thus, international humanitarian law distinguishes ownership of property from use of property, largely disregarding the ownership interests that figure centrally in times of peace, but protecting users' interests.[41]

This is 'good news' for indigenous communities, especially for the WB Bedouin, who by large do not claim ownership of the lands they occupy and use, but the right to reside on them and use them for their survival and livelihood.[42]

IHL does not provide a definition of 'property'. In the absence of such, we can turn to the practice of IHRL to fill the gap.[43] The ECtHR has interpreted the notion of 'possession' more broadly than ownership, to include monetary rights such as entitlements to rent. The Inter-American court of human rights has interpreted the right to property to cover also indigenous peoples' communal property, their right to own natural resources collectively and incorporeal elements and any other intangible object capable of having value.[44] Again this broad interpretation includes the interests of non-owners and community usage of lands.

As for the right of protected persons to stay put, regardless of land title, IHL prohibits the occupant from conducting individual or mass forcible transfers of protected persons,[45] a prohibition considered customary international law.[46] The term 'forcible transfer' has been interpreted to include not only use of physical force but also the taking advantage of coercive circumstances, which pressure people to move and deprive them of real choice.[47]

Finally, also relevant is the occupant's duty under HR, art.43 to 'take all the measures in his power to restore, and ensure, as far as possible, public order and safety, while respecting, unless absolutely prevented, the laws in force in the country.' This general duty of good governance is fundamentally a duty to facilitate normal civil life.[48] As such, it has been interpreted as a channel through which human rights, including economic, social and cultural rights, can be integrated into the occupant's duties.[49] Yet, art.43 can also be interpreted by the occupant to deny its human rights obligations in situations of occupation, based on perceived legal obstacles that limit its legitimacy to introduce changes in the occupied territory (an argument addressed below in section IV).

However, keeping in line with the occupant's obligation to protect the occupied population, it is plausible to argue that changes based on adherence to IHRL and made for the benefit of the inhabitants are not to be considered over-encroaching changes but fulfilment of the occupant's duty to restore and ensure adequate conditions for normal civil life.[50] The longer the occupation subsists, the more proactive intervention may be called for, 'if only to prevent economic, social, and legal stagnation.'[51]

Moreover, implementing IHRL rights, including those associated with social and economic elements, does not necessarily entail far-reaching reforms.[52] For example, in the case of the WB Bedouin what is called for is chiefly to respect their traditional modes of land usage and connect them to essential services. Based on context specific analysis of an occupation, however, the occupant may have a more robust obligation to provide not only 'the humanitarian baseline of protection'[53] but also accommodate long term development.

Thus, the obligation to ensure normal civil life opens the way to include positive obligations which promote tenure security e.g. the right to adequate housing, freedom of movement and choice of residency, and protection from forced eviction.

4. HLP rights under indigenous peoples' rights

Land rights have a central place within indigenous peoples' rights due to the unique bond that indigenous people traditionally have with their lands. Moreover, land is often a source of food and livelihood for indigenous communities.

As noted by Gilbert, '[i]nternationally, no treaty or declaration specifically refers to a human right to land. In fact, strictly speaking there is no human right to land under international law.'[54] For this reason, the explicit incorporation of land rights in indigenous rights instruments is a meaningful step toward the entrenchment of land rights as human rights. Roughly speaking, these are the key contributions of indigenous rights to the protection of HLP rights relevant to the present inquiry:

- Land rights are broader than strict ownership: in a nutshell, not only ownership but also occupation and different forms of land usage (e.g. seasonal cultivation, grazing, hunting, worship) are recognised as conferring rights to specific lands.[55] This recognition pushes back on the approach adopted all too often by modern states, which has hitherto disregarded long-standing land rights that indigenous people have acquired, leading to their disenfranchisement from land they have been occupying and using often for generations back.
- Diversification of procedural mechanisms for resolution of land disputes: in line with the inclusion of a wider array of substantial types of rights to land, the indigenous rights framework broadens the scope of recognised procedural mechanisms by which these rights can be attained. UNDRIP (art.27) acknowledges the power of 'indigenous peoples' laws, traditions, customs and land tenure systems, to recognise and adjudicate the rights of indigenous peoples pertaining to their lands, territories and resources' and calls on states to 'establish and implement, in conjunction with indigenous peoples concerned, a fair, independent, impartial, open and transparent process.'[56]

- Collective nature of rights to land and property: Under ILO 169, the concept of land encompasses the total environment of the areas which either the whole community or individual members occupy and use.[57] UNDRIP further enroots the collective nature of indigenous peoples' land and property rights. This is reflected clearly in the formulation of the articles related to land, all of which constitute the right of indigenous people to land.[58] Jurisprudence of international bodies and tribunals also confirm the emergence of this recognition.[59]
- Cultural value of land: the appreciation of the cultural and spiritual bond that indigenous people often have to land can also be seen as an aspect of the collective nature of the relationship to land.[60] UNDRIP (art.8) articulates the significance of this relationship in a negative way, establishing a right not to be subjected to forced assimilation or destruction of culture through, among other means, dispossession of lands, territories or resources or forced population transfer. This approach to land rights, also referred to as a right to cultural integrity,[61] perceives land rights upon the backdrop of a wider framework of rights, including the rights to culture, subsistence, livelihood, religion and heritage.[62]
- Nomadic peoples' land rights: the protection of nomadic people, as a unique group within indigenous people, did not make it into the UNDRIP, yet has a place in ILO 169, art.14 ('Particular attention shall be paid to the situation of nomadic peoples and shifting cultivators … '). Art.14 protects the right to use land not exclusively occupied, but to which a said group enjoyed access to for their subsistence and traditional activities. Shared use is thus not a ground for recognition of ownership rights, but for usage rights.[63]
- Requirement of due process standards, specifically consultation, where relocation is considered: both ILO 169 and UNDRIP prohibit as a rule forcible removal from lands or territories, yet allow relocation when founded on 'free, prior and informed consent of the indigenous peoples concerned and after agreement on just and fair compensation and, where possible, with the option of return.'[64] This requirement will be further scrutinised in the following section.

5. Incorporating indigenous peoples' rights into the law of occupation

After presenting the relevant HLP protections under the law of occupation (IHL and IHRL) and under the indigenous peoples' rights framework, this section draws attention to the complementing protections, but also to the potential points of friction, between the two legal regimes. The questions guiding the analysis are: whether the incorporation of indigenous rights into the obligations of the occupant could be grounded in the law of occupation? And whether it would enhance the protection of civilians, belonging to an indigenous people, in occupied territory?

5.1. Delimiting the occupant's power to introduce changes into the local legal and political framework

The fundamental tension between the requirement to limit the powers of the occupant to make changes to the local legal or political infrastructure and the need to protect the rights of the civilian population is inherent to the law of occupation. Under the title 'transformative occupation',[65] this has evolved into a central theme in the law of occupation, especially since the 2003 occupation of Iraq. On the one hand, the 'conservationist' principle limits the power of the occupant to alter the legal regime and the institutional structure in the occupied territory only to narrow exceptions derived from HR art.43 and GC IV, art.64 (discussed below). On the other hand, the duty to protect the civilian population, enhanced in protracted occupations, may entail the requirement to introduce new laws and institutions to align with contemporary international human rights standards ('transformative objectives').[66] 'While allegedly benefiting the local population, however, these changes could also further entrench the occupation and serve the interests of the occupying power',[67] what Gross coins 'the double bind of occupation.'[68]

For the moment, it is safe to say that transformative occupation, of the kind which aims to overhaul the legal, political and institutional structures in the occupied territory, is not legally justifiable under IHL.[69] Nonetheless, more minimal changes could be tolerated, or even welcomed, especially when they sincerely serve to enhance the security and welfare of the civilian population.[70] The letter of the law takes us, however, only so far in determining what constitutes a 'minimal' change and a 'benefit' to the civilian population.

Alongside the obligation of the occupant to apply human rights law to the administration of occupied territory, the recognition that self-determination lay within the People rather than the ousted government has clearly left its footprint on the law of occupation.

While a positive development in its own merit, it may be misappropriated in a way that proves detrimental to the interests of the people. An example is the rules of usufruct, discussed above (HR, art.55), which delimit the occupant's scope of use of public land and specifically the profit it may yield from it. Traditionally, art.55's rationale was understood as not only preventing the occupant from depleting natural resources, but also protecting the ousted government's properties from being taken over by local inhabitants.[71] However, once the interests of the ousted government take a backseat in favour of the those of the People, this protection is more prone to misappropriation and more susceptible to legal arguments which conflate the occupant's interests with the People's. The occupant's duty to preserve and save the natural resources still stands regardless of the shift in the identity of the sovereign (the ousted government or the People). Yet, as proven in the case of the oPt, once the interests of the People take centre stage, the occupant is better placed to claim that its use of public resources is beneficial for the local inhabitants.[72]

Turning to the exceptions that permit the occupant to introduce new laws to occupied territory, these are set out in HR, art.43 and GC IV, art.64.

HR, art.43 prescribes that the occupant 'take all the measures in his power to restore, and ensure, as far as possible, public order and safety, while respecting, unless absolutely prevented, the laws in force in the country.' Initially, this provision was formulated with the view that only military necessity could justify deviating from the obligation to respect the laws in force.[73] Yet, as Benvenisti recalls,

> as early as World War I, this test proved to be insufficient as it could not properly conform with the occupant's duty to protect the interests of the local population, interests that at times could be best met by amending the local laws.[74]

In the aftermath of World War II, the recognition that the benefit of the population – also in absence of military justification — could legitimize passing new laws or amending old ones, was further entrenched.[75]

The main contribution of GC IV, art.64 is the permission to introduce new laws 'which are essential' for the occupant to fulfil its obligations under the convention. This permits to introduce laws that implement the bill of rights incorporated in GC IV. Yet, it also restricts the ability to make full blown reforms, since the convention's guarantees are rather minimalistic and do not require the occupant to align the human rights standards in the occupied territory to those in its country.[76]

Returning to the present inquiry, the question is whether incorporation of the indigenous peoples' rights discussed above would require substantial transformative reform, thus overstepping the occupant's authority, or whether such endeavour could be achieved by more modest changes which 'tinker on the edges of societal reform'[77] yet remain within the contemporary reading of the law of occupation?

5.2. Indigenous peoples' rights in a setting of occupation: enhanced protection?

Could, for example, a broader notion of ownership be incorporated into IHL provisions which protect HLP rights? As noted above, the relevant IHL provisions are principally open to such a broader interpretation since the HLP protections they afford are not linked to ownership. Moreover, it is anyway unclear if an occupant has the authority to confer title to land in occupied territory.[78] This, however, does not hinder the occupant from legislating new laws that respect and protect indigenous forms of land usage, the right to housing and cultural integrity or laws that enable the continued application of protective measures that were in place in the territory prior to its military occupation.[79]

This broader notion endorsed by indigenous rights could especially be advantageous to nomadic communities within occupied territories, whose protection requires recognising their access to lands and providing certainty that they can occupy, leave and re-enter lands. Yet, while nomadic peoples' land rights have gained some initial traction under the indigenous peoples umbrella (as indicated by their inclusion in ILO 169), they have since been left out of the current indigenous agenda (as indicated by the absence of their mention in UNDRIP).[80] Thus, a more promising avenue for the protection of their HLP rights in occupied territory could be the occupant's obligation under IHRL. Specifically, ICCPR art.27 is interpreted as covering traditional activities and land usages practiced by indigenous nomadic People.[81]

It is, however, questionable just how broad of an approach to land rights can be protected under the law of occupation. While IHL protections of HLP rights are not limited to ownership, they are linked to the function of the property, namely, its role in assuring the survival of civilians. Incorporating indigenous protections would require a very broad interpretation of 'survival' beyond immediate physical survival of individuals, to encompass cultural survival of Peoples under military occupation. It is noteworthy that IHL provides unique protection of cultural property,[82] but not protection of cultural aspects of land usage as such. In protracted occupation, however, a broader reading of 'survival' may gain more weight.[83]

Another indigenous rights transplant that may be rejected by the body of law of occupation is the procedural requirement of consultation prior to transfer/relocation. In a state framework — at least within a democratic state — the government enjoys fundamental legitimacy. Accordingly, it can be assumed that the citizens give at least implied consent to decisions made by the government, provided that these decisions conform to procedural decision-making requirements. Moreover, when unsatisfied with government decisions, citizens can go to the streets and to the ballots to express their dissatisfaction. From this, stems the citizen's implied consent to accept decisions which promote a collective good, even if made to her personal detriment.

This accepted (even if fictitious) assumption does not apply in a military occupation setting. Even if the occupation itself is legal, the governing power does not enjoy democratic legitimacy. The authority of the occupant is derived from the fact of effective control, not from the popular support.[84] And though it must take measures to protect the occupied population, it in no way represents the people subject to its rule. Implied consent to agree to decisions that serve a greater good thus cannot be assumed. Especially since the protected persons cannot go neither to the streets nor to the ballots to express their discontent.[85] Therefore, in a situation of occupation, it is difficult to assume free consent to relocate, even if negotiations between the people and the military government are seemingly free and transparent. In this respect, the IHL prohibition on transfer of protected persons mentioned above[86] provides a higher threshold of protection for indigenous people than indigenous rights instruments.

Finally, a principle matter that must be addressed is whether incorporation of indigenous protections can be done on a selective basis, without it entailing the occupant to recognise the right of self-determination of the said indigenous people. This should not be problematic when the indigenous people make up the entire population of the occupied territory. Yet, it raises a dilemma when the indigenous people are a sub-group within the population. Recognition of the right to self-determination of a sub-group may have significant social ramifications and create status distinctions among the occupied population (who is/not indigenous?) which are likely to transform the societal fabric of the occupied territory in a way that oversteps the limitations placed on the occupant.

An additional consideration that warrants attention is that while the term self-determination assumes a key role in both the law of occupation and indigenous peoples' rights, its interpretation differs in each legal framework. Under UNDRIP, self-determination is delimited by the principle of territorial integrity,[87] meaning that the realisation of self-determination does not justify - as a rule — succession.[88] The law of occupation also upholds territorial integrity and inalienability of sovereignty by use of force[89], alongside the right to self-determination.[90] Thus, on its face, self-determination, as understood under the law of occupation, does not impinge on the principle of territorial integrity since the occupant anyway does not have a legal claim to sovereignty over the occupied territory. However, when applied to a sub-group within the occupied population, it could potentially pose a threat for the territorial integrity of the future, post-occupation-sovereign-state. This demonstrates how the recognition of the right to self-determination of an indigenous sub-group in occupied territory may ultimately undermine the principle as understood under UNDRIP.

6. Conclusion

The article set out on a theoretical legal inquiry into the potential intersections between the law of occupation and indigenous peoples' rights regime, with a focus on HLP rights. The objective of the inquiry was twofold:

First, to examine whether indigenous peoples' rights could, legally, be incorporated into the obligations of the occupant stipulated by the law of occupation. This was done by specifying the HLP protections afforded by both legal regimes and by examining whether the law of occupation is open to such interpretation that would allow for incorporation of indigenous peoples' rights.

Second, to examine whether such a development would provide an indigenous people living under military occupation more protection than what they are already entitled to as 'protected persons' under the law of occupation. Here the focus of the discussion moved from scrutiny of specific provisions to a broader discussion of the fundaments underlying the legal regimes.

The inquiry posed questions for both legal regimes. Law of occupation: to which extent may the law be stretched to accommodate for rights of indigenous people without tipping the gentle balance underpinning the legal regime, that between the rights of the protected people on the one hand, and the recognised interests of the occupant on the other hand? Indigenous rights: could a rights regime, formulated in a state-centric framework, be transplanted into a non-state setting without it undercutting its fundamental assumptions?

The inquiry also discussed the existing limitations of both regimes which surface when theory is put into practice, as demonstrated by the unique case study of the Bedouin living in the WB under Israeli military occupation. These are rooted in the differing interests, as well as situations, to which each legal regime responds. From the perspective of the law of occupation, its underlying principles seem to offer too narrow of a leeway for the inclusion of a complete indigenous peoples' rights framework, as indicated by the limitations set out on the occupant's power to legislate new laws and by the law's primary focus on immediate humanitarian needs, rather than on long standing cultural survival. From the perspective of indigenous peoples' rights, it is questionable whether it can function outside a state framework, for example in an intermediate political structure which has not yet matured into statehood. This was demonstrated by discussing the difficulty that may arise when affirming the right to self-determination of an indigenous sub-group within a larger political community that has yet to fully realise its right to self-determination.

Concluding, it is fair to say that institutionalizing a completely new framework of indigenous rights into the occupied territory would be overstepping the limits of what is permitted under the contemporary interpretation of the law of occupation and would be considered a 'transformative occupation' that is to date not legally justifiable. Therefore, it is not an obligation that the occupant is committed to fulfil, nor permitted, considering its likelihood to result in a significant transformation to the social institutions and fabric of the occupied population. That said, with respect to the occupant's principle obligation to keep intact and sustain the status quo in the occupied territory pre-occupation, it should keep intact legal, political and social policies and practices which protected indigenous Peoples rights pre-occupation.[91]

Finally, the occupant has the authority to incorporate protections afforded by the indigenous peoples' rights regime through its IHRL obligations.[92] Hence, some indigenous rights could find their way into the occupant's IHRL obligations, especially those that do not require full-blown social or institutional reform. Examples include enabling traditional usage of land or facilitating continuous access to land and natural resources. That stated, IHRL obligations under occupation provide mainly protection for individual members of an indigenous group. The collective group rights of an indigenous people under occupation remain, thus, unduly protected.

Notes

1. An exceptional publication which draws attention to the topic is: Norwegian Refugee Council, Bedouin Rights under Occupation: International Humanitarian Law and Indigenous Rights for Palestinian Bedouin in the West Bank, (November 2015) ('NRC report'). In its advisory opinion on the Western Sahara, the ICJ addressed land rights of nomadic people in occupied territory. Yet, it did not do so in specific reference to the law of occupation nor to the international indigenous peoples framework, whose main instruments (ILO Convention no.169 and UNDRIP) did not exist at the time. See: Western Sahara, Advisory Opinion, ICJ GL No 61, [1975] ICJ Rep. 12 (ICJ 1975), October 16, 1975.
2. International Conferences (The Hague), Hague Convention (IV) Respecting the Laws and Customs of War on Land and Its Annex: Regulations Concerning the Laws and Customs of War on Land, art.43, 18 October 1907, http://www.refworld.org/docid/4374cae64.html ('HR') (visited 30 January 2018).
3. UN General Assembly, United Nations Declaration on the Rights of Indigenous Peoples: resolution / adopted by the General Assembly, 2 October 2007, A/RES/61/295, http://www.refworld.org/docid/471355a82.html [accessed 30 January 2018] ('UNDRIP').
4. NRC report, supra n. 1 at 9; UN Office of the High Commissioner for Human Rights, (24 August 2016), Israeli settlements in the Occupied Palestinian Territory, including East Jerusalem, and the occupied Syrian Golan - Report of the Secretary-General A/71/355, http://ap.ohchr.org/documents/dpage_e.aspx?si=A/71/355 ('Bedouins living in Area C are the most affected by demolitions and at risk of forcible transfer.' (p.22)) (visited 1 February 2018).
5. UN General Assembly, (August 2011) Report of the Special Rapporteur on the Rights of Indigenous Peoples, 24–31, A/HRC/18/35/Add.1.
6. See: NRC report, supra n. 1 at 28–32.
7. International Labour Organization (ILO), Indigenous and Tribal Peoples Convention, C169, 27 June 1989, C169, http://www.refworld.org/docid/3ddb6d514.html (visited 30 January 2018) ('ILO 169').
8. Oslo accord II, concluded in September 1995, divided WB territory into three categories. Area A which includes the Palestinian cities (constituting some 18% of the WB) was assigned to full civil and security Palestinian Authority (PA) control. Area B, most of the built-up areas of the Palestinian villages, (22%) was placed under full Palestinian civil authority, yet remained under Israeli security control. Area C which included the settlements, the main roads, and extensive rural areas (60%), remained under Israeli civil and security authority. Certain civilian powers in Area C were transferred to the Palestinian Authority, yet security and land-related issues (such as planning and building, nature reserves, etc.) remained under full Israeli control. Initially, the division into Areas A, B and C was not intended to last more than five years. Between 1995–2000, the divisions changed multiple times. Since 2000, no official changes to these areas has been made.
9. Bimkom, The Bedouin Communities East of Jerusalem – A Planning Survey: Characteristics of the Bedouin Localities East of Jerusalem, http://bimkom.org/eng/wp-content/uploads/jahalin/character.htm. (visited 1 February 2018).
10. Oxfam, Towards Sustainable Food Security in the Occupied Palestinian Territory: Strengthening rangeland governance (April 2017).
11. For UNRWA's (United Nations Relief and Works Agency for Palestine Refugees in the Near East) eligibility criteria, see: https://www.unrwa.org/ (visited 1 February 2018).
12. IDP protections are developed in soft law documents such as the UN Refugee Agency Guiding Principles on Internal Displacement, (September 2004) E/CN.4/1998/53/Add.2, http://www.unhcr.org/protection/idps/43ce1cff2/guiding-principles-internal-displacement.html

13. Explanation about the annexation of EJ.
14. NRC report, supra n. 1 at 11.
15. International Committee of the Red Cross (ICRC), Geneva Convention Relative to the Protection of Civilian Persons in Time of War (Fourth Geneva Convention), 12 August 1949, 75 UNTS 287, http://www.refworld.org/docid/3ae6b36d2.html (visited 30 January 2018) ('GC IV'), art.4:

    Persons protected by the Convention are those who at a given moment and in any manner whatsoever, find themselves, in case of a conflict or occupation, in the hands of persons a Party to the conflict or Occupant of which they are not nationals …

16. The Israeli High Court of Justice has acknowledged that the HR have a customary status. As to the provisions of GC IV, some have been held by the court to be customary (art. 23 on free passage of humanitarian consignments; art. 64 on penal legislation; and art. 78 on security measures and internment), while others –not (art. 49 is not considered by the court as customary, at least to the degree that it prohibits individual deportations of persons who constitute a security threat).
17. HR, supra n. 2; GC IV supra n. 15; International Committee of the Red Cross (ICRC), Protocol Additional to the Geneva Conventions of 12 August 1949, and relating to the Protection of Victims of International Armed Conflicts (Protocol I), 8 June 1977, 1125 UNTS 3, http://www.refworld.org/docid/3ae6b36b4.html ('AP I'); International Committee of the Red Cross (ICRC), Protocol Additional to the Geneva Conventions of 12 August 1949, and relating to the Protection of Victims of Non-International Armed Conflicts (Protocol II), 8 June 1977, 1125 UNTS 609, http://www.refworld.org/docid/3ae6b37f40.html ('AP II') – (visited 30 January 2018).
18. J.M. Henckaerts and L. Doswald-Beck/ICRC, 'Customary International Humanitarian Law', CUP 2005, (Customary IHL), vol. 1, at 299 *et seq.*
19. Vaios Koutroulis, 'The Application of International Humanitarian Law and International Human Rights Law in Situation of Prolonged Occupation: Only a Matter of Time?' *International Review of the Red Cross* 94, no. 885 (Spring 2012): 165, 194–20 and the sources cited there.
20. E.g.: Meron, *The Humanization of International Law* (Pub Info. 2006); 'The Complex Relationship Between the Geneva Conventions and International Human Rights Law' in *The 1949 Geneva Conventions: A Commentary*, eds. A. Clapham, P. Gaeta and M. Sassòli (Oxford: OUP, 2015) ('Clapham/Gaeta/Sassòli') 701–35; Noam Lubell, 'Human Rights Obligations in Military Occupation', *International Review of the Red Cross* 94, no. 885 (Spring 2012) ('Lubell'); Milanovic, 'The Lost Origins of Lex Specialis: Rethinking the Relationship Between Human Rights and International Humanitarian Law', in *Theoretical Boundaries of Armed Conflict and Human Rights*, ed. Jens David Ohlin, (Cambridge University Press).
21. For a summary of relevant international practice see: Customary IHL, supra n. 18 at vol. 1, 305 *et seq.*
22. ICJ Wall advisory opinion, supra n. 20, paras. 102 *et seq.*
23. HR, art.23; HR, art. 56; GC IV,Art.53 IV GC; AP I, art. 54(2) (which has acquired the status of customary law); GC IV, art.147 enumerates 'extensive destruction and appropriation' as a grave breach. As such, it is also included among the war crimes under the ICC Statute (Art.8(2)(a)(iv)).
24. HR, art. 46: '… Private property cannot be confiscated.' Meaning that only public moveable property of the adversary, or private property that is in the actual service of the adversary, may be subject to confiscation, see; Yutaka Arai-Takahashi, Protection of Private Property, Chapter 71,1522 in: Clapham/Gaeta/Sassòli, supra n. 21 ('Arai-Takahashi').
25. HR, supra n. 2, art.52.
26. HR, supra n. 2, art.55.

27. Those not identical, the two formulations are interpreted as setting out the same standard for exception based on military necessity, see: Yoram Dinstein, *The International Law of Belligerent Occupation* (Cambridge University Press, 2009), 196–7 ('Dinstein').
28. Dinstein, supra n. 28 at 198.
29. Dinstein, supra n. 28, at 230.
30. ICRC, Occupation and international humanitarian law: questions and answers, August 4, 2004, https://www.icrc.org/eng/resources/documents/misc/634kfc.htm
31. Dinstein, supra n. 28 at 231.
32. Dinstein, supra n. 28 at 225.
33. Dinstein, supra n. 28 at 225.
34. HCJ 285/81, El Nazer et al. V. Commander of Judea and Samaria et al., 36(1) PD 701, 704 (in Hebrew).
35. Dinstein, supra n. 28 at 214.
36. Dinstein, supra n. 28 at 215–6.
37. HCJ 9717/03, Na'ale-Association for Settlement in Samaria of Employees of the Israel Aircraft Industry v. the Higher Planning Council in Judea and Samaria, 58(6) PD 97, 102–3 (the Israeli HCJ ruled that the opening of a new quarry in the WB was consistent with HR 55 since its product would be used for local works) ('the Quarry case'). For additional analysis of this trend in Israeli HCJ jurisprudence, see: Kretzmer, *The Occupation of Justice* (2002), 77 ('Kretzmer'), 57–72 and A. Gross, *The Writing on the Wall: Rethinking the International Law of Occupation* (Cambridge University Press, 2017) ('Gross'), 46–51.
38. Dinstein, supra n. 28 at 219, discussion in para. 517.
39. AP I, supra 17, art.54(2).
40. Lea Brilmayer and Geoffrey Chepiga, 'Ownership or Use? Civilian Property Interests in International Humanitarian Law', *Harvard International Law Journal* 49, no. 2 (Summer 2008): 413, 426.
41. Id., 417.
42. Following their 1948 displacement from the Naqab, the Bedouin settled on public lands (which were held at the time by Jordan) or private lands, and typically did not possess ownership title.
43. Arai-Takahashi, supra n. 25 at 1533.
44. E.g. IACtHR, *Mayagna (Sumo) Awas Tingni Community v. Nicaragua*, Judgment, 31 August 2001, Series C, No. 79 (2001), paras. 148–9 (the first time that the Inter-American Court has issued a judgment in favour of the rights of indigenous peoples to their ancestral land). Returning to the setting of occupation, Arai-Takahashi adds that 'in occupied territories, an occupier's exploitation of natural resources may clash with indigenous peoples' collective ownership of such resources, which they deem essential for their ancestral heritage and cultural identity.' (ibid, 1533).
45. GC IV, art.49; See also: AP I, art.17. Commentary to Art.17: 4854 Clearly, imperative military reasons cannot be justified by political motives. For example, it would be prohibited to move a population in order to exercise more effective control over a dissident ethnic group.
46. Customary IHL, supra n 18, vol.1at 462 et seq., Rule 130.
47. Prosecutor v. Krnojelac, ICTY, Trial Chamber, IT-97-25-T, 2002, para. 475 (footnotes omitted) ('Forced' is not to be interpreted in a restrictive manner, such as being limited to physical force. It may include the 'threat of force or coercion, such as that caused by fear of violence, duress, detention, psychological oppression or abuse of power against such person or persons or another person, or by taking advantage of a coercive environment.'). See also *Prosecutor v. Stakic*, ICTY, Appeals Chamber, IT-97-24-T, 2006, para 281.
48. The French version of the provision, which is he only authoritative one, enjoins the occupying power to restore and ensure 'l'ordre et la vie publique', which means that it is obliged to facilitate a normal civil life.
49. Michael Bothe, in Clapham/Gaeta/Sassòli, supra n. 21 at 1469 *et seq.*
50. Gilles Giacca, 'Economic, Social and Cultural Rights in Occupied Territories', Chapter 70, 1493 in: Clapham/Gaeta/Sassòli', id, supra n. XX ('Giacca').

51. Lubell, id, supra n. 21 at 329; Giacca, supra n. 51 at 1503.
52. Giacca, supra n. 51 at 1504.
53. Giacca, supra n. 51 at 1514.
54. Jérémie Gilbert, 'Lands Rights as Human Rights: the Case for a Specific Right to Land', *SUR* 18 (2013): 115–35, 115 ('Gilbert 1').
55. UNDRIP, supra n. 3, arts.25–6.
56. See also ILO 169, supra 7, art.17(1).
57. Ibid, arts.13(2) and 15.
58. UNDRIP, supra n.3, arts. 25–9
59. See examples given in: Jérémie Gilbert, 'Indigenous Rights in the Making: The United Nations Declaration on the Rights of Indigenous Peoples', *International Journal on Minority and Group Rights* 14 (2007): 207–30, 225.
60. ILO 169, supra n. 7, art.13 (1).
61. Gilbert 1, supra n. 55 at 120.
62. Gilbert 1, supra n. 55 at 120.
63. Jérémie Gilbert, 'Nomadic Territories: A Human Rights Approach to Nomadic Peoples' Land Rights', *Human Rights Law Review* (2007) ('Gilbert 2'), 1, 17. This approach was taken by the ICJ in the Western Sahara case. The ICJ acknowledged the relationship of the Sahrawi nomadic people to territories across which they migrated. However, 'the Court did not acknowledge that the nomadic peoples living in the Western Sahara had a legitimate claim to the territory … the ICJ did not consider nomadic peoples as potential owners of their territories.' (there, 9)
64. UNDRIP, supra n. 3, art.10; ILO 169, supra n. 7, art.16.
65. Adam Roberts, 'Transformative Military Occupation: Applying the Laws of War and Human Rights', *American Journal of International Law* 100, no. 580 (2006): 582–5.
66. Gross, supra n. 38 at 38.
67. Gross, supra n. 38 at38
68. Gross, supra n. 38 at 38.
69. ICRC, *Expert Meeting on the Law of Occupation and Other Forms of Administration of Territory* (Geneva: ICRC, 2012). Arguing that also as a matter of practice, unilateral transformative occupation has not been accepted, see: Gregory H. Fox, 'Transformative Occupation and the Unilateralist Impulse', *International Review of the Red Cross* 94, no. 885 (Spring 2012): 237.
70. For a discussion on 'sincerity', see: E. Benvenisit, *The International Law of Occupation.* (Oxford: Oxford University Press, 2nd edn, 2012), 15–6 ('Benvenisti').
71. Benvenisti, supra n. 71 at 28–9, fn.78
72. The quarry case, id., supra n. 38.
73. Benvenisti, supra n. 71 at 14.
74. Benvenisti, supra n. 71 at 14.
75. Benvenisti, supra n. 71 at 14.
76. Benvenisti, supra n. 71 at 105–6.
77. David Scheffer, 'Beyond Occupation Law', *American Journal of International Law* 97 (2003): 842, 851.
78. NRC report, supra n. 1 at 37.
79. NRC report, supra n. 1 at 37 argued there in respect to the WB Bedouin.
80. Gilbert 2, supra n. 64 at 24.
81. Id., 17; General Comment No. 23: Article 27 (Rights of Minorities), para.7, HRI/GEN/1/Rev.7 at 158; 1–3 IHRR 1 (1994).
82. UN Educational, Scientific and Cultural Organisation (UNESCO), Convention for the Protection of Cultural Property in the Event of Armed Conflict, 14 May 1954, (specifically arts.5, 18), http://www.refworld.org/docid/40422c914.html (visited 1 February 2018); AP I, supra n. 17, arts.53, 85(4)(d); AP II, supra n. 17, art.16.
83. In the context of the oPt, the UN Office for the Coordination of Humanitarian Affairs in the oPt refers to the situation in the oPt as a 'protracted protection crisis', encompassing short as

well as long term humanitarian needs, see: 2017 Humanitarian Needs Overview for the occupied Palestinian territory, https://www.ochaopt.org/content/2017-humanitarian-needs-overview-occupied-palestinian-territory (visited 1 February 2018).

84. Giacca, supra n. 51 at 1514.
85. For the severe restrictions on the right to protest in the oPt, making it virtually impossible, see: S. Stein and F. Petersen, 'Protest and Its Suppression in the Occupied Palestinian Territories and in Turkey', *Journal of International Law of Peace and Armed Conflict* 28, no. 1 (2015): 4.
86. together with the prohibition to deprive protected persons of their rights through agreements concluded between the occupant and the ousted government, see: GC IV, supra n. 15, art.47 ('inviolability of rights').
87. UNDRIP, supra n. 3, arts. 3 and 4 read in conjunction with HR, supra n. 2 art.46.
88. International law recognizes a right to secession for people under colonial rule or foreign occupation. Apart from these circumstances, it has been argued that a right to 'remedial secession' *may* in exceptional cases be established when a state is oppressing the people, discriminating against them, violating their human rights and not allowing them freely to be involved in the politics and internal affairs of the state, see: Accordance with International Law of the Unilateral Declaration of Independence in Respect of Kosovo (Request for Advisory Opinion), General List No. 141, International Court of Justice (ICJ), 22 July 2010, http://www.refworld.org/cases,ICJ,4c5151002.html (visited 1 February 2018); Reference Re Secession of Quebec, [1998] 2 SCR 217; Opinio Juris, Ukraine Insta-Symposium: Intervention in the Ukraine by Invitation, http://opiniojuris.org/2014/03/10/ukraine-insta-symposium-intervention-ukraine-invitation/ (visited1 February 2018).
89. Benvenisti, supra n. 71 at 184 and the UN instruments cited there.
90. Occupation per se is not deemed illegal even though the occupant's government in the occupied territory does not represent the People subject to its rule. Nonetheless, an occupation may be considered illegal if the occupant 'holds out in bad faith' and refuses to negotiate the terms of its decline, see: Benvenisti, supra n. 71 at 187.
91. For example, during their occupation of the WB, between 1949–1967, the Jordanian authorities allowed the Bedouin to graze and use state land and practice their traditional lifestyle with minimal disruption. Such Jordanian policies and practices should be respected by the Israel military, in its administration of the oPt.
92. Per the Bedouin case, Israel is not a party to ILO 169, nor has it signed on to UNDRIP. Thus, different to obligations under IHRL treaties to which it is party, it is not legally bound to apply the protections incorporated in these instruments. In cases where the occupant state is a party to these instruments, (particularly ILO 169 as it is of binding legal force) the rationale discussed above re IHRL treaty obligations could apply as well, namely, extraterritorial applicability in territories where the state has effective control over.

Disclosure statement

No potential conflict of interest was reported by the author.

Index